Recht und Verfassung in Afrika – Law and Constitution in Africa

Band/Volume 33

Anne Schmidt

# Public Procurement Law and Reform in Developing Countries: International Best Practices and Lessons Learned

Namibia as a Case Study

Nomos

**The Deutsche Nationalbibliothek** lists this publication in the Deutsche Nationalbibliografie; detailed bibliographic data are available on the Internet at http://dnb.d-nb.de

a.t.: Bremen, Univ., Diss., 2016

ISBN 978-3-8487-3594-5 (Print)
978-3-8452-7902-2 (ePDF)

**British Library Cataloguing-in-Publication Data**
A catalogue record for this book is available from the British Library.

ISBN 978-3-8487-3594-5 (Print)
978-3-8452-7902-2 (ePDF)

**Library of Congress Cataloging-in-Publication Data**
Schmidt, Anne
Public Procurement Law and Reform in Developing Countries: International Best Practices and Lessons Learned
Namibia as a Case Study
Anne Schmidt
608 p.
Includes bibliographic references and index.

ISBN 978-3-8487-3594-5 (Print)
978-3-8452-7902-2 (ePDF)

1. Edition 2017

# Preface

This publication was accepted as dissertation for the doctorate of law by the University of Bremen in January 2016.

My interest in Namibia and its legal system has been persistent since my studies at the University of Namibia in Windhoek in 2008. After completing my LLM studies in London, I decided to write a dissertation on "Chinese investment in Namibia from a legal perspective". Very soon it became clear that this topic was way too complex. But the information on Chinese companies getting blamed for corruptive practices in public procurement led me to the topic of public procurement law and reform.

*Prof. Dr. Manfred Hinz* who has worked at the University in Namibia more than two decades has supported me with my project while giving me the freedom to shape the topic according to my interests. His experience and helpful comments have contributed to the successful finalisation of my dissertation. I also want to thank *Prof. Dr. Andreas Fischer-Lescano* who assisted the dissertation project in particular by helping out with bureaucratic formalities and hindrances.

A very important part of the dissertation is the field study in Namibia. Thanks to a scholarship by the German Academic Exchange Service, I was able to conduct field work in Namibia for 6 weeks in 2014. In this regard I thank *Sevelus, Saave* and *Mathias Nakashole* who hosted and assisted me. Additionally, I thank all the people who were available for an interview and provided information on public procurement in Namibia.

There are many others who have provided academic, financial, linguistic or practical assistance. *Dr. Cornelia Glinz* and my brother, *Jan Schmidt* have read parts of the dissertation while work was in progress and provided helpful critical remarks. My parents supported me financially so that I could invest most of my time into researching and writing.

This study takes into account literature and state practice available until December 2015. The Namibian Public Procurement Bill 2015 has been gazetted shortly after my dissertation was printed, on 31 December 2015. As the Public Procurement Act, 2015 (Act No. 15 of 2015) does not differ from the bill, all references made to the bill can be read as being part of the act.

Sulingen, January 2017 *Anne Schmidt*

# Table of Contents


List of Abbreviations 17

Introduction 19

1. Background 19
2. Problem Statement 21
3. Literature Review 28
4. Research Methodology 35
   a. General Remarks 35
   b. Field Research in Namibia 42
5. General Outline 44

PART I: The Nature and the Regulation of Public Procurement 49

Chapter 1: The Nature of Public Procurement and its general Regulation 51
1. Introduction 51
2. Principles of Public Procurement 52
3. Pillars of Public Procurement Systems 55
4. Stages of Public Procurement Procedures 56
5. Procurement Methods 58
6. E-Procurement 62
7. Organisational Structure and Workforce 65
8. Review Procedures 66

Chapter 2: Transparency and the Problem of Corruption 69
1. Introduction 69
2. Corruption and possible Effects 70
3. Transparency Requirements in Public Procurement 71
4. Additional Instruments to ensure Transparency 76
5. Compromising Efficiency? 78

Chapter 3: Secondary Objectives 81
1. Introduction 81
2. Types of Socio-Economic Objectives 84
   a. Preferential Procurement 85

b. Inclusion of Criteria increasing Social Welfare 91
c. Preferential Procurement from different Viewpoints: Protectionism vs. Liberalisation 93
3. Environmental Procurement 99

Chapter 4: Summary of Findings 105

PART II: International and National Public Procurement Regulations 109

Chapter 1: The WTO Government Procurement Agreement 111
1. Introduction 111
2. The Essentials of the GPA 113
a. Background 113
i. Principles, Objectives and Scope 113
ii. Review of the Agreement 113
iii. Terminology 115
b. Objectives and Principles 116
c. Scope and Coverage of the GPA 121
i. Scope and Coverage 121
ii. General Exceptions 123
3. Procedures 124
a. Procurement Methods and Procedures 124
b. Tender Specification, Award Criteria and Evaluation Methods 127
i. Qualification Criteria 127
ii. Description of the Subject Matter 128
iii. Evaluation Criteria 130
iv. Method of Evaluation 130
4. Institutions: The Committee on Government Procurement 131
5. The Treatment of Developing and Least-developed Countries 131
a. The 1994 Agreement 131
b. The revised Agreement 135
6. Transparency 137
a. General Transparency Provisions 137
b. Procurement Planning 141
7. Secondary Objectives 142
a. The 1994 Agreement 142
b. The revised Agreement 151
c. Rules of Origin and Offsets 154
8. Enforcement 155
a. Introduction 155
b. Challenging Breaches of the Agreement 156

c. Domestic Review Procedures 158
9. The Reluctance of Developing Countries to seek GPA Accession 160
a. The 1994 GPA 160
b. The revised GPA 167
10. Conclusion 169

Chapter 2: UNCITRAL Model Law on Procurement 173
1. Introduction 173
2. About UNCITRAL 174
3. The Essentials of the UNCITRAL Model Law on Procurement 176
a. Background 176
b. Objectives and Principles 178
c. Scope and Coverage 180
4. Tender Procedures 180
a. Procurement Methods and Procedures 180
b. Tender Specification, Award Criteria and Evaluation Methods 184
i. Qualification Criteria 184
ii. Description of the Subject Matter 186
iii. Evaluation Criteria 186
iv. Method of Evaluation 189
v. Rejection of Abnormally Low Submissions 190
5. Institutions and Staff Regulations 190
6. Transparency 190
7. Secondary Objectives 192
a. The Scope of Application of Secondary Objectives 192
b. The Principle of Non-Discrimination 195
8. Review Procedures 198
9. Conclusion 200

Chapter 3: COMESA Procurement Reform – The Example of Mauritius 205
1. Introduction 205
2. COMESA Procurement Reform Project 206
a. Background 206
b. Laws and Regulations 208
i. COMESA Procurement Directive (2003) 208
ii. COMESA Procurement Regulations 208
c. Objectives and Principles 208
d. Scope and Coverage 210
e. Institutions and Staff 211

f. Procedures 213
i. Procurement Methods and Procedures 213
ii. Tender Specification, Award Criteria and Evaluation Methods 216
g. Transparency 217
h. Secondary Objectives 218
i. Review Procedures 219
j. Procurement Planning 220
k. Contract Administration 220
l. Provisions for the Implementation of Reform 220
3. Interim Conclusion 221
4. Mauritian Procurement Law 222
a. Background 222
b. The Framework 223
i. Laws and Regulations 223
ii. Objectives and Principles 224
iii. Scope and Coverage 224
c. Institutions and Staff 226
d. Procedures 230
i. Procurement Methods and Procedures 230
ii. Tender Specification, Award Criteria and Evaluation Methods 236
iii. Procurement Planning 238
iv. Contract Administration 239
e. Transparency 239
f. Secondary Objectives 243
g. Review Procedures 245
5. Conclusion 248

Chapter 4: Public Procurement Law in South Africa 251
1. Introduction 251
2. The Framework 254
a. Laws and Policies regarding Public Procurement 254
b. Objectives and Principles 261
i. Merging Procurement and Financial Management 261
ii. Redressing the Imbalances of the Past 262
c. Scope and Coverage 264
3. Institutions and Staff 266
4. Basics of the Supply Chain Management System 271
a. Procurement Methods 271
b. Tender Specifications, Award Criteria and Evaluation Methods 273

i. Uniformity 276
ii. Electronic Procurement 277
5. Transparency and Strategies to Combat Corruption 278
a. Specific Procurement-related Transparency Provisions 278
b. Non-Procurement Specific Regulations 283
6. Secondary Objectives 289
a. The Preferential Procurement Policy Framework Act and Regulations 289
b. Targeted Procurement 293
c. Pros and Cons of the South African Preferential Procurement System 294
d. South African Preferential Procurement in the International Context 304
7. Review Procedures 306
a. Administrative Review 306
b. Non-Judicial External Review 308
c. Judicial Review 310
d. The main Principles of Public Procurement in South African Case Law 317
e. Problems in the South African Public Procurement Review Mechanisms 319
8. Conclusion 321

Chapter 5: Best Practices in Public Procurement 327
1. Introduction 327
2. Best Practices in Public Procurement Legal Systems 330
a. Objectives 330
b. Institutional and Organisational Form 331
c. Workforce 333
d. Scope 334
e. Procedures and Methods 335
i. Procurement Planning 335
ii. Pre-bidding Phase 336
iii. Bidding Phase 339
iv. Award Phase 339
v. Contract Management 340
f. Secondary Objectives 341
g. Transparency 342
h. Review Mechanisms 343
3. Lessons Learned from Mauritius 344
4. Lessons Learned from South Africa 347

PART III: Namibia as a Case Study: Public Procurement Law and Reform 351

Chapter 1: The Namibian Public Procurement Law 353
1. Introduction 353
2. The Framework 355
   a. Laws and Policies regarding Public Procurement on different Levels of Government Structure 355
   b. Public Procurement-related Development Policies in Namibia: Affirmative Action 357
      i. Introduction 357
      ii. Affirmative Action (Employment) Act 359
   c. Objectives and Principles 360
   d. Scope and Coverage 360
   e. Institutions and Staff 368
3. Basics of the Public Procurement system 373
   a. Procurement Methods 373
   b. Procurement Planning and Contract Management 377
   c. Tender Specification, Award Criteria and Evaluation Methods 379
      i. Contents of Tender Documents 379
      ii. Evaluation of Tenders 382
4. Transparency and Strategies to Counteract Corruption 390
   a. Specific Procurement-related Transparency Provisions 390
   b. Non-Procurement specific Regulations 394
5. Secondary Objectives 401
   a. Price Preference Policy 401
   b. Other Socio-Economic Objectives 403
   c. TIPEEG Tenders 406
   d. Interim Conclusion 407
6. Chinese Construction Companies in the Namibian Public Procurement System 409
7. Review Procedures 420
   a. Introduction 420
   b. Administrative Review 420
   c. Non-Judicial External Review 422
   d. Judicial Review 425
8. The main Principles of Public Procurement in Namibian Case Law 427
   a. Procedural Issues 427
   b. The Principle of Legality 430
   c. The Requirement to provide Reasons under Article 18 438

d. CSC Neckartal Dam Joint Venture v The Tender Board of Namibia & Others 439
i. Background 439
ii. The Court Decision 443
e. Interim Interdicts and the Matter of Urgency 445
f. Summary of Case Law 450
g. Interim Conclusion 451
9. Conclusion 453

Chapter 2: Reform of Public Procurement Law 457
1. Introduction 457
2. The Reform 459
a. Reform Drivers 459
b. Reform Hindrances 460
c. The first Steps of a Public Procurement Reform 463
d. Legal Drafting 466
e. Implementation 466
3. Organisational Issues 471
a. Regulated Process vs. Managerial Task 471
b. Decentralised vs. Centralised Approach 472
c. Institutional Capacity 474
d. Human Resources 475
4. Procedures and Methods 477
5. Transparency 479
6. Secondary Objectives 481
a. Inclusion of Secondary Objectives into Public Procurement Law 481
b. Inclusion of Environmental Criteria 484
7. Review Procedures 485
8. Other Important Considerations 487
a. Procurement Planning 487
b. Contract Management 488
c. E-Procurement 488
9. Conclusion 490

Chapter 3: Procurement Reform in Namibia 495
1. Introduction 495
2. The Reform Project 497
a. Outline of the Reform Process 497
b. Reform Drivers 500
c. Stakeholders Involvement 503
d. Influence of International and Foreign Law 504

e. Reform Hindrances 507
3. Essential Aspects and Recommendations for a new Public Procurement Law 510
a. Scope 510
b. Objectives and Principles 512
c. Organisational Issues 513
i. Institutions 513
ii. Human Resources 519
d. Methods and Procedures 521
e. Transparency 523
f. Secondary Objectives 527
g. E-Procurement 530
h. Procurement Planning 532
i. Contract Management 533
j. Review System 534
4. Learning from Mistakes – an Attempt to make the Reform a Success 537
a. Changes with regard to the Scope 538
b. Institutional and Organisational Structure 540
c. Review Mechanisms 542
d. Interim conclusion 543
5. Conclusion 543

Chapter 4: Lessons Learned and Conclusion 549
1. Conclusion 549
2. Lessons Learned 554

References 559

Bibliography 559
List of Legislation 581
Namibia 581
South Africa 582
Mauritius 583
Others 583
List of International Legal Instruments 585
List of Cases 587
Namibia 587
South Africa 588
WTO Disputes 590

Annexes 591

Annex 1: List of Interview Partners 591
Annex 2: List of Sample Questions 593
Annex 3: Essential Aspects of Public Procurement Reform Processes 595

Index 599

# List of Abbreviations

| | |
|---|---|
| ACC | Anti-Corruption Commission |
| BBBEE | Broad-Based Black Economic Empowerment |
| BEE | Black Economic Empowerment |
| BMZ | Federal Ministry of Economic Cooperation and Development (Bundesministerium für wirtschaftliche Zusammenarbeit und Entwicklung) |
| COMESA | Common Market for Eastern and Southern Africa |
| CoP | Code of Procedure |
| CPPN | Commonwealth Public Procurement Network |
| DoW | Department of Works |
| DSU | Dispute Settlement Understanding |
| EEC | Employment Equity Commission |
| EMEs | Exempted Micro Enterprises |
| EPRCP | Enhancing Procurement Reforms and Capacity Project |
| EU | European Union |
| EXIM | Export-Import Bank of China |
| GATS | General Agreement on Trade in Services |
| GATT | General Agreement on Tariffs and Trade |
| GPA | Government Procurement Agreement |
| HDI | Historically Disadvantaged Individual |
| ILO | International Labour Organisation |
| IMF | International Monetary Fund |
| IPPR | Institute for Public Policy Research |
| ITC | International Trade Commission |
| LGSETA | Local Government Sector Education and Training Authority |
| LRDC | Law Reform and Development Commission |
| LTBR | Local Tender Board Regulations |
| MANWU | Metal Allied Namibian Workers' Union |
| MAPS | Methodology for Assessing Procurement Systems |
| MDGs | Millenium Development Goals |
| MFN | Most-Favoured Nation |
| MNE | Multinational Enterprise |
| NGOs | Non-Governmental Organisations |
| NUNW | National Union of Namibian Workers |
| NQF | National Qualifications Framework |

| | |
|---|---|
| OECD/DAC | Organisation for Economic Cooperation and Development / Development Assistance Committee |
| PAIA | Promotion of Access to Information Act |
| PAJA | Promotion of Administrative Justice Act |
| PFMA | Public Finance Management Act |
| PP | Public Procurement |
| PPPFA | Preferential Procurement Policy Framework Act |
| PPRP | Public Procurement Reform Project |
| RDP | Reconstruction and Development Programme |
| RTBR | Regional Tender Board Regulations |
| SADC | Southern African Development Community |
| SCM | Supply Chain Management |
| SMEs | Small and Medium Enterprises |
| SMMEs | Small, Medium and Micro-sized Enterprises |
| SOEs | State-Owned Enterprises |
| SPP | Sustainable Public Procurement |
| TIC | TIPEEG Implementation Committee |
| TIPEEG | Targeted Intervention Programme for Employment and Economic Growth |
| UK | United Kingdom |
| UN | United Nations |
| UNCITRAL | United Nations Commission on International Trade Law |
| UNCTAD | United Nations Commission on Trade and Development |
| UNDP | United Nations Development Programme |
| US | United States |
| WTO | World Trade Organisation |

# Introduction

## *1. Background*

Public procurement spending is estimated to account for 15% of the world's GDP. Whereas most industrialized countries spend around 10% of their GDP on public procurement, developing countries' public procurement spending amounts to a much higher percentage, in some cases up to 70% of GDP.[1] Procurement rules and practices can, therefore, materially impact the domestic economy. Apart from its economic relevance, efficient and effective public sector procurement is essential to ensure socio-economic development as it depends, inter alia, on qualitative service-delivery and infrastructure development, which in turn is also necessary for economic growth. The poor and the vulnerable are especially dependent on the provision of goods and services in the proper quality and quantity through their governments.[2]

Public procurement is a very sensitive issue because it affects both the private and public sectors and involves consolidating and balancing political interests. The contractor has an economic interest in getting a large and prestigious tender award. Especially in certain branches such as the construction sector a company's outlook can depend on winning government contracts for major infrastructure projects. The government, on the other hand, has to make a difficult decision by choosing the best but also lowest bid in order to fulfil its democratic mandate to spend tax money wisely while pursuing governmental policies. In short, it is a business process within a political system concerning national interests. The way this business process works, both in terms of law and actual practice, has significant implications for the integrity, accountability and effectiveness of pub-

---

1 Development Assistance Committee, 'Strengthening Procurement Capacities in Developing Countries - *Harmonising Donor Practices for Effective Aid Delivery*', (Paris: OECD, 2005), p. 18.

2 Cf. S.J. Evenett, 'Is there a Case for New Multilateral Rules on Transparency in Government Procurement?', in S.J. Evenett, *The Singapore Issues and the World Trading System: The Road to Cancun and Beyond* (Switzerland: SECO, 2003), p. 212.

lic procurement.[3] Public procurement should, hence, be understood not only as discipline in its own right but also in the wider context of good governance.[4] It might also be suggested that the state should invest as much as possible of its already limited funds in policies furthering developing goals such as reducing poverty or increasing and improving health and education. In view of the scarcity of resources, well-conceived procurement decisions can indirectly promote development goals.[5]

Considering the amount of public money being spent in the field of public procurement and the vast sums of money wasted through corruption and inefficiencies one can conclude that the improvement of public procurement systems should be an essential element of initiatives to promote good governance. Good governance is important for the success of public procurement, but also vice versa, since public procurement is a key factor in regard to the efficiency and effectiveness requirement of good governance (that "processes and institutions produce results that meet the needs of society while making the best use of resources of their disposal").[6]

The fact that an efficient and effective procurement system can further socio-economic development has also been emphasised by the OECD/DAC Task Force on Procurement, which noted that effective pro-

3 W.A. Wittig, 'Building Value through Public Procurement: A Focus on Africa', conference paper, 9th International Anti-Corruption Conference, Durban, South Africa, 10-15 October 1999, p. 3.

4 The Cusco Declaration of the OECD/DAC Task Force on Procurement recognises that "efficient and effective public procurement is a fundamental component of good governance." OECD/DAC Task Force on Procurement, 'The Cusco Declaration "Strong Procurement Systems for Effective States"', 2011, available at http://www.oecd.org/dac/effectiveness/48425963.pdf; last accessed: 1 December 2015.

5 Cf. B.C. Basheka, 'Public Procurement Reforms in Africa: A Tool for Effective Governance of the Public Sector and Poverty Reduction', in K.V. Thai, *International Handbook of Public Procurement* (Boca Raton, Florida: Taylor & Francis Group, 2009), p. 133ff; S.J. Evenett; B.M. Hoekman, 'International Cooperation and the Reform of Public Procurement Policies', (World Bank: 2005), p. 4 (available at http://elibrary.worldbank.org/doi/abs/10.1596/1813-9450-3720; last accessed: 26 November 2015).

6 Website of United Nations Economic and Social Commission for Asia and the Pacific, 'What is Good Governance?', http://www.unescap.org/pdd/prs/Project Activities/Ongoing/gg/governance.asp (last accessed: 12 October 2012).

curement systems are a key part of development.[7] Most donor countries, including Germany, actively promote and thereby expedite good governance and the achievement of the above-mentioned development goals – all of which are part of the Millennium Development Goals (MDGs).[8] Public procurement law can therefore be an impetus to achieving these objectives, but can also be an impediment if it is deficient by nature or insufficiently implemented. The creation of an efficient and effective system within the framework of reform is thus in the interest of the donor countries as well as the whole international community that is dedicated to the achievement of the MDGs.

In developing countries, the reform of public procurement law is of particular importance. First because the percentage of the GDP spent on public procurement is often much higher than in developed countries, an efficient and effective public procurement system can be expected to have a significant impact on socio-economic development. Second, the sophistication of the general legal framework and the effectiveness of the implementation of laws in most developing countries differ considerably from that in most western states, and this particularly applies to sub-Saharan African countries, including Namibia. Not only is public procurement law itself very complex, it is also influenced by several other fields of law, which are often not yet well-regulated or at least not effectively implemented in developing countries. The result is that reforming public procurement law poses an exceptional challenge for developing countries.

## *2. Problem Statement*

Increasing discontent in regard to public procurement procedures in Namibia has led to a reform of public procurement law being initiated.[9] Ma-

7 The Second Meeting of the OECD/DAC Task Force on Procurement - Summary of meeting by the UN Procurement Capacity Development Centre, Cusco, Peru, 4th-6th May 2011.

8 United Nations General Assembly, 'United Nations Millennium Declaration ', A/55/L.2 (New York: United Nations, 2000).

9 Corruption Watch Namibia, 'Tender Board swamped by exemptions, reform urgently needed' (Corruption Watch Namibia: 2011), available at http://www.corruption-watch-namibia.com/tender-board.html; last accessed: 3 October 2012; 'Runter von Verliererspur' (Newspaper article), Allgemeine Zeitung (Windhoek, Namibia), 13 September 2011; F. Links; C. Daniels, 'The Tender Board - Need for Root and Branch Reform', Anti-Corruption Research

jor concerns have been the frequent use of exceptions to public infrastructure tender and the granting of tender awards to Chinese companies.[10] Retroactive rectifications of costs, the importation of Chinese employees, and poor working conditions which violate the Namibian labour law, amongst other issues, have led to criticism of tender awards to Chinese companies.[11]

According to the Permanent Secretary of the Tender Board of Namibia, key factors in the reform process are transparency and 'Namibianisation', which refers to the intention to enact a law favouring Namibian over foreign companies in the award process.[12] The introduction of a 51% Namibian ownership criterion for certain tenders has also been suggested.[13]

Although the reform has been ongoing for more than 10 years, [14] it has not led to a satisfying outcome. Different drafts have been shared with research institutions and other stakeholders and it was promised that the bill would be due for approval in 2012.[15] This date was subsequently postponed to 2013.[16] A public procurement bill tabled in parliament in Sep-

---

Programme, Paper 3 (Institute for Public Policy Research: 2011), available at http://www.az.com.na/fileadmin/pdf/2011/az/IPPR-09-12-11.pdf; last accessed: 29 November 2015; 'Tender law needs urgent rewrite' (Newspaper article), Namibian Sun (Windhoek, Namibia), 12 September 2011.

10 Corruption Watch Namibia; Links; Daniels, p. 9,12.

11 'Hat Namibia seine Chancen genutzt? Eine Bilanz (Teil 4a/5)' (Newspaper article), Allgemeine Zeitung (Windhoek, Namibia), 13 April 2012; G. Henrich; V. Truong, 'Das Ende der "Charme-Offensive"? - Der Widerstand kleiner Länder in Südostasien und Afrika gegen die Hegemonialherrschaft Chinas ', (IMS Internationales Magazin für Sicherheit), available at http://www.ims-magazin.de /index.php?p=artikel&id=1330677610,1,gastautor; last accessed: 3 October 2012; H. Jauch, 'Chinese Investments in Africa - Twenty-First Century Colonialism?' (2011) 20(2) New Labor Forum, 49-55 at 52; 'Tender Board tightens rules to protect jobs' (Newspaper article), The Namibian (Windhoek, Namibia), 3 February 2010.

12 F. Links; C. Daniels, 'The Tender Board - Need for Root and Branch Reform; Appendix I - Interview with Tender Board Secretary Welma Enssle', (Institute for Public Policy Research: 2011), available at http://www.az.com.na/fileadmin/pdf/2011/az/IPPR-09-12-11.pdf; last accessed: 29 November 2015.

13 Ibid, 20.

14 Links; Daniels, 'The Tender Board - Need for Root and Branch Reform', p. 1.

15 'Minister lays into Tender Board' (Newspaper article), The Namibian (Windhoek, Namibia), 26 April 2013.

16 'Parlament startet ins Jahresfinale' (Newspaper article), Allgemeine Zeitung (Windhoek, Namibia), 18 September 2012.

tember 2013 was withdrawn after heavy criticism[17] and be re-tabled only in 2015. The 2015 bill was passed in November of the same year and only awaited assent by the president at the time of the finalisation of this dissertation.[18] Reasons for this lengthy reform process seem manifold, including for example a lack of political will.

This dissertation will analyse the tender law in Namibia, putting special emphasis on transparency issues, secondary objectives and protectionist policies, using the WTO Government Procurement Agreement (GPA)[19], the UNCITRAL Model Law,[20] and the South African public procurement legislation as standards for comparison. As it is not intended to provide a comprehensive comparative study of the above mentioned procurement systems not all provisions will be analysed in detail. Rather, the focus will be on key issues that may be helpful for designing public procurement legislation in Namibia with view to sustainable development. Moreover, the reform process itself will be analysed by identifying reform drivers and hindrances, responsibilities in the reform process, external influences and methodologies used in the reform approach. Given that the reasons for the delays and other shortcomings of the reform process might offer an insight into issues that have to be considered in order to carry out a successful and timely reform, the Namibian reform proceedings are critically analysed in the context of best practices recommendations. The lessons learned from the Namibian case study are not only important for other reform projects but also for the general discussion on procurement law.

The reasons for choosing Namibia as case study are manifold. Namibia is classified as one of the most advanced African countries in terms of

17 'Bill Makes Finance Minister 'Too Powerful'' (Newspaper article), The Namibian (Windhoek, Namibia), 24 September 2013; 'Procurement Bill Sparks Heated Debate' (Newspaper article), The New Era (Windhoek, Namibia), 3 October 2013.

18 'Auf das neue Gesetz vorbereiten' (Newspaper article), Allgemeine Zeitung (Windhoek, Namibia), 12 November 2015; 'Six Bills passed' (Newspaper article), The Namibian (Windhoek, Namibia), 17 November 2015. According to Article 56 (1) of the Namibian Constitution, every bill passed by parliament requires the assent of the president in order to acquire the status of an act of parliament.

19 The GPA is a plurilateral WTO agreement that came into force on 1 January 1996. A revised version was adopted in 2012.

20 The United Nations Commission of International Trade Law has adopted the Model Law on Procurement of Goods, Construction and Services in 1994. The primary objectives are to assist reforms and foster harmonization. A revised version was adopted in 2011.

democracy and the rule of law. The 2013 Ibrahim Index of African Governance ranks Namibia 6th of 52 African countries surveyed.[21] The ranking is composed of four different elements: safety and rule of law, participation and human rights, sustainable economic opportunity, and human development.[22] The rule of law and accountability are particularly important in this context. Namibia scored 82.1 out of 100 for the rule of law and 68.1 for accountability[23] and was ranked 4th in both sub-categories.[24] Namibia's democracy is relatively stable, as is confirmed by the 2014 Bertelsmann Transformation Index.[25] In the category political transformation Namibia scores 8.5 out of 10 for stateness,[26] 8,8 for political participation, 7.3 for the rule of law, 7.5 for the stability of democratic institutions and 6.8 for political and social integration, resulting in an overall score of 7.75.[27] Apart from political transformation which is composed only of the sub-categories just mentioned, the index measures economic transformation, meaning the status of a state as a market economy including not only aspects such as economic performance, regulatory or competition policy and property rights but also elements of social justice, such as social safety nets, equality of opportunity and sustainability (6.29).[28] The status index rating is thus 6.99 whereby Namibia ranks 32nd of 128 development and transformation countries studied. In relation to other African countries Namibia is ranked 5th, surpassed only by Mauritius, Botswana,

---

21 Mo Ibrahim Foundation, '2013 Ibrahim Index of African Governance - Summary', (Mo Ibrahim Foundation: 2013), available at http://www.afcgn.org/wp-content/uploads/2013/11/Ibrahim-Index-of-African-Governance-2013.pdf; last accessed: 30 November 2015.

22 Ibid, 3.

23 Ibid, 20.

24 Ibid.

25 See Website of Bertelsmann Foundation, 'Transformationsindex BTI 2014 - Status-Index', http://www.bti-project.de/index/status-index/ (last accessed: 6 September 2015).

26 The study defines "stateness" in reference to the state's monopoly on the use of force and basic administrative structures. See Website of Bertelsmann Foundation, 'Transformation Index BTI 2014 - Methodology', http://www.bti-project.org/index/methodology/ (last accessed: 6 September 2015).

27 Ibid. For a detailed discussion of the Namibian results see Bertelsmann Foundation, 'BTI 2014 - Namibian Country Report' (Gütersloh: Bertelsmann Foundation 2014).

28 Website of Bertelsmann Foundation, 'Transformation Index BTI 2014 - Methodology', http://www.bti-project.org/index/methodology/ (last accessed: 6 September 2015).

Ghana and South Africa. This democratic stability, comparatively good standard of the rule of law and acceptable market economy conditions are essential elements for successfully reforming public procurement law without having to consider other basic good governance or rule of law factors that might influence public procurement.

The analysis of the process leading to the enactment of a new law is one of the main pillars of this dissertation. When conducting the main research for this dissertation, Namibia has initiated a reform but not yet enacted the regulatory framework. Therefore, the timing seems particularly appropriate for this research project. The Namibian discussion can be factored into considerations deriving from the theoretical and comparative analysis. Furthermore, as the enactment of a new public procurement law is envisaged for the near future, its particular elements can be compared with the conclusions drawn from this assessment, providing for a control instrument and opportunities for further research.

'Namibianisation' is a particularly sensitive issue in Namibia and therefore deserves special focus. The inclusion of secondary objectives is a highly controversial issue; but as the objective to reduce the disparities of wealth resulting from colonialism and especially apartheid seems of specific importance in this context, this discussion has become a hot button issue. Although Namibia is not a party to the GPA it is important to note that certain protectionist public procurement policies might violate the General Agreement on Tariffs and Trade (GATT), the General Agreement on Trade in Services (GATS) which are applicable to Namibia as a WTO member state and/or bilateral trade agreements Namibia has signed and ratified. The promotion of socio-economic objectives through public procurement is controversial but many developing countries suffering from stark socio-economic disparities, widespread poverty, unemployment and other socio-economic problems regard public procurement as an opportunity to tackle such problems. The Namibian example might produce lessons in regard to the effectiveness and the possible embodiment of secondary objectives. If pursuing certain secondary objectives is found to be useful in achieving the larger objectives, certain factors important in regard to their application might be identified that can be transferred to projects in other developing countries.

The Namibian reform is not only relevant locally but also for its trading partners. Moreover, it is very important for the general objective of promoting development in Namibia. Germany, for example, has a significant interest in the successful outcome of Namibia's public procurement reform: although Germany is not directly involved in the project, it is deeply committed to promoting socio-economic development. A successful outcome would therefore be in line with Germany's general efforts and confirm its approach to achieving these objectives.

Germany has been an important donor country for Namibia and Namibia is the largest recipient of development aid from Germany in Africa. Since independence, Germany has given Namibia about N$8 billion within the framework of development cooperation.[29] In November 2013, Germany made a commitment to provide about N$2 billion (€147.5 million) for 2014 and 2015.[30] Thematically, the development cooperation between Germany and Namibia addresses three core issues: management of natural resources, sustainable economic development, and transport.[31] For the latter two fields an efficient and effective Namibian public procurement law is of particular relevance. As an aspect of the promotion of sustainable economic development Germany puts special emphasis on the inclusion of private industry[32] because the participation of small and medium-sized enterprises (SMEs) in tenders for public contracts can be an important aspect for development. This can, however, only be ensured if the public procurement system is transparent, fair and accountable. Because the expansion of the transportation infrastructure primarily occurs through public procurement, the efficiency and effectiveness of the public procurement system has a strong impact on the success of infrastructure development. Although the awarding of tenders that are financed by external donors is often governed by special conditions, insufficient procurement practices would thwart the aim of improving infrastructure. The third core area of German-Namibian development cooperation, the management of natural resources, can be influenced by public procurement. The introduction of ecological criteria into procurement criteria, as for example practiced by the European Union,[33] might induce contractors and service providers -

29 Website of Auswärtiges Amt, 'Beziehungen zu Deutschland', http://www.auswaertiges-amt.de/sid_A3C9729CE456796974FEB3D235FE39C8/DE/Aussenpolitik/Laender/Laenderinfos/Namibia/Bilateral_node.html#doc352362bodyText3 (last accessed: 16 April 2014).

30 Ibid.

31 Website of BMZ, 'Namibia - Situation und Zusammenarbeit', http://www.bmz.de/de/was_wir_machen/laender_regionen/subsahara/namibia/zusammenarbeit.html (last accessed: 26 September 2015).

32 Ibid.

33 In 2008 of the European Commission recommended the setting of common criteria for green public procurement in the EU member states and has since then developed more than 20 common criteria. See Communication from the Commis-

and in the wider sense consumers and service recipients – to pay increased attention to environmental and ecological aspects.

Beyond the three key aspects of the German-Namibian development cooperation, the German Federal Ministry of Economic Cooperation and Development (BMZ)[34] is providing assistance to Namibia to overcome social divisions.[35] In particular, Namibia faces the problem of having a predominant white elite and a new black middle class, on the one hand, while the majority of population lives in poverty,[36] on the other. The question of whether the inclusion of secondary objectives in public procurement policy to redress this situation by redistribution through the award of tenders is of general relevant importance in this context and clearly will have implications for German development policy. The reform of public procurement law in Namibia is thus a matter of consequence for the prospects of success of the German development policy goals.

Apart from the specific importance of an efficient and effective public procurement system for the achievement of the German development policy goals, its relevance for the wider goals of good governance and the achievement of the MDGs has to be stressed. An efficient and effective public procurement system is an essential part of good governance and, in particular, of a government's ability to manage resources; it is a key factor for responsible administration and the provision and protection of public goods and services for all members of society.[37] Moreover, governance is only effective and efficient if, among other things, processes and institu-

---

sion to the European Parliament, the Council, the European Economic and Social Committee and the Committee of the Regions Public procurement for a better environment, COM/2008/0400 final and the information on the website of the European Commission: http://ec.europa.eu/environment/gpp/gpp_criteria_en .htm (last accessed: 10 November 2015).

34 Bundesministerium für wirtschaftliche Zusammenarbeit und Entwicklung.

35 Website of BMZ, http://www.bmz.de/de/was_wir_machen/laender_regionen/sub sahara/namibia/zusammenarbeit.html (last accessed: 26 September 2015).

36 For a comprehensive discussion of poverty in Namibia see H. Jauch, 'Poverty, Unemployment and Inequality in Namibia, TEMTI Series of Economic Perspectives on Global Sustainability, EP 02-2013', (Theme On The Environment, Macroeconomics, Trade And Investment (TEMTI) / International Union for the Conservation of Nature (IUCN) / Commission on Environmental, Economic and Social Policies (CEESP): 2012), available at https://cmsdata.iucn. org/.../temti_ep_02_2013.pdf; last accessed: 26th November 2015.

37 Cf. A. Bösl, 'Good Governance als Paradigma moderner Entwicklungspolitik - *Bad Governance und schwierige Partnerschaften: Herausforderungen des 21. Jahrhunderts*' (2007) 2/07 KAS-Auslandsinformationen, 6-34 at 17-18.

tions produce results that meet needs while making the best use of resources.[38] An insufficient public procurement system severely hinders the achievement of these results. As with general efforts to improve good governance, in public procurement transparency, efficiency and effectiveness, responsiveness, forward visions, and rule of law belong to the basic elements that need to be addressed.[39] Hence, there is an interaction between the objective of good governance and the provision of an effective and efficient public procurement system. Furthermore, effective procurement systems are a key part of development.[40] On the one hand, a best possible deployment of resources for public procurement ensures that tax money is not wasted and is available to be spent directly on socio-economic development and, hence, for the achievement of the MDGs. On the other hand, a well-functioning public procurement system is important for guaranteeing that goods and services are delivered in the proper quality and quantity, ensuring infrastructure development and stimulating trade and economy, which are in turn necessary preconditions for socio-economic development. In the broader sense, it can therefore be said that the reform of public procurement law in developing countries is essential for the promotion of good governance and the achievement of the MDGs.

### *3. Literature Review*

The recognition of the importance of an effective and efficient public procurement system has only developed in the past two or three decades and

---

38 UNDP, 'Good governance - and sustainable human development', Governance for sustainable human development, a UNDP policy document (UNDP: 2014), p. 2, available at https://www.google.de/url?sa=t&rct=j&q=&esrc=s&source=web&cd=2&ved=0CC4QFjABahUKEwiLseG64eLHAhXJDiwKHf7FALo&url=http%3A%2F%2Fwww.undp.org%2Fcontent%2Fdam%2Fundp%2Flibrary%2FDemocratic%2520Governance%2FDiscussion-Paper--Governance-for-Sustainable-Development.pdf&usg=AFQjCNEvOh06Nurz-Fh77G0ue_Njz4gvSQ&bvm=bv.102022582,d.bGg&cad=rja; last accessed: 6 September 2015.

39 Cf. Website of OECD Directorate for Public Governance and Territorial Development, 'Principal elements of good governance', http://www.oecd.org/gov/principalelementsofgoodgovernance.htm (last accessed: 12 October 2012).

40 The Second Meeting of the OECD/DAC Task Force on Procurement - Summary of meeting by the UN Procurement Capacity Development Centre, Cusco, Peru, 4th-6th May 2011: 2.

has influenced and stimulated research, government strategies and reform initiatives alike. Public procurement was long regarded as an administrative function and has been paid little attention by most countries.[41] Beyond that it has long been a neglected area of academic research[42] and only gained attention in the recent decades.[43] Since the early 1990s this attitude has changed and the field of public procurement attracted notice by government, public interest groups, international financial institutions and international organisations[44] and has also significantly increased calls for research to investigate, analyse and develop guidance for practice.[45] The growing complexity of public procurement, which, inter alia, arises from increasing globalization of trade and investment, the pressure to cut costs in times of scarce resources and calls for better transparency and accountability might have also been conducive to the increasing interest for public procurement.[46] The World Bank and other development banks, e.g., have assisted developing countries with evaluations of their national public procurement systems and have supported reform processes. Moreover, in the past two decades, several academic conferences regarding public procurement have taken place. Of particular relevance is the "International Public Procurement Conference", which has taken place every two years since 2004 and has brought together academics and researchers from all over the world. These conferences have not only been an important forum for exchanging research findings and experiences from all over the world,

---

41 Wittig, 'Building Value through Public Procurement', p. 4.

42 K.V. Thai, 'Public Procurement Re-Examined' (2001) 1(1) Journal of Public Procurement, 9-50 at 10., see also L. Knight; et al., 'Public Procurement: An Introduction', in L. Knight; et al., *Public Procurement: International cases and commentary* (London and New York: Routledge, 2007 ), p. 1.

43 G. Quinot; S. Arrowsmith, 'Introduction ', in G. Quinot; S. Arrowsmith, *Public Procurement Regulation in Africa* (Cambridge et al.: Cambridge University Press, 2013), p. 1.; see also Knight; et al., 'Public Procurement: An Introduction', p. 1.

44 K.V. Thai, 'International Public Procurement: Concepts and Practices', in K.V. Thai, *International Handbook of Public Procurement* (Boca Raton, Florida: Taylor & Francis Group, 2009), p. 2.

45 Knight; et al., 'Public Procurement: An Introduction', p. 1.

46 Basheka, 'Public Procurement Reforms in Africa', p. 133; N. Caldwell; E. Bakker, 'Procurement Process in the Public Sector: An International Perspective', in K.V. Thai, *International Handbook of Public Procurement* (Boca Raton, Florida: Taylor & Francis Group, 2009), p. 428; Thai, 'International Public Procurement', p. 2.

but have also stimulated research by highlighting the importance of public procurement and the lack of research in this respect.

A number of journal articles has been published in the meantime. Relevant journals in this field of study are the Journal of Public Procurement[47] and Public Procurement Law Review[48], which focus on the legal and policy aspects of public procurement. Most articles deal with one important component of public procurement law, such as transparency or secondary objectives. Several scholars in the field stand out for their extensive contributions in terms of the scope and quality of their research, including Sue Arrowsmith (Nottingham University), John McCrudden (Michigan University), Khi V. Thai (Florida Atlantic University), Louise Knight, Christine Harland (both University of Bath), Jan Telgen (Twente University) and in South Africa Phoebe Bolton und Geo Quinot (both Stellenbosch University). A range of books has been published, which deal with public procurement law in general, going beyond national and regional regulations.[49] There is plenty of literature on the public procurement regulations of the EU, the US and South Africa, but literature analysing the national public procurement legal system of other countries is rare. Only few comprehensive theoretical studies have been conducted[50]on public procure-

47 Editor-in-Chief: Khi V. Thai, Florida Atlantic University; Publisher: PrAcademics Press; first published in 2001.

48 General Editors: Sue Arrowsmith; Adrian Brown; Steen Treumer; Publisher: Sweet & Maxwell; first published in 1992.

49 S. Arrowsmith; R.D. Anderson, 'The WTO Regime on Government Procurement: Challenge and Reform', (Cambridge: Cambridge University Press, 2011); S. Arrowsmith; et al., 'The Regulation of Public Procurement: National and International Perspectives', (Deventer: Kluwer Law International, 2000); J.-C. Gaedtke, 'Politische Auftragsvergabe und Welthandelsrecht', Tübinger Schriften zum internationalen und europäischen Recht - Band 81 (Berlin: Duncker & Humboldt, 2006); C. McCrudden, 'Buying Social Justice - *Equality, Government Procurement, and Legal Change*', (New York: Oxford University Press, 2007); K.V. Thai, 'International Handbook of Public Procurement', (New York: CRC Press, Taylor and Francis Group, 2008); P. Trepte, 'Regulating Procurement: Understanding the Ends and Means of Public Procurement Regulation', (Oxford: Oxford University Press, 2004).

50 In Africa, for example, only the public procurement systems in Ghana and South Africa have been analysed in detail: P. Bolton, 'The Law of Government Procurement in South Africa', (South Africa: Lexis Nexis Butterworths, 2007); D.N. Dagbanja, 'The Law of Public Procurement in Ghana: Law, Policy and Practice', (Germany: LAP LAMBERT Academic Publishing 2011). English-speaking literature covering the public procurement systems of other developing countries has not been found.

ment systems in developing countries and research findings that are based on experiences in developing countries are correspondingly limited.[51] The Namibian system has so far not been analysed in detail and there has been little research into public procurement in Namibia. The literature is limited to one book article of a university professor[52] and reports by the Institute for Public Policy Research (IPPR).[53]

Regarding general literature on public procurement law, the book "The Regulation of Public Procurement: National and International Perspectives" (2000)[54] by S. Arrowsmith, J. Linarelli and D. Wallace is noteworthy. The authors explain how the public procurement process should be managed in order to achieve its objectives in today's global market economy. Reference is made to the whole international system influencing public procurement as strategic economic force, including national regula-

---

51 See e.g. E. Agaba; N. Shipman, 'Public Procurement in Developing Countries: The Ugandan Experience', in G. Piga; K.V. Thai, *Advancing Public Procurement: Practices, Innovation and Knowledge-Sharing* (Boca Raton, US: PrAcademics Press, 2007); R.G. Mamiro, 'Value for Money, the Limping Pillar in Public Procurement - Experience from Tanzania', conference paper, 4th International Conference on Public Procurement, Seoul, South Korea, August 26-28, 2010; V. Mosoti, 'Reforming the Laws on Public Procurement in the Developing World: The Example of Kenya' (2005) 54 International and Comparative Law Quarterly, 621-650; C.K. Sabiiti; E. Muhumuza, 'Second Generation Procurement. Moving from compliance to results in public procurement. Trends, challenges and opportunities from the Uganda experience', conference paper, 5th International Public Procurement Conference, Seattle, Washington, 15-17 August 2012; D.P.R. Teixera, 'The Brazilian Experience of Using Pubic Procurement Policies to Promote the Development of Micro and Small Enterprises from the Legal Point of View', conference paper, 4th International Public Procurement Conference, Seoul, South Korea, August 26-28, 2010.

52 S.K. Amoo; S. Dicken, 'The regulatory framework for public procurement in Namibia', in G. Quinot;S. Arrowsmith, *Public Procurement Regulations in Africa* (Cambridge et al.: Cambridge University Press, 2013).

53 G. Hopwood, 'Comments on the Public Procurement Bill - September 2012', (Windhoek: Institute for Public Policy Research, 2012); Links; Daniels, 'The Tender Board - Need for Root and Branch Reform'; E. Tjirera, 'Public Procurement in Namibia - *The Role of Codes of Conduct in Reducing Corruption*', Anti-Corruption Research Programme, Paper 4 (Windhoek: Institute for Public Policy Research, 2011); F. Links, 'The Public Procurement Bill: A lot of Good some significant Bad, but certainly not Ugly'; Democracy Report, Special Briefing Report No. 9 (Windhoek: Institute for Public Policy Research, 2015).

54 Arrowsmith; et al., 'Regulation of Public Procurement'.

tions, trade agreements and international organisations. The authors focus on the differences between the public procurement practices in industrial, developing and transition countries with respect to both the legal and regulatory framework as well as the actual practice.

The book "Public Procurement – International cases and commentary" (2007),[55] which resulted from the International Research Study on Public Procurement presents case studies of public procurement from different countries but also includes editorial commentary and contextualizing chapters to enable the reader to understand the complex topic of public procurement. The book provides an opportunity to learn from the experiences and lessons of reform initiatives in other countries and other sectors.

Several articles on methods and practices of public procurement, e-procurement and public procurement as a conceptual framework as well as different case studies were contributed to the "International Handbook of Public Procurement" (2008),[56] which was edited by K. Thai.

"Regulating Procurement: Understanding the Ends and Means of Public Procurement Regulation" (2004)[57] by P. Trepte provides a general introduction to the subject, showing why procurement is regulated at all. It considers national, regional as well as international systems of regulation and uses an international and comparative perspective.

The book "Buying Social Justice - Equality, Government Procurement, and Legal Change" (2007)[58] by C. McCrudden provides an overview of the legal basis of pursuing social policies in public procurement. It considers the effect of globalization on achieving social justice by referring to regional and international economic integration through the EC (now the EU) and the WTO and includes a comparative perspective of policies pursued and results achieved in the US, UK, Northern Ireland and South Africa.

The WTO regime on public procurement is dealt with in different books and articles. J. C. Gaedtke, in his book "Politische Auftragsvergabe und Welthandelsrecht" (2006),[59] for example, analyses the latitude given to governments to pursue political objectives in public procurement under the WTO, and in particular the GPA. And "The WTO Regime on Gov-

55 L. Knight; et al. (Eds.), 'Public Procurement: International cases and commentary' (London and New York: Routledge, 2007).
56 Thai, 'International Handbook of Public Procurement'.
57 Trepte, 'Regulating Procurement'.
58 McCrudden, 'Buying Social Justice'.
59 Gaedtke, 'Politische Auftragsvergabe und Welthandelsrecht'.

ernment Procurement: Challenge and Reform" (2011),[60] edited by S. Arrowsmith and R.D. Anderson, contains several articles regarding the development and the future prospects of the GPA, including issues relating to pending accessions, changes in the revised GPA text of 2006 as well as emerging issues such as secondary objectives and the implications of the economic crisis.

There is plenty of literature on EU public procurement regulation.[61] However, public procurement (law) has not yet become a recognised field of study in most African countries,[62] with the exception of South Africa. Research and training programmes in Africa are rare and there are many African states where you cannot find any published study on the domestic public procurement regulatory system.[63] The literature on public procure-

---

60 Arrowsmith; Anderson, 'WTO Regime on Government Procurement'.

61 See e.g. S. Arrowsmith, 'The Law of Public and Utilities Procurement ', Volume 1: Regulation in the EU and the UK (London: Sweet & Maxwell, 2014), 3rd Edition; C.H. Bovis, 'EU Public Procurement Law', (Cheltenham and Northampton Edward Elgar Publishing Ltd., 2013), 2nd Edition; A.N. Erridge, R., 'Public Procurement, Competition and Partnership' (1994) 1(3) European Journal of Purchasing and Supply Management, 169-179; European Commission, 'Modernising European public procurement to support growth and employment', (European Commission: 2011), available at http://europa.eu/rapid/pressReleases Action.do?reference=IP/11/1580&format=HTML&aged=0&language=EN&guiL anguage=en; last accessed: 18 December 2015; J. Koch; M. Kullas, 'EU-Grünbuch - Öffentliches Auftragswesen', (Centrum für Europäische Politik: 2011), available at http://www.cep.eu/Analysen_KOM/KOM_2011_15_OEffen tliches_Auftragswesen/cepAnalyse_KOM_2011_15_OEffentliches_Auftragswes en.pdf; last accessed: 3 October 2012; K. Odendahl, 'Die Berücksichtigung vergabefremder Kriterien im öffentlichen Auftragswesen - *Rechtslage nach EG- und WTO-Recht* ' (2004) 21 Europäische Zeitschrift für Wirtschaftsrecht, 647-653; A. Palmujoki; et al., 'Green Public Procurement: Analysis on the Use of Environmental Criteria in Contracts' (2010) 19(2) Review of European Community & International Environmental Law, 250-262.

62 There are so far only books dealing with the national public procurement systems of Ghana and South Africa: Dagbanja, 'The Law of Public Procurement in Ghana'; Bolton, 'The Law of Government Procurement in South Africa'; G. Quinot, 'State Commercial Activity - *A Legal Framework*', (Claremont: Juta & Co, 2009). Book or journal articles about national African public procurement systems include e.g. Agaba; Shipman, 'Public Procurement in Developing Countries'; B.C. Basheka, 'Procurement Planning and Accountability of Local Government Procurement Systems in Developing Countries: Evidence from Uganda' (2008) 8(3) Journal of Public Procurement, 379-406; Mosoti, 'Reforming the Laws on Public Procurement in the Developing World'.

63 Quinot; Arrowsmith, 'Introduction ', p. 5.

ment in South Africa is of specific relevance for this study. Of particular importance is P. Bolton's "The Law of Government Procurement in South Africa" (2007)[64] which provides a comprehensive analysis of the law of the South African public procurement system. The first book providing a broad overview of several sub-Saharan African national public procurement systems is "Public Procurement Regulation in Africa" (2013)[65] which has resulted from a three-year collaboration of the Universities of Nottingham and Stellenbosch under the British Academy's UK-Africa Academic Partnerships scheme. The project's objective was an analysis of the current state of public procurement regulation in Africa. Quinot and Arrowsmith, two of the leading researchers in the area of public procurement law, have collected nine country studies from Africa, providing doctrinal legal analysis of those countries public procurement systems. Namibia is one of the countries that have been analysed. The book also includes articles on the role of donors in regard to African procurement systems, procurement methods, supplier remedies, corruption and the promotion of social policy in public procurement in the African context. "Public procurement regulation in Africa" provides a comprehensive introduction to sub-Saharan public procurement systems and discusses critical public procurement issues from a comparative point of view. Due to the lack of existing research with respect to African legal systems and the importance of public procurement, the book is an excellent starting point for academic research and debate.

To sum up, there has been plenty of research in the field of public procurement in the past two decades, resulting in an increasing amount of publications. This illustrates both the actual need for research as well as research interest. The constant development and advancement of public procurement law, which is still at its infancy, requires further study on a continuous basis. The focus of research so far has mainly been on the EU public procurement regulations, the international regime on public procurement and the South African procurement regulations. The public procurement regulations in other sub-Saharan African developing countries, such as Namibia, have still not been analysed in detail. The same applies to research on reform processes in the public procurement sector in this geographical area.

---

64 Bolton, 'The Law of Government Procurement in South Africa'.

65 G. Quinot; S. Arrowsmith (Eds.), 'Public Procurement Regulations in Africa ' (Cambridge et al.: Cambridge University Press, 2013).

This study can make an important contribution to existing research by identifying lessons learned from the Namibian experience. Apart from a theoretical analysis of the Namibian public procurement system, important results are derived from field research conducted in Namibia exposing such shortcomings as the ineffective implementation of laws or institutional and organisational defects. This makes it possible to identify specific issues that are of particular importance in developing countries' public procurement systems and that need particular consideration in view of the local context. Moreover, it is the first time a public procurement reform process per se is analysed. This is particularly important since the way a reform is actually carried out is decisive for the later success of the new system. Although many reform initiatives in developing countries have indeed yielded modern and up-to-date public procurement legislation, inadequate implementation has led to public procurement remaining ineffective and inefficient. The lessons learned from Namibia can make a valuable contribution to avoiding reforms from continuing to be carried out without regard for aspects important to the successful implementation of the new system. The Namibian case study can provide a guide to future reform initiatives in other developing countries by developing recommendations based on lessons learned from the Namibian experience. As will be seen below, the Namibian experience provides insight into some essential issues that have to be addressed in developing countries' public procurement systems and the conditions that should be adhered to in order to carry out a successful reform process.

## *4. Research Methodology*

### a. General Remarks

This dissertation uses a comparative approach in order to develop certain best practices and to identify provisions or approaches in international or national public procurement regulations that might be suitable in the Namibian context. The instrument of comparative law can provide helpful clues for reform projects. However, the strengths and weaknesses of a legal system can often only be identified in practice, meaning that studying the actual implementation is essential. References to existing legal norms and practices in other countries with similar conditions or to international norms, which have been implemented, can lead to meaningful and field-tested reform proposals or recommendations.[66] As Lando notes, "legal science has no laboratories, some societies may also serve as testing grounds for experiments in law reform".[67] Comparably, existing laws in other countries can reveal tendencies of success and failure of reform legislation. The success of using of legal transplants – a term introduced by Alan Watson in 1974[68] – cannot be generalized, but varies according to the area or areas of the law concerned and the influence of policy on the respective area of law.[69] In respect of public procurement law, a certain soft power to introduce international best practices can be identified. As Trepte notes, "the similarities in the different regulated systems may suggest some form of universality in the concepts applied in procurement regulation."[70] Certainly, the WTO Government Procurement Agreement (GPA)[71] has not been signed by most of the developing countries, but the UNCITRAL Model Law,[72] the influence of the OECD and the World Bank in respect to public procurement reform and the on-going debate on the international level have a significant impact on public procurement reforms all over the world.

Furthermore, there are certain components of public procurement, where efficiency very clearly demands a certain solution.[73] This includes in particular transparency regulations or the use of open bidding as a general method of tendering. Vice versa, in view to the frequent use of the UNCITRAL Model Law in African reforms, legal transplantation in this area does not seem to be very far-fetched. Additionally, it is important to remark that, as a relatively new field of law, there is the opportunity to

66 Cf. K. Zweigert; H. Kötz, 'An Introduction to Comparative Law', (Oxford et al.: Oxford University Press, 1998), 3rd Edition, p. 15-17.

67 O. Lando, 'The Contribution of Comparative Law to Law Reform by International Organziations' (1977) 25(4) American Journal of Comparative Law, 641-657 at 645.

68 A. Watson, 'Legal Transplants - *An approach to Comparative Law*', (Edinburgh: Scottish Academic Press Ltd., 1974), p. 21ff.

69 Cf. U. Mattei, 'Efficiency in Legal Transplants: An Essay in Comparative Law and Economics' (1994) 14 International Review of Law and Economics, 3-19 at 7.

70 Trepte, 'Regulating Procurement', p. 40.

71 WTO Agreement on Government Procurement, 1994, (signed in Marrakesh on 15 April 1994 and entered into force on 1 January 1996).

72 UNCITRAL Model Law on Public Procurement, 2011, (adopted on 1 July 2011).

73 Cf. Mattei, 'Efficiency in Legal Transplants', 16.

harmonize public procurement law right from the beginning. Many African countries have based their public procurement law on the UNCITRAL Model Law and international best practices;[74] the World Bank has influenced many reform projects.[75] This has led to systems that have a lot in common. Furthermore, the recognition that most public procurement laws have been inefficient in the past not only in developing but also in developed countries lowers the resistance of countries to changing old structures. In contrast to other areas of law such as family law, public procurement is not deeply rooted in society and does not represent a hard-won consensus of the proper balance of essential issues that has evolved throughout a nation's history. The new discovery of public procurement as an important field of government and society allows law-makers to find new solutions that, however, need to be adapted to the local context. The international instruments which have been developed by developed and developing countries alike are far more promising in providing a basis for reform. Nevertheless, it might be worth looking at how countries with similar conditions and problems have modified international best practices in order to suit the local context. These reasons disclose that, in general, a comparative approach can be of great benefit in the field of public procurement law and reform.

Nevertheless, it has to be kept in mind that public procurement law is deeply embedded in the administrative structure. There are several fields of law that have an impact on public procurement, especially state financial regulations, anti-corruption laws, labour rights, etc. A new bill has to

---

74 It has served as basis for legislative texts or inspired legislation in 29 countries so far (For the current status see: Website of UNCITRAL, 'Status - UNCITRAL Model Law on Procurement of Goods, Construction and Services (1994)',http://www.uncitral.org/uncitral/en/uncitral_texts/procurement_infrastructure/1994Model_status.html (last accessed: 6 September 2015). Moreover, many countries have used the UNCITRAL Model Law as guideline for their reforms without notifying the UNCITRAL Secretariat. See E. Caborn; S. Arrowsmith, 'Procurement methods in the public procurement systems of Africa', in G. Quinot; S. Arrowsmith, *Public Procurement Regulation in Africa* (Cambridge et al.: Cambridge University Press, 2013), p. 265.

75 The World Bank has developed instruments and guidelines for improving the public procurement systems of its borrower countries (see Website of World Bank, 'Public Procurement', http://web.worldbank.org/WBSITE/EXTERNAL/PROJECTS/PROCUREMENT/0,,contentMDK:20109646~pagePK:84269~piPK:60001558~theSitePK:84266,00.html (last accessed: 6 September 2015)). See also Caborn; Arrowsmith, 'Procurement methods in the public procurement systems of Africa', p. 268f.

have due regard for these systems in order to have the potential to produce a satisfying outcome. Furthermore, it is important to ensure that the approach to regulating procurement is "[…] consistent with the enacting states' legal and administrative tradition, so that the procurement system operates under a cohesive body of law."[76]

Certain elements of procurement can be adapted more easily than others. Basic transparency requirements and common bidding procedures such as open or selective bidding can, for example, be integrated into most public procurement systems with only minor modification to the local context, whereas e.g. innovative bidding procedures requiring experienced staff able to take qualified decisions are not suitable in all contexts, as such staff is not available in all public procurement systems. The same applies to the establishment of control mechanisms where it can be of great advantage to make use of existing structures that have proven to work effectively rather than establishing new institutions after a foreign model. It is of the utmost importance to always consider the factual constraints facing a public procurement system rather than to simply consider it abstractly as being solely a piece of legislation. Apart from the legislative and regulatory framework of public procurement, the broader national framework, management capacity, organisational structure and the workforce available are important issues in all public procurement systems. Important aspects such as the availability of capacity and resources in order for institutions to function effectively or access to review mechanisms such as to the courts play a decisive role for the successful implementation of public procurement legislation. Moreover, the socio-economic situation prevailing in a national context and its correlation with the national public procurement system should be analysed and considered in order to establish a public procurement system that promotes socio-economic development in the best possible way.

Although certain standards should be reflected in all public procurement systems, the question of how to implement them should be discussed in view of the local context and be embedded into the local structures in order to work efficiently; otherwise the result might be provisions that will never be fully enforced in practice. It can, hence, be said that there is no blueprint approach. Rather, adapting international best practices and other rules and regulations requires a full understanding and consideration of the

---

76 UNCITRAL, 'Guide to Enactment of the UNCITRAL Model Law on Public Procurement', (New York: United Nations, 2012), p. 18, para. 61.

domestic context as well as a clear idea what objectives or rationales are to be pursued.[77] This dissertation, hence, aims to consider the Namibian context as a whole, meaning the public procurement system as embedded in its specific legal, social and economic environment, rather than examining only the legal system.

On the international level, there is an intense debate about public procurement which, amongst other things, concerns the GPA and the UNCITRAL Model Law. The former is of particular importance because a further globalization of public procurement law might also cause Namibia to seek GPA accession in the long run. Considering this scenario it could be beneficial to design a procurement law that adheres to the basic GPA requirements. The GPA was signed in 1994 and came into force in 1996. It has 19 parties covering 47 WTO member states, but not been signed by any African country yet.[78] One question that can be posed is in how far developing countries align their procurement laws with the GPA, inter alia, in order to keep the possibility to join the GPA open without having to redraft their procurement law.

The UNCITRAL Model Law can be seen as another instrument revealing tendencies in international public procurement law; it could provide guidance on public procurement law reform. The Model Law was adopted in 1994 and has the purpose of providing a model for domestic legal reform. It has so far notably influenced 30 states, of which 11 are African countries.[79] It therefore seems to make sense - within the context of the Namibian reform project - to examine the relevant provisions of the Model Law.

When considering influences on public procurement reforms, it is indispensable to refer to the United Nations Convention against Corruption (UNCAC)[80] which contains an article on public procurement requiring its parties to enact measures to prevent corruption in public procurement sys-

---

77 Cf. Trepte, 'Regulating Procurement', p. 40.

78 Website of the WTO, 'Agreement on Government Procurement - Parties, observers and accessions', https://www.wto.org/english/tratop_e/gproc_e/memobs_e.htm (last accessed: 20 December 2016).

79 For further information see the UNCITRAL website: http://www.uncitral.org/uncitral/en/uncitral_texts/procurement_infrastructure/1994Model_status.html (last accessed: 10. November 2015).

80 United Nations Convention against Corruption, 2003 (adopted by the General Assembly by resolution 58/4 of 31 October 2003 and entered into force on 14 December 2005).

tems. The Convention has entered into force in December 2005 and been signed by 140 states.[81] Article 9 read together with Article 65 of UNCAC is binding for all its parties; hence all states that are party to the convention have to ensure that their public procurement systems suffice the requirements of Article 9 and are required to implement adequate measures into their national legal systems.

As the requirements for public procurement systems listed in Article 9 remain vague, additional sources must be consulted for interpretation with view to their implementation on the national level. The United Nations Office on Drugs and Crime (UNODC) which is responsible for overseeing the implementation of the convention[82] has published a guidebook on anti-corruption in public procurement.[83] The information in this guidebook can assist UNCAC member states to implement measures necessary to comply with Article 9. Other instruments referred to in this dissertation, such as by Transparency International or the OECD but also the UNCITRAL Model Law, can be consulted, too.

Globally, the discussion about public procurement law has gone in the direction of following neoliberal trading policies promoting open markets and free trade. It is envisaged to open national procurements to foreign investors and provide more transparent procedures rather than keeping public procurement as internal national matters of the state.[84] This liberal approach is opposed to the protectionist view many developing countries prefer. It is, hence, important to keep in mind Namibia's economic position and its willingness to open its procurement market when testing the suitability of international best practices that have developed under neoliberal policies to liberalize public procurement markets. The divergence

81 See the Website of UNODC 'United Nations Convention against Corruption Signature and Ratification Status as of 12 December 2016', http://www.unodc.org/unodc/en/treaties/CAC/signatories.html (last accessed: 20 December 2016).

82 United Nations Office on Drugs and Crime, 'Reporting on Corruption – A Resource Tool for Governments and Journalists' (New York: United Nations, 2014), p. iii.

83 United Nations Office on Drugs and Crime, 'Guidebook on anti-corruption in public procurement and the management of public finances - *Good practices in ensuring compliance with Article 9 of the United Nations Convention against Corruption*', (Vienna: United Nations in collabaration with the International Anti-Corruption Academy, 2013).

84 R.H. García, 'Introduction: the global challenges of international public procurement', in R.H. García, *International Public Procurement* (London: Lobe Business Publishing Ltd., 2009), p. 10.

between countries that have a competitive advantage in capital and service exports and countries that do not have this advantage is striking, the former following a neoliberal procurement policy and the latter trying to protect their domestic industries and further socio-economic policy goals. This clash of interests has impeded an internationalisation of procurement rules and could be compared to the internationalisation of trade rules, which have, however, so far proved more successful. In view of the efforts to globalize public procurement, the Namibian case study might offer clear indications of what influences states to include protectionist measures.

Reform efforts can be observed in all parts of the world. The EU, for instance, enacted two directives on public procurement in 2004[85] which were repealed in 2014 by two other directives.[86] Moreover, the EU is currently working on additional rules to make public procurement more efficient and enable governments to use procurement to a certain extent as a policy tool.[87] The inclusion of social and ecological criteria in the procurement process has been partly recognised by EU case law.[88] Another example for a regional reform effort, this time in Africa, can be observed within the Common Market for Eastern and Southern Africa (COMESA). It led to the revision of several of its member states' procurement laws on the basis of the UNCITRAL Model Law.[89]

---

85 Directive 2004/17/EC (coordinating the procurement procedures of entities operating in the water, energy, transport and postal services sectors), 2004; Directive 2004/18/EC (on the coordination of procedures for the award of public works contracts, public supply contracts and public service contracts), 2004.

86 Directive 2014/24/EU (on public procurement and repealing Directive 2004/18/EC), 2014; Directive 2014/25/EU (on procurement by entities operating in the water, energy, transport and postal services sectors and repealing Directive 2004/17/EC), 2014.

87 Commission of the European Communities, 'Communication from the Commission to the European Parliament, The Council, The European Economic and Social Committee and the Committee of the Regions: Public procurement for a better environment, COM(2008) 400 final', (Commission of the European Communities: 2008), available at http://eur-lex.europa.eu/legal-content/EN/TXT/PDF/?uri=CELEX:52008DC0400&from=EN; last accessed: 30 November 2015; European Commission; see also Koch; Kullas.

88 Gaedtke, 'Politische Auftragsvergabe und Welthandelsrecht', p. 80f; Odendahl, 'Die Berücksichtigung vergabefremder Kriterien im öffentlichen Auftragswesen', 650.

89 See e.g. S. Karangizi, 'Regional Procurement Reform Initiative', (Dar es Salaam: COMESA, 2003); M. Mampuzhasseril; et al., 'COMESA Public Procurement

A very progressive law in regard to the use of public procurement as a policy tool can be found in South Africa. In the Namibian case a comparative analysis with South Africa is particularly suitable as the shared history and similar conditions have led to requirements that are similar. Furthermore, from a pragmatic perspective public procurement is not solely a national issue since cross-border procurement might be essential for ensuring competition and value for money. In the course of reform it may be worth considering harmonizing public procurement legislation with a view to achieving those objectives: in the long run, harmonizing laws (especially between neighbouring countries) may stimulate competition and thus lead to greater efficiency and effectiveness in public procurement. In South Africa, the explicit policy objectives of public procurement are codified in Article 217 of the Constitution as well as other laws referring to public procurement. Shortly after it achieved independence South Africa has been in the process of substantially reforming its procurement law.

### b. Field Research in Namibia

A field research project in Namibia which forms an essential part of this research project was conducted in February/March 2013. Interviews were conducted with stakeholders in public procurement.[90] The study also examined case-law and media coverage of public procurement in Namibia. Twenty interviews were conducted in Windhoek and Swakopmund with different stakeholders in public procurement.[91] The interviewees were asked a wide range of questions about the then currently applicable procurement legislation and its implementation as well as the reform pro-

Reform and Capacity Building Projects: Project Performance Evaluation Report' (Place: Operations Evaluation Department (African Development Bank Group), 2012).

90 A list of interviews is stated in Annex 1.

91 The stakeholders interviewed include academics and researchers, lawyers and advocates, the director of the German Konrad-Adenauer foundation, a director of a Namibian construction company, a manager of a South African construction company, an architect who is an expert for public procurement infrastructure projects, a member of the Local Tender Board of Khomas Region, staff members of the Tender Board, alternate members of the Tender Board, the General Secretary of the Metal and Allied Namibian Workers Union, and the Namibian Ombudsman.

gress.[92] The interviews were carried out in order to identify problems, strengthens and weaknesses of the public procurement system in force at that time. Questions regarding public procurement procedures, organisational and institutional issues, transparency standards and review mechanisms were asked to expose discrepancies between law and practice and to understand the extent of detrimental effects of shortcomings in public procurement legislation on the achievement of public procurement objectives. With respect to the reform process in Namibia, questions regarding the general approach, reform planning, objectives, responsibilities and involvement of stakeholders were asked to expose hindrances to and drivers of reform as well as shortcomings in the way the reform was addressed. Whereas the ombudsman, lawyers, academics and researcher as well as members from the business community promptly responded to requests for an interview, interviews with the Secretary of the Tender Board, the Minister of Finance or other government officials were not possible, as requests for an appointment by email made far in advance of the journey were not answered. Moreover, in Namibia it was not possible to get through to the senior officials either by phone or in person. Promises by secretaries or clerks to phone back to arrange a meeting were not kept in several instances. The same applies to representatives of Chinese construction companies, who denied any request for an interview. The interviews conducted with staff and alternate members of the Tender Board were organized after a formal request was made to the Secretary of the Board. Regrettably, no interview with a permanent member could be arranged. It can be concluded that no government official was willing to support the research project by providing information on the Namibian public procurement system and reform. Nevertheless, the interviews conducted provided substantial insights into public procurement practices, exposing shortcomings, hindrances and weaknesses, but also strengths of the public procurement system. Hence, this field project yielded a broad picture against which background a qualitative analysis of the national public procurement system could be conducted.

92 For a list of sample questions see Annex 2.

## 5. General Outline

Part I provides a broad overview and understanding of public procurement in general and of ways of regulating public procurement. It entails the importance, development and impact of public procurement. Thereafter, the features of public procurement systems and their regulation are presented to form a theoretical basis. Challenges and critical issues in procurement regulations and policy are identified for further research. Key factors that dominate discussions about public procurement are transparency and secondary objectives. As corruption is a major concern in developing and industrialized countries alike, there is an extensive discussion about how to create more transparent systems. Fundamental elements of a transparent procurement system and essential criteria that can prevent corruption will be discussed in order to establish an overview of critical issues that should be considered in general and especially during the reform process.

Another widely discussed matter is the latitude for pursuing secondary objectives provided by public procurement legislation. Secondary objectives can be distinguished from the primary objective of purchasing goods or services, in that collateral goals pursue socio-economic or environmental policies. Examples include mandates to purchase environmentally-friendly products or the preferential treatment of certain types of businesses to promote their economic activity. Whereas certain policy-goals, such as the inclusion of environmental criteria, are widely accepted as legitimate, the pursuit of other policies and the effect on the efficiency and effectiveness is very controversial. Scholars from various disciplines have addressed this topic with conflicting results. The major issues and views shall be presented and discussed in detail.

A discussion of the gap between liberal and protectionist views is then taken up. Since the liberal position is often attributed to the western states and it would seem biased to simply adopt this approach, both positions shall be presented and discussed.

Part II comprises an overview of the GPA and the UNCITRAL Model Law, the COMESA public procurement directives and regulations as well as the Mauritian and the South African procurement system. These different public procurement systems are analysed by outlining the basic objectives and principles, scope and coverage, procurement methods and procedures, tender specifications, award criteria and evaluation methods, the organisational structure, transparency, secondary objectives and review procedures. This systematic pattern is followed in all three chapters of this part and will also be used to analyse the Namibian public procurement system in Part III.

The GPA has only a limited membership and basically follows the liberal policy of the Washington Consensus.[93] The obligations of the GPA will be presented and critically assessed in order to identify those provisions that could be followed or adopted in Namibia. Additionally, an attempt to explain why countries like Namibia have not become a party to the GPA will be made. In regard to globalization and the wider harmonization of trade rules, an alignment of procurement rules might be essential to guarantee integration into the global trade order.

Whereas the GPA has not yet had an appreciable influence on public procurement systems in Africa, the UNCITRAL Model Law has been taken as a basis for reform in many African countries. Its strong influence has led to a certain degree of harmonization and one cannot get around considering the Model Law during the reform process. In its reform process, Namibia took a closer look at the Mauritian public procurement law which had been reformed under the COMESA public procurement reform. The latter had issued a directive and regulations that were based on the UNCITRAL Model Law. This means that the UNCITRAL Model Law had an indirect influence on the Namibian public procurement draft legislation. The COMESA approach as well as the Mauritian public procurement regulations will therefore also be dealt with briefly.

The procurement system of South Africa deserves special attention in the context of Namibian procurement reform. On the one hand, South Africa's procurement legislation seems quite sophisticated, especially in regard to secondary objectives. On the other hand, the shared history and experience of apartheid has resulted in similar initial situations and has provoked similar problems and obstacles that need to be considered when regulating public procurement.

93 The term "Washington Consensus" was coined in 1989 by John Williamson. It described a list of ten policies where the author found a consensus between the US and International Financial Institutions (IFIs) with respect to Latin American economic policy. The list includes, inter alia, trade liberalisation, liberalisation of interest rates, liberalisation of inward foreign direct investment, and deregulation. The term "Washington Consensus" has been frequently used as a synonym for neo-liberalisation and market fundamentalism. J. Williamson, 'The strange history of the Washington consensus' (2004) 27(2) Journal of Post Keynesian Economics, 195-206 at 195, 196, 201.

Part II concludes with a chapter on the main findings and results of the comparative analysis. After explaining the potential benefits of considering international and foreign public procurement provisions, best practices in public procurement as well as lessons learned from the Mauritian and the South African public procurement systems are presented.

Part III deals with the Namibian procurement system and reform. First of all, the existing law and practices in Namibia are described and analysed according to the same pattern as in Part II. This section will identify and highlight strengths and weaknesses by comparing the Namibian situation with international best practices. Thereafter, critical aspects of public procurement reforms in general will be outlined and practical and strategical recommendations for the implementation of public procurement reforms will be made. This part in turn forms the basis for assessing the Namibian reform efforts. Finally, the Namibian reform process will be outlined and examined.

The analysis of the Namibian public procurement system and its reform is presented in the context of interrelated issues, such as those pursued by secondary policies. These include for example affirmative action and anti-corruption initiatives. Such issues and policies have important effects on the functioning of a procurement system. Practical considerations are drawn from extensive field research in Namibia. As mentioned above, a number of interviews conducted with officials, business people, lawyers, NGOs and research institutes try to give insight into procurement practices in general as well as in the construction sector in particular, and to identify strengths and weaknesses as well as opportunities for improvement. The construction sector is of special importance because infrastructure development is an essential component for socio-economic development. Furthermore, construction includes high-value purchases and represents an essential part of government-spending. It is suspected that corruption is higher in construction than in other economic sector.[94] Moreover, the complexity of such projects as well as the variety of actors/professions involved illustrates many of the challenges and obstacles public procurement potentially faces.

94 N. Stansbury, 'Exposing the foundations of corruption in construction', in T. International, *Global Corruption Report - special focus: Corruption in Construction and Post-Conflict Reconstruction* (Berlin: Transparency International, 2005), p. 36.

In Part IV, the results of the research and the Namibian case study are presented. Recommendations in regard to basic considerations and elements of public procurement regulatory systems that might have a positive effect on the efficiency and the effectiveness of public procurement and socio-economic development in the wider sense are presented. Lessons learned from the Namibian case study are then outlined and lead to the identification of best practices for public procurement reform processes and initiatives.

# PART I: The Nature and the Regulation of Public Procurement

The nature of public procurement systems is anything but straightforward and its regulation is therefore very complex. Several matters influencing public procurement processes must be taken into account. In order to provide a broad overview serving as a theoretical basis for Parts II and III, the nature of public procurement and its regulation are explained. After public procurement has been defined, general principles which should form the basis of any public procurement system are outlined. The first chapter provides an overview of procurement methods, organisational structure and workforce (the latter meaning public procurement officials and staff) as well as review procedures which need to be regulated by law. Basic requirements that are essential in public procurement systems in this respect and their rationales will be discussed in order to provide a general guideline for the analysis of the international and national procurement regulations in Part II. In this respect, not only legal but also economic aspects are considered in order to provide a basis to understand the wider relevance and impact of public procurement. An isolated consideration of legal provisions would not reflect the nature of public procurement, which can only function effectively if the underlying economic reasoning is considered. In Chapter 2 transparency as well as the problem of corruption in public procurement is discussed. Several procurement-specific provisions and general measures that can foster transparency and counteract corruption are identified. The use of secondary objectives in public procurement and the different types of objectives are presented in Chapter 3. Furthermore, benefits and difficulties in pursuing secondary objectives through public procurement as well as the resistance of developing countries to opening their public procurement markets to international competitors are discussed. This part ends with a summary of findings.

## *Chapter 1: The Nature of Public Procurement and its general Regulation*

### 1. Introduction

Public procurement can be defined as the provision of goods and services or awarding work assignments by a state body, organisation, institution or some other legal person regarded as a procuring entity.[95] The scope of government procurement may vary, depending on which procuring entities and which types of procurement contracts are covered. State-owned enterprises (SOEs), for example, are in some countries covered by public procurement legislation whereas in other countries, they are not subject to the national public procurement system but can apply their own procurement strategies and methods. The contractual means usually include methods such as purchase or lease, rental or hire purchase but might also cover other means such as concessions.[96] The extent to what types of contractual means fall under the national public procurement system varies in each jurisdiction. It is, hence, important to consider the scope of public procurement legislation in order to assess the coverage of public procurement systems.

The rationale behind the special importance of an effective public procurement system is the "raison d'être (reasons for existence) of government institutions, which is to achieve, maintain, and enhance the general welfare of society"[97]. Public procurement operates at the interface of a commercial activity and its public function; both have to be balanced in order to guarantee a successful outcome. Key interrelated aspects that govern public procurement systems are value for money, efficiency and effectiveness, transparency, competition, fairness and equality, integrity and accountability. The validity of these principles is widely recognised as being verified by experience and are repeatedly referred to in public procurement legislation.[98]

---

95 See for example Public Procurement Law (Republic of Serbia) 2006 (Official Gazette of the Republic of Serbia, No. 39/02, 43/03, 55/04 and 101/05).

96 Cf. S. Arrowsmith, 'Government Procurement in the WTO ', (The Hague: Kluwer Law International, 2003), p. 100ff.

97 K. Raga; J.D. Taylor, 'Legislative and Administrative Directives governing Procurement Procedures: A Case Study for South Africa', conference paper, 4th International Public Procurement Conference, Seoul, South Korea, August 26-28, 2010.

98 Trepte, 'Regulating Procurement', p. 3f.

The importance of an efficient and effective public procurement system can be attributed to the fact that it accounts for a noteworthy proportion of most countries' GDP, as has been mentioned above. Additionally, the size and volume of government procurement contracts not only affects the market of goods and services but also the budget spending of governments, which are accountable to the public. The multitude of internal and external forces affecting the implementation of public procurement procedures is enormous. Internal factors include interactions between various elements of the system, types of goods and services required, competence of the workforce, staffing levels and budget resources, the organisational structure (such as the issue of centralisation vs. decentralisation), regulations, rules and guidance, and internal controls as well as legislative oversight.[99] External factors comprise the market environment, the legal environment, the political environment as well as social, economic and other environmental forces.[100] An additional factor influencing public procurement is certainly the variety of stakeholders involved, with the government, the procuring entity or entities, the business sector as potential or actual supplier, public interest groups and the wider public having an (often differing) interest in the process and the outcome of public procurement.[101] Moreover, procurement reality, where "imperfectly informed procurers purchase from imperfectly competitive firms on behalf of imperfectly informed tax-payers", makes it hard to design rules which would be perfectly suitable for all situations.[102] These factors exemplify the complexity of the public procurement process and can only indicate the intricacy involved in designing and implementing an efficient and effective procurement (legal) system that serves all policy objectives envisaged.

## 2. Principles of Public Procurement

Value for money can be seen as the overarching principle in public procurement systems. This principle is expressed by the requirements of effi-

99 K.V. Thai, 'Challenges in Public Procurement', in K.V. Thai; et al., *Challenges in Public Procurement: An International Perspective* (Boca Raton, FL, USA: PrAcademics Press, 2004).

100 Ibid.

101 Raga; Taylor.

102 A. Mattoo, 'The Government Procurement Agreement: Implications of Economic Theory' (1996) 19(6) World Economy, 695-720 at 717f.

ciency and effectiveness. It can be defined as "obtaining the best possible balance between price and quality in meeting the customer's requirements".[103] However, in order to achieve the best result not only the final price but the life-time and associated costs have to be considered. This implies a thorough understanding of costs and benefits and environmental impacts.[104] Apart from price reduction, which is probably the most obvious example of better value for money, a greater quantity or quality for the same cost or improved delivery or performance reflect efficiency and effectiveness.[105] Efficiency also implies that the procurement procedure should reflect the value and complexity of the goods or services to be procured.[106] In other words, these principles require that procurement "[...] is carried out without unnecessary or disproportionate delay or waste of resources."[107] Major construction projects, for example, require more time and complex rules than small value purchases. It is much easier to prepare and evaluate bids for small value purchases that do not involve complex technical aspects, such as office stationery. Bid requirements can be easily determined and can be confined to the essentials such price, quantity and design. Comprehensive research and understanding of the matter is not required by the official responsible for carrying out procurement in order to achieve a successful outcome. Moreover, open bidding procedures might not be appropriate as the costs of submitting and evaluating a large number of tenders might be disproportionate to any benefits of open bidding and the objectives achieved thereby, such as competition and value for money.[108] Hence, more simple procurement procedures, as selective tendering, might be more convenient. In contrast, the award of major con-

---

103 A. Korkmaz, 'Benefits and Obstacles of Environmental Social and Sustainable Procurement', conference paper, 4th International Public Procurement Conference, Seoul, South Korea, August 26-28, 2010.

104 Report by the Comptroller and Auditor General, 'Addressing the environmental impacts of government procurement', HC 420 Session 2008-2009 (London: National Audit Office, 2009), p. 7.

105 Erridge, 'Public Procurement, Competition and Partnership', 172.

106 J. Pope, 'Confronting Corruption: The Elements of a National Integrity System, TI Source Book 2000', (Berlin/London: Transparency International, 2000), p. 206.

107 S. Arrowsmith, 'Public Procurement: Basic Concepts and the Coverage of Procurement Rules', in S. Arrowsmith, *Public Procurement Regulation: An Introduction* (Nottingham: EU Asia Inter University Network for Teaching and Research in Public Procurement, 2010), p. 19f.

108 Cf. ibid, 20.

struction projects requires the preparation of higher and more detailed bid requirements according to the planned project details; such projects require higher skills and understanding on the part of public procurement staff and more time for the preparation and evaluation of bids. In addition to the complexity of such projects, the higher amounts of money spent justify increased procurement costs and longer timeframes; the higher degree of competition and transparency required for such projects can only be guaranteed by open bidding procedures.[109]

Transparency is a major issue in public procurement discussion and reform not only because the public has a special interest in the best possible allocation of public money and public officers are accountable for what they do, but also because a lack of transparency potentially undermines the other principles of public procurement, such as non-discrimination, fairness, competition, value for money, etc. and, thereby, might render the procurement process ineffective and inefficient. For example, transparent procedures lower the risk for potential bidders as they can better estimate the probability of success, which is a necessary prerequisite for the attraction of investment.[110] Moreover, transparency is a key priority in addressing corruption, which is a major problem within procurement systems all over the world.

Accountability means ensuring that "the objectives and rules of the procurement system can be monitored and enforced".[111] Holding government officials and procurement agents accountable for their decisions and actions is a very important transparency mechanism in public procurement.

Competition is necessary to achieve best value for money, because it allows for improvements in price, quality, innovation, and execution from the bidder's side. The aim is to encourage as many qualified firms as possible to compete for the tender, which is an essential precondition for attaining value for money.

Fairness aims at ensuring a level playing field and requires an open and equal information policy in regard to all potential bidders.[112] Equal treat-

109 Cf. Pope, 'Confronting Corruption', p. 206f.

110 Wittig, 'Building Value through Public Procurement', p. 6.

111 Arrowsmith, 'Public Procurement', p. 11.

112 OECD, 'Integrity in Public Procurement - Good Practice from A to Z', (Paris: OECD, 2007), p. 29; J.J.D. Read, 'The Road to Hell is paved with Good Intentions', conference paper, 4th International Public Procurement Conference, Seoul, South Korea, August 26-28, 2010, p. 12.

ment in the procurement contexts means the non-discriminatory application of procedures.

Integrity implies the avoidance of conflicts of interest and corruption in public procurement.[113]Any form of corruption is detrimental to the efficiency and effectiveness of public procurement and might have a negative effect on competition, fairness and equity and hence value for money. Corruption is a major problem in public procurement systems in developed and developing countries alike, which will be discussed in detail in Chapter 2 of this part.

### 3. Pillars of Public Procurement Systems

According to the Methodology for Assessing Public Procurement Systems developed by the OECD, public procurement systems are built on four pillars: (1) the legislative and regulatory framework, (2) the institutional architecture meaning the national framework and management capacity, (3) procurement operations and market practices, and (4) the integrity of the procurement system.[114] One must
keep in mind that each pillar needs to function effectively and efficiently in order to facilitate a successful public procurement system that delivers on the key aims, e.g. value for money, transparency, competition, fairness and equity. This requires high quality public governance in terms of transparency and accountability in combination with effective management that can deliver optimum risk management and value-for-money outcomes.[115] According to Hunja,

> "[...] a strong and well-functioning procurement system would be one that is governed by a clear legal framework establishing the rules for transparency, efficien-

113 Arrowsmith, 'Public Procurement', p. 8; see also J. Telgen; et al., 'Public Procurement in perspective', in L. Knight; et al., *Public Procurement: International cases and commentary* (London and New York: Routledge, 2007), p. 17.

114 These elements and several sub-indicators are suggested by the OECD to analyse public procurement systems. OECD, 'Methodology for Assessing Procurement Systems (MAPS)', (Paris: OECD, 2009).

115 P.R. Schapper; et al., 'An Analytic Framework for the Management and Reform of Public Procurement' (2006) 6(1&3) Journal of Public Procurement, 1-26 at 4.

> cy and mechanisms of enforcement, coupled with an institutional arrangement that ensures consistency in overall policy formulation and implementation"[116]

Furthermore, it is essential to have "[...] a professional cadre of staff that implements and manages the procurement function."[117] As mentioned above, a public procurement system cannot be analysed solely by reference to the legislative framework. Rather, other important aspects influencing public procurement systems have to be considered. An isolated consideration of the pillars of public procurement systems would neglect the complex nature of public procurement systems. As all pillars are interrelated only a holistic approach considering all pillars and their interaction can be successful.

## 4. Stages of Public Procurement Procedures

The public procurement procedure can be roughly divided into five stages:[118] procurement planning, the pre-bidding phase, the bidding phase, the selection or award phase and contract management.[119]

Whereas the preparation of bidding documents commences the actual procurement process, the basis for procurement is often set far earlier with the planning of the budget allocated for public procurement at the beginning of the financial year. Including provisions requiring procuring entities and bodies to outline procurements in advance might contribute to achieving the public procurement objectives. Publishing annual public procurement plans at the beginning of each financial year, for example, fosters transparency and enables potential bidders and suppliers to plan their economic activities accordingly. This increases competition and value for money. Additionally, public knowledge about planned procurements well in advance sets a level playing field by providing ample opportunity to participate as not all companies have permanent staff that is re-

116 R.R. Hunja, 'Obstacles to Public Procurement Reform in Developing Countries', in S. Arrowsmith;M. Trybus, *Public Procurement : The Continuing Revolution* (The Hague, The Netherlands: Kluwer Law International, 2003), p. 2.

117 Ibid, 2.

118 Arrowsmith divides the procurement procedure into only three phases: procurement planning, placement of the contract, and contract management. Arrowsmith, 'Public Procurement', p. 1.

119 See for a more detailed description of the procurement process: Caldwell; Bakker, 'Procurement Process in the Public Sector'.

sponsible for and possesses sufficient experience in bid preparation and might need to allocate staff to prepare a bid. Last but not least, it can stimulate innovation and research in specific areas.

In the pre-bidding phase the procuring entity makes a needs-assessment, considers financial arrangements, determines the method of acquisition, chooses the procurement procedure and prepares the bidding documents which include the establishment of criteria according to which the bids will be evaluated.[120] After the tender and the relevant criteria have been published, potential bidders can prepare and tender their bids. In the selection or award phase the bids are evaluated and compared to identify the best bidder in regard to value for money for the award of the tender. After the contract with the award-winning bidder is concluded, effective implementation has to be ensured through monitoring and evaluation mechanisms.[121] Contract management is, hence the final stage of the procurement procedure. Today it is recognised that the public procurement process does not end with the conclusion of the contract but that contract implementation has to be monitored.[122] Problems that may arise in the course of performing the contract, e.g. breaches of contract or non-contractual quality, not only need to be sanctioned but also kept in mind for future bids of the contractor or supplier. Without adequate contract management, there is, for example, the danger that winning tenderers which have handed in the lowest bid later raise their prices or deliver poor quality, which certainly does not meet the objective of value for money.[123] This is also a major reason why the process should be described as a procurement cycle rather than a procurement procedure. Lessons learned should be fed back into the system.

Many current public procurement regulations deal only with the procedures governing the placement of contracts,[124] whereas the phases of pro-

120 Ibid, 429f.

121 Ibid, 435f.

122 See e.g. UNCITRAL, 'Guide to Enactment of the UNCITRAL Model Law on Public Procurement', p. 25, paras. 83 and 85.

123 Cf. ibid, 25, para. 85; see also SIGMA, 'Public Procurement Brief 22: Contract Management, Support for Improvement in Governance and Management - A joint initiative of the OECD and the EU', 2011, p. 2 (available at www.sigmaweb.org/publications/49102599.pdf; last accessed: 29 November 2015).

124 The UNCITRAL Model Law does not include provisions on contract management but it has been emphasized in the Guide that "[t]he enacting State will need to ensure that adequate laws and structures are available to deal with these phases of the procurement process: if they are not in place, the objectives of the Model

curement planning and contract management are not specifically regulated or are regulated in other laws.[125] Nevertheless, the current opaqueness and inefficiency of public procurement systems occurs not only in the bidding, selection and award phase, but already arises in the planning or pre-bidding phase as well as in the contract management or post-bidding phase. This challenges law-makers to widen the scope of public procurement regulation by including detailed provisions on procurement planning and contract management in the statutes and regulations in order to provide a comprehensive body of rules governing the entire procurement cycle.

## 5. Procurement Methods

There are different types of tender procedures for several scenarios. The number, type, value and availability of goods or services procured are main indicators for the decision about what method is used.[126] The procurement of stationery for government offices, for example, differs significantly from the procurement of military equipment due to considerations such as political relevance and confidentiality issues. Generally, open and competitive bidding is the most common and recommended purchasing method. All bidders that meet the tender criteria can file a tender and objective award criteria are used to determine the best bid. This allows a high standard of contestability.[127] Open bidding can also be carried out in two stages. This is often used in highly technical or complex procurements

> "[...] where technically unequal proposals are likely to be encountered or where the purchaser is aware of its options in the market but for a given set of perfor-

---

Law may be frustrated." UNCITRAL, 'Guide to Enactment of the UNCITRAL Model Law on Public Procurement', p. 25, para. 83. Mauritius is one example that has implemented provisions on contract management in its primary public procurement legislation.

125 However, many countries have introduced certain safeguards such as prohibitions of alterations or modifications of contracts. Cf. Arrowsmith, 'Government Procurement in the WTO ', p. 106.

126 Cf. Trepte, 'Regulating Procurement', p. 123. The author notes the following: "Procurement regulation will almost always include provision for the use of varying procedures depending on the value of the contract such that small value contracts will not be seen as justifying the higher implementation costs of employing the open bidding procedures."

127 Ibid, 270.

mance requirements there are two or more equally acceptable technical solutions available."[128]

At the first stage only technical bids without prices are submitted, followed by an evaluation of these bids and discussions and negotiations between the procuring entity and the bidders. Based on the amendments and modifications agreed during the discussions, the bidders are then invited to submit price proposals.[129]

Selective, limited, or restricted procurement procedures predetermine a group of companies that can take part in bidding or provide for the request of quotations from a number of potential suppliers or contractors. This limits competition but might save costs and time. It is usually applied for low-value purchases or in market sectors where only a limited number of suppliers or contractors exist. Another procurement procedure is single source or direct procurement, whereby the procuring entity negotiates the terms and conditions directly with one or more suppliers or contractors. In this negotiated procedures the contractual requirements are open and are, then, negotiated with specific bidders. Negotiation procedures, whether in course of direct procurement or in general after a tender has been awarded, are seen critical, because they might lead to a deficit of accountability and are more difficult to monitor and evaluate. On the other hand, they might increase the possibility of reaching a better value for money outcome,[130] as bids can be improved in consultations with respect to the particular needs of the procuring entity. Such procedures provide the opportunity to adjust the bid proposal to the requirements by reducing unnecessary costs and improving important key factors.

Public procurement systems usually include a general procurement method, favourably open bidding, and different exceptional procedures.[131] Exceptions should, however, be well-defined and only be applied in justified circumstances. In some procurement systems monetary thresholds are applied in determining which procedure should be used.[132] Many public procurement systems set a monetary threshold above which only open and competitive bidding is allowed. Alternative methods can only be applied for low-value contracts and if pre-determined criteria are met in order to

128 Ibid, 97.
129 Cf. Ibid, 97.
130 Erridge, 'Public Procurement, Competition and Partnership'.
131 Namibia is one of the countries not explicitly providing for such classification.
132 Trepte, 'Regulating Procurement', p. 289.

prevent its arbitrary use. Usually, apart from the estimated value of the contract, specific circumstances which make open bidding impractical or impossible justify derogating from the open bidding procedure.[133] This might for example include the procurement of security-related goods or services that require a certain degree of confidentiality and thus can only be procured by using an alternative procurement method.

It is also possible to require prequalification of tenderers, meaning the undertaking of a qualification procedure at the start of an award procedure before tenders are submitted.[134] Prequalification can be used in competitive but also selective procurement methods. Especially in complex or highly-technical procurements bidders without suitable qualifications can be eliminated. Thus, the number of tenders to be evaluated is reduced, which saves time and costs.[135]

A sort of prequalification can also be applied by the introduction of suppliers lists where all suppliers or contractors that fulfil certain requirements such as technical expertise, experience, financial standing, etc. are registered for future procurements. The use of such lists is, however, controversial as it can have a negative effect on competition. However, one must differentiate between mandatory lists that require registration of suppliers in order to be considered for a contract and non-mandatory lists that do not exclude the participation of suppliers not listed. Non-mandatory supplier lists might, for example, solely be used for the purpose of identifying potential suppliers and reducing the bureaucratic burden by recording certain general qualifications in the list.[136] In the latter case, registration is not required by the tenderers in order to participate in bidding.

Beyond conventional public procurement procedures, alternative, non-conventional purchasing methods find their way into government purchasing. One example is public-private partnerships which have become an in-

---

133 See ibid, 271.

134 S. Arrowsmith, 'The conduct of open tendering procedures', in S. Arrowsmith, *Public Procurement Regulation: An Introduction* (Nottingham: EU Asia Inter University Network for Teaching and Research in Public Procurement, 2010), p. 55.

135 UNCITRAL, 'Guide to Enactement of UNCITRAL Model Law on Procurement of Goods,Construction and Services', A/CN.9/403 (New York: United Nations, 1994), Commentary on Article 7.

136 Cf. Arrowsmith, 'Supplier lists and framework agreements', p. 116.

creasingly popular method for procuring large infrastructure projects.[137] Welch notes that there is a move away from the old 'bid and bash' approach to more relationship contracting.[138] According to Gribben et al. a public-private partnership can be described as follows:

> "People and organizations form some combination of public, business and civil constituencies (non-profits) who engage in voluntary, mutually beneficial, innovative relationships to address common societal aims through combining their resources and competencies."[139]

The use of partnership models is a strategy to ensure the delivery and maintenance of goods or products over a longer period of time. The sharing of risks as well as rewards is one important feature of partnership relationships.[140] The construction, operation and management of large infrastructure projects, for example, provides a good example of goods and services that can be procured through a public-private partnership in order to guarantee quality and on-going functionality. The public sector can thereby take advantage of private sector management skills which is incentivized by having private finance at risk.[141] It is, however, disputable how this affects competition and, therefore, has to be carefully implemented and evaluated on a regular basis in order to ensure efficiency and effectiveness.[142]

Framework agreements are agreements concluded between the procuring entity and one or more suppliers or contractors which establish the terms of future procurements. The procuring entity can then place orders

---

137 G.C. Callender; D. Matthews, 'Economic Context of Public Procurement', in K.V. Thai, *International Handbook of Public Procurement* (Boca Raton, Florida: Taylor & Francis Group, 2009), p. 741.

138 B. Welch, 'Best Practices in Federal Acquisition' (2003) 32(3) The Public Manager, 11-17 also available at http://www.thefreelibrary.com/Best+practices+in+federal+acquisition%3A+a+former+senior+procurement...-a0112800160 (last accessed: 14 April 2014).

139 C. Gribben; et al., 'Government as Partners', (Copenhagen: The Copenhagen Center, 2001), p. 8.

140 W.C. Lawther; L.L. Martin, 'Public Procurement Partnerships', in K.V.e.a. Thai, *Challenges in Public Procurement: An International Perspective* (Boca Raton, FL, US: PrAcademics Press, 2004), p. 154.

141 Cf. The Stationery Office, 'Public Private Partnerships: The Government's Appproach', (London: 2000), p. 10.

142 See for further discussion N. Caldwell; et al., 'Promoting Competitive Markets: The Role of Public Procurement', in K.V. Thai; et al., *Challenges in Public Procurement: An International Perspective* (Boca Raton, FL, US: PrAcademics Press, 2004), Vol. 3; Erridge, 'Public Procurement, Competition and Partnership'.

under the terms of the agreement if there is demand for the goods or services covered by the framework agreement. Many (mainly developed) countries use this type of procurement method to purchase commodities or simple services such as vehicle or building maintenance. And in the private sector, framework agreements are a standard procurement method. Despite the fact that framework agreements have several benefits, such as lower transaction costs, stability of costs, foreseeability and security of supply, its application in public procurement raises concerns whether it negatively affects competition, accountability and the principle of non-discrimination.[143] In terms of value for money framework agreements can, nevertheless, provide a better means.[144]

Another trend is outsourcing, whereby less strategic purchases, in particular selected low value, non-critical standard commodity purchases are outsourced to full-service providers.[145] Outsourcing allows more resources for strategic purchasing, which is increasingly recognised as essential for saving money and delivering broader government objectives.[146] However, only purchases in non-critical areas where discretion is limited should be outsourced. It is also important to ensure that the basic principles of public procurement are followed and that processes are transparent and sufficiently monitored.

## 6. E-Procurement

With increasing technical resources a new instrument finding its way into public procurement is electronic procurement or e-procurement which is the "use of web-enabled software systems to enable the purchasing of

143 R.D. Anderson; S. Arrowsmith, 'The WTO regime on government procurement: past, present and future', in S. Arrowsmith; R.D. Anderson, *The WTO Regime on Government Procurement: Challenge and Reform* (Cambridge: Cambridge University Press, 2011), p. 54f.

144 Caborn; Arrowsmith, 'Procurement methods in the public procurement systems of Africa', p. 298.

145 P.L. Carter; et al., 'The Future of Purchasing and Supply: A Ten-Year Forecast' (2000) 36(1) The Journal of Supply Chain Management, 14-26 at 17; J. Zheng; et al., 'An analysis of research into the future of purchasing and supply management' (2007) 13 Journal of Purchasing & Supply Management, 69-83 at 78.

146 Zheng; et al., 'An analysis of research into the future of purchasing and supply management', 78.

goods and services online."[147] Part or all of the purchasing processes are carried out through the use of integrated database systems and wide area network communication systems.[148] E-procurement systems can provide general procurement information on all government departments, tender notices, bidding documents, minutes/records of bidders' conferences, submission of bids, bids received, reports of award proceeding,[149] as well as appeal and review decisions of the review mechanism or other legal institutions. Electronic means can be used in dealing with suppliers, in communication with the public and other public bodies and also in the government's internal administrative processes.[150] The establishment, maintenance and publication of databases of suppliers and contractors enable procuring entities to keep track of potential bidders and their past performance.[151] Providers could be required to register electronically.[152] Certain requirements such as tax statements could be lodged which would decrease the bureaucratic burden for bidders in future procurement procedures. Companies that are blacklisted and the reasons therefore could be accordingly displayed.

Whereas the use of electronic means for communication and information between the procuring entity and potential suppliers involves a basic use of technology that is widely recognised in most countries, carrying out part or all of the purchasing process through electronic means requires more advanced technologies and experience. E-procurement can be seen within the larger framework of e-government and should be considered in the context of the general law on e-commerce applicable in the respective country.

---

147 Caldwell; et al., 'Promoting Competitive Markets', p. 320.

148 S. Croom; J. Brandon, 'Key Issues in E-Procurement: Procurement Implementation and Operation in the Public Sector', in K.V. Thai, *International Handbook of Public Procurement* (Boca Raton, Florida: Taylor & Francis Group, 2009), p. 447.

149 K. Kostyo, 'Handbook for Curbing Corruption in Public Procurement', (Berlin: Transparency International 2006), p. 66.

150 Arrowsmith, 'Electronic Procurement', p. 140.

151 Cf. B.A. Ismahel, 'International Competitiveness: Government Policy and the Development of Competitive Industries', conference paper, 4th International Public Procurement Conference, Seoul, South Korea, August 26-28, 2010, p. 13.

152 Ibid, 13.

By making use of electronic systems, especially the factors cost and time-efficiency as well as transparency can be significantly enhanced.[153] If effectively designed and implemented, e-procurement can provide a substantial improvement of public procurement systems in regard to transparency and accountability, as well as effectiveness and efficiency. It not only removes unnecessary direct interpersonal contacts between suppliers and contracting officers[154] but can also, for example, balance decentralisation of procurement with centralised standards and oversight mechanisms.[155] Moreover, all stakeholders can easily and expeditiously access documents, offers, decisions, etc. which not only saves time and leads to better competition but also facilitates traceability. Especially for international businesses online accessibility diminishes the barriers to access to domestic public procurement systems.[156] Another advantage of e-procurement is that procurement officers have to spend less time on administrative tasks so they can concentrate on more strategic issues of the procurement process. Hence, e-procurement can increase government efficiency and enhance access to public services, while having the additional benefit of building public confidence and strengthening demand.[157] It is assumed that e-procurement leads to efficiency gains of 10 to 20% of the total volume procured.[158]

Nevertheless, e-procurement also involves risks that have to be carefully assessed and addressed in order to ensure authenticity, to protect confidential information and to forestall manipulative interventions that might lead to a flawed public procurement process. Authenticity is important to ensure that submissions by suppliers are final and authoritative, cannot be

153 Carter; et al., 'The Future of Purchasing and Supply', 15; Schapper; et al., 'An Analytic Framework for the Management and Reform of Public Procurement', 19.

154 World Bank, 'Electronic Government Procurement (e-GP) - Opportunities and Challenges', (World Bank: 2006), p. 4, para. 11 (available at http://siteresources.worldbank.org/INTPROCUREMENT/Resources/eGP_Note_V1-1.doc; last accessed: 26 November 2015).

155 Cf. Schapper; et al., 'An Analytic Framework for the Management and Reform of Public Procurement', 19.

156 Kostyo, 'Handbook for Curbing Corruption', p. 67.

157 OECD/DAC, 'ICT and Economic Growth: Evidence from OECD Countries, Industries and Firms', (Paris: OECD, 2004), p. 92.

158 World Bank, 'Electronic Government Procurement (e-GP) - Opportunities and Challenges', p. 4, para. 12.

repudiated and are traceable.[159] On-going exposures of misuse of data protection as well as the vulnerability of web-based systems for hacker attacks exemplify that security risks in regard to the protection of information and functionality have to be a key factor in designing e-procurement systems. Public confidence in the security of the information system and the confidence of procuring entities and bidders that genuine communications are being received[160] are also indispensable for the efficient and effective functioning of e-procurement.

## 7. Organisational Structure and Workforce

Whereas centralised procurement boards have been responsible for carrying out public procurement on behalf of the procuring entities in most states for a long time, this has changed in the past twenty years. There is a tendency to establish procurement units directly within the procuring entities to carry out public procurement, hence to decentralise the operational duties of public procurement and also to separate the operational function from the policy and oversight mechanisms.[161] Central oversight bodies monitor and oversee the tender process and policy offices are responsible for policy formulation, implementing procurement-related policies and monitoring the public procurement system. The lack of such entities, in particular independent oversight bodies, has been identified as one consistent weakness in most developing countries.[162] If there is an adequate system to monitor strengths and weaknesses of public procurement systems, the findings of reviews and studies can be fed back into the public procurement system. Public procurement is an on-going learning process which should be reflected in the structures governing it. Progress has also been made in regard to available review procedures in public procurement

---

159 Arrowsmith, 'Electronic Procurement', p. 147.

160 C. Nicholas, 'Policy Choices in the Implementation of Electronic Procurement: The Approach of the UNCITRAL Model Law on Procurement to Electronic Communications', conference paper, 4th International Public Procurement Conference, Seoul, South Korea, 26-28 August, 2010.

161 Caborn; Arrowsmith, 'Procurement methods in the public procurement systems of Africa', p. 296.

162 Hunja, 'Obstacles to Public Procurement Reform', p. 3.

as many countries have established an independent review panel rather than leaving disputes solely to the courts.[163]

The establishment of institutions providing training for public procurement professionals is a key factor to improving public procurement performance. It is possible to use existing institutions such as universities or other public or private institutes to train public procurement officials or to create a new training centre specifically for public procurement. Apart from basic public procurement training, on-going training programmes that keep officials up to date on new research findings, policy changes and lessons learned are important to ensure a constant improvement of the public procurement system. It is furthermore of utmost importance to ensure that the working conditions of public procurement officials are appropriate in order to attract highly qualified, experienced and motivated professionals. This includes e.g. adequate payment and career opportunities.

Apart from training public procurement officials, it is also advisable to establish assistance centres or units entrusted with assisting companies, especially SMEs, with bid preparation and matters regarding tendering. This can have a positive impact on competition and is, in addition, a way to achieve greater participation of SMEs in the public procurement.

## 8. Review Procedures

The availability of an effective review mechanism is essential for a fair and transparent public procurement system. Unsatisfied bidders that seek clarification of the facts or reasoning of an award, or feel discriminated against need to have access to an (independent) review procedure which provides for effective remedies as appropriate.

Reviews can be carried out by direct supervision, appeal to the procuring entity itself, administrative review, independent agencies, or judicial review.[164] Direct supervision is an internal control mechanism, for example by financial auditors. While it may guarantee adherence to the budget rules, it does not provide regress for unsatisfied bidders. Direct appeals to the procuring entity can in some cases be the easiest and fastest way to

---

163 See e.g. case studies in Quinot; Arrowsmith (Eds.), 'Public Procurement Regulations in Africa'.

164 Trepte, 'Regulating Procurement', p. 51ff.

address alleged irregularities of tender processes and avoid litigation.[165] Administrative review is carried out by superior authorities or specialized services within the hierarchy.[166] It raises questions of transparency and impartiality, though, as such authorities or services are part of the administration itself and may raise the "concern that they act in the favour of the administration rather than of the benefit of tenderers-"[167] Independent review institutions are truly independent of the other government branches and need to have the power to impose sanctions[168] in order to be able to effectively and efficiently meet its purpose to handle procurement disputes and to disclose and sanction irregularities in public procurement processes and, thereby, convey confidence to the stakeholders of public procurement. An example for this kind of review is the establishment of a procurement ombudsman equipped with the required power and functions to handle procurement cases and to impose sanctions against procuring entities. Judicial review might be an effective mechanism and is –as the last resort - "perhaps the highest level system of remedial action which constitutes the greatest incentive for the agent to comply with procurement regulations."[169] However, it carries with it problems as such costs, duration and access. It is possible and recommendable to provide for more than one review mechanism. Whereas direct appeal mechanisms and administrative review might be beneficial in regard to accessibility, costs and time, in the interest of justice it is important to provide an independent review mechanism or direct access to court if the outcome of such appeals is not satisfactory for the applicant. A court can then, for example, declare a decision null and void and might refer the matter back to the procuring entity to be decided again, it can also revise a decision or substitute its decision for a decision by the procuring entity.

Several countries have established an office of procurement ombudsman to serve as an independent and alternative redress mechanism, which can not only serve as a complaint system but also as an information provider on public procurement. A major advantage of having a procurement

---

165 OECD, 'SIGMA Paper No. 30 - Public Procurement Review Procedures, CCNM/SIGMA/PUMA(2000)114', (OECD: 2000), p. 13 (available at http://www.oecd.org/officialdocuments/publicdisplaydocumentpdf/?doclanguage=en&cote=ccnm/sigma/puma(2000)114; last accessed: 1 December 2015).

166 Trepte, 'Regulating Procurement', p. 53.

167 Ibid.

168 See ibid, 54.

169 Ibid, 55.

ombudsman is that it provides an alternative to legal proceedings which is less costly. Furthermore, aggrieved bidders are likely to avoid the complainant-defendant relation of legal proceedings because it might be seen as upsetting procuring entities in view of future tenders.[170] The EU Ombudsman has, for example, been identified as initiator of soft law as e.g. new safeguards like the duty to inform the complainant on the closure of a case or the implementation of transparency rules in procuring entities.[171]

There are a few legal instruments that are of specific importance for the effectiveness of public procurement redress mechanisms. It is, for example, essential to provide injunctive relief or similar instruments to avoid a situation where the tender is executed during the appeals procedure before the tender board.[172] The challenge is to ensure that effective remedies are balanced against the need to minimize disruptions to the procurement process.[173]

170 M.J. Gruppen, 'The Procurement Ombudsman: An Effective National Procurement Mechanism? - Enhancing the Accountability of Procuring entities', conference paper, 4th International Public Procurement Conference, Seoul, South Korea, August 26-28, 2010.

171 Ibid.

172 Mosoti, 'Reforming the Laws on Public Procurement in the Developing World', 629.

173 Quinot, 'A comparative perspective on supplier remedies', p. 323.

## *Chapter 2: Transparency and the Problem of Corruption*

### 1. Introduction

Transparency in public procurement is one of the most discussed aspects in the course of reforms because it is considered as a necessary prerequisite for effective, efficient and, especially, credible public procurement systems.[174] Principals, guidelines and recommendations on transparency standards have been developed by several institutions including OECD, UN and Transparency International in order to provide assistance to countries improving their public procurement systems and minimising corruption.[175] Furthermore, the United Nations Convention against Corruption contains an article on public procurement requiring its member states to implement certain elements in their procurement systems with view to prevent corruption.[176]

Corruption can be identified as one of the major obstacles for the effective and efficient operation of procurement systems.[177] Although developing countries seem to suffer more extensively from this illness, developed countries are not exempted from corruption in procurement and are constantly enacting transparency measures to prevent corruption and the undermining of procurement systems. In most countries corruption is a general rather than a procurement-specific problem. However, the high amounts of money, the variety of vested interests and the complexity involved make public procurement particularly vulnerable to corruption.[178]

---

174 See e.g. Mampuzhasseril; et al., p. 3. See also Evenett; Hoekman, 'International Cooperation and the Reform of Public Procurement Policies'; Hunja, 'Obstacles to Public Procurement Reform'; Mosoti, 'Reforming the Laws on Public Procurement in the Developing World'; Schapper; et al., 'An Analytic Framework for the Management and Reform of Public Procurement'.

175 See eg. Kostyo, 'Handbook for Curbing Corruption'; OECD, 'Integrity in Public Procurement'; OECD, 'OECD Principles for Integrity in Public Procurement', (Paris: OECD, 2009); United Nations Office on Drugs and Crime, 'Guidebook on anti-corruption in public procurement and the management of public finances'.

176 For more information on Article 9 of UNCAC see above (Introduction, Subchapter 4 (a)) and below (Part I, Chapter 2, Subchapter 3).

177 See e.g. Kostyo, 'Handbook for Curbing Corruption', p. 13.

178 OECD, 'Integrity in Public Procurement', p. 10.

## 2. Corruption and possible Effects

Corruption is generally defined as the misuse of public office for personal gain, either at one's own instigation or in response to inducements.[179] Corruption can occur during all different stages of the procurement process and take several forms.[180] There is, for example, the possibility, that specifications or criteria are designed or, in course of the tender process, altered for the benefit of the eventual bid winner process.[181] Another popular corruption method is the tolerance or acceptance of price increases after the tender has been awarded.[182]

From the economic point of view, special importance can be assigned to transparency in the award decision phase. The choice and announcement of the awarding mechanism is seen as decisive for the quality and price of the supplier's bids. Score mechanism can be relative or absolute. Chen[183] demonstrates that relative score methods, where the score of a tender for a specific criterion is determined by comparison with other tenders, thereby leaving a wide discretion to the procurement officials, can create a ranking paradox where the awarding authority has the latitude to make every bidder win. Absolute ranking methods do not entail this paradox since there is no or limited discretion on the procurement official's side. Additionally, absolute ranking methods enable the bidders to submit what they regard as the best possible proposal, as they can clearly identify the weight allocated to the different criteria.[184] Full transparency in regard to the awarding mechanism is a precondition for optimizing bids[185] and

---

179 S. Cavill; M. Sohail, 'Accountability Arrangements to Combat Corruption', 2007, p. 6 (available at http://www.dfid.gov.uk/r4d/PDF/Outputs/Regcomp/WEDC-corruptionlitrev.pdf; last accessed: 26 November 2015).

180 M. Greenwood; J.M. Klotz, 'The fight against corruption in public procurement:an introduction to best practices', in R.H. García, *International Public Procurement* (London: Globe Business Publishing Ltd., 2009); Kostyo, 'Handbook for Curbing Corruption', p. 17.

181 See e.g. Mosoti, 'Reforming the Laws on Public Procurement in the Developing World', 626f.

182 See for a list of corruptive practices in public procurement: Pope, 'Confronting Corruption', p. 208.

183 T.H. Chen, 'An Economic Approach to Public Procurement' (2008) 8(3) Journal of Public Procurement, 407-430 at 408.

184 J. Telgen; F. Schotanus, 'The Effects of Full Transparency in Supplier Selection on Subjectivity and Bid Quality', conference paper, 4th International Public Procurement Conference, Seoul, South Korea, August 26-28, 2010.

185 Kostyo, 'Handbook for Curbing Corruption', p. 44.

can not only lead to better bid quality but also prevent fraud[186] and, thereby, create confidence in the bidding process and provide an incentive to prepare a proposal.

In the broader sense, procurement systems that lack transparency and, thereby, foster corruption undermine development goals. Negative effects of corruption are additional expenses, low quality, ignorance of laws and standards, and distrust in public officials and the government. Corruption can result in the award of a higher but less valuable bid. Money is thereby wasted, which results in less funding for the acquisition of other goods or services or other high priority programmes. Low quality will in many cases affect development not only because the end-users have to cope with the lower quality but also because of follow-on costs which must be borne by the public purse. Awarding contracts to companies that ignore certain laws or standards affects development where employees suffer from low wages, substandard labour standards in regard to health and safety, and excess working hours. If inspectors have been bribed to ignore and construction projects are executed in disregard of planning and building regulations, corruption can even cost lives.[187] Corruption can be said to have severe financial, economic and environmental impacts. Beyond that, it can negatively affect health and human safety. Furthermore, awards based on corrupt activities impede competition and might deter firms from investing in innovation. Moreover, as has been mentioned above, corruption erodes the esteem for officials and the trust in government and harms honest competitors. Finally, corruption causes serious damage to economic development by squandering investment opportunities.[188]

## 3. Transparency Requirements in Public Procurement

Transparency is essential to eradicate corruption and the effects of corruption in public procurement systems illustrate the importance of instruments and measures to improve transparency in order to enable the efficient and effective functioning of public procurement. This has also been

186 Chen, 'An Economic Approach to Public Procurement'; Telgen; Schotanus, 'The Effects of Full Transparency in Supplier Selection on Subjectivity and Bid Quality'.

187 Cavill; Sohail, p. 1. See also Greenwood; Klotz, 'The fight against corruption in public procurement', p. 47.

188 Kostyo, 'Handbook for Curbing Corruption', p. 29ff.

realised by international institutions which have developed certain best practices regarding transparency standards in public procurement. The OECD has for example developed ten basic principles for integrity in public procurement "to guide policy makers at the central government level in instilling a culture of integrity throughout the entire public procurement cycle..."[189] of which two deal with transparency in public procurement procedures. That public procurement is particularly vulnerable to corruptive practices has also been reflected in the United Nations Convention against Corruption as Article 9 (1)[190] requires the member states to take, in accordance with the fundamental principles of its legal system, "[...] the necessary steps to establish appropriate systems of procurement, based on transparency, competition and objective criteria in decision-making, that are effective, inter alia, in preventing corruption."[191] Four aspects that shall be addressed are explicitly referred to in Article 9: the publication of information at all stages of the procurement process, the establishment and publication of conditions to participation, the use of objective and predetermined criteria to allow the scrutinizing of decisions, and effective domestic review systems. It further suggests implementing measures on matters regarding personnel responsible for procurement such as conflict of interest provisions or training requirements. Specific measures to prevent corruption in public procurement systems can further be found in the Handbook for Curbing Corruption in Public Procurement[192] published by Transparency International. Best practices with respect to transparency standards in public procurement are thus well-developed. In the following transparency as principle for public procurement systems will be closer defined.

Transparency requires a certain degree of publicity, documentation and reasoning at all stages of the procurement procedure, while also protecting sensitive data.[193] It is correlated with the right to access of information and the accountability of the government and its representatives.[194] Transpar-

189 OECD, 'OECD Principles for Integrity in Public Procurement', p. 18.

190 For more information on Article 9 see above: Introduction, Subchapter 4 (a).

191 For further information on Article 9 (1) of UNCAC see United Nations Office on Drugs and Crime, 'Guidebook on anti-corruption in public procurement and the management of public finances'.

192 Kostyo, 'Handbook for Curbing Corruption', p. 32ff.

193 See e.g. OECD, 'OECD Principles for Integrity in Public Procurement', p. 23.

194 See for example the definition of transparency in public procurement by the EC as represented in the WTO Working Group on Transparency in Government Pro-

ency in public procurement presupposes publicity of the request for proposals, of all criteria, the evaluation method, and decisions as well as documentation and accessibility to, accountability and traceability of decisions.[195]

Arrowsmith subdivides transparency into four main aspects, namely (1) ensuring adequate publicity for contract opportunities; (2) ensuring public availability and knowledge of the rules governing award procedures; (3) providing the basis for a rules-based procurement system, by limiting the discretionary power of procurement authorities; and (4) providing opportunities for interested parties (including, but not limited to, interested suppliers) to enforce and verify that the rules have been followed.[196] Hence, apart from the necessity of publication requirements, a sufficient degree of accountability is required to provide for a transparent public procurement system. Reducing the discretionary power of procurement authorities to a minimum can indeed foster transparency; however, it is essential to find the right balance without compromising the efficiency of decisions, as will be discussed below in subchapter 5.

The publication of all information on the subject matter, of the evaluation criteria and their weighting allows the potential bidders to assess the risks and costs of their participation.[197] The practice of public bid openings is generally recommended to ensure transparency.[198] Reasoning or the disclosure of the rationale for tender decisions is important for the creation of confidence in the system,[199] especially for the bidders but also the wider public and other stakeholders. This is a major prerequisite for bidders to engage in future biddings, which ensures that the key aspects of value for money and competition are realized in the future. An adequate and comprehensive statement of reasons further enables bidders to improve future bids. In the broader sense, an adequate statement of reasons is essential for a party to be able to effectively institute a review procedure.

---

curement: J. Linarelli, 'The WTO Transparency Agenda: Law, Economics and International Relations Theory', in S. Arrowsmith;M. Trybus, *Public Procurement: The Continuing Revolution* (The Hague, Netherlands: Kluwer Law International, 2003), p. 248.

195 Cf. Kostyo, 'Handbook for Curbing Corruption', p. 50.

196 Anderson; Arrowsmith, 'The WTO regime on government procurement', p. 15.

197 Cf. UNCITRAL, 'Guide to Enactment of the UNCITRAL Model Law on Public Procurement', p. 83, para. 1.

198 See e.g. United Nations Office on Drugs and Crime, 'Guidebook on anti-corruption in public procurement and the management of public finances', p. 20f.

199 Kostyo, 'Handbook for Curbing Corruption', p. 51.

Increased transparency at all stages of public procurement can be facilitated by requirements to publish all relevant documents, the award criteria and the awarding mechanism used in tender selection, and the rationale for tender decisions. It is, however, important to find country-specific measures that suit the countries' circumstances and the cultural setting. Andrew,[200] for example, has suggested the concept of oral debriefing in public procurement for Uganda, which he describes as an 'oral society'. Oral debriefing as envisaged by Andrew means that, after the best evaluated tender has been announced, all bidders are given the opportunity to take part in an informative meeting where details of the public procurement procedure and the decision in that specific case as well as strengths and weaknesses of their individual bids are disclosed. A notice and display period allows bidders to appeal before a contract is concluded, meaning that, after the information and the preliminary award decision have been communicated to the tenderers by way of oral debriefing, unsuccessful tenderers have the opportunity to raise objections to the award decision directly before the decision-making authority or any other authority having jurisdiction. Oral debriefing could create confidence and trust in the procurement system and in the relationship between public purchasers and bidders, be a learning-process for the bidder on how to do business with the government and, in the long-term, reduce the need for (administrative) reviews.

The introduction of public hearings in the procurement system in the first phase of the procurement process in order to discuss the design and the bidding documents is suggested by Transparency International. This might be particularly suitable to assure that public concerns are fully considered and reflected.[201] Especially in large investment projects, information can be disseminated and the stakeholder's commitment, contributions and support can be obtained. This may avoid misguided decisions reflecting manipulative influence of corrupt politicians, consultants, suppliers or contractors,[202] because the involvement of stakeholders already at an early stage and, therefore, increased transparency of the procedure, might deter procurement officials from being manipulated; in other words

200 M. Andrew, 'Accountability and Transparency; Preventing Corruption in Public Procurement: Oral Debriefing Concept', conference paper, 4th International Public Procurement Conference, Seoul, South Korea, August 26-28, 2010.

201 Kostyo, 'Handbook for Curbing Corruption', p. 34. See also Pope, 'Confronting Corruption', p. 213.

202 Kostyo, 'Handbook for Curbing Corruption', p. 90.

it might increase their personal inhibition threshold since corrupt practices are more likely to be detected.

The right to access to information is an important instrument for citizens to hold the government and its representatives accountable. The exercise of this right enables the stakeholders in public procurement procedures to perform the critical function of scrutinizing and challenging tender decisions and can facilitate a culture of justification on the public officials' side.[203] Accountability of the government, civil servants and politicians is important for the functioning of democracy because it allows the citizens to oversee the activities and to understand the reasoning of their elected representatives and other organs of state, in particular the executive. It means that compliance with the rules and regulations of the system is to be achieved.[204] However, accountability not only exists between the government and its citizens but in several other relations. Heeks identifies four types of accountabilities in public procurement: managerial accountability to senior managers within the organisation, political accountability to those institutions that provide the legitimacy of the organisation, financial accountability to those institutions that provide the financing, and public accountability to citizens outside the organisation.[205] This means that a procurement official's decisions are scrutinized from different angles and according to different criteria. Directly in the organisation, there should be a hierarchy allowing a substantive review of decisions by higher ranking officials. The authority of the political institution providing legitimacy for the public procurement office can require information and carry out external reviews. There is also the possibility of establishing an independent institution as an oversight or monitoring mechanism. Moreover, the financial aspects of tender decisions can be scrutinized by the financing institution as e.g. the Ministry of Finance. In the best case, such accountability is transferred to an independent institution such as an auditor-

203 P. Volmink, 'Enhancing Transparency within Public Sector Procurement: The South African Experience', conference paper, 4th International Public Procurement Conference, Seoul, South Korea, August 26-28, 2010, p. 24.

204 C. Nicholas, 'Work of UNCITRAL on government procurement: purpose, objectives and complementarity with the work of the WTO', in S. Arrowsmith; R.D. Anderson, *The WTO Regime on Government Procurement: Challenge and Reform* (Cambridge: Cambridge University Press, 2011), p. 753.

205 R. Heeks, 'Information Systems and Public Sector Accountability', Information Systems for Public Sector Management - Working Paper Series, Paper No. 1 (Manchester: Institute for Development Policy and Management, 1998), p. 6.

general. Last but not least, the public and in particular the stakeholders of public procurement from the business sector play an important role in holding decision-makers accountable; tax-payers have an interest in having their money spent wisely and the business sector wants their business interests to be handled in a respectful and fair manner. However, accountability presupposes the adherence to certain transparency standards. Hence, in order to assure all types of accountability good record keeping, auditing and transparent review procedures have to be carried out appropriately.[206]

4. Additional Instruments to ensure Transparency

An important instrument for improving transparency is the increased monitoring of public procurement.[207] The creation of an independent monitoring institution that supervises all public procuring entities in regard to finances, objectives and procedure can facilitate the improvement of the overall public procurement process and encourage public servants to adhere to the regulations and to best practices in carrying out their office.

There are other substantive criteria that can improve transparency, as, for example, the usage of market based mechanisms, meaning mechanisms that are in conformity with and responsive to the market, and of absolute rather than relative scoring mechanisms as mentioned above.[208] For decentralised procurement systems a standardization of procedure is especially important to facilitate transparency, on the one hand, because bidders do not need to become familiar with a wide range of different procedures and, on the other hand, because it reduces the work involved in monitoring. Furthermore, the use of technology can have a positive impact on transparency in public procurement.[209]

Remedies that directly aim at fighting corruption can be multi-faceted and often require more than the simple enactment of regulations. Nara-

---

206 A.B. Adjei, 'Sustainable Public Procurement: A New Approach to Good Governance', conference paper, 4th International Public Procurement Conference, Seoul, South Korea, August 26-28, 2010.
207 Cavill; Sohail, p. 36.
208 See Subchapter 2 of this chapter.
209 This has been discussed above: Chapter 1, Subchapter 6 of this part.

simham[210] has proposed three dimensions of anti-corruption measures: preventive, punitive and promotional. The preventive measures include electoral and administrative reforms. Punitive instruments cover laws, rules and the mechanism for effective investigation, court trial, departmental disciplinary action and other means to deter corrupt functionaries. The non-existence of punitive instruments also has an ethical impact: if people realise reckless and corrupt behaviour remains without consequences, they easily reduce their own integrity standards.[211] Effective punishment for disobedience of transparency regulations needs to exceed the gains realized through corruption or bribery. One example of such a sanction is the exclusion of firms caught in attempts to engage in bribery from bidding for a number of years (blacklisting).[212] The term promotional measures as used by Narasimham can also be denoted as public awareness or profile-raising campaigns. The encouragement of value-based politics and inculcation of moral and ethical principles can be attributed to promotional measures.

A system is only as good as the people implementing it. Since the effectuation of public procurement depends to a great extent on the workforce, special attention should be given to this aspect. Applying the three dimensions of anti-corruption measures suggested by Narasimham to the workforce, the prevention of corruption begins with the selection and appointment of the staff in order to ensure the necessary degree of independence from political influence. Furthermore, recruitment must focus on candidates with the expertise to be able to deal with the complex system and the challenges of public procurement. In many countries public procurement is carried out by junior officers and clerks that have no special qualification in public procurement. They are not only overly burdened in making qualitative decisions but are also powerless to counteract anomalies and may easily be manipulated by senior officials or politicians.[213] Additional-

---

210 C.V. Narasimhan, 'Prevention of Corruption: Towards Effective Enforcement', in S. Guhan; S. Paul, *Corruption in India: Agenda for Action* (New Dehli: Vision Books, 1997).

211 Greenwood; Klotz, 'The fight against corruption in public procurement', p. 58.

212 Evenett; Hoekman, 'International Cooperation and the Reform of Public Procurement Policies', p. 28.

213 Example of Kenya: N.H. Kimani, 'The Influence of Political Patronage on the Operationalization of Public Procurement Law in Kenya', conference paper, 5th International Public Procurement Conference, Seattle, Washington, 15-17 August, 2012, p. 1612.

ly, comprehensive training of public procurement staff should convey increased awareness and accountability among professionals for technical quality and sound financial management. The introduction of best practice guides and ethical and legal principles in service delivery can further contribute to a diligent work ethos that also takes transparency seriously. Secondly, effective monitoring and enforcement of accountability is essential to guaranteeing the commitment of the public authorities and to creating trust with the stakeholders.[214] These measures are reinforced by the punitive element, which includes effective sanctioning of misbehaviour. Last but not least, there are also promotional instruments that can reduce the likeliness of corruption. The behaviour of the government in general and senior procurement management in particular is crucial because senior officials function as role models; their conduct informs the staff of what is acceptable and what principles guide the system in practice. Apart from the quality of the workforce, staffing levels and budget resources need to be adequate in order to promote a diligent work ethos and guarantee a successful implementation of public procurement.[215]

Certain aspects of transparency in relation to public procurement might be better dealt with in the course of public sector reform rather than as procurement-specific measures.[216] Problems such as inadequate salaries or staffing levels in the public sector can, for example, nurture corruption, thereby frustrating the prescribed procedure. To counteract corruption in public procurement, procurement reform should be accompanied by the enactment of general anti-corruption measures and legislation. This might also include incentives for those who have suffered loss due to corruption to complain and adequate mechanisms to protect whistle-blowers.

## 5. Compromising Efficiency?

There is a growing discontent about the increase of rules and regulations in public procurement in order to achieve transparency, accountability and compliance[217] whereas the promotion of other essential procurement com-

214 Trepte, 'Regulating Procurement', p. 51.

215 Thai, 'Challenges in Public Procurement'. See also Basheka, 'Procurement Planning and Accountability', 399.

216 Cf. Hunja, 'Obstacles to Public Procurement Reform', p. 9.

217 See Mamiro; Read; Schapper; et al., 'An Analytic Framework for the Management and Reform of Public Procurement'; K.F. Snider; R.G. Rendon,

ponents and especially of competition has not received a similar degree of attention.[218] Keeping in mind that probably not even the best system can totally prevent corruption [219] an awareness is needed that an over-complexity of rules and regulations might render the system more inefficient and ineffective and, thereby, contradict such major objectives as value for money and competition. Snider & Rendon, for example, make the following observation:

> "They turn to regulations, laws, and other structural features to govern applications of allocative procurement policies, which may lead to graft, corruption, "pork", and other undesirable outcomes. [...] do structural policies contribute to bureaucratic "red tape"? Do they decrease responsiveness to the costumer of the procurement, and do they sacrifice value-for-money for greater accountability and control? If so, removal of "non-value-added" structural policies ("deregulation") may be preferred."[220]

One example of possible hindrances on the effectiveness of public procurement is the influence of the so-called "heavy-rules-approach"[221] on competition. The more complex the rules, the more cost- and time-extensive it is to prepare bids for public tenders. Often, only large firms which have corporate procurement departments can afford these resources whereas, SMEs lack these resources and are, hence, prevented from taking part in bidding.[222] Beyond these considerations, Trepte notes that,

> "[...] no form of regulation is likely to be wholly comprehensive and cannot address all circumstances likely to arise in the context of economic relationships in the market place."[223]

It is, therefore, questionable whether a very extensive design of legal rules can account for the complexity of a procurement system by trying to cover

---

'Public Procurement Policy: Implications for Theory and Practice' (2008) 8(3) Journal of Public Procurement, 310-333.

218 See Anderson; et al., 'Ensuring integrity and competition in public procurement markets', p. 682.

219 S. Rose-Ackermann, 'The Political Economy of Corruption', in K.A. Elliott, *Corruption and the Global Economy* (Washington: Institute for International Economics, 1997), p. 56.

220 Snider; Rendon, 'Public Procurement Policy', 324, 235.

221 Read, p. 5.

222 Zheng; et al., 'An analysis of research into the future of purchasing and supply management', 75.

223 Trepte, 'Regulating Procurement', p. 7.

all possible scenarios. In fact, it is necessary to balance transparency concerns with those of efficiency and effectiveness of procurement system.[224]

Interestingly, a study performed by Transparency International revealed that the risk of corruption in public procurement associated with the laws is close to 35%. The risk that is associated with how existing laws are implemented was however close to 65%.[225] This discrepancy calls for a stronger focus on improvements in law enforcement rather than sole reforms of existing legal rules. An overall improvement of governance and the strengthening of rule of law might be key factors for fighting corruption. Moreover, the heavy-rules approach might in theory diminish the latitude for corruption, but if the implementation of these rules is flawed their practical effect on fighting corruption is at risk.

224 Cf. Anderson; et al., 'Ensuring integrity and competition in public procurement markets', p. 683.

225 Kostyo, 'Handbook for Curbing Corruption', p. 52.

## 1. Introduction

The inclusion of secondary objectives, also called collateral or horizontal objectives,[226] in public procurement is a highly controversial issue which has been discussed by economic, legal and public policy scholars alike. However, this has not yet led to non-ambiguous evidence whether it is effective, neutral or counterproductive to the rationale of public procurement. The pursuit of secondary objectives often stands in conflict with the primary (economic) concern of procuring goods and services at the best possible terms.[227] Secondary objectives include economic, social and environmental criteria in procurement, whereas the latter can be identified as the less disputed policy goal. Given the outstanding position of and attentiveness to environmental or green procurement, it is worth treating it separately from socio-economic objectives and will be discussed in the final subchapter of this chapter.

In a study undertaken for the EU (then still the European Community), McCrudden[228] provides a list with socio-economic policy goals. Among them are objectives such as the stimulation of economic activity, the protection of national industry against foreign competition, the improvement of the competitiveness of certain industrial sectors, and remedial measures against regional disparities.[229] Further objectives include the facilitation of job creation, promotion of fair labour conditions, promotion of the use of local labour as means to prevent discrimination against minority groups, protection of the environment, encouragement of equality of opportunity between men and women, and promotion of increased utilization of the disabled in employment.[230] In regard to certain societies in which certain groups have been subject to severe economic, social and political discrimination, the promotion of historically disadvantaged groups or people should be added. South Africa, for example, integrates its affirmative ac-

---

226 See Arrowsmith; et al., 'Regulation of Public Procurement'.

227 Ibid.

228 C. McCrudden, 'Public Procurement and Equal Opportunities in the European Community ', A study of contract compliance in member states of the European Community under European Community Law, Contract File No. SOC 9310257105B04 (Oxford: Oxford University 1995).

229 Ibid.

230 Ibid.

tion policy into public procurement. The different types of socio-economic objectives will be discussed in more detail in the following subchapter.

Recently the term sustainability has entered the discussion about collateral objectives of public procurement. The Swiss-led Marrakesh Task Force on Sustainable Public Procurement (SPP) has adopted the definition of SPP as

> "[...] a process whereby organizations meet their needs for goods, services, works and utilities in a way that achieves value for money on a whole life basis in terms of generating benefits not only to the organization, but also society and the economy, whilst minimising damage to the environment."[231]

Interestingly it combines the three types of secondary objectives with the concept of value for money. Whereas it is often criticised that secondary objectives generally contradict the value for money criteria, this approach assumes that consideration of these collateral issues in the long-term accounts for value for money.

Collateral policy objectives, if applied, have to be evaluated not only politically but also legally and economically. As Arrowsmith[232] notes, it is often difficult to accurately estimate, on the one hand, the costs involved in policy promotion and, on the other hand, the benefits that may be achieved thereby. Outcomes are very difficult to measure quantitatively or qualitatively, which makes auditing and verification of the effectiveness of secondary objectives in public procurement nearly impossible.[233] Furthermore, as emphasised by Wittig,[234] pursuing public policies by procuring entities might impede efficiency and value for money and, therefore, hinder the objectives of public procurement. Secondary objectives might have an adverse effect on the primary objective of obtaining value for money and, hence, its benefits would need to be carefully weighed against

---

231 See e.g. Website of United Nations Environment Programme, 'Marrakech Task Force on Sustainable Public Procurement (MTF on SPP)', http://www.unep.fr/scp/marrakech/taskforces/pdf/Procurement2.pdf (last accessed: 6 September 2015).

232 S. Arrowsmith, 'Public Procurement as an Instrument of Policy and the Impact of Market Liberalization' (1995) 111 Law Quarterly Review, 235-285.

233 R. Watermeyer, 'The use of Targeted Procurement as an Instrument of Poverty Alleviation and Job Creation in Infrastructure Projects' (2000) 5 Public Procurement Law Review, 226-250 at 5.

234 Wittig, 'Building Value through Public Procurement', p. 14.

losses in cost-effectiveness.[235] However, as emphasised above, the determination of the benefits of secondary objectives has proven to be very difficult and, hence, makes such an assessment extremely onerous.

Secondary policies can be integrated at different stages in the procurement system e.g. in form of prequalification for bidders, mandatory requirements for the contract or of contractual terms.[236] Despite the ambiguous effect of secondary policies they have been applied by countries with different economic levels and systems.[237]

As Quinot remarks, in most cases the law does not play a significant role in decisions to use public procurement of secondary objectives; it is a policy decision.[238] The law only regulates how much discretion is given to the policy-maker to pursue collateral objectives. In some countries, such as South Africa, the application of preferential procurement is constitutionally required. However, such approaches are exceptions.[239]

In order not to generalize the means to an end, a differentiation between (a) means which require adherence to existing laws, regulations or prescribed standards on the local as well as the international level (contract-compliance) (e.g. the requirement to adhere to the conditions of a collective agreement) and (b) means which prescribe higher standards than generally required (e.g. the requirement to pay employees higher wages than required by a collective agreement in the particular branch) is reasonable. Ideally, bidders should adhere to the former standards as a prerequisite to being awarded the bid; bidders that do not abide by these rules should not in any way be awarded public contracts. Standards that are above the market level, however, might entail additional costs to bidders who otherwise comply with the minimum standards and thereby have a detrimental impact on competition. Trepte uses the terms supplementary policy and additional policy objectives to distinguish between requirements concerning the adherence to existing policies such as national standards and requirements that go beyond such policies.[240]

---

235 See e.g. A. Reich, 'International Public Procurement Law - The Evolution of International regimes on Public Purchasing', Studies in Transnational Economic Law Volume 12 (London: Kluwer Law International 1999), p. 26.

236 Cf. Palmujoki; et al., 'Green Public Procurement', 253.

237 Arrowsmith, 'Public Procurement as an Instrument of Policy'.

238 Quinot, 'Promotion of social policy ', p. 373.

239 Ibid, 373.

240 Trepte, 'Regulating Procurement', p. 138.

## 2. Types of Socio-Economic Objectives

The first type of socio-economic objectives is preferential procurement. As preferential treatment is often discriminatory, the term discriminatory procurement is often used in this context. Examples for such policies are the support of SMEs, the preferential treatment of domestic over foreign bidders, local content requirements, and the promotion of certain groups in society, in particular minorities or historically disadvantaged people (as, for example, the preferential treatment in the context of the Black Economic Empowerment in South Africa today or the US in the 1970s).[241] All these measures mentioned usually aim at economic stimulation, support and protection of certain industries, or are used as remedy for regional inequalities in economic development in order to improve the living conditions for its residents.

The second type of socio-economic policy goals aims exclusively to address social or social welfare considerations, e.g. the inclusion of such criteria as the promotion of fair labour conditions in view of the welfare of society, the use of local labour to provide jobs or the inclusion of disabled or disadvantaged people into economic life or the pursuit of other equality objectives such as gender equality. In contrast to the first type of procurement linkages which try to add welfare aspects by promoting economic activity, public procurement is here used as a tool of social policy.[242] As McCrudden notes, the "modern procurement systems developed alongside the development of the welfare state, and it is hardly surprising that the former was used in part to underpin the latter's goals."[243] Whereas objectives such as the promotion of fair labour conditions can be achieved simply through a requirement to adhere to national laws, most other socio-economic objectives need any kind of preference policy to serve its purpose. This second type of socio-economic policy objectives used in procurement differs from the first type in that preferences are not applied due to the type of company per se (foreign, national, SME, owned by someone from a disadvantaged group) but in regard to company internal methods of operation and policies. As mentioned in the introduction of this chapter all

241 South African approach to Black Economic Empowerement will be discussed in Part II, Chapter 4(6). On the United states approach see McCrudden, 'Buying Social Justice', p. 167ff.

242 Cf. ibid, 41.

243 Ibid, 13.

these criteria can be integrated at different stages of the public procurement system.

Summing up, as a general observation one can say that socio-economic policies usually have various explicit as well as implicit rationales and are affected by different stakeholders with diverse interests. Using public procurement to achieve these socio-economic policies is therefore a highly controversial and complex issue. Furthermore, it is very difficult to measure the effectiveness of socio-economic policies within the public procurement system since it requires long-term monitoring of the market or the impacts on society, which is not only costly but also time-consuming.

In the following subchapters the two types of socio-economic objectives, preferential and purely social (welfare) objectives, will be discussed in detail, followed by a discussion of the clash between protectionist and liberalist views in public procurement and the rationales of governments to pursue preferential procurement and their economic validity.

### a. Preferential Procurement

Discriminatory practices can generally take three different forms: price preferences, cost preferences, and 'entry discrimination' such as the complete exclusion of foreign or a certain type of firms.[244] Price preferences reduce price competition for certain bidders. Cost preferences directly or indirectly increase the cost of bidding for a certain group of bidders.[245] An example is the application of domestic content requirements, meaning that suppliers or contractors are required to use a certain amount of services or material that is produced locally.[246] These different types of discriminatory practices have different effects. Price preferences might induce bidders that do not benefit to substantially lower their bids in order to compete. This might lower the procurement costs. Nevertheless, cost preferences

244 G. Deltas; E. Simon, 'Quantitative Estimates of the Effects of Preference Policies', in B.M. Hoekman; P.C. Mavroidis, *Law and Policy in Public Purchasing: The WTO Agreement on Government Procurement* (Ann Arbor, MI: University of Michigan Press, 2000), p. 74. See also McCrudden, 'Buying Social Justice', p. 117.

245 McCrudden, 'Buying Social Justice', p. 117.

246 Deltas; Simon, 'Quantitative Estimates of the Effects of Preference Policies', p. 74.

and entry discrimination can also lead to less competition and consequently to higher bids and greater overall procurement costs.[247]

The discussion of the use of discriminatory practices in public procurement is generally split in two camps: protectionism and trade liberalisation. However, the application of discriminatory practices also often comes along with crisis situations, which are then used as a justification for the satisfaction of certain interest or lobby groups or, more generally, as a means to maintain political power by satisfying parts of the electorate.[248]

The most substantial argument against the usage of discriminatory practices is that it hinders free trade and an efficient utilization of resources. The effects of trade liberalisation have been discussed quite extensively for some time with different results. Since the matter is basically of economic nature, often based on political reasons or ethical considerations, this point will be dealt with separately in Subchapter c. In general the liberal position will be followed because the assumption that the introduction of liberal market policies has a positive effect on developing countries seems to have broad consensus. However, it should be kept in mind that the best point in time in a state's economic development to begin economic liberalisation is controversial.[249] Nevertheless, a few examples of pros and cons of preferential policies' in public procurement and its influence on procurement objectives will be given in order to understand their controversial nature.

First of all, preferential treatment of certain groups hinders competition. The preferred group of companies or service providers are not encouraged to become competitive which is, however, necessary in order to be successful in the long run. If, for example, domestic companies are chosen over foreign firms not because they have the better offer but simply because of the origin criteria, these domestic firms will not be able to com-

247 S.J. Evenett, 'Multilateral Disciplines and Government Procurement', in P. English, et al., *Development, Trade and the WTO* (Geneva: World Trade Organization, 2002), p. 422.

248 F. Ssennoga; J. Telgen, 'Integrating Socio-Economic Policies into the Public Procurement Framework - An Analysis of the Public Procurement Option Model', conference paper, 4th International Public Procurement Conference, Seoul, South Korea, August 26-28, 2010, p. 17.

249 J.P. Trachtmann, 'The WTO and development policy in China and India', in S. Muthucumuaraswamy; W. Jiangyu, *China, India and the International Economic Order* (Cambridge: Cambridge University Press, 2010), p. 19.

pete on the export markets.[250] Apart from this, the preferential policy enables companies to offer uncompetitive prices, which affects the entire domestic market and, especially, the consumers.[251] In other words, the lack of competition allows domestic or preferred companies to submit higher bids than they would without the preferential policy. For these reasons, it can be said that the promotion of certain bidder groups does not necessarily make them more competitive in the market, which means that their preferment is not sustainable but only profitable for the award-winning company of that specific tender.

Another reason why discriminatory policies might be inefficient is that the resources saved by selecting the best rather than a suboptimal bid of a certain preferred group can be more efficiently and systematically utilized for the support of priority sectors or for advancing socio-economic or environmental policies in general. Not only the winning company but whole sectors or groups of society can thereby benefit. Moreover, it provides much greater latitude for the deployment of resources.

Baldwin and Richardson have analysed the effectiveness of discriminatory policies in a perfectly competitive context and come to the conclusion that, when imported and domestically produced goods are perfect substitutes and government purchases of these goods are only a fraction of domestic supply, discriminatory procurement is completely ineffective for protectionist purposes since it leads to increased domestic prices which would then generate a shift in consumer demand towards imports.[252] Miyagiwa has applied this to the scenario of imperfect markets and reached a similar conclusion.[253]

In contrast to the view that preferential policies are generally economically ineffective, there have also been assumptions that this is not true in all cases. McAfee and McMillan have discussed the effect of discriminatory policies on procurement costs and found the following:

---

250 Cf. F. Ssennoga, 'Examining Discriminatory Procurement Practices in Developing Countries' (2006) 6(3) Journal of Public Procurement, 218-249 at 226.

251 Cf. ibid, 226.

252 R.E. Baldwin; J.D. Richardson, 'Government Purchasing Policies, Other NTB's, and the International Monetary Crisis', in H.E. English; K.A.J. Hay, *Obstacles to Trade in the Pacific Area: Proceedings of the Fourth Pacific Trade and Development Conference* (Ottawa: School of International Affairs, Carleton University, 1972), p. 247f.

253 K. Miyagiwa, 'Oligopoly and Discriminatory Government - *Procurement Policy*' (1991) 81(5) American Economic Review, 1320-1328 at 1327.

> "If the aim of the government is to minimize its procurement costs, it should offer preferences to domestic firms when the industry has a comparative disadvantage; but when the domestic industry has a comparative advantage, the foreign bidders should be favoured. If the domestic firm's profits enter the government's objective function along with procurement cost, the government should always offer preferences to the domestic firms; but these preferences should vary from industry to industry, being smaller in comparative-advantage industries than in comparative-disadvantage industries."[254]

This indicates that discriminatory policies do not necessarily have a negative effect on procurement costs but only when domestic firms with a comparative advantage are granted price preferences. The competitive situation of the beneficiaries of preferential policies would, hence, need to be carefully assessed in order to determine whether a discriminatory policy is cost-effective or not. Such assessment, however, might have negative effects on the costs and the duration of public procurement processes and adds to the complexity of public procurement which is detrimental in regard to transparency, efficiency and effectiveness.

The frequent application of preferential policies in public procurement stands in stark contrast to the academic opinion that they are basically ineffective in an economic sense. Hence, it is important to understand why governments, nevertheless, regard preferential policies as positive means to achieve a certain objective and what validity these arguments have. Governments introducing discriminatory practices often give reasons as that public procurement can essentially contribute to the creation and support of the domestic market and the development of growing enterprises that are able to participate equitably in the global economy as well as to the lowering of bids by competitors. Procurement is used to stimulate increased entrepreneurial activity by certain companies[255] and, thereby, in the wider sense to promote social welfare. And surely, preferential criteria can provide an incentive for certain companies or service providers to participate in bidding. Furthermore, the opportunity to be able to compete with foreign and larger firms might motivate them to become more competitive in the long run. Additionally, public contracts enable companies to accumulate resources which can be reinvested in the company and to raise its reputation through qualitative and satisfactory performance of public

254 R.P. McAfee; J. McMillan, 'Government Procurement and International Trade' (1989) 26 Journal of International Economics, 291-308 at 304.

255 Cf. C. McCrudden, 'Using public procurement to achieve social outcomes' (2004) 28 National Resources Forum, 257-267 at 259.

contracts. Last but not least, competitors can be encouraged to lower their bids in order to be competitive with the preferentially treated bidder groups. Ssennoga & Telgen[256] note in this regard,

> "[g]iven the inadequate capacity in many firms in various sectors in especially developing countries, economic development and transformation cannot be attained without interventions."

SMEs might also find it more difficult to build human and financial capacity to prepare a bid. Larger firms, by contrast, can readily absorb these costs.[257] In this scenario certain potentially competitive bidders might be excluded from the bidding process, thereby diminishing competition per se.[258] However, it is equivocal whether positive discrimination is the right way to tackle this dilemma and, therefore, preferable to an improvement of the initial situation by simplifying and standardising the bidding process and providing information and assistance to SMEs on how to prepare bids. Other possible approaches would be making sub-contracting to local firms obligatory, downsizing contracts to smaller volumes that can be managed by local firms and providing better feedback to local providers and bidders.[259]

To sum up, discriminatory practices might, in a few cases, increase the profitability of domestic firms and thereby generate economic rents which are politically valuable. However, the effect of preferential treatment might also be counterproductive for domestic companies as they might lose its competitiveness on the basis of low incentives to invest in improvement and innovation. Additionally, discriminatory practices usually hardly increase domestic welfare because of increased procurement costs.[260] Moreover, given that these results have been drawn from theoretical considerations rather than practical evaluations the real effect of such practices might be even less convincing.[261] With respect to the situation in

256 Ssennoga; Telgen, 'Integrating Socio-Economic Policies into the Public Procurement Framework - An Analysis of the Public Procurement Option Model', p. 17.

257 J.J.D. Read, 'The Road to Hell is paved with Good Intentions', conference paper, p. 13.

258 Schapper; et al., 'An Analytic Framework for the Management and Reform of Public Procurement', 12.

259 See recommendations for Uganda: Sabiiti; Muhumuza, p. 2046.

260 See Deltas; Simon, 'Quantitative Estimates of the Effects of Preference Policies', p. 83.

261 Cf. ibid, 84.

developing countries, it is also important to consider the probable additional procurement costs of discriminatory practices in regard to limited financial resources. As Trepte notes,

> "[t]he decision to protect [...] has serious economic consequences in terms of economic efficiency and increased costs for the government, a state of affairs which may be particularly harmful to developing economies which are already hindered by a lack of financial resources."[262]

It is important to keep in mind that public procurement is not the only instrument at the disposal of governments; they can use a variety of alternative tools to promote socio-economic policies, including taxes, subsidies, fees or emission permits,[263] which might be more effective to achieving certain objectives.[264] Although public procurement policy objectives are politically appealing and can certainly have some advantages and benefits, their design and implementation is a complex task and has to be carefully balanced and weighed against the benefit of using other economic tools. A welfare analysis comparing gains and losses can ensure that public policies are deployed efficiently.[265] The adoption of a preferential procurement policy can be preferred over other assistance through other means on the grounds that

> "[...] it does not raise public spending directly [...] is less likely to be channelled into the purse of organized crime [...] [and is] more efficient than tax-financed State aid which barely reaches recipients".[266]

---

262 Trepte, 'Regulating Procurement', p. 154.

263 Nevertheless, it has to be remarked that alternative tools might violate other WTO provisions. The grant of subsidies is, for example, not without risk if the country is a WTO Member. Such a programme could be challenged as violating the Agreement on Subsidies and Countervailing Measures (adopted on 15 April 1994 and entered into force on 1 January 1995). Of course, whether or not this is the case will depend on the specifics of the case at hand, e.g. the wording and design of the programme and its implementation. Yet even where it is found that the programme is not inconsistent with the aforementioned Agreement either on its face or as applied, proceedings before the WTO are lengthy and expensive, which means that having to defend such a programme before the WTO could put the country in a worse position than not having it at all and thereby frustrating the objectives the programme was intended to achieve.

264 Cf. Reich, 'International Public Procurement Law', p. 29.

265 Korkmaz; see also Telgen; Schotanus, 'The Effects of Full Transparency in Supplier Selection on Subjectivity and Bid Quality'.

266 J. M. Fernandez-Martin; O. Stehmann, 'Product Market Integration versus Regional Cohesion in the Community' (1991) 16 European Law Review, 216-243 at 238.

Moreover, procurement policies usually do not need parliamentary approval and their costs are often less visible than other forms of assistance.[267]

b. Inclusion of Criteria increasing Social Welfare

Whereas discriminatory practices are rejected by the majority of scholars, the promotion of policies aiming more directly at the welfare of society is considered more favourably.[268] The inclusion of criteria in government procurement to produce certain social effects has a long history, especially in the construction sector.[269] The United States and England already linked policies such as the restriction of working hours or fair wages to government contracts in the 19th century.[270] A famous example of social purchasing is the Davis-Bacon Act of 1931[271] in the United States. It established the requirement that all contracts concluded by the federal government exceeding US$2000 for the construction, alteration or repair of public building or public work projects mandate that prevailing wages be paid.[272] Prevailing wages related to the wages and benefits paid locally paid for similar projects.[273]

Most of the objectives pursued today are tools to promote social responsibility, including refraining from the use of child labour, excessive work hours, paying less than the living wage, gender inequity and other forms of exploitation.[274] Procurement is used as a method of enforcing certain social laws and to advance a broader concept of justice.[275] Such policies can be applied with internal but also with external effect. In the latter case public procurement is used to promote certain social or 'fair-

---

267 S. Arrowsmith, 'Reviewing the GPA: The Role and Development of the Plurilateral Agreement after Doha' (2002) 5(4) Journal of International Economic Law, 761-790 at 781.

268 Arrowsmith, 'Public Procurement as an Instrument of Policy', 247, 248.

269 McCrudden, 'Using public procurement to achieve social outcomes', 259.

270 Ibid, 258.

271 US Public Law No. 403 of 1931.

272 Davis-Bacon Act of 1931 (US Public Law No. 403 of 1931), Sec. 3142 (a).

273 Ibid, Sec. 3142 (b).

274 J.-W. Choi, 'A Study of the Role of Public Procurement - Can Public Procurement make Society better? ', conference paper, International Public Procurement Conference, Seoul, South Korea, August 26-28, 2010.

275 McCrudden, 'Using public procurement to achieve social outcomes', 259.

trade' policies abroad such as the equal treatment of men and women or not using child labour.[276]

EU law provides examples how these objectives can be integrated into the procurement system. At the supplier selection stage, for example, tenderers can be excluded from the procedure if they have been found guilty of grave professional misconduct.[277] Grave professional misconduct includes

> "[…] violations of codes of professional ethics established by professional tribunals, or violations of competition law (anti-trust law) provisions (including collusion in procurement) or legislation on gender or ethnic discrimination (which in some countries involves sanctions of an administrative or civil rather than criminal nature), which have been established by relevant tribunals."[278]

The inclusion of labour standards in the contract award stage is more difficult. Barnard[279] identifies a provision in the EU Procurement Directives which requires the contracting authority to request the details for the constituent elements of the tender including "compliance with the provisions relating to employment protection and working conditions in force at the place where the work, service or supply is to be performed" in cases of abnormally low tenders. Barnard reasons that,

> "[t]his might indicate that only minimum terms and conditions can be requested but the vagueness of the phrase 'place where the work […] is to be performed' might be broad enough to include improved terms and conditions in that particular workplace." [280]

Last but not least, the contracting authority has the opportunity to include requirements for tenderers to take into account minimum terms and condi-

---

276 See McCrudden, 'Buying Social Justice', p. 93.

277 Directive 2004/17/EC (coordinating the procurement procedures of entities operating in the water, energy, transport and postal services sectors), 2004, Art. 45; Directive 2004/18/EC (on the coordination of procedures for the award of public works contracts, public supply contracts and public service contracts), 2004, Art. 45(2) (d). The directives have though been repealed by Directive 2014/24/EU (on public procurement and repealing Directive 2004/18/EC), 2014 and Directive 2014/25/EU (on procurement by entities operating in the water, energy, transport and postal services sectors and repealing Directive 2004/17/EC), 2014.

278 Arrowsmith, 'The conduct of open tendering procedures', p. 58.

279 C. Barnard, 'Using Procurement Law to Enforce Labour Standards', in G. Davidov; B. Langille, *The Idea of Labour Law* (Oxford: Oxford University Press, 2011), p. 263.

280 Ibid.

tions of employment and possibly improved terms and conditions in the contract.[281]

In South Africa and Namibia, certain laws contain provisions that explicitly require suppliers, service providers, and contractors submitting bids for or carrying out public contracts to prove adherence to these laws and to demonstrate adherence to the prescribed standards.[282] Section 53 (1) of the Employment Equity Act of South Africa[283], for example, provides that every employer that makes an offer to conclude an supply, service, hire or lease agreement with any organ of the state must comply with the relevant sections of the Act.[284] Similarly, Section 42 of the Affirmative Action (Employment) Act of Namibia requires any designated employer (25 or more employees) to produce a valid Affirmative Action Compliance Certificate when entering into contracts with the state.[285]

The International Labour Organisation (ILO) provides guidelines and recommendations for labour policies and also recommends adherence to certain standards in government contracts. Although the effect of the ILO's guidelines is limited due to their non-binding nature, they are a useful benchmark and may be considered soft law. Several states have implemented the ILO guidelines and recommendations in their domestic legislation.[286]

### c. Preferential Procurement from different Viewpoints: Protectionism vs. Liberalisation

Although the fact that liberal economic policies and free trade advance economic development will not be challenged in this work, a few objections to the argument that opening public procurement markets generally has a positive impact on economic development need to be considered in

281 Ibid.

282 See e.g. Affirmative Action (Employment) Act 1998 (Act No. 20 of 1998), Sec. 42; Labour Act 2007 (Act No. 11 of 2007), Secs. 138 (2-4); Employment Equity Act 1998 (Act No. 55 of 1998), Sec. 53 (1).

283 Act No. 55 of 1998.

284 It has to attach to the offer a certificate as conclusive evidence for compliance or a declaration by the employer that it complies with the relevant chapters which, when verified by the Director-General, is conclusive evidence of compliance.

285 Affirmative Action (Employment) Act 1998, Sec. 42.

286 Cf. McCrudden, 'Buying Social Justice', p. 56.

order to better understand certain countries' reluctance to open their procurement market and their decision to apply discriminatory policies. As explained above, there are two basic purposes for protectionism: (1) as a compensation for trade imbalances and (2) rectifying social imbalances or improving social welfare. Arguments in favour of discriminatory practices are not found in developing countries alone; they appear in countries experiencing economic crises all over the world.

First of all, the unequal distribution of international economic and political power entails unilateral dependencies on the part of less developed countries; economically powerful actors are able to exert a disproportionate degree of control and influence over them, which adversely affects less developed states. A weaker bargaining position usually leads to unfavourable trade agreements which grant the more powerful party access to the other party's markets but without full reciprocal affect. A famous example is the EU protection of its (declining) agricultural sector against imports, though it should be noted that there are different import duties and restrictions for different countries.[287] Additionally, the asymmetrical economic power also affects the way commercial transactions are carried out and dealt with.[288] The domestic market size and production output of developing countries in key public procurement sectors is often marginal, especially in sectors where demand by the government is large.[289] The political pressure on governments by domestic producers to increase domestic output in these sectors is likely to influence the decision to apply discriminatory policies.[290] And as Jiang rightly observes, in contrast to the taxpayers as the potential beneficiaries of increased foreign competition in public procurement[291] who have too little stake to organize politically to support liberalisation, lobbyists representing national industries exert significant political pressure against market liberalisation.[292]

---

287 J. Francois; et al., 'European Union–Developing Country FTAs: Overview and Analysis' (2005) 33(10) World Development, 1545-1565 at 1548.

288 Ssennoga, 'Examining Discriminatory Procurement Practices', 232.

289 F. Trionfetti, 'Discriminatory Public Procurement and International Trade' (2000) 23(1) The World Economy, 57-76 at 71.

290 Cf. Reich, 'International Public Procurement Law', p. 49.

291 The taxpayers benefit from increased competition as it enhances value for money.

292 L. Jiang, 'Developing multilateral rules on government procurement: the value of soft law', in S. Arrowsmith;R.D. Anderson, *The WTO Regime on Government Procurement: Challenge and Reform* (Cambridge: Cambridge University Press,

The economic consideration might be based on the fact that firms operating in small markets face higher production costs than firms in larger markets and, therefore, have a structural cost disadvantage. Governments might apply discriminatory practices to increase the domestic market size and, thereby, decrease structural costs which can make domestic firms competitive.[293] Given the amount of public procurement spent in developing countries, which provides the states with significant buying power, preferential treatment of local industries is seen as an important means to developing their competitiveness.[294] A lot of sub-Saharan domestic markets are, for example, too small to permit economies of scale that allow a country to be competitive and to integrate into the global economy.[295] Developing countries' markets might, furthermore, "lack an efficient scale of production, which is sometimes insufficient even for the supply of manufactured goods or services for their own domestic market."[296] They may also rely heavily on the export of primary commodities, which, despite a comparative advantage, can hardly compete with highly subsidized equivalents from developed countries.[297] In regard to government procurement the "asymmetry in the distribution of potential import-competing costs and export benefits between developed and developing countries"[298] is a crucial factor for governments resisting liberalisation. Silva[299] brings the general dilemma of equalization of countries' economic situations in regard to free trade to the point by claiming that, "free trade between countries with very different endowments and capabilities, presumably with large asymmetrical commercial power is somehow misleading, to say the least". And he suggests, that

2011), p. 723. See also Evenett, 'Is there a Case for New Multilateral Rules on Transparency in Government Procurement?', p. 210.

293 Trionfetti, 'Discriminatory Public Procurement', 71.

294 See Ismahel, p. 20f.

295 J.W. Musila, 'The common market for Eastern and Southern Africa and Kenya's export trade' (2004) 31(1/2) International Journal of Social Economics, 67-77 at 67.

296 D.L.e. Silva, 'The revision of the WTO Agreement on Government Procurement: to what extent might it contribute to the expansion of current membership?' (2008) 2 Public Procurement Law Review, 61-98 at 80.

297 Ibid.

298 Jiang, 'Developing multilateral rules on government procurement', p. 723.

299 J.R. Silva, 'Trade between asymmetrical democratic countries' (1999) 26(4/5) Journal of Economic Studies, 412-426 at 416.

> "[f]ree trade objectives could be better achieved, i.e., the removal of barriers to trade, whatever they are, would be easier, if the adjustments demanded by the problem of asymmetrical power between countries were more seriously taken into consideration for practical purposes."[300]

In regard to public procurement the disparity of endowments and capabilities might, for example, appear as political support for international firms and for export of goods and services. Ssennoga[301] suggests taking a pragmatic approach to liberalisation and being selective in choosing the manner, time, degree, and sector type to be integrated into the global economy. Gradual liberalisation is also recommended by Trionfetti[302] in order to overcome structural differences in market size. Developing countries should have the opportunity to remove discriminatory procurement over a predetermined period of time while having full access to other countries' procurement markets immediately. Such an approach could overcome structural differences of market size. However, other structural differences such as technological or human capital gaps are not likely to be rectified by discriminatory practices, but rather require other policies such as training, better education and support of research and development initiatives. These shortcomings might even be aggravated by the preference of domestic firms and, therefore, make domestic firms less competitive, which is exactly the opposite of the desired result. Last but not least, discriminatory practices should be applied, if at all, only vis-à-vis industrialized countries: competition between developing countries should be allowed in order to keep a certain degree of competition alive.[303]

It has already been mentioned that the procurement markets of most developing countries account for a significant percentage of the GDP, however, it has to be emphasised that - on the global level - the total amount is marginal. Hence, access to these markets might be desirable for foreign competitors but is by no means essential.[304] Additionally, despite the existence of protectionist measures in many developing countries, foreign companies seem to gain access to the procurement markets through other means such as corruption or existing government channels. Loans or credits by foreign governments, for example, often come with the attached

300 Ibid.
301 Ssennoga, 'Examining Discriminatory Procurement Practices', 234.
302 Trionfetti, 'Discriminatory Public Procurement', 72.
303 Ibid, 72,73.
304 Cf. Evenett; Hoekman, 'International Cooperation and the Reform of Public Procurement Policies', p. 6ff.

condition that a certain project is carried out by a company from that country that otherwise would not have access to that procurement market. This possibility of informal or illegal market access and the relatively marginal size of developing countries' public procurement markets might explain why pressure on developing countries to liberalize their procurement markets has so far been limited.

The second reason why states apply discriminatory policies is to satisfy the social utility function of their people.[305] The rationale behind socio-economic policies in procurement such as the promotion of formerly disadvantaged members of society or SMEs is often just not an economic one, but also based on the government's duty to promote social justice.[306] However, as this is the ideal scenario - perspicuous in theory - it is often misused for political purposes such as for the satisfaction of certain lobby groups or political friends. Whereas policies intended to further social justice can be readily accepted as legitimate, they tend to undermine the fundamental principles of procurement by making it inefficient and ineffective. It can be concluded that a complete renunciation or prohibition of discriminatory policies limits the freedom of governments to act and is only acceptable if the benefits gained by accepting a non-discriminatory framework outweigh this loss of latitude.[307] It is, however, important to put safeguards and restrictions into place which prevent misusing this instrument for political purposes.

The responsibility of satisfying the social utility of the people may not only provoke the application of protectionist policies in less developed countries (where poverty, unemployment and other social policies are at the core of governmental policy) but also in more advanced economies, e.g. in crisis situations.[308] For example, the Buy American Act of 1933, which was passed by the United States Congress during the great depres-

---

305 Cf. Ssennoga, 'Examining Discriminatory Procurement Practices', 233.

306 For a detailed discussion about the social justice component of preferential policies see J. Linarelli, 'The limited case for permitting SME procurement preferences in the Agreement on Government Procurement', in S. Arrowsmith; R.D. Anderson, *The WTO Regime on Public Procurement: Challenges and Reform* (Cambridge: Cambridge University Press, 2011), p. 450-453.

307 M. Dischendorfer, 'The existence and development of multilateral rules on government procurement under the framework of the WTO' (2000) 9(1) Public Procurement Law Review, 1-38 at 7.

308 Cf. C. Barnard, ''British Jobs for British Workers': The Lindsey Oil Refinery Dispute and the Future of Local Labour Clauses in an Integrated EU Market' (2009) 38(3) Industrial Law Journal, 245-277 at 262.

sion and establishes certain discriminatory practices for government procurement, continues to play a central role in US government procurement.[309] Another example is the deviation from competitive public procurement, which could be witnessed in the context of the US procurement response to Hurricane Katrina, the US procurement practice to meet the needs of the 2003 Iraq invasion and of Iraq reconstruction, and, recently, the world financial crisis and recession of 2008-2009 (often referred to as the Great Recession).[310] In response to the latest economic crisis the United States adopted the American Recovery and Reinvestment Act of 2009.[311] Section 1605 prohibits the use of funds allocated under the Act for the "construction, alteration, or repair of public buildings or public works unless all of the iron, steel, and manufactured goods used in the project are produced in the United States."[312] Schwartz concludes that,

> "[t]he pattern appears to be that the advent of a crisis is taken as license by interest groups and political factions to seek the policy changes that they favoured all along. In the case of the global financial crisis, US proponents of protectionism saw an opportunity to add political force to the protectionist positions that they held all along, implicitly daring the proponents of free trade to defend the commitment to trade liberalization in the face of difficult economic conditions."[313]

It can be inferred that there are certain situations favouring and amplifying calls for a return to domestic preferentialism and, thereby, making states vulnerable to deviations from the concept of free trade and non-discrimination. Beyond these domestic calls for protectionism, crisis situa-

309 Buy American Act of 1933 (US Public Law No. 428 of 1933).

310 J.I. Schwartz, 'Procurement as a Tool for Economic Stimulus: The United States' Experience, 2008-2010', conference paper, 4th International Public Procurement Conference, Seoul, South Korea, August 26-28, 2010, p. 4.; see also J.I. Schwartz, 'Procurement in times of crisis: lessons from US government procurement in three episodes of 'crisis' in the twenty-first century', in S. Arrowsmith; R.D. Anderson, *The WTO Regime on Government Procurement: Challenge and Reform* (Cambridge: Cambridge University Press, 2011).

311 American Recovery and Reinvestment Act of 2009 (US Public Law No.111-5 of 2009).

312 See for a comprehensive discussion of this issue: J. Linarelli, 'Global procurement law in times of crisis: new Buy American policies and options in the WTO legal system', in S. Arrowsmith; R.D. Anderson, *The WTO Regime on Government Procurement: Challenge and Reform* (Cambridge: Cambridge University Press, 2011).

313 Schwartz, 'Procurement as a Tool for Economic Stimulus: The United States' Experience, 2008-2010', p. 10.

tions can also be used as justification for the application of discriminatory policies externally.

## 3. Environmental Procurement

In contrast to other secondary objectives, green public procurement has, on the political level, been clearly identified as a legitimate and valuable means to enhance environmental policy goals, although its overall effectiveness has not been clearly ascertained yet and is, in particular, from an economic view point, questionable, as will be seen below. Environmental or green procurement can be seen in the light of the wider goal of promoting sustainable development.[314]

Objectives regarding the environment can be integrated at all different procurement stages: as a prequalification for bidders, as mandatory requirements for the contract, or in the contractual terms.[315] They can aim at the product itself, at production mechanisms or post-production aspects such as maintenance, waste disposal or recycling. The promotion of eco-friendly policies and sustainable growth falls under environmental objectives pursued in public procurement. Environmental objectives can be pursued by introducing mechanisms such as the consideration of life cycle costs of a product, which are derived by considering aspects such as life expectancy, maintenance and disposal or recyclability separately from the actual purchasing price.[316] Other measures used to introduce environmental policies into public procurement include eco-labelling, environmental standards, requirements on the use of specific processes and production methods, and/or performance-based specifications.[317]

It might also be worth considering whether environmental objectives could be achieved by procedural changes in public procurement. An example is the description of a tender in terms of functionality rather than performance requirements in order to stimulate and promote research and

314 McCrudden, 'Using public procurement to achieve social outcomes', 257.

315 Palmujoki; et al., 'Green Public Procurement', 253; see also Korkmaz.

316 Cf. Choi.

317 Cf. R. Brännlund; et al., 'Assessment of Green Public Procurement as a Policy Tool: Cost-efficiency and Competition Considerations', conference paper, 4th International Public Procurement Conference, Seoul, South Korea, August 26-28, 2010.

innovation.[318] The invitation of bids for energy supply, for instance, could then lead to several proposals such as wind or solar energy or other alternative systems, rather than pre-determining a certain solution. This could stimulate research and innovation and, therefore, generate new and alternative forms of energy supply. Although this is certainly not suitable for all types of procurements, it might be worth testing its practicability in several pilot cases. The difficulties in evaluating different bid responses as well as the increased risk exposure by purchasing something that has not yet been tested in a real-world application are factors that need to be analysed and addressed beforehand. Nevertheless, as research and innovation are desperately needed in order to find alternative solutions, the use of functionality criteria could be an effective means in this regard.

Apart from the direct impact environmental policies can have in public procurement, the indirect influence on businesses and markets to create and provide more innovative and environmentally-friendly goods and services is notable.[319] The considerable buying power of the public sector facilitates the incorporation of government policies, such as environmental policies, in supply chains.[320]

The OECD is dedicated to green public procurement and published its "Recommendations of the Council on Improving the Environmental Performance of Public Procurement" in 2002.[321] The recommendations can be broadly summarised in three broad groups: promotional measures, regulatory instruments and monitoring and evaluation measures. The dissemination of information about green public procurement to the public and the provision of information, training and technical assistance to public procurement officials can, for example, be assigned to the promotional measures. Providing an appropriate policy framework to incorporate environmental criteria into public procurement and introducing effective financial, budgeting, and accounting measures to ensure that environmental

318 As suggested by S.-E. Hargeskog, 'Specification, Evaluation and Verification Realising Public Procurement for Innovation', conference paper, ibid.26-28 August, 2010.

319 Website of OECD Environment Directorate, 'Greener Public Purchasing', http://www.oecd.org/document/21/0,3746,en_2649_34281_37414933_1_1_1_1,00.html (last accessed: 5 September 2015).

320 Report by the Comptroller and Auditor General, 'Addressing the environmental impacts of government procurement', p. 20.

321 OECD, 'Recommendation of the Council on Improving the Environmental Performance of Public Procurement (C(2002)3 ), 23 January 2002', (Paris: OECD, 2002).

costs are considered in public procurement policies and practices are recommended regulatory measures. Monitoring and evaluation mechanisms suggested by the OECD include the development of indicators to measure and monitor progress made in greener public purchasing and the evaluation of the economic efficiency and environmental effectiveness of environmental purchasing policies.[322]

A report on the implementation of the aforementioned recommendations found that OECD member states have implemented measures to strengthen greener public procurement in their countries.[323] The degree of implementation was evaluated according to responses to a questionnaire from 19 OECD countries. In order to get an overview of what policies are used to implement environmental procurement, four broader groups of policies were established: financial and contractual instruments, regulatory instruments, information-based measures, and training and education instruments.[324] It was found that most action was taken through information-based measures and training and education instruments whereas financial and contractual as well as regulatory instruments were less often applied.[325] The respondents, for example, raised concerns in regard to financial and budget considerations arguing that the means by which public expenditure decisions are taken make it difficult to integrate lifecycle costing. With respect to legal frameworks, the results of the OECD evaluation revealed that the limited success of environmental procurement is not attributable to legal constraints on the use of environmental criteria, but rather to a high risk aversion by procurement officials in respect of the interpretation of the legal framework.[326]

The fact that indirect measures were chosen to facilitate green public procurement far more often than procedural instruments exemplifies the complexity of integrating environmental policy goals into the public procurement procedure. Integrating green goals poses difficulties for public procurement officials who are, hence, often reluctant to implement environmental objectives. Despite the pursuit of environment objectives

322 Ibid, Section II (2).

323 OECD Working Party on National Environmental Policies, 'Improving the Environmental Performance of Public Procurement: Report on Implementation of the Council Recommendation', ENV/EPOC/WPNEP(2006)6/FINAL (Paris: OECD, 2006).

324 Ibid, 11, para. 31.

325 Ibid, 13, 14, paras. 35, 37.

326 Ibid, 22, para. 59.

through public procurement being politically widely accepted and facilitated, it encounters identical or very similar economic and practical obstacles and problems as the pursuit of socio-economic objectives, as the literature on this issue suggests. From a political viewpoint, the high priority of protecting the environment might justify increased procurement costs and, hence, an exception to the principle that value for money is the highest objective. Nevertheless, environmental policies have an impact on the effectiveness and efficiency of public procurement and should hence be analysed critically. Environmental criteria might bring additional costs to the supplier, which can lead to higher bids and thereby contradict the principle of value for money at least in the short-term, and to the decision of suppliers not to participate in a tender whereby competition is hindered. Lundberg, Marklund & Strömbäck studied the effectiveness of environmental public procurement and found that, in theory, environmental public procurement is objectively ineffective in general and give rise to an environmental policy paradox.[327] Moreover, subjectivity that might come along with environmental criteria and the difficulty of evaluating whether green procurement is environmentally cost-efficient are proving to be major obstacles.

The fulfilment of environmental standards or criteria often implies additional costs for the supplier, which has to consider whether these costs pay off in the long run. In most countries, public awareness about protecting the environment is rising and affects the decision-making of governments, consumers, businesses, and producers. One potential result of this development might be that suppliers decide that investing in the improvement of products, production or post-production methods in the environmental sense might pay off in the long run because of the high social acceptance, rather than solely to have a better chance to win a government contract. This is, however, only speculation and a negative effect on competition cannot be excluded. Extensive research on the effects on competition is needed to be able to draw quantitative and qualitative conclusions about the market-efficiency of green public procurement.[328] It is also important to note that, although environmental public procurement can deter potential suppliers from submitting a bid, it can also stimulate the entry of sup-

327 S. Lundberg; et al., 'Objective Effectiveness of Green Public Procurement', conference paper, 5th International Public Procurement Conference, Seattle, Washington, 15-17 August, 2012, p. 1145.

328 Cf. Brännlund; et al.

pliers in the tender process[329] because suppliers or contractors with a particular pro-environmental strategy might see their opportunity to win a bid on this account.

The subjectivity of environmental policies provides another challenge. Palmujoki[330] accurately notes that there is no universally valid answer to what is the environmental-friendliest solution in the long term. Especially with respect to constantly-changing policies, which are likely to be influenced by lobby groups and the industries concerned, it is a difficult task to balance environmental criteria with general public procurement principles, e.g. equity, transparency, competition, etc. These problems of subjectivity and of political influence on policy-design are accompanied by the difficulties in evaluating the cost-efficiency of environmental public procurement.[331] It is very challenging to assess the life-cycle costs of products or services as the following example illustrates. There are two suppliers, A and B. A has environmental-friendlier products, but B's products are cheaper. However, transportation of A's product produces much more $CO_2$ than transportation of B's product. Is the purchase of A's product still more environmentally-friendly? There are many associated environmental-related components that have to be considered when assessing the overall impact of a product or service on the environment. The environmental assessment therefore requires extensive research and thus financial resources and environmental expertise.

Last but not least, it can be noted that, as in respect of socio-economic objectives, other mechanisms as e.g. taxes, subsidies or tradable permits could have a better overall impact on the environment because all market participants are reached and not only the bidders for public tenders.[332] Brännlund et al[333] note that green public procurement can be an advantage if a decentralised structure enables the consideration of regional variations and adjustments to local conditions and can account for differences in environmental preferences between local authorities. However, the authors come to the general conclusion that green public procurement will never resolve environmental problems cost-efficiently in practice because the

329 Ibid; Korkmaz.

330 Palmujoki; et al., 'Green Public Procurement', 261.

331 Cf. Report by the Comptroller and Auditor General, 'Addressing the environmental impacts of government procurement', p. 24.

332 McCrudden makes a similar argument in regard to social policies: McCrudden, 'Buying Social Justice', p. 119.

333 Brännlund; et al.

costs of implementing the additional environmental control would outweigh its benefits.[334] They therefore recommend that green public procurement should only be considered as an environmental policy tool when the detriments to cost-efficient criteria are negligible.[335]

334 The authors deny that public procurement officials are able to establish optimal environmental objectives because a precise price determination of environmental resources would require perfect information which public procurement officials can hardly have.

335 Brännlund; et al.

# *Chapter 4: Summary of Findings*

The relevance of public procurement to the economy, on the one hand, and socio-development and good governance on the other hand, has been found to be very significant. That is why it has received special attention by governments, interest groups and academics in the last decades. To understand public procurement it is necessary to be aware of its complexity. This intricacy ranges from the variety of stakeholders and vested interests and the interaction of the public sector and private market forces to the embedding of public procurement in financial budget management. The complexity of public procurement can also be highlighted by the fact that academics from various disciplines engage with the topic. Not only public sector specialists, but economists, legal experts as well as political scientists have studied public procurement issues.

Laws and regulations, processes and methods, the workforce and the institutional structure are essential features of a procurement system. There are different procurement methods available which should be carefully selected according to the characteristic, value, complexity and other considerations of the procurement matter. Open bidding is the method generally used, but the costs involved render it ineffective and unsuitable for e.g. low-value purchases. Other methods, however, restrict competition and it is important that the circumstances or conditions justifying the use of alternative tendering methods are clearly outlined. It is worth evaluating new purchasing methods such as framework agreements and public-private partnerships because they may bring significant benefits. Nevertheless, it is always important to ensure that none of the primary objectives of public procurement are sacrificed.

Electronic means, on the other hand, can be used in public procurement systems to quite an extent. E-procurement includes the use of electronic means for communication and information between the procuring entity and potential suppliers as well as the implementation of part or all of the purchasing process. If implemented properly and sufficiently balanced with security and other concerns, it can significantly contribute to the advancement of cost and time-efficiency in public procurement and facilitate transparency and accountability.

For the successful processing of public procurement procedures as well as an effective implementation of public procurement legislation in particular, the design of the organisational structure is decisive. Institutions or offices are required to work independently and to be staffed with sufficient resources and qualified personnel. This will enable a decentralisation of operational duties of public procurement in the procuring entities. Furthermore, there is a recognised need to separate the operational function from the policy and oversight mechanisms.

Moreover, adequate review procedures are a key element for an efficient and effective procurement system. Procedures and remedies that give consideration to the characteristics of public procurement must be put in place. Although court proceedings are often time and cost-consuming, which might affect the procurement outcome, internal administrative review procedures cannot provide the needed independence. The establishment of independent review panels is, hence, strongly recommended.

The creation of a transparent framework is a cornerstone of an efficient public procurement system, not only because corruption represents a major obstacle but also because transparency is a key element of good governance and because it allows market forces to participate in a fair, equal and competitive environment. Comprehensive research has been conducted in this regard and a variety of guidelines and recommendations is available as reference point. Over-regulation should, however, be avoided because it renders public procurement ineffective and at some point the law of diminishing returns kicks in, so that the costs of additional regulation is not commensurate with the gains in fighting corruption. In fact transparency initiatives are only successful if laws are accompanied by a strong political will to combat corruption, effecting a change of attitude within the workforce and the business sector, and inducing civil society to scrutinize public procurement decisions.

The pursuit of secondary objectives through public procurement is a contentious matter. Understanding the rationale behind discriminatory practices and other secondary objectives is essential in order to assess their usefulness; the evaluation must be done on the specific country's domestic level rather than trying to prevent or condemning their application per se. The success of procurement regulation with respect to secondary objectives can only be measured by its ability to satisfy the requirements in the context in which it operates. Although economic rationality might render secondary objectives ineffective, the way a society perceives their application and experiences its impacts might render them politically valuable and generate their acceptance. One can distinguish between discriminatory practices or preferential procurement, socio-economic objectives aiming particularly at improving social welfare and environmental objectives.

Discriminatory practices are generally contrary to the objective of trade liberalisation and are generally regarded as economically ineffective by most scholars. Preferential procurement might have a positive effect in very limited circumstances, but these are difficult to identify. The choice to apply preferential procurement is usually motivated by political rather than economic reasons. Secondary policies to promote social welfare through public procurement have a less severe effect on the efficiency and effectiveness of public procurement. They have a long history and are applied in developed and developing countries alike to achieve certain goals, such as improving labour conditions or promoting social responsibility. Environmental public procurement has gained prominence in recent decades and the EU and the OECD in particular have promoted green public procurement. As it raises procurement costs and complexity, it has a detrimental effect on the efficiency and effectiveness of public procurement in general. This might to be tolerated by governments by referring to the high priority accorded to the protection of the environment. Nevertheless, it is very important to carefully and critically asses the economic impact of such policies and to consider alternative methods to achieving environmental objectives. The same, incidentally, is also true for socio-economic objectives and in particular discriminatory practices where certain objectives might be better and more successfully achieved through other means such as taxes or subsidies. Preferential treatment and other discriminatory measures have been criticised as hindering the liberalisation of trade on the international level. However, despite this criticism preferential treatment has been carried out by industrial and developing countries alike in order to counteract trade imbalances, fight social inequalities and to respond to crisis situations. Although the economic reasons for protectionism of this kind seem to be anything but convincing, the political and social objectives for its application often militate in favour of such measures, which renders the introduction of a general prohibition of preferential policies on the international level in the near future unrealistic.

# PART II: International and National Public Procurement Regulations

Part II comprises a comparative analysis of the GPA, the UNCITRAL Model Law, the COMESA public procurement regulations and the Mauritian national system as well as the case study of the South African public procurement system and its regulation. Apart from the GPA and the UNCITRAL Model Law as international instruments, Mauritius, which reformed its public procurement system in 2006 under the auspices of the COMESA public procurement reform initiative, has been chosen as it has served as a basis for the Namibian reform process, which will be outlined below. The South African public procurement system will be analysed because it is based on a unique approach to regulate public procurement and because of its common history with and the geographic proximity to Namibia. On the basis of findings derived from this analysis, the potential benefits of a comparative approach to public procurement reform and of adhering to international best practices developed from the reviewed international instruments will be assessed. The focus of this section will be on the principles and scope of the regulations in question, the procedures and methods provided, transparency, the discretion to use secondary objectives, the review procedures which are required and which are available as well as other critical relevant aspects such as the regulation of procurement planning and contract management. This analysis will serve as a basis to derive best practices that can serve as a guideline for the Namibian public procurement reform as well as to identify lessons learned so as to prevent Namibia from making the same mistakes as other countries. Hence, in the final chapter, the best practices derived from the comparative analysis of the different public procurement systems are presented. Furthermore, lessons learned from the Mauritian and South African case study which might have explicit implications for other developing countries including Namibia will be outlined.

## *Chapter 1: The WTO Government Procurement Agreement*

This chapter provides a brief overview of the GPA with a special focus on the treatment of developing countries, transparency, secondary objectives and review procedures and tries to find explanations for the limited number of signatories and the negative attitude of developing countries towards the GPA. Reference will also be made to equivalent provisions of the former version of the agreement from 1994, which was amended in 2012, and the modifications in this respect in order to understand why many countries have been unwilling to seek accession to the GPA in the past and to evaluate whether this might change under the revised agreement. The chapter concludes with implications for potential accession states and a short summary of findings.

In this chapter international (best) practices will be presented and discussed in order to derive certain best practices against which the current Namibian public procurement regulations can be evaluated and which can be used as guidelines in the reform process. Simultaneously it aims at giving an overview of the current state of internationalisation of public procurement and its potential influence on reform processes in developing countries. This includes the basic question of whether developing countries, when reforming their public procurement systems, should consider the GPA as guideline in order to be prepared for a future accession.

### 1. Introduction

The GPA was signed in Marrakesh on 15 April 1994 and entered into force on 1 January 1996. It is a plurilateral agreement meaning that the WTO members accede to the agreement on a voluntary basis. This contrasts with the multilateral WTO agreements such as GATT and GATS, where all WTO members are automatically parties to the agreement.[336] Therefore, not all WTO members are automatically parties to the GPA but have an option to join.[337] GATT and GATS explicitly exempt public pro-

336 This treaty regime is also referred to as “single undertaking”. See e.g. Reich, 'International Public Procurement Law', p. 281.

337 Cf. A. Reich, 'The New Text of the Agreement on Government Procurement: And Analysis and Assessment' (2009) 12(4) Journal of International and Economic Law, 989-1022 at 990; see also Linarelli, 'The WTO Transparency Agenda', p. 235.

curement from their coverage. Article III (8) of GATT 1947 exempts government procurement from the national treatment provision. Article XIII (1) of GATS governs the non-applicability of certain key provisions for government procurement.

Only forty-seven countries of the 164 WTO members are so far parties to the agreement and solely very few developing countries.[338] Most of these countries have acceded to the GPA because it had been made a precondition for WTO accession or for the membership of the EU.[339] Twenty-three countries have observer status, as does the International Monetary Fund (IMF), the Organisation for Economic Cooperation and Development (OECD), the United Nations Conference on Trade and Development (UNCTAD), and the International Trade Commission (ITC). Ten countries, including China, are currently negotiating accession.[340]

The agreement has been subject to a substantive revision in the course of on-going negotiations between the member states and the observers. These revisions were accepted through the adoption of the "Protocol amending the Agreement on Government Procurement" on 30 March 2012.[341] One major objective for the revised agreement is to facilitate accessions of new parties. Nevertheless, the major principles of the 1994 GPA were retained in the revised agreement.

---

338 Armenia, for example, has acceded to the GPA on 15th September 2011. Further parties with developing country status are Chinese Taipei, Hong Kong, Singapore and most eastern European countries. No African country has so far become a signatory to the GPA. See on the parties of the agreement: Website of the WTO, 'Agreement on Government Procurement - Parties, observers and accessions', https://www.wto.org/english/tratop_e/gproc_e/memobs_e.htm (last accessed: 20 December 2016).

339 See Silva, 'The revision of the WTO Agreement on Government Procurement', , Arrowsmith, 'Government Procurement in the WTO ', p. 94.

340 Apart from China the following countries are currently negotiating accession: Albania, Georgia, Jordan, Kyrgyz Republic, Moldova, New Zealand, Oman, Panama, and Ukraine.

341 Committee on Government Procurement, 'Adoption of the Results of the Negotiations under Article XXIV:7 of the Agreement on Government Procurement, following their Verification and Review, as required by the Ministerial Decision of 15 December 2011 (GPA/112), Paragraph 5 - Action Taken by the Parties to the WTO Agreement on Government Procurement at a Formal Meeting of the Committee, at the Level of Geneva Heads of Delegations, on 30 March 2012 (GPA/113)' (WTO: 2012), available at http://docsonline.wto.org/imrd/directdoc.asp?DDFDocuments/t/PLURI/GPA/113.DOC; last accessed: 30 November 2015.

## 2. The Essentials of the GPA

### a. Background

#### i. Principles, Objectives and Scope

The main principles of the 1994 version of the GPA were non-discrimination and transparency. It provided procedures and limitations that enabled the greatest possible competition on the international level, thereby liberalising procurement markets. The general procurement procedure was open bidding, which required public tendering available to all potential suppliers or contractors on the national as well as the international level. However, selective tendering was also generally permitted. Limited tendering could be applied only in particular circumstances and for a special type of goods or services. The 1994 agreement foresaw several exemptions for developing as well as least-developed countries. The fact that these exemptions did not induce them to join the agreement tends to support the hypothesis that the 1994 agreement did not actually reflect the particular circumstances and needs of developing and least developed countries.

The scope of the 1994 GPA is very limited. Apart from the fact that only 41 countries have so far become party to the agreement, the de facto application in the member states is determined by bilaterally negotiated criteria between the parties to the agreement, including monetary thresholds, the sectors and entities concerned. These limitations can be found in the annexes of the GPA.

#### ii. Review of the Agreement

The 1994 agreement envisaged on-going negotiations starting not later than the end of the third year from the date of entry into force of the agreement and periodically thereafter, to improve the agreement, extend its coverage and eliminate discriminatory measures.[342] These negotiations were, strictly speaking, not part of the Doha Round, the latest WTO trade negotiation round which was officially launched at the Fourth Ministerial

342 WTO Agreement on Government Procurement, 1994, Art. XXIV (7) (b).

Conference in Doha, Qatar, in November 2001.[343] Negotiations on the latter two elements only started around 2002[344] instead of 1999 as envisaged by the agreement. But, as Reich noted in 2009 in regard to the lack of progress, "one may suspect that the successful conclusion of these negotiations is linked to a successful wrap-up of the entire Doha Round."[345]

The Committee on Government Procurement[346] was aware of the numerous shortcomings of the 1994 GPA and, on the basis of the aforementioned provision providing for a periodical revision of the GPA and a review of its adequacy to achieve the intended objectives, revised the agreement. Negotiations about an improved version of the GPA started about 10 years ago[347] and have finally come to an end in 2012. The new text of the agreement was published for the first time in 2010[348] (in the following: the "new/revised agreement") but most elements had been decided upon in 2006.[349] The coverage of the new agreement was based on the understanding reached in 2006. As a consequence, the final adoption

343 See WTO Website http://www.wto.org/english/tratop_e/dda_e/dda_e.htm (last accessed: 9 June 2014).

344 Committee on Government Procurement, 'Report (2002) of the Committee on Government Procurement (GPA/73), 6 November 2002' (WTO: 2002), para. 39 (available at https://docsonline.wto.org/dol2fe/Pages/SS/DirectDoc.aspx?filename=t%3A%2Fpluri%2Fgpa%2F73.doc&; last accessed: 30 November 2015).

345 Reich, 'The New Text of the Agreement on Government Procurement', 993.

346 The Committee on Government Procurement has been established to oversee the implementation of the Agreement on Government Procurement.

347 Committee on Government Procurement, '"The GPA Renegotiation: Time to Close the Deal" - Statement on Stocktaking and Future Work (Made a the the Informal Closing Session, 18 October 2011)' (WTO: 2011), p. 1 (available at https://www.wto.org/english/news_e/news11_e/gpa_stat_18oct11_e.doc; last accessed: 30 November 2015).

348 Committee on Government Procurement, 'Ministerial-Level Meeting of the Committee on Government Procurement (GPA/112), 15 December 2011', (WTO: 2011), available at https://www.wto.org/english/tratop_e/gproc_e/overview_e.htm; last accessed: 30 November 2015; Committee on Government Procurement, 'Revision of the Agreement on Government Procurement as at 13 December 2010 (GPA/W/313)' (WTO: 2010), available at https://docsonline.wto.org/dol2fe/Pages/FormerScriptedSearch/directdoc.aspx?DDFDocuments/t/PLURI/GPA/W313.doc; last accessed: 30 November 2015.The former version does not include the final provisions but otherwise matches the newer version.

349 Committee on Government Procurement, 'Report of the Committee on Government Procurement (November 2005 - December 2006) (GPA/89), 11 December 2006', (WTO: 2006), para. 20 (available at https://docsonline.wto.org/dol2fe/Pages/FormerScriptedSearch/directdoc.aspx?DDFDocuments/t/PLURI/GPA/89.doc; last accessed: 30 November 2015).

of the text depended on a mutually satisfactory outcome of these negotiations. At the ministerial-level meeting of the committee on 15 December 2011 it was then announced that an agreement had been reached[350] and that the officials would be instructed to

> "[...] work expeditiously to complete the final verification and legal review of the various elements [...] to reflect this Decision, in order that the Committee on Government Procurement can then adopt [the revised text and relevant documents] no later than 31 March 2012."[351]

The revised agreement on government procurement was then adopted on 30 March 2012.[352]

The new agreement differs, at least on the surface, to quite an extent from the 1994 version. Some, but not all, shortcomings of the agreement were addressed during negotiation and led to structural as well as substantive modifications. The revised agreement not only appears to have a better and more clearly defined structure which follows a certain logic but has also been slimmed and written in a clearer sometimes more explicit language.[353] Moreover, the regulation of new issues as e.g. green procurement and e-procurement are included in the agreement. In addition to these amendments, the new agreement modifies and extends the preferential treatment for developing countries. For example, it provides for an extended implementation period for developing countries, the right for parties to object to modifications of the agreement as well as a stronger emphasis on consultation to solve disputes before requesting the formation of a panel under the WTO's Dispute Settlement Understanding (DSU).

### iii. Terminology

The new agreement begins with definitions of relevant terms used in the agreement. This is an important improvement because it ex ante establish-

350 Committee on Government Procurement, 'Ministerial-Level Meeting of the Committee on Government Procurement (GPA/112), 15 December 2011', p. 1.

351 Ibid, 2.

352 Protocol Amending the Agreement on Government Procurement, adopted on 30 March 2012 (GPA/113).

353 Cf. R.D. Anderson, 'The conclusion of the renegotiation of the World Trade Organization Agreement on Government Procurement: what it means for the Agreement and for the world economy' (2012) 3 Public Procurement Law Review, 83-94 at 85.

es and defines the terms and, thus, limits the scope of interpretation which is not only valuable in regard to harmonisation but also simplifies application and implementation of these terms. This can be attributed to the effort to make the agreement more user-friendly. The 1994 GPA does not contain such a provision comprising definitions, but some definitions can be found within particular provisions or in some of the member states' schedules.[354] Despite acknowledging the overall improvement brought about by providing definitions of the terms, Reich criticises certain shortcomings as regards to the content.[355] However, it should be noted that his criticism refers to an older version of the revised agreement which differs to some extent from the final version. His remarks are, hence, only of limited utility. Beyond that, Article II includes a clear definition of government procurement,[356] which closely resembles the definition of government procurement as outlined in Article III (8) (a) of GATT 1947. This provision explicitly exempts government procurement from its national treatment obligation. Hence, it provides an improvement which logically resembles the fact that the GPA is based on and serves to elaborate on the exception provided by GATT.[357] Furthermore, defining the terms contributes to harmonisation since the interpretation of the term government procurement no longer depends on the national definitions but is to be applied uniformly.[358]

### b. Objectives and Principles

The preamble of the 1994 GPA names the principles of transparency and non-discrimination. It further outlines the objectives to liberalise trade and to create a multilateral framework and states the need for effective dispute settlement procedures and to take the development, financial and trade needs of developing countries into account.[359] Apart from these general

354 Reich, 'The New Text of the Agreement on Government Procurement', 1000.
355 For a detailed discussion of the definitions established in Article I see ibid, 1000-1005.
356 WTO Agreement on Government Procurement, 1994, Art. II (2).
357 Reich, 'The New Text of the Agreement on Government Procurement', 1006.
358 Ibid, 1006.
359 Preambles usually outline the main objectives of an agreement and, although, they seem to primarily have declarative or political character, Article 31 (2) of the Vienna Convention on the Law of treaties refers to the preamble as part of the

objectives and remarks, the desire to extend the scope and coverage of the agreement and to encourage acceptance of and accession to the agreement is set out.

The preamble of the revised agreement has been amplified with more specific objectives. Apart from the principles of non-discrimination and transparency, integrity and predictability are explicitly stated as integral parts of government procurement systems. Integrity and predictability are mentioned as key principles for the efficient and effective management of public resources, the performance of the parties' economies and the functioning of the multilateral trading system. In contrast to the 1994 GPA, which only refers to the objective of expanding the conduct of international trade as well as improving its framework, the new agreement includes objectives which focus on the domestic sphere of government procurement or, as Reich notes, it "adds several domestic welfare rationales that are unrelated to the benefits of international trade."[360] This implies that the agreement applies not only to foreign but also to domestic suppliers; products or services and that corruption and good governance are not just matters for domestic law but can also be dealt with by the international community. Whereas the 1994 GPA version only states that the provision of transparency of laws, regulations, procedures and practices regarding government procurement are desirable, the preamble of the new agreement elaborates further on transparency. It recognises

> "[…] the importance of transparent measures regarding government procurement, of carrying out procurements in a transparent and impartial manner and of avoiding conflicts of interest and corrupt practices, in accordance with applicable international instruments, such as the United Nations Convention Against Corruption […]."

Transparency in regard to government procurement is not only amplified by explicitly mentioning that the avoidance of conflicts of interests and corruptive practices is one of the goals but also by expressly referring to international instruments and, particularly, UNCAC which contains certain provisions concerning procurement.[361] This also reflects the fact that non-transparency and most notably corruption have been identified as major obstacles for the efficient and effective functioning of procurement

---

context of the treaty in light of which the treaty should be interpreted and, thereby, assigns a certain legal significance to the content of the preamble.

360 Reich, 'The New Text of the Agreement on Government Procurement', 996.

361 See e.g. Article 9 (1). For more information on Article 9 see above: Introduction, Subchapter 4 (a)) and Part I, Chapter 2, Subchapter 3.

systems worldwide and the view that this problem can only be resolved in accordance with general transparency and anti-corruption initiatives because it is not only a procurement-specific challenge.

The issue of the extent to which the reference to international instruments implies that their provisions are legally binding within the context of the GPA is largely unexplored. Remarkably, few GPA members have signed UNCAC, which raises the question whether the specific reference to that convention implies that it is, at least in regard to the relevant provisions, applicable to all GPA members. Reich suggests that it could mean that even non-members of UNCAC are subject to its provisions in regard to government procurement but the author then elaborates that "applicable" could be understood in the substantive sense and, hence, restrict the application to its members.[362] Applicable might, however, also refer to those provisions of international agreements which are applicable to public procurement, hence attributing legally binding character to those provisions. In any event, UNCAC can be seen as soft power instrument and in the long run its provisions may be accepted as having binding character for non-members to the extent that it has attained the status of customary law. The reference to UNCAC in the GPA is at least an important step in this direction.

The transparency objective as laid out in the preamble is accompanied by substantive and procedural rules within the text of the agreement. Article IV (4) of the revised GPA is especially worth mentioning. This provision states that "[a] procuring entity shall conduct covered procurement in a transparent and impartial manner that: [...] (b) avoids conflicts of interest; and (b) prevents corrupt practices." The matters of corruption and conflict of interest have so far not been amongst the objectives of the GPA.[363] Their inclusion might be a response to the increasing awareness that corruption and conflicts of interests may not only impact market access but also constitute major hindrances for the effectiveness and efficiency of procurement in general.[364] The latter recognition reflects the new, additional focus of the GPA to domestic welfare rationales, as discussed above. Although the provision establishes a new enforceable legal

362 Reich, 'The New Text of the Agreement on Government Procurement', 999f.

363 Cf. Anderson; et al., 'Ensuring integrity and competition in public procurement markets', p. 687.

364 Cf. S. Arrowsmith, 'The Revised Agreement on Government Procurement: changes to the procedural rules and other transparency provisions', p. 289.

obligation for the GPA parties,[365] the vagueness of the provision leaves open what practical and legal implications arise out of it.[366] Nevertheless, it can be said that it sets an example and points the way towards further regulations in this respect.[367]

The inclusion of domestic welfare rationales in the objectives of the agreement, when combined with the transparency disciplines, might further contribute to the promotion of good governance.[368] Since the rule of law is a component of good governance the GPA may not only result in more efficient and effective procurement systems, but also have positive effects on socio-economic development on the national level. The Chairman of the Committee on Government Procurement stressed in regard to the improvements of the revised agreement that it

> "[...] provides an extremely important new tool through which the international community can address the challenges of good governance and promote the effective use of public resources in all participating economies [...]".[369]

The amended GPA is therefore more likely to play a role in advancing domestic procurement systems in general instead of only with regard to the limited scope of the agreement and the liberalisation of public procurement markets. It further increases the potential of GPA provisions to serve as best practices and be a valuable model for countries reforming their public procurement systems.

The preamble, further, envisages flexibility in regard to accommodating the specific circumstances of each party in regard to their procedural commitments under the agreement. This reflects the awareness that national procurement systems might differ to quite an extent and that procedural requirements in the GPA "should not create or impose undue rigidity in the operation of Parties' procurement systems."[370] However, although some provisions have been designed to provide more flexibility, the agreement still sets out detailed procedural rules rather than general prin-

365 R.D. Anderson; et al., 'Ensuring integrity and competition in public procurement markets: a dual challenge for good governance', p. 687.

366 S. Arrowsmith, 'The Revised Agreement on Government Procurement: changes to the procedural rules and other transparency provisions', p. 291.

367 Ibid.

368 Cf. Reich, 'The New Text of the Agreement on Government Procurement', 998.

369 Committee on Government Procurement, '"The GPA Renegotiation: Time to Close the Deal" - Statement on Stocktaking and Future Work (Made a the the Informal Closing Session, 18 October 2011)', p. 1.

370 Arrowsmith, 'The Revised Agreement on Government Procurement', p. 286.

ciples, thereby limiting the flexibility of countries when implementing the agreement. Nevertheless, in comparison to the prior agreement the new version entails several modifications that allow for more flexibility. These include the special and differential treatment of developing countries, the types of procurement, shorter time-periods, etc. Last but not least, the preamble recognises the importance of using, and of encouraging the use of, electronic procurement.

Article IV of the new agreement comprises a summarisation of general principles; these include non-discrimination, transparency and impartiality, rules of origin, offsets, measures not specific to procurement, and the use of electronic means. With the exception of the use of electronic means, all these principles were already contained in the 1994 version. The inclusion of electronic means reflects the increasing use of electronic media in government procurement, which has been identified as an opportunity to improve transparency and efficiency in public procurement.[371] The 1994 article on national treatment and non-discrimination is now simply headed "non-discrimination", which is more definite because national treatment is, in addition to the principle of most-favoured-nation treatment, usually seen as one of the two constituents of the non-discrimination principle underpinning by the WTO.[372]

Non-discrimination can be regarded as the overarching principle of the GPA. It can be assigned to the neoliberal trading policy which supposes that the liberalisation of trade has a positive impact on development and can be ascribed to the prevailing attitude in the WTO. It provides for the equal treatment of domestic and foreign products irrespective of their origin[373] (non-discrimination in terms of the country of origin) and, further, prohibits discrimination of locally established suppliers affiliated or owned by foreigners or producing abroad[374] (non-discrimination in terms of the degree of foreign affiliation or ownership). The provision, however, does not prevent the parties from applying customs duties, import regulations and charges, or measures affecting trade in services unless these concern laws, regulations, procedures and practices regarding government procurement covered by the GPA.[375] Hence, as Arrowsmith notes, "[...]

---

371 See Part I, Chapter 1, Subchapter 6.

372 Cf. Silva, 'The revision of the WTO Agreement on Government Procurement', 82.

373 WTO Agreement on Government Procurement, 1994, Art. III (1).

374 Ibid, Art. III (2).

375 Ibid, Art. III (3).

access to government markets under the GPA remains subject to the limitations and restrictions of these more general barriers."[376]

c. Scope and Coverage of the GPA

i. Scope and Coverage

The 1994 agreement covers procurement of products and services by any contractual means.[377] It applies to any law, regulation, procedure or practice regarding any procurement by entities which are specified in Appendix I if contracts with a value of not less than the relevant threshold, which is likewise specified in Appendix I, are concerned.[378] The definition of procurements in the annexes contains four dimensions: the value of procurement, the identity of the procuring entity, the type of goods or services procured and the origin of the goods or services.[379] Governments can, thereby, define precisely what sectors or entities are subject to the GPA as well as the threshold value for its application. This allows latitude to exclude certain entities or sectors which are significant, e.g. for the development of the domestic market, from the application of the agreement. Article II (now found in Subarticle 6 of Article II) sets out comprehensive guidelines and restrictions for the determination of the value of contracts with the objective of preventing attempts to circumvent the application of the GPA, for example, the splitting of procurement requirements into several individual contracts in order to remain under the monetary threshold.[380]

It is important to note that the determination of entities and sectors which are explicitly made subject to the agreement is carried out through negotiations between the member states. The principle of reciprocity plays an important role in the bilateral negotiations, which means that countries grant or deny the same degree of market access that they have to other parties' market, meaning that they liberalise together.[381] But such negotia-

---

376 Arrowsmith, 'Government Procurement in the WTO ', p. 105.
377 WTO Agreement on Government Procurement, 1994, Art. I (2).
378 Ibid, Art. I (1) and (4).
379 Reich, 'The New Text of the Agreement on Government Procurement', 992.
380 WTO Agreement on Government Procurement, 1994, Art. II (3) and (4).
381 See for example S.J. Evenett; B.M. Hoekman, 'Introduction', in S.J. Evenett; B.M. Hoekman, *The WTO and Government Procurement* (Cheltenham et al.:

tion of coverage also implies that all member states can define different scopes for their relationship with the other parties. The result is a numerousness of bilateral agreements which is only a very small step towards harmonisation of public procurement law because, although this does, indeed, tend towards a convergence of substantive rules, these are only applied reciprocally, instead of universally to all parties to the GPA. The agreement consequently "has the appearance of a series of bilateral agreements based around a common structure of principles and award procedures, rather than a multilateral arrangement."[382]

Beyond that, GPA parties can specify derogations or conditions attached to the coverage of the GPA either by line item, in annex-specific notes, in the general notes, or in a separate note in the party's annexes to Appendix I.[383] Some parties, for example, maintain non-application provisions with regard to the application of domestic policies such as the promotion of SMEs.[384] The bilateral character of the scope of the GPA and the great number of derogations specified by the member states make implementation complicated as it is very difficult to determine which procurements are covered by the GPA and which are not.[385]

The article governing the scope and coverage of the revised GPA is nearly identical to the former respective article but additionally excludes specific contract types which are explicitly mentioned from the new agreement's application. These include public employment contracts and the acquisition or rental of land and immovable property. At this point it is to be noted that the determination of scope of application through negotiations has - despite heavy criticism that such approach undermines its efficiency - not been changed in the new agreement.

---

Edward Elgar Publishers, 2006), p. xiv. Arrowsmith, 'Government Procurement in the WTO', p. 109.

382 S. Arrowsmith, 'Towards a Multilateral Agreement on Transparency in Government Procurement' (1998) 47 International and Comparative Law Quarterly, 793-816 at 796.

383 Anderson; Osei-Lah, 'The coverage negotiations under the Agreement on Government Procurement', p. 158.

384 Ibid, 159.

385 See Reich, 'International Public Procurement Law', p. 316f.

ii. General Exceptions

While the scope of the GPA can be determined by the member states according to the four parameters, there are certain general exceptions allowing the parties to deviate from the terms of the agreement.

With regard to military procurement and procurement indispensable for national security of for national defence purposes the parties are allowed to take any action or to withhold information irrespective of the rights and obligations of the agreement.[386] The exemption of public procurements related to the military, national security and defence is, in particular in the context of the GPA, understandable. As confidentiality in such matters is of the utmost importance for governments, not only within states but in particular with respect to defence alliances, the exemption from the application of the GPA is reasonable.

Article XXIII (2) of the 1994 GPA and Article III (2) of the revised agreement permit the parties to apply measures

> "[...] necessary to protect public morals, order or safety, human, animal or plant life or health or intellectual property; or relating to the products or services of handicapped persons, of philanthropic institutions or of prison labour."

The application of these measures must, however, not

> "[...] constitute a means of arbitrary or unjustifiable discrimination between countries where the same conditions prevail or a disguised restriction on international trade."

Unlike the 1994 GPA where security and general exceptions are only mentioned in Article XXIII, the revised version already sets out these exceptions in Article III. In consideration of the practical meaning of exceptions this structural change seems reasonable as an aid in understanding as well as implementation.

Article III (2) is similar to Article XX of GATT, which is also a general exception clause.[387] It allows governments to protect certain state interests and also to prevent specific standards applied in regard to environmental and social aspects from being undermined. However, it does not provide a blanket exception under which governments may justify any measure. In respect of measures having a discriminatory effect on countries with the

---

386 Revised Agreement on Government Procurement, 2012 (adopted on 30 March 2012 and entered into force on 6 April 2014), Art. III (1); WTO Agreement on Government Procurement, 1994, Art. XXIII (2).

387 This will be discussed in more detail below: see Subchapter 7 of this chapter.

same conditions or where the same standards are applied and such discrimination is arbitrary or cannot be justified, a government cannot invoke Article III (2) of the GPA. The same applies to measures constituting a disguised restriction on international trade. Although the provision is of utmost importance, its application can be problematic in practice as the interpretation of terms such as public morals is vague. In cases where countries invoke their right under Article III (2), this might lead to disputes that can only be solved by a panel established under the WTO Dispute Settlement Understanding, which then has to clarify whether a measure falls under the interpretation of the respective term.

### 3. Procedures

#### a. Procurement Methods and Procedures

A very important improvement in regard to the flexibility of the agreement is that it offers room for the application of other methods of procurement than the three that are explicitly mentioned (open tendering, selective tendering and limited tendering) as long as they comply with the requirements of the agreement. However, instead of providing for a detailed uniform tendering procedure, the tendering procedures outlined in the 1994 GPA were said to be sufficiently flexible to accommodate other related procurement methods.[388] By clarifying that the three methods mentioned are illustrative, the revised agreement clearly permits the use of any other method, provided that it is consistent with the agreement. Article IV (4) (a) provides that a procuring entity shall conduct covered procurements in a transparent and impartial manner consistent with the agreement, using methods such as open tendering, selective tendering and limited tendering. This expressly allows parties to use different kinds of procurement methods that are suitable for the existing needs and circumstances. However, the practical effect of this provision is rather unclear since it is difficult to envisage a more innovative method of procurement that does not fall under the recognised ones but complies with the specific rules of the agreement.[389]

---

388 Arrowsmith, 'Reviewing the GPA', 767.

389 Anderson; Arrowsmith, 'The WTO regime on government procurement', p. 31; Arrowsmith, 'The Revised Agreement on Government Procurement', p. 294.

Articles VII-XV cover the regulations on general procedural requirements and the different procurement types. The sequencing of the provisions according to the procurement cycle is more user-friendly and can thus be considered an improvement over the 1994 agreement. Substantively, however, these provisions do not significantly differ from the provisions of the former version of the agreement.[390]

The GPA explicitly provides for three different tender procedures: open, selective and limited tendering.[391] Open tendering allows all interested suppliers to submit a tender irrespective of their suitability. Selective procedures require a qualification of suppliers whereby the selection of suppliers shall not be applied with the purpose or the effect of creating unnecessary obstacles to the participation of suppliers of another party in its procurement.[392] Open and selective tendering are the prescribed procedures which have to be applied in general circumstances not falling under one of the exceptions laid out in the agreement. They require that a notice of intended procurement be published for all cases of intended procurement.[393] Such notice has to include details about the contact details of the procuring entity, nature and quantity of goods or services, the procedure, delivery date, deadline for the submission of bids, and a description of any conditions for participation of suppliers.[394]

The use of a qualification system as an invitation to participate is governed by Article IX in conjunction with Article VII. Under these procedures interested suppliers have to successfully complete the qualification procedures in order to take part in bidding. The qualification system culls the firms which have the financial, commercial and technical capacity to fulfil the contract in question.[395] It can, therefore, be described as an instrument of selective procurement.

Limited tendering can be applied only under specific circumstances such as the absence of tenders in response to open or selective procure-

---

390 For a discussion about changes in this regard see R.D. Anderson; S. Arrowsmith, 'The WTO regime on government procurement: past, present and future'; Reich, 'The New Text of the Agreement on Government Procurement', 1008.

391 Revised Agreement on Government Procurement, 2012, Art. IV (4) (a).

392 Ibid, Art. IX (3).

393 Ibid, Art. VII (1).

394 Ibid, Art. VII (2); WTO Agreement on Government Procurement, 1994, Art. IX (6).

395 Revised Agreement on Government Procurement, 2012, Art. VIII (3) (a); WTO Agreement on Government Procurement, 1994, Art. VIII (b).

ment, for certain types of contracts such as for the procurement of works of art, and for particular circumstances such as extreme urgency, specific follow-up orders, or goods purchased on a commodity market.[396] All procurements executed under this procedure need to be reported and require a statement indicating the circumstances and conditions that justified the use of limited tendering.[397] The statement has to be disclosed which is important for transparency reasons and allows stakeholders and the wider public to hold the decision-makers accountable. The disclosure criterion and in particular the clear reference to the need of justification is intended to prevent the misuse of limited tendering and the use of this procurement method to unnecessarily limit competition or exclude foreign competitors.

Open as well as selective tendering (including a prequalification procedure) under the GPA allow for a high degree of competition. Given that the GPA covers only procurements above a certain monetary threshold, it is not necessary to consider whether the cost and time expended for a particular procurement under the GPA are disproportionate in regard to the value of the procurement. The approach to generally requiring the use of the most competitive procurement methods while at the same time having due regard to specific considerations that might justify limited tendering procedures can be deemed to be reasonable and adequate. As there are no detailed procedural rules laid down, the GPA member states are provided with enough flexibility to keep or enact rules and regulations that are tailored to the specific local context.

Negotiations between procuring entities and potential suppliers are allowed in two cases.[398] Whereas the 1994 agreement made clear that the practice of negotiation had as its primary objective the identification of the strengths and weaknesses in tenders and required the strict adherence to the principle of non-discrimination and national treatment,[399] the revised agreement contains neither a statement of objectives nor a reference to non-discrimination and national treatment.

The first case where negotiation is allowed under the revised GPA is where such intent has been indicated in the notice of intended procurement.[400] All suppliers that have expressed their interest in participating in

396 Revised Agreement on Government Procurement, 2012, Art. XIII (1).
397 Ibid, Art. XIII (2).
398 Ibid, Art. XII (1).
399 WTO Agreement on Government Procurement, 1994, Art. XIV (2) and (4).
400 Revised Agreement on Government Procurement, 2012, Art. XII (1) (a).

the procedure need to be included in negotiations. If the intent for negotiations has not been indicated beforehand, negotiations are only allowed in cases where it is impossible to determine the most advantageous tender in terms of the specific evaluation criteria set forth in the notice or tender documentation.[401] As negotiations in tendering procedures make monitoring and evaluation more difficult and are, therefore, contested in regard to their effect on accountability the requirements that negotiations can only take place if it was indicated beforehand and with the inclusion of all tenderers having expressed their interest are important safeguards to prevent misuse of negotiation procedures. It is not, however, clear why the objective of negotiations and the requirement to adhere to the principles of non-discrimination and national treatment as outlined in the 1994 GPA have not been integrated into the new version, as these are important factors in regard to the principles of fairness and equity as well as in order to ensure that negotiations are solely used with the purpose of getting better value for the money.

The GPA further allows its parties to keep multi-use lists in order to be used for a certain period of time for procurement covered under the agreement.[402] As such supplier lists can be criticised for limiting competition, certain safeguards are provided for. Suppliers can e.g. apply for inclusion on the list at any time[403] and requests by suppliers not listed for participation in a procurement based on a particular list are to be considered as well.[404] Hence, registration on the list is not absolutely mandatory for participating in the particular procurements. These factors are of utmost importance to prevent the principles of public procurement and, in particular, competition and fairness, from being undermined.

### b. Tender Specification, Award Criteria and Evaluation Methods

#### i. Qualification Criteria

The criteria that can be used in qualification procedures under the GPA include financial, commercial as well as technical aspects regarding poten-

401 Ibid, Art. XII (1) (b).
402 Ibid, Art. IX (7-11).
403 Ibid, Art. IX (10).
404 Ibid, Art. IX (11).

tial suppliers or contractors. In other words, the financial capacity and the commercial and technical abilities of a supplier will be evaluated in order to determine whether or not they are qualified to take part in the bidding.[405] It is not sufficient to assess the supplier's business activities inside the country; its activities abroad also need to be considered.[406] Criteria not falling under financial, commercial or technical matters cannot be used in qualification procedures. This approach prevents the application of subjective criteria not strictly related to the essential capability of suppliers or contractors and, hence, also restricts the application of secondary objectives in this respect.

### ii. Description of the Subject Matter

The description of the subject matter includes the nature and the (estimated) quantity of goods or services. Furthermore, any requirements in regard to the subject matter that have to be fulfilled have to be included in the tender documentation.[407] The requirements include technical specifications, conformity assessment certification, plans, drawings or instructional materials.[408] Technical specifications are to be set out in terms of performance and functional requirements.[409] The use of design or descriptive characteristics shall generally be avoided.[410] If possible, technical specifications shall be based on international standards, otherwise on national standards.[411] In order to ensure the use of fair and objective rather than subjective criteria, the GPA provides for a list of tender requirements that can be used to describe a subject matter as well as further instructions about their contents. The use of international standards in tender specification, for example, fosters competition as it facilitates the participation of foreign bidders. The requirement that technical specifications are to be set out in terms of performance and functional requirements is beneficial in two ways. It not only increases the number of potential bids as products or services can differ to quite an extent in regard to design while fulfilling the

405 Ibid, Art. VIII (3) (c).
406 Ibid.
407 Revised Agreement on Government Procurement, 2012, Art. X (7) (a).
408 Ibid.
409 Revised Agreement on Government Procurement, 2012, Art. X (2) (a).
410 Ibid.
411 Revised Agreement on Government Procurement, 2012, Art. X (2) (b).

same function but can also have a positive effect on research and innovation. In particular the use of functional requirements can stimulate several different proposals or solutions. The promotion of research and innovation through public procurement can be regarded as being of utmost importance for the development of national market and exemplifies that the requirements set forth in the GPA in regard to tender specifications not only benefit the objective of liberalising trade but also objectives pursued on the national level. The naming of a particular trademark or trade name, patent, design or type, specific origin, producer or supplier is generally prohibited. A deviation from this prohibition is permissible only when there is no other possibility of describing the product or service and provided that the tender document states that the reference is solely used to describe the product and that suppliers or contractors of any equivalent product or service can participate.[412] Similarly, Article X (3) requires that, if design or descriptive characteristics are used in the technical specifications, the tender description include an indication that equivalent goods will be considered, too. This prevents any predetermination of suppliers and, thereby, also the indirect promotion of domestic or certain suppliers which would be indirectly discrimination against other suppliers or producers and limit competition. Entities are, additionally, forbidden from seeking or accepting "advice which may be used in the preparation of specifications for a specific procurement from a firm that may have a commercial interest in the procurement."[413]

The objective of the GPA is, hence, to impede any direct or indirect preferential treatment and to enable the highest possible degree of competition. Generally, only neutral criteria that concern the envisaged outcome of procurement and that do not go beyond the officially accepted standards or regulations shall be used in the tender description. As indicated above, this is not only beneficial for international procurements and for liberalising trade but is an essential factor in regard to the principles of national public procurement systems, such as competition, fairness and value for money.

---

412 Ibid, Art. X (4).
413 Ibid, Art. X (5).

iii. Evaluation Criteria

Evaluation criteria and their relative importance need to be published in the tender documentation.[414] Whereas the 1994 GPA did not specify what other criteria beyond the price and other cost factors might be considered in the evaluation of tenders,[415] the new GPA suggests quality, technical merit, environmental characteristics and terms of delivery as evaluation criteria.[416] This reflects the notion that value for money means more than simply the best price. The quality of the product or service is decisive for a satisfying procurement outcome; however, it is also difficult to measure and requires public procurement officials to clearly establish criteria to measure quality on a case-by-case basis. The inclusion of environmental characteristics can be seen as a response to the general notion that public procurement can be used to promote environmental objectives.[417]

iv. Method of Evaluation

The contract award method prescribed by the GPA does not solely focus on price but grants the possibility of awarding tenders according to specific evaluation criteria. The award shall be made to the lowest tender, if price is the sole criterion, or to the tender that in terms of the specific evaluation criteria set forth in the notices or tender documentation is determined to be the most advantageous.[418] The choice of tenders can, hence, follow the principle of lowest price or, if predetermined in the notices or tender documentation, the specific alternative or additional evaluation criteria.

The authority of entities to enquire with the tenderer of abnormally low bids whether it can comply with the conditions of participation and is capable of fulfilling the terms of the contract can also have a positive impact.[419] It constitutes a safeguard against suppliers which misrepresent figures in order to be awarded a contract and, thus, against post-award

414 Ibid, Art. X (7) (c).
415 WTO Agreement on Government Procurement, 1994, Art. VII (2) (h).
416 Revised Agreement on Government Procurement, 2012, Art. X (9).
417 On this topic see above in Part I, Chapter 3, Subchapter 3.
418 Ibid, Art. XV (5).
419 Ibid, Art. XV (6).

price adjustments and shortcomings in or failure of contract implementation.

## 4. Institutions: The Committee on Government Procurement

In regard to national procurement institutions, the only requirement provided by the GPA is to establish a national review mechanism which will be dealt with below in Subchapter 8. Otherwise, the agreement is silent on national institutional matters. On the supranational level, the GPA provides for the establishment of a Committee on Government Procurement (in following: the Committee) which is composed of representatives from each member state. It serves as a consulting body to the parties and has to carry out other responsibilities that may be assigned to it by the member states. It can therefore establish working parties or subsidiary bodies. The Committee has to meet at least once a year but is supposed to meet on an ad hoc basis as necessary. In practice, several formal meetings as well as informal meetings are held each year.[420] Beyond these functions, it is obliged to carry out an annual review of the implementation and operation of the agreement in view of its objectives.[421] The Committee has a policy as well as an oversight function and can have a positive impact in several respects, such as promoting further harmonisation, responding to new findings in regard to future trends of public procurement, assisting member states and ensuring accountability.

## 5. The Treatment of Developing and Least-developed Countries

### a. The 1994 Agreement

The 1994 agreement provided for special and differential treatment of developing and least-developed countries. Article V (1) stated that

> "[p]arties shall, in the implementation and administration of this agreement, through the provisions set out in this article, duly take into account the development, financial and trade needs of developing countries, in particular least-developed countries."

420 Arrowsmith, 'Government Procurement in the WTO ', p. 42.
421 Revised Agreement on Government Procurement, 2012, Art. XXI.

It explicitly mentioned certain factors in respect to supporting developing countries' needs: the balance-of-payments position, an adequate level of reserves, the promotion and establishment of domestic industries, support for industrial units dependent on government procurement, and economic development through regional or global arrangements among developing countries.[422] Article V (2), furthermore, provided that "each party shall, in the preparation and application of laws, regulations and procedures affecting government procurement, facilitate increased imports from developing countries" and, thereby, urged developed countries to grant developing countries preferable market access. A temporary exclusion from any provision of the agreement was not incorporated into the 1994 GPA.[423] Thus, the question arose whether or how these objectives could limit the scope of application of the agreement for developing countries and, thereby, satisfy developing countries' special circumstances. The answer could be found in Article V (3), which required the parties to duly take "into account in the course of negotiations [the aforementioned objectives] with respect to the procurement of developing countries to be covered by the provisions of this Agreement." And Subsection 4 specified that

> "[a] developing country may negotiate with other participants in negotiations under this agreement mutually acceptable exclusions from the rules on national treatment with respect to certain entities, products or services that are included in its coverage lists, having regard to the particular circumstances of each case."

Exclusions for the national treatment principles could therefore be negotiated, even without reciprocal effect. However, there is no "automatic right for developing countries to obtain such concessions."[424] Thus, while it indeed allowed developing countries to include entities or sectors into the coverage of the GPA with exemption of the national treatment provision, to make the effectiveness of special and differential treatment dependent on negotiations between parties with very often unequal economic and political power severely narrowed its practical importance and ignored the fact that most developing countries had a much weaker bargaining power

422 WTO Agreement on Government Procurement, 1994, Art. V (1) (a-d).

423 Art. XXIV (4) excludes the possibility to enter reservations in respect of any of the Agreement's provisions.

424 L. Jiang, 'Regulating Public Procurement in International Trade', in S. Arrowsmith, *Public Procurement Regulation: An Introduction* (Nottingham: EU Asia Inter University Network for Teaching and Research in Public Procurement, 2010), p. 184.

than their counterparts.[425] On the other hand, basing the special and differential treatment provisions on negotiations allowed a regard to individual considerations and specific circumstances of developing countries and could, if effectively conducted, lead to an adequate system of exceptions.[426] Practically it was believed that the provision might convince developing countries to add entities or sectors which benefitted from preferential policies to the coverage list. This had the advantage that procurements in this respect were at least subject to the transparency and procedural rules of the agreement.

Developing countries could also negotiate modifications of its coverage list after accession to the agreement[427] and, furthermore, could request the Committee to "[…] grant exclusions for certain entities, products or services […] in the light of its participation in regional or global arrangements among developing countries."[428]

The 1994 special and differential treatment provision, additionally, provided for technical assistance in regard to procurement[429] and foresaw the establishment of information centres in developed countries which could handle procurement-related requests from developing country parties.[430] Technical assistance included "the solution of particular technical problems to the award of a specific contract" and "any other problem the party making the request and another party agree to deal with in the context of this assistance".[431] Article V (10) explicitly mentioned the translation of qualification documentation and tenders into an official language of the WTO as one component of technical assistance.

With regard to least-developed countries the agreement referred to paragraph 6 of the decision of the contracting parties to GATT 1947 of 28

---

425 Cf. Arrowsmith, 'Government Procurement in the WTO ', p. 113.

426 Cf. A.C. Müller, 'Special and differential treatment and other special measures for developing countries under the Agreement on Government Procurement: the current text and new provisions', in S. Arrowsmith; R.D. Anderson, *The WTO Regime on Government Procurement: Challenges and Reform* (Cambridge Cambridge University Press, 2011), p. 357.

427 WTO Agreement on Government Procurement, 1994, Art. V (5)

428 Ibid, Art. V (5).

429 Ibid, Art. V (8-10).

430 Ibid, Art. V (11). As Arrowsmith noted, until 2003 no such center had been established. Arrowsmith, 'Government Procurement in the WTO ', p. 443.

431 WTO Agreement on Government Procurement, 1994, Art. V (9).

November 1979 on differential and more favourable treatment, reciprocity and fuller participation of developing countries which reads as follows:[432]

> "Having regard to the special economic difficulties and the particular development, financial and trade needs of the least-developed countries, the developed countries shall exercise the utmost restraint in seeking any concessions or contributions for commitments made by them to reduce or remove tariffs and other barriers to the trade of such countries, and the least-developed countries shall not be expected to make concessions or contributions that are inconsistent with the recognition of their particular situation and problems."

The GPA allows for the special treatment of least-developed countries parties and suppliers in those countries according to these guidelines. The special treatment can even be extended to least-developed countries which are not parties to the agreement.[433] Beyond that, developed countries shall, upon request, assist least-developing countries with the application of a tender.[434] This differs from the technical assistance for developed countries in so far as the extent of such technical assistance does not depend on an agreement between the member states. It would be interesting if there has ever been a case where a developed country supported potential tenderers in developing or least-developed countries because it presupposes not only the request from the least-developing countries but also the good will of the developed countries, which is instead of being obliged to provide support, is only supposed to assist. A study of the extent to which technical assistance has generally been provided to developing countries which are parties or potential parties to the GPA would also be interesting.[435]

Under the 1994 GPA, the operation and effectiveness of the special and differential treatment provision was to be reviewed by the Committee every three years. The Committee had the power to modify or extend exclusions from the application of the agreement.[436]

In the course of further rounds of negotiations developing countries were supposed to "give consideration to the possibility of enlarging its

---

432 Decision of the CONTRACTING PARTIES to GATT 1947 of 28 November 1979 on Differential and More Favourable Treatment, Reciprocity and Fuller Participation of Developing Countries (BISD 26S/203-205), 1979.

433 WTO Agreement on Government Procurement, 1994, Art. V (12).

434 Ibid, Art. V (13).

435 Cf. Müller, 'Special and differential treatment and other special measures for developing countries', p. 354f; Silva, 'The revision of the WTO Agreement on Government Procurement', 73.

436 WTO Agreement on Government Procurement, 1994, Art. V (14).

coverage lists, having regard to its economic, financial and trade situation."[437] Hence, developing countries could, theoretically, have decided about the extension of the coverage lists. In practice, the question arises to what extent developed countries exerted their influence and put pressure on developing countries in this regard.

### b. The revised Agreement

The special and differential treatment provision has been substantively modified and entails concrete suggestions for the kind of transitional exemptions developing countries can invoke or negotiate, such as price preference policies, offsets, phased-in addition and higher thresholds (Article V (3)). But as the effectiveness of this provision depends on the parties' agreement and is based on the development needs, its practical relevance is still to be seen. The drafters have thus not totally abided by determining the scope of exemptions through negotiations. Furthermore, developing countries must clearly articulate what specific development needs they have in order to be granted exemptions.

Moreover, although the revised GPA – like the original version of the GPA - does not require parties to grant preferential market access to developing countries,[438] the actual market access for developing countries is greater than under the 1994 GPA. Article V (2) states:

> "Upon accession by a developing country to this Agreement, each Party shall provide immediately to the goods, services and suppliers of that country the most favourable coverage that the Party provides under its annexes to Appendix I to any other Party to this Agreement, subject to any terms negotiated between the Party and the developing country in order to maintain an appropriate balance of opportunities under this Agreement."

Hence, by derogating from the principle of reciprocity developing countries may benefit from full and equal market access despite maintaining certain protectionist policies themselves. Since market access of developing countries has improved under the revised GPA more developing countries may accede to the agreement.

---

437 Ibid, Art. V (15).

438 Silva, 'The revision of the WTO Agreement on Government Procurement', 88. See for a comparison of the respective provisions of the 1996 and the revised GPA Müller, 'Special and differential treatment and other special measures for developing countries', p. 342ff.

A radical modification in regard to the special and differential treatment for developing countries is also the inclusion of an opportunity of delayed application of any specific obligation of the GPA, except the prohibition of discrimination between foreign products or services from parties to the agreement, i.e. the principle of most-favoured-nation treatment.[439] A delayed application of the national treatment principle and, therefore, the application of preferential practices can be negotiated as well as any other delayed application of the provisions of the GPA. This accounts for the special circumstances in developing countries and can certainly be attributed to the effort to make accession more attractive to developing countries. It grants developing countries full and equal access to the procurements covered by the other parties without requiring full reciprocal rights to suppliers of other parties to the agreement, which is the major difference to the 1994 GPA.[440] This responds to the fact that implementation might constitute a major challenge for developing countries. The implementation period is limited to 5 years for least developed countries and to 3 years for developing countries. However, any delayed application needs to be agreed to by the other parties, whereby the practical efficacy depends on the willingness of the other members to allow for this kind of special and differential treatment for a certain time. Again, bargaining power might be decisive for developing countries, which can be usually assigned a weaker standpoint in this respect. Yet at the same time developed countries have a strong interest in new accessions and should be willing to respond to the needs and concerns of developing countries.[441] Beyond this, it might be an opportunity to find adequate ways to deal with the specific and different conditions and circumstances in developing countries. However, the implementation period has been criticised as being too short for small economies to adjust to foreign competition or for developing countries with a low level of bureaucracy to meet the bureaucratic challenges.[442] This argument is, however, only partly convincing, not only because good governance and the rule of law are general accepted and promoted goals rather than procurement-specific objectives and because many developing countries have significantly improved their bu-

439 Revised Agreement on Government Procurement, 2012, Art. V (4).
440 Reich, 'The New Text of the Agreement on Government Procurement', 995.
441 Cf. Müller, 'Special and differential treatment and other special measures for developing countries', p. 374.
442 Silva, 'The revision of the WTO Agreement on Government Procurement', 84f.

reaucratic apparatus in the past years, but also because a transition period which is too long might tempt developing countries not to apply the resources and efforts necessary to adapt their procurement systems.

Nevertheless, strictly speaking developed countries also had such flexibility under the 1994 version of the GPA because it did not restrict the freedom of member states to negotiate coverage.[443] It is therefore not a substantial modification but more of a clarification that developing countries are permitted to derogate from the principle of non-discrimination and other provisions of the agreement for a certain time despite the specific entity or industry being generally covered by the agreement. Although under the 1994 GPA developing countries could have been granted exemptions to the national treatment principle for an unlimited time, the revised GPA - by allowing for delayed application of nearly all the disciplines of the agreement – reduces the burden of the economic as well as administrative implementation costs. It provides the opportunity of gradual implementation, which might constitute an incentive to join the agreement in the first place but also to reach the capacity to implement the agreement in full.[444] Although the possibility of gradual implementation responds both to the implementation difficulties for developing countries and the reluctance to tolerate preferential procurement practices, it remains an open question of whether this approach can provide an incentive for developing countries considering accession.

## 6. Transparency

### a. General Transparency Provisions

Transparency in the GPA is two-fold, with obligations for procuring entities in regard to transparency in the procurement agreement[445] and for the parties with view to the implementation of the agreement.[446] The regulations on transparency have not been substantially altered by the revision of the GPA. A modification of the 1994 agreement that is worth mentioning

443 Cf. Anderson; Arrowsmith, 'The WTO regime on government procurement', p. 45.

444 Cf. Müller, 'Special and differential treatment and other special measures for developing countries', p. 364.

445 Revised Agreement on Government Procurement, 2012, Art. XVI.

446 Ibid, Art. VI.

can be found in Article VII (2) which requires the procuring entity, if applying selective tendering, to state in any notice of intended procurement any limitation of the number of suppliers to be invited as well as the criteria to be used for their selection. This is an important improvement in regard to transparency.

The parties to the agreement are required to submit annual reports to the committee including statistics on its contracts covered by the GPA.[447] If such statistics are accessible through an official website or a single database, a party might be exempted from submitting a report.[448] Apart from the collection and publication of the statistics on procurements under the GPA, the parties to the agreement have an information duty if specific information on a particular tender is requested by a party to the agreement.[449] This may include questions regarding the fairness and impartiality of the tender process or the characteristics and relative advantages of the successful tender.[450] If a negative effect on competition in future tenders can be assumed, the party obtaining the information shall not disclose it to any supplier.[451] Under the GPA, governments have an important role in ensuring accountability of public procurement towards other parties to the agreement. Nevertheless, adherence to these requirements is also essential for every national public procurement system. The establishment of official websites or national databases can e.g. significantly improve transparency and accountability of the public procurement system.

Any notice of intended procurement falling under the scope of the GPA has to be published in an appropriate paper or electronic medium utilised by the parties to the agreement.[452] Further requirements are that the medium is widely disseminated and that the information is accessible to the public at least until the expiry of the time-period indicated in the notice.[453] The publication requirements differ for procuring entities covered under Annex 1 and the ones under Annexes 2 and 3. Notices of the former have to "be accessible by electronic means free of charge through a single point of access."[454] Notices of the latter are required to be, if accessible by elec-

447 Ibid, Art. XVI (4).
448 Ibid, Art. XVI (5) and (6).
449 Ibid, Art. XVII (1).
450 Ibid, Art. XVII (1).
451 Ibid, Art. XVII (1).
452 Ibid, Art. VII (1) read in connection with Appendix III.
453 Ibid, Art. VII (1).
454 Ibid, Art. VII (1) (a).

tronic means, accessible "through links in a gateway electronic site that is accessible free of charge."[455] Apart from the notice of intended procurement, which has to include comprehensive information on the subject matter and the procurement process, procuring entities are obliged to publish a summary notice for each case of intended procurement in one of the WTO languages containing at least the subject-matter of procurement, the final date for submission and the contact details where documents relating to the procurement can be obtained.[456] As mentioned above, comprehensive information and requirements in regard to the subject matter have to be included in the tender documentation.[457] Moreover, the tender documentation has to include the qualification criteria and their relative importance.[458] As has been emphasised in the chapter on transparency in the first part (Chapter 2), the public availability of tender invitations, all criteria regarding the tender and the evaluation method is of utmost importance for the effective and efficient functioning of public procurement systems and should be implemented in any national procurement system.

Procuring entities are obliged to disclose a notice on each contract award within 72 days including certain details on the winning tenderer, the nature and quantity of products or services as provided in the contract and the value of the winning award.[459] If requested from a supplier of a party, each entity is supposed to provide explanations of its practices and procedures and reasons for its decisions.[460] Participating suppliers have to be promptly informed about decisions on contract awards by the entities.[461] Certain exceptions can be justified under Article XVII which regulates the disclosure of information. According to Subarticle 3, confidential information may be withheld if publication would impede law enforcement, be contrary to the public interest, prejudice the legitimate commercial interest of particular enterprises or prejudice fair competition between suppliers.

The aforementioned transparency provisions concern the post-contract award stage. The comprehensive notice on the contract award procedure and outcome enable participants as well as other stakeholders to understand the decision and its basis. Other participants might be able to assess

455 Ibid, Art. VII (1) (b).
456 Ibid, Art. VII (3).
457 Ibid, Art. X (7) (a).
458 Ibid, Art. X (7) (c).
459 Ibid, Art. XVI (2).
460 Ibid, Art. XVI (1).
461 Ibid, Art. XVI (1).

their own bid through comparison with the nature and quantity of products or services and the value of the winning contract. The disclosure of the type of procedure, furthermore, might offer valuable clues to facilitate understanding why the procuring entity decided in favour of the winning tenderer rather than the other participants. For the case that a supplier or unsuccessful tenderer has not been satisfied by the available information and fails to see how the procuring entity reached a certain decision it can request substantive information on the reasons why its application to qualify was rejected and why its tender was not selected. This very important mechanism is an essential feature of a transparent procurement system because it prevents corruption, strengthens trust in the procurement system and facilitates competition. The restriction on the disclosure of information in regard to sensitive information is necessary to protect certain interests, such as the confidentiality of internal company data, which need, for example, to be withheld in order for the company to maintain its competitive advantage. However, application of this provision might prove to be difficult because the decision about the cases where the disclosure of information conflicts with the objectives as laid out in Article XVII (3) is often a balancing act with a variety of interests at stake. The effect of publishing the data is usually hard to estimate beforehand and, therefore, requires a realistic and reasonable assessment by the procuring entity and is, thus, also dependent on skills of the public procurement officials responsible to take such decisions.

Apart from the requirement in regard to the publication of information, the GPA also imposes a duty on procuring entities to keep the records of tendering procedures and contract awards under the GPA for at least three years.[462] Furthermore, the electronic traceability of the conduct of covered procurement by electronic means needs to be ensured.[463] This is essential in order to ensure that decisions and processes can be reproduced, for example, if irregularities are disclosed during contract implementation or at a later stage or if review or court procedures take place. They are, hence, important requirements in regard to transparency and accountability in public procurement.

Another requirement that benefits transparency is the envisaged harmonisation of qualification procedures and registration systems. This provision, which cannot be found in the 1994 version of the agreement, pro-

462 Ibid, Art. XVI (3) (a).
463 Ibid, Art. XVI (3) (b).

vides that each party shall ensure that its procuring entities make efforts to minimise differences in their qualification procedures and, where registration systems are maintained, to minimise differences in this respect.[464] As mentioned in Chapter 2 of Part I, in particular in decentralised systems a standardisation of procedures facilitates transparency, inter alia, because bidders are not forced to familiarise themselves with a variety of procedures and because it alleviates monitoring.

With respect to the transparency requirements as outlined in the GPA, it can be concluded that the requirements represent best practices and can contribute to the achievement of national public procurement objectives. Despite the basic rationale of the GPA to liberalise public procurement markets, it also contains provisions that are of utmost importance for the effective and efficient functioning of national public procurement markets.

### b. Procurement Planning

Apart from the requirement to publish any notice of intended procurement, Article VII (4) of the GPA encourages entities to publish planned procurements. This refers to notices regarding the future procurement plans of procuring entities for the current fiscal year.[465] In contrast to intended procurement notes published in regard to all actual procurements that are announced for open or selective tendering, planned procurement describes procurement which is planned for the future and cannot be understood as an invitation for bids yet. However, it can be considered as an invitation for interested suppliers to express their interest and can be used as a notice of intended procurement if certain criteria are met.[466] Planned procurement is admissible as a notice of intended procurement for the entities outlined in Appendix 3 of the agreement.[467] Each notice of planned procurement is supposed to contain as much of the information required for proposed procurement notices as far as it is available.[468] Furthermore, it needs to include a statement that interested suppliers should express their interest

464 Ibid, Art. IX (2).
465 Ibid, Art. VII (4).
466 Ibid, Art. VII (5); cf. also Arrowsmith, 'Government Procurement in the WTO ', p. 190, 202.
467 Revised Agreement on Government Procurement, 2012, Art. VII (5).
468 WTO Agreement on Government Procurement, 1994, Art. IX (7).

in the procurement to the procuring entity.[469] The recommendation to publish procurement plans can have a positive effect on competition and facilitates the participation of foreign companies in tendering. In addition to this effect, it can contribute to the achievements of national public procurement objectives as it fosters transparency and enables potential bidders and suppliers to plan their economic activities accordingly. Moreover, it can stimulate innovation and research in specific areas.[470]

## 7. Secondary Objectives

### a. The 1994 Agreement

Any practice that discriminates in the course of procurement between domestic and foreign firms is per se prohibited. The application of secondary objectives, however, is not explicitly prohibited by the GPA. Whether or better to what extent it was - within the context of the 1994 GPA - legitimate to pursue objectives that are not directly linked to the subject matter of procurement was always controversial and had to be decided on a case by case basis. Several scholars have interpreted the GPA provisions in respect of the legitimacy of secondary objectives. Many have found that the 1994 GPA allowed for the application of secondary objectives to a limited extent at certain procurement stages provided they did not discriminate against foreign suppliers or contractors or goods or services.[471] Nevertheless, there have also been dissenting views which deny the legitimacy of any secondary objectives under the GPA; this is, however, a minority.[472]

What is non-controversial and has to be stressed beforehand is that any procurement below the threshold value is not subject to the 1994 GPA.

469 Revised Agreement on Government Procurement, 2012, Art. VII (5).

470 On this issue see also above in Part I, Chapter 1, Subchapter 4.

471 Arrowsmith, 'Government Procurement in the WTO ', p. 325ff; Gaedtke, 'Politische Auftragsvergabe und Welthandelsrecht', p. 118ff; McCrudden, 'Buying Social Justice', p. 469ff. See also Odendahl, 'Die Berücksichtigung vergabefremder Kriterien im öffentlichen Auftragswesen', 652.

472 Odendahl, 'Die Berücksichtigung vergabefremder Kriterien im öffentlichen Auftragswesen', 652. The author refers to the following dissenting views: G. Kunnert, 'WTO-Vergaberecht: Genese und System sowie Einwirkungen auf das EG-Vergaberegime ', (Baden-Baden: Nomos, 1998), p. 275. H.-J. Priess, 'Das Übereinkommen über das öffentliche Beschaffungswesen', in C. Pitschas;H.-J. Priess, *WTO-Handbuch* (München: C.H. Beck, 2003), p. 649.

Such procurements can, hence, be legitimately used to pursue certain secondary objectives.[473] The question is, therefore, whether the provisions of the 1994 GPA prohibited or allowed the application of secondary objectives in public procurements covered by the agreement and what has changed under the revised agreement in this respect. The pursuit of secondary objectives might be possible under different provisions of the GPA, including the provisions on technical specifications, qualification criteria and award method, or might be justified by Article XXIII, which allows parties to enact measures that are contrary to the provisions of the GPA for certain purposes, e.g. to protect public morals. In the following the different possibilities to include secondary objectives under the 1994 GPA are analysed and assessed. Thereafter, the modifications in the revised agreement in regard to secondary objectives are presented.

The provision on technical specifications played an important role in regard to measures intended to achieve secondary policy objectives. The agreement required technical specifications laying down the characteristics of the products or services to be designed in such a way that they did not constitute unnecessary obstacles to international trade.[474] Article VI (1) explicitly set out a list of technical specifications: quality, performance, safety and dimensions, symbols, terminology, packaging, marking and labelling, or the processes and methods for their production and requirements relating to conformity assessment procedures prescribed by procuring entities. All technical specifications needed to be performance-related rather than design-related or descriptive[475] and based on international standards, technical regulations or building codes or, in absence of the thereof, national standards, etc.[476] Criteria which lay down rather the characteristics of the supplier or contractor rather than the characteristics of a product or service could not be included as technical specification.[477] This is important for the application of secondary objectives, since socio-economic policies such as affirmative action policies could most likely not be justified as technical specifications because they are not product-related. However, the inclusion of environmental objectives such as the use of environment-friendly materials was conceivable.[478]

473 Silva, 'The revision of the WTO Agreement on Government Procurement', 75.
474 WTO Agreement on Government Procurement, 1994, Art. VI (1).
475 Ibid, Art. VI (2) (a).
476 Ibid, Art. VI (2) (b).
477 McCrudden, 'Buying Social Justice', p. 484.
478 Cf. Gaedtke, 'Politische Auftragsvergabe und Welthandelsrecht', p. 157.

Article XIII (4) (b) states that the procuring entity can award the tender either to the lowest or the most advantageous tender. Any technical specification as outlined in the tender document, including non-economic criteria,[479] can therefore influence the award decision. Socio-economic procurement criteria, e.g. criteria related to racial or gender equality objectives, can, for example, be integrated as contract requirements (technical specification/contract compliance).[480] And Hoekman & Mavroidis have stressed that, in regard to the determination on which tenderer has the best capability to fulfil the contract, the procuring entity is provided wide latitude which is only limited through the specifications in the notices or tender documentations.[481] However, any such requirement that discriminates against foreign suppliers or contractors and especially of foreign goods or services is inconsistent with the GPA. Green procurement, as it is product-related rather than supplier or contractor-related, can be generally pursued through the inclusion of relevant technical specifications. The inclusion of most criteria regarding labour standards and other socio-economic policies might, in contrast, be prohibited because they are not product-related. Nevertheless, much depends on whether the specifications in the notices or tender documentations can be set out in a way that supports certain secondary policies while still complying with the disciplines of the GPA.

Article VIII (b), however, only applies to restricted and limited procurement. This provision provides that "any conditions for participation in tendering procedures shall be limited to those which are essential to ensure

---

479 Although some have argued that Article XII 4 (b) means the most economically advantageous tender and only economic considerations are permitted, this view has been widely neglected and most scholars have agreed upon the view that any criteria, also non-economically evaluation criteria set out in the tender documentation, can influence the decision about the most advantageous tender. For an overview of the discussion and the reasoning see McCrudden, 'Buying Social Justice', p. 486ff.
As, in practice, other than economic evaluation criteria do play a role and McCruddens argumentation is convincing, the prevailing opinion shall be followed. Moreover, it shall be remarked that – with view to the objectives of value for money and the role public procurement plays in practice for the achievement of other than economic objectives – a limitation to economic criteria would not be appropriate.

480 Cf. ibid, 488.

481 B.M. Hoekman; P.C. Mavroidis, 'Basic Elements of the Agreement on Government Procurement', in B.M. Hoekman; P.C. Mavroidis, *Law and policy in public purchasing: the WTO agreement on government procurement* (Ann Arbor: University of Michigan Press, 1997), p. 14.

the firms' capability to fulfil the contract in question." This must be interpreted in light of the non-discrimination requirements of Article VIII, which states that

> "[i]n the process of qualifying suppliers, entities shall not discriminate among suppliers of other Parties or between domestic suppliers and suppliers of other Parties"

and

> "[…] any conditions for participation required from suppliers [...] shall be no less favourable to suppliers of other Parties than to domestic suppliers and shall not discriminate among suppliers of other Parties."

Article VIII (b) seems to constitute a stringent limitation of qualification criteria which excludes or severely restricts the application of most if not all criteria which pursue collateral objectives not directly linked to the contract. The European Community[482] and some scholars[483] have argued that qualification criteria under Article VIII need to be performance related, comprising only financial, commercial, and technical capacity. However, even if only performance-related criteria can be considered, the nature of 'the contract' in question can be determined by the procuring entities and as long as the qualification criteria are performance-related and non-discriminatory they still have the latitude to determine what the product or service is to be and can thereby include certain secondary objectives, as McCrudden argues.[484] He nevertheless contests the presumption that under Article VIII qualification criteria necessarily need to be performance-related, arguing that the final provisions would present examples which would include the notion of professional misconduct for non-performance-related qualification criteria.[485] This controversy exemplifies the difficulty of assessing the legitimacy of secondary objectives under the GPA and poses a difficult task to governments that are parties to the agreement.

---

482 When arguing against the Massachusetts legislation in United States - Measure Affecting Government Procurement, WTO Dispute Settlement, DS 88. For further information in this respect see Odendahl, 'Die Berücksichtigung vergabefremder Kriterien im öffentlichen Auftragswesen', 651.

483 C. Pitschas; H.-J. Priess, 'Secondary policy criteria and their compatibility with E.C. and WTO procurement law - *The case of the German Scientology Declaration*' (2000) 4 Public Procurement Law Review, 171-195 at 189; Kunnert, 'WTO-Vergaberecht', p. 267.

484 McCrudden, 'Buying Social Justice', p. 485.

485 Ibid, 487.

Despite the general ambiguity about the legitimacy of applying secondary objectives, the exceptions of Article XXIII may provide a possibility to justify its application. Article XXIII (1) allows for exceptions that are necessary for the protection of its essential security interests relating to the procurement of arms, ammunition or war materials, or to procurement indispensable for national security or for national defence purposes. Subarticle 2 of Article XXIII reads as follows:

> "Subject to the requirement that such measures are not applied in a manner which would constitute a means of arbitrary or unjustifiable discrimination between countries where the same conditions prevail or a disguised restriction on international trade, nothing in this Agreement shall be construed to prevent any Party from imposing or enforcing measures: necessary to protect public morals, order or safety, human, animal or plant life or health or intellectual property; or relating to the products or services of handicapped persons, of philanthropic institutions or of prison labour."

Measures to safety, human, animal or plant life or health and others can justify the inclusion of socio-economic and environmental objectives as long as they are not applied in a manner which constitutes arbitrary or unjustifiable discrimination between countries where the same conditions prevail or a disguised restriction on international trade. It is not at all difficult to imagine that environmental objectives can fall under a measure to protect human, animal or plant life or health. The protection of disabled persons through government procurement is explicitly stated in Article XXIII (2) as legitimate justification. It refers to measures "relating to goods or services of persons with disabilities, philanthropic institutions or prison labour". Apart from measures necessary to protect intellectual property the clause also allows for the enforcement of measures necessary to protect public morals, order or safety. Although policies addressing unemployment might, for example, be justified by these higher objectives, the fact that such policies would need to be formulated in a way that they do not arbitrarily or unjustifiable discriminate between foreign and domestic suppliers or contractors might render them practically ineffective. In view of countries where severe social, political and economic discrimination has affected a certain group of society the question whether preferential treatment of members of this group through government procurement is legitimate arises. Historically disadvantaged groups are not explicitly named in Article XXIII (2) but it might be possible to declare an affirmative procurement policy as necessary to protect public morals. However, this depends on the interpretation of the term "public morals" and might be challenged by other parties as disguised restrictions on trade or as arbitrarily or unjustified discrimination. The application of socio-economic policies is, hence, a grey area in which is quite controversial: can secondary objectives justify derogations to the non-discrimination principle, and if so to what extent? According to Linarelly, "non-economic policy rationales have no standing in WTO agreements."[486] As the author explains, the WTO is not concerned with the domestic concern of promoting social justice and does not at all claim to promote such objectives, but, quite the contrary, insists on market liberalisation irrespective of such goals.[487] The author points out: "What is one WTO Member's social justice is another's protectionism."[488] This view, however, falls short of the WTO's objectives, which go far beyond trade liberalisation; sustainable development is explicitly mentioned as a central principle of the WTO founding charter[489] and has frequently been referred to in the Doha negotiations.[490] Sustainable development in the WTO context is regarded as a powerful ally of trade, assuming that trade liberalisation and sustainable development go hand in hand. The application of secondary objectives having protectionist character with view to enhancing sustainable development seems to contradict this assumption, meaning that such secondary objections might indeed promote sustainable development but concurrently hinder trade liberalisation. The difficulty of assessing the impact of secondary objectives plus the uncertainty of the success of secondary objectives in public procurement in general might explain why there is neither a clear prohibition nor permission to apply secondary objectives and why there is no explicit scope for its application.

Hindrances on what the benchmark for what these measures comprise might be identified in existing case law or by referring to similar provisions in GATT 1947. Only one of three cases[491] that have been so far initi-

---

486 Linarelli, 'The limited case for permitting SME procurement preferences', p. 455

487 Ibid, 455.

488 Ibid, 455.

489 See the Preamble of the Marrakesh Agreement Establishing the World Trade Organisation (signed in Marrakesh on 15 April 1994 and entered into force on 1 January 1995); Doha Ministerial Declaration, WT/MIN(01)/DEC/1, 20 November 2001, available at http://www.wto.org/english/thewto_e/minist_e/min01_e/mindecl_e.htm (last accessed: 21 October 2015).

490 See Doha Ministerial Declaration, 2001.

491 These are DS73: Japan — Procurement of a Navigation Satellite; DS88/95: United States — Measures Affecting Government Procurement (Massachusetts State Law prohibiting contracts with firms doing business with or in Myanmar); DS163: Korea — Measures affecting Government Procurement (procurement practices of the Korean Airport Construction Authority).

ated under the GPA deals with Article XXIII. The case Massachusetts Burma Law[492] concerned an Act adopted by the Commonwealth of Massachusetts which, in essence, prohibited state authorities from procuring goods or services from any persons who do business with Burma. This was challenged by the European Community and Japan. The case was, however, dropped after the Massachusetts government withdrew the law in question.

The GPA exception provision is very similar to Article XX of GATT and Article XIV of GATS. The introductory clauses, which are referred to as the "Chapeau", are identical:

> "Subject to the requirement that such measures are not applied in a manner which would constitute a means of arbitrary or unjustifiable discrimination between countries where the same conditions prevail or a disguised restriction on international trade, nothing in this Agreement shall be construed to prevent any Party from imposing or enforcing measures [...]."

Therefore, the interpretation of Article XX of GATT and Article XIV of GATS appears to be appropriate reference points for the interpretation of Article XXIII of the GPA.

In US-Gasoline[493] the Appellate Body held that an analysis whether a measure can be justified under Article XX consists of two steps: "first, provisional justification by reason of characterization of the measure under XX (g)"[494] and "second, further appraisal for the same measure under the introductory clauses of Article XX."[495] This was confirmed by the Appellate Body in US – Shrimp[496] which, moreover, held the following:

> "The task of interpreting the chapeau so as to prevent the abuse or misuse of the specific exemption provided for in Article XX is rendered very difficult, if indeed it remains possible at all, where the interpreter [...] has not first identified and examined the specific exception threatened with abuse."[497]

Hence, after it has been established.

---

492 United States - Measure Affecting Government Procurement, WTO Dispute Settlement, DS 88.

493 United States - Standards for Reformulated and Conventional Gasoline, WTO Appellate Body, WT/DS2/AB/R, 29 April 1996.

494 Ibid, 22.

495 Ibid, 22.

496 United States - Import Prohibition of Certain Shrimp and Shrimp Products, WTO Appellate Body, WT/DS58/AB/R, 12 October 1998.

497 Ibid, 44, para. 120.

In the context of the GPA this means that the analysis must begin with the issue of whether the measure (a) is necessary to protect the aim or (b) whether it relates to the product or service in question. If the measure is provisionally justified by one of the exceptions, the panel must assess whether the measure has been applied in a manner which constitutes a means of arbitrary or unjustifiable discrimination between countries where the same conditions prevail or constitutes a disguised restriction on international trade.[498] Certain elements, such as the definition of the term public moral, remain unclear.[499] And since the definitions are not yet clearly outlined by the WTO, the definition of these terms can be determined independently by the member states[500] and, especially, in regard to the yet undefined concepts of public order and morals[501] the justification for secondary objectives remains ambiguous.

It has to be stressed that any secondary objective that is provisionally justified under the GPA cannot be applied in a manner which constitutes arbitrary or unjustifiable discrimination between parties. Any measure to protect domestic industries, such as price preferences, which cannot be justified under the list of exceptions in Article XXIII (2) is therefore prohibited per se. Apart from this it is, however, often difficult to determine whether a certain secondary objective is directly or indirectly discriminatory against foreign suppliers or contractors or goods or services. Moreover, it remains unclear how far derogations from the non-discrimination principle cover policies with extraterritorial effect.[502]

Davies[503] also indicates the scope for considering regulatory purposes and distinguishes between de jure and de facto discrimination. Whereas the former discriminates explicitly between domestic and foreign goods or services, the latter involves "origin-neutral measures which allegedly have

498 Cf. McCrudden, 'Buying Social Justice'; Pitschas; Priess, 'Secondary policy criteria', 193.

499 See for an extensive discussion of this issue McCrudden, 'Buying Social Justice', p. 493-506.

500 Cf. Odendahl, 'Die Berücksichtigung vergabefremder Kriterien im öffentlichen Auftragswesen', 652.

501 Arrowsmith, 'Reviewing the GPA', 780.

502 Ibid, 780.

503 A. Davies, 'The national treatment and exceptions provisions of the Agreement on Government Procurement and the pursuit of horizontal policies', in S. Arrowsmith; R.D. Anderson, *The WTO Regime on Public Procurement: Challenges and Reform* (Cambridge: Cambridge University Press, 2011).

a detrimental effect on foreign suppliers".[504] De facto discrimination is not prohibited per se under the national treatment provision.[505] GPA parties could, for example, align price preferences to comparably situated groups in all other states party to the GPA.[506] Although it would be difficult to find a violation of the national treatment principle such policy might in practice disproportionately affect foreign suppliers or contractors.[507] Such practice would, however, often undermine the rationale behind secondary objectives, namely the promotion of domestic goods or services, suppliers or contractors, thereby rendering it generally impracticable.[508]

It is striking that the GPA came to force with such a strong emphasis on the prohibition of discriminatory policies because a lot of the countries participating in the negotiations had or have actually applied such policies.[509] But, as Arrowsmith remarks with respect to the 1994 agreement, the GPA offers great flexibility in regard to the application of secondary policies even beyond the aforementioned scenarios since parties can exclude particular products, services and entities from the coverage of the agreement and can explicitly authorise policies that might otherwise be at variance with GPA principles.[510] Israel, for example, grants a 15 per cent price preference to domestic firms when competing with firms from non-party states.[511] The US reserved its right to apply "set-asides on behalf of small and minority businesses".[512] Such flexibility, however, rests on the success of negotiations between the parties which might benefit parties with great bargaining power but be unachievable by less powerful countries. The bargaining power rests not only on economic power, but also political international standing of a country. Moreover, a country's bargaining power in general, and its procurement market power in particular,

504 Ibid, 432.

505 See also Arrowsmith, 'Government Procurement in the WTO ', p. 160ff.

506 Davies, 'The national treatment and exceptions provisions of the Agreement on Government Procurement', p. 433, 442.

507 Ibid, 434.

508 Cf. Ibid, 442.

509 Cf. McCrudden, 'Buying Social Justice', p. 225.

510 There is no explicit provision within the GPA but the General Notes in Appendix I of the GPA 1994 allows the parties to establish derogations in respect to the national treatment and MFN-principle. See Anderson; Arrowsmith, 'The WTO regime on government procurement', p. 47f; Arrowsmith, 'Government Procurement in the WTO ', p. 348ff.

511 Evenett, 'Introduction', p. xxi.

512 United States Annex to Appendix 1, General Notes, Note 1.

is decisive because it might allow the country to negotiate a deal which permits it to maintain certain protectionist policies while still liberalising substantial procurement markets.[513] Countries with small procurement markets in contrast have less power to negotiate exceptions to the coverage of the GPA because they are not able to make offers of interest to others.[514] Arrowsmith also recognises that it might be harder for new parties to achieve exclusions.[515] However, the negotiation of exceptions is contrary to the objective of eliminating discriminatory policies and extending the coverage of the agreement and, hence, such practice should be avoided in order not to undermine the foundation of the GPA.[516]

### b. The revised Agreement

In regard to preferential policies and secondary objectives, Arrowsmith made clear that she would prefer a transparency agreement on government procurement over a detailed description of procedures and rules. Such agreement should entail flexible rules on award procedures which allow member states to integrate social and economic policies. She notes the following:

> "The possibility for States to continue with discriminatory policies also raises the question of reciprocity. However, as with a number of other agreements, it appears likely that States may be prepared to accept transparency rules without reciprocal national treatment obligations. This is especially likely if a transparency agreement is seen as a first step to tackling other barriers in public procurement – for example, if it is accompanied by obligations to enter into future negotiations for removing discriminatory measures. It is also more likely if discriminatory policies which do exist are shown to be effective in achieving legitimate social and economic objectives […]."[517]

This reasoning supports the idea of departing from the total ban of socio-economic objectives and discriminatory practices to accelerate the spreading of the GPA; it would create a common ground which clears the way

---

513 Cf. Linarelli, 'The limited case for permitting SME procurement preferences', p. 455.
514 Cf. Silva, 'The revision of the WTO Agreement on Government Procurement', 75.
515 Arrowsmith, 'The Revised Agreement on Government Procurement', p. 321.
516 Cf. Silva, 'The revision of the WTO Agreement on Government Procurement', 74.
517 Arrowsmith, 'Towards a Multilateral Agreement on Transparency', 806.

for negotiations on further steps towards a harmonisation of rules and a gradual renunciation of the application of discriminatory practices. The other notion implied in Arrowsmith' statement is that it is better when discriminatory practices are disclosed than when they are hidden behind non-transparent procedures. This approach has though not been followed in the revised agreement.

The situation of secondary objectives has not substantially changed under the revised agreement since the key provisions outlined above have not been modified. The only matter that was considered during revision and has been altered accordingly is green procurement. As observed in Part I,[518] green procurement has become not only an extensively discussed topic within academia but has also been integrated into the procurement systems in many countries. The provision on green procurement is set out in Article X (6), which reads as follows:

> "For a greater certainty, a Party, including its procuring entities, may, in accordance with this Article, prepare, adopt or apply technical specifications to promote the conservation of natural resources or protect the environment."

GPA members are thus explicitly allowed to include environmental requirements as technical specifications. The provision has to be read in conjunction with the definition of "technical specifications" laid out in Article I (u) which reads as follows:

> "Technical specification means a tendering requirement that (i) lays down the characteristics of goods or services to be procured, including quality, performance, safety and dimensions, or the processes and methods for their production or provision; or (ii) addresses terminology, symbols, packaging, marking or labelling requirements, as they apply to a good or service."

This means that a variety of environmental criteria may be included in the goods- or service-specific criteria or production-related issues. The new GPA also explicitly mentions environmental characteristics as possible evaluation criteria.[519] The provision thus grants procuring entities wide discretion to include environmental policies by appropriately designing the tender document, although it does not exactly determine the kind of environmental measures that can be included.[520] Beyond the inclusion of environmental criteria as technical specifications, evaluation criteria or contract conditions, the application of environmental policies has not been

518 See Chapter 3.
519 Revised Agreement on Government Procurement, 2012, Art. X (9).
520 Arrowsmith, 'The Revised Agreement on Government Procurement', p. 323.

addressed and it remains ambiguous in how far the pursuit of environmental objectives constitutes a legitimate practice within the disciplines of the GPA. Anderson and Arrowsmith note in this regard that

> "[t]he precise impact of these provisions – including the extent to which they extend the flexibility available under the Agreement or merely confirm existing possibilities – is far from clear; but at the very least they do provide an explicit acknowledgement of the potential of procurement in this area and we would expect them to have some impact on the future interpretation of the Agreement in this area."[521]

Moreover, there is no reference to the use of other secondary objectives, e.g. the promotion of labour rights. Reich has harshly criticised this omission: "Given the potential of these important causes to be abused for political purposes, the drafters may have preferred to omit such express permission."[522] However, the Committee has launched the Future Work Programmes to deal with related topics, such as SMEs, sustainable procurement and safety standards in international procurement.[523]

Nevertheless, there is one modification that is of special importance in regard to countries where foreign firms violate local laws such as environmental or labour laws, a circumstance which has been a frequent problem e.g. in Namibia. According to Article VIII (4) suppliers may be excluded from participating in a procurement on grounds such as bankruptcy, false declarations, significant or persistent deficiencies in performance of any substantive requirement or obligation under a prior contract or contracts, final judgements in respect of serious crimes or other serious offences, professional misconduct or acts or omissions that adversely reflect on the commercial integrity of the supplier or failure to pay taxes. Whereas the first two grounds can also been found in the 1994 agreement all the others have been added to the list. Although the wording "such as" has been used in both versions of the agreement the extension of the list explicitly authorises the exclusion of suppliers or contractors who have conducted illegal practices in the past, rendered deficient performance or committed similar types of misconduct, thereby providing greater certainty about "what type of conduct may be considered analogous to the situa-

521 R.D. Anderson; S. Arrowsmith, 'The WTO regime on government procurement: past, present and future', p. 31.

522 Reich, 'The New Text of the Agreement on Government Procurement', 1012.

523 Committee on Government Procurement, '"The GPA Renegotiation: Time to Close the Deal" - Statement on Stocktaking and Future Work (Made a the the Informal Closing Session, 18 October 2011)', p. 2.

tions of bankruptcy and the making of false declarations."[524] Although the provision requires any such decision to be based on supporting evidence, other questions in regard to implementation remain. These include the question of whether performance-related deficiencies or professional misconduct must have been found by a court or any other specific body qualified to do so. Moreover, the question of the time limits for the exclusion based on misconduct remains unsettled, as does the issue of the extension of the exclusion to parent and sister companies which have not been found to be engaged in such conduct.[525] All these matters are essential in regard to the objectives of procurement and need to be regulated by the implementing states.

### c. Rules of Origin and Offsets

Further principles concern rules of origin and offsets. The provisions on these matters have not substantially changed in the revision of the agreement. Rules of Origin can now be found in Article IV (5) and the provision on offsets in Article IV (6), though. Only the rules of origin that are applied in the normal course of trade are admissible. Offsets in the context of government procurement are

> "[...] measures used to encourage local development or improve the balance-of-payments accounts by means of domestic content, licensing of technology, investment requirements, counter-trade or similar requirements [...]"[526]

and, hence, also constitute a certain kind of procurement linkage. Imposing, seeking or considering offsets is prohibited in the qualification and selection of suppliers, products or services as well as in the evaluation of tenders and award of contracts.[527] This follows the notion that offsets constitute an improvement of local suppliers or producers and, thus, represent a form of preferential treatment. The promotion of SMEs, for example, is, therefore, prohibited. Developing countries are free to negotiate exceptions in the regard to offsets concerning the qualification to participate in the procurement process. Offsets in regard to the award contract, however,

---

524 Arrowsmith, 'The Revised Agreement on Government Procurement', p. 309.
525 See ibid, 310f.
526 WTO Agreement on Government Procurement, 1994, Footnote to Art. XVI (1).
527 Ibid, Art. XVI (1).

are non-negotiable.[528] Nevertheless, to what extent developing countries can invoke exemptions from the prohibition to use offsets is determined solely by the outcome of negotiations and rests, hence, solely on the bargaining power of the parties.[529]

## 8. Enforcement

### a. Introduction

Under the 1994 agreement the acceding countries are obliged to

> "[...] ensure, not later than the date of entry into force of this Agreement for it, the conformity of its laws, regulations and administrative procedures, and the rules, procedures and practices applied by the entities contained in its lists annexed hereto, with the provisions of this Agreement."[530]

Despite slightly different wording, Article XXII (4) of the revised agreement has the same effect. Although in countries following the monist approach, which views international and domestic law as forming a single normative legal system and therefore concludes that international law is directly applicable in domestic law, the nature of the GPA requires all member states to enact domestic legislation implementing the provisions of the agreement. In most countries this requires a comprehensive reform of their national public procurement system. Accession to the agreement therefore involves high implementation costs for new member states, and in particular with special regard to the complexity and obscurity of the 1994 agreement. An incomprehensible and sometimes ill-conceived structure and intricate phrasing in combination with the complexity hinder clarity and comprehension, thereby posing a serious challenge to the implementation of the agreement. This may be a contributing factor to the fact that few countries have sought accession to the WTO agreement.

Apart from the acceding countries' duty to ensure that the agreement is fully implemented in national legislation, the GPA also requires the member states to establish a domestic review mechanism and provides for procedures to challenge breaches of the agreement. The agreement requires

528 Ibid, Art. XVI (2).

529 Cf. Silva, 'The revision of the WTO Agreement on Government Procurement', 78.

530 WTO Agreement on Government Procurement, 1994, Art. XXIV (4).

the establishment of a domestic review mechanism for complaints by suppliers in regard to breaches of the agreement in the procurement context.[531] However, if a party has failed to transform GPA provisions into national law, suppliers do not have access to domestic review procedures and can only challenge the government for failing to comply with the agreement. The GPA also allows parties to challenge other parties' breaches of the agreement through the WTO Dispute Settlement Understanding for the resolution of conflicts between parties in regard to the compliance with and the implementation of the agreement, while encouraging the parties to solve disputes by means of consultations.[532] The provisions in regard to breaches of the agreement and in regard to domestic review mechanisms are outlined in the following.

### b. Challenging Breaches of the Agreement

Suppliers may challenge a breach of the agreement that arises in the context of a covered procurement in which the supplier has, or has had, an interest and the parties to the agreement have to ensure that administrative or judicial review mechanisms are provided in this respect.[533] This provision has been inherited from the 1994 version but has been supplemented by Article XVIII (1) (b) which grants the possibility to challenge "a failure to comply with a Party's measures implementing this Agreement" if the breach cannot be challenged directly under domestic law. Thus, if a party has failed to transform certain provisions into national law, suppliers can only challenge the parties' failure to implement the respective provisions of the GPA; it cannot bring an action for non-compliance with them. The provisions of the GPA are therefore not directly applicable even when the failure to implement them can be attributed to the signatory country. Reich criticises the introduction of this provision as adversely and severely undermining domestic challenge procedures.[534] And indeed, requiring a di-

531 For a detailed analyses of the challenge procedure requirements of the GPA see X. Zhang, 'Constructing a system of challenge procedures to comply with the Agreement on Government Procurement', in S. Arrowsmith; R.D. Anderson, *The WTO Regime on Public Procurement* (Cambridge: Cambridge University Press, 2011), p. 485-497.

532 Revised Agreement on Government Procurement, 2012, Art. XX.

533 Ibid, Art. XVIII (1) (a).

534 Reich, 'The New Text of the Agreement on Government Procurement', 1015ff.

rect application of the GPA provisions, whether or not they have been implemented in domestic law, might not only strengthen domestic courts and challenge procedures but also open up a direct channel for suppliers to challenge non-compliance with GPA provisions. With view to strengthening the rule of law in developing countries this might be an important step. In reaction to Reich's criticism, Arrowsmith notes that the approach would be consistent with the position under the previous version of the agreement and, hence, a clarification rather than a modification.[535] In cases where parties have failed to implement GPA provision into national law, suppliers or contractors have no legal remedy. Whereas domestic suppliers or contractors have no opportunity to sue its government, foreign suppliers or contractors that are located in another member state to the agreement can pressure their governments to institute proceedings under the GPA dispute mechanism. Although undesirable, this reflects the nature and the objective of the GPA to regulate international rather than national trade.

In regard to dispute settlement between parties to the GPA the agreement refers in general to the Dispute Settlement Understanding of the WTO.[536] The agreement, however, also stresses that the parties shall

> "[...] accord sympathetic consideration to and shall afford adequate opportunity for consultation regarding any representation made by another Party with respect to any matter affecting the operation of this Agreement."[537]

It requires the parties to first try to find bilateral solutions for matters concerning the operation of the GPA. The provision first included during the revision of the 1994 agreement thus prevents that all conflicting matters are directly transferred to the dispute settlement mechanism of the WTO. Only member state governments can be parties in disputes under the Dispute Settlement Understanding. Consequently, there is no direct access for private parties and they have to rely on their governments to enforce their claim.[538]

So far there have only been three cases concerning the GPA before the DSU.[539] The first case concerned the Act Regulating State Contracts with Companies doing Business with or in Burma (Myanmar) enacted by the

535 Anderson; Arrowsmith, 'The WTO regime on government procurement', p. 32.
536 Revised Agreement on Government Procurement, 2012, Art. XX (3).
537 Ibid, Art. XX (1).
538 Cf. Jiang, 'Regulating Public Procurement in International Trade', p. 186.
539 DS73, DS88/95, DS163.

Commonwealth of Massachusetts on 25 June 1996.[540] This Act basically provided that public authorities of the Commonwealth of Massachusetts are not allowed to procure goods or services from any persons, whether US or foreign, who do business with Burma. This was challenged by the European Communities and Japan as violating several provisions of the GPA. However, the challenge procedure was ceased after a US court ruling barring the implementation of the measure at issue.[541] A complaint against Japan concerning the procurement of a navigation satellite was challenged by the European Communities. The case was not adjudicated by the dispute settlement body as both parties found a mutually agreed solution.[542] The first time that the terms of the GPA were interpreted by a panel of the WTO dispute settlement body was in a case issued by US against Korea in 1999.[543] The US claimed that certain procurement practices of the Korean Airport Construction Authority and other entities concerned with the procurement of airport construction in Korea were inconsistent with Korea's obligations under the GPA. The panel found that the entities responsible for procurement for Korean's Inchon International Airport were not covered entities under Korea's Appendix I of the GPA and are not otherwise covered by Korea's obligations under the GPA and that therefore Korea had not violated the agreement.[544]

### c. Domestic Review Procedures

The parties to the agreement shall encourage complaining suppliers to seek resolution with the procuring entity.[545] The entity is required to

> "[...] accord impartial and timely consideration to any such complaint in a manner that is not prejudicial to the supplier's participation in ongoing or future procure-

540 Act Regulating State Contracts with Companies doing Business with or in Burma (Myanmar) of 1996 ((Chapter 130 of the Acts of 1996), Commonwealth of Massachusetts).

541 World Trade Organisation, United States – Measure Affecting Government Procurement, WT/DS88 and WT/DS95.

542 World Trade Organisation, Japan – Procurement of a Navigation Satellite, WT/DS73.

543 World Trade Organisation, Korea – Measures Affecting Government Procurement, WT/DS163.

544 World Trade Organisation, Korea – Measures Affecting Government Procurement, Report of the Panel, WT/DS163/R, 2000, p. 190, para.VIII.

545 Revised Agreement on Government Procurement, 2012, Art. XVIII (2).

ment or its right to seek corrective measures under the administrative or judicial review procedure."[546]

This is intended not only to encourage suppliers or contractors to lodge complaints about procurement decisions directly with the procuring entity but also to ensure that there are instruments preventing entities from rushing procurement proceedings in order to come to an award decision. An example would be the introduction of a standstill after notification of the award and before the signing of the contract in order to allow an effective bid challenge. In principle this provision stresses that review procedures before specific review bodies or courts should only be the last resort and should usually be preceded by internal complaint procedures. The provision is quite vague and broad, which may hinder effective implementation, but can also be seen as providing more flexibility for member states to find country specific solutions.

The parties are supposed to provide at least one impartial and independent administrative or judicial review body.[547] The challenge procedures must follow the principles of non-discrimination, transparency and efficiency and have to be conducted in a timely manner.[548] A minimum of 10 days must be granted to prepare and file a challenge.[549] If challenges are not directly handled by an impartial and independent administrative or judicial review body, there needs to be a possibility of appeal before such body.[550] Article XVIII (6) outlines procedural requirements for non-judicial review bodies, including the disclosure of relevant documents, the right to be heard and the right to be present.

Furthermore, the agreement requires its parties to adopt or maintain "rapid interim measures to preserve the supplier's opportunity to participate in the procurement" and the correction of the breach of the agreement or compensation for the loss of damages suffered.[551] These are important elements of a procurement review mechanism in view of the commercial and other interests involved. The requirement to establish a domestic review system through which private parties can enforce the GPA provisions (if sufficiently implemented) goes further than other WTO provi-

546 Ibid, Art. XVIII (2).
547 Ibid, Art. XVIII (4).
548 Ibid, Art. XVIII (1).
549 Ibid, Art. XVIII (3).
550 Ibid, Art. XVIII (5)
551 Ibid, Art. XVIII (7).

sions[552] and has the potential to not only "rectify unjustified procurement measures" but also to "deter agencies from employing them."[553] According to Arrowsmith such

> "[...] 'judicialization' of the GPA was possible because of the GPA's plurilateral character and the fact that most original parties were already obliged to provide challenge procedures under regional agreements."[554]

The availability of an impartial and independent review body equipped with the necessary functions and powers is essential for the effective and efficient functioning of public procurement systems. The GPA requires the establishment of at least one such review body, hence, grants its parties great flexibility to design their domestic review mechanism in a way that is suitable in the national context. Important requirements such as the availability of adequate remedies, basic procedural requirements, and a possibility to appeal decisions of the procuring entity under internal complaint procedures are also foreseen by the GPA and can serve as best practices also for countries not party to the GPA.

### 9. The Reluctance of Developing Countries to seek GPA Accession

#### a. The 1994 GPA

The fact that an agreement which was supposed to harmonise public procurement rules on the global level has only 41 signatories after more than 15 years since its coming into force, with 27 of the signatories being EU member states and almost all the rest being developed countries, indicates that it has failed to achieve the objective of liberalising public procurement markets. Arrowsmith recognised only one year after the GPA came into force that the main challenge for policy-makers in regard to the GPA would be

> "[...] to develop an agreement which is effective in improving market access but at the same time avoids the problems afflicting the current GPA which have discouraged accession to that Agreement."[555]

---

552 Arrowsmith, 'Reviewing the GPA', 788. See also P.A. Messerlin, 'Agreement on Public Procurement', in OECD, *The New Wold Trading System: Reading* (Paris: 1995), p. 65.

553 Reich, 'International Public Procurement Law', p. 312.

554 Arrowsmith, 'Reviewing the GPA', 788.

This implies that Arrowsmith accepted the agreement's aim of improving market access but also anticipated that the majority of countries would not accede to the GPA in its original form. There are various reasons for the limited participation which, inter alia, concern the strict application of the national treatment principle, the implementation costs for new members, and the high procedural requirements in regard to transparency and challenge procedures.[556] Despite some improvements the revised agreement does not include substantial modifications. In the following the various aspects possibly accounting for the reluctance of many states to accede the 1994 GPA are outlined and assessed.

The rigorous prohibition of derogations from the non-discrimination principle means relinquishing any possibility of using public procurement above a certain threshold to support certain industries or applying social policies aimed at improving domestic welfare. The last objective, although suspected of being economically inefficient, is a popular political instrument to satisfy particular interests; such policies are often adopted as a response to political pressure.[557] The fact that the GPA pursues an all or nothing approach means that a gradual adaption to the non-discrimination rules and award procedures is not possible. This may deter many countries from acceding to the GPA.[558]

In regard to developing countries, the possibility exists to negotiate derogations and receive preferential treatment which is yet limited due to the often low bargaining power of the developed countries as opposed to that of the generally more powerful western states.[559] The reluctance to abide by the non-discrimination principle in government procurement has been identified as one of the main reasons for the reluctance of developing countries to join the agreement.[560] And if the loss of latitude in applying preferential policies is weighed against improved market access, the former might be preferred, especially in countries which do not yet have

555 Arrowsmith, 'Towards a Multilateral Agreement on Transparency', 794.

556 Cf. Arrowsmith, 'Government Procurement in the WTO ', p. 440f.

557 Arrowsmith, 'Towards a Multilateral Agreement on Transparency', 799f., 802.

558 Arrowsmith, 'Reviewing the GPA', 769. Deltas and Evenett suggest, for example, that the application of price preferences could be gradually abolished rather than being strictly prohibited per se. See Deltas; Simon, 'Quantitative Estimates of the Effects of Preference Policies', p. 82f. or Evenett, 'Is there a Case for New Multilateral Rules on Transparency in Government Procurement?', p. 194.

559 See e.g. Arrowsmith, 'Government Procurement in the WTO ', p. 112.

560 Arrowsmith, 'Towards a Multilateral Agreement on Transparency', 793.

competitive markets for goods or services that are most commonly procured on the international level, as e.g. construction.

The special and differential treatment provision is intended to account for the special economic, legal and bureaucratic challenges developing countries face. In practice, it seems to contain more empty promises than enforceable provisions tailored to the special needs of developing countries.[561] Despite the mandatory requirement for parties to consider the specific circumstances of developing and least-developed countries, there is no reference in regard to the practical effect of this provision. It therefore remains unclear as to how and to what extent parties are to take the special needs of developing countries into account. And as De Lima e Silva noted in 2008, there were no studies on the degree of implementation of this provision by developed countries.[562] In order to gain effectiveness a special and differential treatment provision would need to outline practical specifications rather than mere abstract objectives.

The special and differential treatment provision has also been criticised because it does not require parties to deviate from the principle of reciprocity when negotiating market access with developing countries.[563] This implies that the more protectionist policies developing countries maintain the less market access they might gain, thereby significantly reducing the benefits of acceding to the GPA. Additionally, developing countries, which often have insignificant domestic markets, have few incentives to liberalise their public procurement markets. As Linarelli notes,

> "[c]ountries with smaller economies, particularly developing (and transition) countries with few internationally competitive firms, may find that international competition will lead to greater numbers of procurement awards made to foreign firms, with no compensating offset of awards to their firms in overseas procurement markets."[564]

Beyond this, it is necessary to remark that the benefits of market access in regard to procurement are often limited for developing countries in a significant way by general market restrictions such as tariffs and limits on the

561 Silva states that this is the majority view of the literature. See Silva, 'The revision of the WTO Agreement on Government Procurement', 77. See also Müller, 'Special and differential treatment and other special measures for developing countries', p. 354.

562 Silva, 'The revision of the WTO Agreement on Government Procurement', 77.

563 Arrowsmith, 'Government Procurement in the WTO ', p. 113.

564 Linarelli, 'The WTO Transparency Agenda', p. 237.

movement of natural person,[565] which might also contribute to their reluctance to join the agreement.

It can be concluded that the absolute prohibition of non-discrimination restrains especially countries with weak market power in sectors falling within the scope of the GPA, having corresponding disadvantages in regard to imported goods and services. This helps to explain the reluctance to accede to the GPA. Although there are certain exceptions, such considerations may play a role both for developing as well as least developed countries. Despite the preferential treatment provided by the GPA in this respect, the overall benefits do not appear to outweigh the loss of the ability to pursue specific secondary objectives. In addition, countries in which special interests and lobby groups have a strong influence on political decision-making and where the preservation of power depends on the ability to satisfy this constituency as well as the financial supporters of political parties or candidates (which most notably applies to the US) may want to be free to apply preferential treatment or to use public procurement to pursue certain domestic policy goals through public procurement. The extensive use of the exception clause for crisis situation in the US on several occasions is a significant example in this regard; as mentioned above, this clause allows derogations form the strict prohibition of preferential treatment.[566]

In addition to the concern that they may lose the ability to grant preferential treatment to certain groups, countries might also fear that opening their procurement markets and consequently having to award contracts to foreign firms might result in greater unemployment. This fear is, however, often irrational because foreign firms often sub-contract local firms which could result in a transfer of technology from the foreign firm to the local company, making it more competitive in the long run. Moreover, foreign firms often fill in segments of the market that local firms are in any case unable or unlikely to supply.[567]

As it is clear that any protectionist policy is strictly prohibited the application of other secondary objectives is unclear under the 1994 agreement. Although most scholars argue in favour of the legitimacy of such

565 Arrowsmith, 'Reviewing the GPA', 770; Mattoo, 'The Government Procurement Agreement', 709f.

566 See above: Part I, Chapter 3, Subchapter 2.

567 Anderson; Osei-Lah, 'Forging a more global procurement market', p. 80f.

policies under the agreement, it remains a grey area which potentially deters countries from GPA accession.

Especially for developing countries with limited financial resources, a scarcity of qualified professionals and ineffective or non-existent administrative or legal structures create high barriers to the implementation of the GPA in the national system and thus operate as an obstacle to seeking accession to the GPA in the first place. The bureaucratic burden of implementing the GPA might, moreover, appear disproportionate to the benefits arising from its accession.[568]

Beyond the general implementation of the GPA, the application of some provisions, in particular in regard to transparency and challenge procedures, may constitute a disproportionate burden for certain countries. The requirement to publish a summary of information on procurement opportunities or to implement national challenge procedures can be mentioned in this regard. Arrowsmith ascribes this to the "'hard', or judicialised, approach to enforcement of the GPA"[569] which would prevent any latitude in the application of the GPA's obligation. Particularly states in which public procurement is strongly influenced by political and personal interests might be deterred.[570] Furthermore, politicians might want to avoid being subject to such extensive transparency rules to be able to make contract decisions for personal or political reasons.[571]

The complexity of the language as well as the ambiguity about the application of certain provisions in the 1994 GPA possibly constituted another obstacle for potential accession candidates. As Arrowsmith remarks, some "provisions [...] do not reflect the parties' obvious intentions, or do not reflect those intentions clearly or through consistent language"[572] and concludes that this would result in a "lack of coherence in implementing its [the GPA's] underlying principles."[573] For example: although it was commonly accepted that multiphase procedures were covered by the GPA, it was often not clear how GPA requirements applied in such procedures. Even the obligation of equal treatment was deemed to apply to some procedures but not to others.[574]

568 Arrowsmith, 'Towards a Multilateral Agreement on Transparency', 802.
569 Ibid, 803.
570 Ibid.
571 Ibid.
572 Arrowsmith, 'Reviewing the GPA', 775.
573 Ibid.
574 Ibid.

The high implementation costs also impose a burden, especially for developing countries. The complexity of the agreement requires that extensive resources be expended on the bureaucratic implementation, which in turn presupposes the existence of financial resources as well as expertise. In countries which find it difficult to satisfy the basic needs of the people and face structural problems such as poverty and unemployment, such deployment of resources seems hard to justify in view to the potential benefits. Moreover, compliance with the requirements in regard to transparency and national challenge procedures appears somehow utopian given that in many countries, especially in Africa, corruption is widespread, transparent procedures are rare and seldom at the top of the agenda, and that often not even fundamental legal and juridical structures function efficiently.

Although the GPA envisages that the developed countries support developing and least developed countries in implementing and correctly applying the GPA, an honourable objective with the potential to strengthen and improve the cooperation between developed and developing countries significantly, accession to the GPA is, in the end, not lucrative. However, Anderson and Osei-Lah note that a growing number of WTO members and observers have implemented reforms to their national legislation and procurement policies that potentially make them ready to consider accession.[575]

In light of these shortcomings, namely the obstacles hindering accession of other states and, particularly, developing countries, in 1996 the idea of creating a Transparency Agreement on Government Procurement was proposed. This instrument would require all WTO members to adhere to basic rules of transparency and competition but without making adherence to the non-discrimination principle obligatory.[576] It was intended as preliminary stage of the accession to the GPA and would, therefore, allow for a gradual phase-in.[577] Arrowsmith notes in regard to the potential benefits of such a transparency agreement:

> "A valuable contribution can be made by an agreement which is limited to ensuring predictability, rather than being concerned with the content of the rules applied. Finally, the importance of prescribing detailed rules is minimised by the fact

---

575 Anderson; Osei-Lah, 'Forging a more global procurement market', p. 80.

576 Reich, 'The New Text of the Agreement on Government Procurement', 994. In 1996, the WTO members agreed to establish a Working Group on Transparency in Government Procurement. 'Singapore Ministerial Declaration – Adopted on 13 December 1996', World Trade Organization, document WT/MIN (96)/DEC.

577 Ibid, 994.

> that most States do appear to have procurement rules based on similar principles of competition and transparency, even though they differ in detail."[578]

On the other hand, focusing on detailed procedures and their application was not necessarily seen as beneficial because the principles of competition and transparency seem not to differ extensively in most states anyway. It must though be noted that this might be true for most western countries, but there are still countries whose public procurement systems do not meet international standards of competition and transparency in public procurement, such as Namibia. However, there are also several countries which have enacted up-to-date public procurement rules and procedures, but where the implementation of these rules and procedures is so weak that they can be considered as ineffective. This tends to support the view that the emphasis should not be put on rules and procedures but on the improvement and guarantee of transparency and accountability with view to ensuring that basic principles of public procurement are adhered to in practice. An agreement with the objective of creating a predictable public procurement system, which presupposes transparency, could constitute a more valuable instrument than the GPA. In the course of the Doha Round negotiations this undertaking was, however, abandoned, in part due to strong opposition by developing countries.[579] Nevertheless, the idea of a simplified agreement primarily based on general principles rather than procedural rules was still been argued for even after the termination of negotiations on the transparency agreement.[580] These

> "[...] would not affect the basic transparency goals of the Agreement but would reduce the costs of implementation, including costs in term of loss of discretion in national policy-making; would prevent the Agreement becoming out of date (as has occurred, for example, with the development of electronic procurement); and would remove the scope for unintended anomalies that arise from detailed rules."[581]

It would, however, be important to supplement such a simplified agreement with guidance in order to foster uniform practice, providing infor-

---

578 Arrowsmith, 'Towards a Multilateral Agreement on Transparency', 812.

579 Anderson; Arrowsmith, 'The WTO regime on government procurement', p. 8; Reich, 'The New Text of the Agreement on Government Procurement', 994.

580 See e.g. Arrowsmith, 'The Revised Agreement on Government Procurement', p. 287; Jiang, 'Developing multilateral rules on government procurement', p. 737.

581 S. Arrowsmith, 'The Revised Agreement on Government Procurement: changes to the procedural rules and other transparency provisions', p. 287.

mation on implementation and serving as a guideline for panel or appellate body reviews.[582]

Arrowsmith further suggests that it might be a better approach to "require all policies (discriminatory and non-discriminatory) to be justified, but to remove limitations on the possible *types* of public interest justification."[583] The importance would then lie on the implementation mechanism rather than prohibition. First of all, this approach would require strict transparency rules such as the requirement that secondary policies must be formulated and publicised in advance. Policies which are disguised restrictions on trade or result in arbitrary and unjustified discrimination should still be prohibited. Moreover, secondary policies should only be allowed if they refer to external norms. Beyond this the committee could be given the task of reviewing policies of new members on accession.[584] Such an approach would not restrict the member states' latitude to pursue secondary policies in public procurement as long as there is no arbitrariness or a lack of justification. Although such approach might be detrimental if considered from the economic point of view, it might have many advantages considering the fact that the function of states is not exhausted by their operation as economic entities, but also extends to social and political responsibilities towards the people.

### b. The revised GPA

Although the revised agreement entails several improvements, especially in regard to its complexity, flexibility, structure, phrasing and the inclusion of relevant new concepts, this substantive obstacle has only been addressed in so far as developing countries are allowed an implementation period. During this period only a single provision must be respected; the others may be implemented within a predetermined period from the date of accession. The provision not benefiting from this transition period is the requirement to not discriminate between goods, services and suppliers of any other party. All other forms of discriminatory practices, for example, the preferential treatment of domestic goods, services and suppliers, can be continued till the end of the implementation period. This seems to be a

582 Arrowsmith, 'Reviewing the GPA', 778f.
583 Ibid, 782.
584 Ibid, 781ff.

remarkable advancement but it remains to be seen if it can, in the long run, convince potential candidates to join the agreement. This is because, although the new members do not have to cease all their preferential treatment practices and stop their pursuit secondary objectives through covered government procurement right away, they do commit themselves to renouncing them irrevocable in the long run. Furthermore, whether the option to delay application of provisions of the agreement is given practical effect will depend on the willingness of the current GPA parties to fulfil their promise to grant such an incentive.[585]

However, it should always be kept in mind that the benefits of an application of preferential policies are controversial and that a certain degree of foreign competition is needed in order to enhance the competitiveness of domestic suppliers or contractors.[586] Consequently, it might be preferable for governments to focus on further studying the economic effects of preferential policies and creating awareness about the necessity to constantly challenge preferential policies rather than insisting on their continuing use. Even if a country is not pursuing GPA accession, a stronger focus on assessments and evaluation of applied policies has it benefits in the national context. Moreover, it has to be remembered that any procurement below the determined thresholds are not subject to the rules of the GPA in any event. Hence, secondary objectives are allowed for such procurements and can hence be legitimately used by governments to pursue secondary policies.[587]

The deployment of more precise language and a better structure is a first step towards improving transparency because it makes not only implementation but also monitoring easier. The basis of the agreement is however still the detailed prescription of rules and procedures instead of the provision of guidelines in regard to transparency and predictability, as Arrowsmith suggested for a revised government procurement agreement.[588] Neither the main elements nor the nature of the commitments

585 Cf. Reich, 'The New Text of the Agreement on Government Procurement', 996; see also Silva, 'The revision of the WTO Agreement on Government Procurement', 84.

586 Cf. C.-F. Lo, 'The benefits for developing countries of accession to the Agreement on Government Procurement: the case of Chinese Taipei', in S. Arrowsmith; R.D. Anderson, *The WTO Regine on Government Procurement: Challenge and Reform* (Cambridge: Cambridge University Press, 2011), p. 147.

587 Silva, 'The revision of the WTO Agreement on Government Procurement', 75.

588 Arrowsmith, 'Towards a Multilateral Agreement on Transparency', 812.

made by acceding countries have been fundamentally altered.[589] And although it allows for more flexibility, the practical effect of the modified provisions is not always certain. The implementation costs for the substantive adoption of the procedures and requirements of the GPA may, therefore, still constitute a hindrance to accession to the agreement.

## 10. Conclusion

The GPA puts a strong emphasis on (rule-based) transparency and non-discrimination. Both the rule-based approach to transparency and the principle of non-discrimination have hindered accession, although in different ways. Transparency, in contrast to the absolute application of non-discrimination, is widely accepted as being an elementary part of an efficient government procurement system. Non-discrimination can be classified as one of the pillars of the WTO and its objective to liberalise trade. In regard to public procurement, however, this turns out to be precarious issue because of the diversity and interplay of governmental, public and private interests which may constitute the paramount obstacle for countries considering accession. Nevertheless, the revision of the agreement has led to the expansion of objectives beyond the vision of expanding the conduct of international trade. The GPA's framework was improved by the inclusion of certain objectives aiming at improving domestic welfare. These include integrity, predictability as well as the objective of combating corruption and avoiding conflicts of interest. This indicates, when a country undertakes public procurement reforms, it should consider the GPA not only in respect of a future accession, but also as guideline in regard to international best practices, practices that can have a positive effect on socio-economic development.

The limited but also unclear coverage of the agreement hinders the effect of the agreement. The agreement allows its parties to explicitly exclude certain sectors or industries from the application of the agreement and this shortcoming has not been rectified in the revised agreement. Therefore, states can still protect key sectors or industries. This permits states which have a powerful position to successfully opt out in the negotiations. It might therefore be more advantageous to depart from the strict application of the non-discrimination principle and instead require states

589 Cf. Anderson; Osei-Lah, 'Forging a more global procurement market', p. 87.

to disclose, review and evaluate their discriminatory practices or socio-economic policies related to procurement. Rather than upholding a principle which appears to be practically unachievable, such an approach would not only embrace practical and, particularly, political reality, but also may have the potential to attract many more countries to sign the agreement. The result would lead indeed to a transparent system, including transparency of discriminatory schemes, and possibly promote a substantive extension of coverage and expedite harmonisation. A limited and conditioned allowance of discriminatory practices could, additionally, render the negotiations of the scope of coverage unnecessary but simply include all procuring entities as well as sectors other than the exceptions explicitly mentioned in the GPA. This would also contribute to a widening of the scope of coverage and, moreover, abolish the practice of negotiations which makes the outcome so heavily reliant on the relative bargaining power of the players. It would also eliminate the need for the coexistence of many different bilateral agreements rather than a single multilateral agreement whose application is not only easier to monitor but which also, at least on paper, reflects the notion of equality and, most importantly, harmonisation. It remains to be seen whether future negotiations can lead from a plurilateral to a multilateral agreement on government procurement.

Nevertheless, apart from the character of the GPA itself, growing membership of the current agreement, and in particular the accession of developing countries with greater economic power such as China, might convince developing countries of the benefits of accession and thereby create some sort of soft power.[590] Moreover, the promise to accede the GPA has increasingly been required as accession commitments from countries seeking WTO accession,[591] which can further accelerate GPA accessions. This has, for example, been the case with Chinese Taipei, which has acceded to the GPA in July 2009; several GATT contracting parties had insisted on the commitment to accede to the GPA as a condition to Chinese Taipei's accession to the WTO in 2001.[592]

Benefits of an accession to the GPA might include improved market access, enhanced competition, encouragement of foreign direct investment,

590 R.D. Anderson; S. Arrowsmith, 'The WTO regime on government procurement: past, present and future', p. 35.

591 Ibid, 34.

592 Lo, 'The benefits for developing countries of accession', p. 141.

as well as participation in the further development of the GPA.[593] Moreover, it might help governments to implement public procurement legal reforms as opposed by internal stakeholders.[594]

It is important to keep in mind that the basic rationale behind the GPA differs from the rationales of domestic procurement systems. Nevertheless, benefits that arise from GPA accession can lead to the overall improvement of domestic procurement systems, especially in light of the new focus of the agreement on domestic welfare.[595] A country that is not yet ready to join the GPA might, when reforming its procurement law, design a law that is easy to adapt in case of a future accession. Growing membership as well as further liberalisation of trade and (economic) globalisation might render an accession lucrative in the future. With view to such situation it might be wise to enact a procurement law that can be brought into conformity with the GPA with relative ease.

Additionally, certain provisions of the GPA have been identified as representing best practices and can therefore be regarded as valuable guidelines for domestic reform processes. The transparency requirements, the basic requirements regarding procedures and methods as well as domestic review procedures deserve particular mention in this respect. Transparency is not only required in respect of the publication of the tender invitation, the evaluation criteria, the method as well as the award decisions but other aspects, too, such as the provision of reasons for procurement decisions. Furthermore, the GPA requires procuring entities to collect and publish statistics and to keep records. All these are basic transparency requirements that should be implemented in any public procurement system. Moreover, the encouragement to carry out procurement planning and publish planned procurements might lead to better transparency and, beyond that, have a positive effect on competition, and thus the efficiency and effectiveness of public procurements. The use of open and selective bidding as general procurement methods is also recommendable for domestic public procurement system. However, as the bidding methods in national pub-

593 Anderson; Osei-Lah, 'Forging a more global procurement market', p. 73-79.

594 Arrowsmith, 'Reviewing the GPA', 769. For a discussion about benefits of accession see also: R.D. Anderson; et al., 'Assessing the value of future accessions to the WTO Agreement on Government Procurement: some new data sources, provisional estimates, and an evaluative framework for WTO members considering accession' (2012) 4 Public Procurement Law Review, 113-138.

595 Cf. Anderson; et al., 'Assessing the value of future accessions to the WTO Agreement on Government Procurement', 131.

lic procurement systems have to be applied to a much wider volume of public procurements with a lesser value than the ones falling within the scope of the GPA, the GPA provisions on procedures and methods do not provide an overall solution for domestic systems.

The requirements for domestic review procedures are vague but contain the essential aspects needed to establish an effective and efficient review mechanism. Therefore, the GPA provisions in this respect can be used as general guideline for reform initiatives. It can be concluded that certain provisions of the GPA, and in particular the aforementioned provisions, can - with certain exceptions - be regarded as international best practices and can have a positive impact on socio-economic development and good governance in the countries following these guidelines.

This chapter aims at presenting the basic ideas of the UNCITRAL Model Law (hereinafter referred to also as "the Model Law") regarding objectives and principles, procedures and methods, transparency, the organisational structure and workforce, secondary objectives as well as review procedures. Apart from a presentation of the provisions in respect of these matters the rationale behind these provisions shall be analysed and reference will be made to the GPA where appropriate. As in the previous chapter, best practices as well as shortcomings in the Model Law will be identified and highlighted in order to determine what standards should be followed by developing countries such as Namibia, what provisions should be considered carefully and what approaches should probably be resolved differently.

## 1. Introduction

The original version of the UNCITRAL Model Law on Public Procurement was adopted in 1994 and replaced by the 2011 Model Law. It has served as basis for legislative texts or inspired legal drafting in 29 countries,[596] eleven of which are from Africa. Seven of these African countries have carried out their reform under the auspices of the Common Market for Eastern and Southern Africa. However, many countries have used the UNCITRAL Model Law as guideline for their reforms without notifying the UNCITRAL Secretariat.[597] Therefore the influence is even greater than the official numbers imply.

The intention behind providing a model law on procurement is to increase harmonisation and standardisation to facilitate international trade. In contrast to the GPA, the Model Law presents a more or less comprehensive solution for domestic reform initiatives. It is a framework law providing for "all essential procedures and principles for conducting procurement proceedings in the various types of circumstances likely to be

596 For the current status see the Website of UNCITRAL: http://www.uncitral.org/uncitral/en/uncitral_texts/procurement_infrastructure/1994Model_status.html (last accessed: 26 November 2015).

597 Caborn; Arrowsmith, 'Procurement methods in the public procurement systems of Africa', p. 265.

encountered by procuring entities."[598] Although it entails very detailed rules, it provides sufficient flexibility for adapting it to the domestic context and offers solutions for all types of procurements.[599] It is, however, necessary to enact further regulations, especially regarding the institutional and organisational aspects of public procurement and specifications of procedures and principles. It is also important to remark that procurement planning and contract administration are not dealt with in the UNCITRAL Model Law.

## 2. About UNCITRAL

UNCITRAL was established by the UN General Assembly by its Resolution 2205 (XXI) of 17 December 1966 with the mandate to

> "[…] further the progressive harmonization and modernization of the law of international trade by preparing and promoting the use and adoption of legislative and non-legislative instruments in a number of key areas of commercial law."[600]

UNCITRAL is an intergovernmental body with 60 member states, which include developing as well as developed countries from various regions with different economic and legal systems. It therefore represents a much greater variety of interests than other international organisations and all member states can equally bring forward their proposals and ideas.[601] The member states are selected on a six year basis and the composition changes every three years because the terms of half of the members expire.[602] Namibia, for example, is a member of the UNCITRAL Committee until 2019. UNCITRAL consists of the Commission of the Working Groups and the Secretariat. The Commission meets annually in Vienna or New

598 UNCITRAL, 'Guide to Enactement of UNCITRAL Model Law on Procurement of Goods,Construction and Services', p. 13f., para. 12.

599 Cf. S. Arrowsmith, 'Public Procurement: An Appraisal of the UNCITRAL Model Law as a Global Standard' (2004) 53 International and Comparative Law Quarterly, 17-46 at 22.

600 UNCITRAL, 'The UNCITRAL Guide - Basic facts about the United Nations Commission on International Trade Law', (Vienna: United Nations, 2007), p. 1.

601 Cf. Arrowsmith, 'Public Procurement: An Appraisal of the UNCITRAL Model Law ', 25.

602 Cf. UNCITRAL, 'The UNCITRAL Guide - Basic facts about the United Nations Commission on International Trade Law', p. 3. and the Website of UNCITRAL: http://www.uncitral.org/uncitral/en/about/origin.html (last accessed: 26 Novemer 2015).

York[603] and its work includes the following duties and responsibilities: finalisation and adoption of draft texts referred to the Commission by the working groups; consideration of progress reports of the working groups on their respective projects; selection of topics for future work or further research; reporting on technical assistance activities and coordination of work with other international organisations; monitoring of developments in the "Case Law on UNCITRAL Texts system" and the status and promotion of UNCITRAL legal texts; consideration of General Assembly resolutions on the work of UNCITRAL; and administrative matters.[604] The different working groups are responsible for the preparatory work on their particular topic and comprise members from all UNCITRAL member states as well as staff members from the UNCITRAL Secretariat.[605] The Secretariat is provided by the International Trade Law Division of the Office of Legal Affairs of the Secretariat for UNCITRAL and includes a small number of professional staff members, most of whom are qualified lawyers from different countries and legal traditions.[606] The Secretariat assists the work of UNCITRAL by preparing studies, reports and draft texts on matters that are being considered for possible future inclusion in the work programme, legal research, drafting and revision of working papers and legislative texts on matters already included in the work programme. Beyond this substantial assistance, the Secretariat undertakes a range of administrative services for UNCITRAL and its working groups.[607]

UNCITRAL prepares, adopts and promotes a variety of legal documents such as conventions, model laws, legislative guides and model provisions.[608] Additionally it offers technical assistance and coordination for legal reforms.[609] Part of the mandate of UNCITRAL is also the coordination and promotion of other organisations among them the OECD, the United Nations Conference on Trade and Development, the World Bank and the WTO.[610]

---

603 United Nations Gerenal Assembly, 'General Assembly Resolution 2205 (XXI)' (New York: United Nations, 1996), Sec. II (6).

604 UNCITRAL, 'The UNCITRAL Guide - Basic facts about the United Nations Commission on International Trade Law', p. 3f.

605 Ibid, 4f.

606 Ibid, 6f.

607 Ibid, 7.

608 Ibid, 13.

609 Ibid, 7.

610 Ibid, 10.

## 3. The Essentials of the UNCITRAL Model Law on Procurement

### a. Background

Whereas the first version of the UNCITRAL Model Law, which was adopted in 1993, only covered the procurement of goods and construction, the 1994 version also included the procurement of services.[611] The UNCITRAL Model Law on Procurement of Goods, Construction and Services was adopted with due regard to the fact that procurement constitutes a large portion of public expenditure in most states[612] and that in many countries inadequate or outdated legislation led to inefficiency and ineffectiveness of the procurement process, abuse, and the consequent failure of the public purchaser to obtain adequate value in return for the expenditure of public funds.[613] Moreover, it was recognised that the disparities of national procurement systems might impose a partial limitation on the extent to which governments can access the competitive price and quality benefits available through international procurement.[614] These factors made improvements as well as uniformity of national procurement laws desirable.[615] The rationale behind the adoption of the Model Law is, hence, two-fold with objectives for the domestic as well as the interna-

---

611 Cf. United Nations General Assembly, 'Resolution Adopted by the General Assembly: Model Law on Procurement of Goods and Construction of the United Nations Commission on International Trade Law (A/RES/48/33)' (New York: United Nations, 1994); United Nations General Assembly, 'Resolution Adopted by the General Assembly: Model Law on Procurement of Goods, Construction and Services of the United Nations Commission on International Trade Law (A/RES/49/739)' (New York: United Nations, 1995).

612 United Nations General Assembly, 'Resolution Adopted by the General Assembly: Model Law on Procurement of Goods and Construction of the United Nations Commission on International Trade Law (A/RES/48/33)', p. 2; United Nations General Assembly, 'Resolution Adopted by the General Assembly: Model Law on Procurement of Goods, Construction and Services of the United Nations Commission on International Trade Law (A/RES/49/739)', p. 2.

613 UNCITRAL, 'Guide to Enactment of the UNCITRAL Model Law on Public Procurement', p. 1f., para. 1.

614 Ibid, 2, para. 2.

615 United Nations General Assembly, 'Resolution Adopted by the General Assembly: Model Law on Procurement of Goods and Construction of the United Nations Commission on International Trade Law (A/RES/48/33)', p. 2; United Nations General Assembly, 'Resolution Adopted by the General Assembly: Model Law on Procurement of Goods, Construction and Services of the United Nations Commission on International Trade Law (A/RES/49/739)', p. 2.

tional sphere. These two spheres do not stand in isolation, but rather interact. The latter embraces the desire to contribute - by establishing a model law that is acceptable to all states with different legal, social and economic systems - to the development of harmonious international economic relations.[616] Objectives for the development on the domestic level include the promotion of the economy as well as efficiency and competition in procurement which lead to overall increased economic development.[617] Although developing as well as transition countries are particularly named as addressees of the Model Law, it is intended to assist all states in enhancing their existing procurement laws or formulating procurement laws where none presently exist.[618] The Model Law serves as a framework law which can be used to design legislation at the national level. It provides for essential procedures and principles which can be applied for all types of procurement. It is, however, not extensive but needs further rules or regulations in order to guarantee successful implementation. The enacting states shall, in particular, issue procurement regulations which provide for procedural details. The national governments are free to adapt the Model Law to national circumstances and needs but may not compromise the objectives of the Model Law.[619] A particular problem might be that the Model Law does not provide any suggestions or solutions for the institutional organisation of public procurement systems, which is a decisive factor when it comes to the implementation of procedures and adherence to principles. Especially in developing countries where resources are scarce, the establishment of institutions necessary for the implementation of rules based on the UNCITRAL Model Law could be neglected by putting the focus on the design of rules and procedures rather than following a holistic approach.

The 2011 UNCITRAL Model Law replaced the 1994 UNCITRAL Model Law on Procurement of Goods, Construction and Services and includes new practices such as electronic procurement and framework

---

616 United Nations General Assembly, 'Resolution Adopted by the General Assembly: Model Law on Procurement of Goods and Construction of the United Nations Commission on International Trade Law (A/RES/48/33)', p. 1.

617 Ibid, 1.

618 United Nations General Assembly, 'Resolution Adopted by the General Assembly: United Nations Commission on International Trade Law Model Law on Public Procurement (A/RES/66/95)' (New York: United Nations, 2012), p. 2.

619 UNCITRAL, 'Guide to Enactement of UNCITRAL Model Law on Procurement of Goods,Construction and Services', p. 7, para. 12.

agreements as well as further changes based on experience with the Model Law. Nonetheless, the principles and main procedures have not been changed.[620] The Model Law is supplemented by a "Guide to Enactment of the UNCITRAL Model Law on Public Procurement," which provides background and explanatory information on the policy considerations reflected in the Model Law.[621] The guide primarily aims at supporting policymakers and legislators, but is also designed for regulators and those providing guidance on the implementation of the provisions of the procurement law.[622]

It should be noted that the detailed descriptions and complexity of the UNCITRAL Model Law preclude a comprehensive overview of all the provision. Therefore, only issues that are regarded as crucial in regard to this work will be presented and analysed. Although issues which are not dealt with in this work these should also be considered during the reform of procurement law.

### b. Objectives and Principles

The UNCITRAL Model Law on Procurement promotes economy, efficiency and competition in procurement and fosters integrity, confidence, fairness and transparency in the procurement process.[623] It is founded on the principle of achieving value for money and is designed to prevent abuse.[624] It is worth mentioning that, in contrast to the GPA, which is pri-

620 United Nations General Assembly, 'Resolution Adopted by the General Assembly: United Nations Commission on International Trade Law Model Law on Public Procurement (A/RES/66/95)', p. 1.

621 UNCITRAL, 'Guide to Enactment of the UNCITRAL Model Law on Public Procurement', p. iii, Preface.

622 Ibid.

623 United Nations General Assembly, 'Resolution Adopted by the General Assembly: Model Law on Procurement of Goods and Construction of the United Nations Commission on International Trade Law (A/RES/48/33)'; United Nations General Assembly, 'Resolution Adopted by the General Assembly: Model Law on Procurement of Goods, Construction and Services of the United Nations Commission on International Trade Law (A/RES/49/739)'; United Nations General Assembly, 'Resolution Adopted by the General Assembly: United Nations Commission on International Trade Law Model Law on Public Procurement (A/RES/66/95)'.

624 See Website of UNICTRAL: http://www.uncitral.org/uncitral/en/uncitral_texts/procurement_infrastructure/2011Model.html (last accessed: 26 November 2015).

marily based on non-discrimination, the Model Law does not elevate non-discrimination to an overarching principle.

Whereas all respective General Assembly Resolutions to the different versions of the Model Law express satisfaction with the work of UNCITRAL and recommend that states consider the Model Law and that the text be made widely available, the latest resolution additionally includes calls to improve cooperation and coordination between the Commission and other international organs and organisations, including regional organisations. This is to "[...] avoid undesirable duplication of efforts and inconsistent, incoherent or conflicting results in the modernization and harmonization of public procurement law."[625] Considering specifically the engagement of the World Bank and OECD/DAC as well as regional organisations' efforts to harmonise public procurement law, this can be clearly understood as a call for better cooperation and coordination with these organisations. It is also very important in relation to the 1994 GPA, which has been severely criticised as inadequate for achieving harmonisation by providing procedures and principles that lack flexibility and not living up to the expectation of a majority of countries.[626] Although the revision of both the GPA and the UNCITRAL Model Law has led to a certain level of harmonisation, there are still certain contradicting provisions, in particular in regard to the use of secondary objectives and non-discrimination. The introduction of a procurement law based on the model law of UNCITRAL might lead to conflicts between national law and obligations under the GPA in countries which are signatories to the GPA if there is a heavy emphasis on secondary objectives and preferential treatment. Article 3 of the UNCITRAL Model Law provides that in such circumstances the obligations of the treaty shall prevail. Any UNCITRAL Model Law provision that is inconsistent with the GPA is not only practically ineffectual through the prevalence of the GPA[627] but its adoption or existence would, moreover, be inconsistent with the requirement of the GPA to bring all the laws in conformity with the agreement. However, the

625 United Nations General Assembly, 'Resolution Adopted by the General Assembly: United Nations Commission on International Trade Law Model Law on Public Procurement (A/RES/66/95)', p. 2.

626 See discussion in Chapter 1 of this part. See in particular Subchapter 9.

627 This is because the provisions of the GPA would prevail over any national provisions based on the UNCITRAL Model Law.

revised Model Law takes the requirements of the GPA into account and can therefore be used without major changes by signatories of the GPA.[628]

### c. Scope and Coverage

The UNCITRAL Model Law applies to all public procurement,[629] which is defined as "the acquisition of goods, construction or services by a procuring entity."[630] It neither excludes any form of procurement from the scope of the law nor establishes a threshold below which the Model Law's provisions do not apply. This accommodates the notion that the objectives of the Model Law are best served by the widest possible application of its provision[631] and the fact that it is designed as model for domestic legislation rather than for the regulation of international procurement. In contrast to providing for overall exceptions for certain types of public procurement, the UNCITRAL Model Law provides a variety of procurement methods that are suitable for all types of procurements. This is beneficial as all procurements are subject to the requirements of the Model Law rather than to other rules or standards or even to no regulations at all and thus cannot take place in a legal limbo.

## 4. Tender Procedures

### a. Procurement Methods and Procedures

The general procurement method is open tendering.[632] All other forms of procurement provided by the Model Law can only be applied if justified by one of the situations described in Articles 29 to 31. However, the Model Law emphasises that the selection of other methods of procurement should be carried out in order to accommodate the circumstances of the procurement concerned and with a view to maximising competition to the

---

628 See UNCITRAL, 'Guide to Enactment of the UNCITRAL Model Law on Public Procurement', p. 2, para. 39.

629 UNCITRAL Model Law on Public Procurement, 2011, Art. 1.

630 Ibid, Art. 2 (j).

631 UNCITRAL, 'Guide to Enactment of the UNCITRAL Model Law on Public Procurement', p. 12, para.40.

632 UNCITRAL Model Law on Public Procurement, 2011, Art. 28 (1).

extent practicable.[633] The Model Law further encourages international participation through the default requirement that, with limited exceptions, all procurement proceedings be internationally advertised.[634] The Guide to Enactment of the UNCITRAL Model Law on Public Procurement contains extensive explanations of the circumstances which justify resort to different methods.[635] The alternative methods include restricted tendering, a request for quotations, requests for proposals without negotiation, two-stage tendering, requests for proposals with dialogue, requests for proposals with consecutive negotiations, competitive negotiations, electronic reverse auction, and single-source procurement.[636] They can be classified into three categories with different criteria for their application. Article 29 determines the conditions for the use of restricted tendering, requests for quotations and requests for proposals without negotiation. The conditions for two-stage tendering, requests for proposals with dialogue, requests for proposals with consecutive negotiations, competitive negotiations and single-source procurement are governed by Article 30. Article 31 determines under which condition an electronic reverse auction can be used for procurement.

Article 29 allows the application of restricted tendering in case of a highly complex or specialised subject matter of procurement which is only available from a limited number of suppliers or contractors and for procurements where time and cost for an open tendering procedure are disproportionate to the value of the procurement. Additionally, it provides for procurement by means of a request for quotations for readily available goods or services that can be obtained from an established market if a particular monetary threshold is not exceeded.[637] A request for proposals without negotiation can be used "where the procuring entity needs to consider the financial aspects of proposals separately and only after completion of examination and evaluation of the quality and technical aspects of the proposal."[638]

---

633 Ibid, Art. 28 (2).

634 UNCITRAL Model Law on Public Procurement, 2011, Art. 8. See also UNCITRAL, 'Guide to Enactment of the UNCITRAL Model Law on Public Procurement', p. 38, para. 13.

635 UNCITRAL, 'Guide to Enactment of the UNCITRAL Model Law on Public Procurement', p.128ff.

636 UNCITRAL Model Law on Public Procurement, 2011, Art. 27 (1).

637 Ibid, Art. 29 (2).

638 Ibid, Art. 29 (3).

Article 30 permits engaging in competitive negotiations if there is an urgent need for the subject matter of the procurement or if no other competitive method of procurement is appropriate for the protection of essential security interests of the state. Single-source procurement, which is the procurement method that most extremely contradicts the principle of competition, can be applied if one of the following exceptional circumstances occur: (1) the subject matter of the procurement is available only from a particular supplier or contractor, or a particular supplier or contractor has exclusive rights in respect of the subject matter of the procurement and, thereby, no reasonable alternative or substitute exists;[639] (2) there is an extremely urgent need for the subject matter of procurement due to a catastrophic event;[640] (3) additional supplies must be procured from a supplier or contractor for reasons of standardisation or because of the need for compatibility with existing goods, equipment, technology or services;[641] (4) the use of any other method of procurement is not appropriate for the protection of essential security interests of the state;[642] and (5) procurement from a particular supplier or contractor is necessary in order to implement a socio-economic policy.[643] In summation, the unavailability of alternatives, reference to procurements already made, catastrophic events or the security interests of the state may provide rationales that justify alternative, less competitive methods. Whereas the first four circumstances seem to be non-controversial, the fifth exception needs further assessment which will be conducted below, in the subchapter on secondary objectives.

Apart from the aforementioned general and the alternative procurement methods, the 2011 UNCITRAL Model Law provides for the use of framework agreements. Chapter VII of the Model Law sets out the provisions governing framework agreement procedures, but shall not be discussed in this paper.

The UNCITRAL Model Law also names electronic reverse auctions as possible procurement method. An electronic reverse auction is

> "[...] an online real-time purchasing technique utilized by the procuring entity to select the successful submission, which involves the presentation by suppliers or

639 Ibid, Art. 30 (5) (a).
640 Ibid, Art. 30 (5) (b).
641 Ibid, Art. 30 (5) (c).
642 Ibid, Art. 30 (5) (d).
643 Ibid, Art. 30 (5) (e).

contractors of successively lowered bids during a scheduled period of time and the automatic evaluation of bids."[644]

It is permissible if a detailed description of the subject matter of the procurement is feasible, effective competition is ensured, and the criteria used in determining successful submission are quantifiable and can be expressed in monetary terms.[645] The integration of the electronic reverse auction as procurement method into the revised UNCITRAL Model Law reflects the increasing use of electronic methods in public procurement and the view that electronic methods are beneficial, making procurement more effective and efficient. The conditions exemplify the need to ensure competition, fairness and transparency of decisions. Notwithstanding these potential benefits, especially developing countries need to assess whether the technical conditions and current practices within the country allow for the effective implementation of electronic reverse auctions. However, even if the circumstances at the time of the adoption of a new procurement law do not yet meet those particular needs, the provision might be included with view to its application in the future, because instead of replacing any other forms of procurement methods it poses an additional alternative.

Nevertheless, benefits have to be weighed against risks and costs when considering the introduction of electronic reverse auctions. More competitive offers through the information about other bids and the possibility for a bidder to adjust its tender, limited opportunities for corruption and discrimination and a wider accessibility of the procedure are some of the benefits of electronic auctions.[646] Risks and costs include insufficient attention being given to non-price factors; moreover, suppliers might be hostile to the use of auctions and the facilitation of collusion between suppliers.[647] It is also decisive to clearly outline what type of procurements are eligible for electronic reverse auctions – for example, for procurements where price is not the most important criteria electronic auctions might not be suitable.

The Model Law facilitates and, where appropriate and to the extent possible, encourages the introduction and use of electronic procurement.[648] Articles 5 and 6 provide for e-publication, Article 7 accommo-

644 Ibid, Art. 2 (d).

645 Ibid, Art. 31 (a-c).

646 Arrowsmith, 'Electronic Procurement', p. 150.

647 Ibid, 150f.

648 UNCITRAL, 'Guide to Enactment of the UNCITRAL Model Law on Public Procurement', p. 27. para. 90.

dates electronic means and forms of communication and Article 40 allows for e-tenders. Moreover, the Model Law provides for e-reverse auctions in Chapter VI and for e-framework agreements in Chapter VII. In regard to the potential benefits electronic procurement can have in regard to effectiveness and efficiency,[649] the different provisions outlined in the Model Law are to be commended and countries conducting a procurement reform should consider introducing electronic procurement or providing the necessary legislative arrangements for its future use.

### b. Tender Specification, Award Criteria and Evaluation Methods

#### i. Qualification Criteria

The exhaustive list of criteria which the procuring entities might select to ascertain the qualification of suppliers or contractors include professional, technical and environmental qualifications, professional and technical competence, financial resources, equipment and other physical facilities, managerial capability, reliability, experience and personnel to perform the contract.[650] These criteria are by far more comprehensive than the criteria outlined by the GPA. The inclusion of environmental qualifications, managerial capability, and reliability is especially striking. Environmental qualifications allow the procuring entity to pursue environmental objectives with regard to the supplier or contractor and to use the qualification criteria to carry out green procurement. This has been integrated into many national procurement laws and is consistent with the general environmental agenda. Therefore, the inclusion of environmental qualifications is not at all surprising, but rather a response to actual practices and policies and that environmental sustainability is vital for future living conditions. Managerial capability and reliability, on the contrary, are criteria whose inclusion might raise questions when it comes to their implementation. Although it cannot be questioned that these are important conditions for a successful outcome of procurement, they constitute rather subjective criteria which are difficult to evaluate. In regard to transparency and justiciability of decisions it is preferable to stick to rather objective criteria.

649 For more information on the benefits of e-procurement, see above: Part I, Chapter 1, Subchapter 6.
650 UNCITRAL Model Law on Public Procurement, 2011, Art. 9 (2) (a).

However, the UNCITRAL Guide 2012 explains that while these criteria are exhaustive, only those criteria that are appropriate for the purposes of the particular procurement should be used.[651] For example, managerial capability and reliability would be mainly envisaged for requests for proposals which are traditionally used for the procurement of consulting services.[652]

Beyond these criteria the suppliers or contractors can also be required to meet ethical and other standards applicable within the jurisdiction[653] and to have adhered to their tax and social security contribution obligations.[654] Especially in respect of African countries where Chinese and other countries' firms ignore labour and environmental standards, this requirement provides an essential opportunity to improve adherence to national standards in procurement contracts and beyond and also to impede the evasion of national laws or regulations by foreign but also domestic firms. It is, hence, a provision that can, if effectively used, significantly facilitate legal compliance.

Further criteria include the legal capacity to enter into the procurement contract[655] or that the bidder is insolvent, bankrupt, subject to legal proceedings, etc.[656] and that its directors or officers have, for example, not been convicted of any criminal offence related to their professional conduct.[657] On the one hand, this minimises the failure of the procurement and the performance of the procurement contract. On the other hand, it excludes companies that have been involved in any corrupt or other irregular practices.

The procuring entity is obliged to state all the criteria in the solicitation document, apply them equally to all suppliers or contractors[658] and to evaluate the criteria as specified in the solicitation document.[659] The establishment of any criterion, requirement or procedure with respect to the qualifications of suppliers or contractors that discriminates against or

651 UNCITRAL, 'Guide to Enactment of the UNCITRAL Model Law on Public Procurement', p. 79, para. 5.
652 Ibid, 85f., para. 5.
653 UNCITRAL Model Law on Public Procurement, 2011, Art. 9 (2) (b).
654 Ibid, Art. 9 (2) (e).
655 Ibid, Art. 9 (2) (c).
656 Ibid, Art. 9 (2) (d).
657 Ibid, Art. 9 (2) (f).
658 Ibid, Art. 9 (4).
659 Ibid, Art. 9 (5).

among suppliers or contractors or that is not objectively justifiable is prohibited.[660]

### ii. Description of the Subject Matter

The description of the subject matter of the procurement shall include the relevant technical, quality and performance characteristics[661] and is required to be objective, functional and generic.[662] If possible, standardised features, requirements, symbols and terminology shall be used to formulate the description of the subject matter.[663] Article 10 (4) additionally contains the following sentence:

> "There shall be no requirement for or reference to a particular trademark or trade name, patent, design or type, specific origin or producer unless there is no sufficiently precise or intelligible way of describing the characteristics of the subject matter of the procurement and provided that words such as "or equivalent" are included."

According to the UNCITRAL Guide 2012,

> "[t]he purpose of article 10 is to emphasize the importance of the principle of clarity, sufficient precision, completeness and objectivity in the description of the subject matter of procurement in any pre-qualification or pre-selection documents and in the solicitation documents."[664]

The content of these regulations resembles the provisions of the GPA in this regard and gives little cause for controversial debate.

### iii. Evaluation Criteria

The UNCITRAL Model Law sets out three different types of evaluation criteria: (1) price,[665] (2) criteria aiming, inter alia, at the sustainability of a product or service,[666] and (3) the experience, reliability and professional

660 Ibid, Art. 9 (6).
661 Ibid, Art. 10 (4).
662 Ibid, Art. 10 (4).
663 Ibid, Art. 10 (5) (a).
664 UNCITRAL, 'Guide to Enactment of the UNCITRAL Model Law on Public Procurement', p. 82f., para. 1.
665 UNCITRAL Model Law on Public Procurement, 2011, Art. 11 (2) (a).
666 Ibid, Art. 11 (2) (b).

and managerial competence of the supplier or contractor.[667] The first type of evaluation criteria is indisputable the most important. The inclusion of sustainability criteria makes the procurement process more complex but can extensively contribute to the quality of the product or service, the avoidance of additional costs, the protection of the environment etc. Although sustainability is not directly mentioned as objective by the UNCITRAL Model Law, the Guide to Enactment considers it as an element of processes under the Model Law.[668] Further criteria comprised in the provision are the time and delivery of goods, completion of construction or provision of services, the functional characteristics of goods or construction, the terms of payment and of guarantees in respect of the subject matter of the procurement. All these criteria serve the objective of ensuring the quality, suitability and successful outcome of the procurement. The list of evaluation criteria is illustrative rather than exhaustive, since "it would not be possible to provide for an exhaustive list of evaluation criteria for all types of procurement, regardless of how broadly they are drafted."[669]

With the exception of the criteria set out in Article 11 (3) (see below), all criteria must relate to the subject matter of the procurement. This is, inter alia, to avoid misuse by using other criteria intended to favour a certain supplier or contractor.[670]

In Article 11 (3), the UNCITRAL Model Law also recognises evaluation criteria that serve secondary objectives:

> "In addition to the criteria set out in paragraph 2 of this article, the evaluation criteria may include:
>
> (a) Any criteria that the procurement regulations or other provisions of law of this State authorize or require to be taken into account;
>
> (b) A margin of preference for the benefit of domestic suppliers or contractors or for domestically produced goods, or any other preference, if authorized or required by the procurement regulations or other provisions of law of this State. The

---

667 Ibid, Art. 11 (2) (c).

668 Cf. UNCITRAL, 'Guide to Enactment of the UNCITRAL Model Law on Public Procurement', p. 4, para. 10.

669 Ibid, 85, para. 3.

670 Vgl. M.S. Sabbatini, '2nd (or, from a European Point of View, 3rd) Generation Procurement Law Reform: Principles and Underlying Policies', conference paper, 5th International Public Procurement Conference, Seattle, Washington, 15-17 August 2012, p. 1906.

> margin of preference shall be calculated in accordance with the procurement regulations."

The pursuit of secondary objectives is, hence, explicitly allowed. The possibility of granting a margin of preference by applying evaluation criteria to this effect is a result of the option to include any criteria that the procurement regulations or other provisions of law authorise or require to be taken into account. This exemplifies how flexible the UNCITRAL Model Law is because the states can add any criteria to the list of evaluation criteria stated in Article 11. Although a certain degree of flexibility is desirable in order to facilitate a variety of political, social and economic environments this approach seems to grant a leeway that by far exceeds the margin that is necessary to respond to the needs of the majority of countries and, beyond that, counteracts the attempts to harmonise, standardise and promote international trade. However, while explicitly allowing for preferential procurement and secondary objectives, it makes them subject to the transparency regulations of public procurement law, which is far better than secondary objectives applied in a non-transparent manner. Especially in view of the unwillingness of most countries to give up applying secondary objectives, such approach might be more successful. Nevertheless, it would have been of great advantage to, for example, require that any preference should only be applied once a fair level of competition is achieved, in order to avoid preferences being used to protect a certain group of suppliers or contractors from competition which would be contrary to the objectives of public procurement.

The UNCITRAL Model Law provides that all non-price evaluation criteria shall be objective, quantifiable and expressed in monetary terms.[671] The UNCITRAL Model Law recommends the enacting state to provide regulations or guidance on the way factors are to be quantified in monetary terms.[672] This is, however, restricted by the phrase "to the extent practicable." The UNCITRAL Guide 2012 explains that,

> "[t]he wording "to the extent practicable" has been included in recognition that in some procurement proceedings, such as in request for proposals with dialogue […] expressing all non-price evaluation criteria in monetary terms would not be practicable or appropriate."[673]

---

671 UNCITRAL Model Law on Public Procurement, 2011, Art. 11 (4).

672 UNCITRAL, 'Guide to Enactment of the UNCITRAL Model Law on Public Procurement', p. 86, para. 6.

673 Ibid, 86, para. 6.

The procuring entity has to determine in the solicitation documents whether the award decision is to be made solely on the basis of price or on price and other criteria.[674] All evaluation criteria, their relative weight, the manner of the application of the criteria in the evaluation procedure also need to be stated.[675] These are essential factors for a transparent and fair procurement process and, hence, for its effectiveness and efficiency. Therefore, they can be regarded as best practices and should be implemented in every national public procurement system.

iv. Method of Evaluation

As mentioned above, the UNCITRAL Model Law follows the principle of value for money. This principle is the decisive basis on which procurement contracts are awarded. The award of the procurement to the lowest bid is probably the simplest and most objective decision criterion but it does not allow for the inclusion of any other evaluation criteria than price and hence does not consider procurement concerns, such as the sustainability of the product or service. Consequently, the lowest price does not necessarily guarantee the best value for money. As Article 11 (5) (a) implies, the successful submission can be ascertained on the basis of price or price and other criteria. Further details can be found in Article 43 (3) (b), which defines what the successful tender shall be:

> "Where price is the only award criterion, the tender with the lowest tender price; or where there are price and other award criteria, the most advantageous tender ascertained on the basis of the criteria and procedures for evaluating tenders specified in the solicitation documents [...]."

Decisions made on the basis of the first subparagraph, namely the lowest tender, are unambiguous. The second subparagraph is more challenging because it needs a substantive analysis and assessment of the evaluation criteria, thus leading to decisions that are more difficult to comprehend. Moreover, it poses the risk that the procuring officers misuse evaluation criteria which are less objective than price to favour a particular supplier or contractor. However, as it is, in light of sustainability and the quality of procurement, it is essential to include evaluation criteria other than the price. The challenge is therefore to create a transparent environment that

---

674 UNCITRAL Model Law on Public Procurement, 2011, Art. 11 (5) (a).
675 Ibid, Art. 11 (5) (b-d).

minimises the danger of subjectivity of decision-making which is e.g. facilitated by Article 11 (4-6).

#### v. Rejection of Abnormally Low Submissions

In case the price of a submitted tender seems abnormally low so that the ability of the supplier or contractor to perform the procurement contract might be an issue of concern, the procuring entity can request further details from the supplier or contractor. If, after the consideration of this additional information, the procuring entity continues to have concerns, it can reject the submission. Such decisions as well as the rationale behind them need to be communicated to the supplier or contractor concerned and, in addition to all communications, included in the record of the proceedings.[676] This serves as a safeguard for both suppliers and procuring entities and avoids concluding contracts that cannot be implemented successfully.

### 5. Institutions and Staff Regulations

The UNCITRAL Model Law does not contain any provisions on institutions or regulations for procurement staff. These would need to be independently elaborated within the countries adopting a procurement law based on the Model Law. Provisions of this kind can either be integrated into the procurement law itself or enacted in a distinct law or regulation.

### 6. Transparency

Transparency at all stages of the procurement process is a key principle and the transparency requirements of the UNCITRAL Model Law can be regarded as best practices in this respect, reflecting high standards in regard to publication, documentation and accountability. For example, it not only requires the determination of substantive criteria on disclosure of information but also the provision of rationales for decisions taken by the procuring entity. Additionally, it requires a comprehensive documentary record of all procurements proceedings.

---

676 Ibid, Art. 20.

Article 5 provides for the publication of legal texts which include the procurement law itself, procurement regulations and other texts relevant for public procurement as well as judicial decisions and administrative rulings with precedential value. The procuring entity has to disclose all the requirements in respect to the participation of suppliers and contractors[677] as well as to their qualifications,[678] detailed descriptions of the subject matter of the procurement,[679] evaluation criteria and procedures,[680] and information on the manner, place and deadline of applications.[681] It has to state and record reasons for nearly all decisions taken.[682] Article 28 (3), for example, sets out the requirement to record the reasons and circumstances upon which the procuring entity relied to justify the use of a procuring method other than open tendering and Article 8 (4) and (5) require a statement of reasons for the decision to limit the participation of suppliers or contractors. In general, the statement of reasons has to be published even in the absence of a request. This is of great advantage with view to accountability: public procurement officials know all their decisions and actions need to be justified and can be scrutinized. This not only impedes corrupt activities but might also enhance well-reasoned decision-making.

With due regard to confidentiality, certain information can be excluded from the disclosure if non-disclosure is regarded as necessary for the protection of essential security interests of the state, disclosure would be contrary to law, impede law enforcement, prejudice the legitimate commercial interests of the suppliers or contractor or impede fair competition.[683] Additionally, Article 6 recommends, but does not require, the publication of information on future procurements. This highlights the importance of proper procurement planning for all stakeholders. It is of great advantage for managing the preparation of bids to know as early as possible about future procurements. It also prevents a lack of transparency in procurement plan-

677 Ibid, Art. 8 (3-5).
678 Ibid, Art. 9 (4).
679 Ibid, Art. 10 (1).
680 Ibid, Art. 11 (5).
681 Ibid, Art. 14.
682 Ibid, Arts. 8 (4) and (5), 18 (10), 19 (2), 20 (2), 21 (2), 22 (3) (c), 25 (c-h, k, n, o, q, t, u), etc.
683 Ibid, Art. 24 (1).

ning from leading to unfairness by suppliers gaining access to procurement planning phases and thereby gaining an advantage.[684]

The requirements applicable to documentary records can be found in Article 25. It entails a comprehensive list of information and data that need to be included in the record. Article 15, which regulates clarifications and modification of solicitation documents, is also important to the objective of ensuring transparency. On the one hand, it requires a procuring entity receiving a request by a supplier or contractor for a clarification of the solicitation document to respond to such request within a reasonable time prior to the deadline for presenting submissions.[685] The clarification requested by a supplier or contractor needs to be communicated to all suppliers or contractors to which the procuring entity has provided the solicitation documents.[686] On the other hand, a procuring entity is allowed to modify the solicitation documents by issuing an addendum which needs to be communicated promptly to all suppliers or contractors that have received the solicitation documents.[687] The latter provision is important in order to prevent tenders from having to be cancelled because of false or misleading information in the solicitation document. The possibility of seeking clarifications enables suppliers and contractors to prepare competitive bids that are responsive to the requirements outlined in the solicitation document. It furthermore encourages suppliers or contractors not familiar with tendering for government contractors, e.g. SMEs, to submit a bid. This facilitates competition and, hence, the principle of value for money. Both provisions serve the objective of carrying out procurement in the most effective and efficient way possible.

## 7. Secondary Objectives

### a. The Scope of Application of Secondary Objectives

The UNCITRAL Model Law offers room for the application of socio-economic policies in nearly all phases of the procurement process. Articles

684 UNCITRAL, 'Guide to Enactment of the UNCITRAL Model Law on Public Procurement', p. 67, para. 1. For more information on the importance of public procurement planning see above: Part I, Chapter 1, Subchapter 4.

685 UNCITRAL Model Law on Public Procurement, 2011, Art. 15 (1).

686 Ibid.

687 UNCITRAL Model Law on Public Procurement, 2011, Art. 15 (2).

8-11 on participation, qualification, description of the subject matter and evaluation criteria and procedures are designed in a way which enables the pursuit and implementation of socio-economic policies.[688] The Model Law further explicitly allows using single-sourcing as tendering method in order to achieve a certain socio-economic policy.[689] However, the Guide to Enactment suggests certain safeguards needed in order to ensure that the achievement of the public procurement objectives is not undermined. It stresses the risks and costs of the use of socio-economic policies in public procurement. Socio-economic policies, for example, bring additional costs to public procurement[690] and can have a negative effect if they are applied for an unlimited time.[691] It is recommended that the costs and benefits be weighed and temporarily applied, rather than maintain such measures in perpetuity. The UNCITRAL Guide 2012 also emphasises that socio-economic policies can only be applied as long it does not violate international obligations[692] and if they are set out in other provisions of the law or procurement regulations.[693] This avoids procuring entities having wide discretion in applying socio-economic policies which would increase the risk of abuse and corruption. Stringent transparency requirements in regard to the application of socio-economic policies[694] further the objectives of public procurement while accommodating the state's discretion to use public procurement for policy reasons.

Article 2 (o) defines socio-economic policies as

> "[...] environmental, social, economic and other policies [...] authorized or required by the procurement regulations or other provisions of law [...] to be taken into account by the procuring entity in the procurement proceedings."

It is further noted that this definition may be expanded by providing an illustrative list of such policies. It is somehow surprising that environmental objectives are assigned to socio-economic policies rather than being stated independently since they are generally less disputed objectives but, beyond that, only secondarily affect society and economy. The protection of

688 UNCITRAL, 'Guide to Enactment of the UNCITRAL Model Law on Public Procurement', p. 5, para. 13.
689 UNCITRAL Model Law on Public Procurement, 2011, Art. 30 (5) (e).
690 UNCITRAL, 'Guide to Enactment of the UNCITRAL Model Law on Public Procurement', p. 6, para. 14.
691 Ibid.
692 Ibid, 6, para. 17.
693 Ibid, 7, para. 19.
694 Ibid, 7, para. 20.

the environment is, in most countries, a recognised independent policy objective not belonging to socio-economic policies. It has to be also remarked that UNCITRAL does not differ between socio-economic and preferential policies but considers the latter as part of the former. This may cause confusion because, although there might be an overlap in many cases, not all socio-economic policies are discriminatory. Examples of socio-economic policies can be found in paragraph 28 of the 1994 Guide to Enactment and include, inter alia, encouragement of employment, the transfer of technology and the development of managerial, scientific and operational skills, the development of SMEs, the improvement of the rights of women, the young and the elderly, and people who belong to indigenous and traditional groups.

As mentioned above, single-sourcing can be applied if procurement from a particular supplier or contractor is necessary in order to implement a socio-economic policy. This needs further explanation. Article 30 (5) (e) reads as follows:

> "[Subject to approval by the [name of the organ designated by the enacting State to issue the approval] and,] following public notice and adequate opportunity to comment, procurement from a particular supplier or contractor is necessary in order to implement a socio-economic policy of this State, provided that procurement from no other supplier or contractor is capable of promoting that policy."

The key requirement is that it is necessary to procure the goods or services from a particular supplier or contractor in order to implement a socio-economic policy. Nevertheless, it is hard to imagine what kind of socio-economic policy can be only promoted by the procurement via a particular supplier or contractor and, especially, what kind of socio-economic policy so much depends on the implementation through procurement that it allows for a deviation from the principle of competition, a principle which is assigned special relevance in public procurement. Despite the uncertainty about the practical relevance of this provision and in view of the controversial debate about the effectiveness of such policies it is remarkable that the UNCITRAL Model Law explicitly states it as a rationale for single-source procurement. However, to prevent the misuse of this provision for favouring a particular supplier or contractor, it requires approval by a designated organ as well as issuing a public notice and the provision of an adequate opportunity to comment. It remains unclear what substantive requirements exist for the public notices and in how far the comments affect the decision to procure from the particular supplier or contractor. The only thing that is certain is that a public notice and comments thereon satisfy the principle of disclosure of information and allow stakeholders and the wider public to state their opinion and, thereby, potentially create public awareness and perhaps outrage by one or more interest groups. Whether this will prove to be a mechanism that can deter the procuring entity from using (or abusing) this provision remains unsettled.

### b. The Principle of Non-Discrimination

Although the UNCITRAL Model Law does not refer to non-discrimination as one of the overarching principles, several provisions stress the obligation to treat all suppliers or contractors equally. However, in contrast to the GPA, these provisions are not absolute and allow for exceptions. They also permit for a departure from the national treatment principle, which requires that national and international suppliers or contractors are treated alike. Article 11 (3) (b), for example, allows the evaluation criteria to include a

> "[...] margin of preference for the benefit of domestic suppliers or contractors or for domestically produced goods, or any other preference, if authorized by the procurement regulations or other provisions of law of this State."

Thereafter preferential policies imply not only a departure from the national treatment policy but also allow any other form of unequal treatment of suppliers or contractors. A margin of preference allows the procuring entity to select the lowest-priced local tender if the price difference to the overall lowest-priced tender does not exceed the range of preference. It should be remarked, though, that the application of margins of preference requires an explicit statement of its use in the solicitation documents and in the documentary recording.

The UNCITRAL Model Law generally prohibits discrimination through qualification requirements or examination or evaluation criteria which are set out in Articles 9-11. Article 8, however, provides for an exception:

> "Suppliers or contractors shall be permitted to participate in procurement proceedings without regard to nationality, except where the procuring entity decides to limit participation in procurement regulations or other provisions of law of this State."

This gives leeway to the procuring entities to apply preferential treatment on a case-by-case basis as long as it is covered by other provisions of the procurement law or other provisions of law of this state, but not policies of the procuring entity itself (which is an important safeguard to avoid a conflict of interests). Hence, exceptions that allow for preferential treatment of a group of suppliers or contractors can be found within the procurement law itself or in other national legal provisions. This not only makes it hard to get an overview of possible rationales for preferential treatment but also implies that national governments may legalise protectionist policies by enacting any law as justification for preferential policies. These policies might not be applied for economic but rather for political reasons. Such leeway is, certainly, contrary to the aim to promoting international trade and is inconsistent with the non-discrimination principle as enshrined in the WTO and other organisations. It further undermines the integrity, fairness and public confidence in the procurement process and hinders participation in procurement proceedings by suppliers and contractors regardless of nationality. The latter have both been stated as objectives in the preamble of the Model Law. Nevertheless, this regulation, by requiring a policy to be based in procurement regulation or other laws, prevents the application of ad hoc measures, ensures that preferential policies reflect a countries needs and allows their costs and benefits to be assessed.[695] Additionally, the 1994 Guide to Enactment stresses that it impedes the procuring entity itself from being able to issue such policies or discriminate at its own discretion.[696] Moreover, it has to be stressed that UNCITRAL recommends that they are only applied temporarily as transitory measures and should not be used as a form of protectionism but accommodate a progressive exposure to international competition.[697] As Nicholas suggests, the application of preferential policies on a case-by-case basis is preferable to a general discriminatory procurement system.[698] And the Guide to Enactment explains that Article 8 (1) is "meant to promote transparency and to prevent arbitrary and excessive resort to restriction of foreign participation, and is given effect by a number of provisions."[699] Although this approach is necessary and reasonable to reflect the actual practices of many states, a requirement to explicitly state a list of other provisions of law that allow derogations from the national treatment principle could at least create confidence, enhance predictability and impede an even increasing use of preferential policies, especially because UNCITRAL suggests that socio-economic or preferential policies should ac-

---

695 Nicholas, 'Work of UNCITRAL on government procurement', p. 769.

696 UNCITRAL, 'Guide to Enactment of the UNCITRAL Model Law on Public Procurement', p. 59, para. 8.

697 Ibid, 6, para. 15.

698 Nicholas, 'Work of UNCITRAL on government procurement', p. 769.

699 UNCITRAL, 'Guide to Enactment of the UNCITRAL Model Law on Public Procurement', p. 53, para. 29.

commodate a progressive exposure to international competition rather than an increased use of policies restricting competition.[700]

It can be concluded that this provision not only grants latitude to an extent that is simply not necessary to implement preferential procurement procedures, but also stands in sharp contradiction to the GPA and the general effort to liberalise trade. In view of the fact that cooperation and coordination with other international organisations and organs is a key principle of UNCITRAL this divergence of approaches is striking. However, the ambiguity between promoting free trade, on the one hand, and providing extensive latitude to restrict this general principle, on the other hand, was a controversial issue within the Working Group on Procurement even before 1994.[701] Some even said that it might be better to remain silent on the issue of discrimination than to adopt such an ambiguous provision. Others suggested that the possibility of exclusions should be explicitly limited to the notion of reciprocity and low-value procurements. The working group found, though, that the existing approach was

> "[...] the best possible compromise that could be achieved, in particular from the standpoint of striking a proper balance between the progressive fostering of non-discrimination and the need to recognize that enacting states would, at least for the foreseeable future, continue, to one degree or another, to apply measures designed to favour national suppliers and contractors."[702]

This shows the pragmatic element of the UNCITRAL Model Law, namely to "compromise on ideal standards to take account of political constraints."[703] This would promote wider acceptance of the UNCITRAL Model Law and also ensure that sub-optimal practices are implemented in the least damaging way.[704]

700 Cf. UNCITRAL, 'Guide to Enactment of the UNCITRAL Model Law on Public Procurement', p. 6, para. 15.

701 UNCITRAL, 'Report of the United Nations Commission on International Trade Law on the work of its twenty- sixth session, Official Records of the General Assembly, Forty-eighth Session, Supplement No. 17 (A/48/17)', reproduced in UNCITRAL Yearbook, vol. XXIV: 1993, part one, p. 12,13, para. 56.

702 Ibid, 13, para. 57.

703 Arrowsmith, 'Public Procurement: An Appraisal of the UNCITRAL Model Law ', 24.

704 Ibid, 24.

## 8. Review Procedures

As for the transparency requirements, the requirements in regard to domestic review mechanisms represent best practices. They include all major elements of effective and efficient review procedures and are more detailed than the general guidelines provided by the GPA.

Suppliers or contractors have a right to challenge a decision or action of a procuring entity if it claims to have suffered or may suffer loss or injury because of the alleged non-compliance of that decision or action with the provisions of the procurement law.[705] This includes also the choice of procurement method which was exempted from being challenged under the 1994 UNCITRAL Model Law.[706] The UNCITRAL Model Law provides for three different kinds of challenge procedures: an application for reconsideration to the procuring entity, application for review to an independent body and judicial review.[707] Moreover, there is an optional clause that provides a right to appeal.

Locus standi is restricted to suppliers and contractors. Members of the general public and sub-contractors have no right to challenge a decision, as the 2012 UNCITRAL Guide emphasises. This is

> "[...] to ensure that challenge relate to the decisions and actions of the procuring entity in a particular procurement procedure, and to avoid an excessive degree of disruption to the procurement process through challenges that are based on policy or speculative issues, or based on nominal breaches, and also reflecting that the challenge mechanism is not the only oversight mechanism available."[708]

The UNCITRAL Model Law provides the right to participate for all parties and any governmental authority whose interests are or could be affected.[709] Participants are granted the following procedural rights: the right to be present, represented and accompanied; the right to be heard; the right to present evidence (including witnesses); the right to request that any hearing take place in public; and the right to seek access to the record of the challenge proceedings.[710]

---

705 UNCITRAL Model Law on Public Procurement, 2011, Art. 64 (1).

706 UNCITRAL, 'Guide to Enactment of the UNCITRAL Model Law on Public Procurement', p. 16, para. 57 and p. 378, para. 159.

707 UNCITRAL Model Law on Public Procurement, 2011, Art. 64 (2).

708 UNCITRAL, 'Guide to Enactment of the UNCITRAL Model Law on Public Procurement', p. 306, para. 2.

709 UNCITRAL Model Law on Public Procurement, 2011, Art. 68 (1) and (2).

710 Ibid, Art. 68 (3).

The internal review mechanism, which provides for reconsideration by the procuring entity, and the review by an independent body are governed by Article 66 and Article 67 respectively. The procedural requirements for judicial review are not further specified. It is important to note that any decision that has been made in course of the reconsideration before the procuring entity can be challenged before an independent body or court.[711] An application for reconsideration to the procuring entity is not, however, a mandatory first step before filing an action before an independent body or court. The establishment of an internal review mechanism is rooted in the goal of early resolution of disputes.[712]

The Model Law generally requires procuring entities to provide a standstill period on a case-by-case basis. If, however, no standstill period is applied, it is required to state and record the reasons for this decision.[713] Exemptions from the application of the standstill period are allowed in framework agreement procedures without second-stage competition, where the contract price is less than the threshold amount set out in the procurement regulations and where a standstill period would be contrary to the urgent public interest.[714] The standstill period allows bidders to challenge the decision before the tender is finally awarded. It is to be specified in the solicitation document as well as the notification of the provisional award decision.[715] The length of the standstill period can be established by procuring entities

> "[...] on a procurement-by-procurement basis, depending on the circumstances of the given procurement, in particular the means of communication used and whether procurement is domestic or international."[716]

Challenges regarding other decisions or actions than the terms of solicitation, prequalification or pre-selection or decisions or actions taken in prequalification or pre-selection proceedings which must be submitted prior to the deadline for presenting submissions need to be lodged prior to the expiry of the standstill period. This is a very important mechanism to avoid the problems arising through challenges after a contract has been concluded, such as the annulment of a contract or claims for damages.

---

711 Ibid, Art. 66 (4).
712 Cf. above (Part I, Chapter 1, Subchapter 8).
713 Ibid, Art. 25 (1) (j).
714 Ibid, Art. 22 (3).
715 Ibid, Arts. 22 (2) and 67 (1).
716 UNCITRAL, 'Guide to Enactment of the UNCITRAL Model Law on Public Procurement', p. 115, para. 11.

Article 65 governs the effect of a challenge, namely injunctive relief, which hinders the procuring entity from concluding a procurement contract or framework agreement while the challenge procedure is in progress.[717] Adopting states can independently stipulate the length of time injunctive relief remains in effect after the completion of the challenge procedures or after the applicant and appellant have been informed of the decision.[718] In the exceptional case where the conclusion of the procurement contract is justified by urgent public interest the prohibition on taking any steps that would bring into force a procurement contract or framework agreement can be set aside.[719]

The protection of confidentiality which applies in the general procurement proceedings likewise applies to challenge proceedings.[720]

## 9. Conclusion

The UNCITRAL Model Law offers a good foundation for domestic reform projects and should be considered in all reform processes, at least as guiding instrument. However, taken in isolation as a single instrument it is not sufficient for a holistic approach (as strongly emphasised in the 2012 UNCITRAL Guide), reforming all pillars and stages of procurement, as e.g. the institutional organisation of public procurement systems is not addressed.

The comprehensive Guide to Enactment is a necessary tool in order to understand the Model Law's provisions and to find the most suitable way to regulate procurement in the domestic context. It also provides assistance for downstream regulations which need to be enacted and other aspects of the public procurement system which need to be addressed during reform. The flexibility of the Model Law has benefits as well as disadvantages. It can undermine the aim of harmonising procurement law. However, it might allow for a greater standardisation than if countries create their own rules that are quite different in substance and language.[721] As mentioned above, it was a specific objective to also ensure that states hav-

717 UNCITRAL Model Law on Public Procurement, 2011, Art. 65 (1).
718 Ibid, Art. 65 (2).
719 Ibid, Art. 65 (3).
720 Ibid, Art. 69.
721 Cf. Arrowsmith, 'Public Procurement: An Appraisal of the UNCITRAL Model Law ', 23.

ing international or regional procurement obligations can make use of the Model Law. The UNCITRAL Model Law is well drafted and, therefore, valuable for all countries, developed and developing countries alike.[722] However, the rules-based approach – meaning the very detailed provision of rules and procedures – hampers a state's latitude to integrate the national traditions, customs and usages and to respond to the local circumstances. Moreover, this approach might not be suitable for all countries. As has been seen, there are many countries which have up-to-date public procurement legislation but suffer from irregularities, corruption and other problems due to insufficient implementation of rules and procedures prescribed by law. In such cases, it might be better to first put a strong focus on the principles of transparency and accountability and the institutional aspect and then develop more detailed rules based on practice.

Especially in comparison with the GPA the UNCITRAL Model Law better reflects the variety of interests of developed as well as developing countries. Furthermore, its drafting as well as its implementation and application do not depend on bargaining power.[723] It can, hence, be concluded that the UNCITRAL Model Law has greater potential to harmonise and standardise trade. During revision of the UNCITRAL Model Law the Working Group made specific amendments to ensure greater consistency with the GPA.[724] It can be said that harmonisation efforts are recognisable in both the revised GPA and the revised Model Law. Like the GPA, the Model Law provides for open tendering as the general method and allows for exceptional methods. The GPA, however, is less detailed. This can be attributed to the fact that it only covers public procurements above a certain monetary threshold.

The principles of both texts do not radically diverge. Both texts are generally based on the principle of equal treatment but provide different types of exceptions; the UNCITRAL Model Law certainly provides greater latitude to apply preferential policies. Most exceptions in both texts, however, aim primarily at developing and least-developing countries whose particular circumstances need to find consideration and require special and differential treatment.[725]

---

722 Ibid.

723 See also ibid, 25.

724 See for a comprehensive discussion of these amendments: Nicholas, 'Work of UNCITRAL on government procurement', p. 770f.

725 Cf. ibid, 769.

The Model Law provides a wide range of alternative procurement methods and outlines the requirements for their use. It is strongly recommended that enacting states consult the 2012 UNCITRAL Guide to understand the rationale behind the different methods and their application. The same applies to the provisions on participation, qualification, description of the subject matter, evaluation criteria and methods. The fact that the evaluation criteria of managerial competence should only be used in request-for-proposals and should serve as a minimum requirement is, for example, only outlined in the Guide to Enactment, but it is important that this is followed in order to fulfil the purpose.

The transparency requirements are comprehensive but not over-excessive. It is indispensable to provide for those requirements so as to guarantee the other objectives of public procurement. They reflect international best practices and are similar to the GPA's requirements in this context.

In regard to secondary objectives, the Model Law does not restrict its application, but rather makes the application subject to stringent transparency requirements and requires it to have a basis in law while simultaneously prohibiting policy decisions by procuring entities. Although the wide latitude to apply secondary policies under the UNCITRAL Model Law can be legitimately criticised, it reflects the present view of many countries unwilling to give up its application. And as Arrowsmith notes,

> "[...] taking into account of pragmatic considerations not only promotes wider acceptance of the Model generally but helps ensure that sup-optimal practices are implemented in the least damaging way. Thus, for example, acknowledging domestic preferences means that they are regulated to ensure transparency. The obvious disadvantage of pragmatism is the danger of appearing to legitimize undesirable practices, but this can be mitigated through guidance."[726]

The guide explains the risks and costs of secondary objectives and also recommends safeguards which should be implemented in order to avoid sacrificing the objectives of public procurement through the application of secondary policies. This includes, for example, the temporary application of secondary objectives. The inclusion of a requirement to monitor and evaluate the application of preferential policies can be an additional im-

726 Arrowsmith, 'Public Procurement: An Appraisal of the UNCITRAL Model Law ', 24.

portant instrument in order to measure their effectiveness and ensure that they are not misused for political reasons.[727]

The provisions on challenge procedures provide all the necessary elements that need to be addressed while offering enough flexibility to integrate these elements into existing national dispute resolution mechanisms. The particularity of public procurement challenges is, for example, reflected in the general requirement of a standstill period which avoids the unsatisfactory situation of having to annul a contract in order to rectify a procurement decision.

It can be concluded that the UNCITRAL Model Law to a great extent reflects international best practices and should be studied and considered as guideline in every reform process. However, it is of utmost importance to keep in mind that the UNCITRAL Model cannot serve as single model as it does not provide a holistic approach to public procurement systems. In particular the institutional architecture and the separation of responsibilities within a public procurement system are key factors for effective and efficient public procurement systems and must thus be designed carefully and given appropriate attention during reform processes.

727 Cf. ibid, 44.

This chapter serves as an example of how provisions of the UNCITRAL Model Law can be implemented in national law. Since Mauritius has reformed its public procurement system under the broader framework of the COMESA reform initiative, the latter will be briefly presented. This chapter includes a short overview of the COMESA procurement law reform efforts which is followed by a brief presentation of the Mauritian procurement law and, especially, its critical issues including objectives and principles, scope and coverage, institutions and staff, procedure, transparency aspects, secondary objectives and review procedures. Additionally, the provisions for procurement planning and contract administration, which are not addressed in the UNCITRAL Model Law, will be analysed. As mentioned above, the Mauritian law has been selected as example not only because it has been identified as quite modern and progressive but also because it has had an influence on the draft of the Namibian public procurement bill.[728] Best practices as well as shortcomings of the Mauritian public procurement legislation will be pointed out. Additionally, as the Mauritian example contains, as a national public procurement system, more specific provisions than the general provisions found in the GPA and the UNCITRAL Model Law, it offers practical lessons which will be presented in the final chapter of this part.

## 1. Introduction

The Mauritian procurement law has served as reference point for the reform of the Namibian procurement system.[729] Mauritius has - under the auspices of COMESA - undertaken a substantive reform of its procurement law in 2006. COMESA recommended that its members modify and

728 See below: Part III, Chapter 3, Subchapter 2 (d).

729 The Namibian Tender Board Secretary Enssle said in an interview with the Institute for Public Policy Research that best practices in the public procurement system of Mauritius which had been very robust with their reforms should be looked at by a delegation of Tender Board members. See: Links; Daniels, 'The Tender Board - Need for Root and Branch Reform', p. 20. The Tender Board Control Officer Sipiho confirmed in an interview that a delegation went to Mauritius in 2011. Additionally, the reform process has been assisted by a Mauritian public procurement expert.

adapt their procurement laws with a view to further harmonisation. Its reform suggestions heavily relied on the UNCITRAL Model Law. A closer look at the COMESA example might pose the question whether a regional approach of SADC/SACU might be beneficial for the Southern Africa countries and, especially, for Namibia. It might not only expedite regional integration and facilitate trade between SADC/SACU members but also be beneficial as it could induce further trade liberalisation. This question shall not, however, be dealt with in this dissertation.

It is not obvious why special reference shall be made to Mauritius while other legal systems seem at first sight more appropriate. The common history and especially the experience of the apartheid system, the geographical approximation as well as the very similar legal system of South Africa, which is said to have a very advanced and progressive procurement law, might, for example, be a better choice as guideline for reform. Nevertheless, Mauritius has very modern and progressive, comprehensive procurement laws and regulations. In contrast to the Model Law, it might offer solutions for the institutional and organisational structure and for procurement planning and contract management which is not part of the Model Law. It can, thus, give essential hints in regard to the institutional and organisational architecture of a public procurement system designed according to the Model Law and with respect to the regulation of matters not regulated in the Model Law. The critical review of a public procurement system that has been designed by using the UNCITRAL Model Law therefore represents a reasonable complement to the Model Law itself.

## 2. COMESA Procurement Reform Project

### a. Background

With its 19 member states, COMESA is Africa's largest regional trade area.[730] It was established in 1994 to replace the preferential trade area which had existed since 1981.[731] A free trade area was launched in 2000

730 Mampuzhasseril; et al., p. 1, para 1.1.2.

731 The Treaty Establishing the Common Market for Eastern and Southern Africa was signed in Kampala, Uganda on 5 November 1993 and was ratified in Lilongwe, Malawi on 8 December 1994.

and has so far been joined by fifteen members.[732] With a view to further trade liberalisation COMESA started an initiative to harmonise the procurement systems of its member states in 2001. The reform has been two-phased. The COMESA Public Procurement Reform Project (PPRP), which started in 2001 and was finalised in 2004, and the COMESA Enhancing Procurement Reforms and Capacity Project (EPRCP,) which was begun at 2006, were financed through loans from the African Development Bank.[733] The PPRP primarily aimed at harmonising public procurement rules, regulations and procedures, improving national procurement systems, strengthening the capacity of the member states in public procurement, and enhancing awareness of procurement opportunities in COMESA.[734] One of the key achievements has been the adoption of the Procurement Directive which provided the legislative framework for the public procurement reforms in the member states.[735] The EPRCP, which followed the Procurement Directive, had the objective of further enhancing the public procurement systems of COMESA member states by modernising and harmonising the laws, regulations and procedures, and by strengthening the capacity of countries to manage modern public procurement systems.[736] The Procurement Regulations which establish rules and procedures for cross-border procurement within COMESA was a major achievement resulting from this.[737] Whereas the first project focused on the instrumentality of procurement reforms, the EPRCP relates more to its implementation and capacity building.[738]

---

732 Karangizi, 'Regional Procurement Reform Initiative', p. 2; Mampuzhasseril; et al., p. 1, para. 1.1.1.

733 Mampuzhasseril; et al., p. 2ff., para. 1.2.

734 Karangizi, 'Regional Procurement Reform Initiative', p. 4; Mampuzhasseril; et al., p. 3, para. 1.2.5.

735 Cf. Mampuzhasseril; et al., p. 8, para. 3.2.2.

736 Ibid, vi, para. 2.

737 Ibid, 9, para. 3.2.5.

738 Ibid, 3f., para. 1.2.8.

### b. Laws and Regulations

#### i. COMESA Procurement Directive (2003)

The COMESA Procurement Directive recommends that COMESA members adopt national legislation consistent with certain general international standards based mainly on UNCITRAL model law, such as the adoption of review mechanism and publication requirements for solicitation documents. It contains general guidelines, abstract standards and examples for the regulation of public procurement that are recommended to be implemented into national legislation. However, neither detailed rules on methods and procedures nor on other matters such as the establishment of review mechanisms are outlined in the Directive.[739] COMESA directives are non-binding and the adoption of relevant national legislation to give effect to such directives is voluntarily.[740]

#### ii. COMESA Procurement Regulations

The Procurement Regulations[741] which were adopted in 2009 establish basic rules for regional procurement and give effect to the Directive as they provide for detailed rules on public procurement in COMESA member states.

### c. Objectives and Principles

The main objectives of the COMESA procurement projects are two-fold. One the one hand it is envisaged to liberalise and stimulate trade within COMESA. On the other hand national procurement systems should be improved with a special focus being put on the aspect of good governance.[742]

739 Caborn; Arrowsmith, 'Procurement methods in the public procurement systems of Africa', p. 271.

740 Jiang, 'Regulating Public Procurement in International Trade', p. 197.

741 Published in the Official Gazette of the Common Market for Southern and Eastern Africa, Vol. 15 No. 3 (9 June 2009).

742 Cf. Mampuzhasseril; et al., p. 3, para. 1.2.5.

The primary objective is the liberalisation of the procurement markets of COMESA member states to the suppliers or contractors of other COMESA member states. It has certain analogies with the GPA but differs in scope as procurement market liberalisation is limited to a certain region and, hence, excludes countries from other regions. The GPA, in contrast, is theoretically accessible to all WTO member states. The Procurement Regulations establish that the national treatment and the most-favoured-nation treatment principle are applicable in cases of procurements among the members, but specifically allow for regional preferences and, hence, discrimination against non-members. The GPA, however, strictly prohibits any form of preferential treatment. According to the Regulations, it is prohibited

> "[...] to apply rules of origin to goods imported from another Member State during public procurement proceedings [...] that are different from or inconsistent with the rules of origin the Member States apply in the normal course of trade."[743]

This is similar to the respective GPA provision but as with non-discrimination and the most-favoured-nation treatment principle limited to the member states of COMESA.

The Procurement Regulations contain certain elements which are very similar to GPA provisions. However, in regard to most substantive and procedural rules of the procurement system, the Regulations only provide abstract rules and basic requirements which have to be implemented by the member states. The discretion left to the member states allows the implementation suitable for the domestic context and according to the legal tradition of the member states.

The objectives of the Procurement Regulations are directly linked to the general COMESA objective to enhance trade within the economic zone. These objectives are: the promotion of harmonisation of public procurement laws and practices for the enhancement of intra COMESA trade, fostering competition and openness in public procurement procedures as well as fair management systems, and the promotion of accountability, transparency, and value for money.[744] The Regulations state several general principles which shall be applied and ensured by the member states, name-

743 COMESA Public Procurement Regulations 2009 (Legal Notice No. 3 of 2009, Official Gazette of COMESA, Vol. 15 No. 3), Art. 9.

744 Ibid, Art. 3 (d).

ly, competition and openness, fairness, accountability, transparency, and value for money.[745]

d. Scope and Coverage

The Regulations apply to all regional competitive bidding but name certain exceptions that can justify exclusions or modifications of the prescribed regulations. These include procurement for state security, military related production, defence or international relations and to protect the public interest.[746] The UNCITRAL Model Law emphasises that it is recommendable not to provide exceptions from the Act but rather to provide for methods suitable for particular sensitive procurements such as military related production.[747] This ensures that it is made subject to the basic standards of public procurement legislation such as the transparency regulations. Moreover, the Regulations contain an exception provision which is very similar to Article III (2) of the GPA. It allows for the application of any measure that is necessary for the protection of specific higher objectives such as public morals, life and intellectual property.[748] The reasons that can justify deviation as stated in the GPA have been supplemented by the protection of small and medium enterprises. Although it is not undisputed whether the protection of SMEs also implicates their explicit promotion through procurement and the practical effect is not certain, it constitutes a significant difference between the COMESA and the WTO approach since it might result in and justify preferential treatment.

As with the GPA, the COMESA Regulations require the member states to ensure that procuring entities do not separate a public procurement into two or more smaller procurements in order to remain under the threshold for regional competitive bidding.[749]

The determination of thresholds for the application for regional competitive bidding by the member states, which is established in Article 6, is superficially redolent of the way the GPA established the scope of application. In detail it, however, differs. Whereas the GPA members negotiate

745 Ibid, Art. 3 (a-c).
746 Ibid, Art. 2 (6).
747 Cf. UNCITRAL, 'Guide to Enactment of the UNCITRAL Model Law on Public Procurement', p. 56.
748 COMESA Public Procurement Regulations 2009, Art. 2 (10).
749 Ibid, Art. 5 (4).

the thresholds with the other member states, COMESA members can independently set thresholds under its domestic legislation. The African Development Bank Report states in this regard that

> "[t]his was primarily to accommodate the diversity in the levels of economic development under the principle of 'variable geometry,' which enables a group of member states to move faster in the regional economic integration process than some other member states. The long term objective is to remove the threshold for domestic preference."[750]

COMESA has, hence, decided to allow for gradual liberalisation rather than requiring the immediate removal of all barriers. In this regard the Regulations require the member states to work towards the establishment of a common financial threshold for regional competitive bidding within a period of five years.[751]

The exemption of procurements financed by donors or a funding organisation other than a public body is explicitly allowed. The Regulations provide that procurement rules of a donor or funding organisation be applied when these are mandatory pursuant to an obligation entered into by a member state.[752]

### e. Institutions and Staff

The COMESA Regulations only provide abstract requirements in regard to the organisational and institutional structure of public procurement systems in its member states. They do not prescribe any specific approach of how to allocate tasks and responsibilities in detail. It is, for example, left to the member states whether to take a centralised or decentralised approach. Article 34 requires the establishment of an institution such as a policy office to give guidance to the development and practice of public procurement.[753] Member states furthermore have to ensure that a contact point and information centre on public procurement is established.[754] An oversight institution that monitors and reports, nationally and within the common market, on procurement activities of procuring entities is also to

750 Mampuzhasseril; et al., p. 2, para. 1.1.7.
751 COMESA Public Procurement Regulations 2009, Art. 6 (5).
752 Ibid, Art. 2 (2) and (3).
753 Ibid, Art. 34 (1) (a).
754 Ibid, Art. 34 (1) (b).

be provided for.[755] Last but not least, the member states are required to develop professional capacities.[756] Although not specifically mentioned, this might, apart from training, also include a qualification system ensuring that vacancies are filled with sufficiently qualified people. This aspect is of critical importance for the efficient and effective functioning of public procurement systems. Although these provisions are quite broad and flexible and the exact institutional organisation of public procurement is left to the member states, basic requirements for the institutional organisation of public procurement systems reflecting important public procurement objectives, including transparency, accountability, competition and fairness, might induce the member states to establish an institutional system with adequate capacity to effectively and efficiently enforce all the procurement objectives.

Article 32 of the Regulations requires the development and incorporation of standards of conduct and ethics aimed at the integrity of the workforce.[757] A code of conduct has to provide for impartiality, avoidance of conflict of interest, impropriety and mere appearance of impropriety, confidentiality of certain information, and the prohibition of fraudulent and corrupt practices.[758] It resembles the importance of the integrity of the workforce for the fight against corruption and, hence, for the efficient and effective functioning of procurement systems. Even if it is clear that codes of conduct are not the universal remedy against corruption, the requirement to develop and incorporate codes of conduct and ethics aiming at the integrity of the workforce helps to put corruption on the national agenda and might provoke governments to put a stronger focus on the integrity and quality of the workforce when discussing and reforming public procurement systems.

Apart from the institutional and organisational structures directly linked with the procurement process, there needs to be an appropriate structure set up for contract management.[759] It is emphasised that the execution and monitoring of public procurement contracts require appropriate skills, experience and functions.[760] This can be understood as requirement to ensure that the professional capacity as well as the capacity to act is ensured.

755 Ibid, Art. 34 (1) (c).
756 Ibid, Art. 34 (1) (d).
757 Ibid, Art. 32.
758 Ibid, Art. 32 (3) (a-e).
759 Ibid, Art. 24.
760 Ibid.

Again, the manner of implementation can be chosen by the member states, but it must closely examine the issue of contract management in public procurement and consider adequate ways to set up rules for contract management suitable to achieving the objectives within the local context.

### f. Procedures

#### i. Procurement Methods and Procedures

The COMESA Regulations do not lay down any specific rules in regard to procurement methods. It does, however, require its member states to include international and regional competitive bidding in its domestic legislation.[761] The domestic legislation needs to provide conditions for the procurement methods applied to regional competitive bidding.[762] They are furthermore obliged to make arrangements to ensure that procuring entities do not split up public procurement requirements in order to stay below a certain threshold and, hence, avoid using a particular procurement method.[763]

For regional competitive bidding, the use of standard bidding documents approved by the Council of the Ministers of the Common Market is obligatory.[764] This facilitates harmonisation and, moreover, promotes competition as it allows all potential suppliers and contractors to prepare a bid without much effort, such as familiarising themselves with the bidding documents.

The Regulations allow for prequalification procedures and shortlisting. The rules governing this matter have to be included in the domestic legislation of the member states.[765] In certain circumstances the member states are allowed to conduct post qualification procedures, e.g. in cases of low-value procurement.[766] The objective is to "determine whether the best evaluated bidder has the capability and resources to effectively carry out the public procurement contract."[767] The reason for choosing post-

761 COMESA Public Procurement Regulations 2009, Art. 12 (1).
762 Ibid, Art. 12 (3) (a) and (b).
763 Ibid, Art. 12 (1-3).
764 Ibid, Art. 13 (1).
765 Ibid, Art. 16 (2).
766 Ibid, Art. 20 (4).
767 Ibid.

qualification rather than prequalification is that prequalification requires the determination of all bidders' capability and resources, whereas in post-qualification only the best evaluated bidders' qualification is reviewed. This represents a great advantage in regard to time and resources. The costs of prequalification procedures in, for example, low value procurements might not always be appropriate in regard to the value of procurement.

Article 26 provides regulations on framework agreements which may be provided for in the domestic legislation of the member states. Another striking provision is Article 27, which urges the member states to progressively eliminate the practice of keeping lists of suppliers. Whereas the GPA does not contain any prohibition in regard to keeping lists of suppliers, but rather allows for the use of (non-mandatory) multi-use lists,[768] the UNCITRAL Model Law explicitly recommends not using them. Suppliers lists are not provided for in the Model Law because UNCITRAL believes that the very flexible provisions on framework agreements

> "[...] allow for the benefits of suppliers lists to be achieved, without running the elevated risks to transparency and competition that suppliers lists are considered to raise."[769]

The clear objective of progressively stopping the practice of keeping suppliers lists aims at eliminating entry barriers for potential suppliers or contractors and, hence, facilitating competition. In particular in regard to cross-border procurement, suppliers lists would impede the participation of foreign suppliers and contradict the objective of transparency. In contextual perspective it might be argued that a lot of African countries and, especially, SMEs have neither the experience nor the resources in bidding, which implies that all possible entry barriers should be removed to facilitate their participation. However, a differentiation would be made between mandatory supplier lists which exclude suppliers that are not on the list for particular procurement procedures and lists that are kept for information purposes and in order to reduce the administrative burden in tender procedures. This means that it is possible to save certain information or documentation about suppliers to be available in future tender processes, for example.

---

768 See Arrowsmith, 'Government Procurement in the WTO ', p. 237.

769 UNCITRAL, 'Guide to Enactment of the UNCITRAL Model Law on Public Procurement', p. 254, para. 3.

Article 15, which establishes general obligations of bidders, is very important. Pursuant to this Article bidders have to prove that they have not been

> "[...] debarred from participating in public procurement under domestic legislation of a member state in which the bidder is resident or bidding from and is therefore not debarred from participating in regional competitive bidding under these regulations."[770]

This seems to be an instrument to blacklist companies that have formerly stood out with malpractice and to exclude them from public procurement bidding in all members states of COMESA. The bidder bears the burden of proof that no debarment exists, thereby reducing the burden for procuring entities. It is not only important in regard to jointly combat any irregularities in public procurement involving the external side, but might also encourage companies to adhere to the rules both in their state as well as in other member states. The fact that the bidder must in either case provide a statement verifying that it has not been debarred from participating in public procurement in its own state severely limits the possibility of getting away with irregularities. There is, however, no specification as to how such proof is to be made.

Article 28 provides for periodic assessment of cases where no responsive regional bids are received or bid proceedings are otherwise unsuccessful. It hence includes all procurements carried out through regional competitive bidding where either no supplier or contractor from another member state has submitted a bid or it was not awarded the contract award or the contract was not concluded. This seems to be an adequate and innovative instrument to identify obstacles for regional procurement. Subsection 2 provides a suggestion of matters which might be responsible for the failure of the regional competitive bidding method.

The Regulations generally accommodate the use of e-procurement. Article 17(2), for example, requires procuring entities to "make available a bid box, or other means of receiving regional bids, such as e-procurement."

770 COMESA Public Procurement Regulations 2009, Art. 15 (1) (a).

ii. Tender Specification, Award Criteria and Evaluation Methods

The contents of the bidding documents must include clear instructions on the management of the procurement process and the applicable rules,[771] a clear description of the subject matter[772] and the proposed form and conditions of the contract or a statement of the form and conditions of contract which shall apply.[773] These are important conditions to ensure and facilitate that all potential bidders participate and prepare a responsive bid.

The requirements for technical specifications and for the qualification of bidders seem similar to the respective GPA provisions. Technical specifications shall relate to performance, be based on national or international standards, and not refer to any particular trademark, brand name, patent, type, producer or service provider or to specific origin.[774] However, the COMESA Regulations also stipulate that technical specifications shall refer to descriptive characteristics, which is contrary to the GPA under which its use shall be generally avoided in order not to limit competition. The criteria that can be used to determine the qualification of bidders include the necessary qualifications, capability, experience, resources, equipment and facilities to provide what is being procured.[775] This provides an opening for the application of secondary policies, which has already been discussed within the context of secondary policies and the GPA.

The method for bid evaluation shall be done in accordance with domestic legislation and shall be chosen according to the type, value and complexity of procurement.[776] Bidding documents shall clearly state the methodology and criteria to be used[777] and no other criteria shall be taken into account.[778] The criteria shall be applied equally to all bids.[779]

Although the Regulations were adopted long before the revision of the UNCITRAL Model Law, they provide for a standstill period after the tender notification and the final award. The period is to be specified in do-

771 Ibid, Art. 13 (2) (a).
772 Ibid, Art. 13 (2) (b).
773 Ibid, Art. 13 (2) (c).
774 Ibid, Art. 11 (5).
775 Ibid, Art. 19 (a).
776 Ibid, Art. 20 (1).
777 Ibid, Art. 20 (2).
778 Ibid, Art. 20 (3).
779 Ibid, Art. 20 (3).

mestic legislation and the tender is only to be awarded in the absence of a challenge made by any other bidder within this period.[780] Member states are required to work towards setting unified time frames within a period of 5 years, though.[781]

### g. Transparency

The Regulations do not provide for any requirements in regard to the publication and availability of bid invitations and documents but leaves it to the member states. Other important publication requirements, e.g. the evaluation criteria and methodology have to be clearly outlined in regional competitive bidding documents[782] and a notice of the award decision has to be sent to all regional bidders,[783] are provided for. The provision that unsuccessful bidders can request reasons for which their bids were unsuccessful is just as essential for ensuring transparency.[784] Moreover, Article 18 of the Regulations requires a public bid opening taking place in all cases of regional competitive bidding,

The Regulations provide a comprehensive illustrative list of what steps and actions need to be recorded.[785] It covers all essential steps and actions of the entire procurement process. While the Directive has not provided any specifications on these issues, this shortcoming has been rectified by including comprehensive rules in the Regulations, which specify procedural rules for the disclosure and the keeping of procurement information.[786] The member states are required to provide a complete list of information that needs to be included in the record.[787] All records need to be preserved for a minimum period of time specified in domestic legislation.[788] The records have to be made available to a competent authority carrying out oversight and auditing.[789] Member states are further required

780 Ibid, Arts. 21 (1) and 22 (2) (c).
781 Ibid, Art. 21 (2).
782 Ibid, Art. 20(2).
783 Ibid, Art. 21(1)(a).
784 Ibid, Art. 23.
785 Ibid, Art. 29 (2) (a-k).
786 Ibid, Art. 29.
787 Ibid, Art. 29 (2).
788 Ibid, Art. 29 (1) (b).
789 Ibid, Art. 29 (1) (c).

to ensure that unsuccessful bidders can request that reasons be provided for any unsuccessful bid within a specified period.[790] Thus, the COMESA Directive and Regulations establish basic transparency and accountability requirements that have to be implemented by the member states in order to ensure fairness and competition in public procurement procedures, to impede corrupt practices and enable the review and monitoring of procurement decisions. It, however, does not go as far as the UNCITRAL Model law which promotes very high standards of transparency and accountability, such as by requiring reasoning for most acts and decisions even if no request has been made.[791]

There is, furthermore, an article outlining requirements for the information by member states.[792] This is comparable to the respective GPA provision and shall not be discussed since it is only tangential to the objective of this work.

#### h. Secondary Objectives

As indicated, the Regulations establish the application of the principle of non-discrimination including the MFN-principle as well as national treatment among COMESA Members, but not beyond the borders of COMESA.[793]

Article 7 explicitly requires member states to provide in their domestic legislation that in international competitive bidding procedures preferences in favour of regional bidders are applied.[794] Moreover, preferences shall be granted for goods, works or services manufactured or performed within the common market.[795] The margin of preferences has to be communicated to the secretary general and be posted on their national procurement websites.[796]

The Regulations, furthermore, clarify that suppliers of goods, works, or services of other member states may be denied the benefits of the Regulations

790 Ibid.
791 See Subchapter 6 of the previous chapter.
792 COMESA Public Procurement Regulations 2009, Art. 30.
793 Ibid, Art. 8 (1) and(2).
794 Ibid.
795 Ibid.
796 Ibid.

> "[...] if (a) any foreign bidder owns, produces or performs such goods, works or services or controls that bidder; and (b) that bidder has no substantial business activities in the Member State under whose laws the business enterprise is constituted."[797]

"Business activities" is further specified as requiring a bidder to have its physical business presence in the member state and be an ordinary resident in a member state.[798] This provision constitutes protection from foreigners who merely open a business somewhere in the common market to get access to the market even though in actual fact it is a foreign company.

As mentioned above, apart from preferences for regional bidders the Regulations explicitly allow adopting or maintaining measures necessary to protect small and medium enterprises irrespective of the requirements of the Regulations.[799] There is no other reference to the use of secondary objectives, but there is also no prohibition of the application of secondary objectives through, for example, tender specifications, evaluation criteria or contract requirements.

#### i. Review Procedures

Member states have to provide independent and impartial judicial or administrative challenge procedures. The nature and principal features of the review are outlined in Article 31 (2) and include the right to be heard, transparent procedures conducted in writing, and review institution's authority to apply effective remedies such as set-asides, temporary suspension of the procurement process, etc. The Regulations provide the same degree of discretion to create an appropriate institutional and organisational structure that can effectively implement the requirements set out in the Regulations as for the establishment of institutions responsible for the efficient and effective functioning of the public procurement process according to the law. A shortcoming is that it is not required to provide an appeal mechanism.

As mentioned above, a standstill period between the tender notification and the final award where an application for challenge can be filed is prescribed.[800]

797 Ibid, Art. 8 (4).
798 Ibid, Art. 8 (5).
799 Ibid, Art. 2 (10) (e).
800 Ibid, Arts. 21 (1) (b) and 22 (2) (c).

### j. Procurement Planning

It is worth mentioning that procurement planning regarding regional public procurement, which is not dealt with in the Model Law at all, is addressed by COMESA. It requires member states to include the provision that all procuring entities plan their regional public procurement in a rational manner. Within 60 days after the commencement of the financial year a procurement plan has to be submitted to the secretary general or be made available on the domestic procurement website. This avoids ad hoc procurements at the end of the financial year and promotes competition since suppliers and contractors can plan and prepare their bids in advance.

### k. Contract Administration

In regard to contract administration COMESA requires its member states to set up

> "[...] appropriate structures for the execution and monitoring of the public procurement contract [...] taking into account the skills, experience and functions required for management of the public procurement contract."[801]

It is of great advantage to require coverage of the contract administration stage, because the whole procurement proceedings would be rendered inefficient and ineffective if the contract were not to be executed in a proper way. To ensure that the contract implementation stage is reviewed and properly regulated is, hence, an important part of guaranteeing a successful completion of the procurement cycle.[802]

### l. Provisions for the Implementation of Reform

Finally, the COMESA Regulations provide regulations on legislative procurement reform in member states.[803] Thereafter, member states have to conduct continuously reviews of their public procurement systems "in order to ensure an efficacious legal framework that embraces technological

801 Ibid, Art. 24.
802 On this issue see also above: Part I, Chapter 1, Subchapter 4.
803 Ibid, Art. 33.

advances, corporate governance systems and institutional capacity."[804] This is a very important provision, as it allows countries to identify and rectify shortcomings and to respond to new developments in public procurement. The incorporation of such a provision should generally be considered in every national public procurement system. Article 37 further provides for cooperation among member states in regard to the implementation of the Regulations, the understanding of the procurement systems of member states, capacity building in the public and private sectors, and opportunities to enhance access to procurement markets. The secretary general collects and distributes information on certain aspects of public procurement required to be provided by the member states from and among the member states.[805]

## 3. Interim Conclusion

The COMESA public procurement reform has been based on the UNCITRAL Model Law but contains additional mechanism that were not originally addressed in the 1994 Model Law but only in the revised version, which came into force much later. This includes the requirement to have a standstill period in which it is possible to challenge the decision or a particular act by the procuring entity. Moreover, it makes the regulation of procurement planning and contract administration obligatory, which is desirable and aids in making the whole procurement cycle a success. The comprehensive but flexible approach by COMESA is to be welcomed and in most instances reflects international best practices. The flexibility granted to its member states can have a positive effect on the efficiency and effectiveness of public procurement systems as the system can be designed according to the local context and circumstances as well as the available capacity and resources. The approach to provide general guidelines rather than precast rules as the UNCITRAL Model Law can be regarded as being suitable to balance the objective of harmonisation with efficiency and effectiveness at the national level.

One shortcoming is that it does not require the establishment of an appeal mechanism for the review of procurement decisions. It also fails to require its member states to establish an appropriate system of entry re-

804 Ibid.
805 COMESA Public Procurement Regulations 2009, Art. 37 (2).

quirements for public procurement staff members. A uniform and transparent approach in this respect could make an important contribution to the objective of building professional capacity within the COMESA region.

The potential of regional public procurement approaches such as in COMESA to promote competition within the common market is noteworthy. The COMESA Regulations contain many requirements that facilitate the participation of potential suppliers or contractors, including SMEs, in regional competitive bidding. This includes, for example, the use of standard bidding documents and the stringent transparency requirements. The strong protection of the regional procurement market by making the application of regional preferences in international competitive bidding procedures obligatory should be viewed with scepticism. Although all member states are required to publish the percentage of any margin of preference, there is no uniform preference system in the common market. The lack of a time limit of the preferential treatment of eligible suppliers and contractors is also a major shortcoming; while the objective of granting them a period of transition to become competitive may be supported, the system should not operate to protect them from international competition forever, as that would have negative side-effects for all stakeholders as has been discussed in Part I.[806]

## 4. Mauritian Procurement Law

### a. Background

The Mauritian Public Procurement Law was enacted in 2006 prior to the adoption of the COMESA Regulations. Mauritius strives to constantly review and update its public procurement system. In cooperation with the World Bank, COMESA and UNCITRAL who advised the Mauritian government in the review of its public procurement system, Mauritius issued a White Paper on Modernising the Public Procurement Framework in July 2011.[807] Several amendments have been made and critical issues have been addressed.

---

806 See Chapter 3, Subchapter 2.

807 Ministry of Finance and Economic Development, 'White Paper On Modernising the Public Procurement Framework - Issues and Proposals for Consultation'

### b. The Framework

#### i. Laws and Regulations

The Public Procurement Act[808] was enacted in December 2006 and has been supplemented by the Procurement Regulations of 2008.[809] Further regulations have been enacted in regard to disqualification (2009),[810] debarment and suspension (2008),[811] and framework agreements (2013).[812] Additionally, several directives complementing and clarifying the Act and the regulations have been enacted.

The Mauritius Procurement Law provides a good legal basis or framework, but its efficiency and effectiveness relies to a great extent on the policies of the Procurement Policy Office and on further regulations and directives. Section 61 of the Act establishes in this respect that the Minister to whom responsibility for the subject of finance is assigned may, on the recommendation of the Policy Office, make such regulations as it thinks fit for the purpose of the Act. Subsection 2 reads as following:

> "(2) Regulations […] may provide for
>
> (a) detailed procedures;
>
> (b) competent authorities;
>
> (c) operational thresholds;
>
> (d) time limits and other deadlines; and
>
> (e) the levying of fees or charges by the Policy Office, the Board or the Review Panel; and
>
> (f) the amendment of the Schedule."

A lot of provisions of the Procurement Act which contain the clause "as may be prescribed" need further specification either by directives, procedures, instructions, etc., or standard forms through the Policy Office or by

---

(Ministry of Finance and Economic Development, Mauritius: 2011), available at http://www.govmu.org/portal/goc/pposite/WhitePaper8July2011.doc; last accessed: 30 November 2015.

808 Public Procurement Act 2006 (Act No. 33 of 2006).

809 Public Procurement (Suspension and Debarment) Regulations 2008 (Government Notice No. 8 of 2008).

810 Public Procurement (Disqualification) Regulations 2009 (No. 142 of 2009).

811 Public Procurement (Suspension and Debarment) Regulations 2008.

812 Public Procurement (Framework Agreement) Regulations 2013 (Government Notice No. 177 of 2013).

supplementary regulations made by the Minister on the recommendation of the Policy Office. Not all of these required specifications have been dealt with in regulations nor have they been regulated elsewhere. In some cases they are only dealt with in directives. As they affect substantive issues of the procurement system, such provisions should be mandatory because of their sensitivity. It seems insufficient that such matters have no force in law. Additionally, the situation makes it more difficult for potential bidders and stakeholders to get an overview of how the procurement system functions and interferes with the predictability of decisions.

### ii. Objectives and Principles

The Act does not state any specific objectives or principles. Certain objectives such as transparency, equity, fairness and value for money are, however, stated several times in the Act. The Central Procurement Board is, for example, required to take into account these principles in the execution of its duties.[813] Moreover, there is a strong focus on procurement integrity and accountability. It can also be noted that Mauritius has tried to establish an institutional and organisational structure with sufficient checks and balances to avoid the risks of corruption and the exertion of influence. It has updated its regulations through several amendments, in particular, by including provisions on public-private partnerships, framework agreements and e-procurement.

### iii. Scope and Coverage

The Act provides several exceptions for its application. Procurements undertaken to protect national security or defence can be exempted if the prime minister so determines and the most competitive method of procurement available in the circumstances is used.[814] Procurements undertaken under an agreement or arrangement with a foreign state can only be exempted if the agreement or arrangement allows Mauritius to benefit from the expertise and development experience of that state in a particular

813 Public Procurement Act 2006, Sec. 11 (2).
814 Ibid, Sec. 3 (1) (a).

field.[815] Furthermore, procurements in respect of an information and communication technology project which require interfacing with different existing systems can be exempted where the ministry finds that an entity which has initially developed the system needs to execute the project in order to protect the safety or interests of Mauritius.[816] Additionally, procurements undertaken by diplomatic missions of Mauritius abroad,[817] by any public body in respect of rental or office space,[818] or by any public body in respect of training services[819] are not subject to the application of the Act.

In contrast to the UNCITRAL Model Law which recommends the inclusion of all types of procurement, Mauritius grants several exemptions. The exemptions are also more extensive than the exemptions granted in the COMESA provisions. It is not clear why these types of procurements could not be administered by one of the methods of the Act, for example, direct procurement for security and defence procurements. Furthermore, it is unclear and difficult to imagine what reasons can justify the exemption of, for example, training services. Nevertheless, the restriction of exemptions for agreements or arrangements with foreign states to cases which are beneficial for the state because of a possible transfer of development experience or expertise goes further than the COMESA Regulations and can be of great advantage. It avoids excluding all donor-funded projects, and in particular tied-aid coming with the condition that a project is carried out by a company determined by the donor, from the application of the Act. Such projects have several negative effects on the national economy and the public procurement system in general. First of all, the national economy rarely benefits from such projects. Secondly, the transparency standards otherwise required for public procurement projects are circumvented. Such approach can also be seen as being responsive to international initiatives to untie aid.[820]

815 Ibid, Sec. 3 (1) (b).
816 Ibid, Sec. 3 (1) (c).
817 Ibid, Sec. 3 (1) (d).
818 Ibid, Sec. 3 (1) (e).
819 Ibid, Sec. 3 (1) (f).
820 OECD, 'Aid Effectiveness 2005–10: Progress in implementing the Paris Declaration', (Paris: OECD, 2011). See also Arrowsmith, 'Government Procurement in the WTO ', p. 151.

c. Institutions and Staff

The Public Procurement Act establishes two procurement institutions: the Procurement Policy Office[821] and the Central Procurement Board.[822] The former acts as an independent, though internal, policy institution and is, therefore, not involved in any procurement proceedings. The latter is responsible for the approval of the award of major contracts by public bodies.[823] The Central Procurement Board is a relic of the Central Tender Board Act governing the public procurement system before 2006 and has been retained because "[i]t was felt more appropriate to go for gradual decentralisation while building capacity of public bodies to handle higher value contracts."[824]

The Procurement Policy Office has a variety of functions: policy making, recommendation and facilitation of implementation of measures which lead to the improvement of the functioning of the procurement system, coordination with international institutions and other foreign entities on matters of procurement, monitoring and reporting, and training and advice. Policy-making is, inter alia, to be carried out through the issuance of instructions to public bodies concerning the coordination of their actions with the Policy Office, the Board and the Review Panel, the formulation of policies relating to procurement which are necessary for the implementation of the Act, and the issuance of standard documents such as bidding documents or requests for proposals. The monitoring functions include the collection of information form the Board, the Review Panel and public bodies and the monitoring of their compliance with the Act as well as the monitoring of foreign technical assistance in the field of procurement. In 2009 an amendment was made tasking the Procurement Policy Office with "[attending] to complaints from bidders and suppliers and [advising] the Board or public bodies on the appropriate course of action."[825] This means that internal reviews in cases of major contracts are also to be handled by the Policy Office. In order to be able to carry out these functions effectively, the Policy Office is endowed with specific powers such as the power to request such information, records and other documents as it may require

821 Public Procurement Act 2006, Part II.
822 Ibid, Part III.
823 Ibid, Sec. 8 (1).
824 Ministry of Finance and Economic Development, p. 3, para. 2.2.2.
825 Public Procurement Act 2006, Sec. 7 (db).

from the Board or any public body.[826] Advice is to be given on foreign technical assistance in the field of procurement and to the financial secretary regarding delegation of financial authority to public officers. Apart from the interactions with the public sector side of the procurement system the Board is also required to ascertain the private sector's perception of the effectiveness of the procurement system. The Policy Office is, moreover, required to present an annual report to the Minister on the functioning of the procurement system. Additional functions may be conferred on the Office by the financial secretary.

The institution bears the responsibility for overseeing the procurement system with all stakeholders. It seems very progressive that it is designed so that the Office interacts with the business community. As recognised in the AfDB Report on the COMESA Public Procurement Reform and Capacity Building Projects[827] the capacity of the private sector is key factor for a successfully functioning procurement system. It emphasised the need for strong private sector organisations that advise the business sector.[828] Although establishing such institutions far exceeds the competence of the Office, it, nevertheless, shows how important the business community's acceptance of the procurement system is. And the Policy Office has the possibility to not only take up the business community's criticism and suggestions but also to introduce changes that can overcome existing problems or difficulties. The Procurement Regulations have even extended the Policy Office's responsibilities to providing assistance in the dissemination of information to bidders on the rules and procedures governing public procurement.[829] This might lead to better value for money as it can help to facilitate more competition and also improved bids. It is, moreover, a very important instrument in regard to SMEs which often do not have the capacity and expertise to understand procurement procedures and to prepare bids.

Nevertheless, thee variety of functions to be performed by the Policy Office raises the question of whether the Office has the capacity and resources to execute its responsibilities. Further research would be necessary in order to determine whether the Policy Office successfully implements

826 Ibid, Sec. 7A (1) (a).
827 Mampuzhasseril; et al.
828 Ibid, xi, para. 11.
829 Public Procurement Regulations 2008 (Regulations made by the Minister under Section 61 of the Public Procurement Act 2006) (Government Notice No. 7 of 2008), Reg. 3 (4) (a).

public procurement legislation in practice, in other words, whether it works effectively and efficiently. This reflects the notion that a legal provision, as good as it is on paper, can only be effective if it is properly implemented. The establishment of an institution such as the Policy Office is only valuable if it is ensured that enough capacity and resources are available for its effective functioning.

Notwithstanding that Mauritius has a Central Procurement Board, it does not follow a strict centralised procurement system. As it is not obviously defined to what extent the Board is responsible for the approval of the award of contracts further explanation is required. Section 8 (1) of the Act states that the Board is responsible for the bidding process and award of *major* contracts by public bodies. "Major contract" is defined as a contract for the procurement of goods or services or the execution of works to which a public body is or proposes to be a party, the estimated fair and reasonable value of which exceeds the prescribed amount.[830] "Prescribed amount" means the amount specified in the schedule determining thresholds for the different public bodies and different contract types.[831] According to this scheme, ministries and local authorities can therefore award all type of procurement contracts which do not exceed the amount of 5 million rupees. All contracts that exceed a predetermined level, hence, have to be awarded by the Central Procurement Board; all other contracts can be awarded by the public bodies themselves. The system is, therefore, not centralised in general but ensures that procurements with a certain value are handled by the Central Procurement Board, which may not necessarily have any knowledge of the subject matter, but does have special procurement expertise. Any professional or technical assistance can be requested from any appropriate person.[832] This can remedy the lack of knowledge about the subject matter, especially where complex and highly technical procurements are concerned. What "an appropriate person" means should, however, be defined and there should be guarantees ensuring that such person is impartial.

According to Section 8 of the Act, the Board consists of a chairperson, two vice-chairpersons and three other persons who are supposed to have wide experience in legal, administrative, economic, financial, engineering, scientific or technical matters. Further public officers can be recruited as

830 Public Procurement Act 2006, Sec. 2.
831 Ibid.
832 Public Procurement Act 2006, Sec. 12 (1) (d).

staff members by the head of the civil service or by such persons as may be appointed by the board under contract terms and conditions. No specific entry or qualification requirements have been issued for Board or staff members. It is recommendable to do so in order to ensure professional procurement capacity and restrict possibilities for the exertion of influence for whatever reason in regard to board or staff member selection. The Board does not carry out the bidding process itself but needs to authorise the public body to call for bids or utilise another appropriate procurement method and to approve the award of every major contract. In respect to the Central Procurement Board Section 11 (2) of the Act requires the board to strive to achieve the highest standards of transparency and equity in the execution of its duties. It states that the evaluation and the qualification criteria and methodology disclosed in the bidding documents, equality of opportunity to all bidders, fairness of treatment to all parties, the need to obtain the best value for money in terms of price, quality and delivery, having regard to set specifications, and transparency of process and decisions, must be considered. This explicitly addresses the responsibility to the board members to adhere to the principles of transparency, equality, fairness, and value for money. Although these principles can be found in most current procurement systems, their deliberate mention within the context of the functions of the board might induce a stronger and more conscious identification with them.

Independent evaluation committees carry out a very important function. These are to be set up by the Central Procurement Board or the public body respectively by selecting from a list of qualified evaluators maintained by it. [833] The Board has to select "at least 3 members who are knowledgeable about the goods or services under procurement and the public procurement procedures."[834] Neither any person whose participation would constitute a conflict of interest[835] nor any public officer working in the public body related to the procurement[836] can act as a member of the evaluation committee. For the establishment of evaluation committees for contracts other than major contracts, Regulation 7 (2) of the 2008 Procurement Regulations requires the public body to take into account the proper combination of expertise required and to ensure that the selected

833 Ibid, Sec. 37 (2).
834 Public Procurement Regulations 2008, Reg. 4 (1).
835 Ibid, Reg. 4 (3) (b).
836 Ibid, Reg. 4 (3) (a).

evaluators have the required competence and expertise. The discretion to determine whether evaluation committee members have the required competence and expertise is left solely to the public bodies and there is no requirement concerning the independence of committee members. The term "independent evaluators" was deleted in 2009 and the omission of a definition of "qualified" in regulations is problematic. It seems from the regulations that any public officer from a public body other than the one the procurement is made for can serve as a member of an evaluation committee. The omission of criteria for minimum qualification and experience for the evaluators, the lack of requirements concerning their independence and the eligibility of public office holders are severe shortcomings that leave plenty of room for abuse. It would be of great advantage if, for example, the policy office maintained lists of qualified evaluators instead of the public bodies themselves in order to avoid a situation where the same people responsible for the procurement decision also appoint potential evaluation committee members. Moreover, it is questionable whether the establishment of an evaluation committee for each procurement does not have a negative effect on the efficiency and effectiveness of public procurement. It is not only time-consuming but also costly and might not be appropriate in all cases of procurement, in particular, with regard to procurements with a low value.

### d. Procedures

#### i. Procurement Methods and Procedures

The general bidding method in the case of goods, other services or works is open advertised bidding. All eligible and qualified bidders shall have equal access to the bidding process without discrimination.[837] Another method may be used only in cases where a public body has reason to believe that open advertised bidding will not be efficient or practical for the procurement in question or will be too costly to apply given the value of the procurement.[838] Apart from open bidding, the range of possible procurement methods includes: restricted bidding, request for sealed quota-

837 Public Procurement Act 2006, Sec. 15 (2) (a).
838 Ibid, Sec. 15 (2) (d).

tions, direct procurement, community or end-user participation, or departmental execution.[839]

For the procurement of consultancy services the Act provides a particular procurement method: requests for proposals.[840] While the first three seem to be familiar and are based on the GPA as well as the UNCITRAL Model Law, community or end-user participation and departmental execution are innovative and need further explanation. The procedure of community and end-user participation[841] is not described in detail but needs further policy determination. The UNCITRAL Revised Guide to Enactment addresses community participation, although this method is not contained in the Model Law. It considers community participation as an opportunity to enhance delivery of small-scale projects and warns that their application might be not feasible in larger or more complex projects.[842] It gives the example of community control or public scrutiny of public expenditure.[843] However, other forms of community participation are not excluded. Special reference is made to the application of socio-economic criteria which would allow the involvement of the local community, inter alia, through a requirement to employ local labour or materials.[844] The Guide, however, also indicates that it is necessary to consider the balancing of policy objectives since the limitation of potential participants in the delivery of the project as an inherent feature of community participation threatens to undermine transparency, to add costs or to reduce competition.[845] The Mauritian Procurement Act, on the other hand, establishes when end-users or communities may participate in the delivery of services. Such participation must either enhance the economy, quality or sustainability of the service to be procured, or create employment; the involvement of the beneficiary community is the primary objective of the project.[846] The formulation of the former reason is quite broad and it remains unclear what criteria need to be fulfilled in order to justify or require end-user or community participation. The term "may participate"

839 Ibid, Sec. 15 (1) (a).
840 Ibid, Sec. 15 (1) (b).
841 Ibid, Sec. 15 (1) (a) (v).
842 UNCITRAL, 'Guide to Enactment of the UNCITRAL Model Law on Public Procurement', p. 9, para. 26.
843 Ibid, 9, para. 26.
844 Ibid, 8, para. 25.
845 Ibid.
846 Public Procurement Act 2006, Sec. 22.

suggests, however, that the decision about the participation lies solely within the public body's discretion. The Procurement Regulations set out further details. Regulation 43 (1) states:

> "In the interest of providing employment to local communities, a public body may decide to execute small construction works, including maintenance and repair, through local user committees."

Subregulation 2 then establishes procedural requirements for procurement through a user's committee. The Regulations provide an example for what kind of work can be procured through local user committees. Nevertheless, there is no specification of the circumstances where this procurement method should be chosen and it remains solely in the public body's authority to allow for community participation.

Departmental execution[847] means the effectuation of procurement directly by the public body rather than by any supplier or contractor. There are several cases that allow for departmental execution, including the non-attractiveness of an activity to bidders or emergency situations. This scenario, though, presupposes that necessary competences and skills are available within the public body and hence seems feasible only in a limited number of cases.

All alternative bidding methods are subject to the fulfilment of certain criteria, meaning that there needs to be exceptional circumstances that do not allow for open advertised bidding or open advertised bidding is not adequate or possible. This is very similar to the approach that was taken in the UNCITRAL Model Law.

Open advertised bidding can be conducted either nationwide or worldwide. Open national bidding is, however, only allowed if a limited participation is stated in the invitation to bid or, for prequalification, in the bidding documents and is otherwise in accordance with such criteria as may be prescribed.[848] It has to be kept in mind that the COMESA Regulations restrict such practice in so far as non-discrimination and the MFN-principle apply between all COMESA member states if a certain threshold is exceeded. Member states can still independently determine the financial threshold for procurements that are subject to the COMESA regulations but a common financial threshold is envisaged which would prevent the member states from applying any kind of protectionism in this respect. For open international bidding Section 18 of the Act provides:

847 Ibid, Sec. 15 (1) (a) (vi).
848 Ibid, Sec. 17.

"(1) Open advertised bidding shall be used where-

(a) the estimated value of the procurement exceeds the prescribed threshold;

(b) the goods, works or other services are not available under competitive price and other conditions from more than one supplier in Mauritius; or

(c) there is no response to open national bidding and the goods, other services or works must be obtained from international bidders."

If open bidding is used, there are three possibilities. First of all participation may be limited to citizens of Mauritius or entities incorporated in Mauritius. However this is only possible if the procurement does not fall within the scope of the COMESA Regulations. The second possibility is to advertise bids internationally and allow any supplier or contractor that fulfils the predetermined criteria to participate. There are three scenarios where this method has to be used. First, if the prescribed threshold is exceeded, secondly if the goods, works or other services are not available under competitive price and other conditions from more than one supplier in Mauritius, and, finally, if open national bidding has not been successful. As Mauritius is a COMESA member state, it is required to apply regional competitive bidding if the prescribed threshold is exceeded. Mauritius does not provide for regional competitive bidding as a distinct procurement method, but has taken a more liberal approach by widening the sphere of participation to the international level. However, it has retained the possibility to apply preferential treatment in regard to domestic or regional goods, services or contractors in the case of open advertised bidding in appropriate cases; such preferential procurement is though subject to regulations to that effect.[849]

For large or complex works or high value or complex procurement the Mauritius Procurement Act provides for prequalification proceedings in order to identify bidders that are qualified.[850] The regulations specify that prequalification proceedings shall be carried out for the procurement of any large work above the threshold of 400 million rupees[851] and of works which require specialised expertise.[852] All bidders responding to the invitation to prequalify shall be provided with the necessary prequalification documents to prepare and submit applications for prequalification.[853] After

849 Ibid, Sec. 16 (2).
850 Ibid, Sec. 27 (1) and (2).
851 Public Procurement Regulations 2008, Reg. 6 (1) (a).
852 Ibid, Reg. 6 (1) (b).
853 Public Procurement Act 2006, Sec. 27 (3).

a decision has been taken all applicants shall be provided with a list of successfully pre-qualified applicants.[854]

Moreover, open advertised bidding may be conducted in two-stages if certain exceptional circumstances apply.[855] In the first stage technical bids are submitted and then evaluated and possibly discussed with the bidders.[856] Only those bidders that pass the first stage are invited to submit final bids with prices in the second stage.[857] Negotiations between a public body and a selected bidder are generally prohibited. However, in special circumstances exceptions are allowed, provided such circumstances are foreseen in the legislation.[858] These exceptions are set out in Regulation 8 and include direct and emergency procurement as well as situations in which the lowest evaluated bid is above the estimated costs and a re-invitation of bids is considered impractical.

The use of prequalification procedures or two-stage tendering as well as the leeway to conduct negotiations in particular circumstances can positively contribute to the efficiency and effectiveness of public procurement. Prequalification procedures for highly complicated or technical procurements avoid unnecessary work not only for the procuring entity but also for the potential bidders. Only those passing the prequalification procedures and therefore having a realistic chance to win the bid will put effort in preparing a final bid. Discussing technical details at the first stage of two-stage tendering can provide the procuring entity with an overview of possible technical solutions and help the procuring entity to better formulate the requirements for goods or services to be procured in the second stage. This can lead to a better outcome and stimulates innovation, in particular when the criteria in the bid invitation are functional rather than technical.[859]

Suppliers lists are generally allowed but it is prohibited to exclude firms that meet the eligibility and qualification criteria simply because they are not included in the list.[860] This is similar to the approach taken in the WTO GPA. Similarly to UNCITRAL, COMESA urges its member states

---

854 Ibid, Sec. 27 (4).
855 Ibid, Sec. 29 (1).
856 Ibid, Sec. 29 (2) and (4).
857 Ibid, Sec. 29 (5).
858 Ibid, Sec. 40 (2).
859 UNCITRAL, 'Guide to Enactment of the UNCITRAL Model Law on Public Procurement', p. 188, paras. 4f.
860 Public Procurement Regulations 2008, Reg. 42.

to progressively eliminate the keeping of suppliers lists. The Mauritian approach seems to be a fair balance between keeping lists and not impeding the participation of any potential supplier or contractor.

The restriction of the bid validity to 180 days is also worth mentioning.[861] This ensures that the procurement process does not take longer than the prescribed period, which is in the interest of both the bidders and the public. The 180-day period applies to any complex major contract[862] while local bids should have a bid validity period not exceeding 90 days[863] and international bids 120 days.[864] This is a key element to keeping the public procurement process efficient and effective.

There have been two important amendments in regard to more innovative procurement approaches: public-private partnerships and framework agreements. Public-private partnership projects are regulated in the Public-Private Partnership Act 2004.[865] All stages of the bid procedure in regard to public-private partnerships are required to be carried out or approved by the board.[866] Framework agreements are allowed if certain conditions are fulfilled such as when "the subject matter of a procurement is expected to arise on a repeated basis".[867] However, the Procurement Policy Office has already issued regulations in regard to framework agreements[868] which can be seen as an implying that the Policy Office is successfully meeting its responsibility to facilitate the implementation of measures to improve the functioning of the procurement system.[869]

Electronic procurement is mentioned in Section 50 (5) of the Act which allows public bodies to authorise the use of other forms of communication for publication of invitations to bid, transmission of bidding documents, submission of bids, conclusion of contracts and processing of payment. It explicitly states that electronic communication is an eligible form of communication. Mauritius has strongly supported the introduction of e-procurement and has configured a comprehensive website containing all important information on public procurement in one place accessible by

861 Public Procurement Act 2006, Sec. 34 (1).
862 Public Procurement Regulations, Reg. 30 (3).
863 Ibid, Reg. 30 (2) (a).
864 Ibid, Reg. 30 (2) (b).
865 Public-Private Partnership Act 2004 (Act No. 37 of 2004).
866 Public Procurement Act 2006, Sec. 11A.
867 Ibid, Sec. 29A (a).
868 Public Procurement (Framework Agreement) Regulations 2013.
869 See Public Procurement Act 2006, Sec. 7 (e).

everyone. In 2013, a directive[870] was issued requiring all public bodies to post all invitations to bids undertaken through open advertised biding on the public procurement website. It furthermore obliges all public bodies to post their annual procurement plan, an executive summary of bid evaluation reports and the notices of award of procurement contracts on the website. If successfully implemented, this approach significantly contributes to the achievement of public procurement objectives, in particular transparency, fairness, accountability, competition and hence value for money. Procurement plans and bid invitations are made easily accessible to everyone worldwide and therefore allow everyone to participate in bidding. The publication of the evaluation report and the award decision allows bidders and the public to hold the decision-makers accountable and also allows everyone to understand the formation of the decision and examine alleged irregularities.

What is a very progressive and useful approach in regard to procurement procedures is the provision of a standstill period after the tender notification and before the tender award during which unsatisfied bidders can challenge the decision.[871] The standstill period for international procurement cases is generally 15 days, but is only 7 days for local procurement cases.[872] The revised UNCITRAL Model Law as well as the COMESA Regulations also provide for such a standstill period. However, it is worth mentioning that both of these instruments were adopted after the Mauritian Public Procurement Act was enacted.

### ii. Tender Specification, Award Criteria and Evaluation Methods

The Act neither specifically lays out evaluation or qualification criteria, nor does it explicitly states what the content of the bidding documents is supposed to entail. The Regulations also remain silent on this issue. Section 2 of the Act defines a bidding document as follows: "any document

870 Procurement Policy Office, 'Implementation of e-Procurement - Launching of public procurement website, Directive No. 2 (issued pursuant to Section 7(b) of the Public Procurement Act)' (Procurement Policy Office, Mauritius: 2010), available at http://ppo.govmu.org/English/Directives/Pages/Directives-2013.aspx; last accessed: 1 December 2015.

871 See Public Procurement Act 2006, Secs. 30 (3), 30 (4), 43 (3) (a), see also Sec. 24 (2).

872 Ibid, Sec. 40 (4).

issued by a public body on the basis of which bidders prepare bids" and, more importantly in this respect,

> "[...] any document which contains instructions to bidders, specification, maps, designs, terms of reference, work schedules, evaluation criteria, bills of quantities, conditions of contract or other similar items."

First of all, this list is not exhaustive, as the wording "or other similar items" suggests. Moreover it is a very broad description of what bidding documents might entail instead a limited set of specific criteria. In 2012 the Procurement Policy Office issued a directive concerning technical specifications.[873] It is basically an adaptation of the COMESA requirements in this respect.

Section 37 (9) of the Act provides that,

> "[e]very bid shall be evaluated according to the criteria and methodology set out in the biding documents and the evaluated cost of each bid shall be compared with the evaluated cost of other bids to determine the lowest evaluated bid."

There are no specific requirements either for the design of evaluation criteria or for the evaluation methods used.

It can be concluded from the above that only those evaluation and award criteria as outlined in the bidding documents can be considered but the public bodies have no restrictions on what these criteria may look like. On the one hand, this gives them great discretion to apply socio-economic or environmental objectives, to achieve value for money and also to foster research and innovation but, on the other hand, there is plenty of room for abuse. At least some general criteria such as clarity and objectivity should be included as restrictions limiting the authority's discretion in regard to the tender requirements and evaluation criteria. Currently, there is great latitude provided by law to include socio-economic or environmental or other objectives. Adherence to the principle of non-discrimination is required in open advertised bidding in so far as equal access needs to be provided to all eligible and qualified bidders without discrimination.[874] Hence, it does not include the discrimination of bidders by way of the bidding criteria itself. In practical terms this means that public bodies have several possibilities to design bidding documents in a certain way and,

---

873 Procurement Policy Office, 'Technical Specifications, Directive No 11 (issued pursuant to Section 7 of the Public Procurement Act)' (Procurement Policy Office, Mauritius: 2012), available at http://ppo.govmu.org/English/Directives/Pages/Directives-2013.aspx; last accessed: 1 December 2015.

874 Public Procurement Act 2006, Sec. 15 (1) (a).

thereby, implement secondary objectives, but also to tailor criteria to certain suppliers or contractors. Nevertheless, as the Procurement Policy Office is responsible for the issuance of standard bidding documents and can further formulate policies relating to procurement for the implementation of the Act a more detailed prescription of the content of bidding documents might be determined by the Policy Office. This does not necessarily mean that the latitude to include certain secondary objectives is limited but it can be restricted, controlled or influenced by the Policy Office. As with criteria on technical specifications which have been specified in a directive issued by the Policy Office, the general principles regarding the content of bidding documents, evaluation criteria, etc. should have force of law and be included in the Act or the regulations.

It is also worth mentioning that a public body may, in two-stage proceedings, engage in discussions with any bidder with a view to understanding a technical bid or to indicating changes required to make it acceptable and to seek the bidder's willingness to make such changes.[875] For all other procedures, a public body may seek clarification during the examination of bids from any bidder to facilitate evaluation, but it is prohibited from asking or permitting any bidder to change the price or substance of its bid.[876] The Mauritian law and regulations lack a provision on clarifications of tender documentation by the procuring entity to bidders. This is important in regard to competition and, hence, value for money. In view to the objectives of transparency and fairness, it should also be required to communicate any clarification made to the bidder requesting the information to all other bidders as it is suggested by UNCITRAL.

### iii. Procurement Planning

The Mauritian Public Procurement Act does not contain any provisions on procurement planning. The Procurement Regulations, however, require every public body to prepare an annual procurement plan at the beginning of each financial year. This plan has to be published on its website and be updated and revised periodically.[877] A comprehensive list of what has to be taken into account in planning procurements for major contracts is out-

875 Ibid, Sec. 29 (3).
876 Ibid, Sec. 37 (1).
877 Public Procurement Regulations 2008, Reg. 10 (3) and (4).

lined in Regulation 10 (5). Apart from the annual procurement plan, in respect of investment projects public bodies have to prepare a master procurement plan to cover the entire life of the project.[878] As mentioned for example in Part I,[879] rules governing procurement planning can have several benefits in regard to the achievement of public procurement objectives as such an approach not only improves the transparency of a public procurement system but also can have a positive impact on competition.

iv. Contract Administration

Part VII of the Act establishes criteria for the contents of contracts, payment and termination and breach of contracts. This is essential in order to ensure successful contract implementation and, hence, the effectual completion of the procurement cycle. Furthermore, as mentioned in the subchapter on secondary objectives below, every public procurement contract is required to include clauses regarding working conditions to ensure compliance with certain standards. In order to ensure that the supplier or contractor adheres to these conditions, payment is subject to evidence being furnished proving that the supplier or contractor has complied with these standards. This can be an effective means to protect and promote workers' rights. In contrast to developed countries, where such rights are often effectively ensured through other means, e.g. minimum wages, in several developing countries such safeguards do not exist or are not effectively implemented. In particular, if there is a lack of implementation in this regard, specific contract conditions in public contracts might contribute to the improvement of implementation.

e. Transparency

Transparency features prominently throughout a variety of substantive and procedural specifications. The Mauritian procurement law entails quite a few provisions which can lay a foundation for an efficient and effective procurement system. First of all, as mentioned earlier, the Central Procurement Board is required to strive to achieve the highest standards of

---

878 Ibid, Reg. 10 (2).
879 See Chapter 1, Subchapter 4.

transparency and equity in the execution of its duties taking into account, inter alia, the evaluation and the qualification criteria and methodology disclosed in the bidding documents, the need to obtain the best value for money in terms of price, quality and delivery, having regard to set specifications, and transparency of process and decisions.[880] Hence, disclosure of and adherence to criteria and specifications but also a good balance between the principle of value for money and the requirement to uphold transparency with regard to both procedures and decisions seems an important guideline for the Central Procurement Board. The Central Procurement Board should have sufficient expertise to make quality-based decisions and decide major contracts; it therefore also serves as a role model for the public body's implementation of the procurement process.

Public bodies have to keep records of every procurement proceeding.[881] For example, even the grounds for the choice of an alternative procurement method have to be noted in the record of the procurement proceedings.[882] And transparency about the procurement method to be used is also required in regard to the public as it has to be contained in the announcement or other document used to solicit a bid.[883] This is a useful tool to prevent unjustified limitations of competition by choosing an alternative procurement method over open tendering. Recording and preserving all documentation relating to any procurement proceedings is necessary to create a transparent and accountable system of procurement and is thus indispensable. The requirement of maintaining records might further minimise the temptation of procurement officials to become involved in fraudulent or corrupt practices and facilitates the clarification of facts in court or other review proceedings.

The manner of how to record and preserve such documentation is, however, not specified but needs further regulation by the Procurement Policy Office. The implementation of these "documentation provisions" is thus highly dependent on specifications made by the Policy Office, which stresses the important role assigned to the Policy Office in the Mauritian public procurement system.

Another transparency-related issue is the public opening of bids which is provided for by Section 36 of the Act. Every bidder is allowed to attend

880 Public Procurement Act 2006, Sec. 11 (2).
881 Public Procurement Regulations 2008, Reg. 70.
882 Public Procurement Act 2006, Sec. 15 (2) (e).
883 Public Procurement Regulations 2008, Reg. 22.

the bid opening where the name of the bidder, the total amount of each bid, any discount or alternative offered, and the bid security requirement is read out and recorded. This is important in so far as it prevents the ex post facto modifications or bids or the consideration of non-predetermined criteria and, in case where this nevertheless occurs, it is much easier to detect. Moreover, all bidders get an idea of the bids of their competitors, which enables them to reflect on their own approach, estimate their chance of success and, especially, improve their bids in future procurements. The choice of a public bid opening is very suitable in the Mauritian context as most African countries have, in respect to administrative matters, heavily relied on oral rather than written communication. The bids are supposed to be evaluated according to the criteria and methodology set out in the bidding documents.[884] The lowest evaluated bid is determined by comparing the evaluated cost of each bid.[885] Furthermore, the lowest evaluated bid must meet the qualification criteria specified in the prequalification or bidbidding documents.[886] The evaluation committees are required to issue a report including a detailed description of the examination and evaluation of bids and identifying the lowest evaluated bid.[887] The secretary of the committee has to take minutes of the meeting and keep records of all matters considered by the committee.[888] These are open for inspection by the Policy Office.[889] The successful bidder has to be notified in writing of the selection of its bid for award; all other bidders also need to be informed in writing of the winning bid.[890] Furthermore, prompt public notice of every procurement award is required.[891] Unsuccessful bidders can, additionally, request a reasoned explanation as to why its bid was unsuccessful and why the bid of the successful bidder was chosen. Such a request must be submitted within 30 days of the publication.[892] All these aforementioned regulations ensure that bidders and other stakeholders can understand the award decision and diminish the possibilities for fraudulent and corrupt practices. Article 42 states that the auditor of every public body shall state

884 Public Procurement Act 2006, Sec. 37 (9).
885 Ibid, Sec. 37 (9).
886 Ibid, Sec. 40 (1).
887 Ibid, Sec. 37 (11).
888 Public Procurement Regulations 2008, Reg. 4 (8).
889 Ibid, Reg. 4 (9).
890 Public Procurement Act 2006, Sec. 40 (3).
891 Ibid, Sec. 40 (7).
892 Ibid, Sec. 41. See also Public Procurement Regulations 2008, Reg. 9 (a) and (b).

in his annual report whether the aforementioned and associated provisions have been complied with. Although it remains unclear what information needs to be provided in this regard it might guarantee a minimum of internal oversight.

Whereas the Act remains silent on the issue of confidentiality of information, a very important factor in procurement as often sensitive business data might be involved, the regulations do contain a provision on the matter.[893] Regulation 23 of the Procurement Regulations prohibits the disclosure of information relating to the examination, clarification, evaluation and comparison of bids. Regulation 68 of the Procurement Regulations furthermore prohibits the disclosure of information if such disclosure is contrary to public interest, will prejudice legitimate commercial interests of the parties or will inhibit competition, unless such disclosure is otherwise ordered by a court. Furthermore, the Procurement Regulations stress that public officials involved in public procurement planning or procedures or in contact with such officials are not permitted to disclose to any third party confidential or proprietary commercial information.[894] The Procurement Regulations contain a detailed part on procurement integrity[895] establishing the duties and the conduct of public bodies, the conduct of bidders and suppliers and rules governing the suspension and debarment of bidders and suppliers. Since in procurement a variety of interests and large sums of money are involved, it is very important to ensure that a system of incentives and penalties is established by outlining key principles, best practices and offences. It is beyond the scope of this dissertation to delve deeper into this area but, in view of its importance for the functioning of procurement systems, it certainly merits further research.

The Public Procurement Act requires the Policy Office to provide for disqualification standards and procedures for suppliers, contractors and consultants.[896] Public bodies have to ensure that disqualified suppliers, contractors and consultants are excluded from procurement proceedings and are not permitted to receive a procurement contract.[897] The Policy Office has issued regulations on disqualification of bidders as well as on debarment and suspension of bidders. This is important in order to prevent

893 Public Procurement Regulations 2008, Reg. 78.
894 Ibid, Reg. 78 (1).
895 Public Procurement Act 2006, Part VIII, Secs. 49-53.
896 Ibid, Sec. 35 (2).
897 Ibid, Sec. 35 (1).

and counteract malpractices, corruption, failure to implement a contract, etc. and shows that the Policy Office has put a special focus on combating corruption and keeping the public procurement system efficient and effective.

Other elements worth mentioning in regard to transparency and accountability are requirements for bid security and regulations of cancellation of bidding processes. Other elements include a provision that provides that any person who contravenes the Procurement Act commits an offence and is liable to a fine not exceeding 50,000 rupees and imprisonment for up to 8 years.[898] Furthermore, the Act contains provisions that regulate procurement contracts.

#### f. Secondary Objectives

The Public Procurement Act allows wide discretion to implement secondary objectives. It explicitly provides for preferential treatment and for the protection of labour by requiring the inclusion of respective contract conditions.

Apart from international bidding and the limitation of participation to nationals of the country or entities incorporated in Mauritius, where open bidding is used a public body might confer an advantage or preference to domestic or regional goods, services or contractors. According to the Procurement Regulations the Policy Office can issue instructions relating to the criteria and the applicable percentage preference for domestic or regional goods, services or contractors.[899] Preferential treatment may, hence, be applied to domestic but also to regional goods, services or contractors. The option to apply domestic or regional preferences is acknowledged by Article 8 (1) of the UNCITRAL Model Law. Their application within regional economic integration processes such as those fostered by COMESA has been explicitly recognised by the Revised Guide to Enactment as legitimate.[900] For all cases where the use of open national bidding would be contrary to the COMESA Regulations, the method of open international bidding has to be applied. Nevertheless, a public body can then treat re-

---

898 Ibid, Sec. 60.

899 Public Procurement Regulations 2008, Reg. 5 (1).

900 UNCITRAL, 'Guide to Enactment of the UNCITRAL Model Law on Public Procurement', p. 54, para. 32.

gional goods, services or contractors preferentially and thereby limit the possibility that a contract is awarded to a supplier or contractor from a state which is not a member of COMESA. It is also explicitly stated that bidding documents may provide for an advantage or preference to a bidder. This is limited to appropriate cases and subject to regulations to that effect.[901] The Procurement Regulations establish in regard to domestic and regional margins of preference that they should be applied at the financial evaluation stage, stress that they have to be stated in the bidding document and need to be in accordance with directives issued by the Policy Office.[902] The requirement to apply preferences at the financial evaluation stage is beneficial as it is easier to measure and to comprehend preferences made at that stage. The latter factor is essential as it precludes any public body from being able to apply preferences as they deem appropriate. Thus Directive No. 12 [903] establishes margins of preference for procurements of works for employment of local manpower for international and national bidding procedures. It also entails instructions on monitoring of contactor's employment of local manpower. As it might be detrimental from the strict economic point of view to apply preferences, the restriction on the use of preferences is of the utmost importance and the role played by the Policy Office in this respect is decisive for the success of secondary objectives in the Mauritian public procurement system.

The Act further allows the inclusion of qualifications and evaluation criteria which are based on life cycle costing.[904] This is an important provision as it acknowledges that - in order to determine the best bid in regard to value for money - it is often necessary to consider the costs that might arise through maintenance, life expectancy, etc. in addition to the purchasing costs.

There is no mention of SME's in the Act, but in 2012 the Procurement Policy Office issued a directive on the implementation of budgetary

---

901 Public Procurement Act 2006, Sec. 28 (2).

902 Public Procurement Regulations 2008, Reg. 35.

903 Procurement Policy Office, 'Margin of Preference for Procurement of Works, Directive No 12 (issued pursuant to Section 7 of the Public Procurement Act)' (Procurement Policy Office, Mauritius: 2012), available at http://ppo.govmu.org/English/Directives/Pages/Directives-2013.aspx; last accessed: 1 December 2015.

904 Public Procurement Act 2006, Sec. 28 (2) (b).

measures to promote SME-participation in public procurement.[905] It sets a minimum number of two SMEs which should be considered in informal quotation, restricted bidding and request for sealed quotations procedures.

The Act also refers to secondary objectives during the contract administration stage. According to this every procurement contract shall include a clause ensuring that the workers engaged in the execution of the contract are paid and work under conditions not less favourable than required by collective agreements, arbitration awards, and remuneration regulations or the general level observed in work of the same character in the trade concerned.[906] To ensure that contractors do not simply agree to this on paper, they are only paid if they prove that they have complied with the above mentioned conditions.[907] If remuneration to workers is still outstanding the public body can pay it out of the money payable under the procurement contract.[908] This is a very holistic and direct approach to ensure that labour rights are adhered to in the execution of public contracts. Instead of leaving it to the Ministry of Labour or other institutions, the procuring entity is directly responsible for ensuring compliance.

### g. Review Procedures

The Procurement Act provides for an internal challenge procedure which can be initiated by any bidder who claims to have suffered, or to be likely to suffer, loss or injury because of a breach of duty imposed on a public body or the Central Procurement Board by the Procurement Act.[909] Any challenge has to identify the specific act or omission alleged to contravene the Act and has to be submitted in writing to the Chief Executive Officer of the public body concerned.[910] The reasons for review are not specified but it seems that duties imposed on a public body or the Central Procure-

905 Procurement Policy Office, 'Implementation of Budgetary Measures to promote SMEs participation in Public Procurement, Directive No. 5 (issued pursuant to Section 7 of the Public Procurement Act)' (Procurement Policy Office, Mauritius: 2012), available at http://ppo.govmu.org/English/Directives/Pages/Directives-2013.aspx; last accessed: 1 December 2015.

906 Public Procurement Act 2006, Sec. 46 (5).

907 Ibid, Sec. 46 (6).

908 Ibid, Sec. 46 (7).

909 Ibid, Sec. 43 (1).

910 Ibid, Sec. 43 (2).

ment Board cover all procurement decisions and actions taken under the Act, including, for example, the choice of procurement method.

Locus standi is granted to all bidders, which is the general approach in most countries. Challenges can only be brought before the Chief Executive Officer before the entry into force of the procurement contract.[911] As mentioned above, the Act provides for a standstill period that allows unsatisfied bidders to challenge the award decision of the procuring entity before the tender is finally awarded.[912] The Chief Executive Officer has the power to suspend the public procurement proceedings until the challenge is resolved.[913] Within a specified time period, the Chief Executive Officer has to issue a written decision including the reasoning.[914] If a challenge is upheld, the Chief Executive Officer shall indicate the corrective measures to be taken.[915]

Apart from internal administrative review, the Act requires the establishment of an independent review panel.[916] However, it is not subject to any strict formalities; indeed, it is even supposed to "seek to avoid formality in its proceedings and may conduct them in such manner as it thinks fit."[917] The informality of the procedure might have been chosen in order to avoid lengthy and costly procedures but also in order to not overburden the independent review panel. However, as procedural rights or requirements such as the right to be heard or the requirement to hold public hearings are not mentioned, there is a critical shortcoming in regard to transparency and rule of law. The Procurement Regulations at least determine in this regard that the applicant should have the opportunity to comment on the comments of the public body[918] and that the review panel may conduct a hearing on its own initiative or at the request of the applicant.[919] The applicant as well as the public body shall attend such hearing.[920] Since it is difficult to find the right balance between providing a fair challenge procedure and not impairing the efficiency of public procurement, the dis-

911 Ibid, Sec. 43 (1).
912 Ibid, Secs. 40 (4), 24 (12), 43 (3) (a).
913 Ibid, Sec. 43 (4).
914 Ibid.
915 Ibid.
916 Ibid, Sec. 44.
917 Ibid, Sec. 44 (4).
918 Public Procurement Regulations 2008, Reg. 55 (5).
919 Ibid, Reg. 57.
920 Ibid, Reg. 57 (3).

cretion given to the independent review panel in regard to the challenge procedure combined with the transparency of the procedure and the decision taken by the independent review panel might be a balanced approach to the regulation of public procurement review procedures. However, it might be expedient to ensure that basic procedural rights are nevertheless granted to the parties.

Unsatisfied bidders are entitled to ask the panel to review the procurement proceedings either where the internal challenge does not produce a decision within a specific time or as an appeal against the decision of the Chief Executive Officer.[921] After the standstill period and, therefore, the entry into force of the procurement contract, the value of which is within a certain threshold, a bidder unsatisfied with the procurement proceedings on a ground justifying an internal challenge also has a right to review.[922] It is important to note that the decisions of the independent review panel can be challenged through judicial review. Hence, an appeal against those decisions is possible. This is of the utmost importance, in particular with view to the informality of procedures under the independent review panel.

In cases where the application relates to the bid opening process or the award of a major contract, an amount of 100,000 rupees[923] is required to be deposited.[924] In all other cases the amount of the deposit is 25,000 rupees.[925] Additionally, applicants are required to pay a non-refundable process fee of 50,000 rupees.[926] If the review panel dismisses the application as frivolous the deposit is forfeited.[927] Especially in view to the informality of process of the review panel this might prevent in particular SMEs from seeking review. On the other hand, it reduces the risk of reviews being brought simply to delay the procurement process and can therefore serve as safeguard to ensure the efficiency and effectiveness of public procurement. However, strictly defined standards need to be developed to determine what makes an application frivolous.

---

921 Public Procurement Act 2006, Sec. 45 (1) (a) and (b).

922 Ibid, Sec. 45 (1) (c).

923 One rupee corresponds to approximately US$0,03.

924 Public Procurement Act 2006, Sec. 45 (3) read together with Public Procurement Regulations 2008, Reg. 51 (1) (a).

925 Ibid.

926 Public Procurement Act 2006, Sec. 45 (3) read together with Public Procurement Regulations 2008, Reg. 51 (1) (b).

927 Public Procurement Act 2006, Sec. 45 (3) read together with Public Procurement Regulations 2008, Reg. 51 (2).

The accessibility of all decisions of the independent review panel on the national procurement website is a positive development.

## 5. Conclusion

It makes sense to look at a country that used the UNCITRAL Model Law in order to see how the matters not regulated by the Model Law have been dealt with. This includes especially institutional and organisational matters, procurement planning and contract administration. Furthermore, specific approaches in regard to secondary objectives might offer solutions suitable for other countries.

Mauritius has a comprehensive and modern procurement system. The problems and shortcomings in the implementation of the law and regulations were identified during a review of the system undertaken in cooperation with the World Bank, COMESA, and UNCITRAL. The Policy Office also wanted to respond to new developments and approaches in public procurement such as framework agreements or e-procurement.

The Mauritian procurement law and regulations cover the entire procurement cycle, including procurement planning and contract administration. This is essential to ensure that the whole procurement cycle, from the recognition that something has to be procured until the completion of the contract, becomes a success.

In regard to the scope of the Public Procurement Act and Regulations there are several exceptions which allow procurements for specific matters outside the scope of the Act and the regulations. It might be preferable to use one of the alternative procurement methods and subjecting all procurements to the provisions of the Act so that they take place under the existing transparency standards and public bodies or the Board can be held accountable for procurement decisions in those matters.

In Mauritius the rationale for the decision to let major contracts be awarded by the central procurement board was to decentralise gradually rather than leaving public bodies, which at the time of the enactment of the new procurement did not have any procurement experience, be solely responsible for the award of contracts of high value or complexity. In respect of the capacity needed to carry out public procurement effectively and efficiently, this seems a wise decision. However, the Policy Office or any other authority should have been mandated to periodically review the threshold for major contracts in order to facilitate decentralisation in the best possible way. As a policy and oversight mechanism, the Policy Office plays a very important role in the Mauritian public procurement system. Vested with a variety of functions and responsibilities, it can make an essential contribution to ensure that public procurement is carried out effectively and efficiently. Nevertheless, the comprehensive range of duties raises the question whether the institution lives up to its mandate in practice.

Whereas there are extensive regulations for the code of conduct of officials, it is not specified in detail what qualifications the different officials, staff members and committee members are required to have. This is a significant shortcoming for the successful implementation of public procurement as a system can only be as good as the people implementing it.

The Mauritian public procurement law and regulations comply with the COMESA public procurement requirements. There are several parallels with the UNCITRAL Model Law; in particular the methods of bidding are very similar. The transparency requirements with regard to publication and the maintenance of records meet international best practices, too. Nevertheless, certain provisions that are important for transparency reasons are not included. There are, for example, no specifications in regard to the contents of bidding documents, tender criteria, evaluation criteria, etc. This is deficient as it leaves room for abuse and it should be rectified as soon as possible by including respective requirements in the law or the regulations rather than in directives or the user guide as these instruments have no force in law.

The Mauritian public procurement system provides enough flexibility not to hinder the use of e-procurement. Additionally, the Policy Office has strongly facilitated the implementation of e-procurement, in particular in regard to publication on the national procurement website. All public bodies are required to publish information on its public procurement proceedings on the website, thereby enabling potential bidders, procurement participants and the wider public to get an overview of the situation, stay informed and examine decisions.

Secondary objectives are explicitly pursued through preferential treatment and the protection of labour standards through contract conditions. Preferential treatment is required to be transparent and have a basis in directives issued by the Policy Office. These factors have been marked as preconditions for secondary objectives to be in accordance with the objectives of public procurement. Nevertheless, it can be criticised that preferential treatment has not been indicated as a temporary measure subject to regular review and evaluation with regard to the achievement of its objectives. The requirement to include contract conditions in respect of labour standards and measures to monitor compliance is to be welcomed in the context of a developing country.

The introduction of an independent review panel has a positive impact on the effectiveness and efficiency of public procurement. Mandatory internal review is required as a first step during the standstill period between the tender notification and the final award. The independent review panel serves as an appellant instance for internal review or as the first instance for challenges brought after the conclusion of the contracts. The independent review panel may impose specific remedies, even the payment of damages. The timeframes governing challenges and the provisions on the disclosure of information are adequate. However, the independent review panel is not obliged to follow a formalised procedure. This, on the one hand, bears the risk of sacrificing rule of law standards and, therefore, objectives such as fairness but, on the other hand, is consistent with the goal of keeping public procurement efficient and effective. The difficulty in balancing these objectives is well-known, but there is not yet a tailor-made solution. The success of the Mauritian approach depends to a great extent on the ability of the members of the independent review panel to decide what degree of formality is needed in each specific case. Additionally, in Mauritius these decisions can be appealed before a court of law. This is essential in order to give bidders unsatisfied with the decision of the independent review panel the possibility to appeal against this decision.

## *Chapter 4: Public Procurement Law in South Africa*[928]

In this chapter the South African public procurement system and its regulations will be analysed according to its framework, the organisational structure and staff, procedures and methods, transparency and corruption, secondary objectives as well as review procedures. Moreover, the main principles of public procurement in South African case law will be considered as case law in South Africa has a strong influence on Namibian decisions in this respect.[929] Approaches and organisational patterns that might be suitable in the Namibian context beyond certain international best practices as provided by the GPA and UNCITRAL Model Law shall be identified. Examining South African public procurement law may be of great significance to a successful reform process due to the legal and de facto similarities existing between Namibia and South Africa. Not only might it reveal promising approaches but the South African experience might also be able to be channelled into the Namibian reform process.

### 1. Introduction

South African procurement law could be seen as reference point for Namibian law reform not only because it contains quite progressive elements but also because of the common history of South Africa and Namibia, including the shared experience of the apartheid system. Moreover, there are still some laws which had been enacted before independence and are, hence, the same that were or are applicable in South Africa.[930] Beyond that, certain fields of law have been reformed on the basis of South African laws.[931] It is useful, under these circumstances, to assess the South Af-

---

928 South African case law is generally cited from the Website of the Southern African Legal Information Institute (SAFLII). See www.saflii.org (last access: 16 December 2015).

929 The decisions of the South West African Supreme Court as well as the higher South African courts are still authoritative in Namibia. See H. Sippel, 'Rechtsrezeption in Namibia - Prozesse direkter und indirekter Rezeption des deutschen und südafrikanischen Rechts' (2003) 1 Recht in Afrika, 69-89 at 86.

930 Article 140 of the Namibian Constitution provides that "[s]ubject to the provisions of this Constitution, all laws which were in force immediately before the date of Independence shall remain in force until repealed or amended by Act of Parliament or until they are declared unconstitutional by a competent Court."

931 See Sippel, 'Rechtsrezeption in Namibia'.

rican public procurement system and, in particular, its legislation and to identify difficulties that have arisen in implementing these laws in order to develop an approach that does not lead to similar problems.

It has to be emphasised that South Africa is the only African country whose public procurement system has not been noticeably influenced by any external or international system. Hence, it differs to quite extent from other legal systems and from the provisions of the UNCITRAL Model Law which has served as a basis for many African public procurement systems.[932]

South Africa was the first country that constitutionally established the pillars of its procurement system as well as the application of socio-economic linkages in procurement.[933] Section 217 (1) of the South African Constitution[934] provides for a fair, equitable, transparent, competitive and cost-effective procurement system - these can be referred to as the five pillars of the South African procurement system. Moreover, Section 217 emphasises that the organs of state or institutions can apply schemes of preference and affirmative action. Subsection 3 requires national legislation to prescribe a framework within which the preference policy must be implemented. The public procurement rules have been implemented through the Preferential Procurement Policy Framework Act (PPPFA)[935], the Preferential Procurement Regulations 2011[936] and the introduction of a Supply Chain Management system in accordance with the Public Finance Management Act (PFMA).[937]

In November 2000, a memorandum supported by the Report on Opportunities for reform of Government Procurement in South Africa (also called the Roger Webb report) was brought before the Cabinet to facilitate the reform of the procurement system. The Cabinet then entrusted the Ministry of Finance to address, in consultation with other ministries, the

---

932 P. Bolton, 'The regulatory framework for public procurement in South Africa', in G. Quinot; S. Arrowsmith, *Public Procurement Regulations in Africa* (Cambridge et al.: Cambridge University Press, 2013), p. 186.

933 See e.g. McCrudden, 'Buying Social Justice', p. 250; P. Bolton, 'Overview of the Government Procurement System in South Africa', in K.V. Thai, *International Handbook of Public Procurement* (New York: CRC Press, Taylor and Francis Group, 2008), p. 370. Kenya has with minor changes copied the article on procurement into its new constitution Constitution of Kenya 2010, Art. 227.

934 Constitution of the Republic of South Africa 1996, Sec. 217 (2).

935 Act No. 5 of 2000.

936 Preferential Procurement Regulations 2011 (Government Gazette No. 34350).

937 Act No. 1 of 1999.

central matters of this report.[938] Frequently expressed criticism related to policy incoherence, close-to-chaotic administration, corruption, and the absence of adequate monitoring of outcomes.[939] After conducting a Joint Country Procurement Assessment Review with the World Bank in 2001/02[940] which revealed quite a number of deficiencies South Africa started to substantially reform its procurement system towards a Supply Chain Management (SCM) system with a strong focus on the application of socio-economic linkages. Whereas public procurement had been implemented solely by the State Tender Board and regional tender boards for a long time, the responsibility for public procurement was shifted towards the National Treasury and accounting officers. Each procuring entity is to establish integrated SCM units to implement procurement. The Framework for Supply Chain Management[941] contains regulations on public procurement in terms of the Public Finance Management Act and is the key legal document establishing the SCM system. So far there are - apart from procurement-specific regulations - a variety of other public as well as private law regulations that govern the procurement process, including e.g. the Public Finance Management Act and the Promotion of Access to Information Act.[942] It should also be recalled that certain civil law fields that are regulated by common law such as the law of contract and tort are also applicable to procurement.[943]

---

938 National Treasury, 'Policy Strategy to Guide Uniformity in Procurement Reform Processes in Government ', (National Treasury, South Africa: 2003), p. 11, para. 1.1 (available at http://ocpo.treasury.gov.za/Resource_Centre/Legislation/policy.pdf; last accessed: 30 November 2015).

939 McCrudden, 'Buying Social Justice', p. 255. For a more detailed description of the deficiencies see pp. 611ff.

940 World Bank, 'South Africa - Country Procurement Assessment Report: refining the public procurement system (Vol. 1 of 2): Summary of findings and recommendations (English)', Country Procurement Assessment (CPAR) Report (Washington, DC: World Bank, 2003); World Bank, 'South Africa - Country Procurement Assessment Report: refining the public procurement system (Vol. 2 of 2): Main text (English)', Country Procurement Assessment (CPAR) Report (Washington, DC: World Bank, 2003).

941 Framework for Supply Chain Management (Regulations in Terms of the Public Finance Management Act 1999) 2003.

942 Act 2 of 2000.

943 For a further specification, see G. Quinot, 'Enforcement of procurement law from a South African perspective' (2011) 6 Public Procurement Law Review, 193-207 at 195. See also Bolton, 'Overview of the Government Procurement System in South Africa', p. 368.

## 2. The Framework

### a. Laws and Policies regarding Public Procurement

Section 217, which has been mentioned above, directly refers to procurement. Beyond that Section 216 (1) provides for the establishment of the National Treasury, which has become an important institution in the South African public procurement system. It requires that

> "[n]ational legislation must establish a national treasury and prescribe measures to ensure both transparency and expenditure control in each sphere of government, by introducing - (a) generally recognised accounting practice; (b) uniform expenditure classifications; and (c) uniform treasury norms and standards."

This includes best practices related to procurement and provisioning systems.[944] Other constitutional provisions might come into play in public procurement matters: Section 195 (1) of the Constitution provides that the public administration "must be governed by the democratic values and principles enshrined in the Constitution." This includes the promotion of the "efficient, economic and effective use of resources", the impartial, fair and unbiased provision of services, accountability in public administration and the fostering of transparency.[945]

The first policy paper regarding public procurement after independence was the 10 Point (Interim Strategies) Plan which was issued in November 1995 by the Ministry of Finance and Public Works. The objective pursued by this plan was to provide procurement strategies - which on the one hand do not contradict existing legislation but on the other hand facilitate the objectives of the Reconstruction and Development Programme - for the interim time until the enactment of national procurement legislation.[946] The ten point plan basically aims at increasing participation of small, medium and micro enterprises in the procurement system with a special focus on individuals who belong to a disadvantaged or marginalised sector of

---

944 National Treasury, p. 16, para. 1.2.2.

945 See, for example, Intertrade Two (Pty) Ltd. v. The MEC for Roads & Public Works, Eastern Cape and the Premier of the Eastern Cape (1790/04) [2007] ZAECHC 149; [2008] 1 All SA 142 (Ck) (31 May 2007): para. 4; Total Computer Services (Pty) Limited v. Municipal Manager Ptochefstroom Local Municipality and Others (29416/07) [2007] ZAGPHC 239; 2008 (4) SA 346 (T): para 21.

946 P. Bolton, 'Government Procurement as a Policy Tool in South Africa' (2006) 6(3) Journal of Public Procurement, 193-217 at 204.

society.[947] Participation of small businesses should be achieved, inter alia, by obtaining goods and services in the smallest possible quantities without sacrificing quality, time and cost parameters.[948] The following strategies were chosen to achieve the former objective:

- the improvement of access to tendering information;
- the development of tender advice centres;
- the broadening of a participation base for small contracts (less than R 7,500);
- the waiving of security/sureties on construction contracts with a value less than R 100,000;
- the unbundling or unpacking of large projects into smaller projects;
- the promotion of early payment cycles by government;
- the development of a preference system for small, medium and micro enterprises (SMME) owned by historically disadvantaged individuals (HDI);
- the simplification of tender submission requirements;
- the appointment of a procurement ombudsman; and
- the classification of building and engineering contracts.

In April 1997, the Green Paper on Public Sector Procurement Reform in South Africa further established the ideas of the 10 Point Plan. It was prepared by the Department of Public Works and the Department of Finance in collaboration with the World Bank which provided financial and technical assistance. With reference to the procurement system prior to independence which favoured larger, established companies and made it nearly impossible for newly established businesses to enter the public tendering system,[949] emphasis is put on the promotion of small, medium and micro enterprises. Procurement as envisaged by the Green Paper basically rests on two pillars: good governance and socio-economic objectives. Value for money, good financial control, countering corruption, meeting tax and service charge obligations and adhering to prescribed labour practices were explicitly mentioned as belonging to the aspects of good gov-

947 Cf. National Treasury, p. 11, Sec. 1.1.
948 Raga; Taylor.
949 Ministry of Finance/Ministry of Public Works, 'Green Paper on Public Sector Procurement Reform in South Africa, General Notice No. 691 of 1997' (Ministry of Finance/Ministry of Public Works, South Africa: 1997), para 1.2 (available at http://www.gov.za/sites/www.gov.za/files/17928_gen691_0.pdf; last accessed: 30 November 2015).

ernance. Socio-economic objectives that might be achieved through procurement range from the simplification of tender documents to price preferences to the promotion of employment-intensive practices.

The Green Paper envisaged a public procurement system with two independent arms: procurement offices to carry out day-to-day procurement activities and a Procurement Compliance Office responsible for, inter alia, policy formulation and advice, issuance of instructions, auditing and monitoring of policy-implementation. It was proposed that the Procurement Compliance Office would serve as an independent review panel. All stakeholders and interested groups were invited to comment on the proposals outlined in the Green Paper and, thereby, contribute to the procurement reform process. The planned elaboration of a White Paper never came about since the Department of Public Works and the Department of Finance could not agree on a common basis.[950]

The State Tender Board Act 1968[951] is still in force but is to be repealed as soon as the Supply Chain Management system has been fully implemented.[952] Until this time accounting officers at national governmental level can choose between the application of the State Tender Board Act and the SCM system as regulated in the PFMA.[953] The State Tender Board Act is a holdover from the apartheid system. It has been amended several times and establishes the State Tender Board as well as regional tender boards. According to the Act, the Minister of Finance can appoint 16 to 20 members to the State Tender Board of whom at least half shall be officers or employees.[954] The appointed members shall hold office for the time the Minister serves and any other member for a period of three years.[955] The State Tender Board is, however, apparently defunct.[956]

The regional tender boards consist of 10 to 14 members who are appointed by the Chairmen of the Ministers' Council in the Houses of Assembly, representatives, and delegates and the relevant administrators.[957]

950 McCrudden, 'Buying Social Justice', p. 253.
951 Act No. 86 of 1968.
952 National Treasury, p. 45, Sec. 5.1.1.
953 State Tender Board Act 1968 (Act No. 86 of 1968): Amendment to Regulations of the State Tender Board Act in Terms of Section 13, 2003, Sec. 2.
954 State Tender Board Act 1968 (Act No. 86 of 1968), Sec. 3 (1).
955 Ibid, Sec. 3 (3).
956 Quinot, 'Enforcement of procurement law from a South African perspective', 194.
957 State Tender Board Act 1968, Sec. 3A (1).

Less than half the total number of members is officers or employers.[958] According to Section 5 (2) of the State Tender Board Act the board may delegate any of its powers to the regional tender boards. The power of the board includes the procurement of supplies and services for the state, the arrangement of hiring or letting of anything, the acquisition or granting of any right for or on behalf of the state and the disposal of movable state property.[959] In order to implement these tasks the board has the right to conclude agreements,[960] to invite offers and determine the manner in which and the conditions subject to which such offers shall be made[961] and to inspect and test or cause to be inspected and tested supplies and services[962] and accept or reject any offer for the conclusion of an agreement.[963] The invitation of offers and the determination of the manner of the offer can be made in "any manner deem fit"[964] and the acceptance or rejection of offers can be made without giving reasons.[965] This not only gives the board the greatest possible latitude to configure the bidding process but also creates an atmosphere of non-transparency and non-accountability. It is clear that the old-fashioned procurement system does not satisfy the requirements for an efficient and effective procurement system and, moreover, does not adequately reflect the standards of an open and democratic society or the principle of good governance. Quinot holds in regard to this matter that the "continued presence on the statue book [...] seems curiously at odds with the new approach under the more recent legislation."[966]

The Public Finance Management Act, which applies to the national government and provincial governments, assigns to the accounting officers of departments, trading entities and constitutional institutions and to accounting authorities of public entities the duty to ensure the establishment and maintenance of an appropriate procurement and provision system which is fair, equitable, transparent, competitive and cost-effective.[967]

---

958 Ibid, Sec. 3A (1) (e).
959 Ibid, Sec. 4 (1).
960 Ibid, Sec. 4 (1) (a).
961 Ibid, Sec. 4 (1) (b).
962 Ibid, Sec. 4 (1) (c).
963 Ibid, Sec. 4 (1) (d).
964 Ibid.
965 Ibid.
966 Quinot, 'Enforcement of procurement law from a South African perspective', 195.
967 Public Finance Management Act 1999 (Act No. 1 of 1999), Secs. 38 (1) (a) (iii) and 51 (1) (a) (iii).

This is provided for by the Municipal Finance Management Act[968], which is applicable to local governments, and the Municipal Systems Act[969]. Despite certain similarities the regulations governing procurement differ in detail. An extensive discussion of both Acts is beyond the scope of this dissertation; therefore, only the PFMA regulations will be dealt with.

The PFMA requires accounting officers to report to the relevant treasury as well as the relevant tender board any case of irregular expenditure involving the procurement of goods or services.[970] The National Treasury may make regulations or issue instructions applicable to all institutions to which this Act applies concerning the determination of a framework for an appropriate procurement and provisioning system which is fair, equitable, transparent, competitive and cost-effective.[971] The Public Finance Management Act assigns to the National Treasury the power to make regulations or issue instructions concerning the procurement system. Based on this provision in 2003 the Framework for Supply Chain Management was enacted. It establishes basic principles and procedures of the SCM system. For the interim period, i.e. until the SCM system is fully implemented, Regulation 12 allows for the use of existing procurement processes through the relevant tender boards or other provincial procurement authorities if the capacity to fulfil the framework regulations is not yet available.

The Framework has to be seen in light of the Policy Strategy to Guide Uniformity in Procurement Reform Processes in Government[972] which is intended to give effect to the provisions of the Constitution, the PFMA and the MFMA aiming to promote uniformity in the processes relevant to the transformation of the procurement system and in the interpretation of preferential procurement legislation and policies.[973] It also aims to replace the outdated procurement and provisioning practices with

> "[...] a supply chain management function and a systematic competitive procedure for the appointment of consultants as an integral part of financial manage-

---

968 Local Government: Municipal Finance Management Act 2003 (Act No. 56 of 2003), Secs. 110-119.

969 Municipal Systems Act 2000 (Act No. 32 of 2000 - as amended by Act No. 44 of 2003).

970 Public Finance Management Act 1999, Sec. 38 (1) (g).

971 Ibid, Sec. 76 (4) (c).

972 National Treasury.

973 Ibid, 2 and 18, para. 1.4.

ment in government that conforms to internationally accepted best practice principles."[974]

The National Treasury has issued a number of instruction or practice notes that provide detailed regulations regarding procurement matters, such as on general conditions of contract and standardised bidding documents,[975] appointment of consultants,[976] a code of conduct for SCM practitioners,[977] threshold values for the procurement of goods and services,[978] training of SCM officials[979] and enhancing compliance monitoring and improving transparency and accountability in SCM.[980]

The Preferential Procurement Policy Framework Act[981] establishes basic principles for the implementation of the preferential procurement policy and, thereby, gives effect to Section 217 (3) of the Constitution.

---

974 Ibid, 2.

975 National Treasury, 'Practice Note Number SCM 1 of 2003: General Conditions of Contract (GCC) and Standardized Bidding Documents (SBDs)' (National Treasury, South Africa: 2003), available at http://ocpo.treasury.gov.za/Resource_Centre/Legislation/SCM-PracNote%2003%201.pdf; last accessed: 30 November 2015.

976 National Treasury, 'Practice Note Number SCM 3 of 2003: Appointment of Consultants ', (National Treasury, South Africa: 2003), available at http://www.dedea.gov.za/Practice%20Notes/Practice%20note%20SCM%203%20of%202003%20Appointment%20of%20Consultants.pdf; last accessed: 30 November 2015.

977 National Treasury, 'Practice Note Number SCM 4 of 2003: Code of Conduct for Supply Chain Management Practitioners ' (National Treasury, South Africa: 2003), available at http://ocpo.treasury.gov.za/Resource_Centre/Legislation/SCM-PracNote%2003%204.pdf; last accessed: 30 November 2015.

978 National Treasury, 'Practice Note Number 8 of 2007/2008: Supply Chain Management: Threshold Values for the Procurement of Goods, Works and Services by Means of Petty Cash, Verbal/Written Price Quotations or Competitive Bids ' (National Treasury, South Africa: 2007), available at http://ocpo.treasury.gov.za/Resource_Centre/Legislation/Practice%20note%20SCM%208%20of%202007_8.pdf; last accessed: 30 November 2015.

979 National Treasury, 'Practice Note Number SCM 5 of 2004: Training of Supply Chain Management Officials' (National Treasury, South Africa: 2004), available at http://ocpo.treasury.gov.za/Resource_Centre/Legislation/SCM-PracNote%2004%205.pdf; last accessed: 30 November 2015.

980 National Treasury, 'National Treasury Instruction Note on Enhancing Compliance Monitoring and Improving Transparency and Accountability in Supply Chain Management' (National Treasury, South Africa: 2011), available at http://ocpo.treasury.gov.za/Resource_Centre/Legislation/20110531%20Instruction%20Note%20on%20Enhancing%20Compliance%20Monitoring%20SCM.pdf; last accessed: 30 November 2015.

981 Act No. 5 of 2000.

According to McCrudden the Act "continues the policies developed earlier, but attempts to rationalize the somewhat ad hoc arrangements that had preceded it."[982] The Act establishes a preference point system which has to be applied by all organs of states carrying out public procurement. In addition to the Act, the Minister enacted Preferential Procurement Regulations in 2001,[983] which were in turn replaced by the current version in 2011.[984] An adaption of the Regulations was regarded as necessary because it had several shortcomings and had to be aligned with the Broad-Based Black Economic Empowerment (BBBEE) Act.[985] The Regulations contain technical specifications concerning public procurement and, in particular, the use of preferences.

Implementation of procurement has, however, been unsatisfactory in many respects. Waste and corruption have been widespread and official competitive bidding processes have often been circumvented.[986] One approach to overcome those difficulties has been to urge accounting officers and authorities to develop mechanisms to identify risks and weaknesses in their respective SCM environment and develop strategies to mitigate these risks and weaknesses.[987] This can be found in the "Instruction Note on Enhancing Compliance Monitoring and Improving Transparency and Accountability in Supply Chain Management" which was issued by the National Treasury in terms of Section 76 (4) (c) of the PFMA in 2011.[988] It contains procedural requirements but also determines in a very detailed

982 McCrudden, 'Buying Social Justice', p. 253.
983 Preferential Procurement Regulations 2001 (Government Gazette No. 22549).
984 Preferential Procurement Regulations 2011.
985 Act No. 53 of 2003. See e.g. National Treasury, 'National Treasury Strategic Plan 2004-2007' (National Treasury, South Africa: 2004), p. 53 (available at http://www.treasury.gov.za/publications/strategic%20plan/strat%20plan%202004%20to%202007.pdf; last accessed: 30 November 2015).
986 National Treasury, 'National Treasury Instruction Note on Enhancing Compliance Monitoring and Improving Transparency and Accountability in Supply Chain Management', p. 2, para 2.2; see also National Treasury, 'Practice Note Number 6 of 2007/2008: Procurement of Goods and Services by Means other than through the Invitiation of Competitive Bids' (National Treasury, South Africa: 2007), p. 2, para. 2.4 (available at http://ocpo.treasury.gov.za/Resource_Centre/Legislation/Practice%20note%20SCM%206%20of%202007.pdf; last accessed: 30 November 2015).
987 National Treasury, 'National Treasury Instruction Note on Enhancing Compliance Monitoring and Improving Transparency and Accountability in Supply Chain Management', p. 2, para. 2.3.
988 Ibid.

way what the responsibilities of accounting officers and authorities include and contains measures aimed at counteracting certain malpractices that have been identified as undermining efficiency and effectiveness. The objective is to improve accountability and transparency and to ensure value for money in the procurement of goods, works and/or services.[989]

b. Objectives and Principles

i. Merging Procurement and Financial Management

Unlike the procurement system of the apartheid era the SCM system focuses on the closer integration and interaction between procurement and financial management and pays stronger attention to the commercial aspects of procurement. While intending to introduce international best practice, SCM

> "[…] seeks to breach the gap between traditional methods of procuring goods and services and the balance of the supply chain and at the same time addressing procurement related matters that are of strategic importance."[990]

The supply chain consists of six components including demand management, acquisition management, logistics management, disposal management, risk management, and regular assessment of supply chain performance.[991] The SCM system must provide for the adjudication of bids through a bid committee, for the establishment, composition and functioning of bid committees, the selection of bid committee members, bidding procedures, and the approval of bid committee recommendations.[992] A detailed explanation of the supply chain can be found in the 2003 Policy Strategy Paper.[993] The integration of risk management and supply chain performance measures exemplifies the shift from focusing on inputs towards an outcome-oriented procurement system. This approach might lead to a more efficient and effective public procurement system if its implementation is successful in practice.

989 Ibid, 2, para. 2.8.
990 National Treasury, 'Policy Strategy to Guide Uniformity in Procurement Reform Processes in Government ', p. 19, para. 2.1.
991 Framework for Supply Chain Management 2003, Sec. 2 (c).
992 Ibid, Sec. 6 (2).
993 National Treasury, 'Policy Strategy to Guide Uniformity in Procurement Reform Processes in Government ', p. 19ff., Sec.2.1.

### ii. Redressing the Imbalances of the Past

Public procurement in South Africa basically rests on two general ideas: the promotion of the principles of good governance and the introduction of a preference system to address socio-economic goals. Whereas the former notion is generally acknowledged as the necessary foundation of an efficient and effective procurement system, the strong focus on procurement linkages needs further explanation in the historical context of South Africa in order to understand the particular relevance South Africa assigns to it. During apartheid large parts of the population were excluded from economic, social, and political life, which resulted in huge disparities of wealth, education, ownership, etc. Therefore, the transformation of society has, since independence, been an integral part of South African policy.[994] The provision of services has been identified as a central factor of "transformative constitutionalism".[995] The concept of transformative constitutionalism has been described as

> "[…] a long-term project of constitutional enactment, interpretation, and enforcement committed [...] to transforming a country's political and social institutions and power relationships in a democratic, participatory, and egalitarian direction."[996]

The Constitution is, hence, seen as an essential element to change the political, economic and social structures as well as legal culture in post-apartheid South Africa. Efficiency, in the respect of service provision, is, as Quinot notes,

> "[…] essential in making available the necessary resources to address socio-economic needs, i.e. by reducing spending in other areas and curbing waste, for the achievement of maximum results for the available resources and from a logistics point of view, in getting support and services (in a timely manner) to those in

---

994 This has been confirmed in several court decisions such as Soobramoney v Minister of Health (Kwazulu-Natal) (CCT32/97) [1997] ZACC 17; 1998 (1) SA 765 (CC); 1997 (12) BCLR 1696. In this case the former Chief Justice noted in paragraph 8 that „a commitment […] to transform our society into one in which there will be human dignity, freedom and equality, lies at the heart of our new constitutional order".

995 The term was significantly coined by South African courts and the author Karl Klare who has extensively dealt with the role of constitutionalism in South Africa. See K. Klare, 'Legal Culture and Transformative Constitutionalism ' (1998) 14 South African Journal of Human Rights, 146-188.

996 Ibid, 150.

> need thereof, especially since large numbers of those in need live in rural and isolated parts of the country."[997]

This shows that, in South Africa, the link between procurement and its objective of transformative constitutionalism is undeniable. A key instrument of transformative constitutionalism is affirmative action, which is justified by a particular notion of equality. The right to equality established in Section 9 of the Constitution has been held to refer to a substantive rather than a formal conception of equality.[998] It is accepted that this particular notion of equality - taking account the actual economic and social circumstances of individuals - not only justifies but demands the application of affirmative action strategies.[999] The procurement policy can be fitted into this overall approach and must be recognised as such rather than being simply dismissed as preferential policy applied to exclude foreign competition or promote a certain group of society. It has indeed been recognised as an important tool to redistribute wealth within the South African economy.[1000]

Procurement reform has further been identified as part of the measures to accommodate the objectives of the Reconstruction and Development Programme (RDP).[1001] The RDP policy was implemented in 1994 with the view to promoting transformation by carrying out programmes with the objectives to meet basic needs, develop human resources, build the economy, democratise the state and society and implement the RDP.[1002] The RDP provides, inter alia, for the utilisation of tenders to encourage stakeholder participation in the RDP, to promote workers' rights, human re-

997 Quinot, 'State Commercial Activity', p. 238.

998 See President of the Repulic of South Africa and Another v Hugo (CCT11/96) [1997] ZACC 4; 1997 (6) BCLR 708; 1997 (4) SA 1.

999 See e.g. Bolton, 'The Law of Government Procurement in South Africa', p. 52, 255.

1000 P. Bolton; G. Quinot, 'Social policies in procurement and the Agreement on Government Procurement: a perspective from South Africa', in S. Arrowsmith; R.D. Anderson, *The WTO Regime on Public Procurement: Challenges and Reform* (Cambridge: Cambridge University Press, 2011), p. 464.

1001 African National Congress, 'The Reconstruction and Development Programme - A policy framework', (Johannesburg: Umanyano Publications, 1994). See also Raga; Taylor.

1002 African National Congress, 'The Reconstruction and Development Programme', para 1.4ff.

source development and job creation[1003] and, hence, has had an impact on public procurement in South Africa.

c. Scope and Coverage

The constitutional procurement provision applies to organs of state in the national, provincial or local sphere of government and other institutions identified in national legislation. The term 'organ of state' is defined in Section 239 of the Constitution:

> "'organ of state' means-
>
> (a) any department of state or administration in the national, provincial or local sphere of government; or
>
> *(b)* any other functionary or institution -
>
> (i) exercising a power or performing a function in terms of the Constitution or
>
> (ii) exercising a public power or performing a public function in terms of any a provincial constitution; or legislation,"

Hence, all public entities fall under the scope of Section 217 and have to carry out procurement according to the constitutional requirements. Section 217 applies to contracts for goods or services; there is no reference made to contracts for works.

In contrast, within the ambit of the Regulations tendering includes the provision of services, works or goods.[1004] The PFMA applies to all departments, public entities that are listed in Schedule 2 or 3, constitutional institutions and the parliament.[1005] As Bolton notes, there is a lack of coherence in the scope of application of the Constitution and the Procurement Act and Regulations.[1006]

The PPPFA applies to all organs of states that are specified in Section 1(iii) of the Act. The 2011 Procurement regulations additionally apply to public entities which are listed in schedules of the PFMA and to municipal entities.[1007] According to Bolton the inclusion of public and municipal entities has led to much controversy; major public entities argued that it "un-

1003 Ibid, para. 4.8.11.
1004 Preferential Procurement Regulations 2011, Reg. 2 (1).
1005 Public Finance Management Act 1999, Sec. 3 (1).
1006 Cf. Bolton, 'The regulatory framework for public procurement in South Africa', p. 186.
1007 Preferential Procurement Regulations 2011, Reg. 1 (s).

duly limits their freedom to use procurement for empowerment purposes."[1008] The exemption provided in Section 3 of the PPPFA should also be mentioned. It allows the Minister to exempt organs of state from any or all provisions of the Act for national security reasons, if the likely tenderers are international suppliers, or if it is in the public interest. The approach of allowing the Minister to make exemptions on a case-by-case basis if justified by one of those reasons is preferable to general exemptions for certain types of procurement as in Mauritius. Nevertheless, the latter ground for justification, the public interest, is particularly vague and can be broadly interpreted so that it can justify a variety of exemptions. This is to be criticised as it leaves room for abuse.

The Framework for Supply Chain Management applies to all national and provincial departments and trading entities, constitutional institutions and certain public entities.[1009] It provides for the acquisition of goods and services and the disposal and letting of state assets, including the disposal of goods no longer required.[1010] The integration of the disposal and letting of states assets into public procurement is quite innovative. It is also rational since it is an opportunity to make additional money and to find use for assets which are no longer being used. The people responsible for procuring goods or services have the best overview of what is needed, not needed at the moment or no longer needed and are, therefore, best positioned to manage disposal and letting of states assets in addition to procuring goods and services. Moreover, it seems indispensable that the former follows certain standards and procedures and the principle of good governance in order to achieve the best possible outcome in regard to the financial situation and to guarantee fairness, equity, transparency and competitiveness. The more money earned the more that can be spent or allocated. Moreover, it is essential for the achievement of changing the patterns of the past where procurement contracts were primarily awarded to large, white-owned enterprises. The extension of the procurement scope beyond the procurement of goods and services guarantees that preferential procurement practices can have the widest possible effect.[1011] The Framework does not provide for any exemptions.

1008 Bolton, 'The regulatory framework for public procurement in South Africa', p. 189.
1009 Framework for Supply Chain Management 2003, Reg. 2 (a-c).
1010 Ibid, Reg. 3 (1) (a) and (b).
1011 Cf. Bolton, 'Overview of the Government Procurement System in South Africa', p. 364.

But procurements carried out using foreign assistance can be generally exempted from the otherwise applicable procurement rules.[1012] Practice Note Number SCM 3 of 2005[1013] establishes that no approval is required by the spending agency from the Minister of Finance for the exemption from the PPPFA and its associated regulations if the technical assistance agreement prescribes the use of the donor's own procurement procedures. However, if the technical assistance agreement does not contain any provisions in this respect the South African procurement rules have to be adhered to. The Practice Note encourages accounting officers/authorities

> "[...] to convince donors to utilize the prescripts of the PPPFA and its Regulations as Government is committed towards addressing the inequalities within the South African economy."

This is similar to the approach followed in Mauritius as it seeks to encourage donors to adhere to national public procurement rules. This is an important element of attempts to untie aid, to promote the national public procurement system and ensure transparency and accountability on the national level (cf. Part II, Chapter 3, Subchapter 4 (b) (iii)).

## 3. Institutions and Staff

Prior to the introduction of the SCM system, the State Tender Board was solely responsible for public procurement. It could, though, transfer its power to regional tender boards or other persons or institutions. In general, procurement was not undertaken by the institutions or entities that were in need of the goods or services to be procured but rather by such external tender boards. The SCM system, on the contrary, assigns the task of procurement to the procuring institutions and, in particular, to their financial department. A key role is played by the accounting officer or the accounting authority. They bear the responsibility of establishing and maintaining effective and efficient procurement systems which rest on the five pillars

---

1012 Bolton, 'The regulatory framework for public procurement in South Africa', p. 194.

1013 National Treasury, 'Practice Note Number SCM 3 of 2005: 1. Projects and Services funded by Grandts in accordance with Technical Assistance Agreements / 2. Appointment of Transaction Advisors to assist with Public Private Parternships' (National Treasury, South Africa: 2005), available at http://ocpo.treasury.gov.za/Resource_Centre/Legislation/Practice%20Note%20SCM%203%20of%202005.pdf; last accessed: 30 November 2015.

of procurement set out in the constitution. Accounting officers or authorities are in charge of the training of the procurement staff,[1014] ensuring the correct functioning of bidding processes and the compliance with all relevant laws and regulations[1015] and are responsible for preventing and sanctioning misbehaviour or abuses committed by procurement staff and bidders.[1016] In addition, they have reporting responsibilities towards the relevant treasury.[1017] In short, they are accountable for the whole procurement process within their institution and are not only responsible for their staff but also ensuring that bidders do not abuse the procurement system. The assignment of responsibility to a particular office within the procuring entities might have the advantage that the respective officer does everything possible in order to achieve the objectives of public procurement. Such an officer can guide and instruct procurement officers and staff as well as control all actions and decisions taken. In contrast, if there is no one particular responsible, the personal inhibition threshold of procurement officers and staff to engage in corrupt practices might be higher and the division of labour and cooperation might be more inefficient.

The National Treasury oversees the implementation of the SCM system and its regulations. In response to the 2003 Policy Paper a Supply Chain Management Office has been established within the National Treasury. Its areas of responsibility include administrative functions, policy formulation and advice, monitoring procurement performances as well as policy implementation in general, maintenance of databases, the investigation of complaints received from the public regarding bid procedures and irregularities, etc.[1018] The Green Paper[1019] envisaged the establishment of a Procurement Compliance Office to basically be responsible for the tasks now carried out by the National Treasury; however in contrast to the latter it would have been independent. Although a totally independent office seems to be the better choice as it diminishes the likelihood of political influence on public procurement, the use of existing, well-functioning institutions might be beneficial, especially in developing countries, as available structures, resources and capacities can be used. Nevertheless, it is

1014 Framework for Supply Chain Management 2003, Reg. 5.
1015 Ibid, Reg. 6 (3).
1016 Ibid, Reg. 9.
1017 Ibid, Reg. 11.
1018 National Treasury, 'Policy Strategy to Guide Uniformity in Procurement Reform Processes in Government ', p. 34f., Sec. 3.7.
1019 Ministry of Finance/Ministry of Public Works.

generally recommendable to ensure that there is an independent instance reviewing the work of the respective institution which is not the case in South Africa so far.

The Framework provides for the establishment of separate Supply Chain Management Units within the office of the institution's chief financial officer.[1020] Their entire staff has to follow certain ethical standards which are, inter alia, outlined in Regulation 8 of the Framework. The National Treasury's Code of Conduct for Supply Chain Management Practitioners must also be adhered to.[1021] Subregulation 3 of Regulation 8 requires all persons involved to recognise and disclose any conflict of interest that may arise; to treat all suppliers and potential suppliers equitably; not to use their position for private gain or to improperly benefit another person; to make sure they do not compromise the credibility or integrity of the SCM system through the acceptance of gifts or hospitality or any other act; to be scrupulous in their use of public property; and to assist accounting officers or accounting authorities in combating corruption and fraud in the SCM system. This list shows that the Framework puts a strong emphasis on the prevention of corruption and equitable treatment of suppliers or potential suppliers. All persons involved are urged to avoid intricate situations, resist any form of tortious interference and purely pursue the institutions' benefits. In case a person involved or any of his close family members, partners or associates have any private or business interest in any contract to be awarded, that official must disclose that interest and withdraw from any participation in the procurement of that particular good or service.[1022]

Procurement officials can seek external advice in particular public procurement projects. The authority to engage external consultants can be found in paragraph 3.6.4 of the Policy Strategy to Guide Uniformity in Procurement Reform Processes in Government. The consultants should contribute to the best possible use of resources. The approach acknowledges the fact that the people carrying out procurement tasks cannot oversee and be familiar with the market situation of all goods or services that are to be procured. Specialised services consultants' advice can be selectively considered for particular projects where superior knowledge and

1020 Framework for Supply Chain Management (Regulations in Terms of the Public Finance Management Act 1999) 2003, Reg. 4(1).

1021 Ibid, Reg. 8 (2).

1022 Ibid, Reg. 8 (4).

skills can substantially contribute to the knowledge base and produce a better procurement outcome. Moreover, the rule allows for the provision of independent advice in regard to most suitable approaches, methodologies and solutions of projects.[1023]

Apart from a clear allocation of responsibilities and a code of conduct for procurement officials, the South African SCM system focuses on capacity-building in regard to public procurement officials and staff. The 2003 Policy Paper mentions training as a necessary component for the full implementation of the SCM policy objectives. The provision of general managerial training, financial management training and specialist SCM training is designed to achieve a "dedicated, well-trained, professional supply chain management cadre in government."[1024] The accounting officers or authorities are, in the first place, responsible for adequately training their personnel. The National Treasury is to facilitate the development of appropriate training material in conjunction with other training service providers.[1025] A practice note released by the Supply Chain Management Office of the National Treasury establishes a guide for minimum training and deployment.[1026] The long term development strategy, which envisages formal diploma and degree courses by tertiary institutions, has been implemented successfully as the University of South Africa offers a Programme in Public Procurement and Supply Management. Moreover, the Public Management National Diploma at the Cape Peninsula University includes certain courses on public procurement.

There is also a strong focus on university research on public procurement. The establishment of a new unit on African public procurement regulation research at the University of Stellenbosch facilitates research about public procurement in South Africa and beyond.[1027] It potentially contributes to the improvement of public procurement as it can serve as a basis for reform consideration. Moreover, it has been and will probably contin-

---

1023 National Treasury, 'Policy Strategy to Guide Uniformity in Procurement Reform Processes in Government ', p. 31, Sec. 3.6.4.1.

1024 Ibid, 47, Sec. 5.1.4.

1025 Ibid, 47f., Sec. 5.1.4.

1026 National Treasury, 'Practice Note Number SCM 5 of 2004: Training of Supply Chain Management Officials'.

1027 African Public Procurement Regulation Research Unit, 'Establishment of new unit on African public procurement regulation research announced', 2011, available at http://sun025.sun.ac.za/portal/page/portal/law/index.english/public_proc/News/2011%20News%20Articles (last accessed: 26th November 2015).

ue to be an important source for the interpretation of public procurement legislation by courts.[1028]

In 2008 the National Treasury issued regulations on minimum competency requirements which all municipal financial and SCM officials have to meet.[1029] A supply chain manager, for example, has to hold a National Qualifications Framework (NQF)[1030] level 5 of the National Diploma in Public Finance Management and Administration and have two years work-related experience.[1031] Head of SCM units in high-capacity municipalities have to hold NQF level 6 or a certificate in municipal financial management and are required to have 5 or 7 years of relevant experience.[1032] During the transition period financial and SCM officials were given a 5 years to obtain the required qualifications.[1033] Municipalities must assist their officials by providing resources and opportunities for training.[1034] This approach can serve as a role model for countries lacking public procurement expertise, as it prevents positions from becoming vacant and ensures a certain degree of continuity. The National Treasury has, in cooperation with the South African Qualifications Authority and the Local Government Sector Education and Training Authority (LGSETA), established a training programme to improve the qualifications and skills of municipal financial management officials and help them meet the competency requirements.[1035] The courses are provided by training institutions accredited by the LGSETA which are listed on the National Treasury's website.[1036]

---

1028 Local Government: Municipal Finance Management Act: Municipal Regulations on Minimum Competency Levels 2007 (No. R493 of 2007, Government Gazette 504).

1029 Ibid.

1030 The framework is established by the National Qualifications Framework Act 2008 (Act No. 67 of 2008).

1031 Local Government: Municipal Finance Management Act: Municipal Regulations on Minimum Competency Levels 2007, para 12.

1032 Ibid, para. 11.

1033 Ibid, para. 15.

1034 Ibid, para. 17.

1035 'The Implication of Noncompliance with Treasury's Competency Requirements', Local Tender Bulletin 13(4), 2011.

1036 Ibid.

## 4. Basics of the Supply Chain Management System

### a. Procurement Methods

Procurement is required to comply with the threshold values as determined by the National Treasury.[1037] The South African system provides for the use of different procurement methods "either by way of quotations or through a bidding process".[1038] The threshold values set by the National Treasury determine what processes are generally to be applied: petty cash; verbal/written price quotations or competitive bids.[1039] The petty cash method is allowed for procurements of R 2,000 or less and can be determined by individual internal procedures.[1040] For transaction values between R 2,000 and R 10,000 accounting officers or authorities are required to obtain at least three verbal or written quotations.[1041] Where applicable, lists of prospective suppliers have to be used for this purpose. For procurements up to R 500,000 written quotations should be invited and accepted by as many suppliers from the list of prospective suppliers as possible.[1042] For procurements above the threshold value of R 500,000 competitive bids are generally required.[1043] If tendering is deemed impractical other procurement methods may be used.[1044] The reasons justifying the use of alternative methods must be recorded and approved by the accounting officer or authority.[1045] South African constitutional law does not restrict the application of tendering as only procurement method as Section 217 contains no specific reference in this regard. It has therefore been suggested that any procurement method consistent with the principle of competitiveness is applicable.[1046] The National Treasury suggests the use

1037 Framework for Supply Chain Management 2003, Reg. 6 (1).
1038 Ibid, Reg. 6 (1).
1039 National Treasury, 'Practice Note Number 8 of 2007/2008: Supply Chain Management: Threshold Values for the Procurement of Goods, Works and Services by Means of Petty Cash, Verbal/Written Price Quotations or Competitive Bids '.
1040 Ibid, para. 3.1.
1041 Ibid, para. 3.2.
1042 Ibid, para. 3.3.1.
1043 Ibid, paras. 3.4.1 and 3.4.3.
1044 Framework for Supply Chain Management 2003, Reg. 6 (4).
1045 Ibid.
1046 Cf. Bolton, 'The Law of Government Procurement in South Africa', p. 43.

of price quotations or negotiations as alternatives to competitive bids.[1047] Furthermore, the Regulation 6 (3) (f) of the Framework allows for the procurement of goods or services by means of public private partnerships but requires adherence to Treasury Regulation 16[1048] which contains detailed regulations on public private partnerships. This is generally a positive feature because it recognises that more competitiveness does not necessarily amount to better value for money, but that it is important to consider what approach best balances competitiveness and cost-effectiveness in the situation at hand. Despite this degree of flexibility, the South African approach acknowledges the important insight that the higher the value of contract, the more formal the procedures should be.[1049]

Nevertheless, the provision that other procurement methods can be used, if competitive bidding is deemed to be impractical, lacks clarity and falls short of any requirement to specify reasons that might justify exceptions from competitive bidding. The meaning of "impractical" leaves ample leeway for abuse. Although the regulation is "intended for cases of emergency or where goods and services are available from sole service providers",[1050] legislation has failed to clarify the specific circumstances justifying its invocation. After the National Treasury became aware that institutions were deliberately utilizing the provision to circumvent competitive bidding it issued a practice note regarding "Procurement of Goods and Services by Means other than through the Initiation of Competitive Bids"[1051] pressuring accounting officers and authorities to ensure that the provision in question is "[...] utilized strictly to procure goods and services of critical importance and only in specific cases when it is impractical to invite competitive bids."[1052] However, it contains neither any speci-

---

1047 National Treasury, 'Practice Note Number 8 of 2007/2008: Supply Chain Management: Threshold Values for the Procurement of Goods, Works and Services by Means of Petty Cash, Verbal/Written Price Quotations or Competitive Bids ', p. 2, para 3.4.3.

1048 South Africa Treasury Regulation 16 - Public Private Partnerships, issued in terms of the Public Finance Management Act, 1999 (Gazette No. 25915, 16 January 2004).

1049 Bolton, 'The Law of Government Procurement in South Africa', p. 109; Bolton, 'Overview of the Government Procurement System in South Africa', p. 365.

1050 National Treasury, 'Practice Note Number 6 of 2007/2008: Procurement of Goods and Services by Means other than through the Invitiation of Competitive Bids', para 2.4.

1051 Ibid.

1052 Ibid, para. 2.7.

fication in regard to the exceptions encompassed by impracticalness nor details on what kind of reasons could justify such exceptions. Furthermore, it remains unclear what alternative procurement methods should be used when an exception to competitive bidding is applicable.[1053]

b. Tender Specifications, Award Criteria and Evaluation Methods

Legislation provides no requirements in regard to tender specifications. Paragraph 3.4 of the SCM guide[1054] for accounting officers and authorities, however, states the following in regard to specifications of goods, works or services:

> "Standards and technical specifications quoted in bidding documents should promote the broadest possible competition, while assuring that critical elements of performance or other requirements for the goods, services and/or works being procured are achieved. It is recommended that as far as possible, the institution should specify accepted standards such as those issued by Standards South Africa (the division of the South African Bureau of Standards responsible for standards), the International Standards Organisation or an authority recognised by the South African National Accreditation System (SANAS) with which the equipment or materials or workmanship should comply."

It has to be emphasised that this provision has no legal effect[1055] but rather serves as a guideline on how to implement procurement legislation and "must be seen as a step to assist accounting officers/authorities in the smooth implementation of supply chain management within their institutions."[1056] Beyond this limited effect, guidance provided by this provision remains rather vague; it does not set out explicit requirements about tender specifications. It emphasises competition as a key factor by concomitantly ensuring that the goods, works or services procurement meet its purpose. This is indeed essential for the achievement of value for money and implies that the specifications in bidding documents should be formulated in a way that allows as many suppliers or contractors to participate as possible. This can be interpreted as requiring tender specifications to be objec-

1053 Cf. Bolton, 'The Law of Government Procurement in South Africa', p. 164.

1054 National Treasury, 'Supply Chain Management - A Guide for Accounting Officers/Authorities ', (National Treasury, South Africa: 2004), available at www.treasury.gov.za/divisions/ocpo/sc/Guidelines/SCM%20Jan900-Guidelines.pdf; last accessed: 30 November 2015.

1055 Ibid, 3, Preface.

1056 Ibid, 2, Preface.

tive and related to performance and function rather than to design criteria, but this is not explicitly stated in the SCM Guide. Subparagraph 2 of paragraph 3.4 closely resembles similar provisions in the GPA and the UNCITRAL Model Law.[1057] It provides that specifications should be based on relevant characteristics and/or performance requirements, and that references to criteria such as brand names should be avoided. If it is necessary to make such reference, the words "or equivalent" should be added after such reference. Finally, the guide advices against over-specification in regard to the quality of goods or services as that might limit competition.

The concept of critical elements of performance or requirements for goods, services or works is not defined. As measured by international standards as provided by the GPA or UNCITRAL Model Law on procurement, which lists examples for technical specifications,[1058] the lack of regulations on possible tender specification criteria is a significant shortcoming as it grants procurement officials wide discretion when specifying the goods, work or services to be procured. Although a certain degree of discretion is of the utmost importance, criteria limiting their ability to restrict competition are essential in order to prevent corruption and enhance value for money. The recommendation to refer to national standards is helpful but should be supplemented by general criteria for tender specifications. South African legislation also lacks provisions ensuring that tender specifications are not too restrictive.[1059]

First of all, the contents of paragraph 3.4 of the SCM guide should be placed in legislation in order to prevent accounting officers or the authority from formulating tender specifications to achieve a certain predetermined outcome. Secondly, it should be supplemented by criteria that should be used in order to specify goods, services or works, e.g. that the specifications use objective criteria that are related to performance and

---

1057 Art VI (3) of the GPA and Art 10 (4) of the UNCITRAL Model Law both state the following: „There shall be no requirement for or reference to a particular trademark or trade name, patent, design or type, specific origin or producer unless there is no sufficiently precise or intelligible way of describing the characteristics of the subject matter of the procurement and provided that words such as "or equivalent" are included.“ And Article VI (2) (a) of the GPA provides that technical specifications should be in terms of performance rather than design or descriptive characteristics.

1058 Cf. Art VI (1) of the GPA and Art 10 (3) of the UNCITRAL Model Law.

1059 Bolton, 'The Law of Government Procurement in South Africa', p. 175.

functions. Beyond this, the current legislation provides no clear guidance on how to determine functionality and what weight should be given to different factors. The lack of guidance on criteria determining functionality has been rectified by the introduction of the Implementation Guide on the 2011 Preferential Procurement Regulations.[1060] It stresses that the question whether bids should be invited on the basis of functionality should depend on the nature of the required commodity or service, meaning the quality, reliability, viability and durability of a service and the bidders' technical capacity and ability to execute a contract.[1061] The Implementation Guide also suggests criteria that can be used to determine the latter, such as the consultant's relevant experience, the quality of the methodology, the qualifications of key personnel, transfer of knowledge, etc.[1062] The respective weight given to the criteria is to be determined independently for each bid.[1063] The suggested criteria for evaluation are a major advancement over the previous situation, where the meaning of "the bidders' technical capacity and ability to execute a contract" was left solely to the procurement officers' discretion.[1064]

The ability to provide the goods, services or works required is also one of the evaluation criteria that should be applied in prequalification procedures and the establishment of lists of approved suppliers.[1065]

In practice, tender documentation generally includes the formula which will be used to evaluate the tenders as well as the allocation of points. In *Total Computer Services (Pty) Ltd. v Municipal Manager Potchefstroom Local Municipality*[1066], one of the grounds for review was that the munici-

1060 National Treasury, 'Implementation Guide Preferential Procurement Regulations, 2001 (pertaining to the Preferential Procurement Policy Framework Act, 2000 (Act No. 5 of 2000))', 2001.

1061 Ibid, 10, para. 6.1.

1062 Ibid, 10, para. 6.2 (a).

1063 Ibid, 10, para. 6.2 (b).

1064 Bolton notes in Bolton, 'The Law of Government Procurement in South Africa', p. 103ff., that the only requirement to verify the capability and ability to execute the contract as provided in the SCM guidelines is not further defined and, therefore, does not provide guidance on how to achieve value for money. And, indeed, this not only impinges the implementation of cost-effectiveness on the side of SCM practitioners but also raises transparency issues.

1065 National Treasury, 'Supply Chain Management - A Guide for Accounting Officers/Authorities ', p. 41f.

1066 Total Computer Services (Pty) Limited v. Municipal Manager Ptochefstroom Local Municipality and Others (29416/07) [2007] ZAGPHC 239; 2008 (4) SA 346 (T).

pality erred in the allocation of points. It was argued it did not allocate it according to the preference point system guidelines as outlined in the policy and the tender documentation. Furthermore, the authority erred in not awarding the contract to the tenderer who scored the highest points despite such a clause in the tender documentation.[1067] The court found that the municipality had miscalculated the points and that this was reviewable under the Promotion of Administrative Justice Act (PAJA).[1068] Hence, despite there being no legal requirement that evaluation has to be according to the guidelines as outlined in tender documentation, in practice this is followed and can also be challenged in court.

Bolton's criticism that, in regard to the cost-effectiveness component, current legislation gives little guidance on what factors should be considered when procuring goods or services in order to determine cost-effectiveness[1069] is legitimate. Although certain guidelines have been issued, they do not have the necessary legal effect to ensure the achievement of its objectives.

Although the pursuit of social policies through procurement occupies a prominent position within the procurement system, value for money remains the most important objective and price is the decisive criterion for awarding public contracts. This has been confirmed and emphasised by South African courts.[1070] The award system is dealt with in detail in the paragraph about secondary objectives.

### i. Uniformity

A strong emphasis is put on uniformity and standardisation of bid documents. The National Treasury is the institution responsible for achieving uniformity by enacting a uniform procurement policy, additional regulations or instructions and prescribing pro forma standardised tender docu-

---

1067 Act No. 3 of 2003. See ibid, para. 34.

1068 Ibid, para. 55.

1069 Bolton, 'The Law of Government Procurement in South Africa', p. 129.

1070 See e.g. Cash Paymaster Services (Pty) Ltd. v Eastern Cape Province and Others 1999 (1) SA 324 (CkH): 357; Lohan Civil- Tebogo Joint Venture and Anders v Mangaung Plaaslike Munisipaliteit and Anders (508/2009) [2009] ZAFSHC 46 (6 April 2009): para. 71 (78).

mentation.[1071] Uniformity is supposed to promote a variety of goals, including the stimulation of entry by new entrants/emerging enterprises to government procurement, cost effectiveness, simplification of the bidding process, better risk assessment for (potential) bidders, simplification and improvement of contract management, better value for money and greater transparency in respect of the financial impact of preferential procurement objectives.[1072] The central role the National Treasury plays in this respect is to be welcomed. The clear allocation of responsibility to a single national institution is not only of particular importance for uniformity but also to ensure an adequate system of checks and balances.

### ii. Electronic Procurement

South Africa is one of the first developing countries pursuing an e-government strategy that is seen as part of a larger government modernisation program.[1073] But, apart from a static information provision[1074] and a number of interactive and transactional e-government programmes such as the electronic filing of tax returns of the South African Revenue Service, no considerable progress has been made.[1075] The Electronic Communications and Transactions Act of 2002[1076] is part of the legislative framework that opens the way for e-governance and e-procurement, but there are still several constraints that need to be addressed. Whereas the legislative framework and the governance model required for e-governance are less of a problem, Farelo and Morris identified access, internal efficiency and human resource development as challenges for the implementation of the e-governance strategy.[1077] In most sectors a lack of political will and support, a lack of strong and consistent leadership, a weak and contradictory IT governance framework and continuous political and bureaucratic in-

1071 Cf. National Treasury, 'Policy Strategy to Guide Uniformity in Procurement Reform Processes in Government ', p. 28ff., Secs. 3.6.1 - 3.6.3.1.

1072 Cf. ibid, 29, Sec. 3.6.2.

1073 M. Farelo; C. Morris, 'The Status of E-government in South Africa', conference paper, IST Africa Conference, Pretoria, South Africa 7-9 May, 2006, p. 3.

1074 F. Cloete, 'e-Government Lessons from South Africa 2001-2011: Institutions, State of Progress and Measurement' (2012) 12 The African Journal of Information and Communication Issue, 128-142 at 133.

1075 Ibid, 134.

1076 Act No. 25 of 2002.

1077 Farelo; Morris, p. 11.

fighting have hindered progress towards more mature e-governance in South Africa.[1078]

In public procurement, certain aspects of the procurement process can be conducted electronically. Bid documents, for example, are electronically available and in some cases bids may also be submitted electronically.[1079] However, strategies to make use of e-procurement on the interactive or transactional level have not yet been implemented.

## 5. Transparency and Strategies to Combat Corruption

### a. Specific Procurement-related Transparency Provisions

Explicit statutory provisions that directly provide for mandatory requirements in the procurement process aiming at transparency are rare, if not non-existent. Although the PFMA sets out general provisions, e.g. that accounting officers have to ensure that institutions have and maintain an effective, efficient and transparent system of financial and risk management and internal control and an appropriate procurement and provision system which is fair and transparent,[1080] the Act does not provide further guidance on how to achieve transparency. The Framework though contains certain transparency requirements on bid documentation, including evaluation and adjudication criteria,[1081] the advertisement of bids in at least the Government Tender Bulletin for at least 30 days,[1082] and the publishing of awards.[1083] Conflicts of interest must also be disclosed.[1084]

Additionally, under the authority granted by Section 76 (4) (c) of the PFMA to make regulations or issue instructions concerning a fair and transparent system, the National Treasury has issued an instruction note that contains several more detailed provisions aiming at the improvement of transparency. However, these instructions have limited legal effect

1078 Cloete, 'e-Government Lessons from South Africa 2001-2011', 138.
1079 S. Williams-Elegbe, 'The World Bank's Influence on Procurement Reform in Africa' (2013) 21(1) AFrican Journal of International and Comparative Law, 95-119 at 112.
1080 Public Finance Management Act 1999, Sec. 38 (1) (a) (i) and (iii).
1081 Framework for Supply Chain Management 2003, Reg. 6 (3) (b) and (c).
1082 Ibid, Reg. 6 (3) (c).
1083 Ibid, Reg. 6 (3)(d).
1084 Ibid, Reg. 8 (3).

which severely restricts its relevance and raises the question why this very important topic has not been addressed by a different type of legal instrument. The principal points of the instruction shall, nevertheless, been outlined in the following.

The National Treasury Instruction Note specifies the information required to be published in regard to the successful bid on the institution's website. This information includes the contract numbers and description; the names of the successful bidder(s) and preferences claimed; the contract price(s) and if possible brand names and dates for completion of contracts.[1085] The requirement to keep records of such publications for audit purposes is very important.[1086]

There are no explicit requirements for public bid opening.[1087] As this is an essential and important process of public procurement, the lack of such a requirement is contrary to the objective of transparency. As Bolton notes, there is also "[…] no clarity on the making of changes to tender specifications, the acceptance of alternative or qualified tenders, or the amendment and withdrawal of tenders."[1088] In order to satisfy the required transparency standards for an effective and efficient public procurement system, regulations or instructions in regard to these matters should be made.

The National Treasury Instruction Note establishes different transparency requirements for different threshold values. For example, it requires planned procurements which exceed 500,000 South African Rand to be announced to the relevant treasury by 30 April of each year and to be approved by the accounting officer or his or her delegate prior to its submission.[1089] As mentioned before, the practice of procurement planning is beneficial for the objectives of procurement, especially transparency, competition, fairness and value for money.[1090] However, as there is no requirement to make public procurement plans available to the public, the

---

1085 National Treasury, 'National Treasury Instruction Note on Enhancing Compliance Monitoring and Improving Transparency and Accountability in Supply Chain Management', p. 6f., para. 3.7.2 (a-d).

1086 Ibid, 7, para. 3.7.2.

1087 Cf. Bolton, 'The Law of Government Procurement in South Africa', p. 188.

1088 Ibid, 208.

1089 National Treasury, 'National Treasury Instruction Note on Enhancing Compliance Monitoring and Improving Transparency and Accountability in Supply Chain Management', p. 2f., para. 3.1.1.

1090 See in particular Part I, Chapter 1, Subchapter 4.

effect remains limited in South Africa. An extension of the provision in this respect could have a positive impact on the achievement of public procurement objectives.

For competitive bids above the threshold value of R 500,000 institutions must publish within ten days on their websites the names of all bidders that submitted bids including, if practical, the total price and the preferences claimed by the respective bidders and make them accessible for at least thirty days. This certainly improves the accountability of accounting officers, authorities and procurement staff and allows bidders to compare their bid with the other bidders, enabling them to assess the potential success of their bid. The approach may also have a learning effect and lead to future improved bids.

All contracts with a threshold in excess of R 10 million are subject to the relevant treasury's approval.[1091] The relevant treasury has to ensure that contracts are awarded within the budgetary provisions and that they are aligned with the targets/outputs indicated in the strategic plan of the institution.[1092] Any deliberate splitting of requirements in order to evade the submission requirement is prohibited.[1093] Furthermore, procurement processes involving bids exceeding a value of R 10 million are subject to auditing by internal or external auditors to ensure that the prescribed norms and standards are complied with. The aim of this mechanism is clearly stated in the National Treasury Instruction Note: minimising the risk of possible fraud, corruption and/or litigation.[1094]

The requirements for the conduct of public procurement staff and for transparency in respect of the integrity and accountability of staff members have been outlined above. It shall now be assessed how misconduct is sanctioned. Chapter 10 of the PFMA establishes the elements of financial misconduct by officials in departments and constitutional institutions, by treasury officers, and by accounting officers and officers of public entities.[1095] It also refers to the applicable legal regime for disciplinary proceedings[1096] and requires the Minister to make regulations to specify certain acts constituting misconduct and its consequences.[1097] Last but not

1091 Ibid, 4ff., para. 3.4.
1092 Ibid, 5, para. 3.4.3.
1093 Ibid, 5, para. 3.4.4.
1094 Ibid, 6, para. 3.5.1.
1095 Public Finance Management Act 1999, Secs. 81-38.
1096 Ibid, Sec. 84.
1097 Ibid, Sec. 85.

least, Section 86 declares what specific types of misconduct are criminal offences and establishes what penalties can be imposed. Staff members committing a criminal offence are liable to a fine or to imprisonment.[1098] Misconduct includes failure to comply with certain provisions of the PFMA as well as the wilful or negligent failure to exercise power or perform a duty that has been assigned to the official by law. Making or permitting an irregular expenditure or a fruitless and wasteful expenditure is another form of misconduct under the PFMA.[1099]

Supply Chain Management Officials or other officials involved are required to disclose any conflict of interest that may arise (Regulation 8(3)(a) of the Framework). Subregulation 4 provides the following:

> "(4) If a supply chain management official or other role player, or any close family member, partner or associate of such official or other role player, has any private or business interest in any contract to be awarded, that official or other role player must –
>
> (a) disclose that interest; and
>
> (b) withdraw from participating in any manner whatsoever in the process relating to that contract."

The Code of Conduct for SCM Practitioners[1100] entails general principles, provisions on conflicts of interest, accountability, openness and confidentiality, instructions for bid evaluation/adjudication teams and a provision on combative practices. The instruction on openness is particularly important in this respect. This instruction reads:

> "Practitioners should be as open as possible about all the decisions and actions that they take. They should give reasons for their decisions and restrict information only if it is in the public interest to do so."[1101]

Further recommendations in order to improve transparency in procurement have been the introduction of an independent and external review mechanism, alternative dispute settlement, education programmes to make bidders aware of their rights during the bidding process and the involvement of non-state actors.[1102] Additionally, the reduction of the discretionary nature of calculating preference points through the introduction of the

---

1098 Ibid, Sec. 86.
1099 Ibid, Secs. 81-83.
1100 National Treasury, 'Practice Note Number SCM 4 of 2003: Code of Conduct for Supply Chain Management Practitioners '.
1101 Ibid, 2, para. 4.1.
1102 Volmink.

Black Economic Empowerment (BEE) status level requirement, the requirements on the publication of award criteria and the adherence to such criteria should be emphasised as making a contribution to transparency in the procurement system.[1103]

In order to diminish deficient practice, corruption, fraud etc. several procedural requirements have been added to the SCM system. These include the introduction of the Standard Bid Document "Declaration of Interest" which compels bidders to submit the names of their directors/trustees/shareholders, their individual identity numbers, personal tax reference numbers and state employee/personnel numbers as part of their bid submissions.[1104] Accounting officers or authorities bear the responsibility of verifying the information provided and taking the necessary disciplinary steps in case a bidder/director/trustee or shareholder has given false information.[1105] Beyond this, the accounting officers or authorities have to examine whether the preferred bidder's tax matters are in order and whether they are blacklisted (on the Register for Tender Defaulters or the List of Restricted Suppliers). Finally, they conduct a due diligence investigation as to whether the preferred bidders have the capability and ability to execute the contract.[1106] Those requirements, however, remain vague and guidance on how to conduct such a due diligence investigation is not provided. Under these circumstances it is difficult to see how this requirement can make a contribution to the improvement of the SCM system.

Other instruments to ensure a satisfactory outcome are the requirement of legal vetting of formal contracts or service level agreements and the execution of contract management.[1107] The recognition of the importance of the post-award phase of the procurement process is an important step in the quest to achieve a satisfactory procurement system. First, legal vetting can diminish the risk of litigation. Second, legal vetting and contract management are necessary in order to monitor contract implementation and to guarantee a satisfactory outcome. In the context of the procurement con-

---

1103 Cf. Bolton; Quinot, 'Social policies in procurement and the Agreement on Government Procurement', p. 474.

1104 National Treasury, 'National Treasury Instruction Note on Enhancing Compliance Monitoring and Improving Transparency and Accountability in Supply Chain Management', p. 3f., para. 3.3.1.

1105 Ibid, 4, para. 3.3.2.

1106 Ibid, 4, para. 3.3.4 (a-c).

1107 Ibid, 6, paras. 3.6.1 and 3.6.2.

tract, the National Treasury has instructed that the expansion or variation of contracts is only allowed within a limited monetary range.[1108] Situations in which prices are sharply increased after the award of the contract have occurred frequently in the past. Establishing a threshold for the expansion or variation of orders against the original contract is intended to counteract this practice.[1109] Given the importance of contract management for the successful completion of public procurement processes, the general provisions of the South African SCM system are not sufficient and should be further specified. The Edumbe Local Municipality has, for example, established the possibility to exclude tenderers on ground of poor past performance in its Supply Chain Management Policy.[1110] It also requires the organ of state to inform the tenderer about its bad track record. This includes a duty to continuously monitor the nature of the service and to inform the service provider in good time, frequently and in writing about its unsatisfactory performance. This is important in order to achieve an improvement of performance. A court held in this respect:

> "It is only when a contractor has knowledge about its sub-standard performance that it could improve. The purpose of this proviso must be seen in the background of the history of our country. Potential service providers with no or little business training background should not be visited with a sledgehammer. At best, they should be progressively nurtured and trained by municipalities / state organs to be professional business people of the future."[1111]

Apart from the benefits for the development of economic expertise, in particular in SME's, and performance improvement, a clear benefit is the possibility to sanction shortcomings on the supplier's and contractor's side and to apply lessons learned to future procurements.

### b. Non-Procurement Specific Regulations

Since the specific procurement-related transparency requirements have limited legal effect, the constitutional rights of access to information,[1112] reasoned decisions, the associated implementation laws as well as corre-

1108 Ibid, 7, para. 3.9.3.
1109 Cf. ibid, 7, para. 3.9.2.
1110 Edumbe Municipality Supply Chain Management Policy, 2008, Sec. 38 (1) (d).
1111 Renaissance Security and Cleaning Services CC v Rustenburg Local Municipality and Others (1811/2007) [2008] ZANWHC 29: para. 12.
1112 Constitution of the Republic of South Africa 1996, Sec. 32 (1).

sponding case law play a particular role in regard to the transparency and accountability requirements of the SCM system. The right of access to information and the right to reasoned decisions enable "a person adversely affected by a tender decision to ascertain whether the decision was taken lawfully or not."[1113] The courts are given a special role in ensuring compliance with the constitutional provisions. They have been assigned an important role as guardians of fundamental rights and freedoms and are required to give effect to the spirit, purport and objects of the Bill of Rights when interpreting legislation.[1114] Volmink argues that "[…] the courts have generally given a generous and purposive interpretation to the right to reasons and access to information," noting that "[j]udicial pronouncements on a number of key legal issues have had a significant effect on the promotion of transparency in the arena of public procurement."[1115]

The right of access to information is codified in Section 32 (1) of the Constitution, which reads as follows.

> "Everyone has the right of access to – (a) any information held by the state; and (b) any information that is held by another person and that is required for the exercise or protection of any rights."

In 2000 the Promotion of Access to Information Act (PAIA)[1116] was enacted to give effect to Section 32 (1) of the Constitution. In the context of public procurement, any organ of state that wants to refuse a tenderer access to information "[…] bears the onus of proving that it is entitled to refuse access to the requested information."[1117]

In *Tetra Mobile Radio (Pty) Ltd. v Member of the Executive Council of the Department of Works and Others*[1118] the right of access to information was held to be related to fairness under Section 217 of the Constitution. Tetra Mobile was denied access to certain information which it had requested in order to be able to formulate and pursue an appeal under the Procurement Act. The court held that "[…] the Procurement Act has as its

1113 Volmink.
1114 Constitution of the Republic of South Africa 1996, Sec. 39 (2).
1115 Volmink.
1116 Act No. 2 of 2000.
1117 Bolton, 'The Law of Government Procurement in South Africa', p. 242.
1118 Tetra Mobile Radio (Pty) Ltd. v Member of the Executive Council of the Department of Works and Others (482/2006) [2007] ZASCA 128; [2007] SCA 128 (RSA); 2008 (1) SA 438 (SCA).

object the giving of effect to s 217 of the Constitution […]"[1119] and that fairness is inherent in the tender procedure:

> "Its very essence is to ensure that before Government, National or Provincial, purchases goods or services, or enters into contracts for the procurement thereof, a proper evaluation is done of what is available and at what price, so as to ensure cost-effectiveness and competitiveness."[1120]

It was concluded that

> "[…] s 20 of the Procurement Act, read with s 217 of the Constitution, contemplates a fair system which envisages that, from the time of the award, the appellant has the right of access to information necessary to formulate its appeal properly."[1121]

Chapter 4 of PAIA establishes grounds upon which a request for access to information can be refused. Additionally, Section 36 of the Act provides details on the protection of commercial information of third parties. The question of when information can be withheld for reasons of confidentiality has been discussed in several court cases. Without going into this issue in detail - which is also a matter of general administrative law and has been extensively discussed – a few cases dealing with this matter in the procurement context will be presented.

An important case in this respect is *ABBM Printing & Publishing (Pty) Ltd. v Transnet Ltd.*[1122] where it was established that access to confidential materials should only be given to the unsuccessful tenderer's legal representatives in order to formulate a legal challenge. The case of *Transnet Limited and Inter Waste (Pty) Ltd. v. SA Metal Machinery Company (Pty) Ltd.*[1123] further established that the successful tenderer cannot invoke the confidentiality clause in regard to its tender price after winning the tender award. It was held that if an organ of state

> "[…] enters into a commercial agreement of a public character like the one in issue (disclosure of the details of which does not involve any risk, for example, to State security or the safety of the public) the imperative of transparency and ac-

1119 Ibid, para. 9.

1120 Ibid.

1121 Tetra Mobile Radio (Pty) Ltd. v Member of the Executive Council of the Department of Works and Others (482/2006) [2007] ZASCA 128; [2007] SCA 128 (RSA); 2008 (1) SA 438 (SCA): para. 15.

1122 ABBM Printing and Publishing (Pty) Ltd. v Transnet Ltd 1998 (2) SA 109 (W).

1123 Transnet Limited and Inter Waste (Pty) Ltd. v. SA Metal Machinery Company (Pty) Ltd. (147/2005) [2005] ZASCA 113 (29 November 2005).

countability entitles members of the public, in whose interest an organ of State operates, to know what expenditure such an agreement entails."[1124]

It also emphasised that the confidentiality clause cannot be used to circumvent the terms of the Act.[1125] On the whole, the courts have stressed that a request for access to information cannot be denied per se based on claims of confidentiality. Only where disclosure would probably (not possibly) result in commercial harm can a request for access to information legitimately be refused.[1126]

Section 33 (1) of the Constitution provides that everyone has the right to administrative action that is lawful, reasonable and procedurally fair. Subsection 2 establishes the right of any person whose rights have been adversely affected by administrative action to receive written reasons for the action. The constitutional provision is given effect by the Promotion of Administrative Justice Act.[1127] Section 3 (1) of PAJA requires procedurally fairness for any administrative action which materially and adversely affects the rights or legitimate expectations of any person. The courts have established that most procurement decisions fall under administrative action which is essential as they can be reviewed under PAJA. This will be examined in more detail in the section on review procedures below.

The right to receive written reasons is further specified in Section 5 (1):

> "Any person whose rights have been materially and adversely affected by administrative action and who has not been given reasons for the action may, within 90 days after the date on which that person became aware of the action or might reasonably have been expected to have become aware of the action, request that the administrator concerned furnish written reasons for the action."

If the administrator has not, within 90 days, provided adequate reasons, the courts must presume that the administrative action was taken without good reasons.[1128] The nature of what constitutes "adequate reasons" has been addressed in several court cases. A Canadian case [1129] that has been

1124 Ibid, para. 55.
1125 Ibid.
1126 See Volmink.
1127 Act No. 3 of 2000.
1128 Promotion of Administrative Justice Act 2000 (Act No. 3 of 2000), Sec. 5 (1) and (2).
1129 Rèan International Supply Company (Pty) Ltd. and Others v Mpumulanga Gaming Board (1999) 8 BCLR 918.

cited in several South African court cases[1130] found that "[i]t is impossible to lay down a general rule of what could constitute adequate or proper reasons, for each case must depend upon its own facts."[1131] Case law has, nevertheless, established certain standards that must be met in order to find that the reasoning was "adequate".[1132] What may qualify as adequate reasoning can only be judged on a case-by-case basis. The courts try to achieve a balance between government efficiency and the right of the person seeking reasons; in particular, the state should not be overburdened by this requirement.[1133] Several decisions have dealt with the right to reasons within the procurement context; a few will be outlined in the following.

The Aquafund case[1134] established that the provision of reasons was necessary to enable a bidder to know whether his or her right to fair administrative action was infringed or not. This was confirmed in *Actaris South Africa (Pty) Ltd. v Sol Plaatje Municipality*[1135] where the court held that

> "[...] the reasons to be furnished must be full, and adequate and must be furnished as expeditiously as the circumstances permit to enable the aggrieved party to investigate its case in order to determine what legal recourse he/she intends to take."

The constitutionally protected principles of openness, transparency, justness, fairness and accountability would otherwise be seriously undermined if reasons are not given. In *Cash Paymaster Services (Pty) Ltd. v Eastern Cape Province*[1136] it was found that,

> "[i]t is almost standard practice that an independent tribunal such as the Tender Board would in review proceedings comply with the requirements of Rule 53 of

---

1130 See e.g. Commissioner for the SAPS and Others v Maimela and Another 2003 (5) SA 480 (TPD); Seodigeng v Chief Executive of South African Sucurity Agency (SASSA) (1682/07) [2011] ZANWHC 1.

1131 Rèan International Supply Company (Pty) Ltd. and Others v Mpumulanga Gaming Board (1999) 8 BCLR 918: 927.

1132 For a detailed discussion of the case law on the requirement of adequate reasoning see C. Hoexter, 'Administrative Law in South Africa', (Claremont: Juta & Co, 2012), 2nd Edition, p. 476ff.

1133 Cf. Quinot, 'State Commercial Activity'.

1134 Aquafund Pty Ltd. v Premier of the Province of the Western Cape 1997 (7) BCLR 907 (C): 913 I.

1135 Actaris South Africa (Pty) Ltd. v. Sol Plaatje Municipality and Intelligent Metering Systems (Pty) Ltd (213/2008) [2008] ZANCHC 6; [2008] 4 All SA 168 (NC) (29 February 2008).

1136 Cash Paymaster Services (Pty) Ltd. v Eastern Cape Province and Others 1999 (1) SA 324 (CkH).

> the Uniform Rules of Court by making available the record of its proceedings and its reasons and such documentation as the court may need to adjudicate upon the matter and, if necessary, to file and affidavit setting out the circumstances under which the decision was arrived at."[1137]

The courts have thus made an important contribution to the interpretation of the right of access of information and to reasons in public procurement with due regard to the constitutionally defined objectives of public procurement.

However, it has to be emphasised that the provision of transparency and anti-corruption standards requires further actions and implementation in order to be effective. As Volmink states,

> "[...] despite the lofty standards contained in the Constitution and legislative framework, the *practice* of public procurement in South Africa is often marred by scandal arising from nepotism, corruption and other irregular practices."

With respect to openness and transparency fostered by PAIA, several shortcomings have been identified such as the complexity of legal regulations, lack of alternative dispute settlement mechanisms, unawareness about rights and mechanisms, lack of competency, absence of political support, institutional resistance and a lack of financial resources.[1138] Apart from the enactment of legal provisions, further action is required so as to guarantee a transparent public procurement system. It is crucial to realise that legal provisions are not the sole remedy against corruption and opaqueness in public procurement, but that there are other factors that need to be addressed at the same time; only a holistic approach can be successful. In order to improve transparency in 2011 the National Treasury issued the Instruction Note on Enhancing Compliance Monitoring and Improving Transparency and Accountability in Supply Chain Management[1139] under the authority of Section 76 (4) (c) of the PFMA. Although this Instruction Note contains useful requirements due to its legal nature it has only limited effect.

Another instrument that is relevant in respect to transparency in public procurement is the Prevention and Combating of Corrupt Activities Act[1140] which applies to all levels of government and is also applicable to

---

1137 Ibid, 353G.

1138 See for a detailed description Volmink.

1139 National Treasury, 'National Treasury Instruction Note on Enhancing Compliance Monitoring and Improving Transparency and Accountability in Supply Chain Management'.

1140 Prevention and Combating of Corrupt Activities Act 2004 (Act No. 12 of 2004).

corruption occurring in the course of public procurement. Section 12 establishes offences in respect of corrupt activities relating to contracts, and Section 13 creates offences specifically for corrupt activities relating to procuring and withdrawal of tenders. Several other instruments and institutions play a role and have responsibilities regarding the fight of corruption but the discussion of the general approach to combat corruption is beyond the scope of this dissertation.

## 6. Secondary Objectives

As mentioned above, preferential procurement plays an important role in the South African SCM system and can be attributed to the broader objective of addressing socio-economic inequalities inherited from the apartheid era. The Preferential Procurement Policy Framework Act and Regulations are the key legislative documents in regard to preferential procurement. The basic provisions will be outlined in this section, followed by a brief review of the targeted procurement policy as applied in the construction sector. Thereafter, the South African approach towards secondary objectives in public procurement will be discussed and classified in the international context.

### a. The Preferential Procurement Policy Framework Act and Regulations

According to Section 2 (1) of the PPPFA, any organ of state must determine its preferential procurement policy and implement it by using a preference point system. This preference point system allows the allocation of 10 or 20 of 100 points to specific goals. For contracts above a certain monetary threshold the 80/20 rule applies and for contracts with a value that equals or is below the threshold 10 points can be allocated for specific goals and 90 points are allocated solely by price.[1141] It has to be emphasised that Regulation 6 (3) (b) of the Framework requires that the preference point system which will be applied for evaluating a tender must be stipulated in the bid documents. The tenderer with the lowest acceptable tender, hence, receives up to 80/90 points and might be awarded additional

1141 Preferential Procurement Policy Framework Act 2000 (Act No. 5 of 2000), Sec. 2 (1) (b).

points for specific goals. All other tenderer's points on price are calculated on a pro rata basis in accordance with a prescribed formula.[1142] The contract must be awarded to the tenderer who scores the highest points, unless additional objective criteria justify the award to another tenderer.[1143] Such objective criteria do not need to be stated in the tender document.[1144]

The High Court has stressed, in this respect, that preference points can only be awarded on an objective basis and not from what can be subjectively gleaned from documents.[1145] The successful tenderer was awarded preference points although it did not complete the relevant portions of the tender documentation. It had therefore not provided sufficient information for the procuring authority to award preference points. It was held that

> "[t]he purpose of a preference point system is to award points on an objective basis in accordance with criteria and requirements objectively met and established."[1146]

In another case[1147] the court considered the question of the objective criteria justifying the award to another tenderer. It was found that the objective criteria must be criteria other than those taken account under the preference scheme during scoring. Such criteria could be found in "necessary skills, experience, good financial standing and capacity". In *Simunye Developers CC v Lovedale Public FET College*[1148] poor past performance was found to be a classic example of a criterion that justifies the award to another tenderer.[1149] It was further confirmed that there is no statutory obligation to stipulate such grounds in the tender documents.[1150] And if a tenderer obtains a contract award on account of false information in order

---

1142 Ibid, Sec. 2 (1) (c).

1143 Ibid, Sec. 2 (1) (f).

1144 Road Mac Surfacing (Pty) Ltd. v MEC for the Department of Transport and Roads, North-West Province and Others, Raubex (Pty) Ltd v MEC for the Department of Transport and Roads, North-West Province and Others, High Court (Bophuthatswana Provincial Division), [2006] ZANWHC 54: para. 33.3.

1145 Total Computer Services (Pty) Limited v. Municipal Manager Ptochefstroom Local Municipality and Others (29416/07) [2007] ZAGPHC 239; 2008 (4) SA 346 (T): para. 53.

1146 Ibid, para. 53.

1147 Lohan Civil- Tebogo Joint Venture and Anders v Mangaung Plaaslike Munisipaliteit and Anders (508/2009) [2009] ZAFSHC 46 (6 April 2009).

1148 Simunye Developers CC v Lovedale Public FET College and Another (3059/2010) [2010] ZAECGHC 121.

1149 Ibid, para. 35.

1150 Ibid, para. 33.

to secure preference points, the organ of state may cancel the contract without prejudice to any other remedies available to the organ of state.[1151]

The Act requires any goals for which points can be gained to be measurable, quantifiable and monitored for compliance.[1152] Specific goals are required to be specified in the invitation to submit a tender.[1153] Section 2 (1) (d) states that

> "[…] the specific goals may include – (i) contracting with persons, or categories of persons, historically disadvantaged by unfair discrimination on the basis of race, gender or disability; (ii) implementing the programmes of the Reconstruction and Development Programme as published in Government Gazette No. 16085 dated 23 November 1994."

The former reflects the affirmative action strategy of the government which is supposed to rectify the inequality in society which has resulted from the apartheid system. It needs to be pointed out that the wording "may include" suggests that the list is not conclusive and organs of state can identify other goals to be pursued through procurement. However, it remains unclear as to what exactly "may include" means and how wide the organs of states' discretion is in pursuing secondary objectives of any kind under the PPPFA. The constitutional provision on public procurement does not limit the kind of secondary objectives that may be pursued, either. Furthermore, Section 5 (1) of the Constitution, which requires the state to respect, protect, promote and fulfil the rights in the Bill of Rights, presupposes that any act or policy promoting any of those rights might be legitimately pursued. Section 24 of the Constitution, for example, provides for a right to an environment that is not harmful to human well-being and the protection of the environment for present and future generations. Green procurement might, hence, be possible under the current legislation but is neither required nor explicitly mentioned.[1154] The relevance of environmental procurement was totally disregarded when the PPPFA was drafted.[1155] Considering the importance of sustainability, especially in emergent developing countries, this omission can be heavily criticised.

Section 5 of the Act allows the Minister to make regulations regarding any matter that may be necessary or expedient to prescribe in order to achieve the objects of the Act. Subsection 2, moreover, requires that any

---

1151 Preferential Procurement Policy Framework Act 2000, Sec. 2 (1) (g).
1152 Ibid, Sec. 2 (2).
1153 Ibid, Sec. 2 (1) (e).
1154 Cf. Bolton, 'The Law of Government Procurement in South Africa', p. 281ff.
1155 Cf. Ibid, 282.

draft regulations be published in the Government Gazette and every Provincial Gazette before promulgation. The planning of procurement under the Preferential Procurement Regulations is three-fold; the costs of the provision of services, works or goods which are to be procured need to be estimated, the appropriate preference point system needs to be determined and stipulated, and it has to be determined whether the services, works or goods are designated for local production and content.[1156] The Regulations allow organs of state to evaluate tenders on functionality rather than price.[1157] Functionality means

> "[...] the measurement according to predetermined norms, as set out in the tender documents, of a service or commodity that is designed to be practical and useful, working or operating, taking into account, among other factors, the quality, reliability, viability and durability of a service and the technical capacity and ability of a tenderer."[1158]

The above mentioned 80/20 and 90/10 preference point systems are described in detail.[1159] Section 7 provides that a contract may be awarded to a tenderer that did not score the highest total number of points only if such an award is in accordance with Section 2 (1) (f) of the Act. Moreover, provision is made for the cancellation and re-invitation of tenders.[1160] The Regulations further outline provisions about local production and content in the award of tenders[1161] and about BBBEE Status Level Certificates[1162] and general conditions[1163] such as the qualification of trusts, consortium or joint ventures for BBBEE points.[1164]

Safeguards against misconduct and fraud can be found in Sections 12-14. Section 12 requires the tenderer to make a declaration that the information provided is true and correct, the signatory to the tender document is duly authorised and that, if required, documentary proof is provided. An organ of state has several remedies against tenderers or person which have claimed or obtained their BBBEE status level of contribution on a fraudulent basis or which have failed to fulfil any of the conditions of the con-

1156 Preferential Procurement Regulations 2011, Reg. 3.
1157 Ibid, Reg. 4.
1158 Ibid, Reg. 1 (k).
1159 Ibid, Regs. 5 and 6.
1160 Ibid, Reg. 8.
1161 Ibid, Reg. 9.
1162 Ibid, Reg. 10.
1163 Ibid, Reg. 11.
1164 Ibid, Reg. 11 (6) and (7).

tract.[1165] Remedies include the disqualification of the person from the bidding process, the recovery of all costs, losses or damages, the cancellation of the contract, blacklisting of the tenderer or contractor, its shareholders and directors and forwarding the matter for criminal prosecution.[1166] Section 14 forbids the award of a tender to a person whose tax matters have not been declared by the South African Revenue Service to be in order.

b. Targeted Procurement

The instrument of "targeted procurement" was introduced by the Department of Public Works to achieve socio-economic objectives in a fair, equitable, transparent, competitive and cost effective manner; hence, without compromising efficiency and effectiveness.[1167] The quantification, measurement, verification and auditing of social objectives within the contractual environment set by the public sector procurement regime plays a very important role in achieving positive outcomes.[1168]

Targeted procurement is described as

> "[…] a system of procurement which provides employment and business opportunities for marginalized individuals and communities, enables procurement to be used as an instrument of social policy in a fair, equitable, competitive, transparent and cost-effective manner and permits social objectives to be quantified, measured, verified and audited."[1169]

In addition to technical specifications, the tender documentation outlines the social objectives which are to be realised in the process of delivery and the manner in which they can be achieved, measured and monitored.[1170] These resource specifications

> "[…] enable bidders to quantify the social deliverables which they are prepared to offer during the bidding stage of the procurement process and allow those who

1165 Ibid, Reg. 13 (1).
1166 Ibid, Reg. 13 (2).
1167 Watermeyer, 'The use of Targeted Procurement', 233.
1168 T.E. Manchidi; I. Harmond, 'Targeted Procurement in the Republic of South Africa - An Independent Assessment', (South Africa: Department of Public Works (Republic of South Africa), International Labour Organisation, Development Bank of Southern Africa 2002), p. 1.
1169 Government of the Republic of South Africa, 'Implementation Manual on the Use of Targeted Procurement to Implement and Affirmative Procurement Policy', 2001.
1170 Watermeyer, 'The use of Targeted Procurement', 233.

> administer contracts to audit and verify that such deliverables were in fact delivered in the performance of the contract."[1171]

While the Department of Public Works initiated targeted procurement, many other organs of state have adopted the approach.[1172] The tool of targeted procurement is widely used in the construction industry and has been identified as a best practice by the Interministerial Task Team on Construction Industry Development.[1173] A Targeted Procurement Assessment conducted by national and international consultants was carried out in 2002 in order

> "[...] to assess the effectiveness of TP as a preferential procurement instrument and to determine whether the anticipated socio-economic benefits it was designed to deliver are being realized."[1174]

Although the approach to implementation was found to be unsystematic and fragmented, the impact of targeted procurement and its effectiveness in attaining its stated goals was found to be largely successful.[1175] Emerging enterprises were able to gain access to the construction industry and socio-economic benefits were delivered to the target groups.[1176] The assessment conducted on targeted procurement in South Africa recommended that "the lessons and experiences of TP be incorporated into a simple generic approach and exported regionally and internationally as best practice."[1177]

### c. Pros and Cons of the South African Preferential Procurement System

The public procurement system before 1994 rested almost solely on price considerations. Price was the single decisive criterion on which tenders were awarded.[1178] This changed substantially as the PPPFA makes the inclusion of certain secondary objectives not only possible but mandatory in

1171 Ibid.
1172 Manchidi; Harmond, 'Targeted Procurement', p. 2.
1173 Ibid.
1174 Ibid.
1175 Ibid, 9.
1176 Ibid.
1177 Ibid.
1178 Bolton, 'Government Procurement as a Policy Tool in South Africa', 201; Raga; Taylor.

today's procurement system.[1179] Nevertheless, it has to be emphasised that the price criterion is still the predominant factor influencing the tender award decision.

The South African SCM system generally allows for two different types of preferential treatment: a preference point system for BEE objectives and preferences for the local industry. Both provide for the allocation of preference points at the award stage based on the contractor's or supplier's characteristics rather than the characteristics of the products or services.

The former preference point system basically benefits the groups of persons promoted by the Broad-Based Black Economic Empowerment Act.[1180] The beneficiaries of economic empowerment under the BBBEE Act are all black people comprising Africans, Coloureds and Indians including women, workers, youth, people with disabilities and people living in rural areas.[1181] Section 1 of the Act lists preferential procurement as one socio-economic strategy to achieve BBBEE. The 80/20 (90/10) point system allows the allocation of up to 20 (10) points for the BBBEE status level of contributor. There are eight different status levels as well as non-compliant contributors. The latter receives zero points, contributors with status level eight receive two points and contributors with the status level one receive 20 points. The point allocation occurs in steps with each higher level adding two more points.[1182] In respect to the 90/10 point system status level 1 contributors receive 10 points and each lower level receives one point less.[1183] An important judgement in this respect is *Sizabonke Civils CC t/a Pilcon Projects v Zululand District Municipality*.[1184] The court stressed that any award by organs of state bound by PPPFA where fewer than the prescribed 80 (90) points were allocated to price is null and void because it contradicts the Preferential Procurement Framework Act.[1185] The issue in *Sizabonke* concerned a provision of the 2001 Regulations (Regulation 8) which allowed for a combination of 80 (90) points for

1179 It has to be pointed out, though, that the formulation of Section 217 (2) leaves sufficient leeway to alter the current mandatory towards a voluntary system. Since Section 217 (2) explicitly states that organs of state may apply preferential policies, legislation determines whether it is obligatory.

1180 Broad-Based Black Economic Empowerment Act 2003 (Act No. 53 of 2003).

1181 Ibid, Sec. 1 (Definitions).

1182 Preferential Procurement Policy Framework Act 2000, Sec. 5 (2).

1183 Ibid, Sec. 6 (2).

1184 Sizabonke Civils CC t/a Pilcon Projects v Zululand District Municipality and Others 2011 (4) SA 406 (KZP)) [2010] ZAKZPHC 23; 10878/2009.

1185 Ibid, para. 18.

price and functionality. The court held that Regulation 8 was inconsistent with the Preferential Procurement Act which requires the minimum allocation of 80 (90) points for price.[1186] Regulation 8 was redrafted and the 2011 Regulations specifically allow for the evaluation of tenders on functionality only in a prequalification stage. It allows for the determination of a minimum qualifying score for functionality that needs to be achieved in order for the tenders to be accepted.[1187] All accepted tenders then need to be evaluated in terms of the preference point system.[1188] Despite the legal error being rectified the ruling is very important as it confirms the absolute supremacy of price as the guiding criterion in awarding public contracts under the PPPFA.[1189]

In order to benefit from preferential points tenderers have to submit an original and valid BBBEE status level verification certificate or a certified copy thereof which substantiates their BBBEE rating.[1190] It is the National Treasury's responsibility to issue instructions and guidelines regarding the submission of such certificates. Beyond that the Department of Trade and Industry may publish notices in the Government Gazette in respect of submission requirements of BBBEE status level certificates.[1191] Apart from tenderers holding BBEEE status level certificates tenderers with an annual total revenue of R 5 million or less qualify as Exempted Micro Enterprises (EMEs) in terms of the BBBEE Act.[1192] The introduction of the BBBEE status level certificates in the 2011 Regulations replaces the award of preference points according to the definition of historically disadvantaged individuals (HDI). The rather broad definition has led to confusion and inconsistency and severe abuse of the preference system. The practice of fronting has especially undermined the objectives of affirmaitive procurement.[1193] Fronting describes a practice by which companies either appoint black individuals to senior positions without their knowledge and/or without transferring responsibilities and rewards associated with

1186 Ibid, para. 11.
1187 Preferential Procurement Regulations 2011, Reg. 4 (4).
1188 Ibid, Reg. 4 (5).
1189 G. Quinot, 'Public Procurement - April to June 2010(2) - JQR Public Procurement 2010(2)', Juta's Quarterly Review of South African Law (JQR), 2010, p. 2., para. 2.1.
1190 Preferential Procurement Policy Framework Act 2000, Sec. 10 (2).
1191 Ibid, Sec. 10 (3).
1192 Ibid, Sec. 10 (1).
1193 Cf. Bolton, 'Government Procurement as a Policy Tool in South Africa', 213.

these positions or establishing separate legal entities which fall under the BEE scheme but which factual perform limited or no marketing function.[1194] Fronting has been recognised as a serious threat to the objectives of procurement. It remains to be seen whether the implementation of 2011 Regulations will be effective in supressing fronting. Moreover, the HDI definition had led to some confusion. The definition of HDI has been recast in the light of the 2011 Regulations, thereby harmonising it with the BBBEE Act.

Regulation 3 (1) sets out the remedies that can be taken by an organ of state and states that

> "An organ of state must, upon detecting that –
>
> (a) the B-BBEE status level of contribution has been claimed or obtained on a fraudulent basis; or
>
> (b) any of the conditions of the contract have not been fulfilled, act against the tenderer or person awarded the contract."

The Supreme Court of Appeal established in *Viking Pony Africa Pumps v Hidro-Tech Systems*[1195] that Regulation 15 (1) of the Procurement Regulations 2011 (which can now be found in a slightly modified form in Regulation 13 (1)) imposes an obligation on an organ of state to take action as soon as it becomes aware of an act of fraud. It was held that Regulation 15 "ensures that no organ of state will remain passive in the face of evidence of fraudulent preferment but is obliged to take appropriate steps to correct the situation."[1196] The Supreme Court of Appeal's judgement has been confirmed by the Constitutional Court.[1197]

The BBBEE status is determined according to seven core elements. The direct empowerment elements are equity ownership and management control, which weigh 20% and 10% respectively. Employment equity (15%), skills development (15%), preferential procurement (20%), enterprise development (20%) and socio-economic development initiatives (5%) make up the indirect empowerment components.[1198] In contrast to the strong focus on HDI ownership, this approach gives leeway to award preference

---

1194 Raga; Taylor.

1195 Viking Pony Africa Pumps v Hidro-Tech Systems, unreported, referred to as [2010] ZASCA 23 (25 March 2010).

1196 Ibid, para. 32.

1197 Viking Pony Africa Pumps v Hidro-Tech Systems 2011 (1) SA 327 (CC).

1198 Broad-based Black Economic Empowerment Codes of Good Practice 2007 (Government Gazette No. 29617), para. 8.1.3.

points on a variety of factors aimed at BEE.[1199] This enlarges the number of potential beneficiaries and, therefore, improves competition. Since not only local but also foreign suppliers can obtain preference points under the BEE scheme foreign competitors have been put in a much better position than under the former regulations. Bolton and Quinot conclude that the system "recognizes suppliers' contributions to BEE policies across a much broader front in awarding procurement preference" and that "national social policy is still promoted in South African public procurement, but in a way that allows for much more foreign competition amongst suppliers."[1200]

Preferences for local industry had already been granted under apartheid; they were considered necessary after apartheid, as well.[1201] However, under the New Growth Path and the following Local Procurement Accord, which was signed on 31 October 2011 and sets the ambitious target to achieve a 75% localisation in the procurement of goods and services,[1202] local procurement has been facilitated. The 2011 Preferential Procurement Regulations are seen as an essential part of the strategy to increase local procurement,[1203] thereby contributing to the objective of the New Growth Path to create 5 million jobs by 2020.[1204] Under the 2011 Regulations local production and content requirements can be included as a specific tendering condition. The invitation may therefore stipulate "that only locally produced services, works or goods or locally manufactured goods with a stipulated minimum threshold for local production and content, will be considered."[1205] The application of local production and content requirements differs in designated and in non-designated sectors. Designated sectors are determined by the Department of Trade and Industry and describe sectors, sub-sectors or industries where only locally produced services, works or goods or locally manufactured goods meet the stipulated mini-

1199 Cf. Bolton; Quinot, 'Social policies in procurement and the Agreement on Government Procurement', p. 466.

1200 Ibid, 467.

1201 McCrudden, 'Buying Social Justice', p. 248.

1202 Government of the Republic of South Africa (Economic Development Department), 'New Growth Path: Accord 3 - Local Procurement Accord', (Government of the Republic of South Africa: 2011), p. 6, para. 3 (available at http://www.gov.za/sites/www.gov.za/files/Accord_Procure_3.pdf; last accessed: 30 November 2015).

1203 Ibid, 8, para. 9.

1204 Ibid, 6, para. 1.

1205 Preferential Procurement Policy Framework Act 2000, Sec. 9 (1) and (3).

mum threshold for local production and content.[1206] This means that any organ of state procuring from a designated sector has the obligation to include a specific tendering condition. In non-designated sectors, in contrast, a local production or content requirement may be included only if the condition and threshold(s) are in accordance with specific directives issued for this purpose by the National Treasury.[1207]

Local production or content requirements such as those applied in South Africa are likely to contradict WTO regulations and have attracted the attention of successive WTO Trade Policy Reviews.[1208] In South Africa they form part of the overall strategy to "arrest and reverse industrial decline".[1209] Manufacturing Circle Chairperson Jennings claimed that preferential procurement could be seen as a potential instrument to make people aware of local products, especially with a view to the challenging environment which would, inter alia, be shaped by increasing Chinese exports and administrative price increases.[1210] This is an interesting notion but in view of the fact that set-asides for local products usually do not have the envisaged effect (see Part I)[1211], this has to be considered to be a very optimistic forecast that does not adequately take into account the complexity of the matter.

The application of preferential procurement in South Africa is not without controversy. Criticism has, for example, been expressed in regard to the rigidity of the application of preference policies. Section 2 (1) of the Preferential Procurement Act and similarly Regulation 2 (2) of the 2011 Regulations provides that an organ of state must determine its preferential procurement policy and implement it within the framework provided for

1206 Ibid, Sec. 1 (i).

1207 Ibid, Sec. 9 (3).

1208 See also Government of the Republic of South Africa (Economic Development Department), 'The New Growth Path: The Framework', (Government of the Republic of South Africa: 2010), p. 8 (available at http://www.economic.gov.za/communications/publications/new-growth-path-series/download; last accessed: 30 November 2015); WTO Secretariat, 'Trade Policy Review: Southern African Customs Union - Annex 4 South Africa (WT/TPR/S/114/ZAF), 24 March 2003', (WTO: 2003), p. 248f., paras. 34-40 (available at https://www.wto.org/english/tratop_e/tpr_e/s114-0_e.doc; last accessed: 1 December 2015).

1209 M. Wait, 'SA pins reindustrialisation hopes on new procurement rules', 2012), available at http://www.engineeringnews.co.za/article/sa-pins-reindustrialisation-hopes-on-new-procurement-rules-but-constraints-persist-2012-02-03; last accessed: 17 December 2015.

1210 Ibid.

1211 Chapter 3, Subchapter 2.

in the Act. There is no real discretion left to organs of state in regard to the extent of preference policies, meaning that they are unable to grant either less or more preferential treatment. However, as Bolton recognises in this respect:

> "The "restrictive" nature of section 2(1) and Regulation 2(2), to a large extent, serve to ensure uniformity in the use of procurement as a policy tool in South Africa which, in turn, benefits the integrity and openness of the government procurement system."[1212]

The fact that preferential procurement policies have to conform to national legislation is to be welcomed since uniformity in preferential policies prevents abuse, improves legal predictability and security and makes the preferential procurement system easier for people to understand. The latter is not only important for competition as it might be decisive in encouraging a greatest possible number of bidders but also to evaluate the efficiency and effectiveness of preferential procurement. Furthermore, the obligatory nature of applying a certain preferential policy reflects the particular situation prevailing in South Africa arising from the apartheid system; some believe that preferential policies are essential to transform South Africa and overcome the historical legacy of apartheid.[1213] This notion has been emphasised by the Constitutional Court:

> "Our Constitution recognises that decades of systematic racial discrimination entrenched by the apartheid legal order cannot be eliminated without positive action being taken to achieve that result. We are required to do more than that. The effects of discrimination may continue indefinitely unless there is a commitment to end it."[1214]

The introduction of the awarding of preference points according to the BEE status level has been welcomed as an improvement over the former system in which contracting authorities had broad discretion what specific social policy objectives would earn preference points.[1215]

Bolton supports the South African preference system as price remains the decisive criterion and as the preferential treatment applied

---

1212 Bolton, 'Government Procurement as a Policy Tool in South Africa', p. 274.

1213 See also Bolton, 'The Law of Government Procurement in South Africa', p. 270.

1214 Bato Star Fishing (Pty) Ltd. v Minister of Environmental Affairs and Tourism and Others 2004 (4) SA 490 (CC); 2004 (7) BCLR 687 (CC): para. 74.

1215 Bolton; Quinot, 'Social policies in procurement and the Agreement on Government Procurement', p. 465f.

> "[...] does not amount to an infringement of the right to equality, because [...] the constitutional court has held that Section 9 of the constitution reflects a substantive conception of equality and not a formal conception of equality."[1216]

The strong emphasis on preferential treatment can be understood in the light of the South African history. And as Bolton remarks,

> "[t]here are of course time and cost-premiums involved in using procurement as a policy tool, but this should be regarded as an integral part of South Africa's growth and transformation."[1217]

The "targeted procurement" tool initially used by the Department of Public Works and nowadays applied by many other organs of state, for example, offers a great opportunity to implement secondary policies by measuring their effect contemporaneously with the tender process. Although there have been shortcomings in regard to implementation, it has been found that there is an overall positive effect. Hence, this approach should be further pursued, extended and improved.

However, the ambiguity about what other policies can be pursued through procurement can have a detrimental effect. It is proposed that it should be studied what other policies can be pursued through procurement. For example, a provision that explicitly allows for and encourages environmental procurement may make sense. It is essential to clarify that preferential policies can only be applied in accordance with instructions from the National Treasury and that they are subject to transparency standards.

Furthermore, another severe disadvantage is that there is no phase-out or exit strategy for preferential treatment. It has turned out that the preferential procurement system has "created elite classes of firms that continue to benefit from the preferential procurement policy to the disadvantage of other smaller firms."[1218] Kenya, for example, has placed a time limitation of five years on entitlement to preferences to any given bidder which can

---

1216 Bolton, 'Overview of the Government Procurement System in South Africa', p. 367f.

1217 Ibid, 368.

1218 Williams-Elegbe, 'The World Bank's Influence on Procurement Reform in Africa', 115.

be renewed once.[1219] This might be a suitable option for South Africa as well.[1220]

There have been two studies analysing the practical effect of preferential treatment. Migiro[1221] has carried out a study to explore the perception of Small, Medium and Micro-sized Enterprises (SMMEs) contractors in the Housing Department of the Gauteng Provincial Government toward BEE interventions, to determine the level of compliance with quality assurance regulations and customer needs as well as how service delivery by the Housing Department impacts on the performance of BEE Small, Medium and Micro-sized Enterprises in the industry. He came to the conclusion that the BEE interventions have a positive effect on employment and income distribution but that there were severe shortcomings in regard to service quality. Migiro recommends that "SMME contractors, who do not comply with quality assurance nor committed to the provision of the service tendered for, should be struck off of the service provider's data base."[1222] A study by Watermeyer shows that affirmative public procurement

> "[...] has not only resulted in increased participation by the target group but also in the formalisation of this sector, more structured relationships with the industry and an increase in government's tax base."[1223]

The use of targeted procurement to direct capital flows into underdeveloped or disadvantaged rural communities on conventional construction projects would have also proven successful.[1224]

The studies show that preferential procurement has been successful in achieving the objective of promoting certain groups of society. It can further lead to a formalisation of certain sectors. However, it also disclosed that preferential procurement might lead to a sacrifice in quality and, hence, value for money. This challenges the presumption that a preference

---

1219 Public Procurement and Disposal Act (No. 3 of 2005): (Preference and Reservations) Regulations 2011 (Republic of Kenya) (Legal Notice No. 58), Reg. 22.

1220 Cf. Quinot, 'Promotion of social policy ', p. 402.

1221 S.O. Migiro, 'SMEs and Black Economic Empowerment in the Construction Industry: The Case of Gauteng Provincial Housing Department', conference paper, 4th International Public Procurement Conference, Seoul, South Korea, August 26-28, 2010.

1222 Ibid, para. 1.9.

1223 Watermeyer, 'The use of Targeted Procurement', 245.

1224 Ibid, 246.

system as applied in South Africa promotes SMMEs in a sustainable way. The competitiveness of SMMEs with an inadequate commitment to service quality is probably low and impedes an enduring and successful participation in the market. The question then arises whether those SMMEs benefiting from preferential procurement would have improved the quality of their work if they competed on an equal level rather than being treated preferentially. Nevertheless, it would be possible to provide for safeguards regarding quality, in particular by improved contract administration or rewards for successful and timely contract implementation. This would allow preferential procurement to have a positive impact without sacrificing any of the objectives of public procurement.

Beyond the pursuit of secondary objectives by the use of the preference system, legal provisions specifically require suppliers, service providers and contractors to comply with existing labour standards as defined in various statutes. The Employment Equity Act[1225] for example provides that "every employer that makes an offer to conclude an agreement with an organ of state for the furnishing of supplies or services to that organ of state or for the hiring or letting of anything" must, if it is a designated employer, comply with the chapters on the prohibition against unfair discrimination and affirmative action in the Act, and, if it is not a designated employer, comply with the chapter on the prohibition against unfair discrimination.[1226] As McCrudden concludes, the legal point of these requirements is "to create a link between compliance with the Employment Equity Act, and the award of public contracts."[1227] This will compel compliance with certain standards in order to minimise the costs and thereby obtain a comparative advantage. In contrast to preference systems it does not require any additional measures that go beyond the generally required standard and, hence, does not raise the question whether it hinders competition and is inconsistent with the principle of value for money. In other words, the purchasing power of the government is used to enforce equity legislation.

1225 Act No. 55 of 1998.
1226 Employment Equity Act 1998, Sec. 53.
1227 McCrudden, 'Buying Social Justice', p. 252.

d. South African Preferential Procurement in the International Context

The scenario of joining the GPA was assessed in detail in the Green Paper. It was basically found that at that point South Africa's industries were not ready to compete either locally or on the international level because they would have "not gone through the full development cycle experienced by other developed economies."[1228] It was, however, admitted that price-based preferences that favour locally produced goods over cheaper foreign produced goods might contradict the principle of value for money and that they might contradict international trade agreements.[1229] The accession to the GPA at a later stage was, however, not at all excluded but considered realistic. Potential benefits as well as constraints were specified and analysed.[1230] The most critical issue (and fear) within South Africa is probably that a GPA accession might restrict the application of secondary objectives. Particular reference is made to the objective of the preference system, which aims to promote a more equitable spread of work and entrepreneurial opportunities amongst all sectors of South Africa's population which have been marked with gross inequalities resulting from apartheid and thus cannot be described as merely promoting protectionism.[1231] Loopholes that existed within the former version of the GPA and the limited scope were recognised as potential opportunities to continue the application of secondary policies despite being subject to the rules of the GPA. It was, furthermore, assumed that the pressure to join the GPA might increase in the future, which led to the conclusion that it is important to carefully analyse the costs and benefits of a future accession and its implications.[1232] Pressure has, in practice, been applied less strong than expected, a circumstance which might relate to the fact that the international community has been preoccupied with reforming the GPA, that development assistance has basically been excluded from the scope of the South African procurement system,[1233] and finally that in bilateral negotia-

1228 Ministry of Finance/Ministry of Public Works, para. 4.3.

1229 Ibid.

1230 Ministry of Finance/Ministry of Public Works, para. 4.4.

1231 See S. Shezi, 'Public Sector Procurement as an Instrument of Government Policy', conference paper, 9th International Public Procurement Association Conference, Copenhagen, Denmark, 8 June, 1998.

1232 Ministry of Finance/Ministry of Public Works, para 4.4.

1233 See as discussed above National Treasury, 'Practice Note Number SCM 3 of 2005: 1. Projects and Services funded by Grandts in accordance with Technical

tions a stronger focus was laid on transparency, equitability and fairness than on the discussion of affirmative procurement.[1234] McCrudden came to the conclusion that

> "[it] appears [...] that [...] South Africa has considered that it is able to prosper without joining the GPA, retain its extensive procurement linkages, and that the costs have not been too high."[1235]

Although this statement was made in 2007 it remains valid and future development might strongly depend on the success of the revised version of the GPA, which remains to be seen.

An important question that arises in the context of the South African preference policy is whether it is directly or indirectly discriminatory, or both. If local as well as foreign firms have an equal opportunity to be awarded preference points, it could be found to be only indirectly discriminatory. Whereas the requirements initially were the same for foreign as local companies, it was realised that this might pose an unfair obstacle for foreign firms and a system of "equity equivalent" contributions was introduced.[1236] Although there are certain general conditions, such as that a Multinational Enterprise (MNE) must own and control the entire equity in the local subsidiary or that the MNE would suffer substantial commercial harm if it were to implement the equity ownership requirement that applied locally, the exact requirements are left to the Minister's decision.

---

Assistance Agreements / 2. Appointment of Transaction Advisors to assist with Public Private Parternships'. A specific example is also the SA-EU Trade, Development and Cooperation Agreement (Agreement on Trade, Development and Cooperation between the European Community and its Member States, of the one part, and the Republic of South Africa, of the other part), 1999 (signed on 11 October 1999 in Pretoria and entered fully into force on 1 May 2004) which establishes that „[p]rocedures for procurement or for contracts financed by the Community are laid down in the general clauses attached to the financing agreements." (Art. 74) But it also provides that award and performance of works, supply and service contracts financed by the Community shall follow the regulations of the Agreement and specific regulations adopted by the Coordination Council. (Art. 75)

1234 The SA-EU Trade, Development and Cooperation Agreement (Agreement on Trade, Development and Cooperation between the European Community and its Member States, of the one part, and the Republic of South Africa, of the other part), 1999 provides, for example, that the Parties ‚agree to cooperate to ensure that access to the Parties' procurement contracts is governed by a system which is fair, equitable and transparent'.

1235 McCrudden, 'Buying Social Justice', p. 276.

1236 Ibid.

BBE status can be obtained by local as well as foreign competitors and is, hence, not necessarily directly discriminatory. Bolton and Quinot note in this regard:

> "The [...] approach thus allows for different types of contributions to BEE to be taken into account in relation to foreign firms and sets out how such different contributions are to be equated with the domestic criteria in calculating preference across the board. This ... approach thus at least attempts to level the playing field as far as nationality is concerned [...].[1237]"

The question remains whether it is practically more difficult for foreign competitors to obtain preference points, which would make it indirectly discriminatory under the GPA.

## 7. Review Procedures

### a. Administrative Review

The possibility of administrative enforcement of procurement matters is very limited. The application of general internal remedies to procurement is ambiguous. In general the exhaustion of all internal remedies is a necessary precondition for judicial review in South Africa,[1238] but it is unclear whether this stringently applies to judicial review in public procurement cases, in particular, because there are no clear provisions in respect of internal review procedures. It shall now be analysed whether the PFMA and - because of their specific relevance in this respect - the MFMA and the Municipal Systems Act[1239] entail provisions that establish and regulate internal review procedures.

Regulation 11 (3) of the PFMA Regulations requires National Treasury to establish an internal review mechanism. It reads as follows:

> "The National Treasury and each provincial treasury must establish a mechanism:-
>
> (a) to receive and consider complaints regarding alleged non-compliance with the prescribed minimum norms and standards; and

1237 Bolton; Quinot, 'Social policies in procurement and the Agreement on Government Procurement', p. 472.

1238 Promotion of Administrative Justice Act (South Africa), 2000 (Act No. 3 of 2000), Sec. 7(2).

1239 Act No. 32 of 2000.

> b) to make recommendations for remedial actions to be taken if non-compliance of any norms and standards is established, including recommendations of criminal steps to be taken in the case of corruption, fraud or other criminal offences"

This review mechanism should also consider complaints concerning the SCM system, since the National Treasury has the authority to prescribe norms and standards in this respect. However, there are no further procedural requirements for the review mechanism established by the National Treasury. Therefore, a multitude of questions remain such as who can complain, whether there are any deadlines or whether an internal review procedure has an impact on ongoing procurement procedures. Furthermore, it can be criticised that there is no uniform approach in regard to internal review mechanisms.

Nevertheless, on the municipal level, the applicable Municipal SCM Regulation 49 of the MFMA stipulates that persons who suffer a disadvantage due to a decision or action taken in the implementation of the SCM system are entitled to lodge a written objection of complaint to the municipality or municipal entity against the decision or action. It is explicitly stated that it is not necessary to exhaust internal remedies before seeking judicial review as it provides that a person affected is entitled to approach a court of law for the resolution of the dispute at any time.[1240] The PFMA, however, lacks such provision and it is unclear whether judicial relief may be sought without first exhausting internal remedies.

Furthermore, according to Quinot, Section 62 of the Municipal Systems Act provides a general and comprehensive internal appeal remedy that has been extensively used in the public procurement context at local government level.[1241] However, he remarks that

> "[...] the usefulness in the procurement context of [...] the appeal remedy under s. 62 of the Systems Act aimed at local government procurement, is currently in doubt. If the latest High Court interpretation of this provision stands, it will close down the major avenue of internal redress in public procurement and allow public authorities to simply circumvent internal appeals."[1242]

The High Court decision he refers to is *Loghdey v City of Cape Town* where the judge held that "only the person who has asked or applied for the decision in question may appeal against it in terms of s 62 of the Sys-

---

1240 Municipal Supply Chain Management Regulations (Local Government: Municipal Finance Management Act 2003) 2005 (No. 868 of 2005, Government Gazette No. 27636), Reg. 50 (7).

1241 Quinot, 'Enforcement of procurement law from a South African perspective', 196.

1242 Ibid.

tems Act"[1243] and specifically held that the unsuccessful tenderer would not fall under this group. Other judgements, such as *Groenewald v M5 Development*[1244], however stated that unsuccessful bidders do indeed have the right to appeal under Section 62.[1245] A noteworthy approach has been taken by the Municipality of Transvaal which allows for an appeal period of 21 days before the final award of the tender.[1246] After a decision has been taken the successful as well as the unsuccessful tenderers are notified of the decision. This notification also informs the parties of their right to appeal pursuant to Section 62 of the Systems Act and their right to request reasons pursuant to PAJA. Appeals must be submitted to the Municipal Manager. No award is made until either the expiry of the "appeal period or confirmation in writing that none of the affected parties intend to appeal, or the satisfactory resolution of any appeals." Although this leads to a slight delay of tender procedures, it avoids unsatisfying situations for both the procuring entity and tenderers that arise when judicial review procedures are invoked.[1247]

The lack of clear, unambiguous and uniform requirements and provisions for internal reviews of public procurement decisions on the local and, in particular, on the national level is a severe shortcoming and potentially undermines the effectiveness and efficiency of public procurement.

### b. Non-Judicial External Review

Bolton refers to the possibility to approach non-judicial bodies such as the public protector, the auditor-general, and the national prosecuting authority to review specific procurement aspects. The functions of the public protector are outlined in Section 182 of the Constitution. It provides the power "to investigate any conduct in state affairs, or in the public administra-

---

1243 Loghdey v City of Cape Town and Others, Advance Parking Solutions CC and Another v City of Cape Town and Others (100/09) [2010] ZAWCHC 25: p. 7, para. 12.

1244 Groenewald NO and Others v M5 Developments (Cape) (283/09) [2010] ZASCA 47; 2010 (5) SA 82 (SCA) ; [2011] 1 All SA 17 (SCA).

1245 Ibid, p. 11, para. 21.

1246 Sec. 49 of the Municipality's Procurement Policy. See also Total Computer Services (Pty) Limited v. Municipal Manager Ptochefstroom Local Municipality and Others (29416/07) [2007] ZAGPHC 239; 2008 (4) SA 346 (T): paras. 28, 62ff.

1247 See also Part II, Chapter 2, Subchapter 8.

tion in any sphere of government, that is alleged or suspected to be improper or to result in any impropriety or prejudice" and to take appropriate remedial action in this respect. The auditor-general, having the duty to audit and report on the accounts, financial statements and financial management, inter alia, of all state departments and municipalities might be approached to review budgetary irregularities in procurement procedures.[1248] Furthermore, the National Prosecuting Authority might initiate criminal investigations on behalf of the state, for example under the Prevention and Combating of Corruption Activity Act[1249]. The availability of non-judicial external review is, hence, limited to cases of improper conduct on the part of a public official, cases concerning budgetary issues and criminal matters such as corruption.

An example where these institutions have interfered with a public procurement procedure in order to investigate compliance is an arms deal conducted by the South African National Defence Force. Following a review of the procurement process by the auditor-general, it was decided to conduct joint investigations into a number of issues pertaining to the arms deal. The auditor-general, the public protector, the Directorate of Special Operations of the National Prosecuting Authority, and the Heath Special Investigation Unit were involved.[1250] Although this instance exemplifies that there are institutions that have the power to scrutinise public procurement procedures, it has to be emphasised that these non-judicial bodies are not specifically designed for internal review of procurement issues and may not be able to be approached in all cases. Moreover, there have been doubts about the former public protector office holder concerning his independence and effectiveness.[1251] Furthermore, it has been found that government departments and other public institutions disregard recommendations by the auditor-general.[1252] Since access is free, the general case load already overwhelms the public protector[1253] leading to a situa-

---

1248 Constitution of the Republic of South Africa 1996, Sec. 188 (1).

1249 Act No. 12 of 2004.

1250 See Bolton, 'The Law of Government Procurement in South Africa', p. 314f. .

1251 Hoexter, 'Administrative Law in South Africa', p. 91.

1252 Parliament of the Republic of South Africa, 'Report of the Ad Hoc Committee on the Review of Chapter 9 and Associated Institutions - A report to the National Assembly of the Parliament of South Africa' (Place: Parliament of the Republic of South Africa, 2007), p. 77.

1253 In 2010/2011 16 251 cases were received and 14 148 finalised. See Public Protector South Africa, 'Annual Report 2010/2011', 2011), p. 7 (available at

tion where it does not have the capacity to handle difficult public procurement cases. The lack of competence of existing non-judicial bodies in regard to the complexity of procurement matters coupled with the frequency of procurement issues being brought to court could be counterbalanced by establishing an independent review panel for procurement issues such as the Procurement Compliance Office envisaged in the Green Paper.

### c. Judicial Review

In South Africa public procurement litigation is prevalent and has been increasingly used in the last decade. Most disputes are heard by the High Courts. On appeal they get referred to the Supreme Court of Appeal and a number of cases have been decided by the Constitutional Court. Procurement decisions have been classified as "administrative action"[1254] and can, therefore, be reviewed under general administrative law. Section 33 of the Constitution establishes the right to just administrative action. It reads as follows

> "(1) Everyone has the right to administrative action that is lawful, reasonable and procedurally fair.
>
> (2) Everyone whose rights have been adversely affected by administrative action has; the right to be given written reasons.
>
> (3) National legislation must be enacted to give effect to these rights and must-
>
> (a) provide for the review of administrative action by a court or, where appropriate,
>
> (b) impose a duty on the state to give effect to the rights in subsections (1) and (2); an independent and impartial tribunal; and
>
> (c) promote an efficient administration."

PAJA confirms that administrative actions are subject to judicial review; it gives practical effect and substance to the constitutional rights to administrative justice.[1255] Section 6 (1) of the Act gives any person the right to institute proceedings in a court or a tribunal for the judicial review of admin-

---

http://www.pprotect.org/library/annual_report/PUBLIC%20PROTECTOR%20AR%20FINAL.pdf; last accessed: 1 December 2015).

1254 Hoexter, 'Administrative Law in South Africa', p. 184.

1255 Cf. Total Computer Services (Pty) Limited v. Municipal Manager Ptochefstroom Local Municipality and Others (29416/07) [2007] ZAGPHC 239; 2008 (4) SA 346 (T): para. 22.

istrative action. The Act names several grounds giving a court or tribunal jurisdiction to review administrative action.[1256] Among them is missing authority or bias of the administrator who took the action,[1257] the failure to comply with a mandatory and material procedure or condition,[1258] procedural unfairness,[1259] and errors of law.[1260] Challenges on the grounds of lawfulness, reasonableness, procedural fairness as well as on the basis of reasons justifying procurement decisions are of particular relevance in the public procurement context from an unsuccessful tender's perspective.[1261]

The first question arising is what particular procurement decisions fall under administrative action. The decision to award or reject a tender, the conduct of the procurement process and the evaluation of tenders have been established as falling under administrative action.[1262] The detection of fraud under Regulation 15 of the 2001 Regulations was held to constitute per se administrative action and, hence, could be challenged under PAJA.[1263] In *Chairman of the State Tender Board & Another v Supersonic Tours (Pty) Ltd.*[1264] the court established that the disqualification of a tenderer from future public contracts pursuant to the State Tender Board Act 1968 and the Preferential Procurement Policy Framework Act 2000 amount to administrative action and hence need to follow the requirements of procedural fairness and can be reviewed under PAJA.

The procedure for judicial review is outlined in Section 7 of PAJA. Proceedings for judicial review must be instituted within 180 days after the conclusion of internal remedies[1265] or after the date when

1256 Promotion of Administrative Justice Act 2000, Sec. 6 (2).
1257 Ibid, Sec. 6 (2) (a).
1258 Ibid, Sec. 6 (2) (b).
1259 Ibid, Sec. 6 (2) (c).
1260 Ibid, Sec. 6 (2) (d).
1261 Bolton, 'The Law of Government Procurement in South Africa', p. 19.
1262 See e.g. Logbro Properties CC v Bedderson NO and Others [2002] ZASCA 135; [2003] 1 All SA 424 (SCA); Total Computer Services v. Potchefstroom Local Municipality [2007] ZAGPHC 239; 2008 (4) SA 346 (T); Transnet Ltd. v Goodman Brothers (Pty) Ltd. 2001 (1) SA 853 (SCA).
1263 Viking Pony Africa Pumps v Hidro-Tech Systems, unreported, referred to as [2010] ZASCA 23 (25 March 2010): para. 34.
1264 The Chairman of the State Tender Board v. The Minister of Finance and Supersonic Tours (Pty) Ltd. (389/07) [2008] ZASCA: para. 14.
1265 Promotion of Administrative Justice Act 2000, Sec. 7 (1) (a).

"[...] the person concerned was informed of the administrative action, became aware of the action and the reasons for it or might reasonably have been expected to have become aware of the action and the reasons."[1266]

As mentioned above, it is of particular importance that, in general, judicial review is only possible if all other internal remedies are exhausted[1267] since there are no clear provisions in respect of internal review of public procurement cases. However, Section 7 (2) (c) allows for an exemption if exceptional circumstances apply and the person concerned applied for it and the court deems it in the interest of justice. A review of public procurement decisions might, therefore, also be possible without prior exhaustion of internal remedies.

The Constitution empowers courts deciding on constitutional matters within their power to grant any order that is just and equitable.[1268] The remedies available in proceedings for judicial review of administrative action can be found in Section 8 (1) of PAJA:

"The court or tribunal, in proceedings for judicial review in terms of section 6( 1), may grant any order that is just and equitable, including orders—

(a) directing the administrator—

(i) to give reasons; or

(ii) to act in the manner the court or tribunal requires;

(b) prohibiting the administrator from acting in a particular manner;

(c) setting aside the administrative action and—

(i) remitting the matter for reconsideration by the administrator, with or without directions; or

(ii) in exceptional cases—

*(aa)* substituting or varying the administrative action or correcting a defect resulting from the administrative action; or

*(bb)* directing the administrator or any other party to the proceedings to pay compensation;

(d) declaring the rights of the parties in respect of any matter to which the administrative action relates;

(e) granting a temporary interdictor other temporary relief or

(f) as to costs."

---

1266 Ibid, Sec. 7 (1) (c).
1267 Ibid, Sec. 7 (2) (a).
1268 Constitution of the Republic of South Africa 1996, Sec. 172 (1) (b).

Beyond the remedies provided for in PAJA, there are several other remedies available. Section 24 (c) of the Constitution allows courts to give directions to give reasons. Moreover, courts can grant declaratory orders of rights[1269] or of invalidity.[1270] The question whether or not the remedy of compensation might be available under administrative law is highly controversial and will not be discussed here.[1271]

An important element of public procurement review procedures - also in view to the setting aside of an award decision – is temporary interdicts. Section 8 (1) (e) allows courts or tribunals to grant temporary interdicts or other temporary relief. Interim interdicts and the requirements are well established in South African law in general and can also halt the conclusion or the implementation of a procurement contract.[1272] This prevents further performance or completion of a contract while the award decision is under review. This would render any set-aside of the decisions meaningless or in other words without this, setting aside a decision would become impossible in practical terms. In *Actaris South Africa (Pty) Ltd. v Sol Plaatje Municipality*[1273], for example, the application for an interim interdict to carry out the work under the contract awarded by the tender was granted.[1274] The effect of the judgement is emphasised by Quinot:

> "This judgement should counter the emerging trend in public procurement for contracting authorities to conclude and implement public contracts in a rush and under a protracted veil for secrecy, with the intention of reaching a critical stage of advanced performance beyond which judicial review will no longer be feasible."[1275]

---

1269 Ibid, Sec. 38.

1270 Ibid, Sec. 172 (1) (a).

1271 For detailed discussions of the issue see Bolton, 'The Law of Government Procurement in South Africa', p. 316ff; Hoexter, 'Administrative Law in South Africa', p. 568ff; Quinot, 'State Commercial Activity', p. 167ff.

1272 See, for example, Sizabonke Civils CC t/a Pilcon Projects v Zululand District Municipality and Others 2011 (4) SA 406 (KZP)) [2010] ZAKZPHC 23; 10878/2009: para. 2. Cf. also Quinot, 'Enforcement of procurement law from a South African perspective', 198.

1273 Actaris South Africa (Pty) Ltd. v. Sol Plaatje Municipality and Intelligent Metering Systems (Pty) Ltd (213/2008) [2008] ZANCHC 6; [2008] 4 All SA 168 (NC) (29 February 2008).

1274 Ibid.

1275 G. Quinot, 'Public Procurement - January to March 2008(1) - JQR Public Procurement 2008(1) ', Juta's Quarterly Review of South African Law (JQR), 2008, Sec. 2.1.

Whereas most of the remedies provided by the Constitution and PAJA can be adopted for the judicial review of procurement decisions and do not entail any insoluble problems, the setting aside of an administrative action, in particular at a later stage of the procurement process, can lead to several problems. Furthermore, it raises the question whether the judicial review procedures under PAJA can satisfy the rather complex nature of public procurement disputes. A few court cases revealing the difficulty of set-asides will be outlined in the following. Tender awards that are unreasonable can be set aside upon review. In *Mamlambo Construction CC v Port St Johns Municipality*[1276] the High court held that

> "[i]t is therefore axiomatic that any procurement contract for municipal services concluded in breach of the prescripts of those laudable principles set out above which are after all designed to ensure a transparent, cost effective and competitive tendering process in the furtherance of public interest will virtually in every instance be declared invalid and unenforceable."[1277]

However, as mentioned above, set-asides might be severely harmful for the successful tenderer; especially at an advanced stage of contract implementation, the remedy of setting aside contracts or tender awards needs to be considered critically. It might involve severe losses for the contractor or supplier who, however, has neither any claim to damages under civil law nor any other promising remedy to receive compensation for the financial losses resulting from performance already rendered on the basis of the contract that has been set aside.[1278] Beyond this, it might have significant detrimental effects on the public because it will most probably result in a delay of goods, works or service provision. This might not only cause higher costs but also have direct effects such as a delay in service or infrastructure provision. It can generally be said that set-asides can have severe implications for the efficiency of public procurement.[1279]

In *Steenkamp NO v Provincial Tender Board, Eastern Cape*[1280] the Constitutional Court confirmed that the contracting authority is not liable towards an initially successful tenderer under tort. Steenkamp, which had

---

1276 Mamlambo Construction CC v Port St Johns Municipality and Others (1876/2008) [2010] ZAECMHC 21 (24 June 2010).

1277 Ibid, para. 40.

1278 Quinot, 'State Commercial Activity', p. 288ff.

1279 Ibid, 248f.

1280 Steenkamp NO v Provincial Tender Board, Eastern Cape (CCT71/05) [2006] ZACC 16; 2007 (3) SA 121 (CC); 2007 (3) BCLR 300 (CC) (28 September 2006).

partly performed its duties under the contract awarded under the tender procedure when the contract was set aside, claimed damages for the losses suffered. The judgement is criticised by Quinot as holding "[...] implications for public procurement that may largely undermine some of the very public policy considerations upon which it is based."[1281] However, he acknowledges that the problem is not the judgement itself but "[...] rather [the] hitherto fairly unsophisticated approach to remedies following the judicial review of public tender decisions."[1282] This refers especially to the traditional approach in judicial review proceedings to simply set aside the state action when a reviewable irregularity is found; such orders are considered to be a discretionary remedy in common law and are now enshrined in the Constitution and in PAJA.[1283]

However, in *Millenium Waste Management v Chairperson Tender Board*[1284] the court applied a more careful approach by conditioning the set-aside of a tender award upon an evaluation by the tender board of the appellant's tender, which had been incorrectly excluded from consideration, against the winning tenderer. In other words, the court referred the matter back to the administrator rather than setting the decision aside.

In *Eskom Holdings Limited and Another v New Reclamation Group (Pty) Ltd.*[1285] the court held that there were no public policy considerations which militate against setting aside the award of the tender. It distinguished the situation at hand from another case where the court refused to set the invalid tender award aside due to the fact that, between the launching of the proceedings and the judgement in the court, a quo work had been performed, making it impractical to start the tender process over again for the completion of the remaining work. In contrast, this case concerned a contract to collect material and its subsequent processing and sale, something which could be done by any contractor with the necessary resources, even at this stage.[1286] In *Chairperson: Standing Tender Com-*

1281 G. Quinot, 'Worse than Losing a Government Tender: Winning it' (2008) 19 Stellenbosch Law Review, 101-121 at 101.

1282 Ibid.

1283 Ibid, 118.

1284 Millenium Wast Management (Pty) Ltd. v Chairperson, Tender Board: Limpopo Province 2008(2) SA 481 (SCA); [2007] SCA 165 (RSA).

1285 Eskom Holdings Limited and Another v New Reclamation Group (Pty) Ltd. (358/08) [2009] ZASCA 8; 2009 (4) SA 628 (SCA) ; 2009 (8) BCLR 813 (SCA) ; [2009] 2 All SA 513 (SCA).

1286 Ibid, paras. 16f.

*mittee and Others v JFE Sapela Electronics (Pty) Ltd. and Others*[1287] the court held that

> "[...] the circumstances of the present case [...] are such that it falls within the category of those cases where by reason of the effluxion of time (and intervening events) an invalid administrative act must be permitted to stand."[1288]

A set-aside would give rise to several problems not only in relation to a new tender process but also in relation to the work to be performed since the repair and maintenance components of the contracts were interrelated.[1289]

It can be concluded that a decision to set aside a tender depends on different factors such as the nature of the procured work, products or service, the degree of contract implementation and public policy considerations. Although the courts have tried to balance the different interests and have delivered important judgements in this regard, an assessment of the general suitability of judicial review procedures and remedies under general administrative law for public procurement cases should be conducted, especially with a view to its effect on the principles of value for money and competition. Bidders might, for example, be discouraged from taking part in bidding if they bear the full (financial) risk that the decisions might be set aside a long time after winning the tender. Although it seems that the South African courts have treated the issue of set-asides very sensitively, being aware of the negative impact such decisions might have, the procurement delay and costs that arise if a tender award is set aside are enormous. Hence, additional and alternative approaches such as a standstill period and effective internal review mechanisms might be beneficial to the efficiency and effectiveness of public procurement proceedings and review procedures. Furthermore, it is of the utmost importance to establish an independent review mechanism specifically for public procurement cases to decouple those cases from general administrative law cases and give due regard to the special nature of public procurement challenges. Judicial review should only be seen as last resort.

---

1287 Chairperson: Standing Tender Committee and Others v JFE Sapela Electronics (Pty) Ltd. and Others (511/2004) [2005] ZASCA 90; 2008 (2) SA 638 (SCA) ; [2005] 4 All SA 487 (SCA).

1288 Ibid, para. 29.

1289 Ibid, para. 27.

### d. The main Principles of Public Procurement in South African Case Law

There have been a multitude of court decisions in the field of public procurement, dealing with the clarification of tenders, timeframes in tender procedures, the formulation of tender criteria, and the question of substance vs. form. The courts have constantly referred to the major principles of procurement as stated in the Constitution. Particular emphasis has been put on fairness in tender procedures. A few examples will be outlined in the following in order to provide an impression of how South African courts deal with public procurement cases.

In Metro Projects CC v Klerksdorp Local Municipality[1290] the court held that

> "[…] fairness must be decided on the circumstances of each case. It may in given circumstances be fair to ask a tenderer to explain an ambiguity in its tender; it may be fair to allow a tenderer to correct an obvious mistake; it may, particularly in a complex tender, be fair to ask for clarification or details required for its proper evaluation. Whatever is done may not cause the process to lose the attribute of fairness or, in the local government sphere, the attributes of transparency, competitiveness and cost effectiveness."[1291]

However, the court also recognised that, in certain cases, it might be difficult to assess whether "[…] less than perfect compliance falls on one side or the other of the validity divide."[1292]

Another decision emphasised that "[f]airness entails a consideration not only of the interests of the excluded tenderer […] but also the interests of all the constituents who are effected thereby".[1293] This would include the state as the sole shareholder of the South African Airways, the taxpayer whose taxes to a large extent fund the operations of the airline and the public who have to rely on the services that are tenderer for.[1294] In this case the timeframe to prepare a tender has found to be unfair as it was not sufficient to prepare an adequate proposal.

---

1290 Metro Projects CC and Another v Klerksdorp Local Municipality and Others [2003] ZASCA 91; [2004] 1 All SA 504 (SCA).

1291 Ibid, 10, para. 13.

1292 Ibid, 11, para. 15.

1293 Menzies Aviation South Africa (Pty) Limited v South African Airways (Pty) Ltd. and Others (08/22988) [2009] ZAGPJHC 65 (4 December 2009): para. 38.

1294 Ibid.

In *Minister of Social Development and Pensions v Phoenix Cash and Carry CC*[1295] a tenderer had been disqualified because the form of a proof of financial resources it submitted was not exactly as the examples given in the bid conditions. The court basically drew two conclusions: First, that uncertain bid conditions contradict the principle of fairness not only between the tenderers but also in regard to the relationship between tenderers and the public body.[1296] Secondly, that

> "[...] a process which lays undue emphasis on form at the expense of substance facilitates corrupt practice by providing an excuse for avoiding the consideration of substance; it is inimical to fairness, competitiveness and cost-effectiveness."[1297]

The court stressed that there is a "difference between formal shortcomings which go to the heart of the process and the elevation of matters of subsidiary importance to a level which determines the fate of the tender."[1298]

A similar problem has been discussed in *Millenium Waste Management (Pty) Ltd. v Chairperson, Tender Board: Limpopo Province*[1299]. The appellant in this case had been disqualified for failing to sign a form titled "declaration of interest". From 14 companies that applied for the tender twelve others were also excluded because of failing to comply with administrative or technical requirements. The remaining company was then awarded the tender. Millenium Waste Management applied for an order reviewing and setting aside the decision to award the tender. The court addressed the issue whether the disqualification of the appellant's tender violated its right to procedural fairness. The acceptance of non-compliance with peremptory requirements is permissible if it is not incompatible with public interest, and in this case it would have even served public interest as it would have stimulated competition. The court thus found that

> "[b]y condoning the failure the tender committee would have promoted the values of fairness, competitiveness and cost-effectiveness which are listed in s 217. The appellant had tendered to provide the needed service at a cost of R444 244,43 per month whereas the consortium had quoted and was awarded the tender at the amount of R3 642 257,28 per month."[1300]

---

1295 Minister of Social Development and Pensions v Phoenix Cash and Carry CC [2007] SCA 26 (RSA).

1296 Ibid, para. 2 (1).

1297 Ibid, para. 2 (2).

1298 Ibid.

1299 Millenium Wast Management (Pty) Ltd. v Chairperson, Tender Board: Limpopo Province 2008(2) SA 481 (SCA); [2007] SCA 165 (RSA).

1300 Ibid, para. 17.

The court also suggested that the regulations certainly did not envisage that a tender must comply with conditions which are immaterial, unreasonable or unconstitutional.[1301]

The strong focus on public interest and on the principles of fairness, competitiveness and cost-effectiveness is to be highly welcomed as it furthers the primary goal of public procurement to receive a high quality product or service at a reasonable price. The case law shows that the principle of value for money has priority over minor formal errors. It can be said that procurement officials are granted a certain degree of discretion to accept procedural deficiencies if this helps to achieve value for money. Although such approach bears some risks, such as an abuse of the discretion in decision-making, in contrast to the approach of strictly adhering to formal and procedural requirements, it tends to produce better results in achieving value for money.

Quinot has identified another potential risk of this approach. Although he welcomes the stronger focus on substance than on form, he points out that it would complicate the work of tender committees and open the door to increased litigation in an already litigious field. He explains:

> "All tender committees will hence have to exercise a discretion using the nebulous criterion of compatibility with the public interest to decide whether tenders that do not strictly conform to tender conditions need to be excluded or not."[1302]

And, of course, Quinot's concern is legitimate. Nevertheless, in the long run, it can be expected that the discretion of officials will become less problematic as they gain more experience. The long-term aim of value for money seems to justify a temporary increase of litigation in this field.

### e. Problems in the South African Public Procurement Review Mechanisms

In order to avoid discouraging bidders from bidding for public tenders, it is necessary to create an environment of trust, including the creation of effective, immediate and easily accessible review mechanisms. The South African procurement system does not provide for a procurement-specific complaint system and there is no specific alternative dispute settlement

---

1301 Ibid, para. 19.

1302 G. Quinot, 'Public Procurement - April to June 2008(2) - JQR Public Procurement 2008(2)', Juta's Quarterly Review of South African Law (JQR), 2008, Sec. 2.1.

mechanism, for example an ombudsman who can be approached if a tenderer feels that it has been treated unfairly. The administrative review system in South Africa is highly fragmented and there are several ambiguities in regard to its application. As a result suppliers have relied heavily on judicial review, which is unsatisfactory.[1303] Although it has to be stressed that in general courts have played a crucial role in supervising the activities of administrative agencies[1304] and have delivered important judgements, in view of the problems judicial review entails, such as costs and length, the need to create an alternative and, particularly, independent dispute mechanism, becomes urgent. The 180-day timeframe granted under PAJA for issuing judicial reviews[1305] might not be appropriate for public procurement cases given the fact that most of the contracts are concluded and might even have been performed in the meanwhile. The time and costs involved have severe implications for the stakeholders involved, not only for the successful and unsuccessful bidder but also for the public waiting for its tax money to be properly spent in a timely manner. Additionally, it has to be kept in mind that ordinary courts might lack experience in delivering high-value judgements on procurement matters, which are legally diverse and fragmented. The application of administrative law does not satisfy the complexity and the legal nature of public procurement, which cannot be conceptualised in terms of the public/private law distinction and usually is of a multilateral nature with several stakeholders involved.[1306] A report of the Development of the Working Party on Aid Effectiveness and Donor Practices considers the South African dispute resolution system in regard to public procurement as an area of immediate concern. According to the report two staff members are forced to spend their entire time in court. The report recommends the establishment of an informal dispute resolution mechanism.[1307] Quinot stresses in this respect that it would be necessary to develop remedies that suffice the require-

1303 In *South African Post Office v De Lacy 2009 (5) SA 255 (SCA)* the court held at para. 1: “Cases concerning tenders in the public sphere are coming before the courts with disturbing frequency.” See also Quinot, 'A comparative perspective on supplier remedies', p. 334.

1304 Hoexter, 'Administrative Law in South Africa', p. 64.

1305 Promotion of Administrative Justice Act 2000, Sec. 7 (1).

1306 Cf. Quinot, 'Worse than Losing a Government Tender', 118f.

1307 2nd Joint OECD/DAC - World Bank Round Table on Strengthening Procurement Capacities in Developing Countires - Summary Report (DCD/DAC/EFF/M(2004)3), Kampala, Uganda, 2 April 2004.

ments of Section 217 of the Constitution. He stresses that, in the South African-specific context, which implies a large-scale policy function in redressing the inequalities caused by colonisation and apartheid and the economic realities of South Africa, with its tremendous socio-economic needs and severely limited resources, courts are certainly not the best institutions to act as primary enforcement agents.[1308]

However, as Hoexter remarks, judicial review might even become more prominent than it was in the past, because of the liberalisation of the constitutional rules and the codification of the grounds associated with administrative-law review in PAJA.[1309] The author dashes any hopes for the creation of administrative appeals mechanisms.[1310] The proposal for the establishment of administrative appeal and review mechanisms made by the Law Commission in 1999[1311] did not reflect in PAJA. Hoexter takes the pessimistic view that, "[t]he reform of this area of law is probably as remote a contingency as it has ever been."[1312]

## 8. Conclusion

Despite substantial reform efforts and the enactment of a clear policy, the laws governing public procurement are still highly fragmented. Quinot, for example, notes, "[…] the body of rules that can be said to constitute South African public procurement law is far from coherent or structured in any systematic way."[1313] There is no single comprehensive public procurement statute or code, but several laws from different fields apply. Additionally, there is no uniform scope of application of the rules on public procurement. Moreover, the fact that the State Tender Board Act has still not been repealed is somehow irritating and the status of the Act should be clarified as soon as possible. Nevertheless, procurement-specific regulations, case

1308 Quinot, 'Enforcement of procurement law from a South African perspective', 206f.

1309 Hoexter, 'Administrative Law in South Africa', p. 64.

1310 Ibid, 71f.

1311 South African Law Reform Commission, 'Report on Administrative Justice, South African Law Reform Commission Project 115', (South African Law Reform Commission: 1999), available at http://www.justice.gov.za/salrc/reports/r_prj115_aja_1999aug.pdf; last accessed: 1 December 2015.

1312 Hoexter, 'Administrative Law in South Africa', p. 72.

1313 Quinot, 'Enforcement of procurement law from a South African perspective', 194.

law and academic attention have led to the evolution of public procurement law as distinct discipline.[1314]

Integration of procurement and financial management has been forged in South Africa and this has been assessed positively.[1315] Wittig remarks that

> "[t]he goal of continuous improvement in public sector procurement requires a clear lead and strong commitment through sound management practices. This, together with the basic values and principles governing public administration as enshrined in the new South African constitution, provided a framework to develop sound organisational and institutional arrangements that will result in a public procurement system which becomes more efficient and effective."[1316]

The pillars of procurement as cited in the Constitution are recited in the PFMA/MFMA. Beyond this Section 3 (2) (a) of PAJA requires public procurement procedures which fall under administrative processes to be lawful, procedurally fair and justifiable. The constitutional principles are interrelated and interconnected[1317] and the courts have shown their commitment to enforce the principles of Section 217. Such a strong focus on the basic pillars of procurement is to be welcomed because, although the South African system still discloses many problems and shortcomings, striving for compliance with these principles is a key factor for an efficient and effective procurement system.

The vision to create a Procurement Compliance Office as contemplated in the Green Paper has not been put into practice. Nevertheless, the National Treasury has assumed most functions and responsibilities that were envisaged for the Procurement Compliance Office. The work of the National Treasury, e.g. the Instruction Note on Enhancing Compliance Monitoring and Improving Transparency and Accountability in Supply Chain Management, exemplifies that problems are being addressed and that the National Treasury is taking its responsibility seriously. It might be an indication that the transfer of responsibility for public procurement to the National Treasury was a well-conceived reform that, in the long run, will lead to an effective and efficient public procurement system. In addition, it suggests that the linkage of financial management and public procurement

1314 Cf. ibid, 193f.

1315 See also Development Assistance Committee, 'Strengthening Procurement Capacities ', p. 29.

1316 Wittig, 'Building Value through Public Procurement', p. 16.

1317 See Bolton, 'Overview of the Government Procurement System in South Africa', p. 362.

can be effective as it involves a certain amount of internal control. However, since the National Treasury, in contrast to the originally envisaged Procurement Compliance Office, is not independent, a system of external and independent control should be set up.

South Africa has established a comprehensive system of training public procurement officials. Moreover, the qualifications of public procurement officials and staff are outlined in detail and ensure that only suitably qualified personnel are employed. In order to prevent vacancies and maintaining existing procurement expertise, a transition period of five years allows procurement officials to obtain the necessary qualifications. Apart from training and qualification requirements, provisions to counteract abuse and corrupt practices have been implemented in South Africa, including ethical standards as well as disciplinary measures to sanction misbehaviour.

South Africa follows a very balanced approach by giving effect to cost-effectiveness and competition. Despite a strong emphasis on preferential treatment, procurement price has remained the most important criteria for the award decision. Moreover, principles such as uniformity, sufficient advertising, adequate time frames and designing specifications in an unbiased manner have been implemented in order to ensure competition and cost-effectiveness. [1318] Fairness and transparency have been ensured through several provisions, such as requirements concerning the publication of basic information about the procurement proceedings and providing for the disclosure of conflicts of interests, [1319] but several shortcomings exist if compared with international best practices. It is absolutely necessary to review and amend the current law and regulations in this respect in order to strengthen fairness and transparency.

The pursuit of the two general objectives to promote the principles of good governance and to address socio-economic goals is a different approach than most western countries have chosen but seems appropriate given the particular South African situation, especially, since price remains the major evaluation criterion and the preference system follows basic transparency requirements. Preference schemes and how they work are clearly indicated, thereby making accountability possible. The points system is good in so far as it establishes that 80/90 points are allocated solely on the basis of price. Another positive development is that, under the new regulations, BBBEE status is not only measured by owner-

1318 Cf. ibid, 365f.
1319 Cf. ibid, 366.

ship/management criteria but on the basis of other criteria. BBBEE status can therefore be achieved by anyone and is no longer restricted to a particular type of supplier of contractor. The strong focus on value for money, transparency and fairness is also reflected in the application of preferential procurement. The introduction of a two-stage tender process if tenders are evaluated on functionality is also to be welcomed in this context because it does not undermine the preference points system with 80/90 points exclusive for price and, hence, does not conflict with the principle of value for money. Although preferential procurement as applied in South Africa is per se condemned by many as a protectionist measure, it has to be acknowledged that the preference system is in itself transparent and enables officials to be held accountable. This is a factor that should not to be disregarded. However, objective reasons that might justify the award to another tender are not further defined in legislation and have only been considered in case law. This vagueness gives procurement officials broad discretion. Another problem in regard to the preference system is fronting. It exemplifies that measures have to be found that ensure the effectiveness of the preference system. The regulations requiring bidders to proof compliance with other regulations such as labour laws, tax requirements, etc., is a very positive development. This can strengthen the rule of law and induce companies to comply with the law more scrupulously.

South Africa considered GPA accession but instead has decided to establish an extensive preference system. Considering the limited membership of the GPA and that the South African reservations are shared by many other developing countries this decision is hardly surprising.

Although South Africa's strong focus on preferences is understandable and while admitting that its approach to preferential procurement should not be rejected per se, it is questionable why it is not earmarked as a temporary strategy. This was also proposed by some parties during the drafting process of Section 217, but the proposal was apparently rejected.[1320] Nevertheless – although no explicit reference can be found that signals that preferential procurement might be of a temporary nature - it has to be pointed out that Section 217 (2) – in contrast to the PPPFA - does not make the implementation of preferential policies obligatory, but rather subjects the organs of state's discretion in applying preferential policies application to the disciplines of the applicable implementing legislation.

1320 Report from Theme Committee One, South Africa, Block 5: The Economy, 12 June 1995, Document A 28.

Hence, although not clearly stated, a temporary use of preferential procurement policies is not precluded by the South African Constitution.[1321] It is clear that transformation needs time, but it should be emphasised that preferences are not granted forever in order to incentivise companies to become competitive in the market in the long run.

The review mechanisms available in the procurement system are insufficient. The primary review mechanism available is judicial review, which utilises the South African courts. Although the courts have responded very well to the specific circumstances of public procurement and have delivered judgements that clarify and improve the system, litigation should only be the last resort, especially, in view of the length and costs of judicial proceedings. The internal review mechanisms are ambiguous and limited in scope and should be clarified, improved and extended. There is also a need for alternative, more easily accessible, non-judicial review mechanisms in order to relieve the courts and enable speedy and less costly dispute resolution. It is, therefore, necessary to establish clear and comprehensible regulations on a review mechanism to improve the system, create confidence and satisfy the rule of law standards.

It can be concluded that the SCM, which links financial management and procurement, is potentially very efficient and effective. In particular, the allocation of responsibilities to the National Treasury and financial auditors creates a system of internal control and does not require the establishment of a new institution which might pose a major obstacle in developing countries in view of their capacities and resources. Nevertheless, existing shortcomings still severely hamper the efficiency and the effectiveness of public procurement. On-going revision and enhancements are necessary in order to improve the public procurement system and to achieve the objectives pursued.

---

1321 Cf. Bolton, 'The Law of Government Procurement in South Africa', p. 61, 264.

## *Chapter 5: Best Practices in Public Procurement*

This chapter includes the main findings and results of the foregoing comparative analysis of the GPA, the UNCITRAL Model Law, the COMESA procurement provisions, the Mauritian and the South African public procurement system. In a short introduction, the potential benefits of considering international and foreign public procurement provisions shall be explained. Then, best practices that have been derived from the analysis in the previous chapters are presented. Last but not least, lessons learned from the Mauritian and the South African approaches to the regulation of public procurement are summarised.

### 1. Introduction

Potential benefits for domestic reform processes may be gained from looking at both international best practices, such as contemplated in the GPA and the UNCITRAL Model Law, and at foreign national public procurement systems. It can even be said that such an approach is essential in order to produce a modern public procurement system.

The UNCITRAL Model Law has been specifically designed to be used as a model for national public procurement systems. Additionally, the Guide to Enactment offers a good opportunity to understand the rationale behind the provisions of the Model Law and a solid basis on which to make choices between different approaches. It permits decision-makers to design and implement a successful reform process as it indicates what needs to be considered in the reform processes. The UNCITRAL Model Law offers a range of international best practices in regard to scope, procedures and methods, transparency, secondary objectives, review mechanisms while providing flexibility to adapt the provision to national conditions and circumstances. However, the rules-based approach followed by the Model Law might still be too strict to be suitable for implementation in all countries. As legal traditions and customs vary to quite an extent, the provision of general guidelines and best practices for public procurement systems might be more suitable than such a pre-formulated blueprint. Moreover, the implementation of the provisions of the Model Law might be problematic if the institutional and organisational capacity as well as other components of the public procurement systems necessary for such implementation have not been established or put in place. This is due to the fact that the UNCITRAL Model Law does not offer a holistic public procurement reform solution.

Apart from the best practices provided by the UNCITRAL Model Law, it is also recommendable to consider the basic requirements in regard to transparency, procedures and mechanisms as well as review mechanisms as stipulated in the GPA when reforming national public procurement systems. This is not only because they reflect best practices but also in view to a possible future accession to the GPA which might lead to improved market access and enhanced competition, encourage foreign direct investment and provide the possibility of participating in the further development of the GPA.[1322] An accession might, for example, be induced by growing membership of the GPA. The consideration of the GPA in national reform processes in order to make use of its best practices has become even more worthwhile since the review of the GPA resulting in a new text produced in 2012 led to the inclusion of domestic welfare objectives such as integrity and the fight against corruption. The GPA and the UNCITRAL Model Law have thus been harmonised to a certain extent during their reviews and their principles do not dramatically diverge. Nonetheless, the strong focus on non-discrimination deters many (developing) countries from assessing the possibility of their future accession at all and also from making any reference to it during the reform process. This is unfortunate because it is worth discussing the pros and cons of preferential procurement under the premises of the GPA in the long run rather than generally refusing to liberalise national public procurement markets. If a decision is taken for the application of preferential treatment, it is recommendable to design the law in a way that does not impede a later renunciation of preferential treatment. This is not only beneficial if a country eventually decides to join the GPA but also if it finds preferential treatment no longer feasible or effective to achieve the envisaged objectives and decides to liberalise its national public procurement market.

Moreover, it is highly recommendable to assess the possibility of a regional harmonisation of public procurement during the reform process along the lines taken in the COMESA region. A liberalisation of public procurement markets on the regional level might enhance competition and stimulate cross-border trade. For many developing countries this might be

1322 Cf. Arrowsmith, 'Reviewing the GPA', 769. See also Anderson; et al., 'Assessing the value of future accessions to the WTO Agreement on Government Procurement', 131.

– as a first step - preferable to a complete liberalisation on the international level. And if regional trade agreements or unions exist, the harmonisation of public procurement markets is even more likely to succeed as existing structures and institutions can be used. However, it is necessary to analyse to what extent harmonisation is necessary in order to achieve the envisaged objectives such as to stimulate competition; the objectives do not necessarily require a harmonisation of procurement rules. The use of common standards and procedures, in particular transparency standards, and the provision of assistance in the bidding process might be easier to achieve and might suffice to achieve the envisaged objectives.

As both, the UNCITRAL Model Law and also the GPA do not provide a holistic approach to reform national public procurement systems, the way other countries having implemented the Model Law into national law should be examined in order to ensure that all pillars and stages of public procurement are successfully addressed. The UNCITRAL Model Law does not include provisions on procurement planning and contract management and does not offer solutions in regard to the institutional and organisational structure of public procurement systems. It is desirable to look at such national systems with similar conditions that have been identified as having modern public procurement legislations. An additional benefit is that deficits identified in the application of other countries' public procurement systems based on the Model Law can provide lessons learned, so that similar mistakes are avoided and alternative approaches are implemented. Foreign national public procurement systems should hence be carefully and critically assessed in view of international best practices in order to make use of beneficial provisions and avoid the adoption of deficient provisions. The Mauritian public procurement system, for example, offers certain progressive and useful elements, but also lacks clarity in regard to certain aspects.

Apart from the above mentioned possibilities, the examination of countries following a completely different approach than the UNCITRAL Model Law, for example South Africa, is useful in regard to specific aspects. Certain elements found to be beneficial and suitable to achieve a certain objective might be integrated into a national public procurement system. The integration of procurement and financial management by allocating the responsibilities to the National Treasury and financial auditors, i.e. the approach taken by South Africa, can, for example, lead to innovative and progressive approaches and have a positive effect on the outcome of public procurement. Adherence to international best practices should, however, be ensured. Additionally, if a common situation prevails in two countries, such as the inequalities in South Africa and Namibia resulting from apartheid, possible solutions to address this situation can be found by looking at the other country's approach.

## 2. Best Practices in Public Procurement Legal Systems

The analysis in the foregoing chapters has yielded best practices for public procurement legal systems that can be used as guidelines to draft public procurement legislation. Rather than specific recommendations regarding legal provisions, these best practices are formulated in a general way allowing an adaptation to local circumstances and conditions. To improve clarity, best practices are presented according to the following aspects of public procurement: objectives, institutional and organisational form, workforce, scope, procedures and methods in different phases of procurement, secondary objectives, transparency, and review mechanisms.

The public procurement procedure is divided into five different stages: procurement planning, pre-bidding phase, bidding phase, award phase, and contract management. It should be noted beforehand that it is recommendable that all necessary basic provisions regarding public procurement are established in the public procurement legislative acts rather than other legislation such as those concerning general administrative law. This is important in order to allow stakeholders, including procurement officers and potential bidders, to easily get an overview of the rules and regulations governing the procurement system. It also facilitates challenge procedures. Moreover, important general matters should be dealt with in the primary legislation and details in secondary legislation. This makes it easier to implement new procedures into public procurement legislation without changing primary legislation.

### a. Objectives

There are certain objectives that are commonly accepted as being part of public procurement systems. Although their wording or description is not uniform, the following objectives can be identified as contributing to best practices: transparency and accountability, fairness and equal treatment, value for money, efficiency and effectiveness, and integrity. Mentioning these objectives in the preamble is useful as a reference point; such a technique not only establishes a framework in which provisions are to be interpreted but also makes clear what is envisaged and to be achieved. All institutions and individuals involved in public procurement procedures should be required to adhere to those objectives at all times. There is also the possibility of establishing these objectives in the constitution as South Africa did. However, it should be ensured that such objectives are not only mentioned but are also reflected in the legal provisions themselves.

### b. Institutional and Organisational Form

As the organisation of public procurement heavily depends on the capacity and resources available - which are critical issues in many developing countries – it should be ensured that the institutional design is adequate and appropriate and can be realistically implemented. Strong policy and monitoring institutions with a variety of functions and powers require an adequate number of qualified staff and the availability of resources. If such institutions are established by law despite the absence of those capacities and resources, they will be ineffective and will not be able to fulfil their role. The creation of a smaller institution or the use of an existing institution to assume those functions and powers is probably the better choice leading to a better result. In particular, policy functions can be transferred to relevant institutions such as the national treasury or another department of the ministry of finance while monitoring and review institutions should be independent from political interference.

There are certain guidelines and criteria that should be followed in order to establish an institutional framework serving the aforementioned objectives of public procurement. It is recommended to create procurement units within the procuring entities to be responsible for public procurements at least up to a certain monetary threshold. In general the procuring entities best know what they need and have the best knowledge of the subject matter. This approach is hence more efficient and involves less bureaucratic efforts than having an external institution carry out procurement. It is recommendable to assign the responsibility for public procurements to a certain department or unit within the procuring entity, such as the accounting officer. However, in particular where states have long followed a centralised procurement system and procuring entities lack knowledge and expertise in public procurement processes and practices, it is possible to allow for gradual decentralisation. In this case procurements above a certain value would be procured by a central procurement board in order to ensure that they are carried out effectively and efficiently and for transparency reasons.

It is of great advantage to establish an institution or office with a policy function. The policy function may include the development of public procurement policies, the provision of assistance to bidders, setting standards, issuing standardised bidding documents and guidelines on public procurement procedures for procurement officials and bidders, and interacting with the business community to evaluate procurement procedures and identify possible legislative and practical shortcomings. This is important in order to constantly improve the public procurement system, react to problems arising within the system and to further the objectives of public procurement. Such policy office could also be responsible for dealing with public procurement challenges at the administrative level. While the use of existing structures such as the National Treasury in South Africa might be recommendable in the first place, it is worth considering to gradually transferring the functions and powers to a new, independent institution.

Establishing an oversight institution that closely monitors and reviews the public procurement system is especially important from the perspective of transparency, accountability and in particular the prevention of corruption. Its responsibilities may include the approval of annual procurement plans, the review and validation of procurements above a certain threshold and the review of public procurement procedures on a random basis. Such institutions should be independent and be equipped with the powers necessary to effectively carry out their functions, such as the power to request for information, records and other documents. Given that in many developing countries establishing institutions that operate successfully and efficiently takes some time due to a lack of resources, capacity and political will, it might be preferable to temporary allocate the functions and powers to existing institutions such as anti-corruption bodies or the auditor-general. It is also possible to provide for independent validation by a probity auditor or the involvement of stakeholders with regard to high value procurements in order to ensure a minimum of control.[1323]

The provision for (ad-hoc) independent evaluation committees for certain procurements, for example high value, complex and critical procurements, can also contribute to increased transparency and accountability because the effect of these committees would be to separate the powers in accordance with the different procurement phases. However, it is not rec-

1323 Cf. OECD, 'OECD Principles for Integrity in Public Procurement', p. 25.

ommendable to establish such committees in all procurement cases because the costs and efforts would outweigh the gains. The members of such evaluation committees should be independent, not be involved in decision-making in any form or belong to the procuring entity and should have extensive knowledge and experience with regard to the subject matter.

Apart from the definition of procuring entities and the establishment of a central procurement board, an oversight and policy institution and bid evaluation committees, the creation of independent institutions responsible for handling public procurement challenges is essential. This will be discussed below. The overall objective of the institutions should be to establish a separation of powers with checks and balances. This means that the respective powers and functions are clearly assigned and separated. It also requires that the responsibility for decisions made at key points is shared by at least two persons to guarantee a minimum of control and to ensure impartiality.[1324] It is further important to ensure that institutions can work effectively and efficiently in practice considering the capacities and resources available.

### c. Workforce

As procurement institutions need to be equipped with qualified staff but also, as corruption is a major problem in most public procurement systems, the provisions regarding the workforce have to be ascribed importance and be carefully designed. This includes the establishment of a qualification system and entry requirements as well as the clear allocation of power to recruit staff and of the responsibility for education and training measures. When drafting a law it is recommendable to design a provision granting a transitional period to obtain qualifications. This is important in order to guarantee a certain degree of continuity, to sufficiently qualify existing procurement staff and to avoid vacant positions. Continuing training and education measures are important to keep up with the changing business environment, the development of new ideas and concepts in public procurement and to refresh public procurement knowledge

1324 Cf. ibid, 25; see also United Nations Office on Drugs and Crime, 'Guidebook on anti-corruption in public procurement and the management of public finances', p. 21.

and sensitivity. In order to help attract and retain highly skilled professionals in public procurement, it is of utmost importance to provide adequate employment conditions and incentives.[1325]

With regard to the public procurement workforce, it is also indispensable to establish a framework for action of officials and staff and to clearly outline what kind of conduct is not tolerated and will be sanctioned. This is essential for preventing corruption and can be implemented by adopting a code of conduct. It is further of utmost importance to have legislation in place that protects whistleblowers as this is essential for the disclosure of corruption. However, as corruption and other misconduct is not one-sided and potential bidders and suppliers and other stakeholders of public procurement are likewise susceptible to irregular and corrupt practices, there should also be provisions to make them aware what consequences certain misconduct has by issuing a code of conduct for public procurement stakeholders. In order for such codes of conduct and of public procurement legislation in general to be effective, it should be ensured that any failure to adhere to the law is made an offence and is appropriately sanctioned. This might ensure that provisions are taken seriously, that misbehaviour is sanctioned adequately and further provide deterrence to misconduct. Last but not least, the avoidance of conflicts of interest is important with respect to the prevention of corruption. Consequently, the disclosure of interests and sanctions for the failure to do so should be regulated in public procurement law.[1326]

#### d. Scope

The scope of public procurement law is of essential importance for the effectiveness of public procurement systems. All public procurements should be subject to the basic rules of public procurement and strengthen the rule of law. Exemptions are not necessary if the law is flexible enough to accommodate all types of procurements. If exemptions for certain types of procurements are nevertheless granted, it is important to ensure that exemptions are justified and approved by an oversight authority. For exam-

1325 See OECD, 'OECD Principles for Integrity in Public Procurement', p. 30.

1326 For further mechanisms to prevent risks to integrity in public procurement with respect to the workforce see ibid, 34f.; see also United Nations Office on Drugs and Crime, 'Guidebook on anti-corruption in public procurement and the management of public finances'.

ple, general exemptions for procurements financed by external donors are not recommendable, but exemptions may be justified if there are benefits with regard to expertise and development experience in a particular field and the donor insists on the exemption. This is essential for the prevention of abuse and in order to prevent legal limbos. While most public procurement systems cover the procurement of goods and services, other commercial operations, such as the disposal of state assets, can also fall under the scope of public procurement law. It has to be carefully analysed whether the provisions are generally suitable for the type of operation, if the regulation cannot be better placed in a distinct piece of legislation and if public procurement institutions are equipped to carry out the respective functions.

#### e. Procedures and Methods

When developing procedures and methods, it is important to ensure that the legal provisions cover the whole public procurement cycle. Failures to regulate important steps and phases have negative effects not only on the procurement outcome in the specific case but also for future procurement outcomes. The procurement cycle has five phases, as has been mentioned above.[1327]

##### i. Procurement Planning

In the first phase procurement planning, public procurement legislation should require the publication and approval of annual public procurement plans, at least for public procurements above a certain threshold. It is further recommendable to require the publication of such plans on a national public procurement website which is easily accessible by everyone. Annual public procurement plans not only ensure that there is no rush to spend money at the end of the financial year, but also for other reasons such as predictability and to promote competition. Moreover, unnecessary or excessive procurements can be avoided by way of being identified and unapproved by the institution responsible for approving the annual public procurement plans.

1327 See Part I, Chapter 1, Subchapter 4.

### ii. Pre-bidding Phase

When regulating the pre-bidding phase quite a number of issues have to be considered and clearly and precisely translated into legislation. Apart from open bidding, which should be the general procurement method, there should be alternative procurement methods that can be applied according to the type, value and complexity of procurement. Moreover, prequalification procedures or two-stage procurement can, for example, be used for high value or highly technical and complex procurements, allowing for negotiations in the first stage where only technical bids are considered and only those bidders accepted submit financial bids in the second stage. Negotiation procedures have to be handled carefully as they might lead to a deficit of accountability since they, for example, severely increase the discretion of procurement officials, are more difficult to monitor and evaluate and, hence, should only be possible in specific circumstances, for example, if the lowest evaluated bid is above the estimated costs and a re-invitation is considered impractical. However, there are different procedures available and the most advantageous procedure can only be determined on a case-by-case basis; this should be considered when drafting public procurement legislation. It has to be ensured that the methods are appropriate in the specific circumstances and that the costs, duration and complexity of the procedure is appropriate with regard to the type, value and complexity of public procurement and in view of the objectives. This is essential in order to make a public procurement system efficient and effective. Procedures throwing up bureaucratic roadblocks and thereby unnecessarily limiting competition, such as the use of mandatory supplier lists, should be prohibited. Non-exclusive lists can, however, be used for collecting and saving certain information and therefore limiting bureaucratic costs for officials and also for bidders. If alternative methods are used for procurements above certain thresholds, this should require approval and the recording and publication of reasons. For such cases there should be a requirement that the most competitive method available in the circumstances is used. This not only prevents corruption but also facilitates transparency, accountability and competition. If thresholds are used to determine procurement methods, there should also be a provision prohibiting the splitting of contracts with the intention to evade the threshold in order to avoid abuse in this regard.

To formulate bidding requirements, a needs assessment has to be made. At this stage, the engagement of external experts can be considered and a respective provision can be included in public procurement legislation.

This can lead to an improvement of the knowledge base and to the formulation of bidding documents in the best way according to the law and to the market conditions in order to promote competition and stimulate research and innovation. However, it is necessary to require such experts to be unbiased, independent and have no interest in the specific procurement outcome. It is also possible to make provision for public hearings for certain procurements (high value, critical, complex, e.g. large investment projects) to get input from stakeholders (ideas, suggestions, objections) and to make sure that potential bidders and suppliers best know what the procuring entity wants. Advantages can be better value for money, increased efficiency and fairness, and the prevention of the failure of the procurement.

Bidding documents should be required to entail comprehensive information regarding the subject matter, qualification criteria and their relative importance, and contract conditions. It is recommendable to assign the responsibility to draft standard bidding documents to a suitable institution such as the policy office. Standard bidding documents not only promote participation and hence competition, but also facilitate monitoring and reviewing. Since the nature of the bidding criteria can be crucial for the public procurement outcome, it is necessary to ensure that the selection of criteria is governed by certain requirements allowing for the greatest degree of competition possible. Therefore, it is indispensable that criteria are formulated in an objective and generic way, any reference to any brand name, patent, name, specific origin or other reference that limits competition in an unnecessary way is generally prohibited, national or international standards are used where possible, and that criteria are function- or performance-related rather than descriptive or design-related. If there is no other possibility than referring to a brand name, trademark, etc. or the use of design or descriptive criteria is unavoidable, it has to be required that it is only used to describe the product or service and that anyone can bid. This is of the utmost importance to ensure fairness and to promote competition. It is further recommendable to require weighting methods to be absolute rather than relative in order to limit the discretion of procurement officers during bid evaluation, to prevent abuse and corruption at this stage, and to make decisions more comprehensible. The use of functional rather than design criteria has the additional value that it stimulates research and innovation. Award criteria other than price should also be objective and may include quality, technical merit, environmental characteristics, terms of delivery, etc. The UNCITRAL Model Law sets out an illustrative list of award criteria which can be used as reference point. Award criteria should be quantifiable and expressed in monetary terms, so as to guarantee fairness and prevent abuse. It is recommendable to allow both for the selection of the lowest and the most advantageous tender. The selection method should, however, be required to be stipulated in the bidding document.

Other factors important for the drafting of bidding documents and essential for the efficiency and effectiveness of public procurement are deadlines, bid validity, bid securities, regulations for cancellation of bidding processes, etc. The requirement to determine bid validity within a certain period of time is important to ensuring efficiency and effectiveness. Other requirements such as proof that a bidder is not insolvent, the company is properly registered, complies with the tax laws, safety laws, social security obligations, labour conditions, etc. should also be implemented in legislation. The exclusion of companies not fulfilling such requirements can have many benefits, including the prevention of failure in contract implementation, the punishment of misconduct, securing adherence to laws, and fairness as no one should have an advantage because cost savings are made by disobeying laws or standards. Last but not least, criteria for the contents of contracts, payment and termination and breaches should be required to be included in the bidding documents.

After the bid documents have been drafted, they have to be published. Public procurement legislation should make provision for the place, time and manner of publication. It is recommended to require the publication of bid invitations and all bidding documents on a national procurement website. It is also possible to stipulate that a summary of the procurement invitation is published with reference to the contact details where bidding documents can be obtained in another place such as national newspapers or a tender bulletin. For procurements above a certain level, publication in English or another language used commonly on the international level or in the region concerned should be required to promote competition on the international level. Bidding documents should be made available online and free of charge and be accessible at least until the expiry of the deadline for submission. The publication requirements serve different objectives, including fairness, the promotion of competition, and facilitating participation of bidders and suppliers on the national and international level (including SME's). Provision can also be made for public bid openings for contracts above a certain level or publication of the same information communicated in public bid opening on the national procurement website. Information may include the name of the bidders, the total amount of each bid, any discount or alternative offered, the posting of bid security. This can allow bidders to assess their chances and to let bidders know whether their bid is complete.

### iii. Bidding Phase

During the bidding phase only a few issues require regulation. This includes the alteration of bidding documents which has to be communicated in the same form and manner as the bid invitation. Furthermore, questions by bidders or suppliers with respect to bidding documents or criteria should be required to be answered and communicated to all potential bidders and suppliers in order to guarantee fairness, value for money and to allow bidders to prepare the best bid with view to the envisaged procurement outcome. Another factor that can be stipulated in public procurement legislation is technical assistance in bid preparation. Technical assistance can facilitate the participation of SMEs, ensure that no one is excluded from participating because of bureaucratic hindrances, and create trust and confidence in the public procurement system and institutions. This is of specific importance to SMEs. The policy office can, for example, be mandated to provide such assistance.

### iv. Award Phase

Phase 4, the award or evaluation phase, has to be assigned particular importance as corruption often takes place at this stage. First of all, the evaluation should be required to take place according to criteria and methods as outlined in bidding documents. The criteria should be uniformly applied to all bidders. For procurements above a certain threshold, complex or very technical procurements the establishment of independent evaluation committees can be provided for. This can ensure qualitative, unbiased decision making and therefore prevent corruption. To prevent bids from being excluded because of formal errors, the evaluation committee should be allowed to ask for clarification. However, any financial or substantive amendment of bids should be prohibited to ensure fairness and prevent corruption. It is also recommendable to make provisions for abnormally low tenders, such as the possibility to enquire whether the bidder can comply with the conditions of participation and is able of fulfilling the terms of the contract in order to prevent cost-increases at a later stage, deficits in quality and contract implementation in general. The evaluation process should be comprehensively recorded, including a detailed description of the examination and evaluation of bids and the identification of the bid winner. This is important to ensure transparency and fairness and to facilitate review and monitoring. If the best bidder has been identified, this will need to be communicated to all bidders which should be required by law. Such notification should at least contain the name and price of the winning tender and the nature and quantity of the product or service. The best practices at this stage include the provision of a standstill period to allow challenges by unsatisfied bidders and suppliers before the contract is concluded. The procuring entity should also be obliged to give reasons for its decision and explanations on its practices and procedures if requested by unsatisfied bidders. This can prevent litigation at a later stage and ensure that errors made are identified at an early stage, thereby avoiding implications for contract implementation and guaranteeing fairness. The length of the standstill period can either be fixed by law or decided by the procuring entity on a case-by-case basis, but should be specified in the bidding documents and the provisional award notification. The non-application of a standstill period should only be allowed in specific circumstances, e.g., where there is an urgent public interest, and should require approval and a provision of reasons. This phase ends with the conclusion of a contract according to the contract conditions outlined in the bidding document.

#### v. Contract Management

The final stage is contract management. It is essential to ensure by law that contract implementation is monitored to ensure value for money, quality and adherence to laws, required standards and conditions. Expansions or variations of contracts should generally be prohibited and only be allowed in certain circumstances within a limited monetary range. Otherwise bidders might hand in lower bids in order to be awarded a contract and then increase costs during contract implementation. Appropriate structures have to be set up while taking into account the skills, experience and functions required for the execution and monitoring of public procurement contracts. It is also possible to make provision for certain safeguards such as withholding part of the payment until the contractor has proved that required standards have been complied with. If, for example, workers have not been paid according to the conditions, the money withheld can be used to pay workers the outstanding amount. With regard to the improvement of working conditions and standards and in the wider sense socio-economic development and the rule of law, such an approach can promote such objectives. It is recommendable to make provision for the debarment or blacklisting of bidders involved in corrupt practices and contractors not in compliance with the laws or obligatory standards and conditions as well as for the failure to keep records in order to prevent future failures and to punish and deter misconduct. This should, however, be required to be communicated to the contractors, who should be allowed to submit their opinion and to file an objection. Blacklists should be published and the blacklisting of contractors should be limited to a certain period of time. Problems and shortcomings identified in public procurement procedures should be required to be brought to the attention of a responsible institution such as the policy office. This is an important step to constantly improve the public procurement system. A requirement to issue a report about contract implementation for procurements above a certain threshold, or which are very complex or technical can, for example, facilitate transparency and make it easier to identify lessons learned.

### f. Secondary Objectives

Secondary objectives in public procurement are a controversial issue and their benefits are difficult to determine. Hence, if secondary objectives are pursued through procurement, a public procurement law should include safeguards ensuring that the primary objectives of public procurement are not sacrificed. These include, for example, a requirement that secondary policies have to be based on legal provisions regulating its application or on directives issued by the policy office and are not applied as ad hoc measures. Discrimination through qualification, examination or evaluation criteria should generally be prohibited. Furthermore, there should be certain transparency requirements with respect to secondary objectives. Any such objective or policy should be clearly stated in the bidding documents as well as its weighting which should be in monetary terms if possible in order to ensure fairness and accountability. To ensure that secondary policies are only in place until the desired objectives have been achieved, there should be a requirement that they are transitional measures and that their application is reviewed after a certain period of time. The review of secondary objectives is of the utmost importance as secondary policies can have a severe impact on value for money and on the effectiveness of public procurement procedures. Therefore, it could be required to report on the use and success of secondary policies, at least for procurements above a certain level.

### g. Transparency

Transparency as a key objective of public procurement has to be translated into legislation and there are several requirements and provisions that can be considered best practices in this respect. However, it should also be stressed that the transparency provisions can only be effective if they are accompanied by measures such as the establishment of alternative dispute settlement mechanisms, the creation of awareness of rights and mechanisms, competency of public procurement staff, etc. Transparency in public procurement comprises access to information, the right to request reasons, disclosure of conflicts of interest and accountability. It is recommendable to require the publication of all information on public procurement in a place easily accessible by everyone, such as a national procurement website. The objectives of transparency, accountability and the promotion of competition can be likewise achieved by such regulation. The information necessary to be published basically includes at least the publication of all laws and regulations governing public procurement, judicial decisions and administrative rulings with precedential value, annual procurement plans, bid invitations, bidding documents, reasons for the choice of alternative procurement methods if a certain threshold is exceeded, alteration of and additional information on bidding documents, the provisional award decision, information about initiated challenges, and a report or statement on contract implementation for procurements above a certain threshold. Moreover, the requirement to publish statements of reasons even in the absence of a request can be regarded as exemplary with view to achieving the objectives of transparency and accountability. The provision of the UNCITRAL Model Law and the GPA can be used as references for best practices in this respect. Nevertheless, the right of access to information has to be balanced with the confidentiality of information which must be guaranteed in public procurement in order to protect business interests and to establish confidence and trust in the public procurement system and its institutions. Reasons for withholding information might be that disclosure would impede law enforcement, be contrary to the public interest, prejudice the legitimate commercial interest of particular enterprises or prejudice fair competition between suppliers.

Apart from the publication of information, recording of the whole tender process and of all contract awards for a minimum period of time such as three years is necessary and should be required by law. The form and manner and where those records are kept should be clearly defined.

Furthermore, it is vital for reasons of transparency, effectiveness and the prevention of corruption to create a system of accountability by ensuring that there is an institution responsible for oversight and auditing and the investigation of complaints. Additionally, any misconduct should be sanctioned and non-adherence to public procurement legislation should be made an offence in order to prevent, deter, and punish misconduct and violations. Furthermore, any conflict of interest should be required to be disclosed so as to avoid situations vulnerable to corruption and to ensure transparency and accountability. To facilitate transparency and accountability and, in particular, monitoring but also to render possible an improvement of the system, annual reports should be required to be filed by the procuring entities and other relevant institutions such as the central procurement board for review by the policy office or other oversight institutions.

## h. Review Mechanisms

To ensure effectiveness and fairness in public procurement procedures, certain best practices in regard to challenge procedures should be followed. There should be a right to challenge if someone has experienced or fears a loss or injury because of non-compliance with the public procurement legislation. All decisions or actions under public procurement legislation should be reviewable including the choice of procurement method. In order to prevent unnecessary and inappropriate disturbance of public procurement procedures, provision can be made for a deposit to be paid by a challenger which is forfeited if the challenge is dismissed as frivolous. As indicated above,[1328] there should be a provision requiring a standstill period after the provisional award has been made in order to allow unsatisfied bidders to challenge a decision. This avoids disruptions to the public procurement process after the contract has been signed. Any public procurement legislation should include suitable remedies and specify the institutions having jurisdiction over reviews and make explicit reference to

1328 See Subchapter (e) (iv) of this chapter.

their power to apply the remedies. Remedies important in public procurement systems include rapid interim measures such as injunctive relief, temporary suspension, but also measures for the correction of breach, loss of damages, and the opportunity to participate in ongoing procedures.

Any public procurement legislation should require the establishment of internal review procedures. It is recommendable to follow a uniform approach and be clear and unambiguous about procedures and responsibilities. It is possible to make provision for a direct review by a responsible officer or department in the procuring entity or an administrative review by the policy office. The procedure as well as timelines should be clearly established. Such an internal review mechanism can avoid litigation and increase transparency and accountability as well as trust and confidence. It is important to ensure that there is the possibility to suspend the public procurement procedure until the challenge is resolved. Any internal review procedure decisions need to be challengeable before an independent review mechanism or court. Apart from an administrative review mechanism, an independent review mechanism can significantly contribute to the achievement of the public procurement objectives of fairness and accountability. As the establishment of such an institution requires capacities and resources which are often limited, its form and procedures can be more or less informal. This can also be beneficial in regard to accessibility, costs and duration of challenge procedures. It should, however, be ensured that procedures are transparent, that basic procedural rights are granted and that an appeal to courts is possible. The (political) independence and impartiality of such an institution is a key factor for the objectives fairness and accountability. Judicial review should always be mentioned as last resort rather than as primary instance. Problems such as costs and duration make judicial review unsuitable as sole review mechanism. Judicial review is, however, important for developing the law, establishing guidelines and setting limits on the exercise of discretion.

## 3. Lessons Learned from Mauritius

Mauritius has a quite modern procurement system which can potentially be used as a model for other developing countries. However, a review of the Mauritian system has revealed several shortcomings. These have been addressed through amendments and issuance of regulations and directives. It has also become obvious that certain provisions have been made for a specific reason such as keeping the Central Procurement Board to allow for a gradual decentralisation.[1329] It is of the utmost importance to evaluate secondary legislation and policy documents as well as to understand the motivation and reasons of the lawmakers in order to find suitable solutions for other countries. The fact that shortcomings became evident not long after the enactment of the law and regulations and that amendments or additional, new provisions have been found to be necessary shows that a constant assessment and review of the public procurement system should be provided for. It should be clearly specified who is responsible for the assessment and the review and enough capacities should be raised for such review purposes.

The establishment of a public policy office according to the Mauritian model is generally of great advantage. However, as the Mauritian policy office has a broad field of application and is vested with a variety of functions and duties, it is essential to first conduct further research about the functionality of the policy office in Mauritius and whether the situation regarding capacity and resources is comparable to that of the interested country. The policy office is assigned an important role in the Mauritian public procurement system and the efficiency and effectiveness much depends on whether it can meet its responsibilities. The adoption of the legislative framework in regard to the policy office can only be recommended if it is ensured that there are enough capacities and resources to guarantee the functionality of such an important and influential institution.

The approach of setting up evaluation committees from a list of potential committee members for each procurement case seems to bear advantages but might also have cost-implications and requires the availability of suitably qualified experts. The advantages include that experts having experience and knowledge of the procurement matter can be selected and that the non-permanence of membership in evaluation committees make corruption and abuse less likely. Ideally, the evaluation committee should be independent rather than being members of any public body, especially in high-value projects. Furthermore, it is essential to set up minimum qualification requirements for evaluation committee members. However, the advantages of bid evaluation committees might not be suitable for certain types of public procurements. In particular, in low-value procurements or procurements which are not complex the costs and time involved might not be appropriate. If, for example, procurement decisions are simply taken according the criterion of price and there is not much

1329 See above Part II, Chapter 3, Subchapter 4 (c).

controversy about such decision, it might be more cost-efficient to have the decision taken by a permanent evaluation committee within the procuring entity. It could, hence, be suggested for other developing countries to provide for the establishment of bid evaluation committees for high-value or complex procurements while maintaining internal evaluation committees for other procurement decisions.

In regard to public procurement staff, the provisions on integrity of personnel are very extensive, but the Act and the Regulations remain silent on the required qualifications and expertise of procurement staff. It should be emphasised and ensured that adequate ways are found to build and choose those capacities.

Including certain requirements such as on the content of bidding documents, evaluation procedures, criteria for technical specifications, in the Act or regulations is of the utmost importance. Mauritius has failed to set requirements on most of these issues, and has so far only provided for certain requirements in directives or the user guide which is insufficient because they should have the force of law.

The transparency standards of the Mauritian system are comprehensive and can be regarded as guideline for other countries. However, it might be advantageous to specify how records are made, saved and maintained, especially in view of e-procurement. One example is the establishment of a national procurement website consolidating all necessary information on public procurement, including the invitation to bids by all procuring entities, the evaluation reports, the tender notifications, all laws, regulations, directives, and the decisions of the independent review panel. Any (developing) country reforming its public procurement system should invest all the necessary means in order to guarantee the establishment of such website.

With respect to secondary objectives, other developing countries would be well advised to have a particular look at the contract conditions in regard to labour standards if adherence to labour standards and conditions are a major problem or it is envisaged to promote such standards and conditions through procurement. The transfer of the responsibility of ensuring compliance with those laws from other institutions to those responsible for contract management can be a suitable mechanism to ensure compliance with standards and conditions and to counteract abuses during contract implementation.

The Mauritian Public Procurement Act and Regulations allow for preferential treatment and require it to be transparent and according to the requirements set by the Policy Office. Moreover, preferential treatment is limited to domestic or regional goods, services, suppliers or contractors; hence, the scope for the application of secondary policies is limited. In so far it is in line with best practices. Nevertheless, it is also important to establish clear definitions and guidelines for preferential treatment. Additionally, secondary policies should be implemented only temporarily rather than for an indefinite period and be subject to constant review. Therefore, the Mauritian approach would need to be supplemented by additional provisions and requirements in order to ensure that secondary policies not hinder the efficiency and effectiveness of public procurement system.

The establishment of an independent review panel should be considered by any country reforming its public procurement system. Furthermore, it should be clearly analysed whether the informality of the independent review panel's procedure is suitable in the national context taking into account factors such as the prevailing culture of review mechanisms, transparency standards, the degree of political control as well as capacities and resources. Moreover, it has to be ensured that the panel or tribunal has the appropriate staff and resources to be able to effectively exercise its mandate. The introduction of a standstill period as in Mauritius might be of great advantage in all countries as challenges after the signature of the contract and in particular set-asides of contracts raise additional legal issues such as claims for damages. A review at an early stage makes it easier to rectify any failure or error and minimise damage for all parties involved.

## 4. Lessons Learned from South Africa

First of all it is important to say that the South African system differs to quite an extent from other approaches such as the UNCTIRAL Model Law. Therefore, following the South African model may hinder harmonisation. Nevertheless, the South African approach to decouple public procurement from being purely administrative work and establishing a Supply Chain Management system is very progressive and acknowledges the nature of public procurement. The focus on financial management and efficiency is to be welcomed. Additionally, the constitutionalisation of public procurement emphasises its importance in the course of socio-economic development and its role in the relationship between the state and its people. Any country should ensure that public procurement is no longer regarded as being solely an administrative exercise and that the right of the people to an efficient and effective, fair, transparent and accountable public procurement system is adequately respected and reflected in the legal framework and the whole public procurement system.

It can be beneficial to look at South Africa's public procurement system in several respects. For elements that have not been addressed solutions may be developed on the basis of international best practices.

Decentralisation has been carried out very similarly to the Mauritian approach. While establishing Supply Chain Management units, the institution of the central tender board has temporarily be kept in operation. Nevertheless, similar to the objective of gradual decentralisation followed in Mauritius, the South African approach has from the beginning emphasised that the tender board will be abolished as soon as the procuring entities are able to carry out all procurements. A gradual decentralisation to Supply Chain Management units in the procuring entities is recommendable for other countries which have followed a centralised system and want to decentralise in the long run. Whether the existing central procurement board should be kept in order to carry out public procurement above a certain threshold does not need to be decided until a later stage. Instead, a constant review of the threshold level could be provided for in order to assess whether a further decentralisation is beneficial or whether maintaining the institution of the central procurement board for the award of particular tenders would be advantageous.

In South Africa, the National Treasury functions well and seems to be fulfilling its responsibilities; however, it is not independent as the Procurement Compliance Office envisaged in the Green Paper was supposed to be. Regarding the objective of minimising corruption and political influence in public procurement, it would be recommendable for other countries to create an independent oversight authority and a policy office. Nevertheless, considering the success of assigning the authority of public procurement to the National Treasury in South Africa as well as the limited resources and capacity to establish a completely new institution in other developing countries, it might be worth to consider following the South African approach which might be easier and better implemented in the local context. However, further research should be conducted on the functioning of public procurement institutions in e.g. Mauritius in order to better estimate the potential success of establishing a new independent policy office. Alternatively, responsibilities and functions could be assigned to an existing institution while building an independent institution and gradually transferring powers and responsibilities as the new institution builds its capacities and resources.

South Africa has set out clear requirements for institutions and staff and has ensured that all public procurement officials have the opportunity to get training and receive the minimum qualifications required for staff members and that adequate training facilities are available to qualify procurement professionals. It has also implemented a provision allowing public procurement officials not having the required qualification under the reformed public procurement rules a period of five years to acquire the needed qualifications. This might be an important provision in the context of other developing countries where procurement capacity and expertise is rare. As human capacity is a pillar of a well-functioning procurement system the comprehensive South African approach could be followed or should at least be considered by other countries.

Although the methods and procedures in the South African procurement system have been regulated well, it might be better to look at the UNCITRAL Model Law in order to facilitate trade and foreign investment. Since the procurement methods and procedures as outlined the Model Law are well known within Africa and beyond, such harmonisation might be beneficial in the long run.

The transparency standards are insufficient and it would not be wise to follow the South African approach in this respect. If the publication and documentation of essential public procurement information at all stages of the procurement procedure is not ensured, competition is hampered and procurement officials can hardly be held accountable for their decisions. Certain elements such as the online availability of a government tender bulletin where all tender notices publishes might, however, be taken over.

The South African approach to secondary objectives has to be seen in light of its history and has to be seen as specifically aiming at redressing the imbalances resulting from the apartheid era. The approach to address socio-economic goals can nevertheless serve as a role model for the design of similar laws in countries having experienced strong forms of discrimination in the past which have led to stark socio-economic imbalances. It would, however, be necessary to consider the actual success the South African preferential system has brought. Nevertheless, it has to be noted that it remains a decision of general principle whether preferential procurement can lead to substantive improvement of the socio-economic situation or is rather impeding development (see discussion in Part I, Chapter 3). The strict provisions on the implementation of preferential procurement in South Africa make the process transparent and comprehensible. This is preferable to the approach taken by Mauritius which has failed to implement a comprehensive policy for its preference policy. Especially since preferential treatment seems to be one of the most important issues in reforming its public procurement system, the road South Africa took to promote affirmative action in public procurement should be closely examined. Specific tools such as "targeted procurement" that have proven to be successful in achieving socio-economic objectives can be adopted as best practices. However, the shortcomings identified in South Africa, such as the failure to set a time limit for the application of preferential policies and to make any reference to other specific goals that might be pursued should be addressed when designing a new procurement framework.

The challenge procedure in South Africa, primarily based on judicial review, is insufficient. The courts have played a major role in enhancing the public procurement system, but the time and costs involved as well as the lack of appropriate remedies and time frames are insufficient and do not live up to the requirements for review procedures of a modern, efficient and effective procurement system. In light of these shortcomings it would be more profitable to look at the GPA and the UNCITRAL Model Law or consider the approach taken by Mauritius instead.

# PART III: Namibia as a Case Study: Public Procurement Law and Reform

This part deals with the Namibian public procurement legislation and reform process. First of all, the Namibian public procurement system and regulations applicable prior to the reform are outlined and critically analysed with regard to the best practices developed in the previous part of this dissertation. Thereafter, essential aspects that need to be considered in public procurement reform processes in order to lead to a successful reform outcome are identified and explained, including organisational as well as substantial considerations. These general theoretical observations regarding public procurement reform processes then form the basis for the analysis of the Namibian reform process, which will be examined according to the guidelines developed in the previous chapter. Recommendations for substantive changes when implementing the new public procurement bill will be presented. Lessons learned from Namibia as well as an overall conclusion regarding public procurement law and reform are outlined in the final chapter.

## *Chapter 1: The Namibian Public Procurement Law*[1330]

In this chapter the Namibian public procurement system and regulations are critically analysed and evaluated according to the basic pattern used in Part II and with a view to the best practices developed from the analysis of the GPA, the UNCITRAL Model Law, and the Mauritian and the South African public procurement systems and regulations. Shortcomings as well as positive elements of the Namibian system and legislation are identified in order to highlight required changes and modification as well as provisions that might be worth to be kept in the new public procurement system. After identifying the laws and policies applicable to public procurement, the objectives and principles as well as the scope of the public procurement legislation is outlined. Thereafter, the organisational structure is presented with a focus on the institutions governing public procurement processes and the workforce. After the procurement methods and procedures applicable in the Namibian public procurement system are examined, the regulations regarding tender specification, award criteria and evaluation methods are analysed. This sets the stage for an analysis of general as well as procurement-specific transparency issues and strategies to counteract corruption. Secondary objectives as pursued under the public procurement system before the reform are then presented and evaluated. In this context, the special role of Chinese construction companies in the Namibian public procurement system is laid out. This section discloses many shortcomings of the public procurement as well as in the implementation of the law. Last but not least, the review procedures applicable to public procurement disputes in Namibia are outlined, followed by an analysis of Namibian case law concerning public procurement.

### 1. Introduction

The current Namibian public procurement system and practices have led to severe criticism on a number of different issues. The frequent use of an exemption clause – which allows tender boards to procure goods or services without inviting tenders if it deems it impracticable or inappropriate

---

1330 Unreported Namibian case law is cited from the website of SAFLII (www.saflii.org , last accessed: 16 December 2015).

– has especially caused resentment.[1331] The extreme lack of transparency within the procurement system has also led to criticism.[1332] Moreover, the preferential procurement as provided for in the current procurement system has not led to the expected results, prompting calls for a "Namibianisation" of tenders.[1333] Another critical issue is that tenders in particular in the construction sector have often been awarded to Chinese firms which do not respect existing labour laws.[1334] An increasing number of court applications and cases in the field of public procurement also indicates that the current public procurement system is deficient and lacks the confidence of tenderers.[1335]

1331 Links; Daniels, 'The Tender Board - Need for Root and Branch Reform', p. 3. See also 'Government tender exemptions balloon' (Newspaper article), The Namibian (Windhoek, Namibia), 13 September 2011; 'Bring An End To Tender Exemptions (Editorial)' (Newspaper article), The Namibian (Windhoek, Namibia), 1 February 2013.

1332 Links; Daniels, 'The Tender Board - Need for Root and Branch Reform', p. 9ff. See also F. Links, 'Corruption Prevention: Strengthening Systems, Procedures and Practices', Occasional Paper No. 6/2010 (Hanns Seidel Foundation Namibia: 2010), p. 7f. (available at http://www.hss.de/fileadmin/namibia/downloads/FredericoLinks_CorruptionPrevention.pdf; last accessed: 29 November 2015).

1333 Links; Daniels, 'The Tender Board - Need for Root and Branch Reform; Appendix I - Interview with Tender Board Secretary Welma Enssle', p. 18; Links; Daniels, 'The Tender Board - Need for Root and Branch Reform', p. 12ff. See also Links, 'Corruption Prevention: Strengthening Systems, Procedures and Practices', p. 7; 'Tender Board tightens rules to protect jobs' (Newspaper article), The Namibian (Windhoek, Namibia), 3 February 2010.

1334 See a number of newspaper articles: 'Namibia: "Chinese invasion" - old foes police a new frontier ', Sunday Times (Johannesburg, South Africa), 28 March 2011; 'Construction work at Chinese company at Rundu stopped', The Namibian (Windhoek, Namibia), 14 August 2008; 'Chinese Confronted on Labour Abuse', The New Era (Windhoek, Namibia), 24 August 2006; 'Pohamba Calls for Respect of Labour Laws', The New Era (Windhoek, Namibia), 13 May 2013; 'Rundu road workers sign contracts', The Namibian (Windhoek, Namibia), 10 June 2008;'China should respect labour laws', Informanté (Windhoek, Namibia), 29 August 2012.

1335 Cf. Links, 'Corruption Prevention: Strengthening Systems, Procedures and Practices', p. 6.

## 2. The Framework

### a. Laws and Policies regarding Public Procurement on different Levels of Government Structure

In Namibia public procurement for the national government is carried out by the Tender Board of Namibia. Local and regional tender boards are responsible for public procurement on their respective level. The legal framework is provided by the Tender Board of Namibia Act,[1336] regulations for each of the three different types of tender boards[1337] and code of procedures.[1338] Namibia, like all other sub-Saharan African countries, is neither party nor observer to the GPA.

The public procurement system inherited from South Africa after independence[1339] was superseded by the Tender Board of Namibia Act which came into force on 1 October 1996.[1340] It regulates the procurement of goods and services for the national government, establishes the Tender Board of Namibia and defines its functions. Moreover, it establishes open or competitive bidding through an invitation for tenders as well as prequalification as standard tender procedures. Further instructions for the mandate of the Tender Board can be found in the Tender Board Regulations.[1341] The Tender Board Regulations also establish the price preference system for public procurement and contain an exemption clause for tender procedures. The requirements for tender procedures are defined in the Code of Procedure (CoP).[1342] However, neither the Tender Board nor the procedural requirements differ much from the procurement system under

1336 Tender Board of Namibia Act 1996 (Act No. 16 of 1996), Sec. 5.

1337 Local Authorities Tender Board Regulations: Local Authorities Act, 1992 (No. 29 of 1992, Government Gazette No. 2486); Regional Councils Tender Board Regulations: Regional Councils Act, 1992 (No. 43 of 1992, Government Gazette No. 2492); Tender Board Regulations 1996 (No. 237 of 1996, Government Gazette No. 1403).

1338 Tender Board of Namibia Code of Procedure 1997 (No. 191 of 1997, Government Gazette No. 1692). The Regional and Local Tender Board Regulations each include a code of procedure.

1339 Tender Board Regulations (promulgated in terms of s 26A of Finance and Audit Ordinance 1 of 1926) 1970.

1340 Act No. 16 of 1996.

1341 Tender Board Regulations 1996.

1342 Tender Board of Namibia Code of Procedure 1997.

the apartheid regime.[1343] The only major reform was the introduction of preferential procurement which pursues certain socio-economic objectives such as the promotion of former disadvantaged groups of society.

Namibia is divided in 13 different regions. According to Section 2 (1) of the Regional Councils Act[1344] there shall be a regional council for each region specified. The regional tender boards are established by Tender Board Regulations under the Regional Councils Act.[1345] The Regulations include the description of the mandate of the boards, general procurement requirements and a code of procedure. The Code of Conduct for Members of Regional Councils[1346] is also of particular relevance for the efficiency and effectiveness of public procurement on the regional level. There are local authority councils for municipalities, towns and villages.[1347] The structure of the Local Tender Board Regulations (LTBR) under the Local Authorities Act[1348] resembles the Regional Tender Board Regulations (RTBR).

Apart from the procurement-specific legislation several other statutes have relevance for the effective and efficient functioning of public procurement, such as the Anti-Corruption Act,[1349] the Affirmative Action (Employment) Act[1350] and the Labour Act.[1351] Against the background of the apartheid system, affirmative action plays an important role in the transformation of society and is supposed to be effected through procurement. Hence, a short introduction into affirmative action legislation and policy is given in the following section.

---

1343 Interview Mr Ruppel (LorentzAngula Inc., Director/Chairman), 28th February 2013.

1344 Regional Councils Act 1992 (Act No. 22 of 1992).

1345 Regional Councils Tender Board Regulations: Regional Councils Act, 1992.

1346 Code of Conduct for Members of Regional Councils 2004 (No. 172 of 2004, Government Gazette No. 3255).

1347 Local Authorities Act 1992 (Act No. 23 of 1992), Sec. 2.

1348 Local Authorities Tender Board Regulations: Local Authorities Act, 1992.

1349 Anti-Corruption Act 2003 (Act No. 8 of 2003).

1350 Affirmative Action (Employment) Act 1998.

1351 Labour Act 2007.

### b. Public Procurement-related Development Policies in Namibia: Affirmative Action

#### i. Introduction

With Namibia's independence came the challenge to face the aftermath of years of colonisation and in particular the apartheid system. Large segments parts of its population suffered from racial discrimination in all parts of life. Beyond that, centuries of gender discrimination led to a gender-biased society. This resulted in a society with huge social and economic disparities.[1352] With Namibian's independence a new constitution including a catalogue of fundamental rights and freedoms came into force in 1990. Discrimination on grounds of sex, race, colour, ethnic origin, religion, creed or social of economic status is strictly prohibited.[1353] The catalogue not only establishes a general prohibition of discrimination but also makes possible the criminal punishment for racial discrimination.[1354] However, it is explicitly stressed that groups that have been discriminated against in the past can actually be positively discriminated against, too; meaning that they can be favoured in certain circumstances. In this respect Article 23 (2) of the Constitution allows parliament to enact affirmative action measures for the advancement of persons who have been socially, economically or educationally disadvantaged by past discriminatory laws or practices and to implement policies and programmes aimed at redressing social, economic or educational imbalances in the Namibian society. It is further provided that, in regard to affirmative action legislation, it shall be permissible for parliament to have regard to the fact that women in Namibia have traditionally suffered special discrimination.[1355] Such legislation must, however, comply with Article 22, which stipulates certain criteria that have to be met if fundamental rights or freedoms are limited. This concept of affirmative action creates an opportunity for the prior disadvantaged population group to close the gap that has been created by past discrimination. This means in different fields, as for example employment, measures can be taken to prefer disadvantaged groups in regard to groups

1352 See H. Jauch, 'Affirmative Action in Namibia - *Redressing the Imbalances of the Past?* ' (Windhoek: New Namibia Books, 1998), p. 39ff.
1353 Constitution of Namibia 1990 (Act No. 1 of 1990), Art. 10 (2).
1354 Cf. Ibid, Art. 23 (1).
1355 Ibid, Art. 23 (3).

that have not faced discrimination. Furthermore, Article 63 (2) (i) requires the National Assembly to

> "[...] remain vigilant and vigorous for the purposes of ensuring that the sources of apartheid, tribalism and colonialism do not again manifest themselves in any form in a free and independent Namibia and to protect and assist disadvantaged citizens of Namibia who have historically been the victims of these pathologies."

First of all, it has to be remarked that affirmative action does not have the status of a fundamental right or freedom since it is an exception to the dignity of the person and the right to equality and therefore can be derogated from. The affirmative action provision merely permits affirmative action; it does not mandate it. Hence, the efficiency of the system to redress social and economic inequality resulting from the years of apartheid depends on the implementation of the provision.[1356] Affirmative action is an important tool to address past injustices in Namibia and to restore social and economic balances within the Namibian society. Existing corresponding laws focus mainly on employment and labour relations,[1357] the political participation of women[1358] and land law.[1359] The pursuit of affirmative action through public procurement is possible and might, hence, be endorsed considering the amount of money spent on public procurement. This matter will be discussed in the subchapter on secondary objectives (Subchapter 5 of this chapter). What has been done so far is to include contract conditions requiring suppliers or contractors to adhere to specific provisions of the Affirmative Action (Employment) Act, which will be outlined briefly in the following.

---

1356 Jauch, 'Affirmative Action in Namibia', p. 54.

1357 See Affirmative Action (Employment) Act (Act No. 29 of 1998); see also Labour Act (Act No. 6 of 1992), Sec. 5 (4) (a).

1358 See Public Service Act 1995 (Act No. 13 of 1995), Sec. 18; see also Local Authorities Act 1992 (Act No. 23 of 1992), Sec. 6.

1359 See Agriculturual (Commercial) Land Reform Act 1992 (Act No. 6 of 1995) which has been enacted to provide for the allocation of land to such Namibian citizens who do not own or otherwise have the use of any or of adequate agricultural land, and foremost to those Namibian citizens who have been socially, economically or educationally disadvantaged by past discriminatory laws or practices. (See Preamble of the Act).

ii. Affirmative Action (Employment) Act

As the name of the Act suggests, the Affirmative Action (Employment) Act[1360] regularises the application of affirmative action in employment. It aims to achieve equal opportunity in employment in accordance with Articles 10 and 23 of the Namibian Constitution and, through appropriate affirmative action plans, to redress the conditions of disadvantage in employment experienced by persons in designated groups arising from past discriminatory laws and practices.[1361] It further establishes an Employment Equity Commission[1362] and contains measures to contribute towards the elimination of discrimination in employment.[1363]

The Act not only calls for the elimination of employment barriers against designated groups but also for instituting positive measures for these groups.[1364] Designated groups include racially disadvantaged persons, women, and disabled persons, as defined in Section 18 of the Act. The affirmative action measures established by the Act, first, require existing as well as new training programmes to contribute to furthering the objectives of the Act.[1365] Secondly, it allows preferential treatment in employment decisions to suitably qualified persons from designated groups to ensure equitable representation in the workforce of a relevant employer.[1366] It therefore allows employers to prefer a member of a designated group although he or she is less qualified than another candidate. Of particular relevance in regard to public procurement is that any designated employer (25 or more employees) is required to produce a valid Affirmative Action Certificate when entering into contracts with the state.[1367] Moreover, the standard tender conditions require tenderers who apply for the affirmative action price preferences to attach a valid Affirmative Action Certificate.[1368] An Affirmative Action Compliance Certificate has to

1360 Act No. 20 of 1998.
1361 Ibid, Preamble.
1362 Ibid, Sec. 2ff.
1363 Ibid, Preamble.
1364 Ibid, Sec. 17 (2) (a).
1365 Ibid, Sec. 17 (2) (c) (i) and (ii).
1366 Ibid, Sec. 17 (2) (c) (iii).
1367 Ibid, Sec. 42. See also Identification of Employers as Relevant Employers (in terms of Section 20(1) of the Affirmative Action (Employment) Act 1998) 2006 (No. 95 of 2006, Government Gazette No. 3658).
1368 Ministry of Finance, 'Supply and Delivery of Clothing Material for the Namibian Correctional Service for the Period 01 April 2013 to 31 March 2015: Ministry of

be produced by every relevant employer[1369] and is issued by the Commission if it the relevant employer has submitted a report including statistical data, the employer's administrative action plan and a summary of affirmative action measures it applies.[1370] This report is subject to a review assessing issues such as the compliance and implementation of affirmative action plans[1371] or compliance with relevant sections of the Act[1372] and has to be approved by the Commission in order for an Affirmative Action Compliance Certificate to be issued to the employer.[1373] The end result is that all tenderers are required to adhere to the Affirmative Action (Employment) Act, which will be further discussed below.[1374]

### c. Objectives and Principles

The Tender Board Act does not specifically outline objectives and principles. It can, however, be said that affirmative action and the promotion of the local economy are objectives that are pursued by means of public procurement. The basic principles and objectives of procurement, such as value for money, transparency or fairness, are not mentioned in the Tender Board Act as such.

### d. Scope and Coverage

The scope of the Tender Board Act covers the procurement of all goods and services, the letting or hiring of all things, the acquisition or granting of all rights and the disposal of all property by offices, ministries and agencies for or on behalf of the government.[1375] Regional tender boards are generally responsible for the procurement of goods and services for a regional council, for the arrangement of the hiring or leasing of anything

---

Safety and Security' (Windhoek: Tender Board of Namibia, 2013), Notice to Tenderers - Changes to Tender Conditions.

1369 Affirmative Action (Employment) Act 1998, Secs. 20 and 41.

1370 Ibid, Secs. 27 and 28.

1371 Ibid, Sec. 31 (1) (a).

1372 Ibid, Sec. 31 (1) (b).

1373 Ibid, Secs. 32 (1) (a) and 34 (3).

1374 See Subchapter 5 of this chapter.

1375 Tender Board of Namibia Act 1996, Sec. 21 (1).

or the acquisition or granting of any right for or on behalf of the council, or for the disposal of property of a regional council.[1376] In an analogous manner, local tender boards are responsible to provide tender services to the local authority council for which it is established.[1377]

Whereas the GPA and the UNCITRAL Model Law only provide for the procurement or acquisition of goods and services (the UNCITRAL Model Law also names construction) the South African law goes further and includes the disposal and letting of states assets. The revised GPA, however, even explicitly excludes the acquisition or rental of land and immovable property.[1378] However, this can be explained by the nature of the GPA as a multilateral agreement with the objective of diminishing barriers to trade in goods and services rather than the internationalisation of all government economic activities. As mentioned in Chapter 4 of Part II, expanding the scope to cover other government activities generating revenues or expenditures and providing an opportunity to everyone to apply for the tender is beneficial in many ways. First of all, it allows the government to expand preferential policies to fields other than the procurement of goods and services. Moreover, the Tender Board is generally qualified to conduct the tender procedure and facilitate the objectives of public procurement. The integration of the disposal and letting of state assets makes it subject to transparency standards. Furthermore, it envisages the choice of the best offer by allowing for the greatest possible competition. The inclusion of the acquisition or granting of all rights is even more progressive than the South African approach and is beneficial in two respects: First, the trade of rights to natural resources is of increasing importance in view of the limitation of natural resources and the resulting global struggle for them. Secondly, apartheid has restricted the administration of resources to a minority; the profits earned from the exploitation of natural resource have not been shared with the majority. The application of the preferential policy to the acquisition or granting of rights allows the former disadvantaged groups to acquire rights or concessions they had been excluded from in the past. Additionally, the acquisition or granting of rights might involve huge amounts of money. The United Nations Development Programme

1376 Regional Councils Tender Board Regulations: Regional Councils Act, 1992, Regs. 2 (1) and 6 (1).

1377 Local Authorities Tender Board Regulations: Local Authorities Act, 1992, Regs. 2 (1) and 6 (1).

1378 Revised Agreement on Government Procurement, 2012, Art. II (3) (a).

(UNDP) also states that "[…] good practice suggests that concessions […] should also be awarded according to the fundamental principles of transparency, competition and objectivity" and that a concession would

> "[…] be an arrangement very similar to a regular goods, services or works contract except for the fact that the consideration for the goods, services or works to be carried out usually consists in the right to exploit these goods, services or works together with payment."[1379]

With view to this similarity, it might be a good solution to include the acquisition or granting of rights to the scope of public procurement, in particular where no proper system for the award of concession exists. The Namibian approach in regard to the scope of public procurement could, within a system promoting objectives as transparency, competition and fairness, have great potential to have a positive effect not only on socio-economic development but also the transformation of society.

Goods, services and property which are related to security are exempted from the Act.[1380] Further, the Namibian Defence Force and the Namibian Security Intelligence Agency are explicitly exempted from having to procure, hire, let, or dispose security-related goods, services and property in accordance with the provisions of the Tender Board Act.[1381] Exemptions for security reasons are quite common in public procurement systems and follow a raison d'être. The GPA, the COMESA Procurement Regulations as well as the South African and the Mauritian procurement system, all allow for exemptions from the application of the rights and obligations in cases of procurement indispensable for national security. South Africa does not provide for a general exemption for security-related procurement but allows the Minister to grant exemptions for such procurements. This model is preferable to an overall exemption, permitting goods or services which cannot be procured under the public procurement legislation, for example because of confidentiality or sensitivity, to be procured through other means while still ensuring that all other procurements are covered by the public procurement regulations. The UNCITRAL Model Law offers an alternative approach. It does not allow for exemptions for security reasons but allows the application of single-source procurement if the use of any other method of procurement is not appropriate for the protection of

---

1379 United Nations Office on Drugs and Crime, 'Guidebook on anti-corruption in public procurement and the management of public finances', p. 15.

1380 Tender Board of Namibia Act 1996, Sec. 21 (a).

1381 Ibid.

essential security interests of the state.[1382] This has the advantage that procurement relating to national security does not take place in a legal limbo but is conducted under public procurement legislation and might, hence, be preferable to completely exempting such transactions from procurement legislation.

The Namibian legislation, moreover, provides for exemptions permitting deviations from the generally prescribed open bidding procedure. This includes cases in which the estimated value does not exceed N$10,000 and if the other party is a statutory body, local authority or regional council, a foreign government, etc.[1383] Whereas these exceptions seem reasonable, difficulties arise from Subsection b which exempts "such category of procurement, letting, hiring, rights or disposal as may on the recommendation of the Board, be prescribed". Of particular relevance in this regard is Section 17 (1) (c), which allows the Tender Board to exclude a particular case from the regular tender procedure of the Act if it deems it impracticable or inappropriate to invite tenders. The Tender Board is thereby provided with a carte blanche to conduct transactions without following the tender procedure prescribed in the legislation.

In practice, the grant of exemptions is non-transparent and there are no clearly stated internal criteria when an exemption can be used. It is impossible to comprehend what tenders are exempted from the Act and, especially, for what reasons. According to a director of a Namibian construction company, the Tender Board provides the weirdest reasons for exemptions and its company itself has also been given projects that had not been advertised and thus have been exempted from the application of the Act.[1384]

Whereas all tenders under the Targeted Intervention Program for Employment and Economic Growth (TIPEEG),[1385] an employment creation program initiated in 2011 by the National Planning Commission as a response to the unemployment crisis in 2009, are exempted from the normal procedure, they generally still follow open advertised bidding but with

---

1382 UNCITRAL Model Law on Public Procurement, 2011, Art. 30 (5) (d).

1383 Tender Board of Namibia Act 1996, Sec. 17 (a) and (b).

1384 Interview Mr Schulz (Namibia Construction (Pty) Ltd., Director), 22th March 2013.

1385 National Planning Commission, 'Targeted Intervention Program for Employment and Economic Growth (TIPEEG)' (National Planning Commission, Namibia: 2011), available at http://www.npc.gov.na/publications/TIPEEG.pdf; last accessed: 30 November 2015.

limited time periods.[1386] The exemption of a TIPEEG project still has to be granted by the Tender Board, meaning that the line ministries have to ask the Tender Board for the exemption of those projects.[1387] TIPEEG tenders always follow a two-envelope-system with technical and financial proposals being submitted in separate envelopes.[1388] Moreover, despite the fact that the National Planning Commission deals with TIPEEG tenders, they usually still go through the Tender Board. Nevertheless, certain exceptions seem to exist. According to Tender Board members and staff, exemptions are also granted for urgent procurements and for procurements such as for utilities or travel allowances and for specific items.

Justifying the ballooning of tender exemptions in the 2007/2008 financial year, which experienced an increase of 112,2 % compared to the previous year, the Minister of Trade and Industry, who was the chairman of the Tender Board at that time, said in the report that

> "[t]his increase in exemption approval could be attributed to factors such as urgent construction of and extensions to classrooms due to the exceptionally high demand for classrooms in the Khomas and northern regions for the ever-increasing number of learners."[1389]

It was also mentioned that a lack of financial planning for each year leaves the ministries with money to be spent at the end of the year.[1390] Especially at the end of the year the Tender Board would receive a lot of applications for exemptions by ministries. The Board would mostly grant those exemptions so that the money could be spent. An alternate member of the Tender Board classified the public resentment about exemptions as, at least partly, a problem of misunderstanding because the public would not understand that the above mentioned exemptions "[...] make up quite a big share of the cake."[1391] Another Tender Board member, however, admitted that sometimes exemptions are granted because there is an overload of work.[1392] Additionally, scandals such as the uncovering of an "urgent"

1386 Interview Mrs Jonga (Tender Board, Chief Control Officer), 26th March 2013; Interview Mr Shindinge (Tender Board, Alternate Member), 27th March 2013; Interview Mr Titus (Tender Board, Alternate Member), 28th March 2013.

1387 Interview Mrs Jonga (Tender Board, Chief Control Officer), 26th March 2013.

1388 TIPEEG builds Walvis a new school and Dagbreek new classrooms, Tender Bulletin No. 997 (Windhoek, Namibia), 22-28 February 2013.

1389 Tender Board Namibia, 'Annual Report 2007/2008', (Windhoek: Ministry of Finance 2008).

1390 Interview Mr Isaacs (Tender Board, Chief Control Officer), 26th March 2013.

1391 Interview Mr Titus (Tender Board, Alternate Member), 28th March 2013.

1392 Interview Mr Shindinge (Tender Board, Alternate Member), 27th March 2013.

purchase of alcohol glasses, garden tools and kitchen utensils on Christmas Eve by the Ministry of Defence[1393] exemplify that the broad discretion to grant exemptions is utilized shamelessly to the detriment of the tax payer.

The Act does not provide for any exemptions in respect to international agreements. Many states exclude projects funded by foreign donors from their public procurement legislation. Although the Namibian Tender Board Act is silent on this matter, it might be assumed that donor-funded projects are not dealt with under the Act in practice. However, the interviews with the Tender Board members showed that there is no awareness that projects that have been financed by foreign donors are generally exempted from open bidding.[1394] Nevertheless, members of the construction sector have commented otherwise. They are of the opinion that projects financed by China have indeed attached the condition that it is carried out by their own companies and are, hence, not advertised for tendering.[1395] An example is the construction of the new State House, which was never advertised for tender. The issue is of particular importance in the Namibian context since it is closely related to the role of China; China is known to provide soft-loans for infrastructure projects on the condition that the project is carried out by a Chinese company.[1396] This, however, can have a negative impact on the domestic industry since it diminishes the size of the contestable national procurement market.[1397] It is also known that many other foreign donors and international financial institutions require projects funded by them to be procured according to their own regulations.[1398] An OECD/DAC survey yielded that in 2010 in Namibia only 14

---

1393 'Bring An End To Tender Exemptions (Editorial)' (Newspaper article), The Namibian (Windhoek, Namibia), 1 February 2013.

1394 Interview Mrs Jonga (Tender Board, Chief Control Officer), 26th March 2013

1395 Interview Mr Schulz (Namibia Construction (Pty) Ltd., Director), 22th March 2013; Interview Mr Agenbag (Murray & Roberts Namibia, Commercial Director), 7th March 2013.

1396 F. Buys; S. Hallick, 'The effect of Chinese construction companies on the Namibian construction industry - *a construction and design team members' perspective*' (2010) 17(1) Acta Structilia, 1-24 at 5.

1397 S.J. Evenett, 'Can Developing Countries Benefit from Negotiations on Transparency in Government Procurement in the Doha Round?, Task Force 9 (Open, Rule-Based Trading System) of the United Nations Millennium Project', 2003), p. 1f. (available at https://www.alexandria.unisg.ch/Publikationen/Person/E/Simon_Evenett/22164; last accessed: 30 November 2015).

1398 A. La Chimia, 'Donors' influence on developing countries' procurement sysetms, rules and markets: a critical analysis', in G. Quinot; S. Arrowsmith, *Public*

per cent of aid reported for the government sector used the Namibian procurement system.[1399] It can be assumed that the Tender Board is not informed of such cases, which would explain why the Tender Board members are not aware of any exemptions for externally-funded projects.

The exemption from tender procedures in respect of the procurement of goods and services has become rampant and seems to evade the whole public procurement system. One example is the controversy about contracts regarding the provision of catering to the public hospitals. This has been an on-going issue for more than a decade. Contracts awarded for a year were extended by exemption from formal tender renewal procedure for years. The tender was issued in 2002 and then only in 2009. There is no record that the tender was advertised in 2010, 2011 or 2012.[1400] This exemplifies how exemptions can undermine the objectives of public procurement, especially, transparency, fairness and competition.

Several stakeholders have stated that exemptions are the major problem of the current procurement system. According to the Tender Board Annual Reports for the 2005/2006 financial year tenders worth N$619 million were approved and tenders worth N$170.4 million were exempted from tender procedures.[1401] In the following financial year tender exemptions worth N$1.6 billion by far exceeded awarded tenders, which were valued at N$868.3 million.[1402] The last annual report available so far for the period 2007/2008 states that tenders amounting to N$3.4 billion were exempted and N$624.4 million worth of tenders were awarded.[1403] These financial reports were tabled in the National Assembly in February 2010 and there was no reason given for the delay.[1404] Also the failure to provide the following annual reports has not been commented by the Minister of Fi-

---

*Procurement Regulation in Africa* (Cambridge et al: Cambridge University Press, 2013), p. 235.

1399 OECD, 'Aid Effectiveness 2005–10', p. 125, Appendix A: Country Data, Table A.5.

1400 Hospital catering contract sees the light of day after a decade's procurement obscurity and contractual intrigue, Tender Bulletin No. 998 (Windhoek, Namibia), 01-07 March 2013.

1401 See Links; Daniels, 'The Tender Board - Need for Root and Branch Reform', p. 3. See also N$12 billion worth of tenders exempted' (Newspaper article), The Namibian (Windhoek, Namibia), 13 February 2013.

1402 Ibid.

1403 Ibid.

1404 'N$12 billion worth of tenders exempted' (Newspaper article), The Namibian (Windhoek, Namibia), 13 February 2013.

nance.[1405] The current chairperson of the Board recently said further reports will be published in the near future.[1406] The reason for the absence of annual reports may be a lack of manpower at the secretariat.[1407]

Although the Ministry of Finance is aware of the problem of exemptions it has never issued any regulations in respect of the specification of situations in which exemptions are justified or what alternative tender procedures should be followed if tenders are exempted from the normal procedure, even though the Ministry has the power to issue such regulations.[1408] This is most probably due to a lack of political will; no one wants to commit to anything that could mean a loss of power and influence. Furthermore, the tender exemption clause is assumed to be used by procurement officials and politicians for their own benefit.[1409]

The current legislation on exemptions is insufficient since it is non-transparent, provides no alternative procurement methods for exempted procurements and consequently opens the door to corruption and abuse. It would be necessary to find adequate procurement methods according to the type and value of the products or services to be procured. The UNCITRAL Model Law offers a good solution in this respect; it establishes open bidding as the general procurement method but offers a variety of alternative tendering methods that can be used if certain conditions are met.[1410] The Guide to Enactment of the UNCITRAL Model Law further contains extensive explanations for what circumstances justify the use of different methods.[1411] Mauritius has followed a very similar approach[1412] whereas in South Africa the use of alternative procurement methods in cases where tendering is deemed impractical lacks clarity as well as a requirement to specify reasons that might justify exceptions from competitive bidding. The latter approach is not recommendable because it is contrary to the principles of public procurement, including value for money, competition, fairness and transparency.

---

1405 Ibid.
1406 Ibid.
1407 Ibid.
1408 See Tender Board of Namibia Act 1996, Sec. 20 (c).
1409 Interview Mr Hopwood (IPPR, Director), 26th March 2013.
1410 UNCITRAL Model Law on Public Procurement, 2011, Arts. 27-30.
1411 UNCITRAL, 'Guide to Enactment of the UNCITRAL Model Law on Public Procurement', p. 128f.
1412 See Public Procurement Act 2006, Sec. 15.

e. Institutions and Staff

The key institutions in the Namibian public procurement system are the tender boards. Apart from the national Tender Board, there are tender boards on the regional and on the local level. They carry out public procurement for the government offices, ministries, agencies, departments, sections and divisions and are solely responsible for the award decisions.

The national Tender Board consists of the Permanent Secretary of the Ministry of Finance[1413] and one staff member from each office, ministry and agency. The staff members are nominated by the president, prime minister and ministers.[1414] The agencies include the Namibian Security Intelligence Agency, the National Planning Commission, the Office of the Attorney-General, the Office of the Auditor-General, and the Office of the Parliament. As has become obvious during field research, in practice the permanent secretaries of the Ministries serve as board members. All these people are government employees and legislation does not require them to have any experience or knowledge of public procurement. The nominations can thus be characterised as political appointments for technical jobs.[1415] And indeed, considering the public administration, legal, technical and economic skills and understanding needed to efficiently and effectively carry out procurement, the lack of qualification criteria for tender board members is highly problematic and allows the appointment of members that hinder rather than implement effective and efficient procurement decisions. Apart from internal members, two Namibian citizens who are not staff members are appointed by the Ministry of Finance.[1416] There is again no qualification requirement provided for by legislation. The members of the Tender Board who are employed by the government hold office for the tenure of the Minister and all other members are appointed for a period of three years.[1417] Additionally, the Minister appoints an alternate member for each member of the Board in the case of the member's absence or inability to act.[1418] Usually financial advisors, directors, deputy directors, under-permanent secretaries, permanent secretaries

1413 Tender Board of Namibia Act 1996, Sec. 3 (1) (a).

1414 Ibid, Sec. 3 (1) (b).

1415 Cf. Interview Mr Hopwood (IPPR, Director), 26th March 2013. See also Caldwell; et al., 'Promoting Competitive Markets', p. 329; Mamiro, p. 5.

1416 Tender Board of Namibia Act 1996, Sec. 3 (1) (c).

1417 Ibid, Sec. 4 (1).

1418 Ibid, Sec. 3 (2).

or deputy-permanent secretaries of the ministries are selected as alternate members.[1419] According to the interviews the alternate members attend the tender board meetings more often than the tender board members themselves.[1420] Reappointment is possible[1421] and the Minister has the power to remove members from the board if the person is considered to be unsuitable.[1422] The administrative work of the Board is carried out by staff members designated by the permanent secretary from among the staff of the Ministry of Finance.[1423]

Organisationally, the Tender Board is subdivided into two parts or divisions: administration and the secretariat.[1424] The former division is, according to Section 18 of the Tender Board Act, responsible for all administrative work, including the payment and receipt of moneys. The secretariat is the arm of the board; it prepares the board meetings, notifies the tenders, maintains the contact with the relevant ministries and monitors compliance with the tender documents.[1425] One team is responsible for inspection and training; it trains line ministries and tenderers in tender submission, inspects low-value tenders and is responsible for capacity building. For example, it trains the local and regional offices in public procurement.[1426] In 2013, the whole tender structure consisted of about 50 persons. Several of the interviewees stated that there is an overload of work and that the staff members are overburdened and they have to work overtime.[1427] The institution would need streamlining in order to be able to work more efficiently.[1428] It has to be indicated in this respect that the whole procurement system in Namibia is still solely paper-based which contributes to the overload of work for the tender board staff and its mem-

1419 Interview Mrs Jonga (Tender Board, Chief Control Officer), 26th March 2013; Interview Mr Immanuel (Tender Board, Alternate Member), 27th March 2013.

1420 Interview Mr Titus (Tender Board, Alternate Member), 28th March 2013; Interview Mr Shindinge (Tender Board, Alternate Member), 27th March 2013.

1421 Tender Board of Namibia Act 1996, Sec. 4 (2)

1422 Ibid, Sec. 4 (4).

1423 Ibid, Sec. 18 (1).

1424 See Website of the Ministry of Finance: http://www.mof.gov.na/de/tender-board (last accessed: 18 December 2015).

1425 Interview Mrs Jonga (Tender Board, Chief Control Officer), 26th March 2013.

1426 Ibid.

1427 Interview Mrs Jonga (Tender Board, Chief Control Officer), 26th March 2013; Interview Mr Shindinge (Tender Board, Alternate Member), 27th March 2013; Interview Mr Isaacs (Tender Board, Chief Control Officer), 26th March 2013;

1428 Interview Mrs Jonga (Tender Board, Chief Control Officer), 26th March 2013.

bers.[1429] The IMF noted already in 2008 in the Namibian Country Report that

> "[…] the capacity and professional skills of the tender board staff is limited, half of the established posts are vacant, and there is a heavy workload as a result of low threshold (N$10,000) for issue of tenders; (ii) the tender board still works in a manual mode, as the processes and records are yet to be computerised; (iii) the line ministries may need strengthened guidelines and capacity building on how to screen bids and make recommendations […]."[1430]

One Tender Board member acknowledged that it is problematic that the Tender Board has ordinary clerks for highly difficult but low-paying jobs with a lot of money involved (50% of the GDP).[1431] Public procurement-relevant experience or expertise is not required for board and staff members. There is neither introductory nor regular training for employees of the Tender Board. The previous Permanent Secretary of the Tender Board initiated a training carried out by the Southern Business School, a South African company which offers a diploma course on Supply Chain Management. About four members of the Tender Board attended the training in Namibia which has been accredited by the Qualification Authorities of Namibia.[1432] However, according to an interviewee, this was the only training carried out in the past years.[1433] Neither the University of Namibia nor Polytechnic of Namibia offer any courses or trainings on the subject matter. It might be worth including public procurement in certain fields of study, such as law, business studies, political and economic science or public administration. Moreover, there should be a permanent training institution that offers basic and advanced training for Tender Board members and employees. A lack of expertise and experience not only prevents quality decision-making but it also runs the risk of staff members hesitating to take decisions because they are afraid of making poor decisions and losing their job.[1434]

---

1429 Ibid.

1430 IMF, 'Namibia: Report on Observance of Standards and Codes - Fiscal Transparency Module; IMF Country Report No. 08/184, 2008' (Washington, D.C.), 23, para 58.

1431 Interview Mrs Jonga (Tender Board, Chief Control Officer), 26th March 2013

1432 Interview Mr Isaacs (Tender Board, Chief Control Officer), 26th March 2013.

1433 Ibid.

1434 Cf. Interview Mr Schulz (Namibia Construction (Pty) Ltd., Director), 22th March 2013.

The system of alternate members who serve on the Tender Board if the permanent secretary cannot attend a meeting involves also challenges, such as the exchange of information between the member and the alternate member about preceding meetings. Moreover, the amount of work the Tender Board members face is enormous. Apart from the weekly meetings on Friday the Board meets on an ad hoc basis as required[1435] and the meetings also need to be prepared. Tender documentations have to be reviewed and evaluated in order to take decisions. And, in particular for highly technical tenders, it might be difficult for someone with no knowledge, expertise and experience to follow the technical details of a tender. A qualified assessment might require additional research. It has to be emphasised that the permanent secretaries and the alternate members have other jobs and tasks and that the work for the Tender Board is additional work, since no member is working full-time for the Tender Board. Hence, it is recommendable to establish a Tender Board with permanent and full-time employed members who possess the relevant qualifications. Moreover, establishing procurement units such as the Supply Chain Management Units in South Africa within the procuring entities to ensure that decisions about tenders are taken by people who have the relevant expertise and experience should be considered. The Tender Board could have an oversight function to ensure that rules and procedures and the basic principles of public procurement are followed. It is also possible to make it responsible for public procurements above a certain monetary threshold with view to decentralising gradually.

It also has to be remarked that many permanent secretaries chair ministerial committees which make recommendations to the Tender Board under Article 19 (1) of the CoP. This is deficient since it may lead to a conflict of interest and be contrary to the principle of separated responsibilities meaning that the decision should be taken by another person than the recommendation. Moreover, it is quite common that ministers have been serving in government for quite a long time being shifted from one ministry to another.[1436] The Tender Board can, hence, be characterised as a

1435 Interview Mr Immanuel (Tender Board, Alternate Member), 27th March 2013.

1436 According to Section 4 of the Tender Board Act, the members of the Tender Board who are employed by the government hold office for the tenure of the Minister and all other members are appointed for a period of three years. Reappointment is possible and the Minister has the power to remove members from the board if the person is considered to be unsuitable.

largely exclusive group of people with a disproportionate amount of influence.[1437]

The composition of regional and local tender boards follows a similar pattern as the Tender Board of Namibia. The chairpersons of the regional tender boards are the regional officers or at the local level the town clerks.[1438] Four staff members of the regional/municipal council are appointed by the council.[1439] Additionally, any two residents appointed to the regional council or local authority area belong to the board.[1440] At least two women must be on the board.[1441] The legislation does not provide for such a mandatory gender requirement in regard to the Tender Board of Namibia. This might be due to the fact that the Local and Regional Tender Board Regulations were issued several years later than the Tender Board Act.

The national Tender Board can "[...] require a staff member of any other ministry or of any office or agency to assist the Board with the evaluation of any tender or to make recommendations to the Board in connection with any tender."[1442] This is further specified in Regulation 2 (2) of the Tender Board Regulations, which provides that the Board may, in performing its functions, obtain such expert or technical advice as it may deem necessary. The latter provision can also be found in Regulations 2 (a) of the RTBR and the LTBR.

Whereas the UNCITRAL Model Law and the GPA do not contain provisions regarding institutions and staff, the South African and the Mauritian system substantially differ from the Namibian one. Both have decentralised the public procurement function to units within the procuring entities. In the South African Supply Chain Management system, procurement

1437 See Tjirera, 'Public Procurement in Namibia', p. 5.

1438 Regional Councils Tender Board Regulations: Regional Councils Act, 1992, Reg. 2 (a) (i).

1439 Local Authorities Tender Board Regulations: Local Authorities Act, 1992, Reg. 2 (a) (ii); Regional Councils Tender Board Regulations: Regional Councils Act, 1992, Reg. 2 (a) (ii).

1440 Local Authorities Tender Board Regulations: Local Authorities Act, 1992, Reg. 2 (a) (iii); Regional Councils Tender Board Regulations: Regional Councils Act, 1992 Reg. 2 (a) (iii).

1441 Local Authorities Tender Board Regulations: Local Authorities Act, 1992, Reg. 2 (3); Regional Councils Tender Board Regulations: Regional Councils Act, 1992, Reg. 2 (3).

1442 Tender Board of Namibia Act 1996, Sec. 18 (2).

is carried out by the financial departments of the procuring institutions,[1443] rather than external tender boards. In Mauritius all public bodies carry out procurement with a value below the threshold for major contracts; the latter are still carried out by the Central Tender Board. Such decentralisation has taken place in many public procurement systems in the past decades. The procuring institution knows best what is needed and the procurement procedure might be faster. But such institutional decentralisation might make it more difficult for tenderers to keep track of tenders and might, additionally, imply a loss of transparency. Moreover, the question of integrity has to be posed as the procuring entity is also the contracting party and is thus more likely to be susceptible and to be influenced by subjective rather than objective criteria. However, these concerns can be overcome if sufficient and adequate arrangements are made to prevent the occurrence of these risks. First of all, there needs to be a system of checks and balances, meaning there has to be an oversight mechanism that is responsible for monitoring and auditing public procurement. Secondly, there needs to be a coherent policy and a certain degree of uniformity to ensure transparency and to facilitate monitoring. The establishment of a public procurement policy office with the mandate to issue procurement guidelines and policies, standard bid documents, etc. might be an appropriate way to ensure a consistent policy and uniformity in public procurement proceedings.

## 3. Basics of the Public Procurement system

### a. Procurement Methods

Open or competitive bidding is the standard procurement method in Namibia. Moreover, it is provided for two-stage procurement by means of a prequalification procedure which is, however, in general only conducted nationwide.[1444] The Board may, nevertheless, determine to apply it to companies outside Namibia where circumstances so require.[1445] This provision poses the question of the effects of the prequalification procedure, e.g. whether it is protectionist or promotes preferential treatment. However, the key problem is most probably not the prequalification on the na-

1443 These departments are called the SCM units.
1444 Tender Board of Namibia Code of Procedure 1997, Sec. 2 (1).
1445 Ibid.

tional level per se, but the lack of specification in what circumstances tenders can be invited by means of prequalification. This allows the Tender Board to choose the prequalification procedure in order to exclude the participation of foreign tenders. In practice, there seem to be no criteria when prequalification procedures may be used; this decision is taken at the Tender Board's discretion. According to a Tender Board member prequalification might be used in tenders of highly technical nature in order to select tenderers which have the capability and experience to carry out the procurement in question.[1446]

Under the applicable laws, the invitation of tenders under the competitive bidding method is not restricted to the national level, but open for everyone. Tenders are usually open, meaning that the tender is not restricted to a certain group of companies, for example, Namibian companies. However, the Board has the discretion to specify criteria, e.g. that only bids from local companies will be considered. This will be discussed in more detail in the following subchapter on "Tender specification, award criteria and evaluation methods". Legislation for all three different government levels names the invitation of tenders and prequalification as sole methods to be used for tenders falling under the scope of the Act.[1447] The UNCITRAL Model Law also provides for prequalification procedures but does generally require the invitation to prequalify to be published internationally.[1448]

Although this is not required or provided for by legislation, the Tender Board generally follows a two-envelope system whereby the tenderers hand in a technical and a financial bid.[1449] First, the envelope with the technical bid is opened. The financial bid will only be considered if it complies with the tender requirements.[1450] Whether this practice is strictly followed is questionable, since there have been rumours that tenders have been awarded to companies that turned out to not have the technical capacity and expertise to successfully carry out the project, especially where the construction projects was intended to promote former disadvantaged

1446 Interview Mrs Jonga (Tender Board, Chief Control Officer), 26th March 2013.
1447 Local Authorities Tender Board Regulations: Local Authorities Act, 1992, Regs. 13 and 16; Regional Councils Tender Board Regulations: Regional Councils Act, 1992, Regs. 13 and 16; Tender Board of Namibia Act 1996, Sec. 11; Tender Board of Namibia Code of Procedure 1997, Sec. 2.
1448 UNCITRAL Model Law on Public Procurement, 2011, Art. 18 (2).
1449 Interview Mr Immanuel (Tender Board, Alternate Member), 27th March 2013.
1450 Ibid.

groups. Nevertheless, it is worth to consider the retention of the two-envelope system for complex or high value procurements. First of all, it may be beneficial to maintain certain procedures that have been identified as positive factors in the current system, in particular because all stakeholders are familiar with them. Secondly, it has been suggested that "[…] exposing bid evaluators to bid prices biases the entire comparison process."[1451] Because an exposure to bid prices would bias the judgement in favour of the lower bid, it would be recommendable to conduct a two-stage procedure such as is applied in Namibia.[1452] The UNCITRAL Model Law and the Mauritian procurement law both provide for two-stage procurement for specific cases such as highly technical bids. Other than in Namibia, discussions on the technical part can take place during the first stage. Only those passing the first stage can then hand in a final bid, including a price. This might be appropriate in cases where discussions on the technical bid can ensure quality and that the functional requirements of the procuring entity are met in the best possible way. Additionally, for high value procurements that are not that technically demanding, the two-envelope system without discussion might be suitable for the above mentioned reasons of bid biases.

Transactions conducted by the Namibian Defence Force and the Namibian Security Intelligence Agency and of security-related goods, services and property and transactions that are exempted from the standard procurement method are not subject to any requirements. This means that, e.g. purchases with a value of less than N$10,000 are not subject to any rules; they thus take place in a legal vacuum. It is, as emphasised in Part I, Chapter 1 generally recommendable to provide different types of tender procedures for several scenarios using the number, type, value or availability of goods or services procured as main indicators for the decision about what method is used. The GPA generally requires the use of open or selective tendering.[1453] The latter is conducted in two-stages where invited suppliers have to prequalify in order to participate in a particular procurement. For the use of limited tendering, the GPA provides strict requirements that limit its application to particular cases.[1454] Moreover, the GPA

1451 O. Dekel; A. Schurr, 'The Lower Bid Bias', conference paper, 5th International Public Procurement Conference, Seattle, Washington, 15-17 August, 2012, p. 3352.

1452 Ibid, 3339.

1453 Revised Agreement on Government Procurement, 2012, Arts. IV (4a) and IX.

1454 Ibid, Art. VIII.

allows the use of qualifications systems, such as registrations systems or multi-use lists.[1455] The UNCITRAL Model Law provides for open tendering and several alternative tender methods and strictly regulates what requirements need to be met in order to apply tender methods other than open tendering.[1456] In Mauritius, tender methods other than open advertised bidding can be applied only if certain criteria are fulfilled.[1457] This is very similar to the UNCITRAL Model Law.

Mauritian procurement law differs between open national bidding and open international bidding. The former can, however, only be applied if a certain monetary threshold is not exceeded.[1458] This provision is necessary in order to comply with the COMESA Procurement Regulations. Furthermore, the restriction to national bidding needs to be stated in the tender invitation.[1459]

The South African procurement system uses monetary threshold levels to determine what tender method is to be applied. [1460] The general procurement methods include petty cash, verbal and written price quotations and competitive bids. From a value of
R 500,000 competitive bids are prescribed. [1461] Nevertheless, if tendering is deemed impractical other procurement methods might be used [1462] However, the circumstances making tendering impractical or what the alternative methods should be are not specified. Although certain standards have evolved, such as that the higher the value of contracts, the more formal the procedures should be, and the National Treasury has suggested alternative procurement methods, no legal clarity has been established so far. As in Namibia there remains a legal limbo which opens the door to abuse.

---

1455 Ibid, Art. IX.

1456 UNCITRAL Model Law on Public Procurement, 2011, Arts. 28-31.

1457 Public Procurement Act 2006, Secs. 19-25.

1458 See above in Part II, Chapter 3, Subchapter 4 (e) (i).

1459 Ibid.

1460 Framework for Supply Chain Management 2003, Reg. 6 (1). See also National Treasury, 'Practice Note Number 8 of 2007/2008: Supply Chain Management: Threshold Values for the Procurement of Goods, Works and Services by Means of Petty Cash, Verbal/Written Price Quotations or Competitive Bids'.

1461 National Treasury, 'Practice Note Number 8 of 2007/2008: Supply Chain Management: Threshold Values for the Procurement of Goods, Works and Services by Means of Petty Cash, Verbal/Written Price Quotations or Competitive Bids ', paras 3.4.1 and 3.4.3.

1462 Framework for Supply Chain Management 2003, Reg. 6 (4).

### b. Procurement Planning and Contract Management

Procurement planning is not sufficiently regulated in Namibia. Indeed the preparation of the ministry or agency's annual budgets should include procurement planning and, if possible, the tender documents should be ready from the beginning of the financial year.[1463] If the budget is approved and implemented the ministry of agency should immediately call for tenders.[1464] However, there are no legal provisions in this regard and, in particular, not in the public procurement legislation, which is a severe shortcoming and should be rectified in the new legislation.

The lack of regulations pertaining to contract management and clear assignment of responsibilities in this respect has led to several shortcomings in the effectiveness and efficiency of the Namibian public procurement system. Tenders have, for example, been often awarded to Chinese companies. Such awards have been criticised for not adhering to the Namibian laws and the tender conditions. Not only inadequate labour conditions,[1465] the importation of Chinese workers[1466] but also subsequent price corrections have led to antagonism.[1467] This will be discussed in more detail in the chapter on the role of Chinese companies in the Namibian public procurement system. The Permanent Secretary of the Tender Board justified

1463 See Public Finance Management Act 1999, Sec. 27. See also J. Sankwasa, 'Tender Procedures Presentation', p. 14 (available at http://www.google.de/url?sa=t&rct=j&q=&esrc=s&source=web&cd=1&ved=0CC8QFjAA&url=http%3A%2F%2Funpan1.un.org%2Fintradoc%2Fgroups%2Fpublic%2Fdocuments%2Fcpsi%2Funpan043414.pdf&ei=xzncUcW5GofKtQbwuYFA&usg=AFQjCNGvEAQ4TQbHV7CeW-25ThPyPH5SsQ&bvm=bv.48705608,d.Yms; last accessed: 26th November 2015).

1464 Ibid.

1465 See 'Namibia: "Chinese invasion" - old foes police a new frontier' (Newspaper article), Sunday Times (Johannesburg, South Africa), 28 March 2011; 'Construction work at Chinese company at Rundu stopped' (Newspaper article), The Namibian (Windhoek, Namibia), 14 August 2008; 'Chinese Confronted on Labour Abuse' (Newspaper article), The New Era (Windhoek, Namibia), 24 August 2006; 'Pohamba Calls for Respect for Labour Laws' (Newspaper article), The New Era (Windhoek, Namibia), 13 May 2013; 'Rundu road workers sign contracts' (Newspaper article), The Namibian (Windhoek, Namibia), 10 June 2008; 'China should respect labour laws' (Newspaper article), Informanté (Windhoek, Namibia), 29 August 2012.

1466 'Runter von Verliererspur' (Newspaper article), Allgemeine Zeitung (Windhoek, Namibia), 13 September 2011.

1467 Ibid.

awarding the tenders to Chinese companies because, most of the time, they would "meet all the requirements and they give the best price."[1468] She continued: "Why? We don't know. We have our theories that most of these Chinese companies here are actually state-owned enterprises."[1469] When questioned about Chinese companies not meeting local labour laws, she passed the buck, saying that ensuring legal compliance with labour law was a matter for the Ministry of Labour, not the Tender Board.[1470] This view was also confirmed by the interviewees that are members of the Board. After the award of a tender it is the line ministries responsibility to monitor the implementation of the contract and the Ministry of Labour would be the responsible institution to inspect the labour conditions and ensure compliance with the labour laws.[1471] The Ministry of Works and Transport is responsible for monitoring, evaluating and contract management of capital projects. All TIPEEG projects are carried out under the oversight of the National Planning Commission. The ministries could, nevertheless, if they notice irregularities, approach the Tender Board to decide what to do about the issue and consider cancellation of the contract as well as blacklisting the company.[1472] Such measures have been taken, but usually because of breach of contract.

The IMF found in 2008 that the performance of awarded tenders is not being monitored on a sufficiently regular basis.[1473] Provisions on contract management and remedies in case of breaches of contract should be included in the new tender law to clarify the requirements and responsibilities for contract management. Otherwise, shortcomings in contract implementation, such as low quality or non-compliance with laws or contract conditions, can severely undermine the objectives of public procurement. Furthermore, secondary objectives pursued through public procurement, such as ensuring adherence to certain laws and policies such as labour conditions, can be easily undermined in the contract implementation

1468 Links; Daniels, 'The Tender Board - Need for Root and Branch Reform; Appendix I - Interview with Tender Board Secretary Welma Enssle', p. 19.

1469 Ibid.

1470 Links; Daniels, 'The Tender Board - Need for Root and Branch Reform; Appendix I - Interview with Tender Board Secretary Welma Enssle', p. 20.

1471 Interview Mr Titus (Tender Board, Alternate Member), 28th March 2013; Interview Mr Immanuel (Tender Board, Alternate Member), 27th March 2013.

1472 Interview Mrs Jonga (Tender Board, Chief Control Officer), 26th March 2013; Interview Mr Isaacs (Tender Board, Chief Control Officer), 26th March 2013.

1473 IMF, 23f., para. 58.

phase. Although laws requiring adherence to such policies are in place, these remain ineffective due to a lack of monitoring in the performance stage. Mauritius, for example, has legislation requiring that every procurement contract include a condition that certain labour standards are ensured and that the public bodies or the Central Procurement Board monitor compliance.[1474] This might be a suitable model in the Namibian context.

### c. Tender Specification, Award Criteria and Evaluation Methods

#### i. Contents of Tender Documents

The Tender Board Act contains a provision outlining the minimum requirements for the contents of title of tender:

> "**14.** A title of tender shall as far as practicable contain at least the following information:
>
> (a) Instructions for preparing tenders;
>
> (b) technical and quality characteristics of the goods to be procured or services to be rendered or property to be disposed of or the nature of rights to be acquired or granted, including, where appropriate, technical specifications, plans; and drawings;
>
> (c) currency in which the tender price is to be formulated and expressed;
>
> (d) the manner, place and losing date for submission of tenders;
>
> (e) the period during which tenders shall be in effect; and
>
> (f) tender security to be furnished and conditions for its refund."

Apart from these criteria, the Tender Board usually requires a proof of registration with the Ministry of Trade and Industry and documented evidence that it has paid its taxes and has good standing with the Social Security Commission.[1475] The tender documents usually also include certain standardised documents such as instructions to tenderers (TB 556), general conditions of tender, contract and order (TB489), conditions (TB1288) and special conditions (TB339). Regulations 17 of the RTBR and of the LTBR contain nearly the same provisions, except that they contain the additional requirement that the title of tender shall include a name and reference number by means of which the tender may be identified.

1474 See Part II, Chapter 3, Subchapter 4 (d) (iv).
1475 Links; Daniels, 'The Tender Board - Need for Root and Branch Reform', p. 5.

The requirement to include instructions for preparing tenders is important, especially in developing countries, in order to allow any supplier or contractor to participate in tendering irrespective of prior experience with tendering. Such provisions can also be found in the UNCITRAL Model Law as content requirement for solicitation documents.[1476]

The matter to be procured is to be specified according to technical and quality characteristics and technical specifications where possible. Technical specification is the key specification for goods or services to be procured under the GPA.[1477] In contrast to the Namibian law, the GPA, however, further specifies what falls under technical specifications. [1478] The UNCITRAL Model Law requires that the description of the subject matter of the procurement include the technical, quality and performance characteristics. [1479] Apart from performance characteristics, these description characteristics are identical to the Namibian requirements. Nevertheless, the UNCITRAL Model Law also stresses that the description has to be objective, functional and generic.[1480] The South African and the Mauritian procurement legislation lack specifications of the content of tender.

Section 4 of the CoP is also important in regard to Section 14 of the Namibian Tender Board Act. Section 4 of the CoP reads as follows.

> "A title of tender shall not make reference to any trade mark or trade name or to a specific product, except when used in conjunction or association with the words "similar to" or "equal to" to indicate the style, type or quality of the goods to be procured or services to be rendered."

The RTBR and LTBR contain nearly the same provision.[1481] This is an important issue that is also provided for in the other laws such as Article 10 (4) of the UNCITRAL Model Law, Article X (4) of the GPA and Article 11 (5) of the COMESA Procurement Regulations.

Although certain practical information is required to be stated in the title of tender, an important one has not been included: the manner, place,

---

1476 UNCITRAL Model Law on Public Procurement, 2011, Art. 39 (a).

1477 Revised Agreement on Government Procurement, 2012, Art. X (7) (a).

1478 Ibid, Art. X (1-6).

1479 UNCITRAL Model Law on Public Procurement, 2011, Art. 10 (4).

1480 Ibid, Art. 10 (4).

1481 Local Authorities Tender Board Regulations: Local Authorities Act, 1992, Reg. 34; Regional Councils Tender Board Regulations: Regional Councils Act, 1992, Reg. 34.

date and time for the opening of tenders.[1482] This is important since the public should have the opportunity to attend the public opening of tenders. Everyone must have the possibility to have a certain degree of insight into tender procedures not only because it is the public's tax money that is spent but also because the tender outcome might affect the public. A key condition for this opportunity is the information on the manner, place, date and time for the opening of tenders. Hence, it should be included as a requirement for the contents of title of tenders. Otherwise, transparency is severely restricted. Article 7 (f) of the GPA, for example, requires that, in cases where there will be a public opening, the tender documentation has to include the date, time and place for the opening. Article 39 (p) of the UNCITRAL Model Law also requires the publication of the manner, place, date and time for the opening of tender in the solicitation document. Despite the shortcomings in legislation, the Tender Board has established the practice of carrying out the public bid opening immediately after the tender closes.[1483] The company names the tenderers and the prices are read out and it also announced whether all required documents are attached.[1484]

Additionally, in stark contradiction to transparency standards, it is not required to specify the criteria and procedure for the evaluation of tenders in the title of tender. The disclosure of evaluation criteria and procedures is seen as basic requirement for facilitating transparency and fairness. Moreover, it is important in order to provide the opportunity for potential suppliers or contractors to prepare bids in view of the evaluation criteria and method. The GPA[1485] requires the publication of the evaluation criteria and the relative importance in the tender documentation. The UNCITRAL Model Law[1486] as well as the Mauritian law[1487] require that the evaluation criteria and methodology or weighting of those criteria be stated in the tender document. Furthermore, they stress that only those criteria that have been stated in the tender document can be used for evaluation.

1482 Namibian legislation requires all tenders to be opened in public. See Local Authorities Tender Board Regulations: Local Authorities Act, 1992, Reg. 18 (6); Regional Councils Tender Board Regulations: Regional Councils Act, 1992, Reg. 18 (6); Tender Board of Namibia Act 1996, Sec. 15 (7); Tender Board of Namibia Code of Procedure 1997, Sec. 14 (1).

1483 Interview Mrs Jonga (Tender Board, Chief Control Officer), 26th March 2013.

1484 Ibid.

1485 Revised Agreement on Government Procurement, 2012, Art. X (7) (c).

1486 UNCITRAL Model Law on Public Procurement, 2011, Arts. 39 (r), 11 (5) and (6).

1487 Public Procurement Act 2006, Secs. 2 and 47 (9).

In Namibia, one tender document, for example, states in regard to the evaluation of tenders that tenders will be evaluated inter alia in terms of the tender price, tender specifications, quality of products, period of delivery and preferences.[1488] Through the supplement "inter alia" the Tender Board grants itself wide discretion to establish any additional criteria they want to evaluate the tenders without knowledge of the tenderers. This is strictly against transparency guidelines and the principle of fairness.

Although Section 14 of the Act does not provide that the title of tender must include the contractual terms and conditions of an agreement, this is required under the CoP and the RTBR and LTBR. According to Section 7 (2) of the CoP and Regulation 27 of the RTBR/LTBR the tender boards are obliged to indicate the terms and conditions of a general agreement in the title of tender. This avoids that suppliers or contractors that have won a tender award from being unwilling to sign the contract because they do not want to agree to the contract conditions. Everyone knows from the beginning what to expect, hence, negotiations on the contract terms is precluded in the first place. The UNCITRAL Model Law contains a similar provision requiring the solicitation document to contain "the terms and conditions of the procurement contract, to the extent that they are already known to the procuring entity, and the form of the contract, if any, to be signed by the parties."[1489]

### ii. Evaluation of Tenders

Requirements for the examination, evaluation, comparison and non-acceptance of tenders can be found in Section 15 of the Tender Board Act and Regulations 18 of the RTBR and the LTBR. According to these provisions tenders should only be considered if they comply with all the characteristics, terms, conditions and other requirements set out in the title of tender or the Board regards the non-compliance as a minor deviation not materially altering or departing from the characteristics, terms, conditions or other requirements. This is an important provision as it avoids the exclusion of tenders which might be worth considering for formal reasons. Nevertheless, there is no guidance on what might constitute an "immateri-

---

1488 Ministry of Finance, 'Supply and Delivery of Clothing Material for the Namibian Correctional Service', p. 3, para. 1.4.

1489 UNCITRAL Model Law on Public Procurement, 2011, Art. 39 (e).

al deviation"; this is simply left to the discretion of the Board and, hence, can easily be abused.[1490] Subsection 1 of Section 15, which allows the Board to request any tenderer to clarify his or her tender at any time, is similar. However, the opportunity to influence the Board's decision, especially at the evaluation or comparison stage, is problematic. The Mauritian public procurement law stresses, for example, that the board or public body indeed can request clarifications but it is prohibited to ask or permit a change of substance or price of the tenderer's bid.[1491] The UNCITRAL Model Law also allows the possibility to request further details at all stages in the procurement process,[1492] but does not allow substantive changes, "[...] including changes aimed at making an unqualified supplier or contractor qualified or an unresponsive submission responsive."[1493] It further prohibits negotiations with respect to qualifications, information or submissions and price amendments.[1494] The UNCITRAL Model Law also allows requests for further details from the supplier or contractor in situations where the price of a submitted tender seems abnormally low, thereby raising concerns about the ability to perform the procurement contract. If this concern cannot be removed, then the tender submission can be rejected.[1495]

In Namibia, the non-acceptance of tenders is allowed if the tenderer does not qualify as such in terms of the conditions set out in the title of tender, if the tenderer fails to comply with a request of the Board to clarify his or her tender, and if the tenderer has resorted to corrupt practices with a view to influencing the Board in the selection of tender.[1496] The latter is a necessary provision in order to fight corruption. If a tender is excluded on this ground the reasons have to be kept on record by the Board. However, it is unclear whether this has an effect on future tenders of the same supplier or contractor. According to the interviewed members of the Tender Board, there have been instances where companies have been black-

---

1490 Cf. Amoo; Dicken, 'The regulatory framework for public procurement in Namibia'.
1491 Public Procurement Act 2006, Sec. 37 (1).
1492 UNCITRAL Model Law on Public Procurement, 2011, Art. 16 (1).
1493 Ibid, Art. 16 (3).
1494 Ibid, Art. 16 (4).
1495 Ibid, Art. 20.
1496 Local Authorities Tender Board Regulations: Local Authorities Act, 1992, Reg. 18 (3); Regional Councils Tender Board Regulations: Regional Councils Act, 1992, Reg. 18 (3); Tender Board of Namibia Act 1996, Sec. 15 (3).

listed for failing to implement the contract. However, this has to be preceded by correspondence between the line ministry and the company. Thereafter the ministry has to approach the Tender Board, which takes the decision.[1497] Unfortunately, the whole process is non-transparent. The list is not published and the duration of the blacklisting is unclear. It is not explicitly required to keep the reasons for a blacklisting on record for exclusions on grounds other than corruption. Moreover, it is a severe shortcoming that it is not explicitly stated that decisions and the reasons need to be promptly communicated to the tenderer. [1498] Blacklisting for corrupt practices has not been noted. One tender board member who has served on the board for the last five years stated that she could not recall any case of a company trying to influence the Board.[1499]

Whereas the tender legislation lacks a provision on blacklisting, the Tender Board has included such a provision in the special conditions latest edition (TB339) that is attached to most of the tender documents:[1500]

> "If the Board is satisfied that the execution of a Government contract by a person, firm or company, has been unsatisfactory or that a person, firm or company has offered, promised or given a bribe or any other consideration to any officer in the service of the Government in relation to obtaining or executing of a contract or if the Board is satisfied that a person, firm or company has acted frightened or in bad faith towards either the Government or any public body or company or person or persons, if such person, firm or company withdraws his or its tender after the advertised date and hour or, if when notified that his or its tender has been accepted, he or its fails within the period stipulated in the conditions of tender of such extension as the Government may allow, to sign a contract in terms of the tender form, the Board may after consideration at any time rescind such resolution or may resolve that the period may be reduced. Any restriction imposed upon any person, firm or company shall apply also to any other enterprise under the same or different name with which the person, firm or company restricted is actively associated."

Nevertheless, the interviews lead to the conclusion that this provision is rarely implemented by the Tender Board.[1501] The period of blacklisting is

1497 Interview Mrs Jonga (Tender Board, Chief Control Officer), 26th March 2013.
1498 The UNCITRAL Model, on the contrary, contains such provision (see e.g. Arts. 20 (2) and 21 (2)).
1499 Interview Mrs Jonga (Tender Board, Chief Control Officer), 26th March 2013.
1500 Tender Board of Namibia, 'Special conditions latest edition (TB339) ', Instructions to tenders.
1501 Interview Mrs Jonga (Tender Board, Chief Control Officer), 26th March 2013; Interview Mr Isaacs (Tender Board, Chief Control Officer), 26th March 2013.

not fixed but can be determined by the Board. It is also not required to publish the list. This would be necessary in order to keep the process transparent and fair.

For the examination of tenders, legislation provides that the board shall give consideration to the capacity, experience, integrity and financial status of the tenderer.[1502] The UNCITRAL Model Law and the GPA similarly state a list of conditions that can be applied for the examination of tenders. The former states a list of different criteria that can be laid down by the procuring entity as considered appropriate and relevant in the circumstances of a particular procurement.[1503] The objective of restricting qualification criteria for suppliers or contractors might be to exclude the possibility to pursue secondary objectives through qualification criteria. The UNCITRAL Model Law includes criteria that can be potentially used as secondary objectives, such as environmental qualifications and compliance with ethical and other standards.[1504] Whether the GPA only allows for the usage of commercial, financial and technical capacity criteria is controversial and it has, so far, not been definitely clarified whether secondary objectives can be integrated as qualification criteria or not.[1505] Although the wording of the Namibian Tender Board Act appears to exclude criteria other than the ones explicitly stated, the wording "shall give consideration" could also be understood as being an indication that the criteria list is not exclusive. In practice, it seems to be the common presumption that the Tender Board can come up with own criteria. The Tender Board has, for example, introduced the criteria of 51% Namibian ownership for tenders below N$60 Million which is also envisaged as part of the new bill.[1506] Moreover, something like an equity distribution principle or "share of the cake"- approach has been introduced.[1507] It is basically a list of past tender awards, stating who got what type of tenders with what val-

1502 Tender Board of Namibia Act 1996, Sec. 15 (4).
1503 UNCITRAL Model Law on Public Procurement, 2011, Art. 9 (2).
1504 See above, Part II, Chapter 2, Subchapter 4 (b) (iii).
1505 See above, Part II, Chapter 1, Subchapter 7.
1506 Links; Daniels, 'The Tender Board - Need for Root and Branch Reform; Appendix I - Interview with Tender Board Secretary Welma Enssle', p. 18 and 20; Interview Mrs Jonga (Tender Board, Chief Control Officer), 26th March 2013; Interview Mr Isaacs (Tender Board, Chief Control Officer), 26th March 2013. Interview Mr Titus (Tender Board, Alternate Member), 28th March 2013; Interview Mr Shindinge (Tender Board, Alternate Member), 27th March 2013.
1507 Interview Mrs Jonga (Tender Board, Chief Control Officer), 26th March 2013; Interview Mr Isaacs (Tender Board, Chief Control Officer), 26th March 2013.

ue. The Tender Board then tries to award tenders to companies that have not benefited in the past to give other companies a chance. This practice seems to strictly contradict the principles of public procurement systems, in particular, value for money, fairness and transparency. This also indicates that it is problematic if the Tender Board has the discretion to come up with any type of tender criteria it deems desirable.

Contrary to the wording of the Namibian Tender Board Act ("shall give consideration"), the UNCITRAL Model Law clearly states that tenderers have to have the "necessary" qualifications, competence, resources, etc. This differs from the Namibian approach, which seems to allow for making differences between contractors or suppliers above the minimum threshold. It is not at all clear what this means in practice and what influence the result of such examination can have on the award decision. While it is important to make sure the capacity, experience, integrity and financial status are sufficient to ensure successful performance, any influence of such criteria on the award decision above this level might be subjective and unverifiable, leading to non-transparency in the award decision and unfairness. However, there have been more and more instances where contracts were awarded to companies that did not have the expertise, experience or machinery to carry out the projects. According to the Director of Namibia Construction, there are about 50 projects that have not been finalised because companies lack expertise or have run out of money. His company has been asked a few times to finish those projects, but there are several problems such as the sharing of risks and liabilities. He also told a story about a company that asked him for a concrete mixer for a project in the south of Namibia. After the Director of Namibia Construction asked him a few questions, it became obvious that the contractor did not have enough knowledge to carry out the project. He did not, for example, know how much cement he would need.[1508] The failure by the Tender Board to ensure that the tenderer has the necessary capacity and experience to carry out the project demonstrates that Namibian tender law is insufficient in this respect. It results in a waste of taxpayer's money and might further lead to deficient end products.

1508 Interview Mr Schulz (Namibia Construction (Pty) Ltd., Director), 22th March 2013.

If the Board does not choose the lowest tender, it has to provide reasons which shall be kept on record by the Board.[1509] However, there is no requirement to publish these reasons or make them subject to review. One might draw the conclusion that, generally, the lowest bid should be chosen irrespective of ecological, social or ethical reasons. But the Tender Board of Namibia Act provides that the Board shall adhere to the price preference policy of the government when arriving at its decision about acceptance of tenders. Section 15 (5) of the Tender Board Act provides that

> "[i]n comparing tenders, the Board shall give effect to the price preference policy of the Government to redress social, economic and educational imbalances in a democratic society and to encourage industrial and commercial interests in Namibia."

This has to be read in combination with Section 17 of the CoP (and Regulation 47 of the RTBR/LTBR) which specifically prescribes that tender prices shall be compared before applying price preferences and that delivery and other charges shall be adjusted. Apart from the price preference policy, other criteria might influence the award decision. Section 6 (2) CoP for example states that the Board may give priority to tenderers who tender firm prices for the duration of an agreement and for delivery within a specific period. A very similar provision can be found in Regulation 36 (2) of the Regional and Local Tender Board Regulations.

Additionally, there is a provision which provides for an order of priority in case of equal tenders.[1510] It considers the degree of local input/origin. The first priority shall, for example, be granted to tenders for goods manufactured entirely from raw materials or produced mainly within Namibia. Tenders from overseas suppliers, but preferably suppliers with branches and stock in Namibia, are of least priority. Subsection 2 further provides that "[t]he Board shall as far as practicable in respect of tenders for the furnishing of perishable goods, accept the tender of the tenderer who is at or closest to the place where such goods are required." Although this provision seems to be well thought through, its merit is questionable as a situ-

---

1509 Tender Board of Namibia Act 1996, Sec. 15 (1). According to Regulation 10 (3) (a) of the Local and Regional Tender Board Regulations, local and regional tender boards are also not obliged to accept the lowest tenders. The reasons for the acceptance or rejection of a tender must be kept in the minutes of the meeting records (Regulation 10 (4)).

1510 Local Authorities Tender Board Regulations: Local Authorities Act, 1992, Sec. 50; Regional Councils Tender Board Regulations: Regional Councils Act, 1992, Sec. 50; Tender Board of Namibia Code of Procedure 1997, Sec. 20.

ation where two tenders are equal might rarely occur. Furthermore, it would have a doubling effect of granted preference, since tenders of first priority might have been granted price preferences under the preference scheme already.

The award decision by the Tender Board is usually based on a recommendation obtained from a relevant office, ministry or agency. According to Section 18 (2) of the Tender Board Act, the Board can "require a staff member of any other ministry or of any office or agency to assist the Board with the evaluation of any tender or to make recommendations to the Board in connection with any tender." This is further specified in Regulation 2 (2) of the Tender Board Regulations which provides that the Board may, in performing its functions, obtain such expert or technical advice as it may deem necessary. Furthermore, Section 19 (1) of the CoP states that the board shall, after having opened and listed all tenders, submit the tenders to the relevant office, ministry or agency for its recommendation. The RTB and the LTB shall do that respectively with departments, divisions, or sections. [1511] As suggested above the involvement of the procuring entities through recommendations given to the Tender Boards has turned out to be a thin line between mere rubber-stamping of the recommendation through the Tender Board and the Tender Board members making independent decisions, irrespective of the recommendation. In practice, this provision has turned out to be problematic and has led to several judicial disputes. The courts have clarified that the award decision has to be taken by the Tender Board and not by the advising ministry.[1512] In several cases the award decision was set aside because the Tender Board had acted ultra vires by mere rubber-stamping the recommendation obtained from the respective ministry.[1513] It seems that bid evaluation is often carried out by the ministries rather than the Tender

1511 Local Authorities Tender Board Regulations: Local Authorities Act, 1992, Reg. 49; Regional Councils Tender Board Regulations: Regional Councils Act, 1992, Reg. 49.

1512 See e.g. Disposable Medical Products (Pty) Ltd. v. Tender Board of Nambia 1997 NR 129 (HC).

1513 AFS Group Namibia (Pty) Ltd. v Chairperson of the Tender Board of Namibia and Others (A 55/2011) [2011] NAHC 184; CSC Neckartal Dam Joint Venture v The Tender Board of Namibia and Others 2014 (1) NR 135; Disposable Medical Products (Pty) Ltd. v. Tender Board of Nambia 1997 NR 129 (HC); Minister of Education and Others v Free Namibia Caterers (Pty) Ltd. 2013 (4) NR 1061 (SC).

Board itself.[1514] As indicated by an alternate Tender Board member, the evaluation would be made by the ministries because they have the requisite knowledge and expertise.[1515] Two Tender Board members confirmed that the recommendations by the ministries were usually followed, but it was also stressed that those recommendations would be scrutinised and that the Board was under no obligation to follow the recommendation.[1516] There would be no rubber-stamping of recommendations by the Board.[1517] If, for example, the recommendation was that the higher bid is selected from otherwise two comparable tenders, there would be no substance to the matter and the recommendation would not be followed.[1518] In cases where the recommended tender is not the lowest, the permanent secretary needs to certify that the recommendation is made in the best interest of the government and represents the best value to the government.[1519] There have been also instances where the recommendation has been sent back to the ministry for clarification.[1520] According to one Tender Board member, the reasons for not following recommendations are usually uncertainty, vagueness of the recommendation or non-conformity with the law.[1521] The Board, rather than evaluating the bids itself, would look for inconsistencies in the ministry's recommendation and, if it found irregularities, it would form its own, independent opinion.[1522] An interviewee reported that the recommendations were frequently not followed: "Today [at today's board meeting] at least two of the recommendations were not followed."[1523]

It could be claimed that the fact that the Tender Board relies on the recommendations of the line ministries, especially when it comes to technical tenders, might be better characterised as a systemic issue rather than insufficient implementation. It has to be stressed that most of the members have little knowledge, expertise or experience with the technical issues involved in complex tenders plus an overload of work yet still bear the sole

1514 Interview Mrs Jonga (Tender Board, Chief Control Officer), 26th March 2013.
1515 Interview Mr Immanuel (Tender Board, Alternate Member), 27th March 2013.
1516 Interview Mr Titus (Tender Board, Alternate Member), 28th March 2013; Interview Mr Shindinge (Tender Board, Alternate Member), 27th March 2013.
1517 Interview Mr Titus (Tender Board, Alternate Member), 28th March 2013.
1518 Interview Mrs Jonga (Tender Board, Chief Control Officer), 26th March 2013.
1519 IMF, 23, para. 57.
1520 Interview Mr Titus (Tender Board, Alternate Member), 28th March 2013.
1521 Interview Mrs Jonga (Tender Board, Chief Control Officer), 26th March 2013.
1522 Interview Mr Immanuel (Tender Board, Alternate Member), 27th March 2013.
1523 Interview Mr Titus (Tender Board, Alternate Member), 28th March 2013.

responsibility for the award decision. Indeed, what is most important is that the recommendation by the ministry came about in accordance with the law and is fair and reasonable and this is what the Tender Board currently tries to ensure. If the recommendation by the ministry has not followed the principles of fairness and reasonableness, the Tender Board contests or overrules the recommendation and, according to a member of the Tender Board, this happens on a frequent basis. However, despite the Tender Board members' protestations to the contrary, the rubber-stamping of recommendations seems to happen frequently, as case law reveals. The overload of work of the Tender Board as well as exertion of political influence apparently still lead to mere rubber-stamping of recommendations by the ministries. And the exercise of political influence on the decision-making process often results in the best tender not being selected. It is obvious that the distribution of competences and responsibilities in the current Namibian tender legislation raises difficulties and leads to inadequate and unsatisfactory results.

With respect to the evaluation of tenders it can be concluded that legislation provides different criteria affecting the award decision of tenders and that it is unclear to what degree they influence the award decision and how they are weighed to each other. Moreover, the law neither specifies nor restricts the criteria which can influence the Board's award decision. In combination with the missing requirement of specifying the evaluation criteria in the title of tender, this constitutes a severe breach of the principle of transparency of the evaluation of tenders and the award decision. It can be concluded that the Namibian legislation regarding evaluation, comparison and acceptance of tenders is non-transparent and ambiguous. Neither the tenderers nor the wider public can understand how tenders are evaluated and awarded, nor is the Tender Board provided with clear and unambiguous guidelines. This severely undermines the efficiency and effectiveness of tendering and constitutes a massive breach of the principle of transparency. It creates a range of opportunities for abuse that can hardly be detected and traced.

## 4. Transparency and Strategies to Counteract Corruption

### a. Specific Procurement-related Transparency Provisions

Namibian legislation covers some basic publishing requirements but often does not satisfy a high transparency standard that enables an effective and efficient procurement system. It is required to publish the invitation of tenders once in the Government Gazette and at least once in each of the newspapers that are contracted by the government.[1524] Despite this requirement, it has long been common practice to publish tenders in the Gazette only after the tenders have expired which renders its objective to provide potential bidders with the possibility to hand in tenders ineffective.[1525] However, the tender adverts as well as tender awards are published regularly on the Ministry of Finance's webpage. This is commendable and should be incorporated as publication requirement into the new bill. The regional and local tender boards have to publish tenders not less than once in each newspaper circulating in the local authority's area.[1526] Due to reasons of accessibility, it would be more efficient to create a homepage or national forum on which all invitations of tenders are published. This would allow all potential suppliers or contractors to easily get an overview of all open tenders, facilitate their participation in tendering and, hence, enhance competition. The National Treasury in South Africa, for instance, makes the Tender Bulletin, including all tender notices, available on its website. And Mauritius has a procurement website where all tender notices by all public bodies have to be published. This is important and appropriate in regard to the technical development in Namibia and should be implemented as soon as possible. A new law should include a requirement to publish tender notices respectively.

Another problem regarding tenders is that the complete tender documents can only be collected at the Secretariat of the Tender Board and are subject to a fee. This means that tenderers that are not from Windhoek need to travel or send someone to Windhoek in order to obtain the necessary documents. This requires time and money, potentially preventing potential bidders from tendering and is, hence, an impediment to competition. It should be immediately ensured that all tender documents can be obtained electronically in order to promote competition. As internet access is available in most - if not all - parts of Namibia this would reduce the burden for most potential bidders not from Windhoek.

---

1524 Tender Board of Namibia Act 1996, Sec. 11.

1525 M. Townsend, 'Tendering in Namibia', 2008, available at http://www.tenderscan.co.za/index.php?mod=content&page=8; last accessed: 29 November 2015.

1526 Local Authorities Tender Board Regulations: Local Authorities Act, 1992, Reg. 13; Regional Councils Tender Board Regulations: Regional Councils Act, 1992, Reg. 13.

The provision that all tenders shall be opened in public is a very important one.[1527] However - as mentioned above - Namibian legislation does not provide requirements for publishing the date, time, place and manner for the public opening of tenders. It would, e.g., be possible to require that such information is part of the contents of title of tenders. In addition, Section 14 (2) of the CoP gives the public the right to request the public reading of tender prices for building services and cognate works and for civil engineering services. As high amounts of money are typically spent in this sector and given that corruption is wide spread, transparency in this respect can have a positive effect on the outcome of procurement and impede corrupt practices. It is easier to hold the Board accountable.

The immediate notification of the acceptance or rejection of tenderers and the possibility for tenderers to be provided with reasons for the acceptance or rejection is also important for the effective and efficient functioning of a public procurement system. This is provided for in Section 16 of the Tender Board Act and Regulation 19 of the LTBR/RTBR. The LTBR and RTBR additionally contain a deadline for the statement of reasons of 30 days after receipt of such written request. Nevertheless, it seems that the Tender Board has, in some instances, circumvented the obligation to notify also the rejected tenderers by explicitly stating in the instructions to tenderers that only the successful tenderer will be notified.[1528] There have also been other cases with limited transparency in the process, such as the reluctance to publish prices.[1529] This means that the Tender Board has in some cases not been adhering to the applicable tender legislation, revealing that there are shortcomings not only in the public procurement regulations but also the implementation of the law.

Disclosure of the evaluation criteria and method is another key requirement for an effective and efficient procurement system. It is seen as a basic requirement for facilitating transparency and fairness. Moreover, it is important in order to provide the opportunity for potential suppliers or

1527 Local Authorities Tender Board Regulations: Local Authorities Act, 1992, Reg. 18 (6); Regional Councils Tender Board Regulations: Regional Councils Act, 1992, Reg. 18 (6); Tender Board of Namibia Act 1996, Sec. 15 (7); Tender Board of Namibia Code of Procedure 1997, Sec. 14 (1).

1528 Ministry of Finance, 'Supply and Delivery of Clothing Material for the Namibian Correctional Service', p. 9, para. 10; Tender Board of Namibia, 'TB/556', Instructions to tenderers.

1529 Three TIPEEG tenders awarded, Tender Bulletin No. 996 (Windhoek, Namibia), 15-21 February 2013.

contractors to prepare bids in view of the evaluation criteria and method. As discussed above, Namibian legislation does not require the publication of evaluation criteria. Nevertheless, the boards have to keep record of reasons for accepting tender which is not the lowest tender.[1530] There is, however, no indication that the reasons have to be published and the public can only get access to the records if it requests the board to provide reasons or in the context of court proceedings.

As mentioned above, Section 15 (1) of the Tender Board Act and Regulations 18 (1) of the RTBR and the LTBR allow the board at any time to request tenderers to clarify their tenders in order to assist the boards in the examination, evaluation and comparison of tenders. Although the basic idea of the provision is positive, the actual formulation might lead to abuse. An opportunity for tender boards to raise queries to tenderers for clarification is important in order to avoid excluding tenderers on form rather than on substance. Especially new tenderers that are not that experienced in tendering can benefit from such provision as they are given the chance to clarify information. However, such a clarification should only be allowed in the first phase of the tender procedure, meaning the examination phase, and at any rate before the evaluation stage. Otherwise the tenderer might have the opportunity to influence the board's decision. It should further be explicitly prohibited to alter the tender in regard to substance and price. The information provided to the tenderer seeking clarification should furthermore be communicated to all other tenderers for reasons of transparency and fairness. Additionally, in case that the clarifications are material, it might be necessary to extend deadlines in order to allow prospective bidders to accommodate the new information.[1531]

The transparency standards and requirements in the Namibian public procurement legislation are certainly not in line with international best practices and need to be extensively broadened and specified. Transparency should be acknowledged as a key objective and basic principle of the Namibian public procurement system. The GPA and the UNCITRAL Model Law emphasise transparency as one of the primary principles and objectives of public procurement and offer good guidelines in regard to

1530 Local Authorities Tender Board Regulations: Local Authorities Act, 1992; Regional Councils Tender Board Regulations: Regional Councils Act, 1992; Tender Board of Namibia Act 1996.

1531 Cf. United Nations Office on Drugs and Crime, 'Guidebook on anti-corruption in public procurement and the management of public finances', p. 20.

transparency standards and requirements that should be met in every national public procurement system.

In regard to conflicts of interest, the Tender Board Act requires Board members to disclose a direct or indirect interest in a tender or an agreement. Failure of Board members to disclose such an interest is an offence that can be penalised by a fine of up to N$500,000 and/or an imprisonment for up to 10 years.[1532] On the regional and local level this penalty is limited to N$2,000 and 6 months' imprisonment.[1533] The difference of the amount of the maximum fine and term of imprisonment is astonishing since regional or local procurement might also involve large amounts of money and it is unclear why offences by regional and local officials are less severe. More extensive provisions on the integrity and accountability of public procurement officials are needed. Tjirera from the Institute for Public Policy Research, for example, suggests the introduction of a code of conduct including provisions dealing with the disclosure of assets and interests of procurement officials.[1534] Whereas neither the GPA nor the UNCITRAL Model Law provides any proposals in this regard, the Mauritian and the South African approaches are worth considering. The Mauritian Public Procurement Act contains a comprehensive part on procurement integrity.[1535] And South Africa has introduced a Code of Conduct for SCM Practitioners[1536] which establishes basic principles, provisions on conflict of interest, accountability, openness and confidentiality, instructions for bid evaluation teams and a provision on combative practices.

### b. Non-Procurement specific Regulations

Namibia is part of several regional and international transparency and anti-corruption instruments. It has signed and ratified the UN Convention on

1532 Tender Board of Namibia Act 1996, Sec. 6 (3).

1533 Local Authorities Tender Board Regulations: Local Authorities Act, 1992, Reg. 5 (2); Regional Councils Tender Board Regulations: Regional Councils Act, 1992, Reg. 5 (2).

1534 Tjirera, 'Public Procurement in Namibia', p. 1.

1535 Public Procurement Act 2006, Part VIII, Secs. 49-53.

1536 National Treasury, 'Practice Note Number SCM 4 of 2003: Code of Conduct for Supply Chain Management Practitioners '.

Corruption[1537], the African Union Convention on Prevention and Combating Corruption[1538] and the SADC Protocol against Corruption.[1539] Nevertheless, in 2013 in the Corruption Perceptions Index by Transparency International gave it a score below 50 out of 100 (highly corrupt) which suggests that there are severe shortcomings in transparency and accountability and that corruption is still a major hindrance and has not yet been addressed successfully. Namibia scored 48 and was ranked 57th out of 176 countries.[1540] The UNDP came to the conclusion that

> "while corruption is not endemic in Namibia it is still a serious problem which has the potential to grow apace unless firm action is taken on several fronts which both plug loopholes and demonstrate political will."[1541]

While petty corruption seems not as widespread as in other African countries, "[…] corruption takes place in a grey zone of activity populated by politicians, holders of high offices, parastatals and members of their families."[1542]

The government has repeatedly announced anticorruption campaigns and referred to the need to fight corruption in its policies including Vision 2030 and the Nation Development Plan 4.[1543] However, there seems to be a lack of coordinated response to the threat of corruption and there are still

---

1537 The Convention was adopted on 31 October 2003 and entered into force ion 14 December 2005. It was ratified by the Namibian parliament in 2004.

1538 The Convention was adopted in Maputo on 11 July 2003 and entered into force on 5 August 2006. It was ratified by the Namibian parliament in 2004.

1539 The Protocol was adopted in Blantyre on 14 August 2001 and entered into force on 14 August 2003. It was ratified by the Namibian parliament in 2004.

1540 See Website of Transparency International, 'Corruption Perceptions Index 2013', https://www.transparency.org/cpi2013/results (last accessed: 1 December 2015).

1541 United Nations Development Programme; et al., 'Namibia and the United Nations Convention against Corruption. Gap analysis report' (Windhoek: UNDP/ACC, 2013), p. 8.

1542 Bertelsmann Foundation, 'BTI 2014 - Namibian Country Report'.

1543 See Government of the Republic of Namibia, 'Namibia Vision 2030', Policy Framework for Long-Term National Development (Summary) (Windhoek: Office of the President, 2004), p. 52; National Planning Commission, 'Namibia's Fourth National Development Plan 2012/13 to 2016/17' (Windhoek: Office of the President, 2012), p. 41. See also United Nations Development Programme; et al., 'Namibia and the United Nations Convention against Corruption. Gap analysis report', p. 22f. and Bertelsmann Foundation, 'BTI 2014 - Namibian Country Report', p. 12.

legislative gaps that need to be filled and incompatibilities that need to be addressed in order to successfully fight corruption.[1544]

Apart from domestic procurement specific provisions aiming at transparency and counteracting corruption, there are other laws in this respect. Of particular relevance is Article 94A of the Constitution which was added to the Constitution by the Namibian Constitution Second Amendment Act.[1545] It requires the state to put in place administrative and legislative measures necessary to prevent corruption and provides for the establishment of the Anti-Corruption Commission (ACC). Since, in Namibia, an Anti-Corruption Commission was already established by the Anti-Corruption Act and has been operating since 2006, the Second Amendment Act provides for the continuing existence of the Anti-Corruption Commission. The ACC consists of a director-general, a deputy director-general and other staff members. The director-general and the deputy director-general are nominated by the president and appointed by the National Assembly. According to Section 94A (3) of the Constitution, the Anti-Corruption Commission shall be an independent and impartial body. Nevertheless, while the Constitution establishes the ACC as an independent institution, the de facto independence is questionable as in particular the nomination of the director and deputy-director by the president can be used to undermine the independence of the institution. This gives the president the possibility to appoint "[...] a local party cadre who may not be independent with the appointment then being rubberstamped by a National Assembly nominated by the ruling party."[1546]

The Anti-Corruption Act provides requirements for investigations of corrupt practices and defines penalties. It makes corruption a legal offence and specifies different forms of corruption. A person convicted of such an offence is liable to a fine not exceeding N$500 000 and/or imprisonment for a term not exceeding 25 years.[1547] Section 37 of the Act also determines what practices constitute an offence in relation to tenders:

> "A person commits an offence who, directly or indirectly –

1544 United Nations Development Programme; et al., 'Namibia and the United Nations Convention against Corruption. Gap analysis report', p. 23, 42, 57ff.

1545 Act No. 7 of 2010.

1546 United Nations Development Programme; et al., 'Namibia and the United Nations Convention against Corruption. Gap analysis report', p. 46

1547 Anti-Corruption Act 2003, Sec. 49.

(a) gives or offers to give to any person any gratification as an inducement or a reward for, or otherwise on account of, the withdrawal of, or the refraining from the making of, any tender for a contract invited by any public body, private organisation, corporate body or other organisation or institution to perform any work, provide any service, supply any article, material or substance or for doing anything; or

(b) solicits or accepts or agrees to accept for himself or herself or any other person any gratification as an inducement or a reward for or otherwise on account of the withdrawal of, or the refraining from the making of, a tender for a contract referred to in paragraph (a)."

In fact, the person giving or offering the gratification as well as the person soliciting or accepting it are liable to prosecution. But only corruption with respect to the withdrawal of or the refraining from making a tender is a criminal offence under this section. Any other exertion of influence on the tender procedure does not fall under this provision.

The Anti-Corruption Commission has investigatory, preventive and educational functions which are further determined in the Anti-Corruption Act.[1548] Section 16 of the Act requires the Commission to submit annual reports on the activities of the Commission to the prime minister who then forwards them to the National Assembly. The Commission has though been criticised to be inconsistent in reporting information.[1549] Moreover, the reports do not contain any information on the investigations conducted by the ACC with the exception of a few example cases.[1550] While the Commission has emphasised the need for new public procurement legislation,[1551] there has been no reference to any investigation regarding corruption in public procurement cases. This lack of transparency makes it difficult to assess the effectiveness of the Commission in fighting corruption.

---

1548 See Anti-Corruption Act 2003, Sec. 3.

1549 E. Tjirera; G. Hopwood, 'The ACC in Action. What does the track record say? ', Anti-Corruption Research Programme, Paper 6, November 2011 (Windhoek: Institute for Public Policy Research, 2011), p. 5.

1550 An analysis of the performance of the ACC has been conducted by Tjirera and Hopwood (see previous footnote). The annual reports are available on the ACC'S website: http://www.accnamibia.org/page.php?sid=12&title=Publications&parent=7 (last accessed: 3rd September 2013).

1551 Anti-Corruption Commission, 'Annual Report 2012-2013' (Windhoek: Anti-Corruption Commission, 2013), p. 27. See also Anti-Corruption Commission, 'Annual Report 2011-2012' (Windhoek: Anti-Corruption Commission, 2012), p. 26f.

Although the Commission has a broad mandate to investigate and also to initiate investigations in alleged cases of corruption[1552], its effectiveness is controversial. It is assigned a very important role in the fight against corruption and it has been described as "one of the most positive developments in the legal field undertaken by Government"[1553], but there have been instances where the ACC seemed unwilling to expedite certain investigations. Moreover, it seems to be overburdened[1554] and only takes action on request rather than being proactive on its own. Nevertheless, it has conducted investigations in several tender cases.[1555] Often the allegations have been found not to be true. In other cases it is unclear whether an investigation was conducted. For example, in the tender dispute about the construction of the new headquarters for the Ministry of Lands and Resettlement there were rumours that the ACC conducted a probe of the tender,[1556] but the ACC never published a report about the investigation. There might be different factors that play a role for the success of anti-corruption investigations by the ACC, including the existing structures in the judicial field, the efficiency of the organisational structure, and the quantity and quality of staff.[1557] In particular, the excessive workload for the Commission and the shortage of human resources at the office of the Prosecutor-General who has the prosecution power for corruption cases and causes a delay in the prosecution of corruption cases can be identified as hindering the effectiveness of the ACC.[1558] The Prosecutor-General bears the final responsibility to decide whether prosecution is warranted or

1552 The procedures for investigations by the Commission and the powers vested in the Commission with regard to investigations are outlined in Sections 17ff. of the Act.

1553 B. O'Linn, 'Namibia: The sacred trust of civilization', Ideal and reality. Volume II (Windhoek: Polination Publishers 2010), p. 182.

1554 Interview Mr Ruppel (LorentzAngula Inc., Director/Chairman), 28th February 2013.

1555 See e.g. 'ACC Clears N$2 Billion Namport Tender' (Newspaper article), The Namibian (Windhoek, Namibia), 6 December 2011; 'Ex-NWR-Chef in Erklärungsnot - Schwimmbad-Finanzierung setzt Aupindi dem Verdacht der Bestechlichkeit aus' (Newspaper article), Allgemeine Zeitung (Windhoek, Namibia), 8 February 2012; 'Vorwurf unbestätigt - Keine Korruption bei Namibia Liquid Fuel' (Newspaper article), Allgemeine Zeitung (Windhoek, Namibia), 18 July 2007.

1556 'ACC probes tenders' (Newspaper article), The Windhoek Observer (Windhoek, Namibia), 2008.

1557 O'Linn, 'Namibia: The sacred trust of civilization', p. 182ff.

1558 Ibid, 183.

not. Therefore, after concluding an investigation and finding that a person has committed an offence under the Anti-Corruption Act, the ACC forwards the investigation file to the Prosecutor-General who then may delegate authority to conduct criminal proceeding in court in respect of that matter to any staff member of the Commission who possesses the required legal qualifications to appear in court.[1559] Apart from the staff shortage at the Prosecutor-General's office, the Prosecutor-General has declined prosecutions for lack of evidence and sent dockets back for further information revealing in several cases.[1560] This reveals that the cooperation between both institutions is not as optimal as it should be with regard to the fact that anti-corruption strategies require the consolidated power of all relevant institutions in order to be effective.

An éclat at the Ministry of Works, Transport and Communication, where a senior official allegedly violated tender procedures, led to comprehensive investigations conducted internally and by the ACC.[1561] Money was paid to a company for work that was never carried out. An internal committee mandated to investigate a self-enrichment scam in which several senior people at the Ministry stood accused of pocketing hefty bribes, particularly in the tender procedure for government capital projects had been appointed a few years earlier.[1562] More than 30 cases have been transferred to the prosecutor. In most of these cases poor quality work was delivered and the money saved was shared between the contractor, ministry officials and site inspectors. In other cases the work was not even done yet the inspector nevertheless certified it has been completed.[1563] Investigations by the internal committee, the prosecutor and the ACC carried on for years and some individuals have been found guilty, some have been cleared. The slow pace of investigations has been justified by the prosecutor by pointing to the lack of human resources in her office.[1564] The 300-

1559 Anti-Corruption Act 2003, Sec. 31.

1560 Cf. Tjirera; Hopwood, 'The ACC in Action', p. 1, 7; United Nations Development Programme; et al., 'Namibia and the United Nations Convention against Corruption. Gap analysis report', p. 43.

1561 'Another neverending probe', Corruption Tracker, Insight Magazine, August 2007; see also 'Official Quits, Pockets Millions' (Newspaper article), New Era (Windhoek, Namibia), 12 July 2007; 'ACC Completes Works Probe' (Newspaper article), New Era (Windhoek, Namibia), 19 October 2007; 'ACC Probes Tender Scam' (Newspaper article), New Era (Windhoek, Namibia), 21 September 2007.

1562 Ibid.

1563 Ibid.

1564 Ibid.

pages report of the Committee was finalised in late 2007[1565] but to date no action has been taken based on the findings and the report has not been published.[1566] There has been criticism because there have been cases such as the suspension of an official with full pay.[1567]

There are several other laws referring to the matter of corruption.[1568] The Code of Conduct for Regional Councils[1569] contains for example a list of requirements for the behaviour of members of the regional council as well as for the relationship with communities, between the members and with other staff members. Furthermore, the Code provides for an internal review mechanism which allows the suspension of members if it is found that a member has acted contrary to the code. There is, however, no such official code of conduct for local and the national government authorities. Other examples are the Prevention of Organised Crime Act[1570] and the Financial Intelligence Act[1571] which basically comprise Namibia's anti-money laundering law.

Apart from the ACC, there are other institutions or bodies that can be assigned a role in the fight against corruption including the ombudsman,[1572] the auditor-general,[1573] and the Standing Committee on Public Accounts.[1574] However, according to several of the interviewees, these control committees do not or cannot efficiently carry out their function; reasons might be that they are underfinanced and/or lack competent

1565 'Works Ministry's Pandora's box starts to open', Corruption Tracker, Insight Namibia, October 2007.

1566 'From the Archives', Corruption Tracker, Insight Magazine, September 2009.

1567 K. McNamara, 'Chinese Contractors: Namibian Economist 05.10.2007' (unpublished letter to the Economist).

1568 See for a discussion of all relevant laws: United Nations Development Programme; et al., 'Namibia and the United Nations Convention against Corruption. Gap analysis report', p. 9ff.

1569 Code of Conduct for Members of Regional Councils 2004.

1570 Act No. 29 of 2004.

1571 Act No. 13 of 2012

1572 The role of the Ombudsman will be discussed in Subchapter 7 (c).

1573 Article 127 of the Namibian Constitution provides for the appointment of an Auditor-General who is independent and its functions and duties are specified in the State Finance Act 2001 (Act No. 31 of 1991).

1574 Standing committees are permanent committees established under the Standing Orders of the National Assembly or by resolution of the National Assembly for the duration of a parliament. See Website of the Namibian parliament: http://www.parliament.na/index.php?option=com_content&view=article&id=118&Itemid=1244 (last accessed: 18 December 2015).

staff.[1575] Links recommends in regard to the role of the ACC in corruption prevention

> "[...] that the ACC live out its statutorily mandated role and become more prominent and proactive in advising on, guiding and reforming of public sector practices, processes and institutions, in its efforts to minimise the impacts of corruption on public service delivery."[1576]

In 2008, the IMF country report referred to weaknesses in the functioning of internal audit in the public service.[1577] These are correlated issues that should be addressed within the framework of public procurement reform.

## 5. Secondary Objectives

The Namibian government pursues a price preference policy when carrying out public procurement in order to promote the national economy in regard to foreign competition. Moreover, suppliers or contractors of the government are required to adhere to certain rules and standards.

### a. Price Preference Policy

The price preference policy is specified in the General Notice "Tender Board of Namibia: Preferences"[1578] and names certain socio-economic factors that influence the general decision about the best bid. Preferences are specified as a percentage. The amount equating the granted total preference percentage of the tender price is deducted from the tender price. Hence, the higher the percentage of the price preferences is, the lower is the tender price.

The following preferences or reservations apply in Namibia:[1579]

> "up to 20% preference for goods produced in Namibia

---

1575 Interview Mr Haibach (KAS, Director), 21th February 2013, also Interview Mr Hopwood (IPPR, Director), 26th March 2013; Interview Mr Ruppel (LorentzAngula Inc., Director/Chairman), 28th February 2013.

1576 Links, 'Corruption Prevention: Strengthening Systems, Procedures and Practices', p. 15.

1577 IMF, 24f., paras. 59ff.

1578 General Notice No. 160, Tender Board of Namibia: Preferences, Government Gazette No. 551 of 14 December 1992.

1579 Ibid.

up to 10% preference for goods assembled in Namibia

up to 5% preference to persons domiciled or companies incorporated in Namibia

up to 3% preference for after-sales service provided in Namibia

up to 3% preference for goods conforming to national or international standards

Small scale industries: 2% preference if more than 10 but fewer than 25 workers in small scale industries are employed; 3% if more than 24 but fewer than 50 workers are employed; 5% if more than 50 workers are employed

Employment creation in communal or underdeveloped areas: 2% if more than 10 but fewer than 25 people in communal areas are employed; 3% if more than 24 but fewer than 50 people are employed; and 5% if more than 50 people are employed

up to 2% preference for Namibian manufacturing companies

Implementation of approved affirmative action policy: 2 to 3% preference may be granted, depending on the merits of the case, i.e. structured training programmes, employment of women or handicapped people, or other programmes benefiting disadvantaged Namibian citizens."

The preference system is comprehensible and does not solely restrict preferences to a certain group of people. Although the Namibian input/origin plays an important role, tenderers implementing affirmative action policies or employment creation measures in communal or underdeveloped areas can likewise benefit from the preference scheme. Furthermore, the preference system aims to support the small scale industry and to support the issuance of goods conforming to national and international standards.

Although these preferences criteria allow for a deviation from a decision strictly based on the lowest price, they have proved to be deficient in practice and seem to be detrimental to rather than beneficial to the aim of redressing social, economic and educational imbalances and encouraging industrial and commercial interests in Namibia. With a great number of foreign investors incorporating companies, manufacturing and assembling goods in Namibia, most companies fall under the preference scheme. As the Deputy Minister of Finance stated, this price preference policy has "not produced the required results". And he continued, saying:

> "To the contrary, through the practices of 'fronting' and the like it more often than not caused unsustainable price increases while at the same time gave unintended advantages to non-Namibian enterprises."[1580]

1580 'Tender law needs urgent rewrite' (Newspaper article), Namibian Sun (Windhoek, Namibia), 12 September 2011.

### b. Other Socio-Economic Objectives

The standard tender conditions require tenderers who apply for the affirmative action price preferences to attach a valid Affirmative Action Certificate.[1581] Furthermore, as mentioned above, Section 42 of the Affirmative Action (Employment) Act provides that

> "[n]o contract shall be entered into by or on behalf of the State and any relevant employer [...] unless the relevant employer concerned is in possession of a valid affirmative action compliance certificate."

An Affirmative Action Compliance Certificate has to be produced by every relevant employer (25 or more employees).[1582] There have been cases where this provision has been evaded by way of sub-contracting smaller companies with fewer than 25 employees,[1583] thereby falling outside the scope of the Act. There have also been cases where tenders were awarded to companies that were not in possession of valid Affirmative Action Certificates despite they had more than 25 employees.

The Social Security Act requires any employer to register himself and his employees with the Social Security Commission.[1584] The failure to do so constitutes an offence.[1585] Registered employees shall be members of the Maternity Leave, Sick Leave and Death Benefit Fund; the National Medical Benefit Fund and the National Pension Fund. [1586] Tenders usually require the attachment of original certificates of good standing with the Social Security Commission. The tender documents establish that a tender may be disqualified if the tenderer has neglected its social security contributions, taxes or levies. The emphasis "may disqualify" gives the procuring entity or the Tender Board the discretion to award tenders to companies that do not comply with social security obligations, despite this is required by law.

---

1581 Ministry of Finance, 'Supply and Delivery of Clothing Material for the Namibian Correctional Service', Notice to Tenderers - Changes to Tender Conditions.

1582 Affirmative Action (Employment) Act 1998, Arts. 20 and 41.

1583 Buys; Hallick, 'The effect of Chinese construction companies on the Namibian construction industry ', 11.

1584 Social Security Act 1934 (Act No. 34 of 1994), Sec. 20 (1).

1585 Ibid, Sec. 20 (4).

1586 Ibid, Sec. 21 (1) (a-c).

The instruction to tenderers TB/556 that is usually part of the tender documents[1587] requires companies to certify adherence to Section 138 of the Labour Act of 2007[1588]. This reads as follows:

> "(1) For the purposes of this section, "licence" includes a permit, grant or concession in terms of any law on mining and minerals, wild life, environment and tourism, or fisheries.
>
> (2) The State must not issue a licence to an employer, or enter into a contract with an employer for the provision of goods or services to the State, unless that employer has given a written undertaking as described in subsection (3).
>
> (3) In an undertaking contemplated in subsection (2), the employer must undertake to ensure that every individual directly or indirectly employed for the purpose of exercising rights under the licence, or for the purpose of providing goods or services under the contract, is employed on terms and conditions not less favourable than -
>
> (a) those provided for in a collective agreement in that industry or those prevailing for similar work in the industry and the region in which the employees are employed; or
>
> (b) those prevailing in the nearest appropriate region, if similar work is not performed in the region.
>
> (4) In any dispute about whether an employer is complying with an undertaking given in terms of this section, any person, including the Minister, may make application to the Labour Court to compel compliance, and the Labour Court may make any appropriate order in order to secure compliance."

This concerns the terms and conditions of employment; the state is prohibited from entering into a contract with a company or supplier who does not employ its staff according to the applicable collective agreement or terms and conditions prevailing in the nearest appropriate region. This includes direct as well as indirect employees; hence a sub-contractor would also be subject to the same terms and conditions. This is similar to the Mauritian approach where certain labour standards and working conditions are integrated as contract conditions. However, in contrast to Mauritius there are no provisions for monitoring compliance, which seems to render the provision ineffective.

The objective of protecting and preventing the influx of foreign workers was addressed by the Tender Board in 2010 when it announced in a state-

1587 See, for example, Ministry of Finance, 'Supply and Delivery of Clothing Material for the Namibian Correctional Service', p. 10, Instructions to Tenderers, TB/556, para 17.

1588 Labour Act 2007.

ment to a Namibian newspaper that "100 per cent of all unskilled and semi-skilled labour must be sourced, without exception, from within Namibia."[1589] It was also emphasised that the Ministries of Labour, Works, Home Affairs and Finance would have to work together to implement the new regulation: "The Ministry of Home Affairs will be expected to tighten the criteria for issuing work permits while [the Ministry of] Labour should monitor employers."[1590] The Secretary of the Tender Board also told the newspaper that a review of the public procurement law will also address the monitoring of the winning tenderer's commitment to affirmative action, job creation and the sourcing of local products.[1591]

In April 2013 the then Permanent Secretary of the Ministry of Finance, Erica Shafuda, announced that they "[...] came up with a new intervention that will benefit Namibian companies only when it comes to the awarding of tenders" and further explained that "[t]o make sure that we empower locally owned companies, we will now be sourcing locally, unless the service and products are not available in the country."[1592] Recently many tender invitations contain the following notice:

> "These tenders are restricted to 100 Percent Namibian owned registered SME's and Namibian nationals only. The registration certificate with the Ministry of Trade and Industry must be attached. Tenderers that do not comply with this notice will automatically be disqualified."

Last year the tender board has, moreover, started to try to get local companies to team up with more experienced ones, so that technical expertise can be transferred.[1593] Skills transfer to Namibian companies can be seen as essential component for the development of the local economy.

The support of SME's is another focus of public procurement and fits well into the general objective to promote SMEs. The Namibian government, supported by the German government, financed a tender training programme for SME contractors. This has been carried out by the Ministry of Works in collaboration with the Roads Authority and was attended

1589 'Tender Board tightens rules to protect jobs' (Newspaper article), The Namibian (Windhoek, Namibia), 3 February 2010.

1590 Ibid.

1591 Ibid.

1592 'Stop fronting foreign businesses - Shafudah' (Newspaper article), The Namibian (Windhoek, Namibia), 23 April 2013.

1593 Interview Mr Isaacs (Tender Board, Chief Control Officer), 26th March 2013.

by 360 participants.[1594] The promotion of SME'S participation in public procurement by means of training rather than preferential treatment is to be highly welcomed and should be expanded.

### c. TIPEEG Tenders

According to the outline of TIPEEG by the National Planning Commission[1595] any project identified as falling under TIPEEG, in particular capital projects and projects with a great number of jobs, is exempted from the existing government procurement procedures in order to allow for speedy implementation. The TIPEEG Implementation Committee (TIC) has to recommend on the most effective procurement procedures to be followed to ensure fast implementation of projects, with due regard to good governance, and has the power to approve the procurement of all projects under TIPEEG. Whereas responsibility for the execution of the projects is still vested with the relevant ministries, the decision with regard to procurement is vested solely with the TIC. The Tender Board is not referred to in the paper. The key fields in which TIPEEG is to be active are agriculture, transport and logistics, tourism, housing and sanitation, and public works. It is not clearly specified who decides which projects fall under TIPEEG and which fall under the Tender Board Act.[1596]

TIPEEG is a response to the unemployment crisis which came about in September 2009 and, as a Tender board member explained, since public procurement involves a huge amount of public money this was found as the only and best way to create employment.[1597] Although it was envisaged that TIPEEG is exempted from the Act, it still follows certain rules. A court case questioning whether procurement through TIC is lawful did not, unfortunately, result in a judgement. However, an order setting aside the award of a TIPEEG tender was issued.[1598] As no judgement was ren-

1594 'Labour-based road construction benefits communities' (Newspaper article), The Namibian (Windhoek, Namibia), 19 November 2012.

1595 The establishment of the National Planning Commission is provided for in Article 129 of the Namibian Constitution.

1596 National Planning Commission, 'Targeted Intervention Program for Employment and Economic Growth (TIPEEG)'.

1597 Interview Mrs Jonga (Tender Board, Chief Control Officer), 26th March 2013.

1598 See 'TIPEEG N$100m tender set aside' (Newspaper article), The Namibian (Windhoek, Namibia), 22 December 2011.

dered and, hence, no reasons were delivered for the decision to set aside the award, it is not clear whether the TIC is generally authorised to award TIPEEG tenders. This is very unfortunate because the court could have used the opportunity to clarify what procedure is required for TIPEEG projects.

It seems common practice to involve the Tender Board in the decision to award the tender. A former chairman of the Tender Board said in 2011 that there will not be a wholesale tender exemption for TIPEEG projects. Rather, the TIC will evaluate the tenders; the Tender Board will still take the award decision.[1599] Furthermore, line ministries have to ask for exemptions from the Tender Board (one interviewee stressed that the process has still to be in accordance with the law). Whereas tenderers are usually given 21 days to prepare their bids, TIPEEG projects can be advertised for only 7-14 days to accelerate the project.

Criticism has arisen that under TIPEEG a number of buildings (government offices) have been constructed without calculating the maintenance costs and that there have been numerous instances of procurement decisions which are not far-sighted (no assessment of the product circle/no consideration of follow-up costs).[1600] There have further been allegations that, in order to push affirmative action, companies have been awarded tenders that do not have the necessary expertise.[1601]

### d. Interim Conclusion

The examples show that the failure to regulate the application of secondary policies in public procurement in detail, and especially the exemption from the transparency rules of the Act in respect to TIPEEG tenders lead to obscure practices counteracting the principles of public procurement.

Although the Namibian law does not prohibit the application of secondary objectives, it does not contain any specifications in this respect. Socio-economic and ecological criteria can likewise be applied as tender, evaluation or award criteria. The lack of regulations governing the issue is not only inefficient but also dangerous, since it is up to the tender boards to

1599 'Government tender exemptions balloon' (Newspaper article), The Namibian (Windhoek, Namibia), 13 September 2011.

1600 Interview Mr Ruppel (LorentzAngula Inc., Director/Chairman), 28th February 2013.

1601 E.g. Interview Mr Hopwood (IPPR, Director), 26th March 2013.

decide what collateral objectives, in addition to the preference policy, are to be pursued. Moreover, it makes it very difficult if not impossible for tenderers to adapt to policy strategies. The Tender Board members stated that they have to take decisions in view of (socio-) economic development,[1602] but it seems there are no guidelines or specifications in this respect so that the effect depends on the discretion and the decisions of the Tender Board members. The discretion granted to tender boards could lead to an inconsistent, non-transparent and arbitrary application of secondary policies. It would be better to identify key issues that should be addressed uniformly. The basic requirements that secondary policies need to have a basis in law or be clearly set out by the policy office or a relevant institution and be applied in a transparent manner are necessary in order to ensure that the primary objectives of public procurement are not sacrificed when applying secondary objectives.

The Tender Board Act is currently under review with the intention to "[...] envisage majority Namibian ownership of enterprises to be the most important qualifying criteria for public tender awards."[1603] Hence, a focus would be laid on economic and social factors but not on ecological or ethical factors. Especially ecological sustainability should, however, be a decisive factor also in regard to the development aspect. And in view of compliance with, e.g. labour law, affirmative action law and social security law, ethical criteria could provide a major step in regard to socio-economic development in the long run. The Mauritian approach of implementing adherence to those laws as contract conditions plus ensuring that compliance is monitored and any violation is sanctioned effectively and immediately might be suitable to counteract the problems currently observed in Namibia. The reform of the Act would provide a good opportunity to include ecological and ethical criteria in order to make it sustainable.

1602 As e.g. Interview Mr Immanuel (Tender Board, Alternate Member), 27th March 2013.

1603 'Tender law needs urgent rewrite' (Newspaper article), Namibian Sun (Windhoek, Namibia), 12 September 2011. See also 'Runter von Verliererspur' (Newspaper article), Allgemeine Zeitung (Windhoek, Namibia), 13 September 2011.

## 6. Chinese Construction Companies in the Namibian Public Procurement System

China assisted SWAPO during the liberations struggle and the newly formed Namibian government established diplomatic ties with China straight after independence in 1990.[1604] This relationship has evolved and they now enjoy close economic relations and trade cooperation. Namibian government officials often use references to China's role in the liberation struggle and the close cooperation between the two countries to emphasise the goodwill of its engagement in Namibia.[1605] Whereas China primarily imports raw materials from Namibia, Chinese investments are mainly in the retail and construction sectors.[1606] Grants, interest free loans, credit lines and concessional loans have been granted to Namibia by the Chinese government.[1607] According to a study conducted by the Labour Resource and Research Institute a wide range of projects such as low cost housing, schools, clinics, borehole drilling, irrigation, an aquaculture research centre, and the new State House have been implemented with economic aid from China.[1608] In 2009, it was estimated that between 60 and 70% of the tenders in the construction sector were awarded to Chinese companies.[1609] A Tender Board member stated, however, that nowadays it was rare for a Chinese company to be awarded a tender, in particular because of the equity distribution principle and the 51% Namibian ownership criterion. This, however, contradicts the statements of representatives of the Namibian construction industry, who claim that about 85 or 90% of the public tenders are awarded to Chinese companies.[1610] The Director of the National Union of Namibian Workers (NUNW) also estimated that 75% of the projects were given to Chinese companies.[1611] Public construction projects implemented by Chinese companies include e.g. the Supreme Court build-

---

1604 See for example H. Jauch; I. Sakaria, 'Chinese investments in Namibia', in A.Y. Baah;H. Jauch, *Chinese Investments in Africa - A Labour Perspective* (Accra: African Labour Research Network, 2009), p. 255.

1605 See e.g. 'China means well in Africa: Ngatjizeko' (Newspaper article), The Namibian (Windhoek, Namibia), 3 April 2007.

1606 Cf. Jauch; Sakaria, 'Chinese investments in Namibia', p. 261.

1607 For details of Chinese grants and loans between 1909 and 2009 see ibid, 259.

1608 Ibid, 259.

1609 Ibid, 265.

1610 Interview Mr Agenbag (Murray & Roberts Namibia, Commercial Director), 7th March 2013.

1611 Interview Mrs Jonas (NUNW, Director), 28th March 2013.

ing, the new head office for the Ministry of Lands and Resettlement and the new building for the Ministry of Finance. It has been alleged that the majority of construction projects was awarded to Chinese companies which disregard the legal working standards and thereby gain unfair advantages in competition.[1612] Allegations and observations that Chinese companies do not adhere to the labour laws of the country have been circulating for years, at least since 2006, but despite repeated calls by political officials to Chinese companies to stop these abuses there has so far not been a breakthrough.[1613]

Chinese companies entered the Namibian construction market around 2000. They usually handed in bids with a much lower price but were still able to deliver.[1614] It has been proven that the ability to hand in low bids is at least partly due to savings on labour costs by not adhering to the legal standards and paying wages much lower than the minimum wage in that sector. The Chinese argue they pay their employees according to the grading of skills and labour contribution.[1615] A Chinese manager has also said that Namibians were lazy and therefore did not deserve to be paid highly.[1616] It is also rumoured that those companies are subsidised by the Chinese government.[1617] Bilateral agreements have also played a role in the award of contracts to Chinese companies.

---

1612 'Hat Namibia seine Chancen genutzt? Eine Bilanz (Teil 4a/5)' (Newspaper article), Allgemeine Zeitung (Windhoek, Namibia), 13th April 2012.

1613 See 'Namibia: "Chinese invasion" - old foes police a new frontier' (Newspaper article), Sunday Times (Johannesburg, South Africa), 28 March 2011; 'Construction Work at Chinese company at Rundu stopped' (Newspaper article), The Namibian (Windhoek, Namibia), 14 August 2008; 'Chinese Confronted on Labour Abuse' (Newspaper article), The New Era (Windhoek, Namibia), 24 August 2006; 'Pohamba Calls for Respect for Labour Laws' (Newspaper article), The New Era (Windhoek, Namibia), 13 May 2013; 'Rundu road workers sign contracts' (Newspaper article), The Namibian (Windhoek, Namibia), 10 June 2008; 'China should respect labour laws' (Newspaper article), Informanté (Windhoek, Namibia), 29 August 2012.

1614 Interview Mrs Jonga (Tender Board, Chief Control Officer), 26th March 2013.

1615 'Chinese Embassy breaks wall in construction' (Newspaper article), The Economist (Windhoek, Namibai), 13 September 2007.

1616 'Namibians deserve underpayment, they are lazy - Chinese manager' (Newspaper article), Informanté (Windhoek, Namibia), 29 October 2009.

1617 Interview Mr Isaacs (Tender Board, Chief Control Officer), 26th March 2013.

The findings of a report of the Centre for Chinese Studies at Stellenbosch University[1618] seem to confirm these suspicions. According to this report there are several factors that make Chinese companies in Africa so successful, including cost competitiveness in overall bidding price, access to cheap capital through Chinese state-owned banks, access to skilled low-cost labour, access to cheap building materials through supply chains from China, and political support from the Chinese government channelled through Chinese embassies and Economic and Commercial Counsels in the respective African countries.

Namibia has ratified all core conventions of the International Labour Organisation and the Labour Act of 2007 contains the basic rights enshrined in the ILO conventions.[1619] Nevertheless, despite the existence of protection measures for the local labour market and the local economy in Namibia, evasion appears to be rampant. The law there seems to be ineffective in regard to the achievement of the objective. The illegal advantage Chinese companies gain by violating local laws should not be ignored but scrutinised. Violations should affect future tenders. It seems, however, that certain government officials are willing to subordinate workers' rights and interests to the interests of foreign capital,[1620] but it is also possible that those officials are also pursing their own interests and benefits.

The Namibian construction industry is somewhat perplexed by the situation and shares the common view that the awarding of tenders to Chinese companies is not always according to the rules. The involvement of state institutions in companies investing abroad differs significantly from other states, a fact that becomes obvious when analysing the Chinese foreign investment strategies. The Namibian construction industry assumes that the Chinese companies active in Namibia are state-owned companies or parastatals rather than private companies.[1621] Financial support for outward investments can be obtained from the Export-Import Bank of China (EXIM) which is fully state-owned and has the mandate to facilitate export and import in certain areas, to assist Chinese companies in offshore contract

1618 Centre for Chinese Studies (Stellenbosch University), 'China's Interest and Activity in Africa's Constructrion and Infrastructure Sectors', (Centre for Chinese Studies, Stellenbosch University: 2008), p. 7 (available at www.ccs.org.za/.../DFID%203rd%20Edition.pdf; last accessed: 30 November 2015).

1619 Jauch; Sakaria, 'Chinese investments in Namibia', p. 286.

1620 Ibid, 287.

1621 Interview Mr Agenbag (Murray & Roberts Namibia, Commercial Director), 7th March 2013.

projects and outbound investment, and to promote international economic and trade cooperation in general.[1622] EXIM has representative offices in Paris, St. Petersburg, and in Johannesburg for Southern and Eastern Africa. In fact, loans given by EXIM are a foreign policy tool and concessional loans include the requirement that the infrastructure contract financed by the loan must be carried out by a Chinese contractor.[1623]

In respect to quality of work, the interviews showed that the quality of the work cannot be said to be generally deficient. On the contrary, according to the officials interviewed the Chinese generally produced good quality work and it was normal in construction business that the quality was sometimes worse than usual.[1624] It is, however, alleged that the Chinese companies did not pay minimum wages.

No Chinese construction company is a member of the Construction Industries Federation.[1625] They are therefore not party to the Collective Agreement of the Construction Industries Federation and the Mining & Allied Workers Union[1626], which enforces minimum wages, compulsory pension schemes, health cover, etc. "The Chinese contractors are therefore allowed by the government and by the Union (sadly!) not to contribute to the "compulsory" pension schemes for Namibian workers, nor comply with the minimum wage laws."[1627] This would enable the Chinese companies to save on labour costs and bid lower than companies that are part of the Collective Agreement.[1628] According to McNamara wage-related costs account for almost 50% in the construction sector and companies adhering to the laws cannot compete with companies which often pay less than a third of the minimum wage.[1629] The latter was confirmed by the Labour Resource and Research Institute, whose research demonstrated that hourly wages of N$ 3 instead of the minimum wage of N$8.44 were the norm for

---

1622 Website of EXIM, 'Brief Introduction', http://english.eximbank.gov.cn/profile/intro.shtml (last accessed: 8 September 2011).
1623 L. Corkin, 'The Lion's Share' (2007) icon review 11-14 at 12.
1624 Interview Mr Agenbag (Murray & Roberts Namibia, Commercial Director), 7th March 2013.
1625 The CIF counts more than 250 member companies including construction companies, sub-contractors and builder's merchants.
1626 Collective Agreements are regulated in Sections 70-73 of the Labour Act 2007.
1627 Jauch, 'Chinese Investments in Africa'; K. McNamara, 'Chinese Contractors: Namibian Economist 05.10.2007' (unpublished letter to the Economist).
1628 Ibid.
1629 Jauch; Sakaria, 'Chinese investments in Namibia', p. 269.

Namibian workers at Chinese construction companies.[1630] The research was, however, conducted before 2009 and things might have changed in the meantime. Several very important developments have occurred since the time of the study. For example, Government Notice No. 154,[1631] which extends the application of the Collective Agreement to all employers and employees in the construction industry, has been enacted. Hence, from June 2012 on, the Chinese construction companies have been legally obliged to comply with the provisions, even though they are not members of the Construction Industries Federation.

Besides of the allegation that Chinese companies ignore minimum wages and working conditions standards, Namibian construction companies claim that some Chinese companies import labour despite the fact that the use of foreign labour is prohibited if the work can be done by local workers.[1632] Whereas for Namibian companies are closely monitored as to whether all workers have a work permit (and it would be difficult to obtain a work permit for foreign workers!), it seems that the labour commissioner turns a blind eye on the construction sites of Chinese companies.[1633] As mentioned above, the Tender Board disclaims any responsibility to ensure companies' compliance with the law when implementing contracts from tender awards, instead seeing the respective ministries as bearing responsible for contract administration.

A report of the Ministry of Labour and Social Welfare from 2006 unequivocally demonstrates that the government is aware that most of the Chinese companies were not operating according to the provisions of the Labour Act; they were not paying minimum wages or adhering to other basic conditions of employment.[1634] Furthermore, the Labour Commissioner criticised Chinese companies for their failure to comply with Namibian laws.[1635] Despite this awareness, the government has still not ensured that Chinese companies adhere to local laws.

---

1630 Ibid, 269f.

1631 Extension of Collective Agreement: Construction Industry, 2012 (No. 154 of 2012, Government Gazette No. 4970).

1632 A representative of Murrays & Roberts saw he had seen Chinese doing ceilings in a project where they also did some work and he knew that this work could be done by local workers.

1633 Interview Mr Agenbag (Murray & Roberts Namibia, Commercial Director), 7th March 2013.

1634 Jauch; Sakaria, 'Chinese investments in Namibia', p. 212.

1635 'Chinese Confronted on Labour Abuse' (Newspaper article), The New Era (Windhoek, Namibia), 24 August 2006.

It is also stated that the majority of Namibians employed by Chinese contractors are not registered with the Social Security Commission, although this is required by law.[1636] And McNamara claims that Chinese companies have regularly been awarded tenders since 1998 despite not possessing a compliance certificate in term of the Affirmative Action Act.[1637] As was discovered during the tender evaluation of the new head office of the Ministry of Lands and Resettlement, Chinese companies misrepresented the number of their employees on tender documents to avoid being required to produce Affirmative Action Certificates.[1638] This contradicts the law which prohibits the state from entering into any contract with a relevant employer not holding the certificate. According to members of the construction industry, an apparent collusion between the Chinese contractors and civil servants prevailed in the Employment Equity Commission (EEC), the Tender Board and the Department of Works (DoW) and also between the Chinese contractors and building professionals, who advise the DoW and the Tender Board regarding tender acceptance. “The EEC is under the control of the Chinese contractors who in turn serve the interests of a ‘higher authority’.”[1639] The EEC is alleged to be aware of the facts but nonetheless fails to apply the relevant laws. The same can be said for the officials of the DoW and the Tender Board.

A well-known advocate confirmed the view that laws are strict for Namibian companies but not for the Chinese ones, meaning that the implementation lacks efficiency in respect to Chinese companies.[1640] The certificates that are prescribed for companies entering into contracts with the state were referred to as window dressing by the Director of Namibia Construction.[1641]

---

1636 K. McNamara, 'Chinese Contractors: Namibian Economist 05.10.2007' (unpublished letter to the Economist).

1637 Ibid.

1638 See e.g. 'Chinese contractors accused of dishonesty' (Newspaper article), The Economist (Windhoek, Namibia), 5 October 2009.

1639 K. McNamara, 'Chinese Contractors: Namibian Economist 05.10.2007' (unpublished letter to the Economist).

1640 Interview Mr Tötemeyer (Advocate / Society of Advocates of Namibia, Vice-president), 18th March 2013; Interview Mr Schulz (Namibia Construction (Pty) Ltd., Director), 22th March 2013; Interview Mr Agenbag (Murray & Roberts Namibia, Commercial Director), 7th March 2013.

1641 Interview Mr Schulz (Namibia Construction (Pty) Ltd., Director), 22th March 2013.

The allegation that a Chinese company that won the tender to build the new headquarters of the Ministry of Lands and Resettlement although they did not produce a valid certificate of compliance from the office of the Employment Equity Commissioner as required by the Tender Board regulations was also the issue in the case *Namibia Construction Industries and Murray and Roberts v the Chairman of the Tender Board and the Ministry of Works.*[1642] Namibia Construction Industries and Murray and Roberts were unsuccessful tenderers for the construction of the new headquarters of the Ministry of Lands and Resettlement. The company that won the tender stated that it had fewer than 50 employees. It was probably not aware that threshold had been changed from 50 to 25.[1643] Companies with fewer than 25 employees are exempted from the application of the Affirmative Action Act. However, a survey taken of the site records of past and recent projects by the architects, who were doing the evaluation of tenders, reflected that in 2006 and the first half of 2007 China Nanjing International was employing between 42 and 78 employees at their building sites.[1644] The Employment Equity Commissioner had received no notification from China Nanjing regarding the relevant employer status.[1645]

The quantity surveyor found that China Nanjing International, as the only tenderer, has complied with all other tender conditions and requirements and has submitted a fair and reasonable price at market related rates.[1646] The consultancy report by Kerry McNamara Architects recommended awarding the tender to one of the applicants whose application included formal errors. They considered this to be less severe than the failure to produce compliance certificates of the Employment Equity Com-

1642 Namibia Construction Industries and Murray and Roberts v the Chairman of the Tender Board and the Ministry of Works, unreported Case, A 283/2007, High Court (30 November 2007).

1643 According to Section 20 (1) of the Affirmative Action (Employment) Act, the Minister of Labour has the power to define by notice in the Gazette who is a relevant employer. See Kerry McNamara Architects Inc.; Philip Main Quantity Surveyor 'New Headquarters for the Ministry of Lands and Resettlement in Windhoek, Tender No. F1/10/1 - 08/2007, Evaluation of Tenders and Recommendation' (unpublished), Sec. 2, para. 2.3.

1644 Kerry McNamara Architects Inc.; Philip Main Quantity Surveyor 'New Headquarters for the Ministry of Lands and Resettlement in Windhoek, Tender No. F1/10/1 - 08/2007, Evaluation of Tenders and Recommendation' (unpublished), Sec.2, para. 2.5.

1645 Ibid.

1646 Ibid, evaluation by philip main quantity surveyors, para. 5.4.

missioner, since such omission constituted a violation of the law. The applicants had submitted the contents of the Bill of Quantities as computer printouts although the tender criteria required that tenders must be submitted on the official document and not on the tenderer's own stationary bearing the tenderer's own conditions of tender. Failure to do so was stated as a reason for disqualification of tenders. Kerry McNamara Architects argued that both applicants were substantially compliant with the conditions of tender and that

> "[...] the accuracy, relevance and substance of the information provided by the Bill of Quantities are the issues, and not merely the form in which the vital information was submitted."[1647]

Namibia Construction, however, also failed to submit a valid Certificate of Good Standing from the Receiver of the Revenue. It was recommended to allow the company 3 working days to submit a valid original Certificate of Good-Standing. The evaluator asserted, in Section 4 of the report:

> "5. There are two broad areas of apparent non-compliance in terms of the Tender Form:
>
> 5.1 The Tender Form – with technical requirements concerning non-compliance with the Conditions of Tender: the Tender Board is empowered to exercise its judgement and discretion on judging the value of the tender submissions.
>
> 5.2 Non-compliance with the laws that control equitable procurement in the construction industry – no discretion can be exercised when the laws of the country are not complied with.
>
> 6. The Tender Board has legal power to use their discretion to clarify any doubts when adjudicating tenders. These powers can bus used in the interest of the state and also in ensuring an equitable tender system in the evaluation of tenders. "

They referred to Section 15 (1) of the Tender Board Act which allows the Board to request any tenderer to clarify his or her tender. It was concluded, from the input of the principal agent and the quantity surveyor, that none of the tenders was fully compliant with the tender conditions. This would result in the cancellation of the tender and a new call for tenders. Nevertheless, since this would involve significant cost and loss of public funds, the evaluators stated their opinion that such extreme action would not be justified.[1648] It, instead, recommended that

> "[...] the Bill of Quantities documents of Namibia Construction and Murray & Roberts are legitimised by either allowing the contractor, as a point of clarification

1647 Ibid, Sec. 4, para. A.2.
1648 Ibid, Sec. 6, Conclusion.

> and also as an opportunity for the renunciation, of any possible own Conditions of Tender [...]" or "judging that the documents do in fact provide all the information required to enable the consultants to evaluate their tender effectively."[1649]

The report finally recommended awarding the tender to Murray & Roberts. The Ministry, however, recommended awarding the tender to Chinese Nanjing International, despite the allegations that they did not adhere to the Affirmative Action Act. This recommendation was followed by the Tender Board and it was claimed by the respondents that the Tender Board simply endorsed the decision by the Ministry.[1650] According to the Director of Namibia Construction, the recommendation by the principal agent is often not followed or the agent is asked to change the recommendation. Such requests are generally followed since refusal might result in reprisals, in particular not getting a contract in the future.[1651] This was also confirmed by McNamara, who has served as principal agent in the past.[1652]

The application for urgency by Namibia Construction and Murrays & Roberts was denied and the Chinese company which won the tender commenced work on the project. The case was finally dismissed for procedural reasons[1653] in January 2014 long after the construction of the Ministry of Headquarters had been finished[1654] and the claimants were ordered to pay their opponent's legal costs.[1655]

This case is of special relevance because of increasing Chinese competition in the construction sector, which is highly dependent on public contracts,[1656] and the allegations that Chinese companies do not adhere to local laws. Despite an announcement stressing the importance of employ-

1649 Ibid, Sec. 6, para. 2.

1650 Cf. 'Chinese major beneficiaries of State monies' (Newspaper article), Windhoek Observer (Windhoek, Namibia), 8 March 2008.

1651 Interview Mr Schulz (Namibia Construction (Pty) Ltd., Director), 22th March 2013.

1652 Interview Mr McNamara (Kerry McNamara Architects Inc., Director), 1st March 2013.

1653 The judge held that there is no point in giving Namibia Construction and Murray & Roberts an opportunity to now join the other tenderers as parties to the case. See 'Lands office tender challenge dismissed' (Newspaper article), The Namibian (Windhoek, Namibia), 22 January 2014.

1654 Ibid.

1655 Ibid.

1656 Interview Mr Schulz (Namibia Construction (Pty) Ltd., Director), 22th March 2013.

ment equity and of political will to make it effective[1657] the Tender Board and the Ministry ignored the company's' failure to comply with the Act. This is contradictory and leads to the assumption that there were other motivations to award the tender to the China Nanjing International. Even if the formal error of the two applicants had been found to be too severe to award the tender to them, the Tender Board should have cancelled and re-advertised the tender instead of awarding it to a company that was obviously in breach of the law.

One reason for the lack of successful implementation of laws in respect of Chinese companies might be corruption. One of the interviewees was in possession of a fax by an architecture company to a Chinese company in early 2007. In this fax the director of the company requested the other company to explain what the site manager's intentions were in handing an envelope with N$2,000.00 to the person responsible to test the materials. [1658] The project manager replied and apologised for the behaviour of his site manager. He said he felt it was a big mistake and the site manager would be punished.[1659]

Apart from corruption in form of bribery by Chinese companies there have been rumours that some government officials have shares in Chinese companies.[1660] This would lead to severe conflicts of interest and could explain the alleged favouritism of Chinese companies. The business relations between government officials and Chinese companies are said to be non-transparent and covered up by complex company nettings and changing partner.[1661]

---

1657 The Minster of Labour and Social Welfare Alpheus !Naruseb announced in March 2007 at the opening of the EEC's new offices that Government has requested all law enforcement agencies to ensure speedy prosecution of employers that „dare test" the Government's determination to enforce compliance with the affirmative action law. See 'Affirmative Action Crackdown - Govt to Pursue Offenders' (Newspaper article), The New Era (Windhoek, Namibia), 2 April 2007.

1658 Communication from H. Scheepers to C.J. International: New Offices for DV7: Concrete Test Results, Windhoek, 7 March 2006.

1659 Personal email from Shuohua to Scheepers regarding: *Re: The faxes dated Mar 7, 2006* (Windhoek, 8 May 2006) (unpublished).

1660 Interview Mr Agenbag (Murray & Roberts Namibia, Commercial Director), 7th March 2013.

1661 Interview Mr Tötemeyer (Advocate / Society of Advocates of Namibia, Vice-president), 18th March 2013; Interview Mr Schulz (Namibia Construction (Pty) Ltd., Director, 22th March 203.

Interestingly, the Department of Works Investigation Committee wrote a report[1662] on the anomalies in the evaluation and awarding of construction tenders in general in 2005. Unfortunately, the report is confidential and was not made available to the public. It seems it was carried out in response to the dissatisfaction of the construction industry with the manner in which tenders were awarded. It was, for example, asserted that there were many cases in which the number of employees did not match the number of employees stated on the Certificate of Good Standing issued by the Social Security Commission and that such contradictions were ignored in the evaluation of tenders. Similarly, companies often certified that they were not a relevant employer, but under the organisational strength list the employee numbers were much higher than 50. Strikingly, the report also stated that

> "[...] the Department of Works now requires it to be stated in tender documents that in the event of the tender amount exceeding N$ 5,000,000, tenders will only be accepted from relevant employers and who are in possession of a valid affirmative action compliance certificate."[1663]

It was found that this condition is not adhered to in all instances. The Committee also mentioned that, apparently, there were cases where consultants had been instructed to amend / change their evaluations and recommendations.

The report concluded with the following recommendations:

> "Clear rules must be set out regarding tender evaluations and awards. An attempt was made in 2001 by an employee of the Department of Works regarding the price preference system but these have not been adopted. The rules are generally clear but need adaptation after consultation with the relevant parties and need to be expanded to allow for other factor affecting the award of tenders."[1664]

This leads to several conclusions. First, that there was an awareness of problems and that there were certain people within the institutions that recommended changes. However, it also seems that there was a lack of political will to implement these recommended changes. It also discloses that tenders were indeed awarded irrespective of compliance with the criteria. This shows that is important to find mechanisms that prevent evasion of the law and regulations. Transparency, accountability, control

---

1662 Department of Works Investigation Committee, 'Report on the Anomolies in the Evaluation and Awarding of Construction Tenders in General', Windhoek, 2005.

1663 Ibid, 4.

1664 Ibid, 5.

mechanisms and sanctions for corruption are very important issues to be addressed in the reform. As mentioned above, it is of utmost importance to include substantive provisions on contract management in order to monitor performance and scrutinise non-compliance with tender and contract conditions as well as with the local laws. Unfortunately, the problems and shortcomings of the current system as it is actually practiced have never been fully examined. This would, however, be of great advantage in order to find adequate provisions to counteract these practices.

## 7. Review Procedures

### a. Introduction

Namibian procurement legislation does not refer to review procedures at all. There is, consequently, no procurement-specific external judicial or non-judicial review mechanism. Nor is there an internal review procedure and Namibia does not recognise a general right to administrative review. Hence, the only way to challenge tender decisions is by way of bringing an action before the court or, to a very limited extent, the involvement of the ombudsman. Unsatisfied tenderers can request the Tender Board to clarify its decisions and to provide reasons. "If they are not happy with that, they can only go to court."[1665] Court proceedings are often avoided because of the costs or fear of reprisals, especially in future tenders.[1666] The existing situation can be described as deficient for tenderers and other stakeholders and as hindering rather than contributing to the efficiency and effectiveness of public procurement.

### b. Administrative Review

Public procurement legislation does not provide for administrative review. Unsatisfied tenderers can ask for reasons. If they are not happy with that they have to go to court. But there is no formal procedure and also no gen-

1665 Interview Mrs Jonga (Tender Board, Chief Control Officer), 26th March 2013.
1666 Interview Mr Tötemeyer (Advocate / Society of Advocates of Namibia, Vice-president), 18th March 2013.

erally applicable provision or common law rule that establishes a right to reasons and a right to information.

In contrast to South Africa, the right to reasons is not constitutionally established, but can – to a limited extend - be derived from case law. According to this case law a decision must always be based on reasons. In *Kersten t/a Witvlei Transport v National Transport Commission and Another*[1667], for example, the court at 239H held – with reference to Article 18 – that a body which is required to act fairly and reasonably can in most instances only do so if those affected by its decisions are appraised in a rational manner as to why that body made the decision in question. Giving reasons was implicit in the requirements of Article 18 of the Constitution and the failure would militate against the principle of transparency embodied in the Constitution. And in *AFS Group Namibia (Pty) v Chairperson of the Tender Board of Namibia and Others*[1668] (a procurement case) the judge held:

> "[115] The failure of the Tender Board to give reasons to the applicant based on what it terms to be a legal interpretation of section 16 of the Tender Board also in my view constitutes prima facie an unfair and administrative action and an infringement of the applicant's rights under Article 18 of the Constitution. The giving of reasons is fundamental to fair and administrative decision-making."

In this case the Tender Board failed to give reasons to a tenderer who had not been shortlisted for consideration in the tender process. The unsuccessful tenderer had made a written request for the reasons why it had not been shortlisted. The Tender Board, however, argued that the tender had not been submitted to the Tender Board for award and as a result the Tender Board was not required to, nor could it provide the reasons as yet. Section 16 (1) (b) requires the Tender Board, on the written request of a tenderer, to give reasons for the acceptance or rejection of his or her tender. The decision illustrates that the interpretation of this requirement is not restricted to the acceptance or rejection at the award stage but also in prequalification procedures. The reference to Article 18 of the Constitution and the court's reasoning concerning the relationship between this article and the right to reasons seem to be a great step towards the acknowledgement of a (constitutional) right to reasons. Especially for tenderers re-

---

1667 Kersten t/a Witvlei Transport v National Transport Commission and Another 1991 NR 234 (HC).

1668 AFS Group Namibia (Pty) Ltd. v Chairperson of the Tender Board of Namibia and Others (A 55/2011) [2011] NAHC 184.

questing reasons for the acceptance or rejection of their tender this right can be derived from Section 16 (1) in the light of Article 18 of the Constitution. Nevertheless, there is not yet a general obligation to directly give reasons for a decision.[1669]

The right to information is similarly insufficiently developed. It is only applicable in the sense of the audi alteram partem rule, hence in the course of a judicial hearing.[1670] Nevertheless, even the application of this rule has been criticised as being not stringently enforced and it has been claimed that a culture of secrecy prevails.[1671]

### c. Non-Judicial External Review

The ombudsman's mandate allows for the processing of procurement matters. However, there are several hindrances that might explain why the ombudsman has been approached only a very few times so far and is not suitable to handle procurement cases in general. Chapter 10 of the Constitution and the Ombudsman Act[1672] provide for the establishment of an ombudsman with wide-reaching functions. The Bill of Rights of the Namibian Constitution contemplates that aggrieved persons claiming that a fundamental right or freedom has been infringed or threatened may approach the ombudsman to provide them with such legal assistance or advice as they require.[1673] Since complaints to the Office of the Ombudsman are free of charge, there are no limitations as to who can approach the ombudsman, no requirements of legal representation and no specific formal requirements;[1674] the ombudsman might therefore be an alternative option for tenderers.

The Office of the Ombudsman has, "the duty to investigate complaints concerning alleged or apparent instances of violations of fundamental

1669 C. Glinz, 'Verwaltungsrecht und Rechtsstaatlichkeit in Namibia - *Ein entwicklungspolitisches Reformprojekt*', Recht und Verfassung in Afrika (Baden-Baden Nomos, 2013), p. 180ff.

1670 Ibid, 187.

1671 Ibid, 204.

1672 Ombudsman Act 1990 (Act No. 7 of 1990).

1673 Constitution of Namibia 1990, Art. 25 (2).

1674 Cf. K. Ruppel-Schlichting, 'The independence of the Ombudsman in Namibia', in N. Horn;A. Bösl, *The Independence of the Judiciary in Namibia* (Windhoek: Macmillan Education Namibia, 2008), p. 272f.

rights and freedoms."[1675] This includes the right to administrative justice as contemplated in Article 18 of the Constitution. Since public procurement has been classified as administrative action by the courts[1676] a tenderer may approach the ombudsman if he or she feels that his or her right to administrative justice has been violated in a public procurement matter. The Constitution further provides that the ombudsman has the duty to investigate "manifest injustice, or corruption or conduct by such official which would properly be regarded as unlawful, oppressive or unfair in a democratic society"[1677] and "to investigate vigorously all instances of alleged or suspected corruption and the misappropriation of public monies by officials and to take appropriate steps."[1678] Section 3 (2) (a) of the Ombudsman Act is also important. This provision reads as follows:

> "Without derogation from the provisions of subsection (1), any request or complaint in respect of instances or matters referred to in that subsection, may include any instance or matter in respect of which the Ombudsman has reason to suspect -
>
> (a) that any decision or recommendation taken or made or about to be taken or made by or under the authority of the State, or any local or regional authority, commission, board, corporation, committee, body or institution established or instituted by or under any law, or any act performed or about to be performed or any omission to act on account of any such decision or recommendation, or any act performed or about to be performed by, or any omission to act of, any person in the employment of the State or any such authority, commission, board, corporation, committee, body or institution, or any act performed or about to be performed, or any omission to act, being an act or omission on behalf of the State or such authority, commission, board, corporation, committee, body or institution, or purporting to be any such act or omission -
>
> (i) abolishes, diminishes or derogates from the fundamental rights and freedoms or will abolish, diminish or derogate from any such rights and freedoms;
>
> (ii) is or will be in conflict with any provision of any law or the common law;
>
> (iii) is or will be unreasonable, unjust, unfair, irregular, unlawful or discriminatory or is based on any practice which may be deemed to be as such;
>
> (iv) is based on a wrong interpretation of the law or the relevant facts;
>
> Tenderers can approach the Ombudsman in matters concerning the right to administrative action, public procurement legislation and/or corrupt practices."

---

1675 Constitution of Namibia 1990, Art. 91 (a).

1676 AFS Group Namibia (Pty) Ltd. v Chairperson of the Tender Board of Namibia and Others (A 55/2011) [2011] NAHC 184.

1677 Constitution of Namibia 1990, Art. 91 (a).

1678 Ibid, Art. 91 (f).

The ombudsman cannot only become active in many fields but also has the duty and power to take appropriate action to call for the remedying, correction, and reversal of certain violations of the law.[1679] The Constitution and the Ombudsman Act provide a non-exhaustive list of actions that might be taken by the ombudsman, such as the negotiation and compromise between the parties concerned or referring the matter to the Prosecutor-General. However, the ombudsman can only make recommendations, not issue any orders.[1680] And although he has the legal power to go to court to get an interim interdict to halt a tender, he said he did not have the resources to do so.[1681] Especially in cases where a lot of money is involved this would be unsatisfactory and unsatisfied tenders would choose to go to court directly rather than to approach the ombudsman.[1682] Furthermore, the process might take a long time due to the workload the ombudsman has, and time would be a crucial issue in tender disputes.[1683] Usually tenderers would have enough money to retain a lawyer and only those few that do not have enough financial resources would approach the ombudsman.[1684] But also tenderers who do not have the financial resources to engage a lawyer would have the possibility of applying for legal aid.[1685] Thus, there have only been a few isolated procurement cases that have been handled by the ombudsman.[1686]

So far only the 2007 Annual Report indicates cases concerning corruption or non-transparency in tender procedures. The report contains one case summary relating to public procurement. The complainant, an unsuccessful tenderer, claimed irregularities in the tender process. An investigation by the Office of the ombudsman was unable to substantiate the complainant's allegation. The ombudsman also mentioned another case where an unsuccessful tenderer approached him, and, after looking into the matter, the ombudsman recommended that the Tender Board cancel the award and call for tenders again.[1687] The Tender Board accepted the recommen-

1679 Ibid, Art. 91 (e).
1680 Interview Mr Walters (Ombudsman of Namibia), 27th March 2013.
1681 Ibid.
1682 Ibid.
1683 Ibid.
1684 Ibid.
1685 Ibid.
1686 Ibid.
1687 Ibid.

dation and issued a new call for tenders.[1688] Both of the aforementioned cases concerned relatively small tenders.

It can be concluded that the ombudsman provides a useful external non-judicial review mechanism only in a very few procurement cases. With view to the peculiarities of procurement disputes, such as the importance of interim interdicts, the powers and functions of the ombudsman are insufficient. Additionally, the ombudsman's extensive field of operation and its popularity in other fields lead to an overload of work for his office. This limited institutional capacity further constrains the ombudsman's potential in this respect.

### d. Judicial Review

As mentioned above, public procurement decisions have been generally classified as administrative action and are, hence, reviewable under Article 18 of the Namibian Constitution. Article 18, the right to administrative justice, which provides for a right to judicial review, reads as follows:

> "Administrative bodies and administrative officials shall act fairly and reasonably and comply with the requirements imposed upon such bodies and officials by common law and any relevant legislation, and persons aggrieved by the exercise of such acts and decisions shall have the right to seek redress before a competent Court or Tribunal."

Judicial review in public procurement matters is usually based on Article 18 of the Constitution and common law. Article 18 does not substitute the common law rules but rather supplements them. This has been emphasised in case law.[1689]

Article 18 has to be read in conjunction with Article 12 which establishes the right to a fair trial and Article 5 which requires the executive, legislature and judiciary and all organs of the government and its agencies to respect and uphold the fundamental rights and freedoms and, furthermore, declares them enforceable by the courts. This imperative naturally includes the administrative justice provision of Article 18.

---

1688 Ibid.

1689 See e.g. Frank and Another v Chairperson of the Immigration Selection Board 1999 NR 257 (HC): ;The Medical Association of Namibia Limited and Others v The Minister of Health and Social Services and Others, unreported case, A 199/2009 (28 June 2010): para. 113ff.

As mentioned above, Article 18 constitutionally defines and complements or broadens the applicable common law. Article 66 explicitly provides that the common law of Namibia in force on the date of independence shall remain valid to the extent to which it does not conflict with the constitution or any other statutory law. The same applies for all laws which were in force immediately before the date of independence which are to remain in force until repealed or amended by Act of Parliament or until they are declared unconstitutional.[1690] Moreover, the decisions of the South West African Supreme Court as well as the higher South African courts are still authoritative.[1691] Administrative law consists of the pre-constitutional law and has been extended by relevant provisions of the Constitution, new legislation and the case law of Namibian courts.[1692] Because of the persistence of the pre-constitutional law, Namibian administrative law is materially based on South African administrative law.[1693] However, since the introduction of the Promotion of Administrative Justice Act[1694] in 2000, South Africa has struck out on a new path. A closer examination of this topic and Namibia's administrative law would though be beyond the scope of this dissertation.[1695] It should be sufficient to say that the remedies applied are to a large extent identical. Although the basis in law is different, the main elements remain very similar.

When applying Article 18 the superior courts of Namibia have not only recognised judicial review but also the power to review discretionary decisions. The criteria the courts have applied when reviewing discretionary decisions include the misuse of powers when taking discretionary decision, in particular bad faith, consideration of irrelevant considerations and reasons and unreasonable evaluation of existing facts or law.[1696] There have been several court cases in respect of public procurement issues. Some of those have made a great contribution to the development of public procurement law; others have disclosed the shortcomings of judicial review as the sole review mechanism for public procurement cases.

---

1690 Constitution of Namibia 1990, Art. 140 (1).

1691 Sippel, 'Rechtsrezeption in Namibia', 86.

1692 Glinz, 'Verwaltungsrecht und Rechtsstaatlichkeit in Namibia', p. 205.

1693 Ibid.

1694 Promotion of Administrative Justice Act 2000.

1695 For a detailed discussion of administrative law in Namibia see Glinz, 'Verwaltungsrecht und Rechtsstaatlichkeit in Namibia'.

1696 Glinz, 'Verwaltungsrecht und Rechtsstaatlichkeit in Namibia', p. 289.

## 8. The main Principles of Public Procurement in Namibian Case Law

### a. Procedural Issues

There have been a few cases dealing with procedural issues of judicial review of public procurement issues, including locus standi, the timeframe for review applications and burden of proof. These will be outlined in the following.

The issue of who has locus standi to bring applications to court regarding an award decision by the Tender Board was considered in *Kerry McNamara Architects Inc and Others v Minister of Works, Transport and Communication and Others.*[1697] The two applicants had agreed with one of the tenderers to render services to their company in case the tender was successful. The tender was awarded to another company that tendered a lower price. The question arose as to whether the applicants' rights were of derivative nature or the applicants' interests were directly and substantially affected by the particular administrative actions. The court made clear that "[...] tenderers would be the only persons who have the necessary locus standi to review and insist on compliance with the regulations."[1698] It held that the two applicants "[...] do not fall within that category of persons whose interests were directly and substantially affected by the particular administrative acts."[1699] This strict interpretation of locus standi was, however, modified by later administrative law cases which accorded indirectly concerned persons locus standi.[1700]

The question of what constitutes an unreasonable delay before review proceedings were instituted was dealt with in *Disposable Medical Products (Pty) Ltd. v Tender Board of Namibia and Others*,[1701] which was decided under the former Tender Board Regulations from 1970.[1702] This case concerns an application for review and a prayer to set aside a decision of

---

1697 Kerry McNamara Architects Inc and Others v Minister of Works, Transport and Communication and Others 2000 NR 1 (HC).

1698 Ibid, 11A.

1699 Ibid, 11A-B.

1700 See for an extensive discussion of the matter and the relevant case law: Glinz, 'Verwaltungsrecht und Rechtsstaatlichkeit in Namibia', p. 226ff.

1701 Disposable Medical Products (Pty) Ltd. v. Tender Board of Nambia 1997 NR 129 (HC).

1702 Tender Board Regulations (promulgated in terms of s 26A of Finance and Audit Ordinance 1 of 1926) 1970.

the Tender Board regarding certain items in two different tenders. The first tender was awarded on 6 August 1996 the second one on 20 September 1996. The application for review was served on the first respondent on 29 November and on the other respondents even later than this. The tenders were for products of medical nature for general use in hospitals. The contract period as set out in the tender documents was for a limited period, namely from 1 August, 1996 to 31 July 1998 for the first tender and from 1 July 1996 to 30 June 1998 for the second one. Consequently, the contract period had already started when the application was issued. The court found that the period of about two months elapsing after the award of the second tender would be unreasonable in the circumstances.[1703] The applicant stated the reason that he wanted to wait for the second tender to be awarded before launching proceedings in regard to the first tender. The court rejected the argument as being unfounded as it "was unsure when this would happen or whether there would have been any reason to take those proceedings also on review."[1704] According to the court,

> "[...] in deciding whether a delay was unreasonable two main principles seem to apply. Firstly, whether the delay caused prejudice to the other parties and secondly, the principle applies that there must be finality to proceedings."[1705]

In the ratio decendi the court considered the question of unreasonable delay in the light of the specific nature of public procurement and also referred to potential negative effects and prejudices for public procurement stakeholders that set-asides might cause after the award of tender and the conclusion of the contract.

> "In my opinion there are various factors which should have alerted the applicant to the fact that time was an important factor in the circumstances of this case. The first such indication was that the tender was awarded for a limited time only and for a specific quantity of items. By the time the tender was awarded the contract period had already started to run. Under these circumstances the Applicant must have known that once a tender is awarded the successful tenderer is required to enter into a contract with first or fifth respondents within a specific time. (See the Special Conditions of Tender.) Once such agreement is entered into the successful tenderer is bound to deliver and to sell at the prices so tendered and in terms of the conditions of contract. A step to set aside the award of a tender must have prejudicial consequences for both the tenderer, in this case the second respondent as well

1703 Disposable Medical Products (Pty) Ltd. v. Tender Board of Nambia 1997 NR 129 (HC): 133D-E.

1704 Ibid, 134G.

1705 Ibid, 132C-D.

> as the fifth respondent. In the case of the fifth respondent, and if the tender is set aside, it would mean a complete reversal and again setting in motion the cumbersome process to call for fresh tenders, possibly in a rising market. The prejudice for the second respondent is in my opinion also obvious. One possible result of such a set-aside would be that he will sit with stock which is not readily saleable on the open market or his profit may be tied up in a turnover of the bulk of the items to be delivered by him. The fact of the matter is that a setting aside of the tender affects other prejudicially and this was known to the applicant."[1706]

The argument that the matter was complicated and that it took time to prepare the application was not shared by the court and, in combination with the fact that the application could prejudicially affect the interests of others, it found that the delay was unreasonable.

Another procedural issue that was raised in this case was the question of who bears the burden of proof that the Tender Board acted mala fide. In *Disposable Medical Products (Pty) Ltd. v Tender Board of Namibia and Others*[1707] the court found that the burden of proof that the Tender Board acted mala fide rests on the applicant. In this case, the court made a finding regarding the interpretation of Regulation 8 (5) of the Tender Board Regulations stating that "[n]o resolution of the Board shall be invalid because it is based on an erroneous calculation or a bona fide incorrect application of the regulations." Such a provision can also be found in the procurement legislation currently applicable.[1708] The finding is, hence, still of particular relevance. The Board had granted a preference of 15% instead of the 16% preference the applicant was entitled to. The court found the following:

> "As such it seems to me to fall within the ambit of Reg 8(5) and if it were not for this erroneous calculation applicant, instead of fourth respondent, would have been awarded the tender. This, in my opinion, is precisely what Reg 8(5) had in mind and it can therefore not be said that the resolution of the first respondent by awarding the tender to fourth respondent, was invalid.
>
> Mr Smuts however argued that the figure of 15 was an arbitrary figure which was plucked from the air because neither the first nor fifth respondents anywhere attempted to explain the mistake. I agree with Mr Smuts that if the 15 was an arbitrary percentage just plucked from the air either because those determining it acted mala fide or with an ulterior motive, Reg 8(5) would not assist the respondents.

---

1706 Ibid, 133I-134D.
1707 Ibid.
1708 Tender Board Regulations 1996, Sec. 5 (4).

> But in those circumstances one would expect and require from the applicant to set out grounds for such an allegation. No such grounds were however set out."[1709]

It was clearly established that the applicant bears the onus of proving that the Tender Board acted mala fide. Putting the onus of prove on the applicant is dangerous as it involves the risk that the Tender Board abuses the provision by manipulating the tender award. The Board could, in that case, pretend in court to have made an erroneous calculation, which would be difficult for the loosing tenderer to prove. In particular with respect to the lack of transparency standards in the Namibian public procurement system which makes it difficult to follow Tender Board decisions, it might be difficult to prove that the Tender Board acted mala fide. Thus in such cases a reversal of burden of proof is recommendable.

### b. The Principle of Legality

The principle of legality requires not only that decisions are taken according to the law, but also that the decision-maker is authorised to do so and is properly constituted.[1710] Several decisions have been rendered by the Namibian courts concerning these issues.

The High Court emphasised in *AFS Group Namibia (Pty) v Chairperson of the Tender Board of Namibia and Others* that the mere fact that the EFuel system needs to be overhauled in order to prevent fraud is no reason for a default and illegal tender procedure.

> "[127] Should the Court overlook a tender process that prima facie falls foul of legislation as well as the Constitution, in order to prevent abuse being perpetrated on an EFuel system, when this abuse could have been avoided if decision-makers complied with the law in the first place? Or should this less than perfect EFuel system continue, until the Tender Board has got its house in order? I cannot see that it would be in the public interest to permit a prima facie blatant disregard for the law to continue unabated. Surely illegality cannot be overlooked in the public interest, and in my view, I should at this stage, decline to do so."[1711]

1709 Disposable Medical Products (Pty) Ltd. v. Tender Board of Nambia 1997 NR 129 (HC): 138H-139H.

1710 See on the principle of legality also Glinz, 'Verwaltungsrecht und Rechtsstaatlichkeit in Namibia', p. 223.

1711 AFS Group Namibia (Pty) Ltd. v Chairperson of the Tender Board of Namibia and Others (A 55/2011) [2011] NAHC 184.

In *Minister of Education and Others v Free Namibia Caterers (Pty) Ltd.*[1712] it was established that alterations of tenders in order to qualify are contrary to the law. The court found that "[...] the third appellants' tender was irregularly altered from being disqualified, on proper and valid grounds, to being qualified, for improper and invalid reasons",[1713] in other words, the non-acceptable tender had been changed in order to qualify. Certain documents proved that the members of the evaluation committee "[...] had received unpalatable promptings from higher authorities who wanted the committee to reverse its earlier adverse recommendation against the third appellant."[1714] This is a case disclosing the prevalence of and the scope for corruption in the current organisational and institutional setting. It also exemplifies that the courts can play an important role in challenging public procurement practices and establishing requirements in this respect.

In *New Era Investment (Pty) Ltd. v The Roads Authority 2014*[1715], an unsuccessful tenderer which had the lowest bid price complained that certain criteria and their weighting were applied by the public authority to its disadvantage. This constituted a failure of fairness and reasonableness because the public authority did not apply its mind, meaning that it did not make an objective assessment, and it took into account irrelevant and extraneous considerations in rejecting the applicant's tender. The court rejected these arguments on the basis that the public authority was entitled to collect whatever information and facts and apply whatever criteria and factors in its procurement policy, rules and procedures it desired. It could further put any weight of relevance and importance on any piece of information and fact and any criterion or factor[1716] as long as all these were applied equally to all tenders.[1717] The Roads Authority's decision was based on the fact that the price was 17.76 % below the recommended tender price by the quantitative supplier. It referred to the tender board standards of the Department of Works of the Ministry of Works and Transport which provides for disqualification of tenderers submitting a tender price

1712 Minister of Education and Others v Free Namibia Caterers (Pty) Ltd. 2013 (4) NR 1061 (SC).
1713 Ibid, 1082B.
1714 Ibid, 1073H.
1715 New Era Investment (Pty) Ltd. v Roads Authority and Others 2014 (2) NR 596 (HC).
1716 Ibid, 602G-H.
1717 Ibid, 603E.

more than 15 percent below the cost estimates for the project. The court stressed in this regard:

> "[…] I accept that a tender price below a certain benchmark, in the present case 15 percent, may result in serious prejudice to the first respondent. For instance, it may result in financial strain or insolvency in respect of the particular tenderer. That may in turn result in that tenderer defaulting to carry out the works and the first respondent resorting to the appointment of third parties to complete the works. Additionally, such low tender price may lead to the tenderer cutting corners during the carrying out of the works, resulting in poor workmanship or non-compliance with specifications."[1718]

Although the court's reasoning in general deserve support – tender board regulations should include safeguards to recognise abnormally low tenders and ensure that such low tender prices do not have a negative effect on the procurement outcome – the court did not strengthened but rather undermined the transparency standards regarding the evaluation criteria and its weighting. Although the current legislation does not require publication of all evaluation criteria and their weighting, the court could have derived such a requirement from the principles of fairness and reasonableness under Article 18.

*Serenity Manufacturers v Minister of Health and Social Services and Another*[1719] is an appeal case that concerns the legality of a provision in an agreement for the award of tender A13-4/2000 to Serenity Manufacturing (Pty) Ltd. The agreement was concluded between Serenity Manufacturing (Pty) Ltd. and the Ministry of Health and Social Services for an estimated quantity of 6 million napkins at a price of N$160 per pack of 200 for the first year of the agreement, and N$170 per pack of 200 for the second year of agreement. In fact, a much lesser amount of napkins was ordered. Serenity Manufacturing (Pty) Ltd.'s claim was based on the premise that the defendant was in breach of the agreement to order at least 90% or 80% of the estimated quantity. The court of lower instance dismissed the suit. The issue before the Supreme Court was whether the respective provision of the agreement was in conflict with Section 7 (1) (b) of the CoP. The Supreme Court found that the respective clause fell within the scope of Section 7 (1) (d) which allows an agreement to be concluded for an unspecified quantity or unguaranteed estimated quantity of goods rather than

---

1718 Ibid, 603G-H.

1719 Serenity Manufacturers v Minister of Health and Social Services and Another 2007(2) NR 756 (SC).

within the scope of Section 7 (1) (b).[1720] It further stated that the choice of such an agreement requires a bona fide purpose.[1721] The court dismissed the appeal, arguing that there was every logic in the Ministry opting for estimated quantity contracts rather than fixed contracts in this case.[1722] This was done to ensure that the Ministry reserved its right to place orders commensurate with any shortfall in the stocks available in the Central Medical Store; hence, it acted bona fide.[1723]

> "In addition the economics rule of supply and demand cannot be overstressed in such a situation. It would have been a waste of taxpayers' money to order goods knowing that there was no demand for them."[1724]

The clear reference to economic aspect of public procurement as well as the public interest illustrates that the Supreme Court pursues a careful approach in the interpretation of public procurement cases by considering the specific nature of public procurement.

Several tender board decisions were found to be ultra vires by the courts. In *Skeleton Coast Safaris v Namibia Tender Board and Others*[1725] it was found that the Tender Board acted ultra vires. This case was decided before the Tender Board Act came into force. At that time, procurement law was governed by legislation pre-dating independence: Tender Board Regulations promulgated in terms of Section 26A of Finance and Audit Ordinance 1 of 1926.[1726] The applicant had held a concession to operate safaris in the Skeleton Coast National Park for several years. The concession had been extended several times, most recently in 1992 for another year. In 1993 the Tender Board, created in 1970 by virtue of powers contained in Section 26A of the Finance and Audit Ordinance 1 of 1926, invited tenders for the concession to operate safaris in the Skeleton Coast National Park following a mandate given by the Ministry of Wildlife, Conservation and Tourism.

---

1720 Ibid, 763E.
1721 Ibid, 770A.
1722 Ibid, 769J-770A.
1723 Ibid, 770A.
1724 Ibid, 770B.
1725 Skeleton Coast Safaris (Pty) Ltd. v Namibia Tender Board and Others 1993 NR 288 (HC).
1726 Tender Board Regulations 1970.

It was held that the Tender Board acted ultra vires since the concession is not a service to the state but performed on behalf of the state.[1727] Section 17 of the Nature Conservation Ordinance 4 of 1975 placed the control of game parks in the hands of the Cabinet which, however, did not become involved in the grant of the concession to the third respondent at all. The Tender Board, therefore, acted ultra vires. The court declared the award of the concession to operate Safaris in the Skeleton Coast National Park to the third respondent null and void.[1728]

The case *Disposable Medical Products (Pty) Ltd. v Tender Board of Namibia and Others*,[1729] another case that was decided under the former Tender Board Regulations of 1970,[1730] regards an application for review and prayer to set aside a decision of the Tender Board regarding certain items of two different tenders. The tenders were for products of medical nature to be generally used in hospitals. The applicant alleged that the Tender Board had simply followed the adjudication committee without making an objective assessment of the matter. The court held, in, in this respect,

> "The ratio seems to be that the tenderer knows best what his needs are and must further also foot the bill. It is therefore necessary that the tenderer has a certain amount of freedom when it comes to the awarding of tenders.
>
> At this stage it is necessary to address the allegation made by the applicant in its replying affidavit that the first respondent merely acted as a rubber stamp and that the real decisions were taken by the adjudication committee of the fifth respondent.
>
> When it comes to awarding tenders of a specialised nature it is understandable that a body such as the first respondent will, to a great extent, rely on the recommendations of another body who may be more knowledgeable concerning the items of tender than the first respondent itself."[1731]

And continued,

> "The committee was then also constituted in such a way that various experts served thereon. To this extent the input and recommendations of the committee

1727 Skeleton Coast Safaris (Pty) Ltd. v Namibia Tender Board and Others 1993 NR 288 (HC): 299F.

1728 Ibid, 300G.

1729 Disposable Medical Products (Pty) Ltd. v. Tender Board of Nambia 1997 NR 129 (HC).

1730 Tender Board Regulations 1970.

1731 Disposable Medical Products (Pty) Ltd. v. Tender Board of Nambia 1997 NR 129 (HC): 135D-F.

> must have been of great help to the first respondent. However, as was correctly submitted by Mr Smuts, the first respondent is, in terms of the Regulations, the repository of the power and the recommendations by an outside body can only serve the purpose to assist. The first respondent cannot abdicate its function of decision-maker and, if it should do so, its actions would be subject to review and to be set aside."[1732]

These findings are two-fold: on the one hand, they establish that, especially, if the matter of procurement is of specialised nature, the Tender Board has to rely on external experts. On the other hand, the court stresses that the recommendations by an external body can only serve to assist the Tender Board. The Board has to make the decision on its own authority. Its actions are subject to review. The court set the decision aside. The decision thus outlines guidelines for the relationship between the Tender Board and experts making recommendations on tenders.

The case *R B H Construction and Another v Windhoek Municipal Council and Another*[1733] also concerns the ultra vires doctrine. This case was decided shortly after the LTBR had been promulgated. After establishing the local tender board for the Municipality of Windhoek, but before its proper constitution, the Windhoek Municipal Council invited tenders for the rendering of trenching services and concrete works. The LTBR, however, provided that the tender board had to invite tenders. The court had to decide

> "[...] whether the admitted non-compliance with the regulations impacts on the core requirement of vires to perform an administrative act or simply relates to peripheral considerations of form will ultimately determine whether the subsequent award was void *ab initio* or not."[1734]

The court held as follows:

> "Whilst the manner of publication prescribed in reg 13 may well be said to go to form only (i.e. that it must be published in each newspaper circulating in the local authority area) the identification of the entity obligated with the duty to cause such publication is much more fundamental: it relates to vires.
>
> In the realisation of the regulations' objectives (to which I have referred earlier), the administrative role assigned to local tender boards is pivotal. It is to ensure fairness, impartiality, independence and transparency in the tender process contemplated by the regulations, that local tender boards (and none other) are vested

1732 Ibid, 135G-H.

1733 RBH Construction and Another v Windhoek Municipal Council and Another 2002 NR 443 (HC).

1734 Ibid, 446B-C.

with defined powers, duties and obligations. Within the legislative scheme designed to maintain the integrity of the process, those objectives are as important to the invitation of tenders as they are to the consideration and eventual award thereof. The local tender boards' role in soliciting tenders is not merely a passive or 'mechanical' one.

All of these functions are entrusted by regulation to the local tender board. The underlying legislative purposes for doing so which we have referred to earlier may well be frustrated if another entity (such as the local authority council) were allowed to invite tenders and require of the local tender board simply to award them. So, for example, publication of a tender by the first respondent will deprive the second respondent of the opportunity to first consider whether the invitation should not have been preceded by an invitation for applications to prequalify, whether the invitation should not also be circulated outside Namibia and which conditions should be attached to the tender. While some or all of these considerations may not necessarily apply to the tender invited by first respondent in the circumstances of this case, it is immaterial to the interpretative process aimed at an ascertainment of the legislative intention of the legal consequences attaching to an act of non-compliance."[1735]

The court held that the first respondent acted ultra vires and that the award was a nullity ab initio and had no legal effect.[1736] This case strongly defines the powers and functions of local tender boards and their relationship with the institution it acts on behalf of.

In *Minister of Education and Others v Free Namibia Caterers (Pty) Ltd.*[1737] the court found that the Tender Board ceded its statutory power to other administrative bodies and officials. The Ministry of Education had dealt with the entire tender procedure. The Tender Board had admitted to this in a letter sent to Free Namibia Caterers when it said that the Ministry would be in the best position to give reasons for the decision.[1738]

In *AFS Group Namibia (Pty) Ltd. v Chairperson of the Tender Board of Namibia and Others*[1739] the court found that the applicant had established *prima facie* showing that the Tender Board had abdicated its powers to the Ministerial Tender Committee and that the Ministerial Tender Committee

1735 Ibid, 448C-449C.

1736 Ibid, 450C-D.

1737 Minister of Education and Others v Free Namibia Caterers (Pty) Ltd. 2013 (4) NR 1061 (SC).

1738 Minister of Education and Others v Free Namibia Caterers (Pty) Ltd. 2013 (4) NR 1061 (SC): 1082D-E. See also 'Court stops tender' (Newspaper article), The Namibian (Windhoek, Namibia), 17 November 2010.

1739 AFS Group Namibia (Pty) Ltd. v Chairperson of the Tender Board of Namibia and Others (A 55/2011) [2011] NAHC 184.

acted ultra vires its functions. The court stated with reference to the RBH Construction case and two South African cases:

> "In public law, the perpetrator of an act in question must be legally empowered to perform the act. It is for the administration to justify its acts by reference to the authority of a statute whenever the existence of its powers or the validity of their exercise is in question. In the absence of such power, the act in question would be ultra vires and void."

An order setting aside the award of a TIPEEG tender was issued in *Amswohl & LGA Construction Joint Venture Close Corporation v Permanent Secretary of the National Planning Commission and others.*[1740] The tender was for the construction of infrastructure in Otjomuise Extension 10 in Windhoek. The applicant was informed by a letter from the chairperson of the Local Tender Board that he was being awarded the tender. But the day after this Amswohl & LGA Construction was told that the letter had been withdrawn and the tender would not be awarded to it. The TIPEEG Implementation Committee found that the Local Tender Board had no mandate to award the tender. However, the applicant argued that the TIPPEG Implementation Committee is not a statutory body and does not have the mandate or the power to procure goods and services on behalf of the government. Only the Tender Board had the power to award tenders. Amswohl furthermore claimed that the exemption for TIPEEG projects from existing public procurement procedures was unlawful and contrary to the Tender Board Act.[1741] The court set aside the award of the tender but only issued an order in this respect. No judgement was made; hence it is not clear whether the TIPEEG Implementation Committee is authorised to award TIPEEG tenders. This is also very unfortunate because it could have brought light to the practice of exempting TIPEEG projects from government procurement procedures.

---

1740 Amswohl & LGA Construction Joint Venture Close Corporation v Permanent Secretary of the National Planning Commission, the Windhoek Municipal Council, the Chairperson of the Local Tender Board of the City of Windhoek, The Chairperson of the Tender Board of Namibia, Namibia Construction and Others [no judgement, but court order] (no case no. found).

1741 'TIPEEG N$100m tender set aside' (Newspaper article), The Namibian (Windhoek, Namibia), 22 December 2011.

### c. The Requirement to provide Reasons under Article 18

*AFS Group Namibia (Pty) Ltd. v Chairperson of the Tender Board of Namibia and Others*[1742] concerned an important aspect of public procurement procedure, namely the provision of reasons for decisions. The High Court held:

> "[115] The failure of the Tender Board to give reasons to the applicant based on what it terms to be a legal interpretation of section 16 of the Tender Board also in my view constitutes prima facie an unfair and administrative action and an infringement of the applicant's rights under Article 18 of the Constitution. The giving of reasons is fundamental to fair and administrative decision-making."

In this case the Tender Board failed to give reasons to a tenderer who had not been shortlisted for consideration in the tender process. The unsuccessful tenderer had made a written request for reasons underlying the decision that it had not been shortlisted. The Tender Board had argued that the tender had not been submitted to the Tender Board for award and, as a result, the Tender Board was required to, nor could it provide the reasons as yet. (Section 16 (1) (b) requires the Tender Board, on the written request of a tenderer, to give reasons for the acceptance or rejection of his or her tender.)

In a case before the High Court dealing with irregularities in a hostel catering tender process the applicant claimed that the rule of natural justice was not followed by the Tender Board since it was not provided with reasons for the rejection of its tender despite a timeous written request; the applicant claimed that this omission violated the Tender Board rules.[1743] The judge in this case ruled that there has been a failure of administrative justice and that the failure to give reasons for its decision must result in the decision being set aside.[1744] However, although the appeal was dismissed on other grounds,[1745] the judge therein found that the court a quo had erred in finding that the failure to give reasons must lead to the setting aside of the decision as it is not intrinsic to the actual administrative action

1742 AFS Group Namibia (Pty) Ltd. v Chairperson of the Tender Board of Namibia and Others (A 55/2011) [2011] NAHC 184.

1743 Judgment not found, but see 'Government accused of flouting tender rules' (Newspaper article), The Namibian (Windhoek, Namibia), 11 August 2009.

1744 See appeal case which cites paragraph 15 of the judgement: Minister of Education and Others v Free Namibia Caterers (Pty) Ltd. 2013 (4) NR 1061 (SC): 1066F-G.

1745 Ibid.

of awarding the service contract to the third appellant nor to that of disqualifying the respondents' tender.[1746]

The courts have stressed the importance of the right to reasons in public procurement. Nevertheless, it has also been clarified that the failure to give reasons is not necessarily a justification to set aside a tender. This is essential in respect to thc objectives of public procurement, since the failure to give reasons has no direct effect on the award decision. If the decision to award the tender has otherwise been according to the law, setting aside the award decision would unnecessarily delay the tender process and might have severe cost implications.

### d. CSC Neckartal Dam Joint Venture v The Tender Board of Namibia & Others[1747]

An important case that has been decided recently disclosed many of the shortcomings of the Namibian tender law, and the court made essential and very important remarks on several of these issues. In *CSC Neckartal Dam Joint Venture v The Tender Board of Namibia & Others*[1748] the award decision of the Tender Board was set aside and the matter was referred back to the Tender Board.

#### i. Background

The Neckartal Dam tender award case is probably one of the biggest scandals that has happened in the Namibian public procurement system so far and reveals many of the underlying shortcomings of public procurement legislation, its implementation, institutional capacity and transparency.

The tender for the construction of Neckartal, the biggest dam in Namibia, was awarded to the China Henan International Corporation on 16 December 2011. Five days later, on 21 December 2011, the decision was overturned in an emergency Tender Board meeting, and the tender was

1746 Ibid, 1075H-I.

1747 The following part closely resembles an earlier publication of the author: A. Schmidt, 'The need to reform the Namibian public procurement system: A comment on the Neckartal Dam saga' (2014) 6(1) Namibia Law Journal, 41-50.

1748 CSC Neckartal Dam Joint Venture v The Tender Board of Namibia and Others 2014 (1) NR 135 (HC).

awarded to another bidder, namely Impreglio. It is not known what caused this change of mind, but it is assumed that the Tender Board was evenly split in two camps regarding the tender award, with one half favouring China Henan and the other Impreglio. The reasons for this change of mind are, however, unclear, since the Tender Board has not provided the reasons for its decision. The second decision has been criticised for several reasons. First, when the decision was taken the Tender Board was not properly constituted and, therefore, did not have a quorum when it took the second decision in the emergency board meeting on 21 December 2011. Second, only a handful of permanent members were present at the second meeting, with most of the permanent members being represented by their alternates. Although this is not contrary to the applicable law, it raises questions why so many permanent members did not attend such an important board meeting, sending their representatives instead. The divided camps within the Tender Board in this specific procurement case seem to be part of the problem and might explain the reversal of the first decision. Third, there have also been allegations of corruption and bribery as being the cause for the Tender Board's reversal of its first decision in the second meeting. These allegations were subject to an investigation by the Anti-Corruption Commission,[1749] which was, however, not finally completed until mid-2014. Yet the ACC had already concluded its investigation into suspected irregularities in the tender awards process in September 2012 and forwarded the report to the Prosecutor-General for a decision.[1750] The report was confidential, but it apparently contained recommendations to prosecute several procurement officials.[1751] However, the ACC's Head of Investigations refused to reveal their identities.[1752] The Prosecutor-General sent the Neckartal investigation report back to the ACC in early 2013 with the instruction that it be resubmitted after a further probe.[1753] The instruction asked the ACC to outsource the investiga-

1749 See 'Neckartal heads for court' (Newspaper article), The Namibian (Windhoek, Namibia), 28 March 2013.

1750 'ACC concludes Neckartal probe' (Newspaper article), The Namibian (Windhoek, Namibia), 5 September 2012; 'PSS may face prosecution over Neckartal' (Newspaper article), The Sun (Windhoek, Namibia), 6 September 2012.

1751 'PSS may face prosecution over Neckartal' (Newspaper article), The Sun (Windhoek, Namibia), 6 September 2012.

1752 Ibid.

1753 'ACC gets help with Neckartal probe' (Newspaper article), The Sun (Windhoek, Namibia), 14 March 2013.

tion to a private service company.[1754] In January 2012 it became clear that there had been a disagreement between the Ministry of Agriculture, Water and Forestry and the Tender Board with respect to the Ministry's recommendation to the Tender Board regarding the pre-selection of tenders. This recommendation had been referred back to the Ministry due to vagueness and some technical issues that needed to be resolved. The Ministry was, however, unable to clarify these issues to the Tender Board's satisfaction; thus the documents passed back and forth between them. 20 January 2012 was set as the deadline for the Ministry to rectify the shortcomings of the recommendation.[1755]

This episode exposes the difficulties entailed by the current distribution of competences and powers: whereas the experience and the knowledge about the subject matter are based in the Ministry, the Tender Board is responsible for the award decision in respect to the subject matter. In the case of the Neckartal Dam, the current allocation of responsibilities not only led to confusion between the line ministry and the Tender Board but also to a delay of the tender evaluation and award process. Due to allegations of corruption - the Ministry was alleged to favour the Italian company - the tender was cancelled and re-advertised.[1756]

In early 2013, the tender was finally awarded to Salini – the company which acquired Impreglio, the company who had initially been awarded the contract - despite it only scoring second in the overall evaluation of the tender behind Vinci-Orascom. In a prequalification process, three companies, including Vinci-Orascom, Salini and CSC Neckartal Dam Joint Venture[1757], were found to have the technical capacity and experience to carry out the project.[1758] The Tender Board justified the decision to award the contract to Salini rather than to Vinci-Orascom, which had actually

1754 Ibid.

1755 'Neckartal: Sieben Firmen noch im Rennen - Vergabekommission wartet auf Landwirtschaftsministerium - Entschluss steht noch nicht fest' (Newspaper article), Allgemeine Zeitung (Windhoek, Namibia), 20 January 2012.

1756 'Salini Gets the Nod for Neckartal' (Newspaper article), The Namibian (Windhoek, Namibia), 14 March 2013.

1757 CSC Neckartal Dam Joint Venture is a joint venture of Stefanutti Stocks and CMC de Ravenna (Italy).

1758 CSC Neckartal Dam Joint Venture v The Tender Board of Namibia and Others 2014 (1) NR 135 (HC): 139 E.

achieved the best score, by arguing that the latter had inexperienced key personnel.[1759]

It has to be stressed that the investigation of the ACC was still underway at the time the final award decision was made and that the same people under suspicion of having favoured Impreglio awarded the tender to Salini, which has merged with Impreglio. This raises questions about the role and the efficiency of the ACC which should have finished its investigations long ago. The court documents revealed inconsistencies in the evaluation report which was submitted to the Tender Board by the Ministry. It differed from the consulting engineer's evaluation report, which recommended that Vinci-Orascom be awarded the tender on condition that the three senior site positions[1760] are filled by persons with suitable dam-building experience – especially with respect to the roads contractor company representative.[1761]

Vinci-Orascom approached the court to award the tender to them or, alternatively, to instruct the Tender Board to reconsider the Tender. The company claimed that the

> "[…] agriculture ministry's decision to reject its bid was unreasonable and irrational as it ignored the outcome of a carefully constructed evaluation process just because of false claims of inexperienced personnel."[1762]

Vinci-Orascom also alleged that the Tender Board had simply rubber-stamped the Ministry's recommendation instead of forming its own judgment and that the Tender Board meeting which had approved that Ministry's recommendation had not been properly constituted and, hence, lacked a quorum.[1763] A hearing was subsequently set in the Windhoek High Court for 22 May 2013. Vinci-Orascom also asked the High Court to halt the implementation of the tender pending the outcome of the court hearing.[1764] Both applications were decided around a month later in *CSC*

1759 'Neckartal heads for court' (Newspaper article), The Namibian (Windhoek, Namibia), 28 March 2013.

1760 Site agent, Production Manager for Concrete, and the Roads Contractor Company Superintendent.

1761 'Discrepancies in Neckartal scores' (Newspaper article), The Namibian (Windhoek, Namibia), 12 April 2013.

1762 'Neckartal heads for court' (Newspaper article), The Namibian (Windhoek, Namibia), 28 March 2013.

1763 Ibid.

1764 'Date set for Neckartal challenge hearing' (Newspaper article), The Namibian (Windhoek, Namibia), 26 April 2013.

*Neckartal Dam Joint Venture v The Tender Board of Namibia and Others.*[1765] Although Vinci-Orascom withdrew from the suit at the last minute the third company shortlisted continued to prosecute the case.[1766]

The judgement is decisive for determining the court's role in public procurement and establishing the requirements and criteria that public procurement procedures need to suffice to survive legal scrutiny.

ii. The Court Decision

The High Court set aside the award decision of the Tender Board and referred the matter back to the Tender Board. In regard to the contention that the weightings attached to the technical, financial, risk and social components of the tender evaluations were inconsistent with the principles of fairness, reasonableness, competitiveness and cost-effectiveness because too much weight had been attached to the technical component and too little weight to price,[1767] the court held as follows:

> "Whilst price should in our view always remain an important consideration in a competitive tender process, we do not consider ourselves to be in a position to assess the precise weighting it and the other factors should have received and thus not in a position to find that the weighting of the factors decided upon by the evaluation committee was unfair or unreasonable in the circumstances."[1768]

The court thus refused to make any recommendations regarding the weighting of price and technical criteria while emphasizing that price is always an important criterion in competitive tender processes. Nevertheless, the court found that the identification of four of seventeen designated core positions of personnel for the purpose of evaluation, while one of them was not even specifically listed, was not fair and reasonable.[1769] Requiring adherence to the principles of fairness and reasonableness in the evaluation process, which is not sufficiently regulated in Namibian public procurement legislation, is a great step forward since it limits the Tender

1765 CSC Neckartal Dam Joint Venture v The Tender Board of Namibia and Others 2014 (1) NR 135 (HC).

1766 'Government to answer on Neckartal queries today' (Newspaper article), The Namibian (Windhoek, Namibia), 30 August 2013.

1767 CSC Neckartal Dam Joint Venture v The Tender Board of Namibia and Others 2014 (1) NR 135 (HC): 152 C

1768 Ibid, 155A-B.

1769 Ibid, 160H-161A.

Board's discretion to conduct evaluation in a manner that favours a specific tenderer, and in terms of deviating from the designated evaluation components. The selection of a limited number of designated criteria had been justified by the time constraints, though this justification should never be accepted as a reason for deviating from the law and, particularly, for not considering designated criteria in the evaluation of tenders. The courts' ruling that the evaluation process was unfair and unjustifiable is, therefore, to be welcomed.

Regarding the failure of the decision-maker, the Tender Board, to form its own judgment, the court acknowledged that, especially in highly technical matters, the Tender Board may seek "expert assistance in evaluating, assessing and comparing competing bids as long as it retains its decision making capacity and exercises it."[1770] The court thus considered the Tender Board's difficulty to take a decision in matters requiring technical expertise and experience and, therefore its dependency on the evaluation report from the Ministry. The court thus brought some clarification as to what is required by the Tender Board in order to have applied its mind independently and exercised its discretion fairly and impartially. The court held that

> "[...] where the board seeks and relies upon a summary of the advice of a technical nature, that summary of a technical assessment provided to it must accurately and fairly reflect the views of those who gave it."[1771]

In other words, the evaluation process is obliged to be fully transparent and entirely comprehensible for the Tender Board in order to enable it to make a decision. In this case, first of all, the tender evaluation committee consisted of ministerial staff, on the one hand, and external experts, on the other. The two groups had diverging views on which bid was to be recommended and why. The Tender Board, however, was only informed about the ministerial group's recommendations. The court considered the withholding of the diverging view as material non-disclosure.[1772] Secondly, the Tender Board had not been alerted to the evaluation committee's proposal for the tenders to be clarified in respect of the key personnel.[1773] Thirdly, there were also significant differences between the draft expert

1770 Ibid, 155D.
1771 Ibid, 156A.
1772 Ibid, 158G-H.
1773 Ibid, 158A.

report prepared by the consultants and the ministerial submission.[1774] The court found as follows in this regard:

> "The failure to disclose a matter of a material nature would not in our view amount to a mere internal irregularity in the preceding process which can be overlooked as not affecting the validity of the ultimate decision. The cumulative effect of the failure to disclose those first three facts is in our view devastating to the legality of the decision making and deprived the tender board from being able to apply its mind properly to the enquiry before it."[1775]

The Neckartal Dam tender award case clearly displays the necessity to reform the institutional and organisation structure of the public procurement system, to enact stricter regulations on the use of the evaluation criteria and their weighting as well as to require that comprehensive records be kept and that the evaluation process be fully transparent. It is of special importance that those conducting the evaluation and those taking the decision, respectively, can be held accountable and that there are effective review mechanisms available.

### e. Interim Interdicts and the Matter of Urgency

Considering the nature of public procurement, the remedy of interim interdicts is of particular importance, as the further implementation of a procurement contract while the review is pending might render the final judgment meaningless since, at a later stage of contract implementation, a decision to set aside a contract might be more detrimental to all stakeholders. Furthermore, the negative effects of delayed tendering procedures or contract implementation in respect of the costs involved call for procurement matters to be heard as soon as possible. Hence, applications for urgency are of particular relevance. Relevant case law considering these issues will be outlined in the following.

Rule 73 (4) of the Rules of the High Court of 2014[1776] and the formerly applicable Rule 6 (12) (b) of the Rules of the High Court of 1990[1777] which entail two requirements that need to be fulfilled in order for urgen-

1774 Ibid, 158I.
1775 Ibid, 159C-D.
1776 Rules of the High Court of Namibia: High Court Act, 1990 (No. 4 of 2014, Government Gazette of 17 January 2014).
1777 Rules of the High Court of Namibia: High Court Act, 1990 (No. 59 of 1990, Government Gazette of 10 October 1990).

cy to be granted, are important in regard to urgency. The applicant must demonstrate the circumstances justifying urgency as well as the reasons why he or she could not be afforded substantial redress in due course.

In *AFS Group Namibia (Pty) Ltd. v Chairperson of the Tender Board of Namibia and Others,*[1778] the applicant sought an order suspending, on an urgent basis, the implementation of an agreement concluded between the fourth respondent and Ministry of Works and Transport. The main review application and counter-application regarded the review and the setting aside of the tender award to the fourth respondent. The tender was for "the installation of radio frequency devices and other equipment to Government in-house petrol pumps and Government fuel vehicles, in order to streamline fuelling for Government fleet vehicles". After establishing that there was no culpable remissness or mala fides on the applicants' part and the urgency was not self-created, the court stated that the matter should be heard as a matter of urgency.

In *New Era Investment (Pty) Ltd. v The Roads Authority*[1779] both requirements of Rule 12 (6) (b) of the High Court Rules of 1990 were found to be met and urgency was affirmed. The court stressed the importance of urgency in public procurement cases, reasoning as follows:

> "[13] In my opinion, in a tender to carry out construction works, if the tenderer who did not win the tender and who is aggrieved by the decision of the employer, were to wait for the conclusion of a review application brought in the ordinary course, such aggrieved tenderer would be greatly disadvantaged. He or she would be so disadvantaged in the event of the employer entering into an agreement with the successful tenderer and handing over the site to the successful tenderer who may proceed with the construction works. In such an eventuality it may be difficult to set aside the decision of the employer in due course. If the review application succeeded in the end the aggrieved tenderer may be compensated in damages but the damages of such nature may be difficult to quantify, thereby protracting the suffering of the aggrieved party who may have to incur huge costs involved in employing a financial consultant in his or her attempt to quantify his or her damages. In any case, a claim for damages does not follow as a matter course. In that event, the harm that the aggrieved party would have suffered would be irreparable if the application is heard in the ordinary course."[1780]

---

1778 AFS Group Namibia (Pty) Ltd. v Chairperson of the Tender Board of Namibia and Others (A 55/2011) [2011] NAHC 184.

1779 New Era Investment (Pty) Ltd. v Roads Authority and Others 2014 (2) NR 596 (HC).

1780 Ibid, 600J-601C.

In *AFS Group Namibia (Pty) Ltd. v Chairperson of the Tender Board of Namibia and Others,*[1781] the consideration of the facts according to the four requisites for an interim interdict, including a prima facie right, the apprehension of irreparable harm if interim relief was not granted, a balance of convenience favouring the granting of an interdict, and the lack of an alternative satisfactory remedy, resulted in the decision to suspend the implementation of the agreement, pending the finalisation of the main review application.[1782] Similarly, in *Free Namibia Caterers CC v Chairperson of the Tender Board of Namibia,*[1783] where the court held:

> "[20] In my view, the apprehension which applicant has, is indeed well grounded bearing in mind the background of this matter and the steps that have been taken by respondents so far towards the looming tender process. Applicant has reason to believe that respondents are again manipulating the tender process, hence the need for the court to intervene."

Hence, the court agreed with the applicant's submissions "[…] that a good case has been made for the granting of an interdict having regard to the historical background and current circumstances surrounding the parties' positions."[1784]

Whereas the latter cases have shown that the courts have an important function in interpreting and advancing the law and that the courts are prepared to grant remedies such as interim interdicts or urgency in order to prevent contracts from being implemented while the case is pending and unnecessarily delaying public procurement awards, there have also been cases in which urgency or interdicts were denied and the decision was decided upon after the implementation of the contract. The High Court denied an urgent application in *Shetu Trading CC v Chair, Tender Board of Namibia and Others,*[1785] on the basis of Rule 6 (12) (b). In this case the applicant sought to stop the implementation of the contract. The problem was that the founding affidavit in the urgency application only came before the court more than seven months after the award of the tender and about five month after a review application in the same matter. The appli-

1781 AFS Group Namibia (Pty) Ltd. v Chairperson of the Tender Board of Namibia and Others (A 55/2011) [2011] NAHC 184.

1782 Paras. 70-128.

1783 Free Namibia Caterers CC v Chairperson of the Tender Board of Namibia (A 52/2014) [2014] NAHCMD 103 (27 March 2014).

1784 Ibid, para. 23.

1785 Shetu Trading CC v Chair, Tender Board of Namibia and Others (A 352/2010) [2011] NAHC 188.

cant argued that it acted on the assumption that the contract has not been signed. This, however, contradicted clause 33.2 of the instruction to bidders' manual which provides that the notification of an award will constitute the formation of the contract. It was given to all bidders, including the applicant. Hence, it should have brought the application at the same time as it lodged its review application. The failure to do so meant that the urgency was self-inflicted. An appeal of this decision to the Supreme Court was dismissed. The Supreme Court reasoned that it lacked the element of finality necessary to constitute a judgement or order.[1786] At the time when contract implementation was finalised, the review application was still in court. It seems this could have been avoided if Shetu Trading had applied for urgency at a prior date and it can only be speculated whether it would have been successful or not, because the court did not find it necessary to deal with the merits of the application itself.

In the latter case there was no doubt that the urgency was self-created, but there have been other cases where it was not comprehensible why urgency or interim relief was denied. This second group of cases might be attributable to the fact that judicial review alone with its available remedies is not suitable for all public procurement cases. In *Aurecon Namibia (Pty) Ltd. v The Roads Authority*[1787] an application for urgency was denied. The court reasoned that "in the circumstances of this case the commercial interest of the applicant in this matter is not of such a nature as to render the matter urgent."[1788] The court stressed that "[…] other litigants waiting for their matters to be heard would be prejudiced if priority were afforded to this application as they would have to wait longer."[1789] Matters where a person's safety or liberty is involved, for example, might be more likely to be granted urgency. In court, public procurement cases are competing with other important cases that might have a higher priority. However, this justification can hardly be satisfactory for unsuccessful tenderers seeking judicial review or for the public, since the public has a significant interest in the effective and efficient spending of their tax money and the provision of qualified services.

1786 Shetu Trading v Tender Board of Namibia 2012(1) NR 162 (SC).

1787 Aurecon Namibia (Pty) Ltd. v The Roads Authority, unreported case, A 250/2012, NAHCMD 21 (28 January 2013).

1788 Ibid, para. 16.

1789 Ibid, para. 13.

Another case where urgency was denied is *Namibia Construction Industries and Murray and Roberts v the Chairman of the Tender Board and the Ministry of Works*[1790] which has also been discussed above.[1791] Unfortunately, there is no written judgement available since only a court order was issued. Namibia Construction Industries and Murray & Roberts were unsuccessful tenderers for the construction of the new headquarters of the Ministry of Lands and Resettlement. They did not produce a valid certificate of compliance from the office of the Employment Equity Commissioner as required by the Tender Board regulations. The application for urgency by Namibia Construction and Murrays & Roberts was denied and the Chinese company which won the tender commenced work on the project. The case was finally decided in 2014 and the challenge was dismissed on procedural grounds.[1792] By the time of the dismissal the construction of the Ministry of Headquarters had long been finished. A representative of Murray & Roberts said that the legal costs it and Namibia Construction had incurred were high, amounting to about N$1 million.[1793] A well-known advocate opined that the urgency judgement was not reasonable.[1794] It was also described as an irresponsible decision with the primary objective of allowing the construction project to proceed unhindered.[1795] This raises the question whether the quality of the judgement has a link to the judge's impartiality or the competence of the judge in public procurement matters. Both scenarios could have a detrimental effect on future procurement cases.

In *Premier Construction CC v Chairperson of the Tender Committee of the Namibia Power Corporation Board of Directors and Others*,[1796] an application for interim relief pending a review application in which the

1790 Namibia Construction Industries and Murray and Roberts v the Chairman of the Tender Board and the Ministry of Works, unreported Case, A 283/2007, High Court (30 November 2007).

1791 See Subchapter 6 of this chapter.

1792 Namibia Construction (Pty) Ltd. v The Chairperson of the Tender Board, unreported case, A 283/2007, NAHCMD 6 (21 January 2014).

1793 Interview Mr Agenbag (Murray & Roberts Namibia, Commercial Director), 7th March 2013.

1794 Interview Mr Tötemeyer (Advocate / Society of Advocates of Namibia, Vice-president), 18th March 2013.

1795 'Chinese major beneficiaries of State monies' (Newspaper article), Windhoek Observer (Windhoek, Namibia), 8 March 2008.

1796 Premier Construction CC v Chairperson of the Tender Committee of hte Namibia Power Corporation Board of Directors and Others 2014(4) NR 1002 (HC).

applicant alleged an infringement of Article 18 of the Namibian Constitution was dismissed. It was held that the respondents were not properly cited.[1797] The court also argued that granting the interim relief on the basis that there has been *prima facie* infringement of the applicant's rights would be wrong and unjust because it would set aside the constitutional imperative that the burden of proof lies with the party alleging an infringement of its fundamental rights.[1798] The court also considered the factual circumstances of the case.[1799] The contract had been signed, work had been commenced, contracts for the purchase and supply of machinery and equipment had been concluded, etc. Furthermore, the tender works had to be completed within a period of three months. This led the judge to the conclusion that the company that had been awarded the tender would be more likely to suffer real loss or disadvantage than the applicant.[1800] This contributed to the court's decision to refuse to grant interim relief in the present case. This falls short of the court's duty to establish any violations and irregularities in tender procedures. Indeed the court's approach would render a review application which is heard only after the contract has been implemented meaningless. Moreover, non-transparency in tendering procedures makes it difficult for unsatisfied tenderers to file a well-found review application and to prove an infringement of their rights. Such a system should not be rewarded by allowing the undisturbed completion of the tender process and a denial of interim relief. This case reveals the necessity of immediately introducing a standstill period and establishing both an administrative and an independent review mechanism.

### f. Summary of Case Law

There are several judgements developing the meaning of administrative justice in public procurement, including in particular the right to reasons, which is fundamental for fair administrative decision-making. In a recent case, fairness and reasonableness in the evaluation process and transparency in procurement proceedings have been strengthened. The courts have

1797 Ibid, 1005G-1006F.
1798 Ibid, 1006H-1007I.
1799 Ibid, 1008A-1008E.
1800 Ibid, 1008E.

tried to balance the interest of the public (taxpayer) and of the tenderer, supplier or contractor.

Case law discloses that the practice of seeking recommendations from the Ministries is not adequate and that the tender boards, especially the national Tender Board, often do not comply with their duty to take the award decision but act ultra vires. The courts have clarified the power and responsibilities of the tender boards in several decisions.

Urgency has generally been granted if urgency was not self-created and there was no culpable remissness or *mala fides* on the applicants' part. The courts also considered the nature of the commercial interest when deciding whether a case should be heard as a matter of urgency. Since public procurement cases are competing with all other sorts of cases, including criminal cases and human rights cases, the decision in *Aurecon Namibia (Pty) Ltd. v The Roads Authority*[1801] not to grant urgency is indeed comprehensible but discloses that judicial review as the sole review mechanism is not adequate for public procurement matters. And there has been at least one major judgement where it is not comprehensible why the application for urgency was denied and the review application rendered meaningless since the contract had been implemented at that time. That cases are only decided after the contract has been (partly) implemented exemplifies a major problem and also reveals the necessity of establishing other review mechanisms more suitable for the particular nature of public procurement disputes.

### g. Interim Conclusion

There are several cases that disclose the insufficiency of dispute resolution mechanisms regarding public procurement in Namibia. These cases reveal that there is no effective internal or non-judicial external review mechanism that responds to the specific nature of public procurement. Although judicial review might be an effective mechanism it also involves problems such as cost, duration and access. The lawyers interviewed stated that their clients often give up or shy away from taking court action because they are afraid that it could have an adverse effect on future procurement decisions. "Business prospects are way more important than a single (court)

1801 Aurecon Namibia (Pty) Ltd. v The Roads Authority, unreported case, A 250/2012, NAHCMD 21 (28 January 2013).

case."[1802] Especially in Namibia's small economy this is of particular relevance. This view was confirmed by the Ombudsman of Namibia, who stated that the way to the courts is often avoided because of the costs or fear of consequences such as disadvantages in future tender procedures.[1803]

Public procurement cases are distinguished by the public interest at stake. The urgent clarification is not only relevant for the applicant but for the fairness of the tender procedure and, hence, for its efficiency and effectiveness. If no interdict is granted the application might even be rendered irrelevant if the contract is awarded or implemented in the time passing until the judgement. Where an interdict is issued and the procedure is halted, however, the delay has a negative effect for the whole process because the provision of the goods, services or works is delayed. It shows that, while litigation as last resort is of utmost importance, specific procurement-related review procedures are essential to do justice to tenderers and to the public interest alike.

In Namibia, the courts have rendered some important judgments in respect of public procurement. These judgments have considered the specific nature of public procurement and delivered important clarifications and criteria for public procurement procedures. However, there is an urgent need for internal/administrative review and the creation of an independent review panel. An independent review panel is of great advantage because it is be preferable to judicial review in respect of costs, access and duration. It can hold specific public procurement law expertise and offer remedies and procedures specifically suitable for public procurement disputes. Furthermore, administrative review by way of a direct complaint to the procuring entity or to another administrative authority might be useful in order to prevent delays through challenge procedures. It allows the procuring entity to comment on the allegations, to ease doubts about the fairness and rightfulness of their decision, or to reconsider their decision and make adjustments. This would avoid litigation and corresponding time and costs.[1804]

---

1802 Interview Mr Ruppel (LorentzAngula Inc, Director/Chairman), 28th February 2013.

1803 Interview Mr Walters (Ombudsman of Namibia), 27th March 2013.

1804 Cf. OECD, 'SIGMA Paper No. 30 - Public Procurement Review Procedures, CCNM/SIGMA/PUMA(2000)114'.

## 9. Conclusion

The analysis of the Namibian tender law and regulations discloses that there are several shortcomings that hinder the efficient and effective functioning of the public procurement system. The law on public procurement is insufficient, leaving room for corruption, non-transparent decisions, concealment of facts and other undesirable effects. Nevertheless, the field research also made obvious that the implementation of laws regarding public procurement is deficient, too. Many of the interviewees stated that they consider the implementation of the law as a problem, rather than the law itself.[1805] They also claimed that there was a lack of political will which was a general problem in Namibia.[1806] It seems that implementation is inconsistent but exemptions are granted for certain groups or people. The public procurement system's dysfunction can thus be attributed to shortcomings of the legislative framework but is also caused by institutional weaknesses and a lack of good governance.[1807] These are important factors that have to be paid attention to during reform in order to draft procurement legislation that is adequate and reasonable in the Namibian context. In this regard it is important to design legislation with view to available capacities to implement new procurement legislation and to create ownership for the public procurement system designed by the new bill meaning that the people implementing it can identify with the system.

Exemptions granted from the application of the Act pose a major problem as more than half of public procurement is exempted from the application of the tender law. It is neither clear what criteria need to be fulfilled in respect of exemptions nor is it clear what methods are applied alternatively in the cases of exemptions. It is of utmost importance to enact strict regulations on what method can be applied in what circumstances and to restrict reasons for exemptions rigorously in order to prevent any kind of abuse in this respect and to ensure that the objectives of public procurement are achieved.

---

1805 For example Interview Mr Tötemeyer (Advocate / Society of Advocates of Namibia, Vice-president), 18th March 2013; Interview Mr Schulz (Namibia Construction (Pty) Ltd., Director), 22th March 2013; Interview Mr Hopwood (IPPR, Director), 26th March 2013.; Interview Mr Links (Insight Magazine, Editor), 21th February 2013).

1806 Ibid.

1807 Cf. Links; Daniels, 'The Tender Board - Need for Root and Branch Reform', p. 3.

The institutional and organisational framework has proved to be dysfunctional. The Tender Board and its staff are heavily overburdened and there is a lack of skills and qualification. The political appointment of the Tender Board's members leads to an exclusive circle of politicians with a disproportionate amount of influence. The practice as well as case law has revealed that the separation of responsibilities between the Tender Board and the line ministries leads to practical problems. The Tender Board is required to make an objective assessment but, in particular because a lack of (technical) expertise, it often has to rely on the recommendations obtained from the line ministries in order to make a decision The evaluation of the tenders is basically made by the line ministries and then referred to the Tender Board as a recommendation. The Tender Board therefore is always walking a thin line between acting ultra vires and meeting its responsibilities under the Act. The possible exertion of political influence to follow the recommendation cannot be neglected in this matter. The shortcomings in the institutional and organisational framework should not be underestimated as they severely hinder qualitative and timely decision-making.

The transparency regulations are fragmentary, making it easy to veil corrupt activities. Additionally, there is no effective mechanism to investigate and scrutinise corrupt behaviour. The combination of potential rewards in public procurement, where large amounts of money are spent and a lot of different interests are involved, with a low risk of detection makes it likely that the system is misused for personal benefit.[1808] Transparency regulations are not only insufficiently regulated but also insufficiently implemented as the Tender Board often acts in secrecy and refuses to disclose information unless they are obliged to do so by court. Additionally, there have been cases where the Tender Board did not adhere to the applicable tender legislation, revealing that there are shortcomings in public procurement law implementation and in the wider sense in the application of the rule of law and good governance.

The price preference policy cannot be said to be objectionable per se. It is a good legal basis; however, its implementation lacks transparency and the success has so far not been satisfactory. This might, however, be due to other shortcomings such as the frequent use of exemptions rather than to a weakness of the price preference policy itself. Although there is a legal basis for ensuring that labour law, affirmative action law and social se-

1808 Cf. Quinot; Arrowsmith, 'Introduction ', p. 19.

curity law is adhered to in public procurement, implementation is weak, violations are ignored, and there is a lack of monitoring of compliance. Furthermore, the Tender Board refuses to accept any responsibility for ensuring compliance. The lack of regulating contract management has led to a situation where the Tender Board simply abdicates its responsibilities in regard to abuses after the contract has been awarded. The line ministries, responsible for contract management after the tender has been awarded, and the respective commissioners, responsible to enforce labour, social and affirmative action laws, do not sufficiently interact with the Tender Board. This is inadequate and ineffective; abuses of the law and insufficient contract implementation have occurred quite frequently but have mostly remained without effect on future procurements. This has undermined the efficiency and effectiveness of the whole public procurement system.

The special role of Chinese companies in Namibia's public procurement system discloses numerous weaknesses of the public procurement system and its implementation. The problems actually arising do not exist solely because of an inadequate procurement law but because of general problems such as the lack of transparency, insufficient institutional capacity, etc. All these problems could be solved by introducing a comprehensive and modern public procurement framework and ensuring coherent and efficient implementation.

The review of public procurement proceedings is limited to judicial review and external non-judicial review by the ombudsman. This mechanism has not, however, proven to be adequate for most procurement cases, above all since it does not provide for an administrative review or non-judicial external review procedure that is suitable for public procurement. Judicial review has proven to be inadequate as the sole review mechanism, although courts have rendered some important judgments strengthening the existing public procurement framework. Apart from the practical problem that there often is an unwillingness to take court action because it is feared that it will impinge on business prospects and because of the financial costs involved, the remedies and procedures of judicial review are not suitable to deal with a variety of issues involved in public procurement disputes in an adequate, timely, efficient and effective manner.

The inefficiency and ineffectiveness of public procurement in Namibia severely hinders socio-economic development which depends, inter alia, on qualitative service-delivery and infrastructure development. These in turn also form part of the factors necessary for economic growth. In consideration of the amount of public money being spent in the field of public procurement[1809] and money wasted through corruption and the inefficiency of the current system, the development of an efficient and effective procurement system is essential in order to spend the money wisely.

---

1809 See Introduction.

## *Chapter 2: Reform of Public Procurement Law*[1810]

This chapter outlines general theoretical considerations important in public procurement reform processes. A special focus rests on reform drivers and hindrances, the different stages of reforms and organisational issues, including questions of basic approaches such as whether to establish a decentralised or a centralised system. Then, considerations in regard to procedures and methods, transparency, secondary objectives as well as review procedures that are generally considered to be essential in public procurement reform processes are examined. Additionally, other important aspects of public procurement reform that are essential for a modern and up-to-date public procurement law are presented briefly. These aspects include procurement planning, contract management and e-procurement.

### 1. Introduction

Public procurement law has been reformed in several countries around the globe in the recent decades. This is due to the growing awareness of the size and value of public procurement and the explosiveness of the issue, with many different interests being at stake. Especially developing countries with outdated or non-existent public procurement structures are no longer able to efficiently manage public resources.[1811] In industrial states growing pressure on government budgets has led to calls for an efficient deployment of resources.[1812] The indirect impact public procurement has on governance and the achievement of development goals puts it at the centre of attention. The history of procurement, the state of the public procurement system and public administration in general (institutions, economy, etc.) differ to quite an extent across developing countries. Many former colonised African countries, for example, were subject to a public procurement system imposed by their colonisers for a long time. Transition countries have had to create new purchasing methods for procuring

---

1810 For an overview of the essential aspects of public procurement reform processes see also Annex 3.

1811 Agaba; Shipman, 'Public Procurement in Developing Countries', p. 379; Evenett; Hoekman, 'International Cooperation and the Reform of Public Procurement Policies', p. 4ff; OECD, 'Integrity in Public Procurement', p. 19.

1812 Cf. Evenett, 'Is there a Case for New Multilateral Rules on Transparency in Government Procurement?', p. 172.

from the newly established private sector.[1813] Apartheid South Africa and Namibia have had to overcome the former discriminatory procurement regime. The existing differences have to be considered when analysing reform attempts and, even more importantly, when making use of the instrument of comparative law in order to design a new public procurement law. With a view to further economic globalisation and harmonisation efforts the ideal scenario is to integrate local conditions with international best practice standards.[1814]

There is a tendency to differentiate between first generation and second generation reforms. Whereas the former describes

> "[…] a package that includes legal and regulatory reforms, reform of institutional and organisational frameworks and training procurement officials and other stakeholders on the new arrangements",[1815]

second generation reforms aim at upholding the integrity of the system, the introduction of e-procurement, professionalization of procurement, performance management, etc.[1816] Whereas this correctly describes the recognition that "traditional" reform has not led to the expected results and that further efforts and changes are needed to enhance the efficiency and effectiveness of public procurement, the differentiation might be misleading in so far as it suggests that the two types of reform are consecutive. In the best case a holistic reform process addresses aspects of the so-called first and second generation reforms. Thus such a differentiation is not helpful in this context.

---

1813 Cf. Evenett; Hoekman, 'International Cooperation and the Reform of Public Procurement Policies', p. 19.

1814 Cf. S. Karangizi; I. Ndahiro, 'Public procurement reforms and development in the Eastern and Southern African region', in R.H. García, *International Public Procurement: A Guide to Best Practices* (London: Globe Business Publishing Ltd., 2009), p. 114; see also Trepte, 'Regulating Procurement', p. 4.

1815 Special Steering Committee of the OECD-DAC Task Force on Procurement, 'A Practical Guide to Transforming Procurement Systems ' (Paris: OECD, 2011), p. 8.

1816 Ibid. See also The Second Meeting of the OECD/DAC Task Force on Procurement - Summary of meeting by the UN Procurement Capacity Development Centre, Cusco, Peru, 4th-6th May 2011.

## 2. The Reform

### a. Reform Drivers

In many countries the growing pressure of civil society is inducing the government to take action. Cases of corruption, opaqueness, lack of quality of works or services, delayed project finalisation, and other irregularities cause concern and have provoked calls for reforming existing laws and systems. Additionally, the business sector is increasingly expressing dissatisfaction with existing procurement practices, citing unfair decisions, a lack of competition and other obstacles.[1817] Apart from this internal pressure, international institutions, organisations, donors, regional trade organisations and trading partners might push for reforms in order to liberalise public procurement and improve transparency. Especially donor countries and international financial institutions often make the change of legal settings a precondition for financial support.[1818] The World Bank has, for example, played a major role in the reform processes of public procurement systems in Africa.[1819] In times of economic globalisation companies or businesses with export interests might push their government to negotiate the extension of foreign market access.[1820] Or in other words, bilateral trading partners might have a particular interest in getting access to the national public procurement market in order to sell their products or services. Whereas the external pressure groups usually try to exert influence in regard to non-discrimination, internal pressure groups often request the opposite, i.e. the application of discriminatory practices to treat certain domestic bidder groups preferentially.

---

1817 Cf. Karangizi; Ndahiro, 'Public procurement reforms and development in the Eastern and Southern African region', p. 117.

1818 Agaba; Shipman, 'Public Procurement in Developing Countries', p. 374; OECD, 'MAPS'. See also Karangizi; Ndahiro, 'Public procurement reforms and development in the Eastern and Southern African region', p. 117,118; Silva, 'The revision of the WTO Agreement on Government Procurement', 67f; P. Trepte, 'Building sustainable capacity in public procurment', in S. Arrowsmith; R.D. Anderson, *The WTO Regime on Government Procurement: Challenges and Reform* (Cambridge: Cambridge University Press, 2011), p. 378.

1819 Caborn; Arrowsmith, 'Procurement methods in the public procurement systems of Africa', p. 268f.

1820 Evenett, 'Is there a Case for New Multilateral Rules on Transparency in Government Procurement?', p. 172.

In Africa, several organisations have been involved in setting public procurement on the table for reform. The International Conference on Public Procurement Reform in Africa held in Abidjan in 1998 as well as the High Level Forum on Public Procurement Reform in Africa held in Tunis in 2009 were sponsored by the African Development Bank, African regional trading blocs and organisations, the OECD and the World Bank.[1821] The latter, as international institutions, have been involved in reform efforts all over Africa in the last decades by providing financial as well as technical support. Moreover, the Commonwealth Public Procurement Network (CPPN) holds public procurement workshops and conferences and assists reform processes with technical expertise in Africa. The CPPN is an organisation of the Commonwealth bringing public procurement practitioners together.[1822] The objectives of the Network are the promotion, strengthening and facilitation of information and exchanges of solutions oriented to develop, spread and implement best practices in public procurement.[1823] It has held annual Procurement Conferences in Africa since 2006.

The motivation to initiate a reform process is, hence, often not solely internally driven but enhanced or even imposed by external forces. This is important to keep in mind, since it could be a strong explanation for the lack of political will to finalise reforms and to enforce newly enacted laws and regulations.

### b. Reform Hindrances

In general three major obstacles specific to public procurement reform have been identified: deeply vested interests and lack of political will; paucity of technical knowledge and capacity; and the complexity of the substantive issues involved.[1824]

1821 Quinot; Arrowsmith, 'Introduction ', p. 2.

1822 Records of the Fifth Commonwealth Public Procurement Network (CPPN) Technical Conference 5th Commonwealth Public Procurement Network Technical Conference, Windhoek, Namibia, 6th-8th December 2010.

1823 Ibid.

1824 Hunja, 'Obstacles to Public Procurement Reform', p. 4f.

Deeply vested interests and the lack of political will[1825] to overcome them might not only impede reform efforts from the beginning but also vitiate implementation of new laws and regulations. Governments with a lack of political will often "[...] give lip-service to supporting reforms, but do not follow through in terms of resources, sanctions, etc."[1826] Moreover, the stakeholders of public procurement are often influential, well connected and organised groups of society, and can hence form a strong opposition and resistance to reform efforts.[1827] It is, hence, important to identify and address political influences of that sort and find ways to bring reform obstructers on board rather than trying to carry through the reform without their support. Country ownership and leadership in the design and implementation of public procurement reform have been identified as critical elements of success.[1828]

A second challenge is the paucity of technical knowledge and capacity[1829] and inadequate resources. The rather complex and often ambiguous elements of public procurement require extensive academic and practical research in order to find appropriate country-specific procurement methods and techniques. Since public procurement expertise is, especially in developing countries, still rare – inter alia due to a lack of study and training possibilities – national experts need to be carefully selected and it might be necessary to invite external experts to support the reform process. Furthermore, it is of utmost importance to have enough resources available not only to conduct the reform but also to finance the changes induced by the reform. The establishment of new institutions, for example, requires the availability of budget resources. This has to be considered and evaluated right from the beginning of the reform process.

Last but not least, the complexity of the substantive issues[1830] in itself provides a challenge for the creation of a new system, including such matters as the coordination of different governmental agencies, balancing of vested interests, transparency, institutional capacity, and many more. This

---

1825 See for further discussion on different interests and the lack of political will ibid, 4.

1826 Special Steering Committee of the OECD-DAC Task Force on Procurement, 'A Practical Guide to Transforming Procurement Systems ', p. 29.

1827 Cf. Kimani, p. 1612.

1828 OECD/DAC Task Force on Procurement, 'The Cusco Declaration "Strong Procurement Systems for Effective States"'.

1829 Hunja, 'Obstacles to Public Procurement Reform', p. 5.

1830 Ibid.

intricacy requires a complex analyse of the status quo of a country's economy, administration, and society as well as of the political, economic, societal and environmental objectives but also the inclusion of a variety of stakeholders. A public procurement system can only be effective if it is carefully embedded in the constitutional and administrative structures of a country.[1831] This constitutes a comprehensive task and sometimes includes the treatment of sensitive issues. Moreover, it is very important to realise that public procurement is not a separate and closed system but a fundamental and integrated part of governance and public financial management system of a country.[1832] Public procurement reform has to be seen as an essential feature of a country's broader strategy to improve public financial management systems as well as good governance.[1833] A general approach and commitment to implement and strengthen the rule of law and to reduce corruption are basic conditions for the successful enforcement of a good public procurement system. Beyond that, procurement reform should ideally involve

> "[…] complementary efforts to improve the performance of other parts of the public financial management process, the conduct of executing agencies, and/or other reforms that effect how the public sector operates".[1834]

A reform can therefore only be successful if it follows a holistic approach. The interaction and interdependence of the four pillars of procurement (as described in Part I, Chapter 1, Subchapter 3), for example, requires improvements in all areas rather than simply tackling obvious procurement deficiencies. If the opportunity arises it might be of great advantage to tackle public procurement reform in the course of wider public sector reforms. Because of the close interaction with other fields of law, this might even lead to a more holistic approach and a more satisfying result. According to Hunja, public procurement reform is bound to attract less direct opposition if it is part of a large reform effort.[1835]

There have been many examples of comprehensive legal reforms in African countries which have not led to major improvements. Weak en-

---

1831 Trepte, 'Regulating Procurement', p. 50.

1832 Development Assistance Committee, 'Strengthening Procurement Capacities ', p. 9.

1833 Trepte, 'Building sustainable capacity in public procurment', p. 378.

1834 Development Assistance Committee, 'Strengthening Procurement Capacities ', p. 28.

1835 Hunja, 'Obstacles to Public Procurement Reform', p. 9.

forcement and the persistence of challenges suggest the necessity of following a different approach in order to achieve successful reforms.

### c. The first Steps of a Public Procurement Reform

The reform of public procurement law requires more than merely drafting a new bill. In order to enable improvements of the efficiency and effectiveness of the public procurement system, there is, first of all, an essential need to carry out a comprehensive assessment of the strengths and weaknesses of the current public procurement system as well as to map out the needs and concerns that exist in the specific country context.

The legal reform process should begin with a comprehensive review of the present procurement system.[1836] The review can identify specific legal, institutional, organisational, procedural and professional shortcomings as key priorities for reform. Well-functioning institutions and mechanisms can be adopted, strengthened or modified. The Methodology for Assessing Procurement Systems developed by the OECD might provide a helpful tool to assess the quality and effectiveness of the actual procurement system.[1837]

A lack of data, records and statistics, however, hampers the assessment of procurement systems in many countries and, especially, developing countries. Additionally, it is difficult to determine to what extent the actual procurement practice is consistent with the formal rules and principle,[1838] as has also become obvious during field research in Namibia as outlined in the previous chapter. Existing non-transparency often hampers the will to challenge decisions or practices because of the fear of being blacklisted, on the one hand, and potential own benefits from non-transparent practices, on the other hand. Additionally, the incentives to contest violations might be too low since it requires allocating a significant amount of time and money which is often not outweighed by the result.

There are several tools and standards available that can be consulted to assess and reform a country's procurement system. The joint World Bank and OECD/DAC Procurement Round Table initiative has, together with

---

1836 Wittig, 'Building Value through Public Procurement', p. 17.

1837 OECD, 'MAPS'.

1838 Evenett; Hoekman, 'International Cooperation and the Reform of Public Procurement Policies', p. 32.

developing countries and bilateral and multilateral donors, developed a set of tools and standards that provide guidance for improvements in procurement systems and the results they produce. The probably most important one in this respect is the Methodology for Assessing Procurement Systems (MAPS).[1839] Noteworthy is also the practical guide to transforming procurement systems, which outlines the steps of change management and offers guidance for the entire reform process.[1840] Furthermore, the World Bank has developed the Country Procurement Assessment Report as a tool to assess procurement systems. The Country Procurement Assessment Report has successfully been used in many domestic procurement processes.[1841]

Apart from assessing the status quo, it is essential to discuss what objectives public procurement should achieve. This involves defining general objectives such as value for money, transparency, and fairness, but also specific goals such as pursuance of socio-economic or environmental objectives. Many countries, for example, decide to pursue secondary objectives that may contradict the objectives of non-discrimination and trade liberalisation. It is very important to decide at the beginning of the reform what objectives should be pursued by government procurement. The identification and specification of objectives is a necessary prerequisite for the successful creation of a public procurement system.[1842] That there is no universal procurement system for any type of country is stressed by Trepte: "Procurement systems are not to be analysed or criticised by reference to some universally acceptable and perfect procurement law; they are to be analysed in their context."[1843]

While the UNCITRAL Model Law might offer guidance with legal drafting, it does not relieve the reformers of making arrangements for customs and values of the country's administrative sector, the private sector, civil society and all other stakeholders involved. Country-specific factors that, for example, need to be considered are, inter alia, the institutional architecture, the efficiency of the public sector, the socio-economic situation, the size and nature of the private sector and the size of the country.

---

1839 OECD, 'MAPS'.

1840 Special Steering Committee of the OECD-DAC Task Force on Procurement, 'A Practical Guide to Transforming Procurement Systems '.

1841 Williams-Elegbe, 'The World Bank's Influence on Procurement Reform in Africa', 99.

1842 Cf. Trepte, 'Regulating Procurement', p. 8.

1843 Ibid, 48.

And, as mentioned above, it is an indispensable prerequisite to assess the capacity that is currently available and that can be accumulated as well as other local constraints so as to avoid enacting a law that cannot realistically be implemented. This also includes the establishment of a budget to fund capacity building. A detailed plan of what resources are available for the reform as well as for expenditures for measures necessary to implement change should be drawn up at an early stage and be constantly updated with regard to the envisaged modifications. It is, furthermore, important to identify realistic timelines[1844] so as to prevent reform delays but also discontent and a loss of trust in the achievements of the reform.

The deployment of sufficient human and financial resources to asses and evaluate the procurement system and its environment at the beginning of reform will certainly pay off in the reform outcome. Identifying and then addressing the root causes of problems in public procurement systems is certainly more promising than addressing just the symptoms of the malfunctions. [1845] (Relevant) stakeholders should be involved in this through interviews, workshops or surveys. Since a public procurement reform requires knowledge of public procurement law in general as well as of the country-specific context, it is necessary to find adequate personnel to lead the reform. It might be expedient to consult external experts who have comprehensive knowledge of public procurement reform; however, there should always be a close collaboration with domestic experts. The roles and responsibilities should be clearly assigned[1846] at the beginning of the reform in order to avoid misunderstandings and delays because the lines of authority are unclear. The experts also need to have sufficient knowledge of and experience in the matter as well as enough resources to do the job; the latter includes time and the means to carry out their function.

In countries where reform efforts seem to be never-ending and have not yet led to any result, it is important to identify the obstacles to reform and find ways to deal with them. If this is due to a lack of political will and a change is not in sight, it might be worth introducing intermediate mechanisms that at least deal with the most serious problems in the public pro-

1844 Special Steering Committee of the OECD-DAC Task Force on Procurement, 'A Practical Guide to Transforming Procurement Systems ', p. 55.
1845 Cf. ibid, 52.
1846 Ibid, 55.

curement system.[1847] In Namibia, for example, where the extensive use of exceptions is one of the major problems, the Ministry of Finance could specify the circumstances under which an exception may be applied.

### d. Legal Drafting

Procurement laws should not be over-excessive but provide latitude for qualitative and strategic decision-making of procurement professionals and for regulatory scope to adapt to changing local conditions. It is essential to establish basic principles, procedural details and delegation of powers and responsibilities. Although over-regulation should be avoided, all relevant aspects of the procurement process need to be addressed and determined. However, it is important to keep in mind that what is needed is not an overly complex system of rules but a specific emphasis on transparency, political will, experience and qualification.[1848] It is, moreover, crucial to standardise and align procurement terminology, methods and procedures. This is of special importance in decentralised systems and if there is a multitude of different sources of procurement law.[1849]

Whereas public procurement can be regulated solely by policies, as was formerly the case in many UK-based common law systems, there are several reasons for choosing a comprehensive legal instrument. The major reason is that it is far easier to identify and enforce such rules. It is also important to decide what the law itself should contain and what should be regulated by subsidiary texts. It is recommendable that a public procurement bill includes all essential procedures and methods which can then be specified in regulations.[1850]

### e. Implementation

Public procurement reforms are not sufficiently implemented by simply enacting legislation. There are several basic cornerstones that must be laid and certain preconditions need to be provided for. According to Walk-

1847 Hunja, 'Obstacles to Public Procurement Reform', p. 8.
1848 Interview Mr Ruppel (LorentzAngula Inc, Director/Chairman), 28th February 2013.
1849 Cf. Thai, 'International Public Procurement', p. 8, 9.
1850 Hunja, 'Obstacles to Public Procurement Reform', p. 6.

er,[1851] public procurement reform is most likely to succeed when it follows six basic steps. On this view, a necessary requirement is support from highest political levels or the government's commitment to reform. Then the advantages of a new system need to be made public. The third step is a cooperative dialogue between the public and the private sector in order to better understand each other's problems and needs. Another key priority is good procurement training. Good procurement legislation founds another basis for successful reform. Last but not least, Walker asserts that it is necessary to establish a central public procurement office to determine procurement policy and supervise its implementation.

Agaba and Shipman also stress the importance of enforcement. They also see this as one of the major challenges of the creation of an effective public procurement system:

> "The problems of enforcement and the temptations of malpractice in African countries are greater and consequently a comprehensive public procurement law is an essential requirement to reinforce government policy."[1852]

But "[even] with a procurement law in place, supported by regulations, guidelines and standard bidding documentation, enforcing compliance will continue to be a formidable challenge."[1853] The Task Force on Procurement also notes that in many countries, despite a relatively robust legal and regulatory framework, the level of compliance with remains weak and one of the biggest challenges.[1854] It should always be unequivocal and clearly communicated to all stakeholders that the simple enactment even of a well-designed procurement law is only one step and forms only one pillar of a procurement system; it is the effective implementation of the law that will determine its success.

A very important component for effective implementation of procurement law is capacity building, which encompasses the creation of awareness and understanding of the procurement reform and substantive training programmes for procurement staff. Training measures should, however, not simply aim at ensuring compliance but also at the transfer of

---

1851 C. Walker, 'Setting up a Public Procurement System: the Six Step Method', in S. Arrowsmith; M. Trybus, *Public Procurement: the Continuing Revolution* (Dordretch: Kluwer Law International, 2003).

1852 Agaba; Shipman, 'Public Procurement in Developing Countries', p. 387.

1853 Ibid.

1854 Special Steering Committee of the OECD-DAC Task Force on Procurement, 'A Practical Guide to Transforming Procurement Systems ', p. 34.

knowledge which enables procurement staff to strive for improved procurement outcomes.[1855] This includes assistance in

> "[...] identifying procurement needs, planning procurement activities, assessing market conditions affecting procurement choices, managing their relationship with bidders and contractors or administering contracts."[1856]

Although compliance with rules is an essential component of an efficient and effective procurement system, it does not necessarily ensure a good procurement outcome. The competence of procurement staff is a central component especially for countries which have a principles-based procurement system rather than a system of detailed rules.

Not only the people responsible for the public procurement process to function effectively and efficiently require training, but also the business sector needs to be trained and get assistance with the preparation of bids in the new system.[1857] Assistance should be available on a continuous basis and not only after the introduction of new legislation. Support can be vital especially for small or newly established companies inexperienced in bid preparation, enabling them to compete with more experienced companies and, hence, leading to greater competition. The involvement and training of other stakeholders in public procurement should not be disregarded. Since public procurement is an interaction between public and private players and affects several other groups of people, it is necessary to equip them with the necessary knowledge and skills to play their respective roles.[1858]

Successful and consistent implementation of procurement legislation can further be supported by a user's guide or manual for contracting entities.[1859] This is of special importance if a system becomes more decentralised. It should detail all procedures for the correct administration of procurement legislation and be updated regularly. The responsibility for the drafting and updating of such a manual needs to be clearly established.[1860]

Substantive change in procurement practice can only be achieved if the natural resistance of the majority of stakeholders is overcome. By referring to a formula of change management theory suggested by Beckhard

1855 Cf. Trepte, 'Building sustainable capacity in public procurment', p. 380.
1856 Ibid.
1857 Cf. Walker, 'Setting up a Public Procurement System', p. 7.
1858 Sabiiti; Muhumuza, p. 2049.
1859 OECD, 'MAPS', p. 17f., Sub-indicator 2(e).
1860 Ibid.

and Harris in 1987[1861] the Development Assistance Committee of the OECD names three key factors influencing the natural resistance of systems, organisations and people. First of all, everyone must fully understand that the present situation is unsatisfactory. Then, there needs to be a realistic and positive vision of what the system can and should look like. The third condition is that the change process used to roll out the reform includes some achievable early wins.[1862] The natural resistance of stakeholders that have benefited from the existent procurement system as well as user departments and procurement officers who would face the challenge of becoming acquainted with new rules and processes deserves special attention. Beyond that, government officials who have exploited public procurement for their own benefit, for example by favouring certain companies to ensure political support, might resist change. Another important stakeholder that should be convinced of the potentials of reform should be the agencies responsible for the financial auditing because close coordination with this agency is essential for success. Apart from the internal governmental stakeholders, the reform needs to enjoy overall support from civil society. This includes the business community, the press, academia, NGOs and the wider public.[1863] Walker considers public relations campaigns through different possible means such as briefings, brochures or TV and radio spots as important instrument to make the public familiar with the new system and convince it of its advantages.[1864] However, public campaigns should not only start at a point where legislation has been drafted, but it is essential to engage stakeholders at the very early stages of reform in order to "[...] create ownership and buy-in that will be critical when it comes to implementing changes further on."[1865]

The involvement of stakeholders during public procurement reform can also lead to better legislation, as both the private and the public sector learn about the needs and concerns of the other in regard to public pro-

1861 R. Beckhard; R.T. Harris, 'Organizational Transitions: Managing Complex Change', (Reading, Massachusetts Addison-Wesley Pub. Co., 1987).

1862 Development Assistance Committee, 'Strengthening Procurement Capacities', p. 32.

1863 The Development Assistance Committee provides a list of possible supporters of/stakeholders in procurement reform. See ibid, 33. see also Karangizi; Ndahiro, 'Public procurement reforms and development in the Eastern and Southern African region', p. 114.

1864 Walker, 'Setting up a Public Procurement System', p. 5.

1865 Special Steering Committee of the OECD-DAC Task Force on Procurement, 'A Practical Guide to Transforming Procurement Systems', p. 15.

curement. Whereas the business sector might prefer a less bureaucratic public procurement procedure to save costs and time, the public sector is dependent on rules and regulations in order to suffice the standards of transparency and good governance. Discussions about such concerns can lead to a set of rules that is acceptable for both the public and the private sector.[1866]

With regard to the impact and relevance of public procurement and the variety of ambiguous and unexplored issues connected with procurement, constant monitoring and evaluation of the public procurement system is a key factor for long term success. The effectiveness and efficiency of the existing and post-reform public procurement system depends on the identification of shortcomings and obstacles and their elimination. Elements within the procurement system that are found to be inefficient or ineffective should be modified or abandoned.[1867] This requires comprehensive data collection as well as the definition of success as a benchmark to assess the achievement of commitments and objectives.[1868] It is, hence, of the utmost importance to ensure that the review of the public procurement system is continued even after the successful completion of a public procurement reform. Newly established procurement systems should be constantly assessed in order to identify and address shortcomings and to respond to new developments.

Operational and institutional efficiency, compliance with regulations and procedures and procurement outcomes should be likewise reviewed. Financial and non-financial parameters are of equal importance in indicating the performance of the procurement system. Financial audits should be carried out but on their own are by no means sufficient to evaluate procurement outcomes. The efficiency of secondary objectives should be reviewed regularly and, if necessary, lead to a policy change. It might have a positive impact if good performance were also specifically rewarded, rather than only looking for what goes wrong.[1869]

1866 For the need of cooperation between the public and private sector see also Walker, 'Setting up a Public Procurement System', p. 6f.
1867 Wittig, 'Building Value through Public Procurement', p. 16.
1868 Cf. ibid.
1869 Suggestions for Uganda by Sabiiti; Muhumuza, p. 2049.

### 3. Organisational Issues

#### a. Regulated Process vs. Managerial Task

A public procurement system can be highly regulated and thereby leave very limited scope for managerial decision-making. The adverse performance model relies on regulation "primarily to establish management principles and objectives rather than to micro-manage the process."[1870] The question is whether heavy regulation is adequate to cope with the complexity of public procurement. First of all, the comprehensive specification of all procurement steps and procedures adds to the complexity not only for the executing agents but also all other stakeholders. Knowledge of all substantive and procedural rules is essential for bidders to take part in and oversee the process. Overly complex rules might therefore discourage firms from preparing a bid in the first place and, thereby, reduce competition. Clear and simple rules enable stakeholders and the wider public to engage in an informal peer review of procurement procedures and outcomes.[1871] Additionally, it can be suggested that the more complex the procedure the more time and money it consumes. Complexity of rules also diminishes flexibility to adapt to changes in the market environment and to handle more voluminous or sophisticated procurement.[1872]

The detailed regulation of all steps of procurement reduces the influence of market-based decisions by public procurement officers which consequently minimises their effect on the outcome. Vice versa, the availability of qualified and experienced procurement staff is a major prerequisite for the effective functioning of a procurement system that relies on managerial decision-making rather than on heavy regulation. Reliance on regulation as the primary means of control and implementation of procurement policy might be appropriate where there is a lack of competent procurement staff with adequate managerial skills to make qualitative procurement decisions or to minimise political risks.[1873] The gain in risk minimisation is, however, made at the cost of a loss of effectiveness in terms of value for money. Especially when policy objectives such as the sustaina-

1870 Schapper; et al., 'An Analytic Framework for the Management and Reform of Public Procurement', 14.
1871 Ibid, 12.
1872 Ibid, 6.
1873 Ibid, 5, 6.

bility of products and services are implemented in public procurement, qualitative decision-making is a key success factor. The assessment of life-time costs, for example, requires comprehensive knowledge of the economic, social and environmental character of a specific product or service and cannot be generalised. Bidders might prefer tender awards that are based on qualitative decision-making because it might imply minimising risks in terms of the effectiveness of the outcome. Governments more frequently make use of alternative procurement methods such as partnerships whereby risk and success is shared in order to improve result effectiveness. A highly regulated procurement system, however, impedes such approaches.

In countries where few qualified people are available for the procurement staff the cost of capacity building, including the training of procurement staff, has to be weighed against the choice of more detailed regulation and the attendant compromises in regard to efficiency. In particular, savings could be achieved if there were a shift from accountability for compliance to accountability for outcomes.[1874] Especially in developing countries with a lack of procurement capacity and expertise, clear and detailed rules might be preferable in order to enhance transparency and accountability and not to overburden the public procurement staff. This is important in order to guarantee that procedures are carried out and decisions are taken according to the rules.

### b. Decentralised vs. Centralised Approach

When tackling reform an important decision is whether or to what extent a decentralised procurement system should be designed. There is a universal trend towards decentralisation and this also affects public procurement. Whereas tender laws mainly provided for centralised procurement systems in the past, there is now a shift towards decentralisation.[1875] In many developing countries, it turned out that the increase of the amount and complexity of government purchases under stricter procurement requirements are too unwieldy to be efficiently and effectively carried out by central

1874 Ibid, 14.
1875 Agaba; Shipman, 'Public Procurement in Developing Countries', p. 374.

procurement boards.[1876] Both systems have advantages as well as disadvantages and country-specific factors such as the political system (unitary or federal), a country's size and population density, market size, and the modality of the public service have to be considered in order to find an appropriate way to handle public procurement. Pure centralised or decentralised systems rarely exist in practice. Often agencies are subject to very specific exceptions on a commodity basis, for example, direct procurement of specialised professional services by the user departments.[1877]

In centralised procurement systems most of the rights, powers, duties, and authority relating to public procurement are vested in a central procurement office.[1878] This ensures control and program consistency. Beyond that it facilitates the development of purchasing expertise which has a positive impact on efficiency and economy as well as the integrity of the purchasing system.[1879]

In decentralised procurement personnel is not bound by a hierarchical order and can take procurement decisions unilaterally without the need for a higher authority to delegate power. It is more likely to be well adapted to local needs and peculiarities as well as changing conditions, but mechanisms to link national and sub-national planning processes are nonetheless important in order to guarantee an appropriate reflection of national priorities in regional and local policies.[1880] It is, however, an advantage that procurement is carried out by those responsible for the delivery of services and closer to the end-user than centralised procurement.[1881] Policy coherence is, nonetheless, very important because inconsistency of public procurement practices may constitute a considerable obstacle for bidders to participate in public procurement. Hence, in a decentralised system consistent national standards and a central body monitoring compliance are key factors for success.[1882] Another factor is that decentralised procure-

---

1876 This has been found in Namibia through field research. Agaba and Shipman describe a similar problem for Uganda: Ibid, 374.

1877 Thai, 'International Public Procurement', p. 9.

1878 Ibid.

1879 C.P. McCue, 'Centralized vs. decentralized purchasing: Current trends in governmental procuremen practices' (2000) 12(3) Journal of Public Budgeting.

1880 Cf Basheka, 'Procurement Planning and Accountability', 390; McCue, 'Centralized vs. decentralized purchasing'.

1881 R. Rothery, 'Understanding Public Procurement', The Governance Brief, ADB, Issue 3 (Manila: Asian Development Bank 2000), p. 1.

1882 Ibid, 2. See also Schapper; et al., 'An Analytic Framework for the Management and Reform of Public Procurement', 12.

ment requires more resources that need to be available or generated, especially financial resources and human capacity.

### c. Institutional Capacity

The several duties and responsibilities in public procurement must be devolved to different institutions in accordance with the principle of separation of power.[1883] Different persons should deal with distinct procedural steps to avoid, for example, the same person who determined the award criteria from evaluating the tenders. This ensures the correct application of procedures and diminishes the possibility of corruption. The clash of interests of public policies with efficiency and value for money which might arise within procuring ministries hinders the objectives of public procurement and, therefore, a distinct public body implementing procurement might be expedient.[1884]

Important government stakeholders include the user departments which initiate tendering, procurement units which manage the procurement process and committees which approve the different stages of the procurement process and take the final decision on the best bid and contract award.[1885] Beyond that, there are national institutions that, rather than being directly involved in carrying out procurement, indirectly affect the efficient and effective functioning of public procurement. First of all, the existence or establishment of a procurement oversight organisation which is independent from political interference with regard to operational decisions but an integral part of the government's public financial management system is essential in order to guarantee reporting, monitoring and the evaluation of the procurement system.[1886] Many countries that have recently reformed their procurement systems have decentralised their public procurement system by requiring the establishment of procuring units in any procuring entity. But they have also established central bodies with responsibility for monitoring public procurement and policy formulation.

1883 Development Assistance Committee, 'Strengthening Procurement Capacities ', p. 50.

1884 Wittig, 'Building Value through Public Procurement', p. 14.

1885 Cf. Agaba; Shipman, 'Public Procurement in Developing Countries', p. 379, 380.

1886 Development Assistance Committee, 'Strengthening Procurement Capacities ', p. 49. Walker also argues for the need to establish a central public procurement office. Walker, 'Setting up a Public Procurement System', p. 10ff.

This is important not only to ensure a certain degree of standardisation but also to create a system of accountability and control. The powers and responsibilities of such an entity should be clearly defined and the monitoring body should be able to operate independently without any influence from other governmental offices. The selection and qualification of staff are main components for the efficient and effective functioning of a central monitoring and policy body.

Other institutions carrying out control and enforcement functions are the government's internal audit agency, the parliamentarian oversight committee(s) for the public sector budget, financial management and procurement issues, and the judicial bodies or alternative dispute resolution mechanisms. The quality of the workforce depends to a great extent on the work of the civil service administration, public sector management training institutes and the ministry of education. All these institutions should be already included in the reform process.[1887]

d. Human Resources

A system is only as good as the people implementing it and, therefore, staff competence is a key success factor. Public procurement is not solely an application of certain regulations but requires quality decision-making which includes timely and well-founded decisions motivated by cost and quality and the minimisation of political interference.[1888] This balancing act is a highly sensitive and complex issue whose quality is decisive for effective public procurement.

Public procurement requires not only public administration skills but economic understanding, including knowledge of the market, and the competence to assess and take highly contingent approaches.[1889] Beyond that, sufficient legal and technical understanding and assistance is required. Nowadays IT competence is becoming increasingly important, especially in regard to the use of IT procurement systems and the introduction of e-procurement. Public procurement institutions need public procurement experts, but also a wide range of other professionals including

1887 Cf. Development Assistance Committee, 'Strengthening Procurement Capacities', p. 49, 50.

1888 Rothery, 'Understanding Public Procurement', p. 1.

1889 Caldwell; et al., 'Promoting Competitive Markets', p. 329; Mamiro, p. 5.

accountants, legal officers, project managers, software programmers, computer system analysts, information technology managers, business analysts, research specialists, human resource officers, secretaries, filing clerks, and clerk typists.[1890]

The kind of procurement procedures and mechanism chosen determines the kind of qualifications procurement staff need to have. Capacity building has to be matched to the procurement system, or vice versa: the procurement system has to be reformed in light of the available capacity. Different approaches need different numbers of staff with different skills sets. A public private partnerships approach, for example, may require a smaller number of staff with the appropriate skills set fully dedicated to handling specific procurement transactions.[1891]

There needs to be an effective mechanism to select procurement staff, to establish entry requirements, controls and incentives as well as an educational system catering for the needs of competent procurement staff.[1892] Furthermore, public procurement is more than an administrative function and needs to be recognised as a unique profession within government. This can be accomplished for example by creating a system of certification for suitably qualified officials.[1893] In the short term, there are several national associations and international institutions offering public procurement training and certificates of proficiency.[1894] In the long run, national institutions should be responsible for public procurement training. In some cases the establishment of new institutions such as procurement training centres might be necessary; in other cases existing institutions can be mandated to ensure that the need for qualified procurement staff can be satisfied. A key role can be played by national colleges, universities, management institutes, or other training institutes.[1895] The establishment of a

1890 Cf. Ismahel, p. 19.

1891 Development Assistance Committee, 'Strengthening Procurement Capacities', p. 40. Cf. also Zheng; et al., 'An analysis of research into the future of purchasing and supply management', 77.

1892 Cf. Thai, 'International Public Procurement', p. 11.

1893 OECD, 'SIGMA Paper No. 30 - Public Procurement Review Procedures, CCNM/SIGMA/PUMA(2000)114', p. 9.

1894 See Walker, 'Setting up a Public Procurement System', p. 8. Examples are the Chartered Institute of Purchasing and Supply, the Institute for Supply Management and theSouthern Business School, a South African company which offers a diploma course on Supply Chain Management.

1895 Cf. Trepte, 'Building sustainable capacity in public procurment', p. 388. In the US the National Institute of Governmental Purchasing, Inc. has built up partnerships

national procurement institute that is responsible for the development of a comprehensive long-term curriculum, its coordination and implementation might be beneficial in this regard.

Whereas it is of the utmost important to establish minimum competency levels for procurement staff, this should not lead to unfilled vacancies because no one with the required skills and experience is available. It might be worth following a long-term approach by extensively training incumbent personnel and re-employing qualified staff to fill vacancies. Countries are strongly recommended to create training possibilities and start training at a very early stage of reform in order to build the necessary human resources required for the implementation of the new system.

Especially in developing countries government officials are often not well-paid. This leads many to leave public service to work for the private sector. It is, hence, apart from the provision of training and education on public procurement, very important to increase salaries and to establish well-defined career paths.[1896] A pay-rise can reduce the temptation for officials to engage in corrupt practices to improve their income. And the establishment of well-defined career paths can induce that procurement officials identify with their tasks and responsibilities and demonstrate and develop a leadership function in this respect.[1897]

### 4. Procedures and Methods

As described previously, there are several procurement methods available but in general open competitive bidding should be the primary procurement method. It is also necessary to clearly outline the conditions for the use of alternative procurement methods. The procurement method needs

---

with higher education institutions in 1998. The partnership with the Florida Atlantic University led to the establishment of a specific research center on government procurement and cooperative efforts have produced studies of academic degree programs, the publication of the Journal of Public Procurement as well as national surveys. See K.V. Thai, 'Government Procurement: Past and current developments' (2000) 12(2) Journal of Public Budgeting, Accounting & Financial Management.

1896 OECD, 'SIGMA Paper No. 30 - Public Procurement Review Procedures, CCNM/SIGMA/PUMA(2000)114', p. 9.

1897 G. Callender; J. McGuire, 'People in public procurement', in L. Knight; et al., *Public Procurement: International cases and commentary* (London and New York: Routledge, 2007), p. 321.

to be adequate in regard to the nature, the complexity and the value of the procurement. It is essential that an official who can be held accountable approves the choice of the procurement method. Exceptions can be made by law or administratively; the latter, however, involves a higher risk of abuse. Procurement methods that deviate from conventional methods, such as partnerships or framework agreements, need to be considered in view of the local capacity. More complex and innovative procurement methods such as framework agreements should only be used if there is the necessary institutional capacity.

In regard to the procedures and methods it is important to clearly outline what kind of criteria can be required for the evaluation of tenders and also how much flexibility should be allowed in formulating such criteria. The decision to permit or prohibit the possibility of pursuing secondary objectives in the award phase is of specific importance in this context.

Methods which contribute to efficiency should be evaluated and, where appropriate, adopted. An example is the European Union's initiative to reduce the administrative burden in public procurement. A proposal for a European directive on public procurement suggests reducing requirements that contracting authorities impose on bidders to prove their eligibility to participate in a given procurement procedures. It provides for the acceptance of self-declarations as prima facie evidence; the relevant evidence should, however, be provided by the tenderer winning the contract.[1898] Furthermore, suppliers or contractors bidding for government contracts that have presented certificates or documentary evidence once are not required to produce such evidence again in the following four years provided, of course, the evidence is still valid.[1899] The implementation of such approaches can contribute significantly to the efficiency of a public procurement system; hence, a strong focus of research during reform should be on finding suitable and efficient methods that can facilitate public procurement procedures for all stakeholders. Such facilitations would have a positive impact on the efficiency and the effectiveness of public procurement in general and perhaps lead to greater acceptance.

1898 J.M. Gimeno-Feliú, 'Towards Efficiency in Public Procurement: Simplifying Procedures and Reducing Administrative Burden', conference paper, 5th International Conference on Public Procurement Seattle, Washington, 15-17th August, 2012, p. 1052.

1899 Ibid, 1052f.

## 5. Transparency

Transparency in public procurement is a very important issue. As mentioned in the previous parts, not only developing but also developed countries suffer from corruption, bribery and other friction. It is decisive to ensure the implementation of substantive rules on transparency without over-regulating public procurement and making it too complicated. Stakeholders and the wider public demand clear and understandable rules. Satisfying this need may also give them confidence in the system and public procurement officers.

As mentioned above, the prioritising of transparency issues in public procurement reform while disregarding other factors as value for money has come under increasing criticism. Read, for example, notes that

> "[t]he development of a rule that is designed to make procurement faster, better cheaper, more accessible to suppliers – all those noble purposes – is increasingly rare. Instead, we seem obsessively focussed with fairness, openness and transparency – and with stopping crooks who will subvert the process – and concurrently with making sure that everyone involved in the process is 'safe'."[1900]

This should not imply that the transparency issue is overrated but that it has to be carefully balanced with other principles which are equally significant for effective procurement system. Raga and Taylor explicitly state that the essence of public procurement legislation is "[...] to define and enforce those procedures that will produce a productive and efficient result, while respecting the public nature of the process and the duty of fairness to the supplier."[1901] Hence, improvement of procurement performance should be envisaged in order to generate a better procurement outcome rather than being the objective itself.[1902] This might require a move from traditional bureaucratic procurement processes to a more flexible and managerial style of procurement processes.[1903] Although transparency should be a key priority in public procurement systems, there are other priorities which should be addressed in a balanced way in order to guarantee efficiency and effectiveness.

1900 Read, p. 17.

1901 K. Raga; J.D. Taylor, 'Legislative and Administrative Directives governing Procurement Procedures: A Case Study for South Africa', conference paper.

1902 Cf. Development Assistance Committee, 'Strengthening Procurement Capacities', p. 27.

1903 Basheka, 'Public Procurement Reforms in Africa', p. 136.

There are, however, certain transparency standards that should be followed in order to guarantee transparent procurement including clear and consistent regulations, public tendering as a general rule, widely advertisement of tenders, clear accountability for decision-makers, price-based contract award rather than multiple award scoring mechanisms, full disclosure, standardised bidding documents and general conditions of contracts, a code of conduct for procurement officials, comprehensive data records and a review mechanism for unsatisfied bidders.[1904] Effective sanctions for corrupt actions for the company as well as the public procurement official should be applied. This can not only rectify wrongful acts but deter future corrupt practices. Sanctions might include payment of damages, disciplinary sanctions such as the dismissal from office for the procurement official, the blacklisting of a company taking part in corrupt practices, denial or cancellation of a concluded contract, forfeiture of bids and criminal prosecution.[1905] To prevent corruption in public procurement, Transparency International has suggested the conclusion of an agreement between a government or a governmental department and all bidders for a public sector contract whereby all participants are obliged to renounce any type of corruptive practices. Transparency International also proposes that sanctions be imposed in case of violation. In practice these agreements shall as part of the "Integrity Pact" promote trust and transparency. This approach has proved successful in many countries.[1906]

Beyond procurement-specific standards, general measures to improve governance can indirectly lead to improvements in regard to transparency and accountability and have the potential to create an environment which fosters these objectives. This requires strict anti-corruption legislation and the general attitude and political will to condemn all forms of corruption within the public sector. However, political will not only has to be articulated but also reflect in law enforcement.[1907]

1904 Agaba; Shipman, 'Public Procurement in Developing Countries', p. 376; Rothery, 'Understanding Public Procurement', p. 2.

1905 Pope, 'Confronting Corruption', p. 214; Transparency International, 'The Integrity Pact - The Concept, the Model and the Present Applications: A Status Report' (Transparency International: 2002), p. 7 (available at https://.transparency.hu/uploads/docs/IP-FullStatusReport2002_1_.pdf; last accessed: 1 December 2015).

1906 Transparency International, 'The Integrity Pact - The Concept, the Model and the Present Applications: A Status Report'.

1907 See e.g. Agaba; Shipman, 'Public Procurement in Developing Countries', p. 386.

## 6. Secondary Objectives

### a. Inclusion of Secondary Objectives into Public Procurement Law

Reform discussions should clearly differentiate between policy-adherence and policy-stipulation in regard to collateral objectives of public procurement. Many problems and issues identified in public procurement arise not because of narrow latitudes for the inclusion of secondary policy goals but due to an insufficient implementation of public procurement procedures and disrespect and violation of local, domestic and international laws and regulations. The introduction of discriminatory policies such as the preferential treatment of domestic over foreign bidders is not an adequate solution for removing bidders who, for example, do not adhere to local labour law. The exclusion of foreign bidders does yet not address the fundamental problem of foreign companies violating laws and regulations which should be tackled via other means.

Apart from the realisation of the aforementioned risks in including discriminatory policies in public procurement, a very careful analysis should be made whether policy goals cannot be achieved more effectively through other means, for example, by subsidies, loans or incentives. This may serve to keep the procurement system simple, ensuring that the procedures and manageable system are transparent for all stakeholders. Policies to promote local SMEs, for example, should only be implemented after determining whether a more objective, clear and simplified procedure could not sufficiently facilitate SMEs' access to public procurement, thereby avoiding discriminatory practices and the associated negative side effects. There are other approaches to stimulating SME involvement and success in public procurement such as better feedback, the use of incentives and award procedures for the early and successful completion of projects, new indigenous technologies[1908] and improving funding opportunities.

Ssennoga and Telgen[1909] have developed a Procurement Option Model as a decision tool to determine whether a contract should be awarded to a foreign or a domestic firm. It is an economic model that allows countries

1908 Ismahel, p. 12.

1909 F. Ssennoga; J. Telgen, 'Integrating Socio-Economic Policies into the Public Procurement Framework - An Analysis of the Public Procurement Option Model', conference paper, p. 1.

to institute discriminatory procurement schemes within their procurement framework without compromising the fundamental principle of value for money. The model basically offers a method to calculate whether it is more beneficial to award a contract to a foreign firm with the lower bid and re-channel the money back into priority sectors of the economy or to a domestic firm and thereby achieve a certain policy.[1910] However, this model lacks practical experience and it has to be questioned whether its benefits outweigh the expenditures of its application. Otherwise, if economically feasible it might facilitate an optimal use of discriminatory policies. Nevertheless, as Ssennoga rightly stresses, the margin of preference should never be set at a level that completely shuts out foreign competition. The possibility for foreign firms to win a tender by providing a favourably low bid creates an acceptable level of competition and will eliminate any possible complacency of domestic firms.[1911]

It is also indispensable to consider that the incurrence of enforcement costs of secondary objectives might be disproportionate to the outcome.[1912] However, a cost-benefit analysis is difficult to conduct, especially in light of the budgetary constraints experienced in developing countries. It is, hence, important to consider that measuring and evaluating the effect of secondary objectives in order to determine their practical success requires additional resources beyond the enforcement costs. The effective pursuit of secondary objectives can, hence, be a costly matter tying up resources that might be spent on other measures furthering socio-economic development.

Governments should always critically assess and reflect on the coherence of means and purpose. Whereas temporary applied discriminatory practices[1913] might help to overcome structural differences of market size, other structural differences such as in technology or human capital are even likely to be amplified and should be tackled via other means.[1914] Investments in the education or the research sector are, for example, possible

1910 Ibid, 2.

1911 Ssennoga, 'Examining Discriminatory Procurement Practices', 237.

1912 Cf. UNCITRAL, 'Guide to Enactment of the UNCITRAL Model Law on Public Procurement', p. 6, para 14.

1913 Sec. 22 of the Kenyan Public Procurement and Disposal (Preference and Reservations) Regulations, 2011, for example, provides that enterprises „registered in a target group benefitting from the preference and reservation scheme shall be entitled to such benefits for a period of five years, which may be renewed once."

1914 Cf. Trionfetti, 'Discriminatory Public Procurement', 73.

means to achieve these ends. It is also important to keep in mind that all secondary objectives differ in regard to their effect on economic efficiency and the usefulness of instruments to achieve a certain objective varies with respect to the different industries concerned.

Another issue is the politicisation of discriminatory practices which creates a pattern which is difficult to reverse.[1915] Consequently, if such policies are implemented, they should be considered and applied carefully. This is explained by Ssennoga/Telgen as follows:

> "The problem with discriminatory schemes is that once they are introduced, politically, they are hard to remove. Governments are exposed to various lobby groups that want to ensure they exist in perpetuity. A government fearing to lose an election succumbs to these demands leading to continued perpetuation of inefficiency. A time frame [...] needs to be attached to the programme and progress constantly monitored."[1916]

Moreover, firms might be discouraged from undertaking investment in innovation and restructuring if there is no deadline for discriminatory procurement that marks the date on which direct competition with foreign companies determines success.[1917]

A key factor for the success secondary objectives in public procurement is, furthermore, a transparent and adequate application of policy promotion through public procurement. Criteria implementing such policies should be fully disclosed and designed in a neutral and reasonable way so as not to impede competition. And Quinot explains that

> "[i]t is particularly in relation to horizontal policy influences on public procurement decisions that wide discretionary powers should not be granted to procurement officials. In the absence of clear rules, it is extremely difficult to assess whether a particular procurement decision was properly made in terms of the range of objectives pursued in the procurement system."[1918]

Socio-economic objectives that primarily aim at improving social welfare, e.g. the requirement to adhere to certain labour standards, can be a useful instrument for governments to fulfil their role in the protection and promotion of the economic and social well-being of their citizens. If, for example, the application of poor labour standards in public projects has been

1915 Cf. Reich, 'International Public Procurement Law', p. 50.
1916 Ssennoga; Telgen, 'Integrating Socio-Economic Policies into the Public Procurement Framework - An Analysis of the Public Procurement Option Model', p. 17.
1917 Trionfetti, 'Discriminatory Public Procurement', 73.
1918 Quinot, 'Promotion of social policy ', p. 379.

identified as a major obstacle to socio-economic development, instruments to counteract these trends might be integrated into the public procurement system as policy objectives. Contrary to Trepte's criticism that this could complicate public procurement as regards the administrative burden and costs related to compliance,[1919] the role model function of the government as purchaser as well as the peculiarity of public projects that are often carefully observed by the public can be valid reasons for the inclusion of requirements to adhere to local laws and standards. And, contrary to what Trepte presupposes, adherence can be ensured through respective contract management structures in collaboration between procurement institutions and other law enforcement institutions instead of solely resting on public procurement officials. Additionally, public projects are especially vulnerable to corruption and the cooperation between procurement institutions and other law enforcing institutions in regard to adherence to laws and standards can be a useful means to counteract malpractices, in particular because there is the possible sanction of blacklisting suppliers or contractors that have allegedly violated laws or mandatory standards. In particular in developing countries where law enforcement agencies do not exist or do not work efficiently, the use of public procurement structures to ensure enforcement can be an effective means.[1920]

### b. Inclusion of Environmental Criteria

First of all, it has to be noted that it is easier to introduce environmental objectives through environmentally-friendly product specification than by using award criteria aiming at green production or post-production processes, since the latter are more subjective and difficult to estimate and measure and might, therefore, undermine the transparency objectives of a procurement system. Furthermore, the existing general environmental policy of a country reforming its procurement system should be carefully as-

1919 Trepte, 'Regulating Procurement', p. 171: "[…] this could lead to public purchasers becoming enforcers of a myriad of applicable laws which have little to do with the procurement function. Given the justified concerns both of the purchasers and vendors that increased procurement regulation leads to onerous administrative procedures and increased costs related to compliance, giving purchasers the additional role of enforcers of otherwise enforceable laws is hardly an appropriate means of ensuring procedural efficiency and speed."

1920 Cf. ibid, 189.

sessed and balanced with possible policy goals that can be achieved through government procurement. Nationally accepted environmental standards or labels can, for example, easily be integrated into public procurement.

If environmental criteria are introduced, it is very important to monitor the supplier and impose immediate and predetermined sanctions for breach of contract in order to guarantee that the agreed criteria are honoured. This might reduce the temptation of suppliers to disregard the criteria because of the additional costs thereby incurred.[1921]

As has been emphasised in Part I,[1922] it is very controversial whether green procurement has a positive effect. As with socio-economic objectives it should always be assessed very carefully whether the pursued objectives cannot be better achieved through other means.

## 7. Review Procedures

It has to be noted that the review of public procurement might vary according to a country's conception of public procurement. While some consider it as being solely a public function, some treat procurement contracts as commercial acts and allow, for example, for damages claims covered by private law.[1923] When establishing new review procedures it is important to classify what approach should be pursued. However, there are certain criteria that should be met by all country's public procurement review mechanisms, including that challenges are dealt with promptly and without unnecessary delays, that the costs are kept low and that they are not disruptive to the tender procedures. It is recommendable to allow for internal or administrative review as well as a review procedure to an independent review mechanism and to make judicial review only available as last resort after having exhausted the other available review mechanisms.

It needs to be decided whether and how administrative complaint procedures should be available. This can be a direct complaint to the procuring entity or to another administrative authority. This allows the procuring entity to directly comment on the allegations, to ease doubts about the

1921 Palmujoki; et al., 'Green Public Procurement', 159.

1922 See Chapter 3, Subchapter 3.

1923 For further detail see OECD, 'SIGMA Paper No. 30 - Public Procurement Review Procedures, CCNM/SIGMA/PUMA(2000)114', p. 14.

fairness and rightfulness of their decision, or to reconsider their decision and make adjustments, thereby avoiding litigation and corresponding time and costs.[1924]

In order for review not to rest solely with the courts – which is often unsatisfying because of the long delays and cost involved –, it is also possible and recommendable to establish an independent review body. The type of such a review body has to be determined and specific professional knowledge in dealing with procurement complaints needs to be available or accumulated.[1925]

Moreover, it should be decided whether judicial review should be based on general administrative justice provisions or whether there should be specific public procurement rules for judicial review. It has to be kept in mind that long delays in judicial review might have a negative impact on the objectives of public procurement. Even if courts work relatively fast, this might not be fast enough for public procurement processes and procedures. It further needs to be considered what types of courts are eligible to handle procurement cases. The OECD notes in this respect that

> "[a] legal system that has a network of local courts may be considered to help complainants, while a system where judges specialise in administrative law may provide some assurance of professional competence. However, a centralised system makes review easier to manage and facilitates the training of the judges trying such cases."[1926]

As mentioned in the first part, there is always a trade-off between creating effective remedies and keeping the procurement procedure efficient. "A generous interim relief regime will favour the objective of integrity, while a strict or narrow approach to interim relief will favour efficiency."[1927] The initiation of court proceedings can, for example, result in the automatic suspension of the public procurement process or the implementation of the awarded contract but there is also the possibility of allowing suspension upon application. The challenging supplier then has to show compliance with the conditions for suspension and suppliers challenging a decision simply for the reason of suspension can thereby be avoided.[1928]

To avert the unsatisfying situation of tender awards being challenged and needing to decide whether the contract should be halted pending the

1924 Cf. ibid, 13.
1925 Cf. ibid, 6.
1926 Ibid, 14.
1927 Quinot, 'A comparative perspective on supplier remedies', p. 323.
1928 Ibid, 323f.

outcome of the proceedings, it might be advantageous to make a provisional award, held in abeyance, and allow for an appeal period. Only if no appeal is issued or after appeals have been finalised will the final tender be awarded.[1929] Indeed such a provision protects both the procuring entity and the tenderers; however, it delays the tender process. Nevertheless, this should, if no exceptional circumstances exist, be the lesser of two evils. Although it delays tender procedures in cases where no appeal is lodged, it can avoid judicial review, which usually causes an even longer delay than an administrative appeal. The provision of an appeal mechanism before the tender is finally awarded is of great advantage since at this time no contract has been signed and questions such as compensation and stopping projects or supplies that have started running are avoided.

It has to be emphasised that efficient, well-managed organisational structures and competent and experienced staff as well as effective preventive systems of management control and internal audit[1930] substantively contribute to the avoidance of procurement disputes and irregularities. Efforts to strengthen these factors should always be addressed and considered during reform. Although review procedures constitute an essential component for the effective implementation and enforcement of public procurement legislation, their availability is not in itself sufficient to guarantee the objectives of public procurement.

## 8. Other Important Considerations

### a. Procurement Planning

It is very important to require the preparation of annual procurement plans and estimations of the associated expenditures not only to avoid aggregation of public procurements at the end of the financial year and to enable all stakeholders to pre-plan but also to allow a proper preparation of budgets.[1931] These should be available to the public and updated regularly. Alt-

1929 Section 49 of the Transvaal's Municipality's Procurement Policy provides for such an appeal period. See Total Computer Services (Pty) Limited v. Municipal Manager Ptochefstroom Local Municipality and Others (29416/07) [2007] ZAGPHC 239; 2008 (4) SA 346 (T): paras. 62 ff.

1930 OECD, 'SIGMA Paper No. 30 - Public Procurement Review Procedures, CCNM/SIGMA/PUMA(2000)114', p. 6f.

1931 See OECD, 'MAPS', p. 19f., Sub-indicator 3 (a).

hough general budget planning, including public procurement, is often regulated in other laws, it is of great advantage to include provisions and requirements specifically for procurement planning and, as the case may be, references to the applicable legal provision. This should be considered in every public procurement reform.

### b. Contract Management

It has to be emphasised that public procurement procedures should not be limited to the actual contract award but should also comprise effective contract management in order to guarantee an effective outcome. Hence, procedures for contract management and the allocation of responsibilities in this regard should be discussed in the course of public procurement reforms and suitable structures established in the new legislation. As favourable the contract award can be, loss of value during the implementation phase of the contract reduces effectiveness.[1932] Contract management includes inspection and acceptance procedures, quality control procedures and methods to review and issue contract amendments in a timely manner.[1933] Deficits that might occur due to corruption in earlier procurement stages can be exposed and rectified. If a company has won a contract by paying bribes or offering an unrealistically low bid price, it might try to recover these costs during contract performance, for example, by lower quality or non-compliance with standards or regulations.[1934]

### c. E-Procurement

Despite the advantages identified for e-procurement in Chapter 3 of Part I, it seems that e-procurement has not yet become an operational standard even in developed countries.[1935] With special regard to the situations in developing countries caution has to be exercised. The existence of fast,

1932 Cf. Caldwell; et al., 'Promoting Competitive Markets', p. 329; Mamiro, p. 8.
1933 Development Assistance Committee, 'Strengthening Procurement Capacities ', p. 65.
1934 Pope, 'Confronting Corruption', p. 209.
1935 Cf. F. Garenal, 'Public E-Procurement - Define, Measure and Optimize Organizational Benefits', conference paper, 5th International Public Procurement Conference, Seoul, South Korea, August 26-28, 2010, p. 22.

well-functioning and wide-spread internet connections is a necessary precondition for e-procurement. Otherwise certain bidders might be excluded from the process, competition would be limited and the functioning of the system would be eroded. In many African countries constant supply of electricity is not yet guaranteed and internet connections are still slower than in more developed regions and subject to frequent breakdowns.[1936] Additionally, implementation of e-procurement entails costs for software and infrastructure development, training, advertising, etc. Apart from financial, personnel and technical constraints, there might be cultural barriers, for example, getting SMEs to work with the internet.[1937] Beyond that there might be legal challenges as well as security concerns in regard to the sensitivity of government data and the legal nature of orders and payments.[1938] Developing countries have to carefully assess whether e-procurement is an adequate and realisable instrument that can be deployed in the near future with regard to the development of telecom infrastructure. The objectives of transparency, efficiency, and policy coherence should be closely looked at in view of the introduction of technological processes into public procurement.[1939]

It is recommendable to implement e-procurement in a phased manner with allowing both electronic and paper-based communication until it is found that the using electronic communication as the sole means for procurement has no adverse effect on competition. Furthermore, it is essential to keep in mind that e-procurement might take a long time to pay off financially as well as operationally. High installation costs as well as time needed for all stakeholders to become familiar with the system to tap the full potential might only pay off several years after its introduction.[1940] It requires strong policy leadership and a managerial willingness to innovate in order to successfully implement an e-procurement initiative.[1941]

---

1936 Agaba; Shipman, 'Public Procurement in Developing Countries', p. 384.

1937 Kostyo, 'Handbook for Curbing Corruption', p. 68; M.J. Moon, 'E-Procurement Management in State Governments: Diffusion of E-Procurement Practices and Its Determinants', in K.V. Thai, *International Handbook of Public Procurement* (Boca Raton, Florida: Taylor & Francis Group, 2009).

1938 K. Vaidya; et al., 'Facilitators of Public E-Procurement: Lessons Learned from the U.K., U.S., and Australian Initatives', p. 482.

1939 Cf. Schapper; et al., 'An Analytic Framework for the Management and Reform of Public Procurement', 18.

1940 Vaidya; et al., 'Facilitators of Public E-Procurement', p. 486f.

1941 M.J. Moon, 'E-Procurement Management in State Governments: Diffusion of E-Procurement Practices and Its Determinants', p. 537.

Public procurement systems that have not been designed to facilitate e-procurement are difficult to be adapted since they require a redesign of the purchasing cycle and associated management reform.[1942] Therefore, systematic elements providing for e-procurement should be included and be foreseen in transitional provisions of conventional procurement mechanisms if the use of e-procurement is to be implemented in the near future. The selection of terms should also be made in respect to accommodating traditional paper-based methods as well as other means of communication and information. It is preferable to use rather general terms in primary public procurement legislation and specify them in secondary legislation or instructions that can be more easily adapted.[1943]

## 9. Conclusion

Reform issues have to consider all pillars of public procurement as well as the integration of public procurement into the wider public sector environment. A holistic reform approach, for example in the course of a wider public sector reform, is essential for a successful reform. This, however, requires a substantive analysis of existing procurement methods and structures as well as the commitment of all stakeholders. Furthermore, it is essential to clearly outline certain reform elements at the beginning of a reform; this includes: the general approach, responsibilities and deadlines, budget considerations, and the objectives of the reform. Moreover, hindrances to reform should be identified and adequately addressed. And after strengths and weaknesses have been identified, international best practices and possibilities to adapt them to the local context should be assessed. It is also possible to look at the solutions of other countries that maybe have similar problems, a shared history, cultural commonalities, or a similar societal or economic structure.

Reform efforts should consider all possible procuring scenarios but result in a transparent, clear, efficient and fair procurement system which is carefully embedded in the public sector, economic and political structure as well as responsive to social and cultural peculiarities. Beyond that new developments and ideas with the potential to improve public procurement

1942 Cf. Schapper; et al., 'An Analytic Framework for the Management and Reform of Public Procurement', 21.

1943 Cf. Walker, 'Setting up a Public Procurement System', p. 9.

systems as, for example, e-procurement should be considered as a serious alternative to existing structures.

It is clear that general administrative law provisions and procedures and the traditional public procurement methods and procedures are not always suitable for the increasing complexity of public procurement systems. Alternative approaches need to be found, such as standstill periods allowing for the application of challenges before a public procurement contract is signed.

The focus on the rationale of public procurement should shift from effectiveness of procurement procedures to effectiveness of outcomes.[1944] The age-old focus on the process of buying should be replaced by focusing on what the acquisition is trying to accomplish. This requires a change from administrative, transactional procurement to a more strategic approach. Existing experience and research results[1945] suggest that strategic rather than clerical procurement processes lead to a value-based outcome. However, the decision about the extent of strategic latitude given to procurement officers needs to give adequate consideration to the availability of competent procurement staff and institutional capacities.

Hence, the consideration of available capacity and capacity building should be a key priority in public procurement reforms. This refers not only to the creation of human resources through training and education but also to institutional capacity with independent institutions to implement, monitor and evaluate public procurement. The discussion of the institutional framework, including the separation and allocation of responsibilities and functions as well as the availability of resources and capacity, is essential for a successful public procurement reform. It has to be decided whether or to what extent public procurement should be decentralised and whether new institutions are established or certain functions and duties can be better assigned to existing institutions. Reform considerations should entail a detailed assessment of institutional as well as human capacity to design a law that suits these conditions or in order to determine what modifications are possible and realistic in order to ensure efficient implementation of a new procurement law. At the level of the procuring entities such an assessment should, for example, include analyses of the

---

1944 S. Kelman, 'Procurement - A Time for Statesmanship' (2004) 18(26) Federal Computer Week.

1945 Trepte, 'Building sustainable capacity in public procurment', p. 386; Trepte, 'Regulating Procurement', p. 207.

willingness of those entities to comply, the existence or non-existence of corruption, and the capacity of procuring entities and their procurement officers to implement the legal framework.[1946]

Public procurement officials need sufficient competence and experience. Unlike a clerical job, public procurement requires several skills and qualitative decision-making since there are always trade-offs between different goals of public procurement, such as between collateral objectives and value for money. A public procurement reform should envisage and make provisions for the appointment, employment and training of qualified personnel that is able to fulfil the required functions and to act on their responsibilities. Otherwise no qualified decisions can be made and there might even be a hesitation to take decisions at all because the employees are afraid of making the wrong decisions and, as a consequence, lose their job. It is furthermore an essential issue to pay the personnel adequately in order to reduce the motivation to become corrupt. Institutions, offices and departments not only need to be staffed with qualified but also with a sufficient number of personnel.

With regard to the choice of procedures and methods governing public procurement, it is of utmost importance to legally clearly define fair, effective, efficient and competitive procedures. Adequate procedures considering the nature, the complexity and the value of procurement should be found. Procurement procedures and methods should be appropriate in the local context but always be measured by its efficiency.

Transparency requires more than the simple enactment of rules or better regulations. A change of structure and concept that is suitable in the local context is far more promising in leading to a satisfying result. An example is the oral debriefing concept and introducing a standstill period after the notice of the tender award and the contract formation in order to give bidders the opportunity to challenge the decision. The careful selection and adequate treatment of public procurement staff can also contribute to a working culture promoting transparency. Nevertheless, international best practices of transparency in public procurement should be implemented in every public procurement system. However, the rules should not be overly burdensome in order not to complicate public procurement procedures for the stakeholders involved.

The inclusion of secondary objectives in public procurement should be critically discussed in view of their efficiency. Only if it is found that there

1946 Trepte, 'Building sustainable capacity in public procurment', p. 378.

is no other, preferable way to pursue certain objectives and public procurement is considered as only means promising a successful achievement of certain policy goals, should such approach be pursued. However, it is of utmost importance to balance such an approach with the other principles of public procurement. For example, the application of secondary policies should be transparent and fair and be indicated as temporary measures in order not to limit competition permanently.

The establishment of an adequate review system is indispensable for a well-functioning public procurement system and should therefore be paid special attention during the reform process. As courts have proved to be unsuitable as single review mechanism, it should be carefully assessed what alternative review mechanism can make public procurement challenges more time and cost efficient, are more appropriate in the context of public procurement and easier accessible for unsatisfied bidders. The establishment of administrative or internal review procedures and an independent review body is generally recommendable. Furthermore, suitable and effective remedies should be designed but be carefully balanced with public procurement efficiency.

Although the UNCITRAL Model Law does not entail provisions for procurement planning and contract management, both issues should be incorporated in public procurement legislation. Procurement planning is of specific importance for the proper preparation of budgets and the avoidance of an aggregation of public procurements at the end of the year. It also allows potential bidders and suppliers to take the necessary preparative steps to participate in bidding. The regulation of contract management is necessary in order to guarantee an effective outcome, avoid a loss of value and disclose deficits in contract implementation. Implementing rules and requirements at all stages of the public procurement cycle can have a positive effect on public procurement outcomes and should, therefore, be considered as an important factor in any public procurement reform.

Last but not least, it should be considered whether and to what extent the necessary conditions to implement e-procurement are set out in the reforming country. What is suitable in the national context depends on factors such as the availability of internet access, costs involved, or security concerns. In particular in developing countries, shortcomings in this respect might limit the possibilities to implement comprehensive and innovative e-procurement strategies. However, the use of electronic means for basic communication and information purposes should be provided for in any public procurement system. It is, for example, also possible to implement e-procurement in a phased manner allowing both electronic and paper-based communication in order not to limit competition.

In this chapter, different aspects of the Namibian public procurement reform will be examined, including the reform drivers, the involvement of stakeholders, the instrument of comparative law, the process of legal drafting and major hindrances in order to identify shortcomings that might have contributed to the difficulties in successfully finalising the reform. Since there have been many African reforms, which indeed resulted in enacting a modern and up-to-date legislation but still suffer from ineffective implementation, a special emphasis rests on the question of what aspects of public procurement reforms are important and should be focused on with a view to implementing a new law. Thereafter, specific substantive changes required for the Namibian public procurement system to function efficiently and effectively are highlighted by making reference to a bill introduced in parliament in 2013 and an amended bill that is likely to be enacted in the near future. This is followed by general recommendations. These substantive considerations are made by following the structure of the analysis of the Namibian public procurement system and regulations in the first chapter of this part. Recommendations made in this respect might serve as a general guideline on how to regulate certain elements of the procurement system and what elements deserve particular attention in the Namibian context.

## 1. Introduction

The Namibian government has repeatedly acknowledged the need to reform the existing laws.[1947] The reform process has been going on for quite a while,[1948] but has not yet led to the enactment of a new law. Several

1947 'Runter von Verliererspur' (Newspaper article), Allgemeine Zeitung (Windhoek, Namibia), 13 September 2011; 'Tender Board Review Begins' (Newspaper article), New Era (Windhoek, Namibia), 13 October 2010; 'Tender Board tightens rules to protect jobs' (Newspaper article), The Namibian (Windhoek, Namibia), 3 February 2010; 'Nghimtina Proposes Reform of Tender Board' (Newspaper article), The Namibian (Windhoek, Namibia), 2 April 2012; 'Tender Law law to be amended' (Newspaper article), The Namibian (Windhoek, Namibia), 13 April 2011.

1948 The IPPR assumes that it has been going on for more than a decade. Links; Daniels, 'The Tender Board - Need for Root and Branch Reform', p. 1.

drafts have been shared with research institutes and other stakeholders and the final draft was supposed to be up for approval in the 2013 parliamentary session.[1949] Promises that the draft would be dealt with in parliament had been made in the previous years, but those promises had not been kept.[1950] Finally, in September 2013 a Public Procurement Bill was tabled in the National Assembly.[1951] However, after heavy criticism of the bill, it was finally withdrawn from parliament until further notice in mid-October and the bill was re-tabled for 2014.[1952] But only in 2015 the amended bill was re-introduced in parliament.[1953]

Key reform issues have been the “Namibianisation” of tenders, restricting the application of exemptions from the standard procurement procedure, and transparency.[1954] Moreover, it is envisaged to create an independent review panel and to include greater preferences for SME’s.[1955]

---

1949 'Minister lays into Tender Board' (Newspaper article), The Namibian (Windhoek, Namibia), 26 April 2013.

1950 'Parlament startet ins Jahresfinale' (Newspaper article), Allgemeine Zeitung (Windhoek, Namibia), 18 September 2012.

1951 'Bill Makes Finance Minister 'Too Powerful'' (Newspaper article), The Namibian (Windhoek, Namibia), 24 September 2013.

1952 'Procurement Bill Sparks Heated Debate' (Newspaper article), The New Era (Windhoek Namibia), 3 October 2013.

1953 At the time of the finalisation of this dissertation the 2015 bill has been passed by the Namibian parliament awaiting assent by the president in order to enter into force. (Assent by the president is required by Article 56 (1) of the Namibian Constitution.) See 'Auf das neue Gesetz vorbereiten' (Newspaper article), Allgemeine Zeitung (Windhoek, Namibia), 12 November 2015; 'Six Bills passed' (Newspaper article), The Namibian (Windhoek, Namibia), 17 November 2015.

1954 See e.g. Links; Daniels, 'The Tender Board - Need for Root and Branch Reform; Appendix I - Interview with Tender Board Secretary Welma Enssle'; see also 'N$12 billion worth of tenders exempted' (Newspaper article), The Namibian (Windhoek, Namibia), 13 February 2013; 'Bring An End To Tender Exemptions (Editorial)' (Newspaper article), The Namibian (Windhoek, Namibia), 1 February 2013.

1955 Links; Daniels, 'The Tender Board - Need for Root and Branch Reform; Appendix I - Interview with Tender Board Secretary Welma Enssle'.

## 2. The Reform Project

### a. Outline of the Reform Process

The reform of the tender law in Namibia started more than ten years ago[1956] and the new bill was scheduled to be passed in 2011 and then in 2012.[1957] However, it was not until September 2013 that a bill was tabled in the National Assembly.[1958] After heavy criticism of the bill, it was finally withdrawn from Parliament until further notice in mid-October.[1959] The bill tabled in parliament has been preceded by several other proposals. The first draft did not substantially differ from the current Act but it had meanwhile been realised that the procurement system needed a comprehensive change and the whole structure and procedures of the procurement system had been altered.

The bill introduced in parliament in 2013 was criticised for making the Minister of Finance too powerful as he would have appointed the executive director of the Procurement Policy Office.[1960] Criticism of the bill tabled in parliament was also expressed in regard to the way the bill was drafted. It was also alleged that the role of the government and that of new institutions to be created under the proposed law would not be clear and that the bill might disadvantage businesses run by black Namibians.[1961] Moreover, stakeholders would not have been appropriately enabled to provide their inputs in the reform process.[1962] The SWAPO Party Chief Peter Katjavivi expressed his discontent about the organisational structure foreseen by the bill by saying that

1956 Links; Daniels, 'The Tender Board - Need for Root and Branch Reform', p. 1.

1957 'Minister lays into Tender Board' (Newspaper article), The Namibian (Windhoek, Namibia), 26 April 2013. See also 'Parlament startet ins Jahresfinale' (Newspaper article), Allgemeine Zeitung (Windhoek, Namibia), 18 September 2012.

1958 'Bill Makes Finance Minister 'Too Powerful'' (Newspaper article), The Namibian (Windhoek, Namibia), 24 September 2013.

1959 'Procurement Bill Sparks Heated Debate' (Newspaper article), The New Era (Windhoek, Namibia), 3 October 2013; 'Public Procurement Bill Withdrawn' (Newspaper article), The New Era (Windhoek, Namibia), 17 October 2013.

1960 'Procurement Bill Sparks Heated Debate' (Newspaper article), The New Era (Windhoek, Namibia), 3 October 2013.

1961 'Public Procurement Bill Withdrawn' (Newspaper article), The New Era (Windhoek, Namibia), 17 October 2013.

1962 Ibid.

> "[...] the multiplicity of entities within the Bill creates a worry over bureaucratic delays. If you have the Procurement Policy Office, the Central Procurement Board, the Procurement Committee, the Procurement Management Units and Bid Evaluation Committee, probably we do not need the bid evaluation committees, because procurement committees can as well evaluate bids."[1963]

The bill was promised to be re-tabled in 2014 parliamentary session.[1964] But the Ministry of Finance only introduced another public procurement bill in 2015 which has been passed by parliament in late November 2015 awaiting assent by the president.[1965] As the bill does not substantially differ from the bill introduced in parliament in 2013, the former bill shall be taken as a basis for discussion in this chapter and important amendments in the 2015 bill will be highlighted subsequently. Although the delay of the reform process is probably due to several factors, the major reason seems to be the lack of political will to finalise the reform.

The Ministry of Finance, in particular the Tender Board itself is in charge of the reform.[1966] According to one of the interviewees there has also been communication with the Office of the Prime Minister about the reform.[1967] The Law Reform and Development Commission (LRDC) of the Ministry of Justice have not been involved.[1968] The LRDC has been established by Section 2 of the Law Reform and Development Commission Act[1969]. It is, however, not clear what kind of reform projects are drafted by the relevant ministers themselves and what is done by the Ministry of Justice or the LRDC. In the case of the public procurement reform, it might have been of great advantage for the reform process if it had been drafted by experts that are not part of and have thus no interests in the public procurement system itself. It can further be assumed that neither the Ministry of Finance nor the Tender Board have sufficient knowledge of public procurement law and reform in order to be able to successfully

---

1963 Ibid.

1964 'Procurement Bill Sparks Heated Debate' (Newspaper article), The New Era (Windhoek, Namibia), 3 October 2013.

1965 See also above in Footnote 18.

1966 Interview Mr Schulz (Namibia Construction (Pty) Ltd., Director), 22th March 2013; Interview Mr Isaacs (Tender Board, Chief Control Officer), 26th March 2013; Interview Mr Titus (Tender Board, Alternate Member), 28th March 2013.

1967 Interview Mr Issacs (Tender Board, Chief Control Officer), 26th March 2013.

1968 Interview Mr Hopwood (IPPR, Director), 26th March 2013.

1969 Act No. 29 of 1991, as amended by the Law Reform and Development Commission Amendment Act 2004 (Act No. 2 of 2004).

draft a new bill. For example, two lawyers are members of the Tender Board but without any qualifications in public procurement law.

The reform process was accelerated in 2010 when the Commonwealth got involved. Prior to this external assistance, the Tender Board members and the Ministry of Finance were solely responsible for the reform project. In 2010 the Fifth CPPN Technical Conference was hosted by Namibia, particularly the Ministry of Finance and the Tender Board of Namibia.[1970] At the conference, the Deputy Minister of Finance at that time stressed the need for a review of Namibian's public procurement legislation. He stressed that a successful procurement process has to be transparent and predictable, cost effective, accountable and there needs to be consequences for wrong-doing. Sustainable procurement outcomes could be ensured by procurement mainstreaming, capacity development, benchmarking, monitoring and evaluation. Mrs Shafudah, Chairperson of the Tender Board at that time, presented an overview of the legislative review. Further presentations about the Namibian public procurement system were made by a CEO of the Namibia Chamber of Commerce and Industry (Namibia's Current Public Procurement Practices: The Private Sector's Perspective), by the Director of the Construction Federation Industry (Challenges in the Namibian Construction Industry) and by the Director of Capital Project Management of the Ministry of Works and Transport of the Republic of Namibia (Stakeholder's engagement – Merits of a progressional approach). Problems and weaknesses of the Namibian public procurement system were, however, at the most glossed over. It was, for example, stated twice that there are exemptions for price preferential considerations[1971] and that there are "some exceptions from normal tender procedure".[1972] However, that quite a big share of tenders are exempted from the normal procedure and that this process is rather non-transparent and applied randomly and, hence, constitutes a major problem in the Namibian public procurement system, was not mentioned. It seems that the chance to receive recommendations from public procurement experts at the conference about how to deal with the shortcomings of the Namibian

1970 Records of the Fifth Commonwealth Public Procurement Network (CPPN) Technical Conference 5th Commonwealth Public Procurement Network Technical Conference, Windhoek, Namibia, 6th-8th December 2010, available at http://www.publicprocurement.gov.sl/files/Namibia_CPPN_Report.pdf (last accessed: 1 December 2015).

1971 Ibid.

1972 Ibid.

public procurement system was blown by not wanting to admit the basic but severe shortcomings. Nevertheless, after this conference, which was held in Namibia, it was realised that something urgently needed to be done in regard to the Namibian procurement system.[1973] An expert from Mauritius was thus invited to Namibia to provide his technical expertise in drafting a new bill and a Namibian delegation went to Mauritius to take a closer look at their public procurement system.[1974] In 2012 a group of procurement experts from the Commonwealth Secretariat came to Namibia to assess its public procurement system,[1975] but the report is apparently not available to the public. The interviewed Tender Board members did not know about the existence of such report and the IPPR had not even heard that such an assessment took place.

Further actors entered the stage to assist and facilitate the Namibian reform process. According to the Commonwealth Secretariat, this has been catalysed by the report of the Commonwealth.[1976] The EU's support included a €250,000 diagnostic review of public procurement. Additionally, in early 2013 the European Union sent three procurement experts, one legal and one IT expert as well as an accountant.[1977] According to the Control Officer of the Tender Board, the World Bank also expressed its interest in assisting the reform project.[1978] He also said that from mid-2013 the government would employ three procurement experts (one IT expert, one public procurement expert and one legal expert) for a three-year project on the reform and the implementation of the public procurement system.[1979]

### b. Reform Drivers

The role of the IPPR as reform driver has to be highlighted since it is the only Namibian institution that has carried out (qualified) academic research about public procurement. Although its influence on the project

---

1973 Interview Mr Sipiho (Tender Board, Control Officer), 26th March 2013.

1974 Ibid.

1975 Commonwealth Secretariat, 'Commonwealth review leads to increased support for Namibia's Public Procurement Systems', Governance Matters - Newsletter of the Governance and Institutional Development Division, Spring 2013.

1976 Ibid.

1977 Interview Mr Sipiho (Tender Board, Control Officer), 26th March 2013.

1978 Ibid.

1979 Ibid.

was limited, which can be attributed to the government's unwillingness to involve external experts and stakeholders, it might have inspired the Ministry of Finance to press ahead with the reform. The Namibian delegation to Mauritius, for example, only went after a paper of the IPPR has referred to the Mauritian public procurement law.

The Tender Bulletin, a weekly newsletter that has been published since 1990, has also played an important role in exposing problems in the Namibian public procurement system. It contains a variety of information on tenders, including tender invitations and award decisions, and publishes detailed background information regarding tender procedures. The Tender Bulletin does not get financial support from the government. Because it is not a daily newspaper, it was not allowed to tender for the publishing of bid averts.[1980] However, it is an important source of information and even newspapers often obtain their information from the Tender Bulletin. The Tender Bulletin has an important function in creating transparency, providing an overview of and scrutinizing public procurement practices. It seems it has become more critical in recent times; they might have found that the system has become more corrupt.[1981]

Several stakeholders, especially from the construction sector, have called for the reform of the public procurement system. The discontent of the public and, especially, of local companies, which is also represented in the media seems, however, not to have had a significant effect on government action. The analysis of this phenomenon would be beyond the scope of this dissertation, but it can be guessed that the following factors play a role: the strength of SWAPO, the lack of a strong middle income sector and of a civil society that is "outside the system" or in opposition to the political leaders.

When thinking about strategies to scrutinise the government's non-action in regard to Chinese companies breaking labour laws, the trade unions could play a major. According to Advocate Tötemeyer, they would be the only ones that could break the cycle.[1982] They are said to have become more independent from government in the last years and are starting to criticise government action.[1983] Nevertheless, another interviewee stated

1980 'No interest in Govt advertising tender' (Newspaper article), The Namibian (Windhoek, Namibia), 18 March 2013.

1981 Interview Mr Hopwood (IPPR, Director), 26th March 2013.

1982 Interview Mr Tötemeyer (Advocate / Society of Advocates of Namibia, Vice-president), 18th March 2013.

1983 Ibid.

that they are still close to government; they would be afraid of the Chinese and might be called off by government officials in respect to certain issues and they can only act hand in hand with the Labour Commissioner.[1984] The development of the trade unions in Namibia and especially the question whether they can gain further strength in the future might be a decisive issue in stopping government officials from disregarding the law. The Director of NUNW[1985] said that between 2007 and 2011 they had fought the violation of worker's rights by Chinese companies hard. Since then they have started to collect information in order to understand the system and the culture better, some changes have occurred and some companies have started to comply. One instrument has been threatening Chinese companies (which often receive Chinese government support, but are managed by private persons) with informing the Chinese government. Companies not adhering have been also exposed to the media in order to get the government to send inspectors and conduct on-site inspections. The Namibian trade unions have built up connections in Africa and on the international level in order to address issues that are not solely national but global ones.[1986]

In 2010 the NUNW has presented the Namibian president with a letter stating their concerns on labour issues in the construction industry.[1987] As a result, the president has reiterated that Chinese companies must adhere to the laws.[1988] The Metal Allied Namibian Workers' Union (MANWU) called for peaceful demonstration over the issue of Chinese construction companies. Because fewer and fewer government tenders are being awarded to Namibian construction firms, large numbers of workers in the construction sector are becoming unemployed. Moreover, MANWU raised the concern of worker exploitation by Chinese construction companies.[1989]

The engagement of civil society groups such as trade unions is a necessary driver for change. It is only if the government feels scrutinised by in-

1984 Interview Mr Schulz (Namibia Construction (Pty) Ltd., Director), 22th March 2013.

1985 Interview Mrs Jonas (NUNW, Director), 28th March 2013.

1986 Ibid.

1987 Ibid. See also 'Pohamba Calls for Respect for Labour Laws' (Newspaper article), The New Era (Windhoek, Namibia), 13 May 2013.

1988 Ibid.

1989 'Builders fed up with Chinese firms' (Newspaper article), The Namibian (Windhoek, Namibia), 9 February 2011.

fluential organisations that it might be willing to expedite reforms and change its attitude with respect to the implementation of existing laws. Although there has not been a substantial change yet, according to the Director of the NUNW the Chinese companies are starting to comply.[1990]

c. Stakeholders Involvement

During the whole reform there has not been a formal consultation process of relevant stakeholders. In respect of reform processes in other fields of laws, workshops are held or letters sent out with the call for comment.[1991] In this case, certain individuals were approached for comment but formal consultation did not take place.[1992] The director of a Namibian construction company stated that the government once or twice asked the company what it would like to be changed in the new bill.[1993] He also stressed that this consultation took place more than a year ago (early 2012); they have not heard anything from the government again and so far nothing has changed.[1994]

According to a Tender Board member, stakeholders such as companies, SOEs and parastatals were invited to meetings to give their input.[1995] Moreover, the first draft would have been sent to the parastatals to obtain their input.[1996] Another member admitted that consultation did not happen to the extent as it should have.[1997] Several stakeholders have been approached but there has not been a full engagement of stakeholders. Only a few that were proactive were involved in the discussion to a limited extent.[1998]

The Institute for Public Policy Research has done intensive research about the Namibian procurement system. It has analysed the strengths and

1990 Interview Mrs Jonas (NUNW, Director), 28th March 2013.
1991 Interview Mr Hopwood (IPPR, Director), 26th March 2013.
1992 Interview Mr Hopwood (IPPR, Director), 26th March 2013; Interview Mrs Jonga (Tender Board, Chief Control Officer), 26th March 2013; Interview Mr Schulz (Namibia Construction (Pty) Ltd., Director), 22th March 2013
1993 Interview Mr Schulz (Namibia Construction (Pty) Ltd., Director), 22th March 2013
1994 Ibid.
1995 Interview Mr Isaacs (Tender Board, Chief Control Officer), 26th March 2013.
1996 Ibid
1997 Interview Mrs Jonga (Tender Board, Chief Control Officer), 26th March 2013
1998 Ibid.

weaknesses of the system and identified critical elements that have to be attended to. The IPPR was given two different drafts by the Ministry of Finance. The first one, from June 2010, did not differ much from the current Act. Another draft was given to the IPPR in 2012, though not as an electronic version and with some missing pages. This draft has changed significantly and resembled the Mauritian procurement law. Some believe that the 2012 version might be close to the actual version of the draft bill to be put before parliament. The Ministry of Finance thanked the IPPR for its comments and said it would consider them.[1999] The Tender Bulletin was also given a draft but it is not clear whether this is the same draft the IPPR received. It can be concluded that consultation has only taken place to a very limited extent and in a non-transparent way.

d. Influence of International and Foreign Law

In how far a state is bound by obligations deriving from international law on public procurement is an important factor that should be considered during a reform process. Namibia follows a generally positive attitude towards international law and accepts its responsibilities arising from being a member of the international community. According to Article 144, "the general rules of public international law and international agreements binding upon Namibia under [the] Constitution shall form part of the law of Namibia", unless the Constitution or an act of parliament provides otherwise. Moreover, Article 96 of the Constitution urges the state to ensure that international law and treaty obligations are respected. As a member of UNCAC, Namibia is required to ensure that certain standards in public procurement are adhered to. There is no hint that the obligations arising from Article 9 of UNCAC[2000] were considered during the reform process and that the meaning of international law on public procurement has been critically reflected. Thus, Namibia falls not only short of its international obligations, in particular deriving from Article 9 of UNCAC, but also of its constitutional mandate to foster the respect for international law.[2001]

1999 Interview Mr Hopwood (IPPR, Director), 26th March 2013.

2000 For more information on Article 9 of UNCAC see above (Introduction, Subchapter 4 (a); Part I, Chapter 2, Subchapters 1 and 3).

2001 For more informationon on the reception of international in Namibia see M. Hinz; A. Schmidt; C. Mapaure, 'Namibia', In International Encyclopaedia of Laws: Constitutional Law, edited by A. Alen; D. Haljan (Alphen aan den Rijn,

In contrast to international law, foreign legal public procurement systems have played a major role in the reform process. The legal systems of Tanzania, Botswana and Mauritius were given particular consideration as models for the new bill.[2002] Those laws were identified as the most progressive public procurement laws within Africa. The influence of the Mauritian law might also be attributed to the fact that one of the experts assisting the reform project is from Mauritius. And, as mentioned above, in 2010 a Namibian delegation went to Mauritius to take a closer look at its public procurement system.[2003] Mauritius introduced its tender law in 2006 within the context of reform efforts by COMESA.[2004] The law considers best practice recommendations of the UNCITRAL model law and the COMESA Public Procurement Regulations.[2005]

However, the UNCITRAL model law or the COMESA Public Procurement Regulations have not been examined at all. Since the UNCITRAL Model Law provides general rules and procedure that can be aligned to each country's situation, it would make sense to look at the Model Law rather than solely at a domestic procurement system which is to be seen within the setting of the particular country. It is distressing that most of the interviewed board members have not even heard from the UN-UNCITRAL Model Law. The same applies to the GPA. The lack of knowledge about the international discussion on public procurement law and reform not only indicates that the Tender Board members have not conducted much research about public procurement law and reform, but also that the reform process, including the conferences and workshops, have not considered the all possibilities of tackling reform.

The initiation or consideration of potential future regional procurement rules in the SADC or SACU region is also not on the table. Botswana, for example, has designed its procurement regulation flexibly enough to integrate external trade obligation into its public procurement system, if nec-

---

NL: Kluwer Law International), p. 80f. The state's constitutional obligation to consider international public procurement law, both hard and soft law, has been discussed further in A. Schmidt, 'Public Procurement - A Constitutional Perspective', forthcoming.

2002 Interview Mr Isaacs (Tender Board, Chief Control Officer), 26th March 2013.

2003 Interview Mr Sipiho (Tender Board, Control Officer), 26th March 2013.

2004 Special Steering Committee of the OECD-DAC Task Force on Procurement, 'A Practical Guide to Transforming Procurement Systems '.

2005 On the COMESA and the Mauritian procurement regulations see above (Part II, Chapter 3).

essary.[2006] And, as Amoo notes, "the recent free trade agreement between SACU, SADC, COMESA and EAC may bring the liberalisation of procurement markets to the fore in the near future."[2007]

Despite the common history of apartheid and certain legal similarities, the South African public procurement system was not considered as model. After independence Namibia has been geared to the South African legal system, simply because Namibia has not had enough capacity to originate own progress.[2008] Article 140 (1) of the Namibian Constitution states that

> "[...] subject to the provisions of this Constitution, all laws which were in force immediately before the date of Independence shall remain in force until repealed or amended by Act of Parliament or until they are declared unconstitutional by a competent Court."

Hence, many laws have been inherited from the pre-independence area and some new laws[2009] are similar to South African Law.[2010] Furthermore, there is a similar legal culture in Namibia and South Africa. This makes it even more astonishing that the South African system has not even been looked at. In particular, in view to affirmative action strategies within the public procurement system, it might have been worth looking at their approach, since they face similar problems resulting from decades of discrimination under the apartheid system. It was reasoned that South Africa had its own challenges and was not really a benchmark in public procurement.[2011] Additionally, Namibia wanted to move away from the South African system.[2012] However, the fact that the South African system was not even examined can, based on the above mentioned similarities of the legal systems and the social context, be deemed to be a defect.

It also has to be emphasised that coherence of legal rules plays a significant role when using foreign laws as basis for reform. It is insufficient to simply copy provisions used in other countries without adapting them to

---

2006 R.A. Kumar; E. Caborn, 'The regulatory framework for public procurement in Botswana', in G. Quinot; S. Arrowsmith, *Public Procurement Regulations in Africa* (Cambridge et al. : Cambridge University Press, 2013), p. 37.

2007 S.K. Amoo; S. Dicken, 'The regulatory framework for public procurement in Namibia', p. 131.

2008 Glinz, 'Verwaltungsrecht und Rechtsstaatlichkeit in Namibia', p. 133.

2009 See e.g. Competition Act 2003 (Act No. 2 of 2003).

2010 Cf. Sippel, 'Rechtsrezeption in Namibia',

2011 Interview Mr Titus (Tender Board, Alternate Member), 28th March 2013.

2012 Ibid.

the domestic context. The non-critical examination of foreign legal systems in the field of public procurement, and especially neglecting to look at South Africa's approach to preferential procurement, suggests that it has not been seriously attempted to find regulations that are appropriate for the Namibian setting. Nevertheless, this might not necessarily be due to ignorance or unwillingness, but rather the fact that there is a lack of qualified legal procurement experts and a general intention to establish independence from South Africa.

### e. Reform Hindrances

The fact that the leadership of the Tender Board has changed three times since the start of the reform has been emphasised as a major obstacle to reform.[2013] Moreover, it can be assumed that there has been a lack of communication and collaboration between responsible people in the Ministry of Finance and the Tender Board and also within the Tender Board itself, which is split into two camps.[2014]

The fact that the involvement of the CPPN accelerated the reform process might be an indication that there is a lack of expertise and experience to review and address the public procurement system within Namibia. Moreover, there has been no proper strategy to carry out the reform. It would have been necessary to first analyse in detail what the major shortcomings of the current system are. According to one of the interviewees the unwillingness to make an analysis of errors in their own house is a common problem in Namibia. Instead of working on the roots of a problem and improving existing legislation a completely new bill is passed. Reasons for this would be the lack of expertise, not enough people who could identify the shortcomings, unwillingness to admit errors, lack of political will and political interference in administrative decision-making.[2015]

Nevertheless, an assessment of the Namibian public procurement system was conducted by the Commonwealth in 2012. However, the scope and results of this assessment are unknown as the report is not available. This is a severe shortcoming as regards transparency in the reform process

2013 Interview Mrs Jonga (Tender Board, Chief Control Officer), 26th March 2013

2014 Interview Mr Links (Insight Magazine, Editor), 21th February 2013.

2015 Interview Mr Schulz (Namibia Construction (Pty) Ltd., Director), 22th March 2013.

which is important in order to involve stakeholders and build ownership. Instruments such as the OECD/DAC Methodology for Assessing Procurement Systems could have been used to assess the quality and effectiveness of the presently applicable Namibian public procurement system. Furthermore, comprehensive research of international best practices and foreign systems with a similar legal system and similar problems, such as South Africa, would have been indispensable to finding qualitative and suitable solutions for Namibia.

Namibia has not set out the responsibilities, deadlines and objectives of reform. When the Tender Board Secretary Welma Enssle was asked in 2011 whether there is a timeline for reform, she responded that "[w]e would like to see it this year still, and I think the minister would like to see it this year."[2016] Additionally, the complexity of the matter has not been adequately recognised. A review of non-procurement specific public service functions such as internal audits in regard to their impact on public procurement and their efficiency should take place since they can make an important contribution to the transparency of the public procurement system.

The length of the reform and non-transparency and the comments of several interviewees show that there is clearly a lack of political will to finalise and pass the bill. The fact that the reform initiative has been internally driven rather than imposed by external pressure groups seems to contradict the assumption that there is a lack of political will. Indeed it shows that there are certain groups or actors that can put issues on the political agenda and that there are political elements that want change and improvement. However, the pressure does not seem to be strong enough to finalise the reform initiative. Statements from the highest governmental levels, such as from the then president Pohamba, who said, in early 2011 that he would had instructed the Ministry of Finance to finalise the reform of the public procurement bill as soon as possible,[2017] seem to be empty rhetoric rather than resolute determination. It can be assumed that vested interests of government officials are the major reason for the continuing resistance of decision-makers. The fact that the main focus on Namibianisation rather than transparency in the tender reform process might be an

2016 Links; Daniels, 'The Tender Board - Need for Root and Branch Reform; Appendix I - Interview with Tender Board Secretary Welma Enssle', p. 17.

2017 'Pohamba: "Werden mehr tun"' (Newspaper article), Allgemeine Zeitung (Windhoek, Namibia), 16 February 2011.

indication that government, and in particular the Ministry of Finance and the Tender Board, does not realise or does not want to admit that non-transparency is hindering the efficiency and effectiveness of the procurement system. Corruption in tender procedures is not seen as a major issue. Hence, there is ignorance in respect to this matter and, hence, a lack of political will to address it.

Especially the permanent secretaries, who have a great deal of power in regard to public procurement decisions in the current system, would try to block any changes simply because it would mean a loss of influence and power.[2018] The relationship of government officials with Chinese companies might also play a role. As loans or other assistance coming from China often come with conditions such as the award of projects to Chinese companies, a more transparent public procurement system might interfere with such obscure deals, which are probably used by procurement officials for their own personal benefit, as well. Furthermore, favouritism in respect to relatives, friends or even ethnic groups as well as other forms of corruption remain undetected and without consequences in the current system. As this might change after a successful reform, officials or politicians that benefit from the actual situation might try to impede the reform progress. Especially in this situation - where the Tender Board itself is in charge of the reform - the reformer is identical with or closely related to the group of people that have a significant personal interest in maintaining the status quo. The situation in Namibia is a real world example of the scenarios described by Hunja. He refers to scenarios where, despite public commitments to reforms by governments, endless and circular discussions are used as a means of forestalling progress or finalisation.[2019]

It has also been suggested that Namibia lacks a public/civil society demanding change. With a low population and high income inequalities, there is no strong, established middle class that challenges government action. Many of the well-educated young people are recruited by the government and, hence, become part of the system rather than opposing it.

A lack of financial resources to carry out reform and restructuring the public procurement system is, according to the Director of the IPPR, not an issue. The government has enough resources; they just need to be used.[2020]

---

2018 Interview Mr Hopwood (IPPR, Director), 26th March 2013.

2019 Hunja, 'Obstacles to Public Procurement Reform', p. 5.

2020 Interview Mr Hopwood (IPPR, Director), 26th March 2013.

With view to parliament's rejection of the 2013 public procurement bill, it can be concluded that, although the reform process finally delivered a bill, the proposed law has been dismissed because the reform process was so flawed, non-transparent and exclusive. There is no ownership of the proposed bill, the majority of members of parliament, who are probably representative for the wider public, cannot relate to the new bill and the parliamentarians are also not aware of the ideas and the reasons behind the new organisational structure and the new public procurement system. This might be partly due to the fact that the underlying problems of the current tender board system were never really understood, as only the negative effects of such problems were revealed and caught outrage without pointing out the roots of the problems. Stakeholders were never properly consulted. Information about the reform progress and the involvement of foreign experts were never published. Although several government officials repeatedly stressed the importance and the priority of the reform, this was not reflected in the way the reform has been handled. When conducting a public procurement reform delivering a good piece of legislation cannot be the only aim. It needs to be ensured that specific government leaders own the legislation and that such ownership is known in the private sector and in the wider public. This has been totally disregarded in Namibia and will probably have a negative effect on its implementation, assuming that a new bill is passed.

## 3. Essential Aspects and Recommendations for a new Public Procurement Law

### a. Scope

The bill tabled in parliament in 2013 was to be applied to all procurements of goods and services undertaken by a public body as well as to all procurements of non-security-related goods by the Namibian Defence Force, the Namibia Central Intelligence Service and the Namibian Police Force.[2021] However, the bill emphasised that security-related goods had to be managed according to a method outlined in the Act, the president had to approve the category of items as security-related goods and services and

2021 Public Procurement Bill (As read a First Time) 2013, Sec. 2 (1).

the Tender Board needed to be informed of such.[2022] Such approach is meritorious as it balances the need to protect confidential information and the need to avoid a public procurement from take place in a legal limbo. Furthermore, it ensures that only those procurements are exempted that individually have been found to be unsuitable to be procured under the Act rather than providing a general exception. The bill further established different procurement methods and the conditions for their applicability.[2023] Exemptions that allow for public procurements to be conducted in a legal limbo would have therefore not been possible under the 2013 bill.

The 2013 bill interpreted the term "public bodies" broadly, so that it included state-owned enterprises and entities declared to be public bodies by the Minister of Finance.[2024] This is important because non-transparent and obscure procurement practices by parastatals have led to increasing criticism and have proven inefficient and hindering a successful outcome. One such example is Namport's tender for the construction of a container terminal in Walfis Bay.[2025] This case is of particular importance for Namibia and has dragged on for about three years.

In contrast to the Tender Board Act 1996, the bill only applied to procurement - which means the acquisition by any means, including by purchase, rental, lease or hire-purchase, of goods or services – but not to the acquisition or granting of rights. Such restriction limits the complexity and the workload for public procurement institutions, which can be an advantage with respect to the capacity of those institutions. However, it is necessary to ensure that the acquisition or granting of rights is regulated elsewhere.

The bill was responsive to Namibia's international obligations. All treaties and agreements that are in conflict with the Act would have prevailed, so would have conditions of grant agreements with international financial institutions in which the government is a beneficiary.[2026] Nevertheless, it was emphasised that, if there were no regulations and requirements made

2022 Ibid, Sec. 2 (2).
2023 Public Procurement Bill (As read a First Time) 2013, Secs. 37ff.
2024 Public Procurement Bill (As read a First Time) 2013, Sec. 1 read together with Sec. 4.
2025 See e.g. More questions than answers in Namport's Walvis Harbour container terminal tender, Tender Bulletin No. 997 (Windhoek, Namibia), 22-28 February 2013.
2026 Ibid, Sec. 5(1).

in regard to public procurement, Namibian law would be applicable.[2027] Such approach is beneficial as it promotes the application of Namibian law, allows the public to scrutinise the procedure by ensuring a coherent and transparent approach to these types of projects and provides the greatest benefit for the national economy. And indeed, if the public procurement system follows international best practices and is flexible enough, nothing should stand in the way of its application.

The approach of not allowing any exemptions from the scope of the Act while also ensuring that there are alternative procurement methods that can be applied to all possible procurement methods had to be warmly endorsed. Specifying procurements that can be exempted by the Minister upon request was also conceivable. The Mauritian approach grants several general exemptions for procurements of particular nature; this approach should not be followed because it is of utmost importance that all procurements follow a fair and transparent procedure.

The solution of giving prevalence to international treaties or agreements including requirements in regard to public procurement as suggested in the 2013 bill would be in line with Article 144 of the Namibian Constitution and reflect the position of Namibia as responsible nation within the system of international law. A provision that Namibian law applies if the treaty or agreement is silent on the matter of procurement is also commendable. This is necessary in order to clarify what procurement rules are used for projects funded by external donors. The UNCITRAL Model Law generally exempts aid projects from its application whereas the South African and the COMESA approaches are similar to the approach followed in the 2013 bill.

b. Objectives and Principles

The 2013 bill stated harmonisation, competition, integrity and accountability, fairness, transparency and value for money as objectives.[2028] It additionally stated certain secondary objectives, such as the promotion of the empowerment of Namibian women and youth, job creation, sourcing of local products, industrialisation, local entrepreneurial development as well as the building of procurement capacity in Namibia and the promotion of

2027 Ibid.
2028 Ibid, Sec. 3 (a-d).

preferential treatment in regard to formerly disadvantage persons or groups of person.[2029] This would have clearly revealed the focus on Namibianisation and the recognition of preferential treatment as a legitimate means to achieve collateral objectives.

Outlining the basic principles of the national public procurement system, including value for money, transparency, accountability, integrity, competition, fairness and equity, is highly recommended. Nevertheless, it is not sufficient to name the objectives; they need to be backed by substantial and procedural requirements in the Act that actually promote those objectives. It is important to remark that the inclusion of secondary objectives with view to disadvantaging foreign bidders can deter foreign bidders from participating in Namibian public procurement procedures and, hence, limit competition and impact the objective of value for money; thus undermining primary objectives of public procurement. Additionally, with respect to the above made findings, it is generally questionable if preferential treatment is a useful instrument to advance the national economy in the long run and it is thus of particular importance to apply preferential treatment with utmost care and as a transitional measure. It is not recommended to decide against the incorporation of a preferential treatment scheme at all. However, the inclusion of secondary objectives as objectives of the Act might have a detrimental effect on public procurement efficiency and effectiveness and is, therefore, not recommended.

### c. Organisational Issues

#### i. Institutions

The 2013 bill established a variety of institutions not known under the Tender Board Act 1996. This included the Public Procurement Policy Office, procurement committees, procurement management units, bid evaluation committees as well as an independent review panel. The bill basically established - as in Mauritius - four procurement bodies: a Public Procurement Policy Office, a Central Procurement Board, Public Procurement Entities, and an Independent Review Panel. The Tender Board would have still existed but its structure, functions and power would have changed radically. The bill provided for a decentralisation of public pro-

2029 Ibid, Sec. 3(e-i).

curement by establishing procurement units within the ministries to carry out procurement under a certain threshold. Whereas the public procurement entities would have been responsible for establishing procurement committees and procurement management units within their respective public body, the Central Procurement Board would have no longer been responsible for the whole tender procedure, but would have continued to examine bidding documents and oversee the conduct of bidding processes.

Namibia now follows a centralised system; which results in an overload of work for the Tender Board.[2030] The bill envisaged the increase of the threshold for tenders that are procured through the Central Procurement Board. All tenders falling below these thresholds should have been carried out by procurement units within the ministries.

According to the 2013 bill, the Procurement Policy Office was designed as a procurement policy and monitoring body. It would have had a variety of functions and powers, including policy-making, monitoring and reviewing, training and capacity building, developing of procurement performance assessment systems, facilitating e-procurement, and investigating whether the provisions of the Act have been complied with.[2031] The executive director and the directors of the Office would have been appointed by the Minister of Finance after consultation with the Public Service Commission and they were required to possess suitable qualifications.[2032] It is important to remark that the directors would have been not allowed to engage in any business, profession, occupation or paid employment elsewhere, except with approval of the Minister.[2033] The Policy Office's staff members would have been appointed by the executive director and had to be persons of high integrity, knowledge and experience in the fields relevant to the functions of the Policy Office.[2034]

In regard to the Central Procurement Board, there would have no longer been an automatic membership for permanent secretaries and the board would have been much smaller, with only 9 members – a chairperson, a deputy chairperson and seven other members who have knowledge and experience relevant to the work of the Board.[2035] Further recruitment criteria, conditions and vetting procedures might have been prescribed by the

2030 Interview Mrs Jonga (Tender Board, Chief Control Officer), 26th March 2013.
2031 Public Procurement Bill (As read a First Time) 2013, Sec. 7.
2032 Ibid, Sec. 8 (1) (a).
2033 Ibid, Sec. 8 (4).
2034 Ibid, Sec. 10 (1).
2035 Ibid, Secs. 11 (2) and 11 (3).

Minister of Finance.[2036] The Minister of Finance would have appointed the members, who would have served for three years.[2037] The system of appointing alternate members would have continued, but subject to the restriction that not more than three alternate members are present and voting at a meeting of the Board.[2038] The Board would have been responsible to appoint persons of high integrity with substantial knowledge, experience and appropriate skills in the field of procurement as its professional staff.[2039] The Board would have had the power to appoint persons to act as members of bid evaluation committees of the Board, including representatives nominated by the relevant public bodies.[2040] The Board would have been funded with money appropriated by Parliament, prescribed fees of levies charged to the benefit of the Board, and donations, grants and bequests accrued to the Board from any source approved by the Minister.[2041]

The procurement committees of the ministries would, according to the bill, have been responsible for overseeing the procurement processes in public bodies.[2042] The members of the committees would have not been appointed by the ministries, but by the accounting officers of public bodies who would have borne the overall responsibility for the execution of the procurement process.[2043] Committee members would have been appointed with regard being had to their technical and professional competence, procurement skills and knowledge as well as integrity and sound decision-making abilities.[2044] The accounting officer would have been required to establish a balanced structure of gender and skills among the members.[2045] The procurement management units would have been responsible for managing all procurement activities for their public body.[2046] The management unit staff members would have been appointed according to requirements similar to those governing the appointment of the procurement committee members.[2047]

---

2036 Ibid, Sec. 11 (4).
2037 Ibid, Sec. 11 (2) (c).
2038 Ibid, Sec. 15 (10) and (11).
2039 Ibid, Sec. 19 (1).
2040 Ibid, Sec. 12 (1) (j).
2041 Ibid, Sec. 20 (1).
2042 Ibid, Sec. 28 (1).
2043 Ibid, Secs. 27 (1) and 29.
2044 Ibid, Sec. 29 (2).
2045 Ibid, Sec. 29 (3).
2046 Ibid, Sec. 32 (1).
2047 Ibid, Sec. 33 (1, 2).

Moreover, the 2013 bill provided for the establishment of bid evaluation committees. They would have been responsible for the evaluation of prequalifications, bids, proposals or quotations that are within the prescribed threshold for a public body.[2048] The number and level of expertise of members of a bid evaluation committee would have depended on the value and complexity of the procurement requirement concerned.[2049] The number of members would have had to be an odd number in order to enable majority decisions.[2050] Members of a bid evaluation committee would have had to possess skills, knowledge and experience relevant to the procurement requirements.[2051] Bid evaluation committees would have been composed of one or more members from the user department, the person involved in the preparation of the bidding document if considered beneficial depending on the type and complexity of the procurement as well as one or more persons who are not staff members of the public body concerned.[2052]

It is of the utmost importance to ensure the independence of the institutions and to clearly separate and define responsibilities and powers. The bill establishes an organisational structure which clearly defines roles and responsibilities and separates powers but raises questions in regard to successful implementation in view of limited capacities and, in particular, qualified public procurement officers and staff. Although the bill is quite clear about the separation of powers and responsibilities, which is recommendable per se, the multitude of entities created raises concerns about the possibility of implementing the provisions in practice. The Procurement Policy Office, for example, plays a very important role for the efficient and effective functioning of the public procurement system envisaged. However, whether the necessary capacity and resources are available to establish a strong institution that can embrace the multitude and variety of functions assigned to it, is more than questionable. It might be beneficial to slim the functions of the Procurement Policy Office and outsource certain activities such as capacity building or guidance on operational matters. It might be beneficial to use existing structures rather than establishing giant institutions that will not be operative in practice. It would, for

2048 Ibid, Sec. 36 (1), 36 (3) (a).
2049 Ibid, Sec. 36 (6).
2050 Ibid.
2051 Ibid, Sec. 36 (5).
2052 Ibid, Sec. 36 (2).

example, be conceivable to (transitionally) transfer certain policy functions to a special group in the Ministry of Finance, as the National Treasury in South Africa. The Procurement Policy Office could then focus on monitoring public procurement processes. If the institution then works efficiently and effectively, its functions can later be broadened. Consequently, the functions outlined in the Public Procurement Act should be restricted to basic provisions and regulate details in secondary legislation.

Apart from the public procurement institutions, other external institutions have important oversight functions. These include the auditor-general and the ACC. Under the 2013 bill, the auditor-general would have been responsible for the annual auditing of the accounts and records of the Tender Board. In cases of alleged corruption, the public policy office, the Tender Board as well as the public bodies would have been required to refer the matter to the Anti-Corruption Commission. The involvement of external actors, in particular financial auditing by the auditor-general and the clear reference to the Anti-Corruption Commission as the authority responsible for investigations, is recommendable. In the light of the practical experience and especially the inefficiency of the ACC, it is also commendable that certain requirements regarding the investigation procedures, such as a time limit in which a report has been submitted, are included.

The decentralisation of public procurement under a certain threshold as suggested by the draft and as practiced in Mauritius and also in South Africa is in line with the approaches followed in most countries and can have a positive effect and solve several problems existing in the current public procurement system. In particular, the inefficiency of the Tender Board due to an overload of work can be rectified. The bill gave the Central Tender Board sole responsibility for the awarding of contracts above a determined threshold. However, it would be recommendable to provide for a constant review of the threshold for contracts awarded by the Central Tender Board in order to facilitate further decentralisation. The decisions of a Central Tender Board should also be subject to the review of the Procurement Policy Office, as foreseen in the latest draft.

The 2013 bill required the accounting officer bearing the sole responsibility for the execution of public procurement processes within the public body to appoint members to the bid evaluation committees as or the procurement management units and procurement committees. The allocation of responsibility to the accounting officers within the procuring entities is similar to the South African approach in this respect. And indeed, it is important to clearly assign responsibilities in order to be able to hold someone accountable for public procurement decisions.

Similarly, the Minister of Finance would have been responsible for appointing the executive director of the Procurement Policy Office and the members of the Tender Board. Therefore the Minister of Finance would have had a strong personal influence on the institutions responsible for public procurement. It would be preferable for such key positions to be filled by independent committees such as the public service commission or the personnel board in accordance with the accounting officer.

Abolishing the system that composes the Tender Board of influential politicians who may have a conflict of interest where the outcome of public procurement procedures is concerned has to be seen as a top priority. In regard to the composition of the Tender Board, it should not be enough that the members be sufficiently qualified. It is also necessary to ensure that the Tender Board's staff members are sufficiently qualified, as was foreseen in the latest draft. The limited number of board members avoids camp building[2053] and facilitates decision-making. However, as the Director of the IPPR notes, it is still a challenge to find independent, qualified people who are eligible for the job.[2054] It would have been a great improvement, however, that the Board members were employed full-time and could only carry out other jobs if the Minister had given its approval. The restriction that not more than three alternate members can be present and voting at a Board meeting is important in order to prevent situations in which decisions are basically taken by alternates instead of permanent members, as it has been the case under the Tender Board Act 1996.

The Tender Board needs an adequate substructure in order to be able to meet its responsibilities. It is very important to equip the Board with sufficient capacity and this should be also regulated in law. Since the Tender Board still plays an important role by being responsible for high-value procurements, there should be certain requirements ensuring independence in this respect. The bill indeed contained certain qualification requirements for Board members but it was not required that they be independent. This was a severe shortcoming.

The provision that the funds of the Tender Board consist, inter alia, of donations, grants and bequests from any source approved by the Minister, is more than questionable. Such approach provides great latitude for the exertion of influence and should not be adopted. The Tender Board should be financed solely by money appropriated by parliament in order to avoid

2053 Interview Mr Hopwood (IPPR, Director), 26th March 2013.
2054 Ibid.

any possibility of exercising influence on the Board. Additionally, in case such a provision is regarded as necessary in order to ensure the efficient functioning of the Central Tender Board with regard to the available resources, donations, grants or bequests should not only require the approval of the Minister of Finance, who has a lot of influence already and cannot be regarded as independent, but also of an independent organ such as the auditor-general. Grants from international financial institutions, for example, would then be conceivable, but any donation, grant or bequest from the business sector or other stakeholders cannot be justified.

The provision for bid evaluation committees as they exist in Mauritius is laudable. However, this might not be appropriate in all procurement cases, as the system should generally be not too complex. Such an approach might indeed be appropriate in regard to high-value or highly technical procurements but not in other circumstances. The establishment of ad hoc evaluation committees might not be suitable in all public procurement procedures, especially low-value procurement. Furthermore, it should be borne in mind that the procurement management units are monitored by the procurement committees. The involvement of bid evaluation committees not only makes the process more complex but more time consuming and more costly, which is contrary to the principle of value for money. It is also questionable as the establishment of ad hoc committees "does nothing to encourage the development of a rational accumulation of specialised procurement knowledge", as the appointed members "face recurring learning curves which are often too steep to be mastered in the time available for the completion of the procurement at hand."[2055] In particular, in the Namibian circumstances, where persons with the required expertise are rare to find, this poses a major problem and casts doubts on the possible efficiency and effectiveness of such ad hoc committees. The involvement of ad hoc committees should therefore be limited to specific procurements requiring an evaluation by a particular committee such as high-value or complex public procurements.

### ii. Human Resources

Building and developing human capacity and procurement expertise have not been extensively discussed in the course of the reform. It should be re-

2055 Trepte, 'Regulating Procurement', p. 269.

alised that even a good law needs to be accompanied by measures ensuring its successful implementation. As the current system discloses, the shortcomings of the current public procurement system is not only a result of outdated and incomplete legislation but also of insufficient implementation of existing legal provisions. The bill required all relevant procurement officers and staff to have certain qualifications. However, it did not provide for the establishment of a proper qualification system. The qualification requirements remained vague, allowed for political appointments and did not ensure that the staff members were adequately qualified for the job in question. A stronger involvement of the public service commission is possible and recommendable. It could, for example, be commissioned with developing qualification criteria in consultation with the Minister.

The Tender Board would have been required to use its best efforts to provide adequate training and technical skills to its staff members.[2056] The bill required the Procurement Policy Office

> "[...] to set mandatory training standards, capacity building and competence levels, certification requirements and professional development paths for procurement practitioners in Namibia with the consent of the Minister."[2057]

Although this would be an important provision, it is questionable whether a Procurement Policy Office with a variety of functions has enough resources and capacity to ensure its implementation. The creation of procurement expertise in Namibia could, for example, be entrusted to existing training institutes such as the Namibia Institute of Public Administration and Management, which could be commissioned to establish training programmes for public procurement. Moreover, integrating public procurement into the curricula of certain study fields such as law could also be pursued. Research on public procurement should be encouraged and facilitated. The law could, for example, commission one of the research institutes with assisting with constant monitoring and review of the public procurement system. It would have been of great advantage if such external institutions were included at a very early stage of reform to build procurement capacity and expertise. And it has to be recognised that the use of existing institutions in building procurement capacity and expertise as well as facilitating research can be a great advantage and be far more efficient than establishing new institutions.

2056 Public Procurement Bill (As read a First Time) 2013, Sec. 19 (2) (b).
2057 Ibid, Sec. 7 (1) (h).

Additionally, it is of the utmost importance to recognise the public procurement profession and implement an adequate qualification system for public procurement professionals. All procurement officials currently employed should be given a certain period of time to obtain the required qualifications. With respect to the lack of procurement expertise, the employment of persons not yet suitably qualified might be necessary to avoid unfilled vacancies and, thereby, the non-functioning of a whole institution. Continuous training of such persons could contribute to the creation of sufficient qualified procurement staff. It is worth looking at the South African strategy in this respect.

It has to be emphasised that the existence of a lack of qualified public procurement personal needs to be considered when establishing new institutions with a variety of functions and powers. The 2013 bill assumed that this had not been done in Namibia. Additionally, a heavy-rules approach with several new and independent institutions to be established as provided by the latest draft might be advantageous in view of objectives such as transparency and the fight against corruption. However, regarding the lack of capacity and experience, it might be preferable to design the public procurement law in a way that allows a gradual broadening of responsibilities of those institutions and, therefore, allow time to create and establish procurement knowledge. One solution would be the enactment of a tender law, which establishes new public procurement institutions but outlines only the important general principles of the public procurement system and its procedures. Detailed rules can then be placed in regulations and directives and be adapted progressively. In other words, the functions of new institutions should be slimmed down while responsibilities should be assigned to existing institutions for a transitional period of time until the new institutions have been successfully established and can work efficiently and effectively.

### d. Methods and Procedures

The 2013 bill provided for alternative tendering methods if certain conditions are met, which is very similar to the Mauritian approach. There would have been no broad discretion to apply exemptions but detailed provisions explicitly stated when public bodies can deviate from open bidding.[2058] The bill required that the Board or public body had to note in the record of the procurement proceedings the grounds for the choice of the procurement method.[2059] Considering the abuse of the current Tender Board in regard to exemptions and, hence, renunciation of open bidding procedures, it is strongly advised that, in addition to the requirement to give reasons for the decision in the record, the Procurement Policy Office has to approve the choice of the procurement method in public procurement processes carried out by the Central Tender Board.

As foreseen in the bill, the Namibian public procurement system should provide for alternative procurement methods for all possible types of procurement. A look at the UNCITRAL Model Law or the Mauritian approach is better than taking the South African approach as a model because, although the South African model is not per se detrimental, it does hinder harmonisation. Allowance of a certain degree of flexibility in regard to procurement methods is preferable to a system of general exemptions. Modern procurement methods such as framework agreements, electronic reverse auctions or public-private partnership should be carefully assessed and implemented in the Namibian context. The provisions as found in the bill were quite progressive in this regard. And it is advisable to keep certain procedures of the current Namibian system such as the two-envelope system, which could be used for complex and high-value procedures for the reasons mentioned above. The bill provided for two-stage bidding, which is also quite acceptable.[2060] Two-stage bidding permits discussions of the technical bid in order to ensure that the bidders are not restricted in their flexibility of how to achieve the desired outcome and allows for unconventional and progressive technical approaches. This is particularly advantageous where highly technical procurements are concerned and can be an important means of promoting innovation. The possibility of seeking clarification from the bidders regarding their bids as well as from the bidders regarding the tender documents should be granted. However, it should be transparent and fair. Bidders should not, for example, be allowed to alter the substance and price of their bids. This has been sufficiently provided for in the latest draft.

---

2058 Hopwood, 'Comments on the Public Procurement Bill', p. 5.
2059 Public Procurement Bill (As read a First Time) 2013, Sec. 37 (4).
2060 Ibid, Sec. 54.

e. Transparency

Transparency has not been mentioned as a particular core area of reform by the Namibian government. This might be attributed to the fact that the Tender Board itself does not view transparency and corruption as major problems of the current system.

Nevertheless, in practice, apart from technical shortcomings of the public procurement legislation, corruption is a major concern. The Institute for Public Policy Research has, in contrast to the government, stressed the need to improve the transparency and accountability of the Tender Board. Despite the fact that transparency has not been emphasised as a core area of reform, the bill was an improvement with respect to transparency standards and accountability; it did not, however, suffice international best practices.

Transparency was mentioned as an objective of public procurement in the bill,[2061] but according to Hopwood this did not reflect in the bill.[2062] Certain publication requirements had been included but lack specification such as the nature and timing of such publication. According to Hopwood, there were

> "[...] piecemeal mentions of 'transparency' and 'publication' in the bill, but not an overall approach in keeping with the principle of access to information."[2063]

Indeed, several publication requirements such as the evaluation criteria and methodology which have to be set out in the bidding document were included.[2064] However, there was, for example, no detailed provisions governing tender specification and evaluation criteria. Although a balance needs to be found between outlining criteria for tender specification and flexibility in order not to hinder innovation, the provision of basic guidelines in this respect is recommendable to facilitate public procurement officers' work, limit discretion and to foster transparency.

Moreover, in open bidding procedures, tenders would have had to be published in a national newspaper of wide circulation and in cases of international bidding, in selected international publications with wide circulation. There was no requirement to publish tenders electronically in the internet, for example, on a national procurement website. Yet such a re-

2061 Ibid, Sec. 3 (d).
2062 Hopwood, 'Comments on the Public Procurement Bill', p. 6.
2063 Ibid.
2064 Public Procurement Bill (As read a First Time) 2013, Sec. 62 (9).

quirement is highly recommendable for Namibia and facilitates access to tender invitations and, hence, competition. Barriers such as unstable or slow internet connections do not exist. It is also to be criticised that certain requirements, including the requirement to publish evaluation criteria and methodology, were not clearly pointed out as such but instead are hidden between other provisions and therefore could not be easily identified.

The publishing of all necessary information during the whole public procurement process should be obligatory and defined in detail; enabling the public to scrutinize public procurement decisions. It is, for example, of the utmost importance to specify the criteria for the title of tender and the nature of the evaluation criteria that can be used. The UNCITRAL Model Law can serve as guideline in respect of transparency requirements. Additionally, the use of electronic means should be considered in order to make information easier to access. The establishment of a national procurement website containing all information, including the announcement of all open tenders accompanying the announcement in a national newspaper, is highly recommendable.

Apart from publication requirements, all public procurement institutions were required to keep records of public procurement procedures. The bill, for example, required that the reasons for using an alternative bidding method had to be recorded by the Board.[2065] The Chief Executive Officer of the Tender Board was obliged to keep full and proper accounts and records of the Tender Board's financial transactions, and cause them to be inspected by the auditor-general.[2066] The Board was further obliged to prepare and submit annual reports to the Minister of Finance for tabling in the National Assembly. This is an important aspect to enable the public to hold the Board accountable.[2067] Moreover, procurement committees and procurement management units were generally required to properly record procurement proceedings. The recording of all public procurement proceedings is an indispensable requirement. The records should be maintained and kept available for inspection by the responsible oversight authority at all times. The bill conferred to the Procurement Policy Office the power to require any information, documents, records or reports with respect to any aspect of public procurement procedures.[2068]

2065 Ibid, Sec. 37 (4).
2066 Ibid, Sec. 23.
2067 Ibid, Sec. 24.
2068 Ibid, Sec. 7 (2) (a).

It can be summarised that the institutions are indeed required to record most acts and decisions; however, the public has no opportunity to access that information.[2069] For example the ground for the choice of the procurement method has to be recorded but not published.[2070] Additionally, certain important information such as a list of suppliers and bidders that have been blacklisted were not required to be published which is contrary to transparency standards. Moreover, while the Board is required to submit annual reports, there are no explicit requirements regarding their content and their publication.[2071] Hence, there is no possibility for the public to demand access to the reports in a timely manner.[2072] With special regard to the fact that public procurement officers and staff members are strictly prohibited from disclosing "any information that comes into [their] possession relating to procurement proceedings and bids, including proprietary information of bidders"[2073] and that all information in challenge procedures are strictly confidential and disclosure is an offence,[2074] one must assume that any form of public scrutiny is not intended.[2075]

The bill included provisions on codes of conduct and disclosure of interests. The Public Procurement Policy Office would have had to investigate alleged non-compliances with the Act and would have therefore been provided with a variety of powers, such as to require that any information documents, records or reports be handed over and to summon and examine witnesses.[2076] If it was established that the Act had been infringed, the Procurement Policy Office might have referred the matter to the appointing authority of the staff member, to the Namibian Police, Anti-Corruption Commission or any other competent authority for investigation.[2077] Any appointing authority that would have received a referral and recommendations regarding alleged non-compliance of a staff member would have had to acknowledge receipt thereof within seven days and ensured that the recommendations were attended to promptly and report progress the Poli-

2069 Cf. Links, 'The Public Procurement Bill', p. 13.
2070 See Public Procurement Bill (As read a First Time) 2013, Sec. 37 (4).
2071 Ibid, Sec. 24 (2).
2072 Cf. Schmidt, 'Public Procurement – A Constitutional Perspective'.
2073 See Public Procurement Bill (As read a First Time) 2013, Sec. 81 (1) (d).
2074 Ibid, Sec. 75 (1).
2075 Cf. Schmidt, 'Public Procurement – A Constitutional Perspective'.
2076 Ibid, Sec. 7 (1) (u) and 7 (2).
2077 Ibid, Sec. 7 (3).

cy Office within 30 days of receipt.[2078] The Tender Board similarly would have had the power and obligation to report non-compliance and could have examined witnesses and request information under the latest draft.[2079]

Failures to disclose interests or to provide records or documents as well as acts such as disclosing confidential information or corruption, for example, were liable to a fine between not exceeding amounts between N$500 000 and N$2 000 000 and imprisonment up to 10 years.[2080] Bidders or suppliers caught being involved in corrupt activities could have likewise been punished under the latest draft.[2081] Moreover, the bill provided for the blacklisting of potential bidders and suppliers for certain acts.[2082] However, debarment would have been only possible if a certain procedure was followed and was limited to a period of 5 years.[2083] Unfortunately, as mentioned above, there was no requirement in regard to the publication of a list of suspended bidders and suppliers.

It should be clearly defined what institution is responsible for accepting, investigating and sanctioning illegal or improper conduct of public procurement officials and institutions. The bill did clearly define the lines of responsibility. Nevertheless, in particular the provisions on disclosure of interests can be criticised as not going far enough. First of all, the "[...] narrow defining of relational bonds is highly problematic in the interest of closing all avenues for corrupt insider dealing around public contracts."[2084] The scope of Section 81 (2) covers only interests by close relatives, meaning parent, sibling, spouse, child or grandchild; not those of other relatives or family friends. Secondly, there is a provision allowing the Board to decide that a person in a conflict of interest with view to a public procurement matter can still participate in the proceedings if the conflict of interest is found to be "[...] frivolous to affect the impartiality of the staff member."[2085] This approach leaves room for abuse, as the conflict of interest in fact still exists, even if a person is excused.[2086] Moreo-

2078 Ibid, Sec. 7 (3) and (4).
2079 Ibid, Sec. 12 (4).
2080 Ibid, Sec. 2 (4), see also Secs. 7 (5) and 12 (5).
2081 Ibid, Sec. 81.
2082 Ibid, Sec. 83 (1)
2083 Ibid, Sec. 83 (2) and (3).
2084 F. Links (2015), p. 15.
2085 Public Procurement Bill (As read a First Time) 2013, Sec. 81 (2) (b).
2086 Cf. Links (2015), p. 15.

ver, it is unclear what kind of constellation or circumstances would constitute "frivolity".[2087] It can also be criticised that the requirements and the procedure for blacklisting should have been outlined in detail. Additionally, it is necessary to require publication of the list of companies excluded from tendering due to past irregularities and illegal conduct as well as the period of exclusion. Blacklisting should be applied in cases of corruption and other violations as well as in cases of insufficient contract implementation.

### f. Secondary Objectives

As mentioned above, several secondary objectives had been included as objectives of the Public Procurement law in the 2013 bill. Specific secondary objectives, including preferential treatment, had, hence been assigned a particular importance and position in the Namibian public procurement system. The five secondary objectives that were explicitly mentioned were the empowerment of Namibian women and youth in the Namibian economy, the promotion of job creation, the promotion of domestic manufacturing and entrepreneurship, the building of procurement capacity and affirmative action.[2088] The bill included a whole section on preferences; limiting preferences to the specific objectives outlined in the Act, requiring the Minister to issue codes of good practices on preferences and determining certain requirements for the application of preferences.[2089] Preferences and weightings were, for example, required to be clearly stated in the bidding documents.[2090] This would have been a great improvement over current practice. However, although the bill provided that codes of good practice might include indicators to measure empowerment through preferential treatment and the weight attached to these indicators,[2091] this would have not been obligatory and the authorities would have continued to retain broad discretion with respect to preferential treatment. Moreover, it had been suggested that a code of good practice include the targets and the period within which those targets must be

---

2087 Ibid.
2088 Ibid, Sec. 3 (e-i).
2089 Ibid, Sec. 84ff.
2090 Ibid, Sec. 87 (2).
2091 Ibid, Sec. 85 (1) (c) and (d).

achieved.[2092] Nevertheless, this was – in the bill - not obligatory and a review and an evaluation of preference policies was not required. Additionally, it can be criticised that preferences seemed not to be intended as transitional and temporary measures that are applied only as long as necessary to achieve the objectives. The requirement imposed in the bill that the Minister published the draft of code of good practice and invited any interested person to comment or make representation in connection therewith within a specified period would have been a positive development. However, the requirement to involve stakeholders did not apply if the Minister was of the opinion that it was in the public interest that it was issued without delay, which severely watered the provision down. It should also be remarked that the Minister of Finance who has wide-ranging powers under the bill is responsible for drafting the code and therefore can strongly influence public procurement policies.[2093]

It can be concluded that the Namibian law should emphasise that preferential procurement should not be contrary to the objectives of non-discrimination, competition, equity and fairness. Secondary objectives should be required to be based on policies issued by the Minister of Finance after consultation with other institutions, including the Public Procurement Policy Office and respective ministries rather than left to the discretion of procuring entities. They should further be applied in a transparent manner. It is important to continually review the application of secondary objectives since the socio-economic situation is constantly changing. A respective provision should be included in the new law and responsibilities should be clearly assigned. It would e.g. be recommendable to establish a term limit for companies benefiting from preferential treatment, such as has been done in Kenya. Their preference regulations provide that eligible enterprises can benefit from the preferential and reservation schemes for five years. This period can be renewed once.[2094]

Namibia has problems similar to South Africa. These problems are truly relicts of the apartheid system. The approach to address socio-economic goals and specifically the PPPFA and its regulations can serve as a model for the design of an equivalent law in Namibia. It would, however, be nec-

2092 Ibid, Sec. 85 (2) (a) and (b).

2093 See ibid, Sec. 70 (1).

2094 Public Procurement and Disposal Act (No. 3 of 2005): (Preference and Reservations) Regulations, 2011 (Republic of Kenya) (Legal Notice No. 58), Reg. 22.

essary to consider the actual success of the South African preferential system in practical terms. Nevertheless, it should first be assessed whether preferential procurement can lead to substantive improvement of the socio-economic situation or is rather impeding development (see also the discussion in Part I, Chapter 3). However, considering the specific Namibian situation, which is very similar to South Africa's, preferential procurement might be justified and constitute an important element of the transformation process, even if its practical effects are limited.

The strict provisions on the implementation of preferential procurement make the process transparent and comprehensible. This is preferable to the approach taken by Mauritius, which has failed to implement a comprehensive policy for its preference policy yet. Especially given that preferential treatment seems to be one of the most important issues in reforming its public procurement system, the road South Africa took to promote affirmative action in public procurement should be closely examined. Specific tools such as "targeted procurement" that have proven to be successful in achieving socio-economic objectives can be adopted as best practices. Nevertheless, the shortcomings identified in South Africa, such as the failure to set a time limit for the application of preferential policies and to make any reference to other specific goals that might be pursued, should be addressed when designing a new procurement framework and alternative solutions should be found. In this respect Namibia should find alternative approaches.

In respect to the problem of (construction) companies disregarding labour, social security and affirmative action laws, it would make sense to include contract conditions such as requiring that the employees be paid the minimum wage as stated in the collective agreement or otherwise paid the average remuneration in that sector in that region. Although this is currently usually stated in the tender documentations it might be more effective and more difficult to be disregarded if this is stated in the central piece of legislation. It is also necessary to ensure that compliance is monitored and violations sanctioned. It has to be clearly defined who is responsible in this regard. The Mauritian approach in this respect could serve as a model.

The inclusion of environmental criteria has not been discussed as being included in the bill. It seems that currently there is a common understanding that the ministries should consider these issues when planning projects, but that they are not relevant as evaluation criteria. The ministries usually carry out a feasibility study to assess the impacts of a project on the environment.[2095] It is hence the line ministries' responsibility to ensure that a project is environmentally feasible.[2096] However, the use of environmental requirements in the evaluation of tenders could have a much bigger impact on the promotion of environmentally sustainable products and production. However, in regard of the controversial nature of the efficiency of green public procurement and the fact that the more secondary objectives pursued the more complex public procurement becomes, it does not make sense to address this issue at this stage. Nonetheless, the reform process should consider aligning public procurement with existing environmental policies, in particular because the government is obliged to protect the environment under the Namibian Constitution.[2097] Certain standards could, for example, be required to be adhered to by contracting parties of the state.

### g. E-Procurement

The Tender Board is currently developing a database since the whole system is still paper-based, which delays the process and produces a lot of work. The operation of the database started on 1 April 2013 and further steps towards e-procurement are planned for the future.[2098] The arrival of an IT expert from the EU to help introduce electronic procurement and to implement the database can be seen as major step towards restructuring the paper-based system towards an electronic procurement system. Furthermore, the Permanent Secretary of the Ministry of Finance went to the Seychelles for a conference on e-governance.[2099] Although this concerns e-governance in general rather than e-procurement, it shows that there is certainly something happening in regard to the use of technology in governance. Additionally, there are initiatives at the local level to make use of electronic means in public procurement. For example, the Local Tender Board of Windhoek has offered an online subscription service since 2005. People can tick what type of tenders they want to be informed of and regu-

2095 Interview Mr Immanuel (Tender Board, Alternate Member), 27th March 2013.
2096 Ibid.
2097 Constitution of Namibia 1990, Art. 95 (i).
2098 Interview Mrs Jonga (Tender Board, Chief Control Officer), 26th March 2013; Interview Mr Isaacs (Tender Board, Chief Control Officer), 26th March 2013.
2099 Interview Mr Isaacs (Tender Board, Chief Control Officer), 26th March 2013.

larly receive emails containing the requested information. This is an advantage as no tender information can be missed. Approximately 35 subscribers had registered in 2013. [2100]

However, frequent problems with the government's email-system and insufficient updating of websites are either signs that there is a lack of IT expertise or a lack of willingness to use electronic means. Nevertheless, within Africa, Southern Africa was regarded as the region with the highest e-government readiness in 2008[2101] and the technical developments in recent years have make the option of using electronic means in public procurement even more promising.

The bill indeed required the Procurement Policy Office to issue guidelines regarding e-procurement. Nevertheless, there were only a few provisions in the latest draft that could be interpreted as promoting the use of electronic means instead of paper-based means. The Board or a public body might have authorised the use of other forms of communication for publication of invitations to bid, transmission of biddings, submission of bids, conclusion of contracts and processing of payment. Electronic communication was specifically mentioned as a possible alternative form of communication.[2102] It was further provided that, whereas bids were usually to be submitted in writing, duly signed and in a sealed envelope, the bidding documents could authorise other methods for the submission of bids.[2103] As mentioned above, it would be feasible to at least require the publication of invitations of bids online as well as make available the bid documents by electronic means.

Furthermore, it is strongly recommended to design the new law in such a way that it does not forestall the use of electronic means in public procurement but instead provides enough flexibility to accommodate a gradual development towards e-procurement. The establishment of a website with comprehensive information about the entire procurement cycle as available in Mauritius should be expedited straight away. The tender notices, dates and deadlines, award notices, notices about contract implementation, jurisprudence and if possible an explanation of practical impli-

2100 Interview with Mrs David (Local Tender Board of the City of Windhoek, Accounting Assistant: Tender Invitations), 11th March 2013.

2101 See Townsend.

2102 Public Procurement Bill (As read a First Time) 2013, Sec. 80 (5).

2103 Ibid, Sec. 56 (3).

cations of judicial verdicts, acts, policies, regulations, institutions and the latest research results (articles, etc.) should be published.

### h. Procurement Planning

It is important to regulate procurement planning in an adequate way. In Namibia the delayed implementation of allotted projects at the end of the financial year has contributed to the excessive use of exemptions for public tenders. In 2012 the Finance Minister stressed that there are severe shortfalls regarding the financial planning of public procurement and arranged a meeting to instruct officials about basic rules of financial administration.[2104] These shortfalls need to be addressed and be reflected in the new bill. The 2013 bill only provided for a general requirement to issue procurement plans.[2105] For example, the Tender Board was required to submit to the Minister of Finance for approval an annual plan at least 60 days before the commencement of its next financial year, or a later date determined by the Minister.[2106] However, there were no criteria and requirements concerning what the annual plan should have included. The provisions providing that the accounting officer was responsible for the submission of an annual procurement plan to the Board and that the procurement management units had to prepare reports on the implementation of annual procurement plans were equally imprecise.[2107]

Procurement planning should be required for all procuring entities at the beginning of each financial year. Requirements in regard to the contents of procurement plans should be clearly outlined. The annual plans should be available to the public on the national procurement website and be updated regularly. The Mauritian approach could serve as a model. However, it is necessary to ensure that the approach is suitable in the context of public budget management and in line with the laws governing state finances. It should be ensured that procurement (financial) planning is reviewed and audited from an external expert. The institution of the auditor-general, for example, lends itself to carrying out this task.

2104 'Minister gehen in die Finanzschule - Premier Angula und Finanzchefin Kuugongelwa-Amadhila bestehen auf strengere Haushaltsbestellung' (Newspaper article), Allgemeine Zeitung (Windhoek, Namibia), 12 June 2012.

2105 Public Procurement Bill (As read a First Time) 2013, Secs. 22, 27 (1) (j), 34 (f).

2106 Ibid, Sec. 22.

2107 Ibid, Secs. 27 (1) (j), 34 (f).

i. Contract Management

Although the problems experienced in the current public procurement system call for the establishment of effective and efficient structures of contract management, the latest draft failed to clearly regulate contract management in a comprehensive way. There were specific requirements in regard to the contents of procurement contracts but not in respect to contract management. Under the latest draft the Procurement Policy Office would have had the power to and responsibility of developing and implementing procurement performance assessment systems, inspecting or causing to be inspected any procurement activity to ensure compliance with a procurement award as well as instituting contract and performance audits.[2108] The Tender Board would have further had the power to suspend, debar and disqualify suppliers in the prescribed manner and form.[2109] The Policy Office could have also blacklisted suppliers for different reasons, including misconduct relating to execution of procurement contracts.[2110] The procurement committees would have been responsible for the review of applications for variations, addenda or amendments to ongoing contracts.[2111] There were, however, no requirements in regard to the cooperation between the different institutions with respect to contract management and consequences of deficiencies in this respect.

As the public procurement cycle does not end with the tender award or the signing of a contract, contract management needs to be regulated as well. It is necessary to clarify the responsibilities of contract management in the new public procurement system in order not only to ensure successful contract implementation and feedback about possible deficiencies or misconduct on the part of the company carrying out the contract but also to ensure consistency and cooperation between institutions in contract management. Especially in contracts of special importance such as high-value or complex contracts, the requirement for the Tender Board to write a report after the completion of a contract and publish it on the national procurement website might improve transparency and confidence in the procurement system. It is also important to establish strong cooperation between the institution responsible for tendering and the labour commis-

2108 Ibid, Sec. 8 (1) (k,n,o)
2109 Ibid, Sec. 12 (1) (n).
2110 Ibid, Sec. 83 (1).
2111 Ibid, Secs. 69 and 72.

sioner, employment equity commissioner, ACC, etc. The current situation where the Tender Board simply abdicates any responsibilities in regard to abuses of the law after the contract has been awarded is inadequate and ineffective. Although only the respective commissioners can enforce the laws, there should still be close cooperation with the procuring entity. Following the Mauritian approach and including contract conditions requiring compliance with the law and regulating monitoring and sanctioning of violations should also be considered. A whole article or section on contract management - as incidentally should also be done in regard to procurement planning – should be included instead of including certain requirements hidden under different headings.

### j. Review System

To avoid the courts being the sole venue for settling public procurement disputes the latest draft established an internal review procedure as well as an independent review panel. Most basic requirements for an effective review mechanism could be found in the 2013 bill. A standstill period of 14 days was required after the notification of the bidders about the tender award.[2112] The bill required the exhaustion of all available domestic remedies under the Act before instituting any judicial remedy.[2113] Internal challenges could have been made by way of an application to the Board or the public body for reconsideration of their decision or action,[2114] whereas the Review Panel would have been responsible for reviewing decisions and actions in procurement proceedings or failures to take a decision in internal challenging proceedings in this respect by the Board or public body.[2115] According to the 2013 bill, it seems that any decision or action in the procurement proceedings is reviewable. This means that also decisions of the Board or a public entity such as the choice of the procurement method can be subject to review. This is recommendable in order to increase accountability. The procurement process would have been immediately halted if any challenge procedure had been initiated.[2116] Procedural rules were provided in respect to internal challenge procedures as well as

2112 Ibid, Sec. 65 (5).
2113 Ibid, Sec. 69 (4).
2114 Ibid, Sec. 69 (3).
2115 Ibid, Sec. 73 (1).
2116 Ibid, Sec. 70 (1).

challenges to the review panel.[2117] Moreover, the participants' basic rights were protected in the challenge procedures.[2118] In this regard, the 2013 bill basically reflected international best practices. However, it is questionable how independent the review panel really would have been, since it would have been appointed by the Ministry[2119] and there were no requirements in regard to the independence of its members. Moreover, the chairperson and four members of the review panel were required to have qualifications, wide knowledge and experience in legal, administrative, economic, financial trade, engineering, scientific or technical matters and would have been appointed on such terms and conditions as the Minister thinks fit.[2120] The requirements were very broad and, hence, vague; the Minister had broad discretion to appoint any person he deemed suitable.

Additionally, the 2013 bill made all information in challenge proceedings confidential and the disclosing of information to a third party an offence.[2121] The bill further listed several reasons which allowed challenge proceedings to be conducted behind closed doors, excluding the public.[2122] The parties to challenge proceedings had though the right to request any hearing to be public.[2123] According to Section 75 (2) no public hearings had to be held if they impair the protection of essential security interests of the state, are contrary to the law, impede law enforcement, prejudice the legitimate commercial interests of the bidder or supplier or impede fair competition. In particular the latter reasons can be interpreted broadly and can be used as reasons to exclude the public in nearly all procurement cases. Moreover, there seems no possibility to challenge such a decision. This approach does not at all satisfy the requirements inherent in the principle of the rule of law.

It is recommendable to create an internal review mechanism as well as an independent review panel, but it is not acceptable to exclude the public from challenge proceedings if there are no reasons that make this strictly necessary. The UNCITRAL Model Law and the Mauritian law offer guidelines on establishing an adequate review mechanism for public pro-

---

2117 Ibid, Secs. 71 and 73.
2118 Ibid, Sec. 74.
2119 Ibid, Sec. 72 (1) and also Interview Mr Hopwood (IPPR, Director), 26th March 2013.
2120 Public Procurement Bill (As read a First Time) 2013, Sec. 72 (1).
2121 Ibid, Sec. 75 (1).
2122 Ibid, Sec. 75 (2).
2123 Ibid, Sec. 74 (3) (d).

curement. In Namibia, the establishment of an administration tribunal such as suggested by the constitution[2124] and found in several fields such as tax or land matters[2125] could, however, be a possible country-specific way. Such tribunals have been established by special administrative law to review administrative decisions in the relevant area of legislation. These tribunals function independently and have different competencies and responsibilities.[2126] Ensuring that the independent review panel or tribunal has the necessary resources, capacity and powers is indispensable. It is also of the utmost importance to ensure its independence; members should not be appointed solely by the Minister and they must be totally independent from the government. It is also important to establish adequate remedies and timeframes for public procurement challenges. An independent review panel needs to have the power to enforce remedies such as interim interdicts in order to efficiently and effectively carry out reviews.

As foreseen in the latest draft, judicial review of decisions of such independent review panel should be explicitly allowed if all other remedies are exhausted. The provision for a standstill period after the tender notification and before the tender is finally awarded is recommendable in order to avoid challenges being brought after the conclusion of a contract, a circumstance that can have severe implications for the award winner and which can complicate the whole procurement proceedings. It is, however, necessary to find adequate timeframes in relation to the value and complexity of procurements in order to not unnecessarily delay procurement proceedings. It might be possible to establish a minimum timeframe and leave discretion to the procuring entities to specify the length of the standstill period in the tender documents. It is not necessarily suitable to provide for a common standstill period for all contracts, as foreseen in the latest draft.

2124 Constitution of Namibia 1990, Art. 18.

2125 See Section 73A (2) of the Income Tax Act, 1981 (Act No. 24 of 1981) as amended by the Income Tax Amendment Act, 2005 (Act No. 4 of 2005) and Section 63(1) of the Agricultural (Commercial) Land Reform Act, 1995 (Act No. 6 of 1995).

2126 Glinz, 'Verwaltungsrecht und Rechtsstaatlichkeit in Namibia', p. 249ff.

## 4. Learning from Mistakes – an Attempt to make the Reform a Success

In early 2015, the Tender Board of Namibia issued a document containing information on the public procurement reform process as well as challenges and achievements.[2127] This seems to be an attempt to make up for the lack of transparency that had prevailed during the reform process in the past. It is also the first time that explicit references was made to international best practices, in particular the UNCITRAL Model Law, and to tools available for the conducting of reforms such as MAPS.[2128] It, furthermore, emphasises the need to ensure successful implementation of the law, including for example the provision of training not only for public procurement officials but also for other stakeholders.[2129]

Considering this different approach, one can assume that a process of rethinking took place within the institutions responsible for reform, in particular within the Tender Board and the Ministry of Finance. This change of attitude within the Tender Board and the Ministry of Finance has, to my mind, been necessary in order to create ownership for the bill and is a first step for the improvement of the Namibian public procurement system. However, only future will tell whether the good intentions expressed by the Tender Board are put into practice.

The bill that was withdrawn from parliament in 2014 "for further consultations with stakeholders"[2130] has been amended and has been re-introduced in parliament in September 2015.[2131] This bill, however, does not reflect the change of attitude which the Tender Board's statement about the reform suggests. Despite a few minor improvements, there are some amendments to the 2013 bill which even constitute a step backwards with regard to international best practices. In the following the most important examples of negative but also positive amendments shall be given.

Improvements of the bill include for example the provision for a threshold for the establishment of ad hoc evaluation committees as it is not suitable in all cases of procurement such as low-value procurements to establish such committees. Additionally, the 2015 bill is a bit more responsive to e-procurement and provides for the establishment of a public pro-

---

2127 Tender Board of Namibia, 'Public Procurement Reforms 2012/13-2013/14 - *Challenges and achievements*', (Windhoek Tender Board of Namibia, 2015).

2128 Ibid, 15.

2129 Ibid, 1, 5, 17.

2130 See ibid, 1.

2131 Public Procurement Bill (As read a First Time) 2015.

curement portal – however: without stating any details. [2132] Positive is also the provisions for gender balance in public procurement,[2133] that there are no alternate board members anymore, and that the criteria on disqualification of bidders are specified.[2134]

However, there are also negative aspects such as that, despite the explicit naming of transparency as objective of public procurement,[2135] this still does not reflect in the substance of the bill. As in the 2013 bill institutions are indeed required to record information but there have been no measures taken to enable the public to get access to that information in order to scrutinize public procurement decisions.[2136] Moreover, there are several provisions, in particular with view to scope, institutional and organisational structure and review mechanism, that are insufficient as measured by the objectives of transparency and accountability.

### a. Changes with regard to the Scope

The revision of the 2013 bill included the widening of the scope in so far that the letting and hiring of anything and the acquisition or granting of rights and the important aspect of contract management falls under the scope of the 2015 bill.[2137] As has been mentioned above,[2138] this might be preferable as it is ensured that the acquisition or granting of rights follows certain procedures and transparency standards. Moreover, it makes the regulation of the acquisition or granting of rights in another piece of legislation as well as the creation of institutions dealing with these issues obsolete. The inclusion of contract management into the scope of the bill is of utmost importance to guarantee a good procurement outcome, as the public procurement process does not end with the award decision.[2139] However, although the bill states that the scope of public procurement covers

2132 Ibid, Sec. 28 (c).
2133 See e.g. ibid, Secs. 11 (1) (a) and 58 (1) (b).
2134 Ibid, Sec. 50 (2).
2135 Ibid, Sec. 2 (a).
2136 See above in Part III, Chapter 3, Subchapter 3 (e).
2137 Public Procurement Bill (As read a First Time) 2015, Sec. 3 (1) (b) and (c).
2138 See Chapter 1, Subchapter 2 (d) of this part.
2139 See e.g. in Part I, Chapter 1, Subchapter 4.

contract management,[2140] it must be stressed that there are no specifications made for its implementation.

The 2015 bill falls short of many of the positive aspects of the 2013 bill with regard to the scope. The biggest setback is the inclusion of the provision allowing the Minister of Finance to grant exemptions. The practice of granting exemptions has been recognised as one of the main problems under the currently applicable public procurement system; disclosing the need to abide by this provision. The frequent abuse of the exemption provision in the past has not only undermined transparency but also contravened the other principles of public procurement, such as value for money and fairness. In particular, if there are no safeguards for the allowance of exemptions like a requirement to justify such decisions and make them subject to scrutiny of an oversight institution such approach can undermine the basic principles of a public procurement system enormously and is not recommendable. It gives plenty of room for abuse and deprives all stakeholders of public procurement but also the wider public of the possibility to comprehend and scrutinize decisions. And as has been emphasised above,[2141] there is no need for exemptions if a public procurement law is wisely drafted.

The bill allows the Minister to grant general and specific exemptions from the application of certain provisions for procurements by the Namibian Defence Force, the Namibian Police Force, the Namibia Correctional Services and the Namibia Central Intelligence Service.[2142] Moreover, the Minister can, by way of a directive, exempt specific types of procurement or disposal from the application of certain provisions "[...] that are not practical or appropriate for the purpose for which such goods are let, hired or disposed of [...]."[2143] It remains unclear what provisions can and whether there are any provisions that cannot be departed from. That the power to grant exemptions has been shifted from the Tender Board to the Minister of Finance does not alter the fact that such approach is insufficient with view to the achievement of public procurement objectives. The power to decide upon exemptions is centralised within one person and it does not underlie any transparency requirements. Thus, the Minister of Finance is prone to corruption and there is no possibility to scrutinize his or

2140 Ibid, Sec. 3 (1) (b).
2141 For example in Part II, Chapter 3, Subchapter 2 (d).
2142 Ibid, Sec. 4(1).
2143 Public Procurement Bill (As read a First Time) 2015, Sec. 4(2).

her decisions. It is questionable what kind of procurements would need exemptions from the application of the Act and for what reason. The procurement methods outlined in the bill should be designed in a way that their application is practical and appropriate for all possible types of procurements. It can be concluded that this approach not only does not satisfy best practices, which recommend providing no exemptions from the Act, but also by far does not suffice with regard to the objectives of transparency and accountability.

The provision acknowledging international obligations has been deleted in the 2015 bill, which, on the contrary, determines that the provisions of the bill prevail if there is a conflict with any other law, regulations, rules or directives.[2144] With view to Article 144 of the Namibian Constitution, this decision is difficult to comprehend.[2145] However, the fact that Namibian public procurement legislation would prevail over the provisions on public procurement in grant agreements could have a positive effect, namely that procurements financed by grants from foreign donors would be subject to the transparency standards of the Act, thus could be scrutinized by the public. But there is still the possibility that the Minister of Finance makes use of his power to exempt procurements of such kind from the application of the Act and thereby avoids the need to follow transparency, accountability, competition and fairness standards. This would render the positive effect of the provision on conflict of laws void.

### b. Institutional and Organisational Structure

The 2015 extends the responsibilities of accounting officers with view to the 2013 bill. Accounting officers bear the sole responsibility for setting up internal organisational structures in their public entities and are accountable for compliance with legislation.[2146] This is very similar to the South African approach and can have several benefits as has been outlined above.[2147] The extensive provisions on procurement committees and procurement management units have been deleted in the 2015 bill and will be

2144 Public Procurement Bill (As read a First Time) 2015, Sec. 3(2).
2145 See Part III, Chapter 3, Subchapter 2 (d).
2146 Public Procurement Bill (As read a First Time) 2015, Sec. 25(1).
2147 See Part II, Chapter 4, Subchapter 3.

dealt with by regulations.[2148] This slims down the comprehensive bill and makes it easier to implement lessons learned with regard to the functioning of procurement management units and committees without having to change the Public Procurement Act.

The establishment of a Procurement Policy Unit within the Ministry of Finance might be appropriate with regard to the availability of resources and capacities.[2149] However, an independent institution that is responsible for oversight and monitoring is not provided for anymore which is a severe detriment; in particular with view to the wide-ranging powers of the Minister of Finance. The Minister is e.g. the only person that can refer matters of alleged non-compliance with the Act to the Namibian Police, the ACC or any other competent authority for investigation.[2150] The Central Procurement Board cannot call upon those institutions directly, but has to refer the matter to the Procurement Policy Office, located in the Ministry of Finance.[2151] The only mechanism making the Minister accountable is through the annual reports which are tabled in the National Assembly.[2152] But, since the content requirements for those reports remain vague and the Minister can, to a great extent, influence the content of the reports, the possibility to hold the Minister accountable for his or her decisions is weak.

Besides, under the 2015 bill the Minister of Finance's powers and competences in the public procurement system have been further extended. The Minister of Finance can e.g. determine the rate for margin of preferences.[2153] Notable is further that the Minister of Finance can grant general or specific exemptions for specific types of procurement from the application of certain provisions of the bill.[2154]

It can be summarised that the role the Minister of Finance would play within the public procurement system under the 2015 bill must be seen critically with view to the objectives of transparency and accountability. The Minister's powers are wide-ranging and he or she can make decisions

---

2148 See Sec. 25 (3) which provides that „[t]he powers and functions of the internal sturcutres of a public entity are exercised and performed in accordance with the prescribed procedure and processes."
2149 See Public Procurement Bill (As read a First Time) 2015, Secs. 6 and 7.
2150 Ibid, Sec. 7 (4).
2151 Ibid, Sec. 9 (4).
2152 Ibid, Sec. 24.
2153 Ibid, Sec. 52 (10).
2154 Ibid, Sec. 4 (2). See above in Subchapter 4 (a) of this chapter.

regarding key elements of the public procurement procedure without having to justify such decisions while no mechanisms exist to challenge or scrutinize its decision.

c. Review Mechanisms

Amendments made to the provisions on review mechanisms must be assessed critically, too.[2155] While it is not such a big issue that the independent review panel under the 2015 bill would no longer be a permanent institution but an ad hoc tribunal (meaning that the Minister of Finance could, if he thinks it is necessary, appoint five persons from a list of 15 persons to constitute a review panel), there have been other revisions that are contrary to best practices und severely undermine public procurement objectives including transparency and accountability. In contrast to the 2013 bill, the 2015 bill e.g. does not provide for an internal review mechanism which is not recommendable, as this is the most direct, less bureaucratic and often fastest way to resolve an issue.[2156] Furthermore, there is no mentioning of procedural rights for the participants of challenge procedures. This also includes the right to request any hearing to be public which was, as provided in the 2013 bill, the only way participants could challenge a decision to exclude the public for several reasons based on Section 75 (2) of the 2013 bill and Section 61 (2) of the 2015 bill. As mentioned above, this approach does not suffice rule of law standards. Another setback is that, under the 2015 bill, only decisions or actions taken by the Board or a public entity for the award of a procurement contract are reviewable and not all other decisions or actions taken in the procurement proceedings.

Another amendment is that public procurement procedures are not immediately halted, if a challenge has been initiated, but only suspended if an application has been made in this regard and resolved in favour of the suspension.[2157] Considering the fact that, in the past, several court cases were only decided after the implementation of the contract in question, this approach is not reasonable. It unnecessarily burdens not only the challenging party but also the review panel. It would be preferable to provide

2155 See ibid, Secs. 58 - 61.

2156 See above in Part I, Subchapter 1 (8); Part II, Chapter 2, Subchapter 8; Part II, Chapter 4, Subchapter 7 (c); Part II, Chapter 5, Subchapter 2 (h).

2157 Public Procurement Bill (As read a First Time) 2015, Sec. 59 (2).

for automatic suspension and allow for derogation thereof if justified by urgent public interest; as suggested by Article 65 (3) of the UNCITRAL Model Law. Assuming that the approach in the 2015 bill has the intention to ensure that unsatisfied tenderers do not use challenge procedures with no prospect of success to delay the public procurement process, it should be noted that this concern can be dealt with in other ways; for example by following the Mauritian approach to require the deposit of a certain amount of money which is forfeited if the review panel dismisses the application as frivolous.[2158]

It can be summarised that, compared to the 2013 bill, the 2015 bill weakens the right to review extensively and does not suffice best practice requirements.

### d. Interim conclusion

Although the 2015 bill contains several improvements in comparison with the State Tender Board Act, there are still several shortcomings, in particular with regard to transparency and accountability. The 2015 bill includes several amendments to the 2013 bill which are not in line with international best practices. The passing of the 2015 bill will thus most probably not result in an overall efficient, effective and especially transparent public procurement system and is not recommendable with view to the objectives a public procurement system shall achieve.

## 5. Conclusion

The Namibian reform process has been running for more than 5 years without success. A lack of political will could be identified as major hindrance, but there are other problems impeding reform progress as well. These include a lack of capacity and expertise, the fact that the same people who are responsible for running daily public procurement proceedings are responsible for the reform (which not only leads to conflicts of interest but also to time constraints), a lack of a coherent reform strategy, and the rapid change of ministers in the responsible Ministry. Namibia has fur-

---

2158 See above in Part II, Chapter 3, Subchapter 4 (g).

thermore failed to conduct a substantive assessment of the current public procurement system in order to identify strengthens and weaknesses.

With respect to the substantive part of a new public procurement framework, Mauritius was selected as a model. No substantive research on public procurement has been conducted and none of the interviewed Tender Board members had even heard about the UNCITRAL Model Law or the GPA. Mauritius seems to have been chosen for the basic reasons that its public procurement system is quite modern and progressive and that a Commonwealth expert from Mauritius assisted the Tender Board with the reform. There has been a general unwillingness to look at the South African approach, something which might have proven beneficial in regard to certain elements. It seems that the reform team has not selected the Mauritian law as a basis because of factual considerations and of the similarity of factors of influence – since these have not been analysed in detail - but on the basis of the reputation of the Mauritian law and the reluctance to consider the South African legal system for political reasons. This seems to be a very subjective approach and cannot necessarily be considered appropriate.

Whereas in many countries external assistance has led to the enactment of new public procurement legislation, Namibia has not produced results in a timely manner despite the involvement of several external experts. Unfortunately, it is unclear what institutions have been involved to what degree. The World Bank, the European Union and the Commonwealth Public Procurement Network have all apparently played a role in the Namibian reform process but there has been no transparency about this involvement. Additionally, communication between the Tender Board and the responsible persons in the Ministry of Finance has been insufficient, which makes the reform process even more obscure.

With exception of the Institute for Public Policy Research, there is no academic debate about public procurement and no expertise challenging current procurement practices. However, there is huge public discontent about the way public procurement is carried out and the media deals with this issue frequently. Unfortunately, this does not seem sufficient to inspire political resolve to finalise the reform. Public procurement stakeholders have not been involved in the reform process properly and adequately. Nor has it been possible for any stakeholder to track reform proceedings as the whole process has been non-transparent. This has led to a lack of understanding and ownership of the proposed law, which contributed to its being withdrawn from the National Assembly because of severe criticism.

Despite major improvements, the bill that was withdrawn from parliament in 2013 after heavy criticism did not address all the key issues that need to be considered and effectively regulated in order to lay a good foundation for a new public procurement system. The draft posed different problems, including shortcomings in regulation as well as in regard to implementation. The same accounts for the 2015 bill which on some points even contains deteriorations in comparison with international best practices.

The organisational structure clearly established responsibilities and a separation of powers, but the lack of capacity and resources leads one to believe that the establishment of these institutions and their efficient and effective functioning might have been difficult to be achieved in practice under the current circumstances. The lack of procurement expertise, qualified independent staff and financial resources are major hindrances in this regard, but have so far not been addressed in the reform process. The wide and comprehensive variety of functions and powers assigned to the Procurement Policy Office would require a well-organised and well-staffed institution whose constitution would need time and resources before being able to work effectively and efficiently. Moreover, the Minister of Finance would have been granted an extraordinary degree of power and allowing him to exert a great extent of influence by making him responsible for appointing key persons in key institutions and for determining key policies and regulations. The 2015 bill even extended the power of the Minister of Finance. The functions and powers assigned to the Procurement Policy Office were, though, assigned to a special unit in the Ministry of Finance which might be preferable with view to limited resources and capacity. Nevertheless, in the 2015 bill there is no independent monitoring and oversight institution as it would have existed under the 2013 bill. This is a severe detriment with view to the objectives of transparency and accountability.

Although there were several qualification requirements for public procurement officials and staff, the requirements basically remained vague and, hence, did not necessarily ensure that procurement officials and staff is adequately qualified for the job in question. Furthermore, the qualification procedures allowed for political appointments. The assignment of comprehensive functions in regard to capacity building in public procurement rested with the Procurement Policy Office, which might have been detrimental with respect to its own capacity to handle such matters. It might be suitable to outsource most of these functions to an external institution with the necessary expertise and experience. The document issued by the Tender Board in early 2015 reveals that the Board realised that qualified staff and training measures are key factors for the success of public procurement. This is an important step in the reform process but dedepends on immediate and effective implementation.

The procedures and methods provided for in the 2013 bill sufficed international best practices. The use of exemptions – that has been one of the major problems under the current Act – would have been sharply restricted. Although alternative methods were foreseen, they could have only been applied if certain requirements were met. With regard to the scope, the 2015 bill, however, constitutes a massive retrograde step as it allows for the granting of general and specific exemptions which has been identified as a severe shortcoming in the public procurement system applicable before the reform.

Although transparency has not been a core area of reform, the 2013 and the 2015 bill contained several transparency requirements that are not contemplated by the current Act. However, there are still requirements which are regarded as best practises and have not been integrated. A major point of criticism is that it is nearly impossible for tenderers but also the wider public to hold procurement officials accountable as a great part of information on procedures and decision-making is not accessible.

Moreover, apart from the organisational structure, the over-detailed rules might have caused confusion amongst procurement officials, staff members as well as other stakeholders of the procurement system and thereby hindered transparency. Priorities should be set in respect of the need for and importance of rules, requirements and provisions to make the public procurement system more transparent, easier to understand and implement.

Secondary policies, and in particular preferential treatment, play an important role under the 2013 and the 2015 bill and have been identified as one of the objectives of the public procurement system. This might have a detrimental effect on the achievement of other public procurement objectives such as cost-effectiveness, competition, fairness and equity. Moreover, it is necessary to reconsider the approach to preferential treatment under the 2013 and also the 2015 bill in order to establish sufficient safeguards to ensure that secondary objectives are only applied if they have a positive effect and for as long as needed.

Procurement planning as well as contract management, which have been identified as very important issues that require effective and efficient regulation in the Namibian public procurement system in order to avoid the occurrence of problems that have frequently occurred before the reform, had only been mentioned in the bills, not regulated in a proper and efficient way. The same applies to e-procurement, in particular the use of electronic means of communication and the establishment of a national procurement website, which had not been appropriately considered and implemented in the bill in light of the technical possibilities existing in Namibia. Despite general efforts to implement e-procurement, the 2013 did not reflect this endeavour and was not formulated in a way that allowed for a gradual implementation of e-procurement. The 2015 bill constitutes a slight improvement as it provides for the establishment of an online public procurement portal, however, without stating any details.

The review mechanisms established by the 2013 bill were encouraging. Moreover, the provision for effective instruments and remedies such as a standstill period or the halting of procurement procedures during challenges would have constituted a major improvement. Under the 2013 bill judicial review would have been only available as last resort and the difficulty of providing adequate review mechanisms accommodating the specific nature of public procurement had been addressed. Nevertheless, the fact that the Minister would have appointed the review panel members and that there were insufficient requirements in regard to the independence of the members as well as a vague description of qualification requirements would have significantly undermined the credibility, efficiency, effectiveness and independence of the review panel. Reconsideration in this respect would be urgently needed. The 2015 bill constitutes a retrograde step rather than an improvement with regard to review mechanism, for example because an internal review mechanism is not provided for, the scope is limited and no procedural rights are mentioned.

The enactment of the 2015 bill is likely as the parliament has passed the bill and it only requires assent by the president. Finally, the reform process would have produced a result – however, with regard to international best practices and the principles of public procurement, the result would be very unsatisfactory. Major problems of the current public procurement system would continue to exist. Not only the detection of corruption would still be difficult as basic transparency and accountability requirements have not been included into the bill but the allowance for exemptions would leave massive room for abuse. Moreover, the strong focus on preferential treatment without implementing appropriate safeguards for its application is of concern and the review procedures available, lacking an internal review mechanism, would not be adequate for public procurement challenges. Thus, despite the long reform process and the appearance that lessons learned during the process found consideration, the result is unsatisfactory.

It should finally be emphasised that many aspects that have been identified as essential for successful reform processes in this dissertation have not been complied with in Namibia. A stronger commitment to the manner of the reform process considering the essential aspects and strategy proposals made in this dissertation might have led to a different and more promising result. With regard to the substance of the new law, international best practices as defined in this dissertation have not been sufficiently considered and the request for a more transparent and accountable public procurement system has not been complied with.

*Chapter 4: Lessons Learned and Conclusion*

This chapter forms the closing part, including a conclusion of the major results from all different parts as well as an outline of the lessons learned from the Namibian case study. The conclusion also outlines recommendations for substantial issues that should be considered when drafting a new public procurement bill as well as for aspects that should be given special attention during reform processes. The lessons learned from Namibia are used to identify and highlight best practices for public procurement reform processes and initiatives.

## 1. Conclusion

The nature of public procurement, especially its complexity and the money and interests involved, pose specific problems for reform efforts. This applies particularly to developing countries where corruption is a major problem and resources and capacity are rare. Many countries have successfully enacted a new public procurement framework but whether it is effective and efficient will only be seen if implementation is measured. There is a general desire among developed and developing countries alike as well as international institutions to improve public procurement systems and to facilitate harmonisation. However, it has to be noted, there is a lack of will to renounce the application of preferential policies. The insistence on preferential policies, in particular by developing countries, is thus one reason for the low signature rate of the GPA.

The institutions and organisations concerned with public procurement include the World Bank, the OECD, the Commonwealth, UNCITRAL, the African Development Bank, COMESA and many more. Several instruments exist that can be used when developing and implementing public procurement reforms. These include manuals for the assessment of public procurement systems and frameworks, best practices, reform guides, etc. This enormously facilitates domestic reform efforts as well as harmonisation. Because public procurement law has, in contrast to other fields of law, only recently developed as distinct area of law and the provisions are not deeply rooted in society, the consideration of international and foreign approaches or the use of comparative law is easier than in other fields. There are certainly international best practices that should be followed. However, it is very important to find approaches that are suitable to the country's specific situation in order to ensure that the public procurement system turns out to be efficient and effective. Special consideration has to be given to the administrative, legal and economic structure and framework of the respective countries. A public procurement framework has to be integrated into the wider public sector environment. Only a holistic approach can be successful.

Regional approaches such as by COMESA might have several benefits including harmonisation, facilitation of trade between the member states, increased availability of resources and capacity. The exchange of experiences and personnel might also be beneficial.

In the recent decades approaches to public procurement have changed from a purely administrative approach to one which acknowledges the specific nature of public procurement, taking also the particular financial, economic, and managerial aspects into account. There has been a shift towards strategic approaches and towards measuring the success of public procurement according to the effectiveness of procurement outcomes rather than the procedures per se. However, in developing countries a lack of skills requires carefully balancing detailed, comprehensive regulation with enough flexibility to accommodate all possible procurement scenarios in the best possible way.

In many countries procurement has been decentralised from national tender boards to procuring entities within public bodies. Additional institutions have been established in order to give consideration to the specific nature and importance of public procurement for states and particularly for their development. The establishment of institutions responsible for monitoring and policy-making as well as an effective review mechanism is necessary to ensure a system of sufficient checks and balances, the achievement of the objectives of public procurement and to allow for a constant improvement of public procurement systems.

The lack of qualified procurement staff is a problem in many countries and in nearly all developing countries. This is due inter alia to the fact that public procurement has only been accepted as distinct field and as a profession in the last decades. In most developing countries it still has not been recognised as such, though. The creation of public procurement capacity should be one of the important elements of reform. It needs to be promoted with sufficient resources and energy as soon as possible at a very early stage in the reform process.

A public procurement framework with the widest scope possible should be designed. General exemptions should be avoided or be provided for in a very limited context and with detailed justification criteria. Open bidding as the primary procurement method should be complemented by a range of alternative procurement methods. It is necessary to grant enough flexibility to accommodate all possible procurements but the scope for abuse through the choice of procurement methods should be restricted as much as possible. What method can be used under what circumstances should be stipulated in the legislation and decisions to use an alternative procurement method might be made subject to review. The applicability of progressive and modern procurement methods should be considered and regulated according to the context of each country. E-procurement should be promoted but be introduced step by step according to the country's capacity to use electronic means in public procurement. The law should be designed flexibly enough to accommodate such technological progress and other developments in public procurement.

Transparency is one of the key objectives of public procurement systems and is more important than an overly complex regulation of the matter. The GPA and the UNCITRAL Model Law outline a comprehensive list of transparency standards whereas the Mauritian and the South African approach have some deficits in this respect. Considering the Model Law as the foundation is especially advantageous, since the Guide to Enactment provides comprehensive and extensive explanations and suggestions for the enactment of all provisions contained in the Model Law and might also be a basis for decisions to regulate certain matters differently. The whole public procurement process should be recorded and be available for inspection to the respective oversight authorities. All necessary information needs to be communicated to the tenderers and the public. Information should be made easily accessible. Tenderers should have the right to request reasons for procurement decisions.

A code of conduct for procurement officials is an important element in public procurement since there are several interests at stake and usually large amounts of money are involved. Any misconduct or corrupt activities of procurement officials or tenderers need to be sanctioned. Corruption cannot, however, be counteracted solely by stricter rules. A strong political will to condemn corruption, a change of attitude of the workforce and the business sector, and a civil society that scrutinises decisions are needed as well.

As mentioned above, overly complex regulations or a heavy-rules approach might limit the scope for corruption but it may also have severe negative effects on the efficiency and effectiveness of public procurement. A balance needs to be struck between flexibility and the limitation of discretion of public procurement officials. It is essential to consider the available capacity; more discretion requires better qualified and available staff members. Furthermore, it might be of great advantage to focus on outcomes rather than procedures when designing public procurement legislation. On the one hand, such design indeed requires staff qualified and experienced enough to take qualified decisions in regard to the outcome of procurement. Nevertheless, it can be an essential means to promote innovation and value for money. An example is the use of outcome-related or functionality criteria rather than product- or service-related criteria and design specification in tender specifications which allow bidders to hand in innovative bid proposals. Innovation can, for example, also be promoted by negotiations or dialogue as in two stage or competitive dialogue procedures.

The pursuit of secondary objectives in public procurement has been the subject of extensive debates about its validity and effectiveness. Several developing countries put a special emphasis on preferential procurement to promote their local economy. Other secondary objectives such as the pursuance of environmental goals through public procurement so far do not play a major role in developing countries. It should in any case be carefully assessed whether objectives cannot be better achieved by other means and whether the quality of the public procurement outcome is adversely affected. If secondary objectives are applied, they should be constantly reviewed for their validity and effectiveness and adapted or modified accordingly. It is generally recommendable to require that all secondary objectives have a basis in policies or regulations made by the responsible institution and that they be applied in a transparent manner. It is also strongly recommended to mark all secondary policies as transitional measures so as to be able to stop their application as soon as they are no longer needed or have been identified as inefficient.

The inclusion of contract conditions to respect certain labour or other standards should be considered as an important means to set an example for best practices in this respect. In particular, in countries where law enforcement is weak, this approach can be an effective instrument to ensure adherence to national rules and standards. Monitoring of adherence to such conditions as well as sanctioning of violations is, however, of the utmost importance to make such conditions effective. The effective and efficient regulation of contract management plays a key role in this respect and, in particular, issues such as the allocation of responsibilities for contract management should be addressed.

In contrast to a general administrative review mechanism, a public procurement review mechanism requires a specific approach. Timeframes, remedies and accessibility need to be attuned to the nature of public procurement. A standstill period after the notice of the tender award but before the conclusion of a contract should be provided to allow unsatisfied bidders to complain to the procuring entity or another institution responsible for such reviews. An independent review panel should be established consisting of independent members with the necessary qualifications in public procurement law to hear public procurement complaints in a timely manner. Such an institution needs to have the necessary powers to prevent the procuring entity from rushing into a contract. It is also of the utmost importance to grant basic procedural rights to the complainant and to ensure that the process follows certain transparency standards. The provision of an internal/administrative review mechanism is recommendable in order to create the possibility to defuse allegations as quickly as possible and avoid litigation and corresponding time and costs. Judicial review can be of great importance but should only be available as a last resort after the exhaustion of all other remedies.

Public procurement reforms have often led to modern and up-to-date legislation. Unfortunately, there is a low success rate in implementing such legislation. This might indicate that reform processes need to be framed differently, with a stronger focus on aspects important for implementation. Moreover, in particular in developing countries there are several obstacles to reform which impede reform efforts and, therefore, have to be considered and addressed during the reform process. There are certainly best practices and general phases that should be followed when conducting public procurement reforms. The details of the execution during these phases, however, differ and execution needs to be adapted to the local circumstances, e.g. the availability of resources and capacity, state of governance, legal and economic environment, etc.

In developing countries several shortcomings such as a lack of public procurement expertise hinder the effective implementation of reform. The Namibian example shows that public procurement expertise, which is rare in developed countries, is even scarcer in developing countries. Establishing a team of external and internal experts to work together with national public procurement officials to analyse the existing law, its strengths and weaknesses and prepare a new law/system is a key factor for successful reform. This should be the first step after the decision to reform public procurement law.

After assessing the current system to identify strengths and weaknesses it is essential to outline a clear reform strategy, to make a budget plan, to allocate responsibilities, to set deadlines, and to formulate the objectives of reform. Reform drivers should be involved in the reform process in a transparent way. The stakeholders of public procurement should be involved right from the beginning of the reform process. This is important not only in regard to the success in enacting legislation to accommodate the particular situation within the country but also to create ownership and acceptance of the new system.

People and institutions that have an interest in keeping the status quo and oppose any reform efforts should not be responsible for the reform in any way; however, a strategy to overcome the inevitable opposition and include these parties is nonetheless important. Likewise, the reform strategy should include elements sufficient to overcome other identified hindrances to reform. This is of specific importance in order to give consideration to the complexity of public procurement and to counter political opposition to reform progress. Last but not least, the institution responsible for the reform should be independent from the institutions carrying out day-to-day procurement.

## 2. Lessons Learned

The assessment of the Namibian public procurement system and reform process has disclosed many shortcomings which can be used as examples for other public procurement reform processes.

It has not only become obvious during the field research in Namibia that the powers and responsibilities need to be clearly assigned, but also that there needs to be a clear separation of powers and responsibilities in order to prevent corruption. The evaluators should be independent from the people directly involved in the procurement matter (e.g. special units within the ministries) and there needs to be an external monitoring of procurement decisions in order to avoid any kind of exertion of influence on the decisions motivated by reasons other than the pursuit of the procurement objectives.

It has also become apparent that the decentralisation of public procurement and an institutional restructuring along the lines - as implemented in many public procurement systems in the recent years - is also urgently needed in Namibia. Although it is clear that there needs to be an effective institution with oversight responsibilities, staffed with qualified and independent personnel, public procurement decisions might be taken more efficiently and effectively by a special unit in the procuring entities, providing such unit possesses the relevant knowledge and experience of public procurement in general as well as in the specific procurement matter. The development of procurement expertise and capacity is therefore important as are the recognition of public procurement as a profession and the provision of well-defined career-paths.

The analysis of the scope of application of the Namibian law, which allows for general exemptions that are not bound to any specific criteria and have severely undermined the transparency and the effectiveness of the public procurement system, reveals that the scope of application needs to be as extensive as possible. The provision for alternative procurement methods for all possible scenarios is preferable to exemptions which allow public procurement to take place in a legal limbo in a non-transparent way.

A public procurement law needs to be designed in a way that does not leave room for non-transparent and corrupt practices or other kinds of abuse. Therefore, transparency in all procurement stages is essential. Moreover, effective oversight mechanisms need to be created. A general oversight mechanism might be overburdened with procurement cases, so it may be a better solution to establish a specific procurement oversight body. This, however, needs to be decided according to the particular local context. Additionally, it is strictly advisable to establish an independent review panel and the possibility for administrative review as judicial review alone is not suitable for the specific nature of public procurement cases. Nevertheless, as the Namibian example has shown, courts have an important function in developing and interpreting the law through their judgments.

The objective of supporting the national economy and certain groups in society should not lead to the introduction of unchallenged and unlimited preferential treatment. The possibility of applying preferential treatment existed in the Namibian public procurement system before the reform, but it was found that the approach did not to lead to the expected results. However, the reasons for the failure to achieve the objectives were not investigated. It seems that the general suitability of preferential treatment to achieve the envisaged objectives was not questioned during the reform and led to the inclusion of preferential treatment provisions without ensuring that their effectiveness is constantly reviewed and without earmarking them as transitional measures. This can have a negative impact on competition and value for money as well as restrain national companies from becoming competitive in the foreign market in the long run. Additionally, strong political interest groups might counteract any attempt to limit preferential treatment in the future, which might make it hard to create a level playing field when the time is ripe.

The assessment of the Namibian procurement system has disclosed that new legislation has to include the regulation of contract management. This is a key instrument to ensure successful contract implementation and the adherence to the laws of a country. It is not only important for the reliance on the rule of law by potential tenderers, investors, companies and other stakeholders but in a wider sense for socio-economic development, too. Likewise, there should be requirements to outline and publish annual procurements plans. In Namibia, a large number of exemptions were granted at the end of the financial year because the money needed to be spent urgently. This is unsatisfactory and contrary to the principles of public procurement. Hence, public procurement planning should be regulated in a proper way – this includes the requirement for all public bodies and the Tender Board to provide and publish annual public procurement plans, specific content requirements thereto and the allocation of responsibilities to review these plans by a qualified institution.

As the Namibian case study discloses, although implementation is indeed of the utmost importance, if the existing law has too many loopholes only a new law can foster a radical improvement of the situation. Deficient public procurement legislation such as in Namibia has a severe negative effect on socio-economic development. A reform is hence urgently needed. However, the operation of the reform process with the aim to adopt a new law is of particular relevance for the success of new legislation and its implementation. Simply replacing one deficient act with a modern and up-to-date piece of legislation is not enough for a successful reform outcome. In order for a public procurement system that does not reveal the same problems as the previous system, an assessment of the old system has to be carried out. Strengths and weaknesses need to be identified. The Namibian case study, furthermore, reveals that is necessary to clearly assign responsibilities and to commission qualified, experienced and unbiased experts with the reform. Nevertheless, it has to be ensured that an adequate proportion of those experts knows the local context. Additionally, the allocation of adequate resources and capacity is a key condition to carry out a public procurement reform successfully.

Namibia has had external assistance in the past few years of its reform process. It has shown that external involvement can accelerate and support domestic reform efforts; however, it should be ensured that local people are equally involved in the reform project. Otherwise there will be a lack of domestic context in the new legislation and a lack of ownership, too. The involvement of foreign actors should be treated as transparently as possible to counteract a rejection of the new law as a product being imposed by foreign actors.

The Namibian example further reveals that it is essential to do comprehensive and substantive research on public procurement. Other legal systems and especially international best practices should be looked at. Yet it is also important not to be led by subjective motivations in the choice of other legal systems as models. In Namibia, apart from the Mauritian law, the UNCITRAL Model Law should have been carefully studied; it could have served as a benchmark for Namibian best practices. The UNCITRAL Model Law is, in particular after its revision, an up-to-date model of public procurement legislation. The Guide to Enactment offers the possibility to understand the rationales behind the law and help to adapt the model provisions to the national context. Furthermore, the GPA can be consulted in reform processes in view of a possible future accession and, for example, in regard to best practices such as transparency requirements. In Namibia, the South African approach should have been considered in regard to its approach to affirmative action in procurement as well as the integration of the public procurement system with financial management. Countries with similar problems and a common history that have recently reformed their procurements system might provide the opportunity to identify certain approaches suitable in the local context but might also provide clues as to the shortfalls that might accompany certain approaches. All provisions and approaches should be considered with regard to the local context instead of being adopted one to one.

A key result of the analysis of the Namibian reform process is that transparency and the inclusion of stakeholders already at an early stage of the reform are of the utmost importance to create ownership of the new law; this is the first step towards successful implementation of new public procurement legislation. For a successful reform process, consultation of stakeholders should be comprehensive, start at an early point of the reform process and be transparent. A lack of political will can only be overcome if the stakeholders are convinced of the advantages of the reform, understand the need for reform and no one is left behind.

In Namibia, the outcome of the reform process is a bill that leaves room for abuse and is not responsive to the problems identified in the public procurement system applicable prior to reform. This result indicates that the lack of political will has not been overcome but been persistent throughout the whole reform process. It should be emphasised again that the lack of political will can be a major hindrance to public procurement reform process and lead to an unsatisfactory outcome if not overcome during the reform process. In Namibia, in particular the resistance to change towards a more transparent and accountable public procurement system and the prevalence of the intention to keep the status quo have blocked the necessary changes. A public procurement system that allows for personal enrichment, nepotism and other forms of corruption could thus not be overcome. This leads to the question what can be done against these hindrances during reform processes. It can be assumed that, in Namibia, the allocation of responsibilities for the reform process to people who have no particular interest in keeping the status quo would have facilitated a more transparent reform process. Additionally, a stronger involvement of stakeholders and a deeper consideration of international best practices would have been key factors to overcome the lack of political will and led to a different and more satisfactory outcome of the reform process.

# References

## *Bibliography*


Adjei, A.B., 'Sustainable Public Procurement: A New Approach to Good Governance', 4th International Public Procurement Conference, Seoul, South Korea, August 26-28, 2010

African National Congress, 'The Reconstruction and Development Programme - A policy framework', (Johannesburg: Umanyano Publications, 1994)

Agaba, E.; Shipman, N., 'Public Procurement in Developing Countries: The Ugandan Experience', in Piga, G.;Thai, K. V., *Advancing Public Procurement: Practices, Innovation and Knowledge-Sharing* (Boca Raton, US: PrAcademics Press, 2007)

Amoo, S.K.; Dicken, S., 'The regulatory framework for public procurement in Namibia', in Quinot, G.;Arrowsmith, S., *Public Procurement Regulations in Africa* (Cambridge et al.: Cambridge University Press, 2013)

Anderson, R.D., 'The conclusion of the renegotiation of the World Trade Organization Agreement on Government Procurement: what it means for the Agreement and for the world economy' (2012) 3 Public Procurement Law Review, 83-94

Anderson, R.D.; Arrowsmith, S., 'The WTO regime on government procurement: past, present and future', in Arrowsmith, S.;Anderson, R. D., *The WTO Regime on Government Procurement: Challenge and Reform* (Cambridge: Cambridge University Press, 2011),

Anderson, R.D.; Kovacic, W.E.; Müller, A.C., 'Ensuring integrity and competition in public procurement markets: a dual challenge for good governance', in Arrowsmith, S.;Anderson, R. D., *The WTO Regime on Government Procurement: Challenge and Reform* (Cambridge: Cambridge University Press, 2011)

Anderson, R.D.; Müller, A.C.; Osei-Lah, K.; Pelletier, P., 'Assessing the value of future accessions to the WTO Agreement on Government Procurement: some new data sources, provisional estimates, and an evaluative framework for WTO members considering accession' (2012) 4 Public Procurement Law Review, 113-138

Anderson, R.D.; Osei-Lah, K., 'The coverage negotiations under the Agreement on Government Procurement: context, mandate, process and prospects', in Arrowsmith, S.;Anderson, R. D., *The WTO Regime on Government Procurement: Challenge and Reform* (Cambridge: Cambridge University Press, 2011)

Anderson, R.D.; Osei-Lah, K., 'Forging a more global procurement market: issues concerning accessions to the Agreement on Government Procurement ', in Arrowsmith, S.;Anderson, R. D., *The WTO Regime on Government Procurement: Challenge and Reform* (Cambridge: Cambridge University Press, 2011)

Andrew, M., 'Accountability and Transparency; Preventing Corruption in Public Procurement: Oral Debriefing Concept', 4th International Public Procurement Conference, Seoul, South Korea, August 26-28, 2010

Anti-Corruption Commission, 'Annual Report 2011-2012', (Windhoek: Anti-Corruption Commission, 2012)

Anti-Corruption Commission, 'Annual Report 2012-2013', (Windhoek: Anti-Corruption Commission, 2013)

Arrowsmith, S., 'The conduct of open tendering procedures', in Arrowsmith, S., *Public Procurement Regulation: An Introduction* (Nottingham: EU Asia Inter University Network for Teaching and Research in Public Procurement, 2010)

Arrowsmith, S., 'Electronic Procurement and Electronic Reverse Auction', in Arrowsmith, S., *Public Procurement Regulation: An Introduction* (Nottingham: EU Asia Inter University Network for Teaching and Research in Public Procurement, 2010)

Arrowsmith, S., 'Government Procurement in the WTO ', (The Hague: Kluwer Law International, 2003)

Arrowsmith, S., 'The Law of Public and Utilities Procurement ', Volume 1: Regulation in the EU and the UK (London: Sweet & Maxwell, 2014), 3rd Edition

Arrowsmith, S., 'Public Procurement as an Instrument of Policy and the Impact of Market Liberalization' (1995) 111 Law Quarterly Review, 235-285

Arrowsmith, S., 'Public Procurement: An Appraisal of the UNCITRAL Model Law as a Global Standard' (2004) 53 International and Comparative Law Quarterly, 17-46

Arrowsmith, S., 'Public Procurement: Basic Concepts and the Coverage of Procurement Rules', in Arrowsmith, S., *Public Procurement Regulation: An Introduction* (Nottingham: EU Asia Inter University Network for Teaching and Research in Public Procurement, 2010)

Arrowsmith, S., 'Reviewing the GPA: The Role and Development of the Plurilateral Agreement after Doha' (2002) 5(4) Journal of International Economic Law, 761-790

Arrowsmith, S., 'The Revised Agreement on Government Procurement: changes to the procedural rules and other transparency provisions', in Arrowsmith, S.;Anderson, R. D., *The WTO Regime on Government Procurement: Challenge and Reform* (Cambridge: Cambridge University Press, 2011)

Arrowsmith, S., 'Supplier lists and framework agreements', in Arrowsmith, S., *Public Procurement Regulation: An Introduction* (Nottingham: EU Asia Inter University Network for Teaching and Research in Public Procurement, 2010)

Arrowsmith, S., 'Towards a Multilateral Agreement on Transparency in Government Procurement' (1998) 47 International and Comparative Law Quarterly, 793-816

Arrowsmith, S.; Anderson, R.D., 'The WTO Regime on Government Procurement: Challenge and Reform', (Cambridge: Cambridge University Press, 2011,

Arrowsmith, S.; Linarelli, J.; Wallace, D., 'The Regulation of Public Procurement: National and International Perspectives', (Deventer: Kluwer Law International, 2000)

Baldwin, R.E.; Richardson, J.D., 'Government Purchasing Policies, Other NTB's, and the International Monetary Crisis', in English, H. E.;Hay, K. A. J., *Obstacles to Trade in the Pacific Area: Proceedings of the Fourth Pacific Trade and Develop-*

*ment Conference* (Ottawa: School of International Affairs, Carleton University, 1972)

Barnard, C., "British Jobs for British Workers': The Lindsey Oil Refinery Dispute and the Future of Local Labour Clauses in an Integrated EU Market' (2009) 38(3) Industrial Law Journal, 245-277

Barnard, C., 'Using Procurement Law to Enforce Labour Standards', in Davidov, G.;Langille, B., *The Idea of Labour Law* (Oxford: Oxford University Press, 2011)

Basheka, B.C., 'Procurement Planning and Accountability of Local Government Procurement Systems in Developing Countries: Evidence from Uganda' (2008) 8(3) Journal of Public Procurement, 379-406

Basheka, B.C., 'Public Procurement Reforms in Africa: A Tool for Effective Governance of the Public Sector and Poverty Reduction', in Thai, K. V., *International Handbook of Public Procurement* (Boca Raton, Florida: Taylor & Francis Group, 2009)

Beckhard, R.; Harris, R.T., 'Organizational Transitions: Managing Complex Change', (Reading, Massachusetts Addison-Wesley Pub. Co., 1987)

Bertelsmann Foundation, 'BTI 2014 - Namibian Country Report', (Gütersloh: Bertelsmann Foundation 2014)

Bolton, P., 'Government Procurement as a Policy Tool in South Africa' (2006) 6(3) Journal of Public Procurement, 193-217

Bolton, P., 'The Law of Government Procurement in South Africa', (South Africa: Lexis Nexis Butterworths, 2007)

Bolton, P., 'Overview of the Government Procurement System in South Africa', in Thai, K. V., *International Handbook of Public Procurement* (New York: CRC Press, Taylor and Francis Group, 2008)

Bolton, P., 'The regulatory framework for public procurement in South Africa', in Quinot, G.;Arrowsmith, S., *Public Procurement Regulations in Africa* (Cambridge et al.: Cambridge University Press, 2013)

Bolton, P.; Quinot, G., 'Social policies in procurement and the Agreement on Government Procurement: a perspective from South Africa', in Arrowsmith, S.;Anderson, R. D., *The WTO Regime on Public Procurement: Challenges and Reform* (Cambridge: Cambridge University Press, 2011)

Bösl, A., 'Good Governance als Paradigma moderner Entwicklungspolitik - *Bad Governance und schwierige Partnerschaften: Herausforderungen des 21. Jahrhunderts*' (2007) 2/07 KAS-Auslandsinformationen, 6-34

Bovis, C.H., 'EU Public Procurement Law', (Cheltenham and Northampton Edward Elgar Publishing Ltd., 2013), 2nd Edition

Brännlund, R.; Lundberg, S.; Marklund, P.-O., 'Assessment of Green Public Procurement as a Policy Tool: Cost-efficiency and Competition Considerations', 4th International Public Procurement Conference, Seoul, South Korea, August 26-28, 2010

Buys, F.; Hallick, S., 'The effect of Chinese construction companies on the Namibian construction industry - *a construction and design team members' perspective*' (2010) 17(1) Acta Structilia, 1-24

Caborn, E.; Arrowsmith, S., 'Procurement methods in the public procurement systems of Africa', in Quinot, G.;Arrowsmith, S., *Public Procurement Regulation in Africa* (Cambridge et al.: Cambridge University Press, 2013)

Caldwell, N.; Bakker, E., 'Procurement Process in the Public Sector: An International Perspective', in Thai, K. V., *International Handbook of Public Procurement* (Boca Raton, Florida: Taylor & Francis Group, 2009)

Caldwell, N.; Walker, H.; Harland, C.; Knight, L.; Zehng, J., 'Promoting Competitive Markets: The Role of Public Procurement', in Thai, K. V.;al., e., *Challenges in Public Procurement: An International Perspective* (Boca Raton, FL, US: PrAcademics Press, 2004), Vol. 3

Callender, G.; McGuire, J., 'People in public procurement', in Knight, L.;Harland, C.;Telgen, J.;Thai, K. V.;Callender, G.;McKen, K., *Public Procurement: International cases and commentary* (London and New York: Routledge, 2007)

Callender, G.C.; Matthews, D., 'Economic Context of Public Procurement', in Thai, K. V., *International Handbook of Public Procurement* (Boca Raton, Florida: Taylor & Francis Group, 2009)

Carter, P.L.; Carter, J.R.; Monczka, R.M.; Slaight, T.H.; Swan, A.J., 'The Future of Purchasing and Supply: A Ten-Year Forecast' (2000) 36(1) The Journal of Supply Chain Management, 14-26

Cavill, S.; Sohail, M., 'Accountability Arrangements to Combat Corruption', 2007), available at http://www.dfid.gov.uk/r4d/PDF/Outputs/Regcomp/WEDC-corruption litrev.pdf (last accessed: 26 November 2015)

Centre for Chinese Studies, S.U., 'China's Interest and Activity in Africa's Constructrion and Infrastructure Sectors', (Centre for Chinese Studies, Stellenbosch University: 2008), available at www.ccs.org.za/.../DFID%203rd%20Edition.pdf (last accessed: 30 November 2015)

Chen, T.H., 'An Economic Approach to Public Procurement' (2008) 8(3) Journal of Public Procurement, 407-430

Choi, J.-W., 'A Study of the Role of Public Procurement - Can Public Procurement make Society better? ', International Public Procurement Conference, Seoul, South Korea, August 26-28, 2010

Cloete, F., 'e-Government Lessons from South Africa 2001-2011: Institutions, State of Progress and Measurement' (2012) 12 The African Journal of Information and Communication Issue, 128-142

Commission of the European Communities, 'Communication from the Commission to the European Parliament, The Council, The European Economic and Social Committee and the Committee of the Regions: Public procurement for a better environment, COM(2008) 400 final', (Commission of the European Communities: 2008), available at http://eur-lex.europa.eu/legal-content/EN/TXT/PDF/?uri=CELEX:5200 8DC0400&from=EN (last accessed: 30 November 2015)

Committee on Government Procurement, 'Adoption of the Results of the Negotiations under Article XXIV:7 of the Agreement on Government Procurement, following their Verification and Review, as required by the Ministerial Decision of 15 December 2011 (GPA/112), Paragraph 5 - Action Taken by the Parties to the WTO

Agreement on Government Procurement at a Formal Meeting of the Committee, at the Level of Geneva Heads of Delegations, on 30 March 2012 (GPA/113)', (WTO: 2012), available at http://docsonline.wto.org/imrd/directdoc.asp?DDFDocuments/t/PLURI/GPA/113.DOC (last accessed: 30 November 2015)

Committee on Government Procurement, '"The GPA Renegotiation: Time to Close the Deal" - Statement on Stocktaking and Future Work (Made a the the Informal Closing Session, 18 October 2011)', (WTO: 2011), available athttps://www.wto.org/english/news_e/news11_e/gpa_stat_18oct11_e.doc (last accessed: 30 November 2015)

Committee on Government Procurement, 'Ministerial-Level Meeting of the Committee on Government Procurement (GPA/112), 15 December 2011', (WTO: 2011), available at https://www.wto.org/english/tratop_e/gproc_e/overview_e.htm (last accessed: 30 November 2015)

Committee on Government Procurement, 'Report (2002) of the Committee on Government Procurement (GPA/73), 6 November 2002', (WTO: 2002), available at https://docsonline.wto.org/dol2fe/Pages/SS/DirectDoc.aspx?filename=t%3A%2Fpluri%2Fgpa%2F73.doc& (last accessed: 30 November 2015)

Committee on Government Procurement, 'Report of the Committee on Government Procurement (November 2005 - December 2006) (GPA/89), 11 December 2006', (WTO: 2006), available at https://docsonline.wto.org/dol2fe/Pages/FormerScriptedSearch/directdoc.aspx?DDFDocuments/t/PLURI/GPA/89.doc (last accessed: 30 November 2015)

Committee on Government Procurement, 'Revision of the Agreement on Government Procurement as at 13 December 2010 (GPA/W/313)', (WTO: 2010), available at https://docsonline.wto.org/dol2fe/Pages/FormerScriptedSearch/directdoc.aspx?DDFDocuments/t/PLURI/GPA/W313.doc (last accessed: 30 November 2015)

Corkin, L., 'The Lion's Share' (2007) icon review 11-14

Corruption Watch Namibia, 'Tender Board swamped by exemptions, reform urgently needed', (Corruption Watch Namibia: 2011), available at http://www.corruption-watch-namibia.com/tender-board.html (last accessed: 3 October 2012)

Croom, S.; Brandon, J., 'Key Issues in E-Procurement: Procurement Implementation and Operation in the Public Sector', in Thai, K. V., *International Handbook of Public Procurement* (Boca Raton, Florida: Taylor & Francis Group, 2009),

Dagbanja, D.N., 'The Law of Public Procurement in Ghana: Law, Policy and Practice', (Germany: LAP LAMBERT Academic Publishing 2011),

Davies, A., 'The national treatment and exceptions provisions of the Agreement on Government Procurement and the pursuit of horizontal policies', in Arrowsmith, S.;Anderson, R. D., *The WTO Regime on Public Procurement: Challenges and Reform* (Cambridge: Cambridge University Press, 2011)

Decision of the CONTRACTING PARTIES to GATT 1947 of 28 November 1979 on Differential and More Favourable Treatment, Reciprocity and Fuller Participation of Developing Countries (BISD 26S/203-205), 1979

Dekel, O.; Schurr, A., 'The Lower Bid Bias', 5th International Public Procurement Conference, Seattle, Washington, 15-17 August, 2012

Deltas, G.; Simon, E., 'Quantitative Estimates of the Effects of Preference Policies', in Hoekman, B. M.;Mavroidis, P. C., *Law and Policy in Public Purchasing: The WTO Agreement on Government Procurement* (Ann Arbor, MI: University of Michigan Press, 2000),

Department of Works Investigation Committee, 'Report on the Anomolies in the Evaluation and Awarding of Construction Tenders in General', Windhoek, 2005

Development Assistance Committee, 'Strengthening Procurement Capacities in Developing Countries - *Harmonising Donor Practices for Effective Aid Delivery*', (Paris: OECD, 2005),

Dischendorfer, M., 'The existence and development of multilateral rules on government procurement under the framework of the WTO' (2000) 9(1) Public Procurement Law Review, 1-38

Doha Ministerial Declaration, WT/MIN(01)/DEC/1, 20 November 2001, available at http://www.wto.org/english/thewto_e/minist_e/min01_e/mindecl_e.htm (last access: 21 October 2015)

Erridge, A.N., R., 'Public Procurement, Competition and Partnership' (1994) 1(3) European Journal of Purchasing and Supply Management, 169-179

European Commission, 'Modernising European public procurement to support growth and employment', (European Commission: 2011), available at http://europa.eu/rapid/pressReleasesAction.do?reference=IP/11/1580&format=HTML&aged=0&language=EN&guiLanguage=en (last accessed: 16 December 2015)

Evenett, S.J., 'Can Developing Countries Benefit from Negotiations on Transparency in Government Procurement in the Doha Round?, Task Force 9 (Open, Rule-Based Trading System) of the United Nations Millennium Project', 2003), available at https://www.alexandria.unisg.ch/Publikationen/Person/E/Simon_Evenett/22164 (last accessed: 30 November 2015)

Evenett, S.J., 'Is there a Case for New Multilateral Rules on Transparency in Government Procurement?', in Evenett, S. J., *The Singapore Issues and the World Trading System: The Road to Cancun and Beyond* (Switzerland: SECO, 2003)

Evenett, S.J., 'Multilateral Disciplines and Government Procurement', in English, P.;Hoekman, B. M.;Matto, A., *Development, Trade and the WTO* (Geneva: World Trade Organization, 2002)

Evenett, S.J.; Hoekman, B.M., 'International Cooperation and the Reform of Public Procurement Policies', (World Bank: 2005), available at http://elibrary.worldbank.org/doi/abs/10.1596/1813-9450-3720 (last accessed: 26 November 2015)

Evenett, S.J.; Hoekman, B.M., 'Introduction', in Evenett, S. J.;Hoekman, B.M., *The WTO and Government Procurement* (Cheltenham et al.: Edward Elgar Publishers, 2006),

Farelo, M.; Morris, C., 'The Status of E-government in South Africa', IST Africa Conference, Pretoria, South Africa 7-9 May, 2006

Fernandez-Martin, J.M.; Stehmann, O., 'Product Market Integration versus Regional Cohesion in the Community' (1991) 16 European Law Review, 216-243

Francois, J.; McQueen, M.; Wignaraja, G., 'European Union–Developing Country FTAs: Overview and Analysis' (2005) 33(10) World Development, 1545-1565

Gaedtke, J.-C., 'Politische Auftragsvergabe und Welthandelsrecht', Tübinger Schriften zum internationalen und europäischen Recht - Band 81 (Berlin: Duncker & Humboldt, 2006)

García, R.H., 'Introduction: the global challenges of international public procurement', in García, R. H., *International Public Procurement* (London: Lobe Business Publishing Ltd., 2009)

Garenal, F., 'Public E-Procurement - Define, Measure and Optimize Organizational Benefits. ', 5th International Public Procurement Conference, Seoul, South Korea, August 26-28, 2010

Gimeno-Feliú, J.M., 'Towards Efficiency in Public Procurement: Simplifying Procedures and Reducing Administrative Burden', 5th International Conference on Public Procurement Seattle, Washington, 15-17th August, 2012

Glinz, C., 'Verwaltungsrecht und Rechtsstaatlichkeit in Namibia - *Ein entwicklungspolitisches Reformprojekt*', Recht und Verfassung in Afrika (Baden-Baden Nomos, 2013)

Government of the Republic of Namibia, 'Namibia Vision 2030', Policy Framework for Long-Term National Development (Summary) (Windhoek: Office of the President, 2004)

Government of the Republic of South Africa, 'Implementation Manual on the Use of Targeted Procurement to Implement and Affirmative Procurement Policy', 2001

Government of the Republic of South Africa (Economic Development Department), 'New Growth Path: Accord 3 - Local Procurement Accord', (Government of the Republic of South Africa: 2011), available at http://www.gov.za/sites/www.gov.za /files/Accord_Procure_3.pdf (last accessed: 30 November 2015)

Government of the Republic of South Africa (Economic Development Department), 'The New Growth Path: The Framework', (Government of the Republic of South Africa: 2010), available at http://www.economic.gov.za/communications/publicatio ns/new-growth-path-series/download (last accessed: 30 November 2015)

Greenwood, M.; Klotz, J.M., 'The fight against corruption in public procurement:an introduction to best practices', in García, R. H., *International Public Procurement* (London: Globe Business Publishing Ltd., 2009)

Gribben, C.; Pinnington, K.; Wilson, A., 'Government as Partners', (Copenhagen: The Copenhagen Center, 2001)

Gruppen, M.J., 'The Procurement Ombudsman: An Effective National Procurement Mechanism? - Enhancing the Accountability of Procuring entities', 4th International Public Procurement Conference, Seoul, South Korea, August 26-28, 2010

Hargeskog, S.-E., 'Specification, Evaluation and Verification Realising Public Procurement for Innovation', 4th International Public Procurement Conference, Seoul, South Korea, 26-28 August, 2010

Heeks, R., 'Information Systems and Public Sector Accountability', Information Systems for Public Sector Management - Working Paper Series, Paper No. 1 (Manchester: Institute for Development Policy and Management, 1998)

Henrich, G.; Truong, V., 'Das Ende der "Charme-Offensive"? - Der Widerstand kleiner Länder in Südostasien und Afrika gegen die Hegemonialherrschaft Chinas ', (IMS Internationales Magazin für Sicherheit: available at http://www.ims-magazin.de/index.php?p=artikel&id=1330677610,1,gastautor (last accessed: 3 October 2012)

Hinz, M.; Schmidt, A. and Mapaure, C. , 'Namibia', In International Encyclopaedia of Laws: Constitutional Law, edited by Alen, A.; Haljan, D. (Alphen aan den Rijn, NL: Kluwer Law International, 2016)

Hoekman, B.M.; Mavroidis, P.C., 'Basic Elements of the Agreement on Government Procurement', in Hoekman, B. M.;Mavroidis, P. C., *Law and policy in public purchasing: the WTO agreement on government procurement* (Ann Arbor: University of Michigan Press, 1997)

Hoexter, C., 'Administrative Law in South Africa', (Claremont: Juta & Co, 2012), 2nd Edition

Hopwood, G., 'Comments on the Public Procurement Bill - September 2012', (Windhoek: Institute for Public Policy Research, 2012)

Hunja, R.R., 'Obstacles to Public Procurement Reform in Developing Countries', in Arrowsmith, S.;Trybus, M., *Public Procurement : The Continuing Revolution* (The Hague, The Netherlands: Kluwer Law International, 2003)

IMF, 'Namibia: Report on Observance of Standards and Codes - Fiscal Transparency Module; IMF Country Report No. 08/184, 2008' (Washington, D.C.)

Ismahel, B.A., 'International Competitiveness: Government Policy and the Development of Competitive Industries', 4th International Public Procurement Conference, Seoul, South Korea, August 26-28, 2010

Jauch, H., 'Affirmative Action in Namibia - *Redressing the Imbalances of the Past?* ', (Windhoek: New Namibia Books, 1998)

Jauch, H., 'Chinese Investments in Africa - Twenty-First Century Colonialism?' (2011) 20(2) New Labor Forum, 49-55

Jauch, H., 'Poverty, Unemployment and Inequality in Namibia, TEMTI Series of Economic Perspectives on Global Sustainability, EP 02-2013', (Theme On The Environment, Macroeconomics, Trade And Investment (TEMTI) / International Union for the Conservation of Nature (IUCN) / Commission on Environmental, Economic and Social Policies (CEESP): 2012), available at https://cmsdata.iucn.org/.../temti_ep_02_2013.pdf (last accessed: 26th November 2015)

Jauch, H.; Sakaria, I., 'Chinese investments in Namibia', in Baah, A. Y.;Jauch, H., *Chinese Investments in Africa - A Labour Perspective* (Accra: African Labour Research Network, 2009)

Jiang, L., 'Developing multilateral rules on government procurement: the value of soft law', in Arrowsmith, S.;Anderson, R. D., *The WTO Regime on Government Procurement: Challenge and Reform* (Cambridge: Cambridge University Press, 2011)

Jiang, L., 'Regulating Public Procurement in International Trade', in Arrowsmith, S., *Public Procurement Regulation: An Introduction* (Nottingham: EU Asia Inter University Network for Teaching and Research in Public Procurement, 2010)

Karangizi, S., 'Regional Procurement Reform Initiative', (Dar es Salaam: COMESA, 2003)

Karangizi, S.; Ndahiro, I., 'Public procurement reforms and development in the Eastern and Southern African region', in García, R. H., *International Public Procurement: A Guide to Best Practices* (London: Globe Business Publishing Ltd., 2009)

Kelman, S., 'Procurement - A Time for Statesmanship' (2004) 18(26) Federal Computer Week

Kerry McNamara Architects Inc.; Philip Main Quantity Surveyor 'New Headquarters for the Ministry of Lands and Resettlement in Windhoek, Tender No. F1/10/1 - 08/2007, Evaluation of Tenders and Recommendation' (unpublished)

Kerry McNamara, 'Chinese Contractors: Namibian Economist 05.10.2007' (unpublished letter to the Economist)

Kimani, N.H., 'The Influence of Political Patronage on the Operationalization of Public Procurement Law in Kenya', 5th International Public Procurement Conference, Seattle, Washington, 15-17 August, 2012

Klare, K., 'Legal Culture and Transformative Constitutionalism ' (1998) 14 South African Journal of Human Rights, 146-188

Knight, L.; Harland, C.; Telgen, J.; Caldwell, N., 'Public Procurement: An Introduction', in Knight, L.;Harland, C.;Telgen, J.;Thai, K. V.;Callender, G.;McKen, K., *Public Procurement: International cases and commentary* (London and New York: Routledge, 2007)

Knight, L.; Harland, C.; Telgen, J.; Thai, K.V.; Callender, G.; McKen, K., 'Public Procurement: International cases and commentary' (London and New York: Routledge, 2007)

Koch, J.; Kullas, M., 'EU-Grünbuch - Öffentliches Auftragswesen', (Centrum für Europäische Politik: 2011), available at http://www.cep.eu/Analysen_KOM/KOM_2011_15_OEffentliches_Auftragswesen/cepAnalyse_KOM_2011_15_OEffentliches_Auftragswesen.pdf (last accessed: 3 October 2012)

Korkmaz, A., 'Benefits and Obstacles of Environmental Social and Sustainable Procurement', 4th International Public Procurement Conference, Seoul, South Korea, August 26-28, 2010

Kostyo, K., 'Handbook for Curbing Corruption in Public Procurement', (Berlin: Transparency International 2006)

Kumar, R.A.; Caborn, E., 'The regulatory framework for public procurement in Botswana', in Quinot, G.;Arrowsmith, S., *Public Procurement Regulations in Africa* (Cambridge et al. : Cambridge University Press, 2013)

Kunnert, G., 'WTO-Vergaberecht: Genese und System sowie Einwirkungen auf das EG-Vergaberegime ', (Baden-Baden: Nomos, 1998)

La Chimia, A., 'Donors' influence on developing countries' procurement sysetms, rules and markets: a critical analysis', in Quinot, G.;Arrowsmith, S., *Public Procurement Regulation in Africa* (Cambridge et al: Cambridge University Press, 2013)

Lando, O., 'The Contribution of Comparative Law to Law Reform by International Organziations' (1977) 25(4) American Journal of Comparative Law, 641-657

Lawther, W.C.; Martin, L.L., 'Public Procurement Partnerships', in Thai, K. V. e. a., *Challenges in Public Procurement: An International Perspective* (Boca Raton, FL, US: PrAcademics Press, 2004)

Linarelli, J., 'Global procurement law in times of crisis: new Buy American policies and options in the WTO legal system', in Arrowsmith, S.;Anderson, R. D., *The WTO Regime on Government Procurement: Challenge and Reform* (Cambridge: Cambridge University Press, 2011)

Linarelli, J., 'The limited case for permitting SME procurement preferences in the Agreement on Government Procurement', in Arrowsmith, S.;Anderson, R. D., *The WTO Regime on Public Procurement: Challenges and Reform* (Cambridge: Cambridge University Press, 2011)

Linarelli, J., 'The WTO Transparency Agenda: Law, Economics and International Relations Theory', in Arrowsmith, S.;Trybus, M., *Public Procurement: The Continuing Revolution* (The Hague, Netherlands: Kluwer Law International, 2003)

Links, F., 'Corruption Prevention: Strengthening Systems, Procedures and Practices', Occasional Paper No. 6/2010 (Hanns Seidel Foundation Namibia: 2010), available at http://www.hss.de/fileadmin/namibia/downloads/FredericoLinks_CorruptionPrevention.pdf (last accessed: 29 November 2015)

Links, F., 'The Public Procurement Bill: A lot of Good some significant Bad, but certainly not Ugly'; Democracy Report, Special Briefing Report No. 9 (Windhoek: Institute for Public Policy Research, 2015)

Links, F.; Daniels, C., 'The Tender Board - Need for Root and Branch Reform', Anti-Corruption Research Programme, Paper 3 (Institute for Public Policy Research: 2011), available at http://www.az.com.na/fileadmin/pdf/2011/az/IPPR-09-12-11.pdf (last accessed: 29 November 2015)

Links, F.; Daniels, C., 'The Tender Board - Need for Root and Branch Reform; Appendix I - Interview with Tender Board Secretary Welma Enssle', (Institute for Public Policy Research: 2011), available at http://www.az.com.na/fileadmin/pdf/2011/az/IPPR-09-12-11.pdf (last accessed: 29 November 2015)

Lo, C.-F., 'The benefits for developing countries of accession to the Agreement on Government Procurement: the case of Chinese Taipei', in Arrowsmith, S.;Anderson, R. D., *The WTO Regine on Government Procurement: Challenge and Reform* (Cambridge: Cambridge University Press, 2011)

Lundberg, S.; Marklund, P.-O.; Strömbäck, E., 'Objective Effectiveness of Green Public Procurement', 5th International Public Procurement Conference, Seattle, Washington, 15-17 August, 2012

Mamiro, R.G., 'Value for Money, the Limping Pillar in Public Procurement - Experience from Tanzania', 4th International Conference on Public Procurement, Seoul, South Korea, August 26-28, 2010

Mampuzhasseril, M.; Kumbi, G.E.; Tan, M.H., 'COMESA Public Procurement Reform and Capacity Building Projects: Project Performance Evaluation Report' (Tunis: Operations Evaluation Department (African Development Bank Group), 2012)

Manchidi, T.E.; Harmond, I., 'Targeted Procurement in the Republic of South Africa - An Independent Assessment', (South Africa: Department of Public Works (Republic of South Africa), International Labour Organisation, Development Bank of Southern Africa 2002)

Mattei, U., 'Efficiency in Legal Transplants: An Essay in Comparative Law and Economics' (1994) 14 International Review of Law and Economics, 3-19

Mattoo, A., 'The Government Procurement Agreement: Implications of Economic Theory' (1996) 19(6) World Economy, 695-720

McAfee, R.P.; McMillan, J., 'Government Procurement and International Trade' (1989) 26 Journal of International Economics, 291-308

McCrudden, C., 'Buying Social Justice - *Equality, Government Procurement, and Legal Change*', (New York: Oxford University Press, 2007)

McCrudden, C., 'Public Procurement and Equal Opportunities in the European Community ', A study of contract compliance in member states of the European Community under European Community Law, Contract File No. SOC 9310257105B04 (Oxford: Oxford University 1995),

McCrudden, C., 'Using public procurement to achieve social outcomes' (2004) 28 National Resources Forum, 257-267

McCue, C.P., 'Centralized vs. decentralized purchasing: Current trends in governmental procuremen practices' (2000) 12(3) Journal of Public Budgeting

Messerlin, P.A., 'Agreement on Public Procurement', in OECD, *The New Wold Trading System: Reading* (Paris: 1995)

Migiro, S.O., 'SMEs and Black Economic Empowerment in the Construction Industry: The Case of Gauteng Provincial Housing Department', 4th International Public Procurement Conference, Seoul, South Korea, August 26-28, 2010

Ministry of Finance, 'Supply and Delivery of Clothing Material for the Namibian Correctional Service for the Period 01 April 2013 to 31 March 2015: Ministry of Safety and Security', (Windhoek: Tender Board of Namibia, 2013)

Ministry of Finance and Economic Development, 'White Paper On Modernising the Public Procurement Framework - Issues and Proposals for Consultation', (Ministry of Finance and Economic Development, Mauritius: 2011), available at http://www.govmu.org/portal/goc/pposite/WhitePaper8July2011.doc (last accessed: 30 November 2015)

Ministry of Finance/Ministry of Public Works, 'Green Paper on Public Sector Procurement Reform in South Africa, General Notice No. 691 of 1997', (Ministry of Finance/Ministry of Public Works, South Africa: 1997), available at http://www.gov.za/sites/www.gov.za/files/17928_gen691_0.pdf (last accessed: 30 November 2015)

Miyagiwa, K., 'Oligopoly and Discriminatory Government - *Procurement Policy*' (1991) 81(5) American Economic Review, 1320-1328

Mo Ibrahim Foundation, '2013 Ibrahim Index of African Governance - Summary', (Mo Ibrahim Foundation: 2013), available at http://www.afcgn.org/wp-content/uploads/2013/11/Ibrahim-Index-of-African-Governance-2013.pdf (last accessed: 30 November 2015)

Moon, M.J., 'E-Procurement Management in State Governments: Diffusion of E-Procurement Practices and Its Determinants', in Thai, K. V., *International Handbook of Public Procurement* (Boca Raton, Florida: Taylor & Francis Group, 2009)

Mosoti, V., 'Reforming the Laws on Public Procurement in the Developing World: The Example of Kenya' (2005) 54 International and Comparative Law Quarterly, 621-650

Müller, A.C., 'Special and differential treatment and other special measures for developing countries under the Agreement on Government Procurement: the current text and new provisions', in Arrowsmith, S.;Anderson, R. D., *The WTO Regime on Government Procurement: Challenges and Reform* (Cambridge Cambridge University Press, 2011)

Musila, J.W., 'The common market for Eastern and Southern Africa and Kenya's export trade' (2004) 31(1/2) International Journal of Social Economics, 67-77

Narasimhan, C.V., 'Prevention of Corruption: Towards Effective Enforcement', in Guhan, S.;Paul, S., *Corruption in India: Agenda for Action* (New Dehli: Vision Books, 1997)

National Planning Commission, 'Namibia's Fourth National Development Plan 2012/13 to 2016/17', (Windhoek: Office of the President, 2012)

National Planning Commission, 'Targeted Intervention Program for Employment and Economic Growth (TIPEEG)', (National Planning Commission, Namibia: 2011), available at http://www.npc.gov.na/publications/TIPEEG.pdf (last accessed: 30 November 2015)

National Treasury, 'Implementation Guide Preferential Procurement Regulations, 2001 (pertaining to the Preferential Procurement Policy Framework Act, 2000 (Act No. 5 of 2000))', 2001

National Treasury, 'National Treasury Instruction Note on Enhancing Compliance Monitoring and Improving Transparency and Accountability in Supply Chain Management', (National Treasury, South Africa: 2011), available at http://ocpo.treasury.gov.za/Resource_Centre/Legislation/20110531%20Instruction%20Note%20on%20Enhancing%20Compliance%20Monitoring%20SCM.pdf (last accessed: 30 November 2015)

National Treasury, 'National Treasury Strategic Plan 2004-2007', (National Treasury, South Africa: 2004), available at http://www.treasury.gov.za/publications/strategic%20plan/strat%20plan%202004%20to%202007.pdf (last accessed: 30 November 2015)

National Treasury, 'Policy Strategy to Guide Uniformity in Procurement Reform Processes in Government ', (National Treasury, South Africa: 2003), available at http://ocpo.treasury.gov.za/Resource_Centre/Legislation/policy.pdf (last accessed: 30 November 2015)

National Treasury, 'Practice Note Number 6 of 2007/2008: Procurement of Goods and Services by Means other than through the Invitiation of Competitive Bids', (National Treasury, South Africa: 2007), available at http://ocpo.treasury.gov.za/Resource_Centre/Legislation/Practice%20note%20SCM%206%20of%202007.pdf (last accessed: 30 November 2015)

National Treasury, 'Practice Note Number 8 of 2007/2008: Supply Chain Management: Threshold Values for the Procurement of Goods, Works and Services by Means of Petty Cash, Verbal/Written Price Quotations or Competitive Bids ', (National Treasury, South Africa: 2007), available at http://ocpo.treasury.gov.za/Resource_Centre/Legislation/Practice%20note%20SCM%208%20of%202007_8.pdf (last accessed: 30 November 2015)

National Treasury, 'Practice Note Number SCM 1 of 2003: General Conditions of Contract (GCC) and Standardized Bidding Documents (SBDs)', (National Treasury, South Africa: 2003), available at http://ocpo.treasury.gov.za/Resource_Centre/Legislation/SCM-PracNote%2003%201.pdf (last accessed: 30 November 2015)

National Treasury, 'Practice Note Number SCM 3 of 2003: Appointment of Consultants ', (National Treasury, South Africa: 2003), available at http://www.dedea.gov.za/Practice%20Notes/Practice%20note%20SCM%203%20of%202003%20Appointment%20of%20Consultants.pdf (last accessed: 30 November 2015)

National Treasury, 'Practice Note Number SCM 3 of 2005: 1. Projects and Services funded by Grandts in accordance with Technical Assistance Agreements / 2. Appointment of Transaction Advisors to assist with Public Private Parternships', (National Treasury, South Africa: 2005), available at http://ocpo.treasury.gov.za/Resource_Centre/Legislation/Practice%20Note%20SCM%203%20of%202005.pdf (last accessed: 30 November 2015)

National Treasury, 'Practice Note Number SCM 4 of 2003: Code of Conduct for Supply Chain Management Practitioners ', (National Treasury, South Africa: 2003), available at http://ocpo.treasury.gov.za/Resource_Centre/Legislation/SCM-PracNote%2003%204.pdf (last accessed: 30 November 2015)

National Treasury, 'Practice Note Number SCM 5 of 2004: Training of Supply Chain Management Officials', (National Treasury, South Africa: 2004), available at http://ocpo.treasury.gov.za/Resource_Centre/Legislation/SCM-PracNote%2004%205.pdf (last accessed: 30 November 2015)

National Treasury, 'Supply Chain Management - A Guide for Accounting Officers/Authorities ', (National Treasury, South Africa: 2004), available at www.treasury.gov.za/divisions/ocpo/sc/Guidelines/SCM%20Jan900-Guidelines.pdf (last accessed: 30 November 2015)

Nicholas, C., 'Policy Choices in the Implementation of Electronic Procurement: The Approach of the UNCITRAL Model Law on Procurement to Electronic Communications', 4th International Public Procurement Conference, Seoul, South Korea, 26-28 August, 2010

Nicholas, C., 'Work of UNCITRAL on government procurement: purpose, objectives and complementarity with the work of the WTO', in Arrowsmith, S.;Anderson, R. D., *The WTO Regime on Government Procurement: Challenge and Reform* (Cambridge: Cambridge University Press, 2011)

O'Linn, B., 'Namibia: The sacred trust of civilization', Ideal and reality. Volume II (Windhoek: Polination Publishers 2010)

Odendahl, K., 'Die Berücksichtigung vergabefremder Kriterien im öffentlichen Auftragswesen - *Rechtslage nach EG- und WTO-Recht* ' (2004) 21 Europäische Zeitschrift für Wirtschaftsrecht, 647-653

OECD, 'Aid Effectiveness 2005–10: Progress in implementing the Paris Declaration', (Paris: OECD, 2011)

OECD, 'Integrity in Public Procurement - Good Practice from A to Z', (Paris: OECD, 2007)

OECD, 'Methodology for Assessing Procurement Systems (MAPS)', (Paris: OECD, 2009)

OECD, 'OECD Principles for Integrity in Public Procurement', (Paris: OECD, 2009)

OECD, 'Recommendation of the Council on Improving the Environmental Performance of Public Procurement (C(2002)3 ), 23 January 2002', (Paris: OECD, 2002)

OECD, 'SIGMA Paper No. 30 - Public Procurement Review Procedures, CCNM/SIGMA/PUMA(2000)114', (OECD: 2000), available at http://www.oecd.org/officialdocuments/publicdisplaydocumentpdf/?doclanguage=en&cote=ccnm/sigma/puma(2000)114 (last accessed: 1 December 2015)

OECD Working Party on National Environmental Policies, 'Improving the Environmental Performance of Public Procurement: Report on Implementation of the Council Recommendation', ENV/EPOC/WPNEP(2006)6/FINAL (Paris: OECD, 2006)

OECD/DAC, 'ICT and Economic Growth: Evidence from OECD Countries, Industries and Firms', (Paris: OECD, 2004)

OECD/DAC Task Force on Procurement, 'The Cusco Declaration "Strong Procurement Systems for Effective States"', 2011), available at http://www.oecd.org/dac/effectiveness/48425963.pdf (last accessed: 1 December 2015)

Official Gazette of the Common Market for Southern and Eastern Africa, Vol. 15 No. 3 (9 June 2009)

The Second Meeting of the OECD/DAC Task Force on Procurement - Summary of meeting by the UN Procurement Capacity Development Centre, Cusco, Peru, 4th-6th May 2011

Palmujoki, A.; Parikka-Alhola, K.; Ekroos, A., 'Green Public Procurement: Analysis on the Use of Environmental Criteria in Contracts' (2010) 19(2) Review of European Community & International Environmental Law, 250-262

Parliament of the Republic of South Africa, 'Report of the Ad Hoc Committee on the Review of Chapter 9 and Associated Institutions - A report to the National Assembly of the Parliament of South Africa' (Cape Town: Parliament of the Republic of South Africa, 2007)

Personal email from Shuohua to Scheepers regarding: *Re: The faxes dated Mar 7, 2006* (Windhoek, 8 May 2006) (unpublished)

Pitschas, C.; Priess, H.-J., 'Secondary policy criteria and their compatibility with E.C. and WTO procurement law - *The case of the German Scientology Declaration*' (2000) 4 Public Procurement Law Review, 171-195

Pope, J., 'Confronting Corruption: The Elements of a National Integrity System, TI Source Book 2000', (Berlin/London: Transparency International, 2000)

2nd Joint OECD/DAC - World Bank Round Table on Strengthening Procurement Capacities in Developing Countires - Summary Report (DCD/DAC/EFF/M(2004)3), Kampala, Uganda, 2 April 2004

Priess, H.-J., 'Das Übereinkommen über das öffentliche Beschaffungswesen', in Pitschas, C.;Priess, H.-J., *WTO-Handbuch* (München: C.H. Beck, 2003)

Procurement Policy Office, 'Implementation of Budgetary Measures to promote SMEs participation in Public Procurement, Directive No. 5 (issued pursuant to Section 7 of the Public Procurement Act)', (Procurement Policy Office, Mauritius: 2012), available at http://ppo.govmu.org/English/Directives/Pages/Directives-2013.aspx (last accessed: 1 December 2015)

Procurement Policy Office, 'Implementation of e-Procurement - Launching of public procurement website, Directive No. 2 (issued pursuant to Section 7(b) of the Public Procurement Act)', (Procurement Policy Office, Mauritius: 2010), available at http://ppo.govmu.org/English/Directives/Pages/Directives-2013.aspx (last accessed: 1 December 2015)

Procurement Policy Office, 'Margin of Preference for Procurement of Works, Directive No 12 (issued pursuant to Section 7 of the Public Procurement Act)', (Procurement Policy Office, Mauritius: 2012), available at http://ppo.govmu.org/English/Directives/Pages/Directives-2013.aspx (last accessed: 1 December 2015)

Procurement Policy Office, 'Technical Specifications, Directive No 11 (issued pursuant to Section 7 of the Public Procurement Act)', (Procurement Policy Office, Mauritius: 2012), available at http://ppo.govmu.org/English/Directives/Pages/Directives -2013.aspx (last accessed: 1 December 2015)

Public Protector South Africa, 'Annual Report 2010/2011', 2011), available at http://www.pprotect.org/library/annual_report/PUBLIC%20PROTECTOR%20AR %20FINAL.pdf (last accessed: 1 December 2015)

Quinot, G., 'A comparative perspective on supplier remedies in African public procurement systems', in Quinot, G.;Arrowsmith, S., *Public Procurement Regulation in Africa* (Cambridge et al.: Cambridge University Press, 2013)

Quinot, G., 'Enforcement of procurement law from a South African perspective' (2011) 6 Public Procurement Law Review, 193-207

Quinot, G., 'Promotion of social policy through public procurement in Africa', in Quinot, G.;Arrowsmith, S., *Public Procurement Regulation in Africa* (Cambridge et al. : Cambridge University Press, 2013)

Quinot, G., 'Public Procurement - April to June 2008(2) - JQR Public Procurement 2008(2)', Juta's Quarterly Review of South African Law (JQR), 2008

Quinot, G., 'Public Procurement - April to June 2010(2) - JQR Public Procurement 2010(2)', Juta's Quarterly Review of South African Law (JQR), 2010

Quinot, G., 'Public Procurement - January to March 2008(1) - JQR Public Procurement 2008(1) ', Juta's Quarterly Review of South African Law (JQR), 2008

Quinot, G., 'State Commercial Activity - *A Legal Framework*', (Claremont: Juta & Co, 2009)

Quinot, G., 'Worse than Losing a Government Tender: Winning it' (2008) 19 Stellenbosch Law Review, 101-121

Quinot, G.; Arrowsmith, S., 'Introduction ', in Quinot, G.;Arrowsmith, S., *Public Procurement Regulation in Africa* (Cambridge et al.: Cambridge University Press, 2013)

Quinot, G.; Arrowsmith, S., 'Public Procurement Regulations in Africa ' (Cambridge et al.: Cambridge University Press, 2013)

Raga, K.; Taylor, J.D., 'Legislative and Administrative Directives governing Procurement Procedures: A Case Study for South Africa', 4th International Public Procurement Conference, Seoul, South Korea, August 26-28, 2010

Read, J.J.D., 'The Road to Hell is paved with Good Intentions', 4th International Public Procurement Conference, Seoul, South Korea, August 26-28, 2010

Records of the Fifth Commonwealth Public Procurement Network (CPPN) Technical Conference 5th Commonwealth Public Procurement Network Technical Conference, Windhoek, Namibia, 6th-8th December 2010, available at http://www.publicprocurement.gov.sl/files/Namibia_CPPN_Report.pdf (last accessed: 1 December 2015)

Reich, A., 'International Public Procurement Law - The Evolution of International regimes on Public Purchasing', Studies in Transnational Economic Law Volume 12 (London: Kluwer Law International 1999)

Reich, A., 'The New Text of the Agreement on Government Procurement: And Analysis and Assessment' (2009) 12(4) Journal of International and Economic Law, 989-1022

Report by the Comptroller and Auditor General, 'Addressing the environmental impacts of government procurement', HC 420 Session 2008-2009 (London: National Audit Office, 2009)

Rose-Ackermann, S., 'The Political Economy of Corruption', in Elliott, K. A., *Corruption and the Global Economy* (Washington: Institute for International Economics, 1997)

Rothery,R., 'Understanding Public Procurement', The Governance Brief, ADB, Issue 3 (Manila: Asian Development Bank 2000)

Ruppel-Schlichting, K., 'The independence of the Ombudsman in Namibia', in Horn, N.;Bösl, A., *The Independence of the Judiciary in Namibia* (Windhoek: Macmillan Education Namibia, 2008)

Sabbatini, M.S., '2nd (or, from a European Point of View, 3rd) Generation Procurement Law Reform: Principles and Underlying Policies', 5th International Public Procurement Conference, Seattle, Washington, 15-17 August 2012

Sabiiti, C.K.; Muhumuza, E., 'Second Generation Procurement. Moving from compliance to results in public procurement. Trends, challenges and opportunities from the Uganda experience', 5th International Public Procurement Conference, Seattle, Washington, 15-17 August 2012

Schapper, P.R.; Malta, J.N.V.; Gilbert, D.L., 'An Analytic Framework for the Management and Reform of Public Procurement' (2006) 6(1&3) Journal of Public Procurement, 1-26

Schmidt, A., 'The need to reform the Namibian public procurement system: A comment on the Neckartal Dam saga' (2014) 6(1) Namibia Law Journal, 41-50

Schmidt, A., 'Public Procurement – A Constitutional Perspective', forthcoming

Schwartz, J.I., 'Procurement as a Tool for Economic Stimulus: The United States' Experience, 2008-2010', 4th International Public Procurement Conference, Seoul, South Korea, August 26-28, 2010

Schwartz, J.I., 'Procurement in times of crisis: lessons from US government procurement in three episodes of 'crisis' in the twenty-first century', in Arrowsmith, S.;Anderson, R. D., *The WTO Regime on Government Procurement: Challenge and Reform* (Cambridge: Cambridge University Press, 2011)

Shezi, S., 'Public Sector Procurement as an Instrument of Government Policy', 9th International Public Procurement Association Conference, Copenhagen, Denmark, 8 June, 1998

SIGMA, 'Public Procurement Brief 22: Contract Management, Support for Improvement in Governance and Management - A joint initiative of the OECD and the EU', 2011), available at www.sigmaweb.org/publications/49102599.pdf (last accessed: 29 November 2015)

Silva, D.L.e., 'The revision of the WTO Agreement on Government Procurement: to what extent might it contribute to the expansion of current membership?' (2008) 2 Public Procurement Law Review, 61-98

Silva, J.R., 'Trade between asymmetrical democratic countries' (1999) 26(4/5) Journal of Economic Studies, 412-426

Sippel, H., 'Rechtsrezeption in Namibia - *Prozesse direkter und indirekter Rezeption des deutschen und südafrikanischen Rechts*' (2003) 1 Recht in Afrika, 69-89

Snider, K.F.; Rendon, R.G., 'Public Procurement Policy: Implications for Theory and Practice' (2008) 8(3) Journal of Public Procurement, 310-333

South African Law Reform Commission, 'Report on Administrative Justice, South African Law Reform Commission Project 115', (South African Law Reform Commission: 1999), available at http://www.justice.gov.za/salrc/reports/r_prj115_aja_1999 aug.pdf (last accessed: 1 December 2015)

Special Steering Committee of the OECD-DAC Task Force on Procurement, 'A Practical Guide to Transforming Procurement Systems ', (Paris: OECD, 2011)

Ssennoga, F., 'Examining Discriminatory Procurement Practices in Developing Countries' (2006) 6(3) Journal of Public Procurement, 218-249

Ssennoga, F.; Telgen, J., 'Integrating Socio-Economic Policies into the Public Procurement Framework - An Analysis of the Public Procurement Option Model', 4th International Public Procurement Conference, Seoul, South Korea, August 26-28, 2010

Stansbury, N., 'Exposing the foundations of corruption in construction', in International, T., *Global Corruption Report - special focus: Corruption in Construction and Post-Conflict Reconstruction* (Berlin: Transparency International, 2005)

Teixera, D.P.R., 'The Brazilian Experience of Using Pubic Procurement Policies to Promote the Development of Micro and Small Enterprises from the Legal Point of

View', 4th International Public Procurement Conference, Seoul, South Korea, August 26-28, 2010

Telgen, J.; Harland, C.; Knight, L., 'Public Procurement in perspective', in Knight, L.;Harland, C.;Telgen, J.;Thai, K. V.;Callender, G.;McKen, K., *Public Procurement: International cases and commentary* (London and New York: Routledge, 2007)

Telgen, J.; Schotanus, F., 'The Effects of Full Transparency in Supplier Selection on Subjectivity and Bid Quality', 4th International Public Procurement Conference, Seoul, South Korea, August 26-28, 2010

Tender Board Namibia, 'Annual Report 2007/2008', (Windhoek: Ministry of Finance 2008),

Tender Board of Namibia, 'Public Procurement Reforms 2012/13-2013/14 - *Challenges and achievements*', (Windhoek Tender Board of Namibia, 2015)

Tender Board of Namibia, 'Special conditions latest edition (TB339) ', Instructions to tenders

Tender Board of Namibia, 'TB/556', Instructions to tenderers

Thai, K.V., 'Challenges in Public Procurement', in al., K. V. T. e., *Challenges in Public Procurement: An International Perspective* (Boca Raton, FL, USA: PrAcademics Press, 2004)

Thai, K.V., 'Government Procurement: Past and current developments' (2000) 12(2) Journal of Public Budgeting, Accounting & Financial Management

Thai, K.V., 'International Handbook of Public Procurement', (New York: CRC Press, Taylor and Francis Group, 2008)

Thai, K.V., 'International Public Procurement: Concepts and Practices', in Thai, K. V., *International Handbook of Public Procurement* (Boca Raton, Florida: Taylor & Francis Group, 2009)

Thai, K.V., 'Public Procurement Re-Examined' (2001) 1(1) Journal of Public Procurement, 9-50

The Stationery Office, 'Public Private Partnerships: The Government's Appproach', (London: 2000)

Tjirera, E., 'Public Procurement in Namibia - *The Role of Codes of Conduct in Reducing Corruption*', Anti-Corruption Research Programme, Paper 4 (Windhoek: Institute for Public Policy Research, 2011),

Tjirera, E.; Hopwood, G., 'The ACC in Action. What does the track record say? ', Anti-Corruption Research Programme, Paper 6, November 2011 (Windhoek: Institute for Public Policy Research, 2011)

Townsend, M., 'Tendering in Namibia', 2008), available at http://www.tenderscan.co.za/index.php?mod=content&page=8 (last accessed: 29 November 2015)

Trachtmann, J.P., 'The WTO and development policy in China and India', in Muthucumuaraswamy, S.;Jiangyu, W., *China, India and the International Economic Order* (Cambridge: Cambridge University Press, 2010)

Transparency International, 'The Integrity Pact - The Concept, the Model and the Present Applications: A Status Report', (Transparency International: 2002), available at transparency.hu/uploads/docs/IP-FullStatusReport2002_1_.pdf (last accessed: 1 December 2015)

Trepte, P., 'Building sustainable capacity in public procurment', in Arrowsmith, S.;Anderson, R. D., *The WTO Regime on Government Procurement: Challenges and Reform* (Cambridge: Cambridge University Press, 2011)

Trepte, P., 'Regulating Procurement: Understanding the Ends and Means of Public Procurement Regulation', (Oxford: Oxford University Press, 2004)

Trionfetti, F., 'Discriminatory Public Procurement and International Trade' (2000) 23(1) The World Economy, 57-76

UNCITRAL, 'Guide to Enactement of UNCITRAL Model Law on Procurement of Goods,Construction and Services', A/CN.9/403 (New York: United Nations, 1994)

UNCITRAL, 'Guide to Enactment of the UNCITRAL Model Law on Public Procurement', (New York: United Nations, 2012)

UNCITRAL, 'Report of the United Nations Commission on International Trade Law on the work of its twenty- sixth session, Official Records of the General Assembly, Forty-eighth Session, Supplement No. 17 (A/48/17)', reproduced in UNCITRAL Yearbook, vol. XXIV: 1993, part one

UNCITRAL, 'The UNCITRAL Guide - Basic facts about the United Nations Commission on International Trade Law', (Vienna: United Nations, 2007)

UNDP, 'Good governance - and sustainable human development', Governance for sustainable human development, a UNDP policy document (UNDP: 2014), available at https://www.google.de/url?sa=t&rct=j&q=&esrc=s&source=web&cd=2&ved=0CC4QFjABahUKEwiLseG64eLHAhXJDiwKHf7FALo&url=http%3A%2F%2Fwww.undp.org%2Fcontent%2Fdam%2Fundp%2Flibrary%2FDemocratic%2520Governance%2FDiscussion-Paper--Governance-for-Sustainable-Development.pdf&usg=AFQjCNEvOh06Nurz-Fh77G0ue_Njz4gvSQ&bvm=bv.102022582,d.bGg&cad=rja (last accessed: 6 September 2015)

United Nations Development Programme; Anti-Corruption Commission; Institute for Public Policy Research (London), 'Namibia and the United Nations Convention against Corruption. Gap analysis report', (Windhoek: UNDP/ACC, 2013)

United Nations General Assembly, 'Resolution Adopted by the General Assembly: Model law on Procurement of Goods and Construction of the United Nations Commission on International Trade Law (A/RES/48/33)', (New York: United Nations, 1994)

United Nations General Assembly, 'Resolution Adopted by the General Assembly: Model Law on Procurement of Goods, Construction and Services of the United Nations Commission on International Trade Law (A/RES/49/739)', (New York: United Nations, 1995)

United Nations General Assembly, 'Resolution Adopted by the General Assembly: United Nations Commission on International Trade Law Model Law on Public Procurement (A/RES/66/95)', (New York: United Nations, 2012)

United Nations General Assembly, 'United Nations Millennium Declaration ', A/55/L.2 (New York: United Nations, 2000),

United Nations Gerenal Assembly, 'General Assembly Resolution 2205 (XXI)', (New York: United Nations, 1996),

United Nations Office on Drugs and Crime, 'Guidebook on anti-corruption in public procurement and the management of public finances - *Good practices in ensuring compliance with Article 9 of the United Nations Convention against Corruption*', (Vienna: United Nations in collabaration with the International Anti-Corruption Academy, 2013)

United Nations Office on Drugs and Crime, 'Reporting on Corruption – A Resource Tool for Governments and Journalists' (New York: United Nations, 2014)

Vaidya, K.; Callender, G.C.; Sajeev, A.S.M., 'Facilitators of Public E-Procurement: Lessons Learned from the U.K., U.S., and Australian Initatives', in Thai, K. V., *International Handbook of Public Procurement* (Boca Raton, Florida: Taylor & Francis Group, 2009)

Volmink, P., 'Enhancing Transparency within Public Sector Procurement: The South African Experience', 4th International Public Procurement Conference, Seoul, South Korea, August 26-28, 2010

Wait, M., 'SA pins reindustrialisation hopes on new procurement rules', 2012), available at http://www.engineeringnews.co.za/article/sa-pins-reindustrialisation-hopes-on-new-procurement-rules-but-constraints-persist-2012-02-03 (last accessed: 17 December 2015)

Walker, C., 'Setting up a Public Procurement System: the Six Step Method', in Arrowsmith, S.;Trybus, M., *Public Procurement: the Continuing Revolution* (Dordretch: Kluwer Law International, 2003)

Watermeyer, R., 'The use of Targeted Procurement as an Instrument of Poverty Alleviation and Job Creation in Infrastructure Projects' (2000) 5 Public Procurement Law Review, 226-250

Watson, A., 'Legal Transplants - *An approach to Comparative Law*', (Edinburgh: Scottish Academic Press Ltd., 1974)

Welch, B., 'Best Practices in Federal Acquisition' (2003) 32(3) The Public Manager, 11-17

Williams-Elegbe, S., 'The World Bank's Influence on Procurement Reform in Africa' (2013) 21(1) African Journal of International and Comparative Law, 95-119

Williamson, J., 'The strange history of the Washington consensus' (2004) 27(2) Journal of Post Keynesian Economics, 195-206

Wittig, W.A., 'Building Value through Public Procurement: A Focus on Africa', 9th International Anti-Corruption Conference, Durban, South Africa, 10-15 October 1999

World Bank, 'Electronic Government Procurement (e-GP) - Opportunities and Challenges', (World Bank: 2006), available at http://siteresources.worldbank.org/INTPROCUREMENT/Resources/eGP_Note_V1-1.doc (last accessed: 26 November 2015)

World Bank, 'South Africa - Country Procurement Assessment Report: refining the public procurement system (Vol. 1 of 2) : Summary of findings and recommendations (English)', Country Procurement Assessment (CPAR) Report (Washington, DC: World Bank, 2003)

World Bank, 'South Africa - Country Procurement Assessment Report: refining the public procurement system (Vol. 2 of 2) : Main text (English)', Country Procurement Assessment (CPAR) Report (Washington, DC: World Bank, 2003)

WTO Secretariat, 'Trade Policy Review: Southern African Customs Union - Annex 4 South Africa (WT/TPR/S/114/ZAF), 24 March 2003', (WTO: 2003), available at https://www.wto.org/english/tratop_e/tpr_e/s114-0_e.doc (last accessed: 1 December 2015)

Zhang, X., 'Constructing a system of challenge procedures to comply with the Agreement on Government Procurement', in Arrowsmith, S.;Anderson, R. D., *The WTO Regime on Public Procurement* (Cambridge: Cambridge University Press, 2011)

Zheng, J., Knight, L., Harland, C., Humby, S. and James, K., 'An analysis of research into the future of purchasing and supply management' (2007) 13 Journal of Purchasing & Supply Management, 69-83

Zweigert, K.; Kötz, H., 'An Introduction to Comparative Law', (Oxford et al.: Oxford University Press, 1998), 3rd Edition

# List of Legislation

## Namibia

Affirmative Action (Employment) Act 1998 (Act No. 20 of 1998)

Agricultural (Commercial) Land Reform Act, 1995 (Act No. 6 of 1995)

Anti-Corruption Act 2003 (Act No. 8 of 2003)

Code of Conduct for Members of Regional Councils 2004 (No. 172 of 2004, Government Gazette No. 3255)

Competition Act 2003 (Act No. 2 of 2003)

Constitution of Namibia 1990 (Act No. 1 of 1990)

Edumbe Municipality Supply Chain Management Policy, 2008

Extension of Collective Agreement: Construction Industry, 2012 (No. 154 of 2012, Government Gazette No. 4970)

Finance and Audit Ordinance 1 of 1926

Financial Intelligence Act 2012 (Act No. 13 of 2012)

General Notice No. 160, Tender Board of Namibia: Preferences, Government Gazette No. 551 of 14 December 1992

Identification of Employers as Relevant Employers (in terms of Section 20(1) of the Affirmative Action (Employment) Act 1998) 2006 (No. 95 of 2006, Government Gazette No. 3658)

Income Tax Act 1981 (Act No. 24 of 1981) as amended by the Income Tax Amendment Act 2005 (Act No. 4 of 2005)

Labour Act 2007 (Act No. 11 of 2007)

Law Reform and Development Commission Act, 1001 (Act No. 29 of 1991), as amended by the Law Reform and Development Commission Amendment Act, 2004 (Act No. 2 of 2004)

Local Authorities Act 1992 (Act No. 23 of 1992)

Local Authorities Tender Board Regulations: Local Authorities Act, 1992 (No. 29 of 1992, Government Gazette No. 2486)

Namibian Constitution Second Amendment Act 2010 (Act No. 7 of 2010)

Nature Conservation Ordinance 4 of 1975

Ombudsman Act 1990 (Act No. 7 of 1990)

Prevention of Organised Crime Act 2004 (Act No. 29 of 2004)

Public Procurement Bill (As read a First Time) 2013

Public Procurement Bill (As read a First Time) 2015

Public Service Act 1995 (Act No. 13 of 1995)

Regional Councils Act 1992 (Act No. 22 of 1992)

Regional Councils Tender Board Regulations: Regional Councils Act, 1992 (No. 43 of 1992, Government Gazette No. 2492)

Rules of the High Court of Namibia: High Court Act, 1990 (No. 59 of 1990, Government Gazette of 10 October 1990)

Rules of the High Court of Namibia: High Court Act, 1990, (No. 4 of 2014, Government Gazette of 17 January 2014)

Social Security Act 1934 (Act No. 34 of 1994)

State Finance Act 2001 (Act No. 31 of 1991)

State Tender Board Act 1968 (Act No. 86 of 1968)

State Tender Board Act 1968 (Act No. 86 of 1968): Amendment to Regulations of the State Tender Board Act in Terms of Section 13, 2003

Tender Board of Namibia Act 1996 (Act No. 16 of 1996)

Tender Board of Namibia Code of Procedure 1997 (No. 191 of 1997, Government Gazette No. 1692)

Tender Board Regulations (promulgated in terms of s 26A of Finance and Audit Ordinance 1 of 1926) 1970

Tender Board Regulations 1996 (No. 237 of 1996, Government Gazette No. 1403)

## South Africa

Broad-Based Black Economic Empowerment Act 2003 (Act No. 53 of 2003)

Broad-based Black Economic Empowerment Codes of Good Practice 2007 (Government Gazette No. 29617 )

Constitution of the Republic of South Africa 1996

Employment Equity Act 1998 (Act No. 55 of 1998)

Framework for Supply Chain Management (Regulations in Terms of the Public Finance Management Act 1999) 2003

Local Government: Municipal Finance Management Act 2003 (Act No. 56 of 2003)

Local Government: Municipal Finance Management Act: Municipal Regulations on Minimum Competency Levels 2007 (No. R493 of 2007, Government Gazette 504)

Municipal Supply Chain Management Regulations (Local Government: Municipal Finance Management Act 2003) 2005 (No. 868 of 2005, Government Gazette No. 27636)

Municipal Systems Act 2000 (Act No. 32 of 2000 - as amended by Act No. 44 of 2003)

National Qualifications Framework Act 2008 (Act No. 67 of 2008)

Preferential Procurement Policy Framework Act 2000 (Act No. 5 of 2000)

Preferential Procurement Regulations 2001 ((Government Gazette No. 22549))

Preferential Procurement Regulations 2011 (Government Gazette No. 34350)

Prevention and Combating of Corrupt Activities Act 2004 (Act No. 12 of 2004)

Promotion of Access to Information Act 2000 (Act No. 2 of 2000)

Promotion of Administrative Justice Act 2000 (Act No. 3 of 2000)

Public Finance Management Act 1999 (Act No. 1 of 1999)

South Africa Treasury Regulation 16 - Public Private Partnerships, issued in terms of the Public Finance Management Act, 1999 (Gazette No. 25915, 16 January 2004)

## Mauritius

Public Procurement (Disqualification) Regulations 2009 (No. 142 of 2009)

Public Procurement (Framework Agreement) Regulations 2013 (Government Notice No. 177 of 2013)

Public Procurement (Suspension and Debarment) Regulations 2008 (Government Notice No. 8 of 2008)

Public Procurement Act 2006 (Act No. 33 of 2006)

Public Procurement Regulations 2008 (Regulations made by the Minister under Section 61 of the Public Procurement Act 2006) (Government Notice No. 7 of 2008)

Public-Private Partnership Act 2004 (Act No. 37 of 2004)

## Others

Act Regulating State Contracts with Companies doing Business with or in Burma (Myanmar) of 1996 ((Chapter 130 of the Acts of 1996), Commonwealth of Massachusetts)

American Recovery and Reinvestment Act of 2009 (US Public Law No.111-5 of 2009)

Buy American Act of 1933 (US Public Law No. 428 of 1933)

COMESA Public Procurement Regulations 2009 (Legal Notice No. 3 of 2009, Official Gazette of COMESA, Vol. 15 No. 3)

Constitution of Kenya 2010

Davis-Bacon Act of 1931 (US Public Law No. 403 of 1931)

Directive 2004/17/EC (coordinating the procurement procedures of entities operating in the water, energy, transport and postal services sectors), 2004

Directive 2004/18/EC (on the coordination of procedures for the award of public works contracts, public supply contracts and public service contracts), 2004

Directive 2014/24/EU (on public procurement and repealing Directive 2004/18/EC), 2014

Directive 2014/25/EU (on procurement by entities operating in the water, energy, transport and postal services sectors and repealing Directive 2004/17/EC), 2014

Public Procurement and Disposal Act (No. 3 of 2005): (Preference and Reservations) Regulations, 2011 (Republic of Kenya) (Legal Notice No. 58)

Public Procurement Law (Republic of Serbia) 2006 (Official Gazette of the Republic of Serbia, No. 39/02, 43/03, 55/04 and 101/05)

# *List of International Legal Instruments*

African Union Convention on Combating Corruption, 2003 (adopted in Maputo on 11 July 2003 and entered into force on 5 August 2006)

Agreement on Subsidies and Countervailing Measures (adopted on 15 April 1994 and entered into force on 1 January 1995)

Marrakesh Agreement Establishing the World Trade Organisation, 1994 (signed in Marrakesh on 15 April 1994 and entered into force on 1 January 1995)

Revised Agreement on Government Procurement, 2012 (adopted on 30 March 2012 and entered into force on 6 April 2014)

SADC Protocol against Corruption, 2001 (adopted in Blantyre on 14 August 2001 and entered into force on 14 August 2003)

Trade, Development and Cooperation Agreement (Agreement on Trade, Development and Cooperation between the European Community and its Member States, of the one part, and the Republic of South Africa, of the other part), 1999 (signed on 11 October 1999 in Pretoria and entered fully into force on 1 May 2004)

Treaty Establishing the Common Market for Eastern and Southern Africa (signed in Kampala on 5 November 1993 and ratified in Lilongwe on 8 December 1994)

UNCITRAL Model Law on Public Procurement, 2011 (adopted on 1 July 2011)

United Nations Convention against Corruption, 2003 (adopted by the General Assembly by resolution 58/4 of 31 October 2003 and entered into force on 14 December 2005)

WTO Agreement on Government Procurement, 1994 (signed in Marrakesh on 15 April 1994 and entered into force on 1 January 1996)

# *List of Cases*

## Namibia

AFS Group Namibia (Pty) Ltd. v Chairperson of the Tender Board of Namibia and Others (A 55/2011) [2011] NAHC 184

Aurecon Namibia (Pty) Ltd. v The Roads Authority, unreported case, A 250/2012, NAHCMD 21 (28 January 2013).

CSC Neckartal Dam Joint Venture v The Tender Board of Namibia and Others 2014 (1) NR 135

Frank and Another v Chairperson of the Immigration Selection Board 1999 NR 257 (HC)

Amswohl & LGA Construction Joint Venture Close Corporation v Permanent Secretary of the National Planning Commission, the Windhoek Municipal Council, the Chairperson of the Local Tender Board of the City of Windhoek, The Chairperson of the Tender Board of Namibia, Namibia Construction and Others [no judgement, but court order] (no case no. found)

Disposable Medical Products (Pty) Ltd. v. Tender Board of Nambia 1997 NR 129 (HC)

Kerry McNamara Architects Inc and Others v Minister of Works, Transport and Communication and Others 2000 NR 1 (HC)

Kersten t/a Witvlei Transport v National Transport Commission and Another 1991 NR 234 (HC)

The Medical Association of Namibia Limited and Others v The Minister of Health and Social Services and Others, unreported case, A 199/2009 (28 June 2010)

Minister of Education and Others v Free Namibia Caterers (Pty) Ltd. 2013 (4) NR 1061 (SC)

Namibia Construction (Pty) Ltd. v The Chairperson of the Tender Board, unreported case, A 283/2007, NAHCMD 6 (21 January 2014)

Namibia Construction Industries and Murray and Roberts v the Chairman of the Tender Board and the Ministry of Works, unreported Case, A 283/2007, High Court (30 November 2007)

New Era Investment (Pty) Ltd. v Roads Authority and Others 2014 (2) NR 596 (HC)

Premier Construction CC v Chairperson of the Tender Committee of hte Namibia Power Corporation Board of Directors and Others 2014(4) NR 1002 (HC)

RBH Construction and Another v Windhoek Municipal Council and Another 2002 NR 443 (HC)

Serenity Manufacturers v Minister of Health and Social Services and Another 2007(2) NR 756 (SC)

Shetu Trading CC v Chair, Tender Board of Namibia and Others (A 352/2010) [2011] NAHC 188

Shetu Trading CC v Chair, Tender Board of Namibia and Others 2012 (1) NR 162 (SC)

Skeleton Coast Safaris (Pty) Ltd. v Namibia Tender Board and Others 1993 NR 288 (HC)

## South Africa

ABBM Printing and Publishing (Pty) Ltd. v Transnet Ltd 1998 (2) SA 109 (W)

Actaris South Africa (Pty) Ltd. v. Sol Plaatje Municipality and Intelligent Metering Systems (Pty) Ltd (213/2008) [2008] ZANCHC 6; [2008] 4 All SA 168 (NC) (29 February 2008)

Aquafund Pty Ltd. v Premier of the Province of the Western Cape 1997 (7) BCLR 907 (C)

Bato Star Fishing (Pty) Ltd. v Minister of Environmental Affairs and Tourism and Others 2004 (4) SA 490 (CC); 2004 (7) BCLR 687 (CC)

Cash Paymaster Services (Pty) Ltd. v Eastern Cape Province and Others 1999 (1) SA 324 (CkH)

Chairperson: Standing Tender Committee and Others v JFE Sapela Electronics (Pty) Ltd. and Others (511/2004) [2005] ZASCA 90; 2008 (2) SA 638 (SCA) ; [2005] 4 All SA 487 (SCA)

Commissioner for the SAPS and Others v Maimela and Another 2003 (5) SA 480 (TPD)

Eskom Holdings Limited and Another v New Reclamation Group (Pty) Ltd. (358/08) [2009] ZASCA 8; 2009 (4) SA 628 (SCA) ; 2009 (8) BCLR 813 (SCA) ; [2009] 2 All SA 513 (SCA)

Groenewald NO and Others v M5 Developments (Cape) (283/09) [2010] ZASCA 47; 2010 (5) SA 82 (SCA) ; [2011] 1 All SA 17 (SCA)

Intertrade Two (Pty) Ltd. v. The MEC for Roads & Public Works, Eastern Cape and the Premier of the Eastern Cape (1790/04) [2007] ZAECHC 149; [2008] 1 All SA 142 (Ck) (31 May 2007)

Logbro Properties CC v Bedderson NO and Others [2002] ZASCA 135; [2003] 1 All SA 424 (SCA)

Loghdey v City of Cape Town and Others, Advance Parking Solutions CC and Another v City of Cape Town and Others (100/09) [2010] ZAWCHC 25

Lohan Civil- Tebogo Joint Venture and Anders v Mangaung Plaaslike Munisipaliteit and Anders (508/2009) [2009] ZAFSHC 46 (6 April 2009)

Mamlambo Construction CC v Port St Johns Municipality and Others (1876/2008) [2010] ZAECMHC 21 (24 June 2010)

Menzies Aviation South Africa (Pty) Limited v South African Airways (Pty) Ltd. and Others (08/22988) [2009] ZAGPJHC 65 (4 December 2009)

Metro Projects CC and Another v Klerksdorp Local Municipality and Others [2003] ZASCA 91; [2004] 1 All SA 504 (SCA)

Millenium Wast Management (Pty) Ltd. v Chairperson, Tender Board: Limpopo Province 2008(2) SA 481 (SCA); [2007] SCA 165 (RSA)

Minister of Social Development and Pensions v Phoenix Cash and Carry CC [2007] SCA 26 (RSA)

President of the Repulic of South Africa and Another v Hugo (CCT11/96) [1997] ZACC 4; 1997 (6) BCLR 708; 1997 (4) SA 1

Rèan International Supply Company (Pty) Ltd. and Others v Mpumulanga Gaming Board (1999) 8 BCLR 918

Renaissance Security and Cleaning Services CC v Rustenburg Local Municipality and Others (1811/2007) [2008] ZANWHC 29

Road Mac Surfacing (Pty) Ltd. v MEC for the Department of Transport and Roads, North-West Province and Others, Raubex (Pty) Ltd v MEC for the Department of Transport and Roads, North-West Province and Others, High Court (Bophuthatswana Provincial Division), [2006] ZANWHC 54

Seodigeng v Chief Executive of South African Sucurity Agency (SASSA) (1682/07) [2011] ZANWHC 1

Simunye Developers CC v Lovedale Public FET College and Another (3059/2010) [2010] ZAECGHC 121

Sizabonke Civils CC t/a Pilcon Projects v Zululand District Municipality and Others 2011 (4) SA 406 (KZP)) [2010] ZAKZPHC 23; 10878/2009

Soobramoney v Minister of Health (Kwazulu-Natal) (CCT32/97) [1997] ZACC 17; 1998 (1) SA 765 (CC); 1997 (12) BCLR 1696

Steenkamp NO v Provincial Tender Board, Eastern Cape (CCT71/05) [2006] ZACC 16; 2007 (3) SA 121 (CC); 2007 (3) BCLR 300 (CC) (28 September 2006)

South African Post Office v De Lacy 2009 (5) SA 255 (SCA)

Tetra Mobile Radio (Pty) Ltd. v Member of the Executive Council of the Department of Works and Others (482/2006) [2007] ZASCA 128; [2007] SCA 128 (RSA); 2008 (1) SA 438 (SCA)

The Chairman of the State Tender Board v. The Minister of Finance and Supersonic Tours (Pty) Ltd. (389/07) [2008] ZASCA

Total Computer Services (Pty) Limited v. Municipal Manager Ptochefstroom Local Municipality and Others (29416/07) [2007] ZAGPHC 239; 2008 (4) SA 346 (T)

Total Computer Services v. Potchefstroom Local Municipality [2007] ZAGPHC 239; 2008 (4) SA 346 (T)

Transnet Limited and Inter Waste (Pty) Ltd. v. SA Metal Machinery Company (Pty) Ltd. (147/2005) [2005] ZASCA 113 (29 November 2005)

Transnet Ltd. v Goodman Brothers (Pty) Ltd. 2001 (1) SA 853 (SCA)

Viking Pony Africa Pumps v Hidro-Tech Systems 2011 (1) SA 327 (CC)

Viking Pony Africa Pumps v Hidro-Tech Systems, unreported, referred to as [2010] ZASCA 23 (25 March 2010)

## WTO Disputes

Japan — Procurement of a Navigation Satellite, WT/DS73

Korea — Measures affecting Government Procurement (procurement practices of the Korean Airport Construction Authority), WT/DS163

United States - Import Prohibition of Certain Shrimp and Shrimp Products, WTO Appelate Body, WT/DS58/AB/R, 12 October 1998

United States - Measure Affecting Government Procurement, WTO Dispute Settlement, DS 88

United States — Measures Affecting Government Procurement (Massachusetts State Law prohibiting contracts with firms doing business with or in Myanmar), WT/DS88/95

United States - Standards for Reformulated and Conventional Gasoline, WTO Appelate Body, WT/DS2/AB/R, 29 April 1996

# Annexes

## *Annex 1: List of Interview Partners*

Interview Mr Agenbag (Murray & Roberts Namibia, Commercial Director), Windhoek, 7th March 2013

Interview Mr Haibach (Konrad Adenauer Stiftung (KAS), Director), Windhoek, 21st February 2013

Interview Mr Hopwood (Institute for Public Policy Research (IPPR), Director), Windhoek 26th March 2013

Interview Mr Immanuel (Tender Board, Alternate Member), Windhoek, 27th March 2013

Interview Mr Isaacs (Tender Board, Chief Control Officer), Windhoek, 26th March 2013

Interview Mr Links (Insight Magazine, Editor), Windhoek, 21st February 2013

Interview Mr McNamara (Kerry McNamara Architects Inc., Director), Swakopmund, 1st March 2013

Interview Mr Ruppel (LorentzAngula Inc., Director/Chairman), Windhoek, 28th February 2013

Interview Mr Schulz (Namibia Construction (Pty) Ltd., Director), Windhoek, 22nd March 2013

Interview Mr Shindinge (Tender Board, Alternate Member), Windhoek, 27th March 2013

Interview Mr Sipiho (Tender Board, Control Officer), Windhoek, 26th March 2013

Interview Mr Titus (Tender Board, Alternate Member), Windhoek, 28th March 2013

Interview Mr Tötemeyer (Advocate / Society of Advocates of Namibia, Vice-president), Windhoek, 28th March 2013

Interview Mr Walters (Ombudsman of Namibia), Windhoek, 27th March 2013

Interview Mrs Jonga (Tender Board, Chief Control Officer), Windhoek, 26th March 2013

Interview Mrs David (Local Tender Board of the City of Windhoek, Accounting Assistant: Tender Invitations), Windhoek, 11th March 2013

Interview Mrs Jonas (National Union of Namibian Workers (NUNW), Director), Windhoek, 28th March 2013

*Annex 2: List of Sample Questions*

*A selection of questions regarding the current public procurement system*

- Is there a restriction of open or competitive bidding to the national level? Or do they have to be open to everyone?
- Are there internally any standards which are used in order to decide whether tenders are invited through prequalification?
- Tenders are usually open, meaning that there is no restriction to a certain group of companies that can apply as, for example, Namibian companies. Can the Board specify in the title of tender that only Namibian companies can apply?
- What criteria need to be met in order to find it impracticable or inappropriate to invite tenders?
- Why are the latest annual reports of the Tender Board not available at the homepage?
- Where are the date, time and place of the public bid opening published?
- Who and how are the evaluation criteria determined and weighed against each other?
- What are reasons for the non-acceptance of tenders?
- Another factor that might influence the award decision is a recommendation obtained from a relevant office, ministry or agency. According to Sec 19(1) of the CoP, the board shall after having opened and listed all tender, submit the tenders to the relevant office, ministry or agency for its recommendation. The RTB and the LTB shall do that respectively with departments, divisions, or sections. What influence has the recommendation for the decision of the board?
- What happens if a tender price is increased after it has been awarded and before an agreement has been concluded?
- Considering the public administration, legal, technical and economic skills and understanding needed to efficiently and effectively carry out procurement the lack of qualification criteria for tender board members is highly problematic and allows the appointment of members that hinder rather than implementing effective and efficient procurement decisions. Are there any criteria for the selection of tender board members and staff?
- How long have the tender board members been in office? What qualifications do they have? Is there any training provided?

- With reference to the right to administrative action, public procurement legislation and/or corruptive practices, tenderers can approach the ombudsman. How often does it happen?
- Do you think the factors hindering efficient and effective procurement procedures are based on deficits in tender legislation or on the failure of implementing that law?
- What do you think could be done to improve implementation?
- Does national procurement law apply when the financing of a work or service is done through loans from foreign donors? Is there a provision somewhere?
- Since the biggest problem is the exemption of tender procedures, why is the Ministry of Finance not issuing a regulation that lays down stricter criteria for exemption until the new tender bill is issued?

*A selection of questions regarding the reform process*

- Why is the draft of the new tender bill not available online?
- Is e-procurement considered as essential component of the new tender legislation?
- Why was the Mauritian law chosen as model law? And not, for example the South African law?
- Have the provisions of the GPA been considered during the reform progress? Keeping in mind, that one day it might be beneficial to seek accession to the GPA.
- Has there been the consideration to initiate regional procurement regulations as on SADC level?
- Does the draft contain review procedures for public procurement?

*Annex 3: Essential Aspects of Public Procurement Reform Processes*

Different phases of a strategic and transparent approach to conduct PP reforms with view to create ownership and to create a PP system that is adequate with regard to the local possibilities and constraints

| Phase of procurement reform | Matters to be addressed | Possible assistance/interventions by foreign actors/experts |
|---|---|---|
| ***During all Phases*** | • *strategic planning*<br>• *be transparent about the reform strategy, the process and the involvement of stakeholders* | |
| **Phase I: Preparation** | • identify unbiased, experienced and qualified experts that can lead the reform (not only external experts)<br>• allocate responsibilities<br>• set out deadlines and general objectives that are to be achieved<br>• prepare detailed roadmap<br>• accumulate resources and capacity for reform<br>• inform stakeholders about reform process and create platform for exchange with stakeholders<br>• start building procurement expertise → identify or establish institution that can carry out PP education/training | • hold workshop about PP-systems<br>• provide resources and capacity<br>• training of PP staff |
| **Phase II: Execution of Assessment of Status Quo** | • assess current PP system (here: involve stakeholders already/ identify strengths and weaknesses; compare with best practices and international standards)<br>• assess what other legislation/policies/restraints interact with the PP-Systems and what are potential hindrances → decide whether other areas also require reform (holistic approach) | • provide expertise to assess PP system together with local experts |

| | | |
|---|---|---|
| **Phase II: Execution of Assessment of Status Quo** | • also consider the historical development and role of public procurement within society (to be aware of local particularities and challenges)<br>• identify reform drivers and obstacles (→ develop strategy to involve actors and to overcome obstacles)<br>• assess capacities and resources available in view of the objectives (being realistic what can be achieved in the local context as e.g. availability of workforce) BE AWARE: more discretion requires better qualified and available staff members | |
| **Phase III: Assessment of Aims and Objectives** | • What shall be achieved by PP? (consider issues such as secondary objectives, regulatory vs. discretionary approach, institutional design, decentralisation vs. centralised approach, harmonization with neighbouring countries, possible accession to GPA)<br>• What has to change? What can be kept?<br>• collect opinions from different stakeholders what they expect (=>create ownership, create a system that is suitable for all needs)<br>• consider international best practices and identify possible legal solutions of other countries suitable in the local context | • organize and fund workshops/conferences bringing stakeholders together |
| **Phase IV: Execution Phase** | • draft law<br>• discuss law with stakeholders<br>• improve law<br>• table it in parliament<br>• establish institution that can monitor and evaluate PP systems<br>• draft guide on PP system | • assist with legal drafting<br>• assist with the establishment of institutions |

| | | |
|---|---|---|
| **Phase V: Post-processing Phase** | • monitor and evaluate PP system to identify weaknesses and shortcomings in legislation as well as in implementation<br>• correct deficits | • assess PP reform process and its success in order to develop best practices |

# Index


abnormally low tenders 92, 339, 432
ACC 395-400, 440, 442, 517, 534, 541
access to information 75, 283-286, 342, 523
accountability 19, 24, 29, 33, 51, 54f., 59, 62, 64, 68, 72f., 74f., 78f., 105, 127, 131, 138, 140, 166, 190, 201, 209, 212, 218, 224, 236, 243, 254, 257, 259-261, 266, 279-282, 284, 286-288, 322f., 330, 332, 336, 341-344, 394f., 419, 472f., 475, 480, 512f., 523, 534, 538, 540-543, 545, 547
administrative action 286f., 310-312, 314, 360, 421, 423, 425, 438
administrative burden 214, 478, 484
administrative justice 310, 423, 425, 438, 450, 486
administrative law 285, 310, 313, 316, 320, 330, 426f., 486, 491, 536
administrative review 66, 106, 246, 320, 344, 420, 452, 455, 485, 552, 555
affirmative action 46, 82, 143, 252, 263, 291, 303, 350, 356-360, 402f., 405, 407f., 418f., 454, 506, 527, 529, 557
Affirmative Action Compliance Certificate 93, 359, 403
affirmative public procurement 302
alternative bidding methods 232 *see also alternative procurement method*
alternative procurement method 60, 240, 551 *see also alternative bidding methods*
American Recovery and Reinvestment Act of 2009 98
annual procurement plans 56, 332, 335, 342, 487, 532, 556
annual public procurement plans *see annual procurement plans*
apartheid 25, 45, 206, 251, 256, 261f., 289, 291, 298, 300, 304, 321, 330, 349, 356-358, 361, 506, 528
audi alteram partem rule 422
award decision 70, 74, 144, 159, 189, 199, 217, 236, 241, 246, 295, 313, 323, 342, 386-388, 390, 407, 427, 439, 441-443, 451, 538
award phase 56-58, 282, 330, 478
best practices 23, 35, 37, 46f., 70, 72, 76, 109, 111, 119, 141, 160, 171, 173, 189f., 198, 205, 242, 254, 327f., 330, 340, 342f., 347, 350f., 353, 460, 529, 540, 542, 549, 552f., 557 *see also international best practices*
bidding phase 56, 58, 330, 339
blacklisting 77, 293, 341, 378, 384, 480, 484, 526f.
Buy American Act of 1933 97f.
centralised procurement 228, 331, 472f.
China 86, 112, 170, 354, 365, 377, 409-411, 415, 418, 439, 509
Chinese companies 22, 377, 409-414, 417f., 455, 501-503, 509

choice of the procurement method 478, 522, 525, 534
civil society 106, 459, 464, 469, 501f., 509, 551
code of conduct 212, 249, 259, 269, 334, 394, 400, 480, 525, 551
codes of conduct *see code of conduct*
COMESA 41, 44f., 109, 205f., 208-211, 213, 215f., 218, 220-222, 225, 227, 232-234, 236f., 243, 248f., 327f., 362, 376, 380, 505, 512, 549, 550
commercial interests 191, 242, 387, 402, 535
community participation 231
comparative law 35, 458, 495, 549
competition 24, 42, 51, 53-56, 59-62, 64, 66, 71-73, 79-81, 83, 85f., 89, 92, 94, 96, 102f., 105, 113, 118f., 126-129, 136, 138-140, 142, 162, 165f., 168, 170f., 177f., 180, 182f., 188, 191f., 194, 196, 199, 209, 212-214, 216, 218, 220, 222, 227, 231, 236, 238-240, 242, 263, 273f., 279, 298, 300, 303, 316, 318, 323, 328, 335-338, 342, 349, 361, 366f., 391, 401, 410, 417, 459, 468, 471, 482f., 489, 493f., 512f., 524, 528, 535, 540, 546, 555
competitive bidding 58f., 210f., 213, 215, 217f., 222, 233, 260, 272, 355, 367, 373f., 477
competitiveness 81, 89, 95, 168, 265, 271, 285, 303, 317-319, 411, 443
complexity 29, 46, 52f., 69, 79, 88, 101, 105, 107, 155, 164f., 167, 178, 216, 248, 288, 299, 310, 320, 336, 460f., 471f., 478, 491f., 508, 511, 516, 536, 549, 554
compliance 31, 40, 75, 78, 81, 83, 92f., 144, 156, 165, 185, 198, 226, 239, 245, 250, 259, 267, 284, 291, 302f., 306f., 309, 317f., 322, 324, 341, 343, 346, 360, 369, 378, 382, 385, 403f., 408, 413-416, 418f., 427, 432, 435f., 449, 455, 467, 470, 472f., 484, 486, 488, 525, 529, 533f., 540f.
confidential information 64, 139, 511, 526
confidentiality 58, 60, 123, 140, 191, 200, 212, 242, 281, 285f., 342, 362, 394
conflict of interest 55, 72, 117f., 169, 212, 229, 268, 278, 281, 334, 342f., 371, 394, 418, 518, 526, 543
conflicts of interest *see conflict of interest*
construction 19, 42f., 46, 53, 61, 71, 91, 98, 158, 162, 176, 180, 187, 232, 255, 289, 294, 302, 353f., 361, 363-365, 374, 398, 403, 406, 409-417, 419, 437, 439, 446, 449, 501-503, 511, 529
construction sector *see construction*
contract administration 174, 205, 220f., 239, 245, 248, 303, 413 *see also contract management*
contract management 56-58, 109, 206, 212, 277, 282, 329f., 340, 346, 377f., 420, 455, 457, 484, 488, 493, 533, 538, 546, 552, 556 *see also contract administration*
corruption 20, 34, 37, 39, 40, 44, 46, 49, 54f., 69-73, 76-80, 96, 106, 117f., 140, 165, 169, 183, 193, 201, 212, 224, 243, 251, 253, 255, 260, 268, 274, 280,

282, 288f., 307, 309, 328, 332-334, 336f., 339, 343, 345, 348, 353, 362, 367, 383, 392-398, 400, 418, 420, 423f., 431, 440, 453, 456, 459, 462, 474, 479, 480, 484, 488, 492, 509, 517, 521, 523, 526f., 539, 547, 549, 551, 554, 558
cost-effectiveness 83, 276, 323
Davis-Bacon Act of 1931 91
decentralisation 52, 64, 105, 226, 248, 331, 345, 348, 373, 472, 513, 517, 554
democracy 24, 75
developing countries 19, 21, 25, 28f., 30f., 34-37, 39f., 49, 55, 65, 69, 86, 89, 90, 94-96, 107, 109, 111f., 115f., 120, 131-137, 155, 157, 161f., 164-168, 170, 173, 177, 183, 201, 239, 267, 277, 291, 324f., 328, 331f., 344, 346, 348f., 365, 380, 457, 461, 463f., 472, 477, 482, 484, 488, 493, 549f., 552f.
direct procurement 59, 225, 231, 473
disclosure of information 139f., 190, 194, 242, 250
discretion 62, 70, 83, 109, 152, 166, 193, 196, 209, 219, 230, 232, 237, 243, 247, 274f., 291, 300, 319, 324, 336f., 344, 365, 374, 382f., 386, 403, 408, 416, 444, 521, 523, 527f., 535f., 551
discrimination 81, 85, 89, 92, 120, 123f., 126, 129, 136, 146, 148f., 161, 167, 169, 179, 183, 195, 197, 209, 230, 237, 291, 300, 303, 349, 357, 359, 506
discriminatory policies 87f., 94, 97, 99, 150f., 481f.
Dispute Settlement Understanding 115, 124, 156f.
disqualification 223, 242, 293, 311, 318, 416, 431, 538
Doha Round 113, 166
domestic firms 86, 88f., 95f., 150, 185, 482
donors 26, 34, 211, 266, 335, 365, 459, 464, 512, 540
economic empowerment 295
economic globalisation 458f.
effectiveness 19-21, 25f., 28, 42, 44, 47, 51, 53, 55, 61, 64, 68, 79f., 82, 85, 87f., 99, 101f., 107, 118, 132, 134f., 162, 171, 184, 189, 194, 203, 221, 223, 227, 230, 234, 247, 250, 261, 272, 275-277, 285, 293f., 300, 308f., 316-319, 323-325, 330, 334, 338, 341, 343, 345, 347, 356, 377, 390, 397f., 420, 443, 452, 455, 458, 463, 470f., 478f., 488, 491, 508f., 513, 519, 546f., 550-552, 555
efficiency 20, 26, 28, 36, 42, 44, 47, 51, 53, 55f., 61, 64, 73, 80, 82, 88, 90, 99, 101-103, 105, 107, 118, 120, 122, 159, 171, 177f., 184, 189, 221, 223, 230, 234, 246f., 250, 261, 277, 287, 293, 300, 308, 314, 316, 325, 330, 337f., 345, 347, 356, 358, 377, 390, 398, 414, 420, 442, 452, 455, 458, 463, 470, 472-474, 478f., 483f., 486, 489, 492f., 508f., 513, 519, 530, 547, 551
electronic procurement 62, 120, 166, 177, 183, 530 *see also e-procurement*
electronic reverse auction 181-183
England 91
environmental objectives 99, 101, 104, 106, 130, 143, 146, 153, 184, 193, 237, 462, 464, 484 *see also environmental policies*
environmental policies 44, 87, 99f., 102f., 152, 530 *see also*

*environmental objectives*
e-procurement 32, 62, 64, 115, 215, 224, 235, 248f., 277f., 346, 457f., 475, 488-491, 493, 514, 530f., 537, 547 *see also electronic procurement*
equal treatment 92, 120, 164, 201, 330
equality 24, 51, 81, 84, 144, 170, 229, 262f., 301, 358
EU 30, 32, 33, 34, 41, 53, 60, 68, 81, 92, 94, 97, 107, 112, 132, 160, 305, 500, 530
evaluation committee 229, 241, 332f., 339, 345, 431, 443f., 498, 513, 515-517, 519, 537
evaluation criteria 73, 127, 130, 144, 152, 171, 186-189, 191, 193, 195, 202, 217, 219, 237, 244, 249, 275, 341, 381, 390, 392, 432, 445, 523f., 529
evaluation process 340, 442-445, 450
exceptions 22, 83, 123, 125, 133, 139, 146, 149-151, 154, 163, 170, 172, 180f., 195, 201, 210, 224, 234, 248, 272, 363f., 367, 466, 473, 499 *see also exemption*
exemption 123, 132, 148, 211, 225, 265f., 312, 335, 353, 355, 362-364, 366f., 407, 437, 539 *see also exceptions*
fairness 51, 54f., 127, 129, 138, 178, 183, 196, 210, 212, 218, 224, 229, 236, 238, 250, 265, 279, 284, 286f., 305, 311, 317-319, 323f., 330, 337-339, 341, 343f., 360, 362, 366f., 381, 386, 390, 392f., 431f., 435, 443, 450, 452, 464, 479, 486, 512f., 528, 539f., 546
favouritism 418, 509
field research 35, 42, 46, 368, 453, 463, 473, 554
foreign assistance 266
framework agreement 60, 62, 105, 178, 182, 184, 199, 200, 214, 223f., 235, 248, 478, 522
fraud 71, 268, 280, 282, 292, 297, 307, 311, 430
free trade 40, 86, 93, 95, 98, 197, 206, 506
functionality 61, 65, 99, 275, 292, 296, 324, 345, 552
GATS 25, 111, 148
GATT 25, 111, 116, 123, 133f., 147f., 170
GDP 19, 21, 52, 96, 370
good governance 20f., 25, 27, 105f., 117, 119, 136, 172, 208, 255, 257, 262, 265, 323, 406, 453f., 462, 470
GPA 23, 25, 32, 36, 39, 44f., 91, 109, 111-132, 134-138, 140-142, 144f., 148-153, 155-157, 159-173, 178f., 184, 186, 195, 197f., 201f., 205, 209f., 214, 216, 218, 231, 234, 251, 274, 304, 306, 324, 327-329, 342, 350, 353, 355, 361f., 372, 375, 380f., 385, 393f., 505, 544, 549, 551, 557
green procurement 81, 99, 102, 115, 152, 184, 485 *see also green public procurement*
green public procurement 99-103, 107, 530 *see also green procurement*
harmonisation 116, 122, 131, 140, 152, 170, 173, 179, 201, 206, 209, 213, 221, 328, 347, 349, 458, 512, 522, 549f.
heavy-rules approach 80, 521, 551
hindrances 23, 43, 79, 118, 339, 422, 457, 490, 495, 545, 554, 558
holistic approach 56, 177, 200, 203, 288, 329, 462, 550

ILO 93, 411
independent review body 160, 486, 493 *see also independent review panel*
independent review panel 66, 246-248, 250, 256, 310, 346f., 452, 496, 513, 534f., 542, 553, 555 *see also independent review body*
injunctive relief 68, 200, 344
innovation 54, 57, 71, 89, 100, 129, 142, 234, 237, 337, 483, 522f., 552
institutional and organisational form 331 *see also institutional and organisational structure; organisational and institutional structure*
institutional and organisational structure 206, 219, 224, 329, 538 *see also institutional and organisational form; organisational and institutional structure*
integrity 19, 51, 55, 72, 77, 79, 80, 117-119, 153, 169, 178, 196, 212, 224, 242, 268, 280, 300, 328, 330, 334, 346, 373, 385f., 394, 436, 458, 473, 486, 512-515
interim interdict 313, 424, 447 *see also interim measures*
interim measures 159, 344 *see also interim interdict*
internal challenge procedure 245
international best practices 36-38, 40, 46, 109, 169, 172, 202f., 221, 249, 251, 323, 327, 329, 348, 393, 490, 492, 508, 512, 523, 535, 537, 543, 545-549, 557f. *see also best practices*
international law 155, 504f., 512
international obligations 193, 504, 511, 540
internationalisation of procurement rules 41
judicial review 66, 156, 159, 198f., 247, 306-308, 310-316, 320f., 325, 344, 350, 420, 425-427, 448, 451f., 455, 485-487, 536, 547, 555
labour conditions 81, 84, 107, 338, 377f. *see also working conditions*
labour laws 153, 324, 354, 377f., 410, 501
labour rights 37, 153, 245
labour standards 71, 92, 144, 249, 303, 346, 379, 404, 483
lack of political will 23, 277, 367, 419, 453, 460f., 465, 498, 507f., 543, 557
law enforcement 80, 139, 191, 342, 418, 480, 484, 535, 552
least-developed countries 113, 131, 133f., 162
legal drafting 173, 464, 495
legal limbo 180, 363, 376, 511, 555
legal transplants 36
lessons learned 47, 57, 351
liberalisation 45, 86, 94-96, 107
lists of suppliers 214
litigation 67, 280, 282, 310, 319, 325, 340, 344, 452, 486, 553
locus standi 198, 246, 427
market access 97, 118, 121, 132, 135, 160-162, 170, 328, 459
Mauritius 24, 58, 109, 205f., 222-225, 228, 233, 235, 243, 248, 250, 265f., 344-350, 367, 373, 376, 379, 391, 404, 500f., 505, 513, 517, 519, 529, 531, 544
Methodology for Assessing Procurement Systems (MAPS) 55, 459, 463f., 468, 487, 508, 537
military procurement 123
Millennium Development Goals (MDGs) 21, 27

minimum competency levels 477
misconduct 92, 145, 153, 280, 292, 334, 338, 341, 343, 533, 551
Model Law 23, 37, 39, 45, 58, 109, 173, 176-183, 187-190, 196-202, 205f., 214, 220f., 231, 248, 327-329, 347, 349, 361, 367, 380, 385, 505, 551, 557
monetary thresholds 59, 113
monitoring 57, 65, 75f., 78, 85, 100, 127, 141, 168, 175, 212, 218, 220, 226, 244, 253, 256, 259, 267, 331, 337, 340, 343, 373, 378f., 404f., 455, 470, 473f., 499, 514, 517, 520, 534, 541, 545, 550, 554
most-favoured-nation treatment 120, 136, 209
Namibia 21-23, 25-27, 31, 34f., 39f., 42, 45f., 59, 93, 109, 153, 166, 173f., 206, 251, 330, 351, 353-358, 360, 362-370, 372-377, 381, 383-388, 391-396, 398-402, 405-418, 420-427, 429-431, 433f., 436-449, 451-453, 455, 458, 460, 463, 466, 473, 495-504, 506-512, 514, 520f., 524, 528, 530, 532, 536f., 539, 543f., 547-549, 554, 556f.
national defence 123, 146
national security 123, 146, 224, 265, 362
national treatment 112, 116, 120, 126f., 132, 136f., 149-151, 161, 195f., 209, 218
negotiation 113, 115, 122, 126, 151, 181, 424
neoliberal 40, 120
non-discrimination 54, 62, 98, 113, 116f., 120, 126f., 137, 145, 147, 149, 159, 161, 163, 165, 169, 179, 195-197, 209, 218, 232, 237, 328, 459, 464, 528
OECD 19-21, 28, 36, 40, 54f., 64, 69, 72, 100f., 107, 112, 160, 175, 179, 225, 332, 334, 365f., 452, 457-461, 463-465, 467-469, 476f., 485-487, 505, 508, 549
ombudsman 42f., 68, 320, 400, 420, 422, 423f., 452, 455 *see also procurement ombudsman*
open bidding 36, 53, 58f., 113, 230, 233, 243, 336, 363, 365, 367, 522f.
oral debriefing 74, 492
organisational and institutional structure 38, 44, 49, 52, 105, 173, 211, 251, 353, 398, 497, 510, 516, 545, 546 *see also institutional and organisational form; institutional and organisational structure*
organisational structure *see organisational and institutional structure*
outsourcing 62
over-regulation 466
oversight 52, 64f., 75, 106, 131, 198, 211, 217, 242, 248, 332-334, 343, 348, 371, 373, 378, 474f., 517, 524, 539, 541, 545, 551, 554f.
ownership 22, 120, 262, 297, 305, 324, 385, 408f., 453, 461, 469, 508, 510, 537, 544, 554, 556f.
pillars of public procurement systems 56
planned procurement 141
policy office 211, 230, 332, 337, 339, 341, 343-345, 348, 373, 408, 517
pre-bidding phase 56-58, 330, 336
preference policy 84, 252, 305, 349, 387, 401f., 408, 454, 529 *see also preferences; preferential procurement; preferential treatment*

preferences 84f., 88, 97, 103, 147, 149-151, 161, 188, 202, 218f., 244, 256, 260, 279f., 295, 301, 304, 324, 359, 382, 387f., 401-403, 496, 527, 541 *see also preference policy; preferential procurement; preferential treatment*
preferential procurement 83-85, 90, 106, 137, 188, 197, 233, 258f., 265, 277, 289, 294f., 297, 299, 300-302, 324, 328, 349, 354, 356, 507, 528f., 552 *see also preference policy; preferences; preferential treatment*
preferential treatment 44, 84, 86, 89, 95, 107, 115, 129, 146, 154, 161, 163, 167, 179, 195, 209f., 222, 233, 243, 249, 295, 300-302, 323, 328, 346, 350, 359, 373, 406, 481, 513, 527-529, 546f., 555 *see also preference policy; preferences; preferential procurement*
prequalification 60, 83, 99, 126, 186, 199, 213, 232-234, 241, 296, 336, 355, 373f., 421, 441 *see also prequalification procedures*
prequalification procedures 214, 275 *see also prequalification*
principle of legality 430
procedural rights 198, 246, 344, 542, 547, 553
procurement costs 54, 85, 87-89, 102, 107
procurement cycle 57f., 72, 125, 220f., 239, 248, 335, 493, 531, 533
procurement methods 34, 44, 49, 105, 124, 126, 171, 180, 182f., 202, 213, 230, 248, 271f., 336, 342, 349, 353, 367, 376, 461, 472, 477, 490f., 511f., 522, 540, 551, 555
procurement ombudsman 67, 255 *see also ombudsman*
procurement planning 56, 58, 109, 171, 174, 191, 205f., 220f., 238, 242, 248, 279, 329f., 335, 377, 457, 488, 493, 532, 534, 556
procurement website 220, 236, 248f., 335, 338, 342, 346, 391, 523f., 532f., 547
protectionism 86, 94, 98, 107, 147, 196, 232, 304
public bid openings 73, 338
public hearings 74, 246, 337, 535
public procurement officials 49, 66, 100f., 104, 130, 140, 269, 323, 349, 394, 484, 526, 537, 545, 551, 553
publication 63, 72f., 138-140, 171, 183, 190f., 208, 217, 235, 241, 249, 282, 323, 335f., 338, 342f., 349, 381, 391, 393, 432, 435f., 439, 477, 523-527, 531
publication of reasons 336
public-private partnership 60f., 105, 224, 235, 522
qualification system 125, 212, 333, 520f.
reasonableness 311, 390, 431f., 443, 450
reform 21-23, 25, 27-29, 32, 34f., 37, 39, 41f., 44-47, 54, 78, 109, 111, 155, 171-173, 178, 184, 200, 203, 205-207, 220f., 251f., 256, 263, 269, 321f., 327-329, 351, 353, 356, 401, 408, 420, 439, 445, 453, 457-465, 467, 469, 470, 472, 475, 477-479, 487f., 490-493, 495-501, 503-510, 519f., 523, 530, 537, 543-550, 553-557
reform drivers 23, 457, 495, 500
reform hindrances 460, 507
regional integration 206

regional preferences 209, 222, 243
remedies 34, 66, 68, 106, 160, 219, 250, 291f., 297, 306f., 311-316, 320, 343, 350, 378, 426, 447f., 452, 455, 486, 493, 534, 536, 547, 552
restricted procurement 59 *see also restricted tendering*
restricted tendering 181 *see also restricted procurement*
review mechanism 63, 66f., 131, 155, 159f., 172, 199, 208, 281, 306f., 316, 325, 344, 400, 420, 425f., 450f., 455, 480, 485, 493, 534f., 538, 542, 547, 550, 552 *see also review procedure*
review procedure 66, 73, 159, 307, 344, 420, 455, 485, 534 *see also review mechanism*
right to a fair trial 425
right to administrative justice 423, 425
right to appeal 198, 308
right to information 421f.
right to reasons 284, 287, 421, 439, 450 *see also right to request reasons*
right to request reasons 308, 342, 551 *see also right to reasons*
Roger Webb report 252
rule of law 24, 28, 80, 119, 136, 157, 246, 250, 324f., 334, 341, 454, 462, 535, 542, 556
SADC 206, 395, 505
scope 30, 44, 51, 58, 109, 113, 116f., 119, 121-123, 132, 135, 138, 147, 149, 163, 166, 170, 172, 180, 192, 205, 209f., 224, 233, 242, 248, 258, 264f., 289, 304, 321, 325, 327, 330, 334, 347, 353, 360-362, 374, 403, 426, 431f., 466, 471, 501, 507, 510, 512, 526, 538f., 546f., 550f., 555
secondary objectives 23, 25, 27, 30, 33, 44f., 49, 81-83, 99, 106, 109, 111, 128, 142f., 145-147, 149-153, 163, 168, 173, 179, 182, 187f., 202, 205, 219, 238f., 243-245, 248f., 251, 276, 289, 291, 294, 303f., 327, 330, 341, 346, 349, 358, 378, 385, 407, 457, 464, 470, 478, 482f., 492, 512f., 527f., 530, 546, 552
selective procurement 60, 125f. *see also selective tendering*
selective tendering 53, 113, 124-126, 138, 141, 375 *see also selective procurement*
set aside 200, 314-316, 388, 407, 427f., 434f., 437-439, 443, 445f., 450
small value purchases 53
SMEs 26, 66, 79, 84, 89, 97, 122, 153f., 192, 194, 210, 214, 222, 227, 245, 247, 302, 339, 405, 481, 489
social welfare 84, 88, 94, 106, 483
socio-economic development 19-21, 26, 28, 38, 46f., 119, 169, 172, 297, 341, 347, 362, 408, 455, 482, 484, 556
socio-economic linkages 252f. *see also socio-economic objectives; socio-economic policies*
socio-economic objectives 25, 81f., 84f., 102f., 106, 151, 255, 293, 350, 356, 485, 529 *see also socio-economic linkages; socio-economic policies*
socio-economic policies 85, 90, 97, 143f., 147, 170, 192f. *see also socio-economic linkages; socio-economic objectives*
SOEs 51, 503
solicitation documents 186, 189, 192, 195, 208, 380

South Africa 20, 25, 30, 32-34, 42, 45, 51, 81, 83f., 93, 206, 251-255, 262-266, 268f., 271-280, 283f., 287f., 291, 293f., 296, 299-306, 309-313, 317, 320-325, 329, 331f., 347-350, 354f., 362, 367, 371, 377, 391, 394, 410, 421, 426, 458, 479, 506-508, 517, 528
special and differential treatment 120, 131-136, 162, 201
stakeholders 22, 42, 52, 64, 67, 73-75, 78, 85, 105, 126, 139, 171, 191, 194, 222, 224, 227, 241, 256, 320, 330, 332, 334, 337, 366, 375, 420, 428, 445, 458, 461f., 464f., 467-469, 471, 474, 478, 481, 487, 489f., 492, 495-497, 501, 503, 508, 519, 528, 537, 539, 544, 546, 554, 556-558
standard bidding documents 213, 222, 238, 337
standardisation 141, 173, 182, 200, 276, 475
standstill period 199, 203, 216, 219, 221, 236, 246f., 250, 316, 340, 343, 347, 450, 492, 534, 536, 547, 553
suppliers lists 60, 214, 235
Supply Chain Management system 252, 256, 347, 372
sustainability 24, 82, 184, 186, 189, 231, 291, 408, 472
sustainable development 23, 99, 147
targeted procurement 289, 293f., 301f., 350, 529
tax money 19, 28, 320, 381, 448
technical specifications 128, 143, 144, 152, 216, 237f., 260, 273f., 293, 346, 379f.
temporary interdicts 313 *see also temporary relief; temporary suspension*
temporary relief 312f. *see also temporary interdicts; temporary suspension*
temporary suspension 219, 344 *see also temporary interdicts; temporary relief*
TIPEEG 363f., 378, 392, 406f., 437
trade liberalisation 45, 86, 98, 106, 147, 206f., 464
trade unions 501f.
training 33, 66, 72, 78, 96, 100f., 212, 225f., 259, 267, 269f., 283, 323, 333, 349, 359, 370, 402, 405, 458, 461, 467f., 472, 475-477, 486, 489, 491f., 514, 520, 537, 546
transparency 22f., 28-30, 36, 38, 43f., 49, 51, 54-56, 64, 67-74, 76-78, 80, 88, 103, 105f., 109, 111, 113, 116-120, 126, 133, 137-142, 151, 159, 161, 164-171, 173, 178, 183f., 188, 190-193, 196, 198, 201f., 205, 209f., 212, 214, 217f., 222, 224f., 229, 231, 236, 238-240, 243, 246, 248f., 251, 254, 257, 259, 261, 265f., 275, 277-281, 283, 285, 287f., 301, 305, 317, 323, 327-330, 332, 336, 340-344, 346f., 349, 353f., 360f., 366f., 373, 381, 386, 390, 392-397, 407, 421, 424, 430, 432, 435, 439, 450, 454f., 457, 459, 461, 463f., 466, 470, 472, 479f., 484, 489, 492, 496, 501, 507f., 512f., 521, 523-525, 533, 537-547, 551, 553, 555, 557
Transparency International 40, 46, 53, 63, 69, 72, 74, 80, 395, 480
two-stage procurement 336, 373, 375 *see also two-stage tendering*
two-stage tendering 181, 234 *see*

*also two-stage procurement*
ultra vires 388, 433-437, 451, 454
UN 21, 28, 69, 174, 394, 458
UNCAC 39, 40, 69, 72, 117f., 504
UNCITRAL Model Law 23, 36, 38-41, 44f., 57, 60, 65, 73, 109, 173f., 176-190, 192f., 195-203, 205f., 210, 214, 216, 221, 225, 231f., 234, 243, 249, 251f., 274, 327-329, 342, 349f., 353, 361-363, 367, 372, 374-376, 380-383, 385f., 393f., 464, 482, 493, 505, 512, 522, 524, 535, 537, 543f., 551, 557
uniformity 176, 258, 276, 300, 323, 373
United States 91, 97f., 145, 147f., 150, 158
UNODC 40
urgency 126, 417, 445-449, 451
value for money 42, 51, 53-57, 59, 62, 73, 79, 82, 94, 102, 129f., 144, 178, 189, 192, 209, 224, 227, 229, 236-238, 240, 244, 261, 272-277, 279, 302-304, 316, 319, 324, 330, 337, 339-341, 360, 367, 386, 464, 471, 474, 479, 482, 492, 512f., 519, 539, 552, 555
Washington Consensus 45
welfare 51, 84, 85, 89-91, 107, 117-119, 161, 169, 171, 328
workforce 38, 49, 52, 77, 105f., 173, 212, 330, 333f., 353, 359, 475, 551
working conditions 22, 66, 92, 239, 341, 404, 413 *see also labour conditions*
World Bank 29, 36f., 64, 175, 179, 222, 248, 253, 255, 278, 301, 459f., 463f., 500, 544, 549
WTO 23, 25, 30, 32f., 36, 39, 51, 58, 62, 72f., 75, 85f., 90, 94f., 97f., 111-113, 115f., 120-126, 130-137, 139, 141-145, 147-151, 153-159, 161f., 165f., 168-171, 175, 196, 209f., 214, 225, 234, 263, 299, 328, 459